The
Unfinished
Nation

A CONCISE HISTORY
OF THE AMERICAN PEOPLE

Volume Two: From 1865

The Unfinished Nation

A CONCISE HISTORY
OF THE AMERICAN PEOPLE

Volume Two: From 1865

Alan Brinkley
Columbia University

OVERTURE
BOOKS

McGraw-Hill, Inc.
New York St. Louis San Francisco Auckland Bogotá
Caracas Lisbon London Madrid Mexico City Milan
Montreal New Delhi San Juan Singapore
Sydney Tokyo Toronto

THE UNFINISHED NATION: A Concise History of the American People
Volume Two: From 1865

Copyright © 1993 by McGraw-Hill, Inc. All rights reserved. Printed in the United
States of America. Except as permitted under the United States Copyright Act of
1976, no part of this publication may be reproduced or distributed in any form or
by any means, or stored in a data base or retrieval system, without the prior written
permission of the publisher.

Adapted from *American History: A Survey*, by Brinkley, Current, Freidel, and
Williams.

5 6 7 8 9 0 DOC DOC 9 0 9 8 7 6 5 4

ISBN 0-07-007872-6

This book was set in Janson by Black Dot, Inc.
R. R. Donnelley & Sons Company was printer and binder.
Maps were prepared by David Lindroth Inc.

Publisher: Roth Wilkofsky
Sponsoring Editor: Peter Labella
Associate Editor: Niels Aaboe
Editing Supervisor: Larry Goldberg
Designer: Wanda Siedlecka
Production Supervisor: Kathryn Porzio
Photo Editor: Elyse Rieder

Cover photo: Maxine Albro, *California Agriculture*, 1934. Left panel, Public Works
of Art Project, Coit Tower, San Francisco, CA. Photo by Don Beatty © 1981.

Library of Congress Cataloging-in-Publication Data

Brinkley, Alan.
   The unfinished nation: a concise history of the American people /
Alan Brinkley.
      p.   cm.
   "Overture books."
   Includes bibliographical references and index.
   Contents: v. 1. to 1877—v. 2. From 1865.
   ISBN 0-07-007871-8 (v. 1)—ISBN 0-07-007872-6 (v. 2)
   1. United States—History.   I. Title.
E178.1.B827   1993
973—dc20   92-44995

Contents

AMERICAN VOICES

DEBATING THE PAST

APPENDICES

List of Illustrations

List of Maps

Preface

The story of the American past, which is the subject of this book, is as contested today as it has been at any moment in its history. As the population of the United States becomes ever more diverse and as groups that once stood outside the view of scholarship thrust themselves into its center, historians are revealing the immense and, until recently, inadequately understood complexity of their country's past. The result has been the slow emergence of a richer and fuller history of the United States, but also a more fragmented and contentious one. That history offers a picture of a highly diverse people. It also provides a picture of a great nation.

Threading one's way through the many, conflicting demands of contemporary scholars and contemporary readers is no easy task. But I have tried in this book to find an acceptable middle ground between the claims of diversity and the claims of unity. The United States is, indeed, a nation of many cultures. We cannot understand its history without understanding the experiences of all the different groups that have shaped American society, without understanding the particular worlds that have developed within it based on race, gender, ethnicity, religion, class, or region.

But the United States is more than just a collection of different cultures. It is also a nation. And as important as understanding its diversity is understanding the forces that have drawn it together and allowed it to survive and flourish despite division. The United States has constructed a remarkably stable and enduring political system that touches the lives of all Americans. It has developed an immense, highly productive national economy that affects the working and consuming lives of virtually everyone. It has created a mass popular culture that colors the experiences and assumptions of almost all the American people, and the people of much of the rest of the world as well. One can admire these unifying forces for their contributions to America's considerable success as a nation, or condemn them for the ways they have contributed to inequality, injustice, and failure. But no one proposing to understand the history of the United States can afford to ignore them.

In the great historical narratives of the nineteenth and early twentieth centuries, the story of America moved smoothly and triumphantly from one clearly defined era to another, focusing on great events and great men and tracing the rise of national institutions. The late twentieth century has produced a different narrative, with frequent, sometimes jarring, changes of focus and direction. It devotes attention to private as well as public events, to failure as well as success, to difference as well as to unity. And yet it remains, in the end, a narrative, a story—newly complicated, perhaps, by our understanding of the many worlds of historical experience that once eluded us—but no less remarkable and compelling for those complications.

This book is an effort to tell this newer story of America for students of history and for general readers in a single, reasonably concise volume. It has its origins in a considerably larger book by Alan Brinkley, Richard N. Current, Frank Freidel, and T. Harry Williams, *American History: A Survey*, now in its eighth edition. But it is not simply an abridgment of that longer work. I have tried here to craft a new, more thematic, and more selective narrative that preserves the central elements of the larger text but presents a clearer and more readily accessible story. In addition to the central narrative (and the maps and illustrations that accompany it), readers will also find a collection of essays examining major interpretive debates among scholars; and they will find a series of excerpts from important or emblematic American autobiographies, journals, memoirs, and other works. Together, I hope, these elements will serve to introduce readers to enough different approaches to and areas of American history to make them aware of its extraordinary richness and diversity. I hope they will also give readers some sense of the shared experiences of Americans.

The title of this book, *The Unfinished Nation*, is meant to suggest several things. It is a reminder of America's exceptional diversity: of the degree to which, despite all the many efforts to build a single, uniform definition of the meaning of American nationhood, that meaning remains contested and diverse. It is a reference to the centrality of change in American history: to the way in which the nation has continually transformed itself and to how it continues to do so in our own time. And it is a description of the writing of American history itself, of the way historians are engaged in a continuing, ever unfinished, process of asking new questions of the past.

Many people contributed to this book: Chris Rogers, David Follmer, Niels Aaboe, Larry Goldberg, Roth Wilkofsky, and Peter Labella at McGraw-Hill; Ashbel Green at Knopf; Yanek Mieczkowski, my research assistant at Columbia; and several anonymous scholars who read and commented on the manuscript and saved me from many errors and inelegancies. I am grateful to them all. I will also be grateful to any readers who wish to offer comments, criticisms, and corrections as I prepare future editions. Suggestions can be sent to me in care of the Department of History, Columbia University, New York, NY 10027; I will respond to them as fully and constructively as I can.

ALAN BRINKLEY

CHAPTER FIFTEEN

Reconstructing the Nation

The Problems of Peacemaking ~ *Radical Reconstruction*
The South in Reconstruction ~ *The Grant Administration*
The Abandonment of Reconstruction

EW PERIODS in the history of the United States have produced as much bitterness or created such enduring controversy as the era of Reconstruction—the years following the Civil War during which Americans attempted to reunite their shattered nation. Those who lived through the experience viewed it in sharply different ways. To many white Southerners, Reconstruction was a vicious and destructive experience—a period when vindictive Northerners inflicted humiliation and revenge on the prostrate South and unnecessarily delayed a genuine reunion of the sections. Northern defenders of Reconstruction, in contrast, argued that their policies were the only way to prevent unrepentant Confederates from restoring Southern society as it had been before the war; without forceful federal intervention, there would be no way to forestall the reemergence of a backward aristocracy and the continued subjugation of blacks—no way, in other words, to prevent the same sectional problems that had produced the Civil War in the first place.

To most black Americans at the time, and to many people of all races since, Reconstruction was notable for other reasons. Neither a vicious tyranny, as white Southerners charged, nor a drastic and necessary reform, as many Northerners claimed, it was, rather, an essentially moderate, even conservative program that fell far short of providing the newly freed slaves with the protection they needed. Reconstruction, in other words, was significant less for what it did than for what it failed to do. And when it came to an end, finally, in the late 1870s, black Americans found themselves once again abandoned.

CHARLESTON, 1865 Not until 1864 did substantial fighting and destruction begin to take place in the urban South. But in the last year of the war, several major cities (and many towns and smaller communities) experienced devastation at the hands of the Northern armies—among them Richmond, Atlanta, and (as seen here) Charleston.

THE PROBLEMS OF PEACEMAKING

In 1865, when the Confederacy finally surrendered to the North, no one in Washington knew quite what to do in response. Abraham Lincoln could not negotiate a treaty with the defeated government; he continued to insist that that government had no legal right to exist. Yet neither could he simply readmit the Southern states into the Union as if nothing had happened.

The Aftermath of War

The South after the Civil War was a desolate place. Towns had been gutted, plantations burned, fields neglected, bridges and railroads destroyed. Many white Southerners—stripped of their slaves through emancipation and stripped of the capital they had invested in now worthless Confederate bonds and currency—had no personal property. More than 258,000 Confederate soliders had died in the war, and thousands more returned home wounded or sick. Many families had to rebuild their fortunes without the help of adult males. Many white Southerners faced starvation and homelessness.

If conditions were bad for Southern whites, they were far worse for Southern blacks—the 4 million men and women now emerging from bondage. As soon as the war ended, hundreds of thousands of them—young and old, many of them ill and feeble—left the plantations in search of a new life in freedom. But most had nowhere to go. They trudged to the nearest town or city or roamed the countryside, camping at night on the bare ground. Few had any possessions except the clothes they wore.

The response of many white Southerners to this desolation was an effort to restore their society to its antebellum form. Slavery had been abolished in some areas in 1863 by the Emancipation Proclamation and in all areas as of December 1865 by the Thirteenth Amendment. But many white planters wanted to continue slavery in an altered form by keeping black workers legally tied to the plantations. Blacks, of course, had a very different vision of the postwar South. They wanted, above all, to know and feel their freedom and to be assured that they were not again to lose it. They wanted to own land, to educate their children, and to gain the right to vote. The struggle between Southern blacks and whites over these competing visions was an unequal one, but for a time blacks had the benefit of at least some support from the federal government.

The government kept troops in the South to preserve order and protect the freedmen. And in March 1865, Congress established the Freedmen's Bureau, an agency of the army directed by General Oliver O. Howard. The Freedmen's Bureau distributed food to millions of former slaves. It established schools, staffed by missionaries and teachers who had been sent to the South by Freedmen's Aid Societies and other private and church groups in the North. It tried to settle blacks on lands of their own. (The bureau also offered considerable assistance to poor whites, many of whom were similarly destitute and homeless after the war.)

But the Freedmen's Bureau was not a permanent solution. It had authority to operate for only one year; and it was, in any case, far too small to deal effectively with the enormous problems facing Southern society. It remained up to the federal government to determine whether the hopes of Southern whites or those of Southern blacks would prevail.

Issues of Reconstruction

The terms by which the Southern states rejoined the Union had important implications for both major political parties. The Republican victories in 1860 and 1864 had been a result, in large part, of divisions within the Democratic party and, later, the removal of the South from the electorate. Leaders of both parties believed that readmitting the South would reunite the Democrats and weaken the Republicans. In addition, the Republican party had taken advantage of the absence of the South from Congress to pass a program of nationalistic economic legislation—railroad subsidies, protective tariffs, and other measures of benefit to Northern business leaders and industrialists. Should the Democratic party regain power with heavy Southern support, these programs would be in jeopardy. Complicating these practical questions were emotional concerns. Many Northerners believed the South should be punished for the suffering and sacrifice its rebellion had caused. And many Northerners believed, too, that the South should be transformed, made over in the North's urban-industrial image.

Even among the Republicans in Congress, there was considerable disagreement about the proper approach to Reconstruction—disagreement that reflected the same factional division (between the party's Conservatives and Radicals) that had created disputes during the war over emancipation. Conservatives insisted that the South accept the abolition of slavery, but they proposed few other conditions for the readmission of the seceded states. The Radicals, led by Representative Thaddeus Stevens of Pennsylvania and Senator Charles Sumner of Massachusetts, urged that the civil and military chieftains of the late Confederacy be punished, that large numbers of Southern whites be disenfranchised, that the legal rights of blacks be protected, and that the property of wealthy white Southerners who had aided the Confederacy be confiscated and distributed among the freedmen. Some Radicals favored granting suffrage to the former slaves. Others hesitated, since few Northern states permitted blacks to vote. Between the Radicals and the Conservatives stood a faction of uncommitted Republicans, the Moderates, who rejected the punitive goals of the Radicals but supported extracting at least some concessions from the South on black rights.

Plans for Reconstruction

President Lincoln's sympathies lay with the Moderates and Conservatives of his party. He believed that a lenient Reconstruction policy would encourage Southern Unionists and other former Whigs to join the Republican party and thus prevent the readmission of the South from strengthening the Democrats. More immediately, the Southern Unionists could become the nucleus of new, loyal state governments in the South. Lincoln was not uninterested in the fate of the freedmen, but he was willing to defer questions about race relations for the sake of rapid reunification.

Lincoln's Reconstruction plan, which he announced in December 1863, offered a general amnesty to those white Southerners—other than high officials of the Confederacy—who would pledge loyalty to the government and accept the elimination of slavery. When 10 percent of the number of voters in 1860 took the oath in any state, those loyal voters could set up a state government. Lincoln also hoped to extend suffrage to those blacks who were educated, owned property, and had served in the Union army. Three Southern states—Louisiana, Arkansas, and Tennessee, all under Union occupation—reestablished loyal governments under the Lincoln formula in 1864.

The Radical Republicans were astonished at the mildness of Lincoln's program. They persuaded Congress to deny seats to representatives from

ABRAHAM LINCOLN Lincoln was the subject of many photographic portraits, of which this one, by Matthew Brady, is one of the most famous.

the three "reconstructed" states and refused to count the electoral vote of those states in the election of 1864. But for the moment, the Radicals were uncertain about what form their own Reconstruction plan should take.

Their first effort to resolve that question was the Wade-Davis Bill, passed by Congress in July 1864. By its provisions, the president would appoint a provisional governor for each conquered state. When a majority (not Lincoln's ten percent) of the white males of the state pledged their allegiance to the Union, the governor could summon a state constitutional convention, whose delegates were to be elected by voters who had never borne arms against the United States (again, a major departure from Lincoln's plan). The new state constitutions would be required to abolish slavery, disenfranchise Confederate civil and military leaders, and repudiate debts accumulated by the state governments during the war. After these conditions were met, Congress would readmit the states to the Union. Like the president's proposal, the Wade-Davis Bill left up to the states the question of political rights for blacks.

Congress passed the bill a few days before it adjourned in 1864, and Lincoln disposed of it with a pocket veto. His action enraged the Radical leaders, and the pragmatic Lincoln realized he would have to accept at least some of the Radical demands. As a result, he began to move toward a new approach to Reconstruction.

The Death of Lincoln

What plan he might have produced no one can say. On the night of April 14, 1865, Lincoln and his wife attended a play at Ford's Theater in Washington. As they sat in the presidential box, John Wilkes Booth, an unsuccessful actor obsessed with aiding the Southern cause, entered the box from the rear and shot Lincoln in the head. Early the next morning, the president died.

The circumstances of Lincoln's death earned him immediate martyrdom. They also produced something close to hysteria throughout the North. There were accusations that Booth had acted as part of a great conspiracy—accusations that contained some truth. Booth did indeed have associates, one of whom shot and wounded Secretary of State William Seward the night of the assassination, another of whom abandoned at the last moment a scheme to murder Vice President Andrew Johnson. Booth himself escaped on horseback into the Maryland countryside, where, on April 26, he was cornered by Union troops and shot to death in a blazing barn. Eight other people were convicted by a military tribunal of participating in the conspiracy (at least two of them on the basis of virtually no evidence). Four were hanged.

To many Northerners, however, the murder of the president seemed evidence of an even greater conspiracy—one masterminded and directed by the unrepentant leaders of the defeated South. Militant Republicans exploited such suspicions relentlessly in the ensuing months, ensuring that Lincoln's death would help doom his plans for a relatively generous peace.

Johnson and "Restoration"

Leadership of the Moderates and Conservatives fell to Lincoln's successor, Andrew Johnson, who was not well suited, either by circumstance or personality, for the task. A Democrat until he had joined the Union ticket with Lincoln in 1864, he became president at a time of growing partisan passions. And Johnson himself was an intemperate and tactless man, filled with resentments and insecurities.

Johnson revealed his plan for Reconstruction—or "Restoration," as he preferred to call it—soon after he took office, and he implemented it during the summer of 1865 when Congress was in recess. Like Lincoln, he offered amnesty to those Southerners who would take an oath of allegiance. (High-ranking Confederate officials and all white Southerners with land worth $20,000 or more would have to apply to the president for individual pardons.) In most other respects, however, his plan resembled that of the Wade-Davis Bill. For each state, the president appointed a provisional governor, who would invite qualified voters to elect delegates to a constitutional convention. Johnson did not specify how many qualified voters were necessary, but he implied that he would require a majority (as had the Wade-Davis Bill). In order to win readmission to Congress, a state had to revoke its ordinance of secession, abolish slavery and ratify the Thirteenth Amendment, and repudiate Confederate and state war debts—essentially the same stipulations that had been laid down in Wade-Davis. The final procedure before restoration was that a state would elect a state government and send representatives to Congress.

By the end of 1865, all the seceded states had formed new governments—some under Lincoln's plan, some under Johnson's—and were ready to rejoin the Union, *if* Congress chose to recognize them when it met in December 1865. But Radicals in Congress vowed not to recognize the Johnson governments, just as they had previously refused to recognize the Lincoln regimes; for by now, Northern opinion had become more hostile toward the South than it had been a year earlier when Congress passed the

Wade-Davis Bill. Many Northerners were disturbed by the apparent reluctance of some delegates to the Southern conventions to abolish slavery and by the refusal of all the conventions to grant suffrage to any blacks. They were astounded that states claiming to be "loyal" should elect as state officials and representatives to Congress prominent leaders of the recent Confederacy. Particularly hard to accept was Georgia's choice of Alexander H. Stephens, former vice president of the Confederacy, as a United States senator.

RADICAL RECONSTRUCTION

Reconstruction under Johnson's plan—often known as "presidential Reconstruction"—continued only until Congress reconvened in December 1865. At that point, Congress refused to seat the senators and representatives of the states the president had "restored." Instead, it set up a new Joint Committee on Reconstruction to investigate conditions in the South and to advise Congress in devising a Reconstruction policy of its own. The period of "congressional" or "Radical" Reconstruction had begun.

The Black Codes

Meanwhile, events in the South were driving Northern opinion in even more radical directions. Throughout the South in 1865 and early 1866, state legislatures were enacting sets of laws known as the Black Codes, modeled in many ways on the codes that had regulated free blacks in the prewar South and designed to guarantee white supremacy. Although there were variations from state to state, all codes authorized local officials to apprehend unemployed blacks, fine them for vagrancy, and hire them out to private employers to satisfy the fine. Some of the codes forbade blacks to own or lease farms or to take any jobs other than as plantation workers or domestic servants. To the white South, the Black Codes were a realistic approach to a great social problem. To the North, and to most African-Americans, they represented a return to slavery in all but name.

Congress first responded to the Black Codes by passing an act extending the life of the Freedmen's Bureau and widening its powers. The bureau could now establish special courts for settling labor disputes; the courts could nullify work agreements forced on freedmen under the Black Codes. In April, Congress struck again at the Black Codes by passing the first Civil Rights Act, which declared blacks to be citizens of the United States and empowered the federal government to intervene in state affairs when necessary to protect the rights of citizens. Johnson vetoed both the Freedmen's Bureau and Civil Rights Acts, but Congress eventually overrode him.

The Fourteenth Amendment

In April 1866, the Radicals acted again. The Joint Committee on Reconstruction submitted a proposed Fourteenth Amendment to the Constitution, which Congress approved in early summer and sent to the states for ratification. Eventually, it became one of the most important of all the provisions in the Constitution.

The amendment offered the first constitutional definition of American citizenship. Everyone born in the United States, and everyone naturalized, was automatically a citizen and entitled to all the "privileges and immunities" guaranteed by the Constitution, including equal protection of the laws by both the state and national governments. There could be no other requirements. The amendment also imposed penalties—reduction of representation in Congress and in the electoral college—on states that denied suffrage to any adult male inhabitants. (This was the first time the Constitution had made reference to gender, and the wording clearly reflected the prevailing view in Congress and elsewhere that the franchise was properly restricted to men.) Finally, it prohibited those who had aided the Confederacy after having taken an oath to support the Constitution (that is, members of Congress and other federal officials) from holding any state or federal office unless two-thirds of Congress voted to pardon them.

Congressional Radicals made it clear that if Southern legislatures ratified the Fourteenth Amendment, their states would be readmitted to the Union. But of the former Confederate states, only Tennessee did so. The refusal of others to ratify, along with the refusal of Kentucky and Delaware, denied the amendment the necessary approval of three-fourths of the states and temporarily derailed it.

In the meantime, however, the Radicals were growing stronger, in part because of Northern anger at the South's and Johnson's recalcitrance. When bloody race riots broke out in New Orleans and other Southern cities—riots in which blacks were the principal victims—Radicals cited the incidents as evidence of the inadequacy of Johnson's policy. In the 1866 congressional elections, Johnson actively campaigned for Conservative candidates; but he did his own cause more harm than good with his intemperate speeches. The voters returned an overwhelming majority of Republicans, most of them Radicals, to Congress. In the Senate, there were now 42 Republicans to 11

Democrats; in the House, 143 Republicans to 49 Democrats. (The South remained largely unrepresented in both chambers.) Nothing now prevented the Republicans in Congress from devising a Reconstruction plan of their own.

The Congressional Plan

The Radicals passed three Reconstruction bills early in 1867. Johnson vetoed them all, but Congress overrode him. Finally, nearly two years after the end of the war, the federal government had established a coherent plan for Reconstruction.

That two-year delay had important effects on the way the South reacted to the program. In 1865, with the South reeling from its defeat and nearly prostrate, the federal government could probably have imposed almost any plan on the region without provoking much resistance. But by 1867, the South had already begun to reconstruct itself under the reasonably generous terms Lincoln and Johnson had extended. Measures that might once have seemed moderate now seemed radical, and the congressional Reconstruction plan created deep resentments and continuing resistance.

Under the congressional plan, Tennessee, which had ratified the Fourteenth Amendment, was promptly readmitted. But Congress rejected the Lincoln-Johnson governments of the other ten Confederate states and, instead, combined them into five military districts. Each was assigned a military commander who—in preparation for the readmission of the states—was to register qualfed voters, defined as all adult black males and those white males who had not participated in the rebellion. After the registration was completed, voters would elect a convention to prepare a new state constitution, which had to include provisions for black suffrage. Once voters ratified the new constitution, elections for a state government could be held. Finally, if Congress approved the constitution, if the state legislature ratified the Fourteenth Amendment, and if enough states ratified the amendment to make it part of the Constitution, then the state was to be restored to the Union.

By 1868, seven of the eleven former Confederate states (Arkansas, North Carolina, South Carolina, Louisiana, Alabama, Georgia, and Florida) had fulfilled these conditions (including ratification of the Fourteenth Amendment, which now became part of the Constitution) and were readmitted to the Union. Conservative whites held up the return of Virginia and Texas until 1869 and Mississippi until 1870. By then, Congress had added an additional requirement for readmission—ratification of another constitutional amendment, the Fifteenth, which forbade the states and the federal government to deny the suffrage to any citizen on account of "race, color, or previous condition of servitude." Several Northern and border states refused to approve the Fifteenth Amendment, and it was adopted only with the support of the four Southern states that had to ratify it in order to be readmitted to the Union.

To stop the president from interfering with their designs, the congressional Radicals passed two remarkable laws in 1867. One, the Tenure of Office Act, forbade the president to remove civil officials, including members of his cabinet, without the consent of the Senate. The principal purpose of the law was to protect the job of Secretary of War Edwin M. Stanton, who was the only Lincoln appointee still in Johnson's cabinet and who was cooperating with the Radicals. The other law, the Command of the Army Act, prohibited the president from issuing military orders except through the commanding general of the army (General Grant), whose headquarters were to be in Washington and who could not be relieved or assigned elsewhere without the consent of the Senate.

The congressional Radicals also took action to stop the Supreme Court from interfering with their plans. In 1866, the Court had declared in the case of *Ex parte Milligan* that military tribunals were unconstitutional in places where civil courts were functioning, a decision that seemed to threaten the system of military government the Radicals were planning for the South. Radicals in Congress immediately proposed legislation to require a two-thirds majority of the justices to overrule a law of Congress, to deny the Court jurisdiction in Reconstruction cases, to reduce its membership to three, and even to abolish it. The justices apparently took the hint. Over the next two years, the Court refused to accept jurisdiction in any cases involving Reconstruction.

The Impeachment of the President

Although President Johnson had long since ceased to be a serious obstacle to the passage of Radical legislation, he was still the official charged with administering the Reconstruction programs; and as such, the Radicals believed, he was a serious impediment to their plans. Early in 1867, they began looking for a way to get rid of him. According to the Constitution, only "high crimes or misdemeanors" in office were grounds for impeaching a president and removing him from office. Republicans could find nothing on which to base such charges until Johnson gave them what they considered a plausible reason for action. He deliberately violated the Tenure of

Office Act—in hopes of bringing a test case of the law before the courts. ... dismissed Secretary of War Stanton even though the Senate had already refused to consent to the removal.

In the House of Representatives, elated Radicals impeached the president on eleven charges and sent the case to the Senate for trial. The first nine counts dealt with the violation of the Tenure of Office Act. The tenth and eleventh charged Johnson with slandering Congress and with not enforcing the Reconstruction Acts.

The trial before the Senate lasted throughout April and May 1868. The president's accusers argued that Johnson had defied Congress and was indeed guilty of high crimes and misdemeanors. His defenders claimed that he had acted properly in challenging what he considered an unconstitutional law. The Radicals put heavy pressure on all the Republican senators, but the Moderates (who were losing faith in the Radical program) vacillated. On the first three charges to come to a vote, seven Republicans joined the twelve Democrats to support acquittal. The vote was 35 to 19, one short of the constitutionally required two-thirds majority. After that, the Radicals dropped the impeachment campaign.

THE SOUTH IN RECONSTRUCTION

When white Southerners spoke bitterly in later years of the effects of Reconstruction, they referred most frequently to the governments Congress imposed on them—governments that were, they claimed, both incompetent and corrupt, that saddled the region with enormous debts, and that trampled on the rights of citizens. When black Southerners and their defenders condemned Reconstruction, in contrast, they spoke of its failure to guarantee to freedmen even the most elemental rights of citizenship—a failure that resulted in a new and cruel system of economic subordination. Both complaints had some justification, but most historians would now agree that the black criticisms of Reconstruction had a much stronger basis than the white ones.

The Reconstruction Governments

In the ten states of the South that were reorganized under the congressional plan, approximately one-fourth of the white males were at first excluded from voting or holding office, which produced black majorities among voters in South Carolina, Mississippi, and Louisiana (where blacks were also a majority of the population) and in Alabama and Florida (where they were not). But most suffrage restrictions were soon lifted so that nearly all white males could soon vote. After that, Republicans maintained control only with the support of many Southern whites.

Critics labeled these Southern white Republicans with the derogatory term "scalawags." Many were former Whigs who had never felt comfortable in the Democratic party. Some were wealthy (or once wealthy) planters or businessmen. Others were farmers who lived in remote areas where there had been little or no slavery and who hoped the Republican program of internal improvements would help end their economic isolation. White men from the North, known to their opponents as "carpetbaggers" (after the cheap suitcases some of them carried as they moved into the region), also served as Republican leaders in the South. Most of the carpetbaggers were veterans of the Union army who looked on the South as a new frontier, more

THE BURDENED SOUTH This Reconstruction-era cartoon expresses the South's sense of its oppression at the hands of Northern Republicans. President Grant rides in comfort in a carpetbag as the South staggers under the burden in chains.

promising than the West. They had settled there at war's end as hopeful planters, businessmen, or professionals.

The most numerous Republicans in the South were the black freedmen, most of whom had no previous experience in politics and tried, therefore, to build institutions through which they could learn to exercise their power. In several states, African-American voters held their own conventions to chart their future course. One such "colored convention," as Southern whites called it, assembled in Alabama in 1867 and announced: "We claim exactly the same rights, privileges and immunities as are enjoyed by white men—we ask nothing more and will be content with nothing less." Black churches also helped give unity and political self-confidence to the former slaves. After emancipation, most blacks withdrew from the white churches they had been compelled to attend on the plantations and formed their own—institutions based on the elaborate religious practices they had developed (occasionally surreptitiously) under slavery.

African-Americans played a significant role in the politics of the Reconstruction South. They served as delegates to the constitutional conventions. They held public offices of practically every kind. Between 1869 and 1901, twenty blacks served in the United States House of Representatives, two in the Senate. They served, too, in state legislatures and in various other state offices. Southern whites complained loudly (both at the time and for generations to come) about "Negro rule" during Reconstruction, but no such thing ever actually existed in any of the states. No black man was ever elected governor of a Southern state (although P. B. S. Pinchback, the African-American lieutenant governor of Louisiana, was acting governor briefly). Blacks never controlled any of the state legislatures (although African-Americans did once win a majority of seats in South Carolina's lower house). In the South as a whole, the percentage of black officeholders was far lower than the percentage of blacks in the population.

Expanding Budgets and Services

The record of the Reconstruction governments was mixed. Critics at the time and since have denounced them for corruption and financial extravagance, and there is some truth to both charges. Officeholders in many states enriched themselves through graft and other illicit activities. State budgets expanded to hitherto unknown totals, and state debts soared to previously undreamed-of heights. In South Carolina, for example, the public debt increased from $7 million to $29 million in eight years.

The corruption in the South, real as it was, was hardly unique to the

Reconstruction governments. Corruption was at least as rampant in the Northern states. The end of Reconstruction, moreover, did not end corruption in Southern state governments. In many states, in fact, corruption grew worse. And the state expenditures of the Reconstruction years were huge only in comparison with the meager budgets of the antebellum era. They represented an effort to provide the South with desperately needed services that antebellum governments had never offered: public education, public works programs, poor relief, and other costly new commitments. There were, to be sure, graft and extravagance in Reconstruction governments; there were also positive and permanent accomplishments.

Perhaps the most important of those accomplishments was a dramatic improvement in Southern education—an improvement that benefited both whites and blacks. In the first years of Reconstruction, much of the impetus for educational reform in the South came from outside groups—from the Freedmen's Bureau, from Northern private philanthropic organizations, from many Northern white women who traveled to the South to teach in freedmen's schools—and from African-Americans themselves. Over the opposition of many Southern whites, who feared that education would give blacks "false notions of equality," these reformers established a large network of schools for former slaves—4,000 schools by 1870, staffed by 9,000 teachers (half of them black), teaching 200,000 students (about 12 percent of the total school-age population of the freedmen). In the 1870s, Reconstruction governments began to build a comprehensive public school system in the South. By 1876, more than half of all white children and about 40 percent of all black children were attending schools in the South. Several black "academies," offering more advanced education, also began operating. Gradually, these academies grew into an important network of black colleges and universities.

Landownership

The most ambitious goal of the Freedmen's Bureau, and of some Republican Radicals in Congress, was to make Reconstruction the vehicle for a fundamental reform of landownership in the South. The effort failed. In the last years of the war and the first years of Reconstruction, the Freedmen's Bureau did oversee the redistribution of substantial amounts of land to freedmen in a few areas. By June 1865, the bureau had settled nearly 10,000 black families on their own land—most of it drawn from abandoned plantations. By the end of that year, however, the experiment was already collapsing. Southern plantation owners were returning and demanding the

AFTER SLAVERY Although many freed slaves remained agricultural laborers after Emancipation, a considerable number moved off the land in search of new occupations and new homes. For many, that meant living for some time without stable employment or a permanent home. This photograph from the late 1860s shows a group of former slaves at a county almshouse in the South.

restoration of their property, and President Johnson was supporting their demands. Despite the resistance of the Freedmen's Bureau, most of the confiscated land was eventually returned to the original white owners. Congress, moreover, never had much stomach for the idea of land redistribution. Very few Northern Republicans believed that the federal government had the right to confiscate property. Even so, the distribution of landownership in the South changed considerably in the postwar years. Among whites, there was a striking decline in landownership, from 80 percent before the war to 67 percent by the end of Reconstruction. Some whites lost their land because of unpaid debt or increased taxes; some left the marginal lands they had owned to move to more fertile areas, where they rented. Among blacks, during the same period, the proportion who owned land rose from virtually none to more than 20 percent.

Still, most blacks, and a growing minority of whites, did not own their own land during Reconstruction; and some who acquired land in the 1860s had lost it by the 1890s. Instead, they worked for others in one form or another. Many black agricultural laborers—perhaps 25 percent of the total—simply worked for wages. Most, however, became tenants of white landowners—that is, they worked their own plots of land and paid their landlords either a fixed rent or a share of their crop (hence the term "sharecropping"). The new system represented a repudiation by blacks of the gang-labor system of the antebellum plantation, in which slaves had lived and worked together under the direction of a master. As tenants and sharecroppers, blacks enjoyed at least a physical independence from their landlords and had the sense of working their own land, even if in most cases they could never hope to buy it. But tenantry also benefited landlords in some ways, relieving them of the cost of purchasing slaves and of any responsibility for the physical well-being of their workers.

Incomes and Credit

In some respects, the postwar years were a period of remarkable economic progress for blacks. If the material benefits they had received under slavery are calculated as income, then prewar blacks had earned about a 22 percent share of the profits of the plantation system. By the end of Reconstruction, they were earning 56 percent. Measured another way, the per capita income of blacks rose 46 percent between 1857 and 1879, while the per capita income of whites declined 35 percent. This represented one of the most significant redistributions of income in American history.

But these figures are somewhat misleading. For one thing, while the black share of profits was increasing, the total profits of Southern agriculture were declining—a result of the dislocations of the war and a reduction in the world market for cotton. For another thing, while blacks were earning a greater return on their labor than they had under slavery, they were working less. Women and children were less likely to labor in the fields than in the past. Adult men tended to work shorter days. In all, the black labor force worked about one-third fewer hours during Reconstruction than it had been compelled to do under slavery—a reduction that brought the working schedule of blacks roughly into accord with that of white farm laborers. Nor did the income redistribution of the postwar years lift many blacks out of poverty. Black per capita income rose from about one-quarter of white per capita income to about one-half in the first few years after the war. After this initial increase, it rose hardly at all.

For blacks and poor whites alike, whatever gains there might have been as a result of land and income redistribution were often overshadowed by the ravages of the crop lien system. Few of the traditional institutions of credit in the South—the "factors" and banks—returned after the war. In their stead emerged a new system of credit, centered in large part on local country stores—some of them owned by planters, others owned by independent merchants. Blacks and whites, landowners and tenants—all depended on these stores for such necessities as food, clothing, seed, and farm implements. And since farmers do not have the same steady cash flow as other workers, customers usually had to rely on credit from these merchants in order to purchase what they needed. Most local stores had no competition (and went to great lengths to ensure that things stayed that way). As a result, they were able to set interest rates as high as 50 or 60 percent. Farmers had to give the merchants a lien (or claim) on their crops as collateral for the loans (thus the term "crop-lien system," generally used to describe Southern farming in this period). If a farmer suffered a few bad years in a row, as often happened, he could become trapped in a cycle of debt from which he could never escape.

This burdensome credit system had a number of effects on the region, almost all of them unhealthy. One was that some blacks who had acquired land during the early years of Reconstruction gradually lost it as they fell into debt. So, to a lesser extent, did white small landowners. Another was that Southern farmers became almost wholly dependent on cash crops—and most of all on cotton—because only such marketable commodities seemed to offer any possibility of escape from debt. Thus Southern agriculture, never sufficiently diversified even in the best of times, became more one-dimensional than ever. The relentless planting of cotton, moreover, was contributing to an exhaustion of the soil. The crop-lien system, in other words, was not only helping to impoverish small farmers; it was also contributing to a general decline in the Southern agricultural economy.

The African-American Family in Freedom

One of the most striking features of the black response to Reconstruction was the effort to build or rebuild family structures and to protect them from the interference they had experienced under slavery. A major reason for the rapid departure of so many blacks from plantations was the desire to find lost relatives and reunite families. Thousands of blacks wandered through the South looking for husbands, wives, children, or other relatives from whom they had been separated. Former slaves rushed to have their marriages, previously without legal standing, sanctified by church and law. Black families resisted living in the former slave quarters and moved instead to small cabins scattered widely across the countryside, where they could enjoy at least some privacy.

Within the black family, the definition of male and female roles quickly came to resemble that within white families. Many women and children ceased working in the fields. Such work, they believed, was a badge of slavery. Instead, many women restricted themselves largely to domestic tasks— cooking, cleaning, gardening, raising children, attending to the needs of their husbands. Still, economic necessity often compelled black women to engage in income-producing activities: working as domestic servants, taking in laundry, or helping their husbands in the field. By the end of Reconstruction, half of all black women over the age of sixteen were working for wages. And unlike white working women, most black female income earners were married.

THE GRANT ADMINISTRATION

Exhausted by the political turmoil of the Johnson administration, American voters in 1868 yearned for a strong, stable figure to guide them through the troubled years of Reconstruction. They did not find one. Instead, they turned trustingly to General Ulysses S. Grant, the hero of the war and, by 1868, a revered national idol. Grant was a disastrous president. During his two terms in office, he faced problems that would have taxed the abilities of a master of statecraft. Grant, however, was a dull and unimaginative man with few political skills and little vision.

The Soldier President

Grant could have had the nomination of either party in 1868. But believing that Republican Reconstruction policies were more attuned to public opinion than the Democratic alternatives, he accepted the Republican nomination. The Democrats nominated former governor Horatio Seymour of New York. The campaign was a bitter one, and Grant's triumph was surprisingly modest. He carried twenty-six states, Seymour eight. But Grant's popular majority was a scant 310,000 votes, a result of some 500,000 black votes in the reconstructed states of the South.

Grant entered the White House with no political experience of any kind, and his performance in office was clumsy and ineffectual from the start. Except for Hamilton Fish, whom Grant appointed secretary of state and who served for eight years with great distinction, most members of the cabinet were as dull and inept as the president. Grant relied chiefly, and increasingly, on the machine leaders in the party—the group most ardently devoted to the spoils system.

Grant used the spoils system even more blatantly than most of his predecessors. In doing so, he provoked the opposition of Senator Charles Sumner and other Republican leaders, who joined with reformers to agitate for a new civil-service system to limit the president's appointive powers. Nothing came of their efforts. Grant soon attracted the hostility of other Republicans as well. Many Northerners were growing disillusioned with Reconstruction. Disgusted by stories of corruption, extravagance, and incompetence in the South, they opposed Grant's continuing support of Radical programs there. Some Republicans suspected, too, that there was also corruption in the Grant administration itself. Still others criticized Grant because he did not support a tariff reduction.

By the end of Grant's first term, therefore, members of a substantial faction of the party—who referred to themselves as Liberal Republicans—had come to oppose what they called "Grantism." In 1872, hoping to prevent Grant's reelection, they bolted the party and nominated their own presidential candidate: Horace Greeley, veteran editor and publisher of the New York *Tribune*. The Democrats, somewhat reluctantly, named Greeley their candidate as well, hoping that the alliance with the Liberals would enable them to defeat Grant. But the effort was in vain. Grant won a substantial victory, polling 286 electoral votes and 3,597,000 popular votes to Greeley's 66 and 2,834,000. Greeley had carried only two Southern and four border states. Three weeks later, apparently crushed by his defeat, Greeley died.

The Grant Scandals

During the 1872 campaign, the first of a series of political scandals came to light that would plague Grant and the Republicans for the next eight years. It involved the French-owned Crédit Mobilier construction company, which had helped build the Union Pacific Railroad. The heads of Crédit Mobilier had used their positions as Union Pacific stockholders to steer large and fraudulent contracts to the construction company, thus bilking the Union Pacific (and the federal government, which provided large subsidies to the railroad) of millions. To prevent investigations, the directors had transferred some Crédit Mobilier stock to key members of Congress. But in 1872, Congress did conduct an investigation, which revealed that some highly placed Republicans—including Schuyler Colfax, now Grant's vice president—had accepted stock.

One dreary episode followed another in Grant's second term. Benjamin H. Bristow, Grant's third Treasury secretary, discovered that some of his officials and a group of distillers operating as a "whiskey ring" were cheating the government out of taxes by filing false reports. Then a House investigation revealed that William W. Belknap, secretary of war, had accepted bribes to retain an Indian-post trader in office (the so-called Indian ring). Other, lesser scandals added to the growing impression that "Grantism" had brought rampant corruption to government.

The Greenback Question

Compounding Grant's, and the nation's, problems was the financial crisis known as the Panic of 1873. It began with the failure of a leading investment banking firm, Jay Cooke and Company, which had invested too heavily in postwar railroad building. There had been panics before—in 1819, 1837, and 1857—but this was the worst one yet. The depression it produced lasted four years.

Debtors now pressured the government to inflate the value of their currency, which would have made it easier for them to pay their debts. More specifically, they urged the government to redeem its war bonds with greenbacks, paper currency of the sort printed during the Civil War, which would increase the amount of money in circulation. But Grant and most Republicans wanted a "sound" currency—based solidly on gold reserves—which would favor the interests of banks and other creditors.

The greenback question would not go away. There was, for one thing, the approximately $356 million in paper currency issued during the Civil War that was still in circulation. And in 1873, when the Supreme Court ruled in *Knox* v. *Lee* that greenbacks were legal, the Treasury issued more in response to the panic. The following year, Congress voted to raise the total further. But Grant, under pressure from Eastern financial interests, vetoed the measure.

In 1875, Republican leaders in Congress, in an effort to crush the greenback movement for good, passed the Specie Resumption Act. This law provided that after January 1, 1879, the greenback dollars, whose value constantly fluctuated, would be redeemed by the government and replaced with new certificates, firmly pegged to the price of gold. The law satisfied creditors, who had worried that debts would be repaid in debased paper currency. But "resumption" did little for debtors, because the gold-based money supply was never able to expand as much as they wanted.

In 1875, the "greenbackers," as the inflationists were called, formed their own political organization: the National Greenback party. Active in the next three presidential elections, it failed to gain widespread support. But it did keep the money issue alive. And in the 1880s, the greenback forces began to merge with another, more powerful group of currency reformers—those who favored silver as the basis of currency—to help produce a political movement that would ultimately attain enormous strength. The question of the proper composition of the currency was to remain one of the most controversial and enduring issues in late-nineteenth-century American politics.

Republican Diplomacy

The Johnson and Grant administrations achieved their greatest success in foreign affairs. The accomplishments were the work not of the presidents themselves, who displayed little aptitude for diplomacy, but of two outstanding secretaries of state: William H. Seward, who had served Lincoln and who remained in office until 1869; and Hamilton Fish, who served throughout the two terms of the Grant administration.

An ardent expansionist and advocate of a vigorous foreign policy, Seward acted with as much daring as the demands of Reconstruction politics and the Republican hatred of President Johnson would permit. Seward agreed to a Russian offer to sell Alaska to the United States for $7.2 million. Only with great difficulty was he able to persuade Congress to authorize the purchase, and he faced criticism from many who considered Alaska a useless frozen wasteland and derided it as "Seward's Folly" or "Seward's icebox." But Seward knew that Alaska was an important fishing center and a potential source of valuable resources such as gold. In 1867, Seward also engineered the American annexation of the tiny Midway Islands west of Hawaii.

In contrast with its often shambling course in domestic politics, the diplomatic performance of the Grant administration under Hamilton Fish was generally decisive and firm. Fish's first major challenge was resolving a burning controversy with England. Many Americans believed that the British government had violated the neutrality laws during the Civil War by permitting English shipyards to build ships (among them the *Alabama*) for the Confederacy. American demands that England pay for the damage these vessels had caused became known as the "Alabama claims."

Seward had tried to settle the Alabama claims through the Johnson-Clarendon Convention of 1869, which would have submitted the matter to arbitration. But the Senate rejected it because it contained no British apology. In 1871, Fish succeeded in forging a new agreement, the Treaty of Washington, which provided for international arbitration and in which Britain expressed regret for the escape of the *Alabama* from England.

THE ABANDONMENT OF RECONSTRUCTION

As the North grew increasingly preoccupied with its own political and economic problems, interest in Reconstruction began to wane. The Grant administration continued to protect Republican governments in the South, but less because of any interest in ensuring the position of freedmen than because of a desire to prevent the reemergence of a strong Democratic party in the region. But even the presence of federal troops was not enough to prevent white Southerners from overturning the Reconstruction regimes. By the time Grant left office, Democrats had taken back (or, as white Southerners liked to put it, "redeemed") seven of the governments of the former Confederate states.

For three other states—South Carolina, Louisiana, and Florida—the end of Reconstruction had to wait for the withdrawal of the last federal troops in 1877, a withdrawal that was the result of a long process of political bargaining and compromise at the national level.

The Southern States "Redeemed"

In the states where whites constituted a majority—the states of the upper South—overthrowing Republican control was relatively simple. By 1872, all but a handful of Southern whites had regained suffrage. Now a clear majority, they needed only to organize and elect their candidates.

In other states, where blacks were a majority or the populations of the two races were almost equal, whites used intimidation and violence to undermine the Reconstruction regimes. Secret societies—the Ku Klux Klan, the Knights of the White Camellia, and others—used terrorism to frighten or physically bar blacks from voting or otherwise exercising citizenship. Paramilitary organizations—the Red Shirts and White Leagues—armed themselves to "police" elections and worked to force all white males to join the Democratic party and to exclude all blacks from meaningful political activity. Strongest of all, however, was the simple weapon of economic pressure. Some planters refused to rent land to Republican blacks; storekeepers refused to extend them credit; employers refused to give them work.

In the meantime, Southern blacks were losing the support of many of their former advocates in the North. After the adoption of the Fifteenth Amendment in 1870, some reformers convinced themselves that their long campaign in behalf of black people was now over; that with the vote, blacks ought to be able to take care of themselves. Former Radical leaders such as Charles Sumner and Horace Greeley now began calling themselves Liberals, cooperating with the Democrats, and at times outdoing even the Democrats in denouncing what they viewed as black-and-carpetbag misgovernment. Within the South itself, many white Republicans joined the Liberals and moved into the Democratic party.

The Panic of 1873 further undermined support for Reconstruction. In the congressional elections of 1874, the Democrats won control of the House of Representatives for the first time since 1861. Grant took note of the changing temper of the North and stopped using military force to prop up the Republican regimes that were still standing in the South.

By the end of 1876, only three states were left in the hands of the Republicans—South Carolina, Louisiana, and Florida. In the state elections that year, Democrats (after using terrorist tactics) claimed victory in all three. But the Republicans claimed victory as well and were able to remain in office because of the presence of federal troops. If the troops were to be withdrawn, the last of the Republican regimes would fall.

The Compromise of 1877

Grant had hoped to run for another term in 1876, but most Republican leaders—shaken by recent Democratic successes, afraid of the scandals with which Grant was associated, and worried about the president's failing health—resisted. Instead, they sought a candidate not associated with the problems of the Grant years, one who might entice Liberals back and unite the party again. They settled on Rutherford B. Hayes, a former Union army officer and congressman, three times governor of Ohio, and a champion of civil-service reform. The Democrats united behind Samuel J. Tilden, the reform governor of New York, who had been instrumental in overthrowing the corrupt Tweed Ring of New York City's Tammany Hall.

Although the campaign was a bitter one, there were few differences of principle between the candidates, both of whom were conservatives committed to moderate reform. The November election produced an apparent Democratic victory. Tilden carried the South and several large Northern states, and his popular margin over Hayes was nearly 300,000 votes. But disputed returns from Louisiana, South Carolina, Florida, and Oregon, whose total electoral vote was 20, threw the election in doubt. Tilden had undisputed claim to 184 electoral votes, only one short of the majority. But Hayes could still win if he managed to receive all 20 disputed votes.

The Constitution had established no method to determine the validity of disputed returns. It was clear that the decision lay with Congress, but it was not clear with which house or through what method. (The Senate was Republican, and the House was Democratic.) Members of each party naturally supported a solution that would yield them the victory.

Finally, late in January 1877, Congress tried to break the deadlock by creating a special electoral commission to judge the disputed votes. The commission was to be composed of five senators, five representatives, and five justices of the Supreme Court. The congressional delegation would consist of five Republicans and five Democrats. The Court delegation would include two Republicans, two Democrats, and the only independent, Justice David Davis. But when the Illinois legislature elected Davis to the United States Senate, the justice resigned from the commission. His seat went instead to a Republican justice. The commission voted along straight party lines, 8 to 7, awarding every disputed vote to Hayes. Congress accepted the verdict on March 2. Two days later, Hayes was inaugurated.

Behind the resolution of the deadlock, however, lay a series of elaborate compromises among leaders of both parties. When a Democratic filibuster threatened to derail the commission's report, Republican Senate leaders met secretly with Southern Democratic leaders to work out terms by which the Democrats would support Hayes. According to traditional accounts, Republicans and Southern Democrats met at Washington's Wormley Hotel. In return for a Republican pledge that Hayes would withdraw the last federal troops from the South, thus permitting the overthrow of the last Republican governments there, the Southerners agreed to abandon the filibuster.

Actually, the story behind the "Compromise of 1877" is somewhat more complex. Hayes was already on record as favoring withdrawal of the troops. The real agreement, the one that won the Southern Democrats over, was reached before the Wormley meeting. As the price of their cooperation, the Southern Democrats (among them some former Whigs) exacted several pledges from the Republicans: the appointment of at least one Southerner to the Hayes cabinet, control of federal patronage in their areas, generous internal improvements, federal aid for the Texas and Pacific Railroad, and withdrawal of the troops. Many powerful Southern Democrats supported industrializing the region. They believed that Republican programs of federal support for business would aid their region more than the states' rights policies of the Democrats.

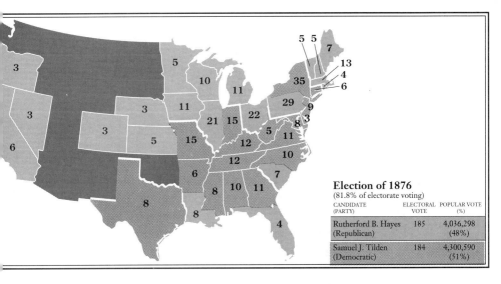

Election of 1876
(81.8% of electorate voting)

CANDIDATE (PARTY)	ELECTORAL VOTE	POPULAR VOTE (%)
Rutherford B. Hayes (Republican)	185	4,036,298 (48%)
Samuel J. Tilden (Democratic)	184	4,300,590 (51%)

In his inaugural address, Hayes announced that the South's most pressing need was the restoration of "wise, honest, and peaceful local self-government"—a signal that he planned to withdraw the troops and let white Democrats take over the state governments. The statement, and Hayes's subsequent actions, supported the widespread charges that he was paying off the South for acquiescing in his election and strengthened those who referred to him as "His Fraudulency." But the election had already created such bitterness that there was probably nothing Hayes could have done to mollify his critics, not even his promise to serve only one term.

The president and his party hoped to build up a "new Republican" organization in the South drawn from Whiggish conservative white groups and committed to modest support for black rights. But all such efforts failed. Although many white Southern leaders sympathized with Republican economic policies, resentment of Reconstruction was so deep that supporting the party was politically impossible. The "solid" Democratic South, which would survive until the mid-twentieth century, was taking shape. And the withdrawal of federal troops was a signal that the national government was giving up its attempt to control Southern politics and to improve the lot of blacks in Southern society.

The Legacy of Reconstruction

Reconstruction was not a complete failure in its effort to help African-Americans. There was a significant redistribution of income, from which blacks benefited. There was a more limited but not unimportant redistribution of landownership, which enabled some former slaves to acquire property. There was both a relative and an absolute improvement in the economic circumstances of most African-Americans.

Nor was Reconstruction as disastrous an experience for Southern whites as most believed at the time. The region had emerged from a prolonged and bloody war defeated and devastated; and yet within little more than a decade, the white South had regained control of its own institutions and, to a great extent, restored its traditional ruling class to power. Former Confederate leaders received no severe punishments. The federal government imposed no drastic economic reforms on the region and indeed few lasting political changes of any kind other than the abolition of slavery. Not many conquered peoples fare as well.

Yet for all that, Americans of the twentieth century cannot help but look back on Reconstruction as a tragic era. For in those years the United States failed in its first serious effort to resolve its oldest and deepest social problem—the problem of race. What was more, the experience so disappointed, disillusioned, and embittered white Americans that it would be nearly a century before they would try again in any serious way.

Why did this great assault on racial injustice end so badly? In part, it was because of the weaknesses and errors of the people who directed it. But in greater part, it was because attempts to produce solutions ran up against conservative obstacles so deeply embedded in the nation's life that they could not be dislodged. Veneration of the Constitution sharply limited the willingness of national leaders to infringe on the rights of states and individuals. A profound respect for private property and free enterprise prevented any real assault on economic privilege in the South. Above all, perhaps, a pervasive belief among many of even the most liberal whites that the black race was inherently inferior served as an obstacle to equality. Given the context within which Americans of the 1860s and 1870s were working, what is surprising, perhaps, is not that Reconstruction did so little but that it accomplished even as much as it did.

Given the odds confronting them, therefore, African-Americans had reason for pride in the limited gains they were able to make during Reconstruction. And future generations had reason for gratitude for two great charters of freedom—the Fourteenth and Fifteenth amendments to the Constitution—which, although largely ignored at the time, would one day serve as the basis for a "Second Reconstruction" that would renew the drive to bring freedom and equality to all Americans.

DEBATING THE PAST

Reconstruction

DEBATE OVER THE nature of Reconstruction has been unusually intense, not only among historians but among much of the larger public as well. Indeed, few issues in American history have raised such deep and enduring passions.

Beginning in the late nineteenth century and continuing well into the twentieth, a relatively uniform and highly critical view of Reconstruction prevailed among historians—a reflection of a broad consensus among white Americans about the inferiority of blacks and of a yearning in both the North and the South for sectional reconciliation. William A. Dunning's *Reconstruction, Political and Economic* (1907) was the principal scholarly expression of this prevailing view. Dunning portrayed Reconstruction as a corrupt and oppressive outrage imposed on a prostrate South by a vindictive group of Northern Republican radicals. Unscrupulous carpetbaggers flooded the South and plundered the region. Ignorant African-Americans were thrust into political offices for which they were unfit. Reconstruction governments were awash in corruption and compiled enormous levels of debt. The Dunning interpretation dominated several generations of historical scholarship. It also helped shape such popular images of Reconstruction as those in the novel and film *Gone with the Wind*.

Among historians, at least, the Dunning interpretation gradually lost credibility in the face of a series of challenges. W. E. B. Du Bois, the great African-American scholar, offered one of the first alternative views in *Black Reconstruction* (1935). To Du Bois, Reconstruction was an effort by freed blacks (and their white allies) to create a more democratic society in the

(continued on next page)

South, and it was responsible for many valuable social innovations. In the early 1960s, John Hope Franklin and Kenneth Stampp, building on a generation of work by other scholars, published new histories of Reconstruction that replaced, and radically revised, the Dunning interpretation. Reconstruction, they argued, was a genuine, if flawed, effort to solve the problem of race in the South. The Reconstruction governments were not perfect, but they were bold experiments in interracial politics. Congressional radicals were not saints, but they were genuinely concerned with protecting the rights of former slaves. Reconstruction had brought important, if temporary, progress to the South and had created no more corruption there than governments were creating in the North at the same time. What was tragic about Reconstruction, the revisionists claimed, was not what it did to Southern whites but what it failed to do for Southern blacks. It was, in the end, too weak and too short-lived to guarantee African-Americans genuine equality.

In more recent years, some historians have begun to question the assessment of the first revisionists that, in the end, Reconstruction accomplished relatively little. Leon Litwack argued in *Been in the Storm So Long* (1979) that former slaves used the protections Reconstruction offered them to carve out a certain level of independence for themselves within southern society: strengthening churches, reuniting families, and resisting the efforts of white planters to revive the gang labor system.

Eric Foner's *Reconstruction: America's Unfinished Revolution* (1988) also emphasized how far African-Americans moved toward freedom and independence in a short time, how much of lasting value they were able to accomplish despite imposing obstacles, and how important they were in shaping the execution of Reconstruction policies. Reconstruction, he argues, "can only be judged a failure" as an effort to secure "blacks' rights as citizens and free laborers." But it "closed off even more oppressive alternatives. . . . The post-Reconstruction labor system embodied neither a return to the closely supervised gang labor of antebellum days, nor the complete dispossession and immobilization of the black labor force and coercive apprenticeship systems envisioned by white Southerners in 1865 and 1866. Nor were blacks, as in twentieth-century South Africa, barred from citizenship, herded into labor reserves, or prohibited by law from moving from one part of the country to another. . . . The doors of economic opportunity that had opened could never be completely closed."

CHAPTER SIXTEEN

The New South and the Far West

The South in Transition ∼ *The Conquest of the Far West*
The Dispersal of the Tribes ∼ *The Rise and Decline of the Western Farmer*

M UCH OF THE United States in the years following Reconstruction was preoccupied with the expansion and development of an already advanced urban-industrial society. In two regions of America, however, the experience was quite different. In the South, the first region of the country to have been settled by English-speaking Europeans, and in the Far West, the last such region, the late nineteenth century was a time of new beginnings and important changes. For many residents of both regions, it was also a period of decline relative to the rest of the nation—a decline that would ultimately produce major social and political upheavals.

THE SOUTH IN TRANSITION

The Compromise of 1877—the agreement between Southern Democrats and Northern Republicans that helped settle the disputed election of 1876—was supposed to be the first step toward developing a stable, permanent Republican party in the South. In that respect, at least, it failed. In the years following the end of Reconstruction, white Southerners established the Democratic party as the only viable political organization for the region's whites.

By the end of 1877—after the last withdrawal of federal troops—every Southern state government had been "redeemed." That is, political power had been restored to white Democrats. Many white Southerners rejoiced at the restoration of what they liked to call "home rule." But in reality, political power in the region was soon more restricted than at any time since the Civil War. Once again, the South fell under the control of a powerful, conservative oligarchy, whose members were known variously as the "Redeemers" or the "Bourbons."

The "Redeemers"

In a few places, this post-Reconstruction ruling class was much the same as the ruling class of the antebellum period. In Alabama, for example, the old planter elite—despite challenges from new merchant and industrial forces—retained much of its former power and continued largely to dominate the state for decades. In most areas, however, the Redeemers constituted a genuinely new class. Merchants, industrialists, railroad developers, financiers—some of them former planters, some of them Northern immigrants who had become absorbed into the region's life, some of them ambitious, upwardly mobile white Southerners from the region's lower social tiers—combined a commitment to "home rule" and social conservatism with a commitment to economic development.

Whatever their differences, the various Bourbon governments of the New South behaved in many respects quite similarly. Conservatives had complained that the Reconstruction governments fostered widespread corruption, but the Redeemer regimes were, if anything, even more awash in fraud and waste. (In this, they were little different from governments in every region of the country.) Virtually all the new Democratic regimes, moreover, lowered taxes, reduced spending, and drastically diminished state services—including many of the most valuable accomplishments of Reconstruction. In one state after another, for example, state support for public school systems was reduced or eliminated.

By the late 1870s, dissenting groups were challenging the Bourbons: protesting the cuts in services and denouncing the commitment of the Redeemer governments to paying off the prewar and Reconstruction debts in full, at the original (usually high) rates of interest. There were demands as well for greenbacks, debt relief, and other economic reforms. (A few of the independent movements included significant numbers of blacks in their ranks, but all consisted primarily of lower-income whites.) By the mid-1880s, however, conservative Southerners—largely by exploiting racial prejudice—had effectively destroyed most of the dissenting movements.

Industrialization and "the New South"

Some Southern leaders in the post-Reconstruction era hoped to see their region become the home of a vigorous industrial economy. The South had lost the war, many argued, because its economy had been unable to compete with the modernized manufacturing capacity of the North. Now the region must "out-Yankee the Yankees" and build a "New South." Henry Grady, editor of the *Atlanta Constitution*, and other prominent spokesmen for a New South seldom challenged white supremacy. But they did advocate other important changes in Southern values. Above all, they promoted the virtues of thrift, industry, and progress—the same qualities that prewar Southerners had so often denounced in Northern society.

Partly as a result of their efforts, Southern industry expanded significantly in the years after Reconstruction and became a more important part of the region's economy than ever before. Most visible was the growth in textile manufacturing, which increased ninefold in the last twenty years of the century. In the past, Southern cotton had usually been shipped out of the region to manufacturers in the North or in Europe. Now textile factories appeared in the South itself—drawn to the region from New England by the abundance of water power, the ready supply of cheap labor, the low taxes, and the accommodating conservative governments. The tobacco processing industry, similarly, established an important foothold in the region, largely through the work of James B. Duke of North Carolina, whose American Tobacco Company established for a time a virtual monopoly over the processing of raw tobacco into marketable materials. In the lower South, and particularly in Birmingham, Alabama, the iron (and, later, steel) industry grew rapidly. By 1890, the Southern iron and steel industry represented nearly a fifth of the nation's total capacity.

Railroad development increased substantially in the post-Reconstruction years—at a rate far greater than that of the nation at large. Between 1880 and 1890, trackage in the South more than doubled. And the South took a giant step toward integrating its transportation system with that of the rest of the country when, in 1886, it changed the gauge (width) of its trackage to correspond with the standards of the North. No longer would it be necessary for cargoes heading into the South to be transferred from one train to another at the borders of the region.

Yet Southern industry developed within strict limits, and its effects on the region were never even remotely comparable to the effects of industrialization on the North. The Southern share of national manufacturing doubled in the last twenty years of the century, to 10 percent of the total. But that percentage was the same share the South had claimed in 1860; the region had, in other words, done no more than regain what it had lost during the war and its aftermath. The region's per capita income increased 21 percent in the same period. But at the end of the century, average income in the South was only 40 percent of that in the North; in 1860 it had been more than 60 percent. And even in those areas where development had been most rapid—textiles, iron, railroads—much of the capital had come from the North.

The growth of industry in the South required that the region recruit a substantial industrial work force for the first time. From the beginning, a high percentage of the factory workers (and an especially high percentage of textile workers) were women. Heavy male casualties in the Civil War had helped create a large population of unmarried women who desperately needed employment. Factories also hired entire families, many of whom were moving into towns from failed farms. Hours were long (often as much as twelve hours a day) and wages were far below the Northern equivalent; indeed, one of the greatest attractions of the South to industrialists was that employers were able to pay workers there as little as one-half what Northern workers received.

Life in most mill towns was rigidly controlled by the owners and managers of the factories. They rigorously suppressed attempts at protest or union organization. Company stores sold goods to workers at inflated prices and issued credit at exorbitant rates, and mill owners ensured that no competitors were able to establish themselves in the community. At the same time, however, the conditions of the mill town helped create a strong sense of community and solidarity among workers (even though they seldom translated such feelings into militancy).

Some industries, such as textiles, offered virtually no opportunities to black workers. Others—tobacco, iron, and lumber, for example—did provide blacks with some employment, usually the most menial and lowest-paid positions. Some mill towns, therefore, were places where black and white cultures came into close contact.

At times, industrialization proceeded on the basis of no wage-paying employment at all. Through the "convict-lease" system, Southern states leased gangs of convicted criminals to private interests as a cheap labor supply. The system exposed the convicts to brutal and at times fatal mistreatment. It paid them nothing (the leasing fees went to the states, not the workers). And it denied employment in railroad construction and other projects to the free labor force.

The Crop-Lien System

Despite significant growth in Southern industry, the region remained primarily agricultural. The most important economic reality in the post-Reconstruction South, therefore, was the impoverished state of agriculture. The 1870s and 1880s saw an acceleration of the process that had begun in the immediate postwar years: the imposition of systems of tenantry and debt peonage on much of the region; the reliance on a few cash crops rather than on a diversified agricultural system; and the increasing absentee ownership of valuable farmlands (many of them purchased by merchants and industrialists, who paid little attention to whether the land was being properly used). During Reconstruction, perhaps a third or more of the farmers in the South were tenants or sharecroppers; by 1900 the figure had increased to 70 percent.

At the center of the Southern agricultural system was the crop-lien system, which had emerged in the aftermath of the Civil War and had kept most small farmers (black and white) trapped in an endless cycle of debt. (See pp. 418–419.) Farmers who owned their own land often lost it as merchants seized it for payment of unpaid liens. Farmers who were already tenants or sharecroppers found themselves increasingly under the control of merchants and landlords, whom they had little hope of ever paying off completely.

The collapse of antebellum financial institutions and the increasing scarcity of banks and currency in the South meant that credit—always important to farmers, with their seasonal production—was very difficult to obtain. Control of credit often fell into the hands of "furnishing merchants": the owners of the local stores from which farmers bought their tools, seed, and other necessities. Few farmers ever had enough money to pay cash for what they needed, so they bought their supplies on credit, promising the merchant a share of their crop (or giving him a "lien" on it) when it was harvested.

Furnishing merchants (who were also often important landowners) seldom had competitors; indeed, they went to considerable lengths to ensure they retained a monopoly. So farmers had little choice but to pay the high prices and exorbitant interest the local merchants charged them. By the time farmers harvested their crops, they were often so deeply in debt that they had to turn over the entire harvest to the merchant. Even that was generally not enough. Thus year after year, their indebtedness grew.

The crop-lien system was one of several factors contributing to a social and economic transformation of the Southern back country, the piney woods and mountain regions where cotton and slavery had always been rare and where farmers lived ruggedly independent lives. Subsistence agriculture had long been the norm in these areas; but as indebtedness grew, many farmers now had to grow cash crops such as cotton, instead of the food crops they had traditionally cultivated, in order to make enough money to pay their debts. Opportunities for families to live largely self-sufficiently were declining; at the same time, opportunities for profiting within the market remained slim. The people of the back country would be among the most important constituents for the populist protests of the 1880s and 1890s.

The crop-lien system was particularly devastating to Southern blacks, few of whom owned their own land to begin with. Already dependent on landowners as tenants and sharecroppers, they were especially vulnerable to the economic tyranny of the furnishing merchant. These economic difficulties were compounded by social and legal discrimination, which in the post-Reconstruction era began to take new forms and to inspire new responses.

African-Americans and the New South

The "New South creed" was not the property of whites alone. Many African-Americans were attracted to the vision of progress and self-improvement as well. Some blacks succeeded in elevating themselves into a distinct middle class—one economically inferior to the white middle class, but nevertheless significant. A cardinal tenet of this rising group of blacks was that education was vital to the future of their race. With the support of Northern missionary societies and, to a far lesser extent, a few Southern state governments, they expanded the network of black colleges and institutes that had taken root during Reconstruction into an important educational system.

The chief spokesman for this commitment to education, and ultimately the major spokesman for his race as a whole, was Booker T. Washington, founder and president of the Tuskegee Institute in Alabama. Born into slavery, Washington had used his education (at Virginia's famous Hampton Institute) to pull himself out of poverty. He urged other blacks to follow the same road to self-improvement.

Washington's message was both cautious and hopeful. African-Americans should attend school, learn skills, and establish a solid footing in agriculture and the trades. Industrial, not classical, education should be their goal. Blacks should, moreover, refine their speech, improve their dress, and adopt habits of thrift and personal cleanliness; they should, in short, adopt the standards of the white middle class. Only thus, he claimed, could they win the respect of the white population, the prerequisite for any larger social gains. In a famous speech in Georgia in 1895, Washington outlined a philosophy of race relations that became widely known as the Atlanta Compromise. Blacks should forgo agitating for political rights, he said, and concentrate on self-improvement and preparation for equality.

Washington offered a powerful challenge to those whites who strove to discourage blacks from acquiring an education or winning any economic gains. But his message was also an implicit promise that blacks would not challenge the system of segregation that whites were then in the process of erecting. "In all things that are purely social," he once said, "we can be separate as the fingers yet one as the hand in things that relate to mutual progress."

The Birth of Jim Crow

Few white Southerners had ever accepted the idea of racial equality. That the former slaves acquired any legal and political rights at all after emancipation was in large part the result of federal support. That support all but vanished after 1877. Federal troops withdrew. Congress lost interest. And the Supreme Court effectively stripped the Fourteenth and Fifteenth amendments of much of their significance. In the so-called civil-rights cases of 1883, the Court interpreted the Fourteenth Amendment narrowly, ruling that it prohibited state governments from discriminating against people because of race but did not restrict private organizations or individuals from doing so. Thus railroads, hotels, theaters, and the like could legally practice segregation.

Eventually, the Court also validated state legislation that discriminated against blacks. In *Plessy* v. *Ferguson* (1896), a case involving a Louisiana law that required separate seating arrangements for the races on railroads, the Court held that separate accommodations did not deprive blacks of equal rights if the accommodations were equal, a decision that survived for years as part of the legal basis of segregated schools. In *Cumming* v. *County Board of Education* (1899), the Court ruled that laws establishing separate schools for whites were valid even if they provided no comparable schools for blacks.

Even before these decisions, white Southerners were working to strengthen white supremacy and to separate the races to the greatest extent possible. One illustration of this movement from subordination to segregation is black voting rights. In some states, disfranchisement had begun almost as soon as Reconstruction ended. But in other areas, black voting continued for some time after Reconstruction—largely because conservative whites believed they could control the black electorate and use it to beat back the attempts of poor white farmers to take control of the Democratic party.

In the 1890s, however, franchise restrictions became much more rigid. During those years, some small white farmers began to demand complete black disenfranchisement—both because of racial prejudice and because they objected to the black vote's being used against them by the Bourbons. Many members of the conservative elite, at the same time, began to fear that poor whites might unite politically with poor blacks to challenge them. They too began to support further franchise restrictions.

In devising laws to disenfranchise black males (black females, like white women, had never voted), the Southern states had to find ways to evade the Fifteenth Amendment, which prohibited states from denying anyone the right to vote because of race. Two devices emerged before 1900 to accomplish this goal. One was the poll tax or some form of property qualification; few blacks were prosperous enough to meet such requirements. Another was the "literacy" or "understanding" test, which required that voters demonstrate an ability to read and to interpret passages from the Constitution. Even those African-Americans who could read found it hard to pass the difficult tests white officials gave them.

Such restrictions affected poor white voters as well as blacks. By the late 1890s, the black vote had decreased by 62 percent, the white vote by 26 percent. One result was that some states passed so-called grandfather laws, which permitted men who could not meet the literacy and property qualifications to be enfranchised if their ancestors had voted before Reconstruction began, thus barring the descendants of slaves from the polls while allowing poor whites access to them. In many areas, however, ruling elites were quite content to see poor whites, a potential source of opposition to their power, barred from voting.

The Supreme Court proved as compliant in ruling on the disfranchising laws as it was in dealing with the civil-rights cases. The Court eventually voided the grandfather laws, but it validated the literacy tests (in the 1898 case of *Williams* v. *Mississippi*) and displayed a general willingness to let the Southern states define their own suffrage standards as long as evasions of the Fifteenth Amendment were not too glaring.

Laws restricting the franchise and segregating schools were only part of a network of state statutes—known as the "Jim Crow laws" (after a popular cartoon character of the day)—that by the first years of the twentieth century had institutionalized an elaborate system of segregation reaching into almost every area of Southern life. Blacks and whites could not ride together in the same railroad cars, sit in the same waiting rooms, use the same washrooms, eat in the same restaurants, or sit in the same theaters. Blacks were denied access to parks, beaches, and picnic areas; they were barred from many hospitals. Much of the new legal structure did no more than confirm what had already been widespread social practice in the South since well before the end of Reconstruction. But the Jim Crow laws also stripped blacks of many of the modest social, economic, and political gains they had made in the more fluid atmosphere of the late nineteenth century. They served, too, as a means for whites to retain control of social relations between the races in the newly growing cities and towns of the South, where traditional patterns of deference and subjugation were more difficult to preserve than in the countryside. What had been maintained by custom in the rural South was to be maintained by law in the urban South.

More than legal efforts were involved in this process. The 1890s witnessed a dramatic increase in white violence against blacks, which (along with the Jim Crow laws) served to inhibit black agitation for equal rights. The worst such violence—lynching of blacks by white mobs, either because the victims were accused of crimes or because they seemed somehow to have violated their proper station—reached appalling levels. In the nation as a whole in the 1890s, there was an average of 187 lynchings each year, more than 80 percent of them in the South. The vast majority of victims were black.

Those involved in lynchings often saw their actions as a legitimate form of law enforcement; and indeed, some victims of lynchings had in fact committed crimes. But lynchings were also a means by which whites controlled the black population through terror and intimidation. Thus, some lynch mobs killed blacks whose only "crime" had been presumptuousness. Others chose as victims outsiders in the community, whose presence threatened to disturb the normal pattern of race relations. Whatever the circumstances, the victims of lynch mobs were denied the protection of the laws and the opportunity to prove their innocence.

The rise of lynching shocked the conscience of many white Americans in a way that other forms of racial injustice did not. Almost from the start there was a substantial antilynching movement. Ida B. Wells, a committed black journalist, launched what became an international antilynching crusade with a series of impassioned articles in 1892 after the lynching of three of her friends in Memphis, Tennessee, her home. The movement gradually gathered strength in the first years of the twentieth century, attracting substantial support from whites (particularly white women) in both the North and the South. Its goal was a federal antilynching law, which would

LYNCH MOB, 1893 White Southerners sometimes traveled many miles to watch a lynching, such as this one of a black man accused of killing a three-year-old white girl. More common than these large public lynchings, however, were less conspicuous vigilante murders by small groups of whites.

allow the national government to do what state and local governments in the South were unwilling to do: punish those responsible for lynchings.

But the substantial white opposition to lynchings in the South stood as an exception to the general white support for suppression of the black race. Indeed, just as in the antebellum period, the shared commitment to white supremacy helped dilute class animosities between the poorer whites and the Bourbon oligarchies. Economic issues tended to take a subordinate role to race in Southern politics, distracting people from the glaring social inequalities that afflicted blacks and whites alike. The commitment to white supremacy, in short, was a burden for poor whites as well as for blacks.

The Origins of African-American Protest

Not all African-Americans were content with Booker T. Washington's cautious approach to racial progress. By the turn of the century a powerful challenge was emerging—to the philosophy of Washington and, more important, to the entire structure of race relations. The chief spokesman for this new approach was W. E. B. Du Bois.

Du Bois, unlike Washington, had never known slavery. Born in Massachusetts, he was educated at Fisk University in Atlanta and at Harvard, where he became the first African-American to earn a Ph.D. He grew to maturity with a far more expansive view than Washington of the goals of his race and the responsibilities of white society to eliminate prejudice and injustice. In *The Souls of Black Folk* (1903), he launched an open attack on the philosophy of the Atlanta Compromise, accusing Washington of encouraging white efforts to impose segregation and of unnecessarily limiting the aspirations of his race. Rather than content themselves with education at the trade and agricultural schools, Du Bois argued, qualified African-Americans (what he and others called the "talented tenth") should accept nothing less than a full university education. They should aspire to the professions. They should, above all, fight for the immediate restoration of their civil rights, not simply wait for them to be granted as a reward for patient striving.

In 1905, Du Bois and a group of his supporters met at Niagara Falls in Canada and launched what became known as the Niagara Movement. Four years later, after a race riot in Springfield, Illinois, they joined with white progressives sympathetic to their cause to form the National Association for the Advancement of Colored People (NAACP). Whites held most of the offices; but Du Bois, its director of publicity and research, was the guiding spirit.

Within less than a decade, the NAACP began to win some important victories in the federal courts in its drive to achieve equal rights. In *Guinn v. United States* (1915), the Supreme Court supported the association's position that the grandfather clause in an Oklahoma law was unconstitutional. (The statute denied the vote to citizens whose ancestors had not been enfranchised in 1860.) In *Buchanan v. Worley* (1917), the Court struck down a Louisville, Kentucky, law requiring residential segregation. The NAACP was not a radical, or even an egalitarian, organization. It relied, rather, on the efforts of the most intelligent and educated members of the black race, the "talented tenth" as Du Bois called them. Ultimately, its members believed, such efforts would benefit all blacks. By creating a trained elite, blacks would, in effect, be creating a leadership group capable of fighting for the rights of the race as a whole.

THE CONQUEST OF THE FAR WEST

By the time of the Civil War, the Western edge of English-speaking settlement in North America had already moved well beyond what it had been even twenty years before. White civilization had crossed the Mississippi and established a permanent foothold in the next tier of states—Minnesota, Iowa, Missouri, and Arkansas—as well as in the eastern parts of Nebraska, Kansas, and Texas. There had been a white settlement in Oregon since the early 1860s. And largely as a result of the great gold rush that began in 1849, there was a substantial English-speaking population (and a small but growing population of Chinese and other Asian immigrants) in California. But vast areas of the Far West remained free of any substantial numbers of English-speaking settlers. Living there was a significant population of Hispanics (some were immigrants from Mexico; others, long-standing residents who had lived in the region even before the United States acquired it). Above all, the lands were the homes of Indian tribes.

Delayed Settlement

Early white explorers had dubbed the Great Plains west of the Mississippi the "Great American Desert," and in the 1840s English-speaking migrants had hastened through it on their way to California and Oregon. By the 1860s, however, whites were beginning to move into the region in great numbers. They were attracted by gold and silver deposits, by the short-grass pasture for cattle and sheep, and by the sod and mountain meadowlands that seemed suited for farming or ranching. They were attracted, too, by the completion of the great transcontinental railroad lines and their feeders, which opened up the plains both to settlement and to commerce. The railroad companies themselves actively solicited new settlers (to create customers for their lines) by, among other things, selling company lands to them at low prices.

The federal government also encouraged settlement. The Homestead Act of 1862 permitted settlers to buy plots of 160 acres for small fees if they lived on them for five years. But 160 acres was too small for the grazing and grain farming of the arid Great Plains, so Congress eventually increased the allotments through a series of other measures passed between 1873 and 1878, which ultimately made it possible for settlers to acquire as much as 1,280 acres of land at little cost. Some got much more through the rampant fraud in the administration of the acts.

After Kansas became a state in 1861, the remaining Western territories of Washington, New Mexico, Utah, and Nebraska (all of which originally included much more territory than those states do today) were divided into smaller units. By the end of the 1860s, Nevada and Nebraska had become states; and white governments were operating in the new territories of Colorado, Dakota, Arizona, Idaho, Montana, and Wyoming. Colorado became a state in 1876; North and South Dakota, Montana, and Washington, in 1889; Wyoming and Idaho, in 1890. In 1896, Utah was admitted, after its Mormon leaders had convinced the government that polygamy (the practice by which men take several wives) had been abandoned. By 1900, only three territories—Arizona, New Mexico, and Oklahoma (formerly Indian Territory), in all of which nonwhites formed a majority of the populations—still awaited statehood.

The Arrival of the Miners

White settlement of the Far West moved in three distinct stages. The first was the development of mining, and hence the first part of the area to be extensively settled was the mineral-rich region of mountains and plateaus, where white settlers hoped to make quick fortunes by finding precious metals. The mining boom was brief. It began suddenly in about 1860, flourished until the 1890s, and then abruptly declined.

News of a gold or silver strike would spark several stages of settlement. First, individual prospectors would flock to the area to exploit the first ores largely by hand, with pan and placer mining. After the shallower deposits had been depleted by these methods, corporations moved in to engage in lode or quartz mining. Then, as those deposits dwindled, commercial mining either disappeared or contracted.

The first great mining boom began in 1858, when gold was discovered in the Pike's Peak district of what would soon be Colorado; the following year, 50,000 prospectors stormed into the region. Almost overnight Denver and other mining camps blossomed into instant "cities." A year later, miners from California began flocking to Nevada, where gold had been found in the Washoe district and silver in the great Comstock Lode. When the surface deposits dwindled, California investors bought up the claims of many prospectors and began quartz mining. From 1860 to 1880 the Nevada lodes yielded gold and silver bullion worth $306 million. More than a decade later, in 1874, gold was found in the Black Hills of southwestern Dakota Territory, sparking another, even briefer boom. With the inevitable fading of surface resources, corporations again took over from the miners, and the white population declined. Gold and silver created the most excitement, but the extraction of other, less glamorous minerals was more important to white development of the Far West in the long run: copper (launched in 1881 by the great Anaconda copper mine in Colorado), lead, tin, quartz, and zinc.

The mining communities were the home of people of many races and cultures. Indians, Mexicans, African-Americans, and Chinese lived along-

COLORADO BOOM TOWN After a prospector discovered silver nearby in 1890,
miners flocked to the town of Creede, Colorado. For a time, 150 to 300
people arrived there daily. Like other such boom towns, however, Creede's
prosperity was short-lived. In 1893 the price of silver collapsed, and Creede
was soon almost deserted.

side whites, although seldom entirely harmoniously. White settlers tried to
place boundaries on the acceptable social and economic behavior of nonwhites, who generally had difficulty gaining ownership of land or finding
any but menial jobs. Yet nonwhites were essential to the functioning of the
mining economy as laborers in the mines and as providers of vital services
in the towns.

Men greatly outnumbered women in the mining towns; and younger
men, in particular, had difficulty finding female companions of comparable
age. Those women who did gravitate to the new communities often came
with their husbands, and their activities were generally (although not always)
confined to the same kinds of domestic tasks that Eastern women performed. Single women, or women whose husbands were not earning enough
money, sometimes worked for wages as cooks, laundresses, and tavern
keepers. And in the sexually imbalanced mining communities, there was
always a substantial market for prostitutes.

The Cattle Kingdom

Even while the mining empire was flourishing, the second stage of white
settlement of the Far West was under way: the growth of cattle ranching.
The open range—the unclaimed grasslands of the public domain—pro-

vided a huge area on the Great Plains where cattlemen could graze their herds free of charge and unimpeded by private farms. The railroads provided access to markets in the East.

The Western cattle industry was Mexican first. Long before citizens of the United States invaded the Southwest, Mexican ranchers had developed the techniques that the white cattlemen and cowboys of the Great Plains later employed: branding, roundups, roping, and others. They had also created the equipment of the herders—lariat, saddle, leather chaps, and spurs. Americans in Texas adopted the Mexican methods and carried them throughout the cattle kingdom. Texans also developed the largest herds and bred the horses—small, muscular broncos or mustangs—that enabled cowboys to control them.

At the end of the Civil War, an estimated 5 million cattle roamed the Texas ranges, and prices in Northern markets were rising. In 1866, some Texas cattle ranchers began driving their combined herds, some 260,000 head, north to Sedalia, Missouri, a market on the Missouri Pacific Railroad. Much of the total herd was lost along the way to outlaws and Indians. But the drive proved that cattle could be driven to distant markets and pastured along the trail, and that they would even gain weight during the journey. From that point on, the "long drive" became the basis of the cattle kingdom. Combined herds on the drives usually numbered from 2,000 to 5,000 head. Cowboys representing each of the major ranchers accompanied them. Many cowboys in the early years were veterans of the Confederate army. The next largest group consisted of blacks, followed by white Northerners, Mexicans, and others.

Abilene, Kansas, on the Kansas Pacific Railroad, was the first capital of the cattle kingdom. Between 1867 and 1871, cattlemen drove 1,460,000 head there along the Chisholm Trail. By the mid-1870s, however, farmers were beginning to occupy the open rangelands in western Kansas, impeding the drives, so new cattle centers developed farther west, in Nebraska, Wyoming, and Montana, as railroad lines moved out to meet them.

Open-range cattle ranching was risky business. "Texas fever"—a disease transmitted to cattle by ticks—could decimate a herd. Rustlers and Indians could seize livestock. And cattlemen faced increasing competition from other whites for use of the plains. Sheep ranchers from California and Oregon brought their flocks onto the range to compete for grass. Farmers ("nesters") from the East threw fences around their claims, blocking trails and breaking up the open range. A series of violent "range wars"—between sheepmen and cattlemen, between ranchers and farmers—erupted out of the tensions between these competing groups.

The Cattle Kingdom, c. 1866–1887

Open range

——— Railroads

CATTLE TRAILS

Sedalia and Baxter Springs Trail

Chisholm Trail

Western Trail

Goodnight-Loving Trail

As the cattle industry became more profitable, it overexpanded. By the 1880s, there was no longer enough grass on the open range to support the enormous herds or sustain the long drives. Even nature turned hostile. Two severe winters, in 1885–1886 and 1886–1887, with a searing summer between them, devastated the plains, driving many ranchers out of business. The open-range industry and its long drives soon largely disappeared. But established cattle ranches—with fenced-in grazing land and stocks of hay for winter feed—survived and prospered.

Although the cattle industry was overwhelmingly male in its early years, there were always a few women involved in ranching and driving. As ranching became more sedentary, the presence of women greatly expanded.

By 1890, there were more than 250,000 women who owned ranches or farms in the Western States. Indeed, the region provided women with many opportunities that were closed to them in the East—including the opportunity to participate in politics. Wyoming was the first state in the Union to guarantee woman suffrage; and throughout the West, women established themselves as an important political presence (and occasionally as significant officeholders).

The Romance of the West

The West had always occupied a special place in the American imagination. But the vast regions of the Far West had a particularly strong romantic appeal. That was partly because the landscape, with its brilliant diversity and spectacular grandeur, was so different from anything white Americans had encountered before.

Even more appealing than the landscape, perhaps, was the rugged, free-spirited life style that many Americans associated with the West—a life style that stood in sharp contrast to the increasingly stable and ordered world of the East. Particular public interest attached to the figure of the cowboy, who was transformed remarkably quickly into a powerful and enduring figure of myth. Admiring Americans seldom thought about the dreariness of the cowboy's life: the tedium, the loneliness, the physical discomforts, the relatively few opportunities for advancement. Instead, in Western novels such as Owen Wister's *The Virginian* (1902), the cowboy became one of the most powerful symbols of what had long been an important ideal in the American mind—the ideal of the natural man.

But the Far West was particularly important to the nation's imagination because many Americans considered it the last frontier. One of the clearest and most influential statements of this vision of the West came from the historian Frederick Jackson Turner, of the University of Wisconsin. In 1893, at a meeting of the American Historical Association, the thirty-three-year-old Turner delivered a paper entitled "The Significance of the Frontier in American History." Westward expansion, he said, had stimulated individualism, nationalism, and democracy; it had defined American civilization. But now, Turner argued, the great unsettled lands were gone, "and with its going has closed the first period of American history."

In fact, Turner's concerns were both inaccurate and premature. A vast public domain still existed in the 1890s; during the forty years after Turner's address, the government was to give away many more acres than it had given as homesteads in the past. But if the "passing of the frontier" was largely a myth, it was a powerful one. And it kept the romantic image of the West alive for many decades to come.

THE DISPERSAL OF THE TRIBES

White Americans liked to think of the Far West as a vast unpeopled land awaiting settlement. In fact, the West already had a substantial population, mostly of Indians, before the white settlers arrived. Some were members of Eastern tribes—Cherokee, Creek, Winnebago, and others—who had been forcibly resettled west of the Mississippi in Indian Territory (later Oklahoma) before the Civil War. But most were members of tribes indigenous to the West.

The Western Tribes

The Western tribes had developed several different patterns of civilization. The Pueblo of the Southwest lived largely as farmers and had established permanent settlements. They continued to occupy lands guaranteed them by the Spanish before the annexation of the Western territories by the United States. They grew corn; they built towns and cities of adobe houses; they practiced elaborate forms of irrigation.

Other tribes in that region—the Navajo and Apache of western Texas and eastern New Mexico—lived less rooted lives and combined hunting with farming and sheep herding, moving their settlements from place to place. The most numerous Indian groups in the West, however, consisted of the plains Indians—the Sioux, the Blackfoot, the Cheyenne, the Kiowa, the Apache, the Comanche, the Crow, and others—who occupied large parts of what became Minnesota, the Dakotas, Nebraska, Idaho, and Montana. The plains Indians lived a largely nomadic life, because the semiarid, treeless plains encouraged a culture based on hunting. When a band halted, it constructed tepees as temporary dwellings; when it departed, it left the landscape almost completely undisturbed, a reflection of a reverence for nature central to Indian culture and religion.

The chief target of these Indian hunters was the buffalo, or bison—a huge grazing animal that provided the economic basis for the plains Indians' way of life. Its flesh was their principal source of food, and its skin supplied clothing, shoes, tepees, blankets, robes, and utensils. "Buffalo chips," dried manure, provided fuel; buffalo bones became knives and arrow tips; buffalo tendons formed the strings of bows.

Tribes (which sometimes numbered several thousand) were generally subdivided into "bands" of up to 500 men and women, often consisting of interrelated families. Each had its own governing council. Within each band, tasks were generally divided by gender. Women performed domestic and artistic roles: raising children, cooking, gathering roots and berries, preparing hides, and creating the artworks of tribal culture. They also tended fields and gardens in those places where bands settled long enough to raise crops. Men worked largely as hunters and traders and supervised the religious and military life of the band.

The plains Indians were proud and aggressive warriors, the most formidable foes white settlers had yet encountered. But they also suffered from several serious weaknesses that in the end made it impossible for them to prevail. Perhaps the most crippling was the inability of the various tribes (and often even of the bands within tribes) to unite against white aggression. Indeed the plains Indians were frequently distracted from their battles with whites by conflicts among the tribes themselves.

White Policies Toward the Tribes

The Western tribes were also victimized by the incompetence and duplicity of the white officials charged with protecting them. The policy of the federal government was to regard the tribes simultaneously as independent nations and as wards of the president in Washington, and to negotiate treaties with them that were solemnly ratified by the Senate. Seldom, however, did treaties or agreements with the tribes survive the pressure of white settlers eager for access to Indian lands. The history of relations between the United States and the Native Americans is, therefore, one of broken promises.

By the early 1850s, the idea of establishing one great territory in which all the tribes could live (the idea that had led to the creation of the Indian Territory in what is now Oklahoma) was in retreat. In the face of white demands for access to lands on the "One Big Reservation," the federal government created a new policy, known as "concentration." In 1851, each tribe was assigned its own reservation, confirmed by separate treaties (many of them illegitimately negotiated with unauthorized representatives, chosen by whites, known as "treaty chiefs"). The new arrangement had many benefits for whites and few for the Indians. It separated the tribes from one another and made them easier to defeat. It allowed the government to force tribes into scattered locations and to take over the most desirable lands for white settlement. But it did not survive as the basis of Indian policy for long.

In 1867, in the aftermath of a series of bloody conflicts, an Indian Peace Commission established by Congress recommended yet another "permanent" Indian policy. The commission recommended abandoning the policy of scattering the tribes and proposed relocating all the plains Indians in two large reservations—one in Indian Territory (Oklahoma), the other in the Dakotas. Government agents cajoled, bribed, and tricked the Arapaho, Cheyenne, Sioux, and other tribes into agreeing to treaties establishing the new reservations.

This policy worked no better than the previous ones. In part that was because the Bureau of Indian Affairs, the government agency responsible for administering the reservations, was appallingly incompetent and corrupt. Even the most honest and diligent of the Bureau's agents in the West were woefully unprepared for their jobs and had no understanding of tribal ways.

But the problem was also a result of the relentless slaughtering by whites of the buffalo herds that supported the tribes' way of life. Even in the 1850s, white migrants in the West had been killing buffalo to provide themselves with food and supplies. After the Civil War, white demand for buffalo hides became a national phenomenon—partly for economic reasons and partly as a fad. Professional hunters swarmed into the plains to gather hides they could sell in the East. Amateur hunters traveled to the plains to shoot buffalo for sport. Railroads organized large shooting expeditions to thin the herds, which were obstructions to traffic. The Southern herd was virtually exterminated by 1875, and within a few years the smaller Northern herd had met the same fate. In 1865, there had been at least 15 million buffalo; a decade later, fewer than a thousand of the great beasts survived. The army and the agents of the Bureau of Indian Affairs condoned and even encouraged the killing.

Indian Resistance

There was almost incessant fighting between whites and Indians on the frontier from the 1850s to the 1880s, as Indians struggled against the growing threats to their civilizations. Indian warriors, usually traveling in raiding parties of thirty to forty men, regularly attacked wagon trains, stagecoaches, and isolated ranches, often in retaliation for earlier attacks on them by whites. As the United States Army became more deeply involved in the fighting, the tribes began to focus more of their attacks on white soldiers.

At times, this small-scale fighting escalated into something resembling a war. During the Civil War, the eastern Sioux in Minnesota, cramped on an inadequate reservation and exploited by corrupt white agents, suddenly rebelled. Led by Little Crow, they killed more than 700 whites before being subdued by a force of regulars and militiamen. Thirty-eight of the Indians were hanged, and the tribe was exiled to the Dakotas.

At about the same time, the Arapaho and Cheyenne in eastern Colorado were in conflict with white miners settling in the region. Bands of Indians attacked stagecoach lines and settlements in an effort to regain territory they believed was theirs. In response to these incidents, whites called up a large territorial militia and the army issued dire threats. The governor urged all friendly Indians to congregate at army posts to protect themselves against retribution. One Arapaho and Cheyenne band under Black Kettle, apparently in response to the invitation, camped near Fort Lyon on Sand Creek in November 1864. Some members of the party were warriors, but Black Kettle believed he was under official protection and exhibited no hostile intention. Nevertheless, Colonel J. M. Chivington, apparently encouraged by the army commander of the district, led a volunteer militia force—much of it consisting of unemployed miners, many of whom were apparently drunk—to the unsuspecting camp and massacred perhaps 200 men, women, and children. Black Kettle and his Cheyennes escaped the Sand Creek massacre and moved south toward Texas. Four years later, a United States Army force under Colonel George A. Custer caught up with them near the border, killed Black Kettle, and slaughtered his people.

The treaties of 1867 brought a temporary lull in the conflicts. But in the early 1870s, more waves of white settlers, mostly miners, began to penetrate some of the lands in Dakota Territory supposedly guaranteed to the tribes in 1867. At the same time, the federal government, responding to the recommendations of another commission, decided that it would no longer recognize the tribes as independent entities or negotiate with tribal chiefs. It was a step intended to undermine the collective nature of Indian life and to force the Indians to assimilate into white culture—a goal cherished by many white reformers, who believed that only through assimilation could Indians thrive.

Indian resistance flared anew. In the Northern plains, the Sioux rose up in 1875 and left their reservation. When white officials ordered them to return, bands of warriors gathered in Montana and united under two great leaders: Crazy Horse and Sitting Bull. Three army columns set out to round

A M E R I C A N V O I C E S

Two Indian Leaders Face Conquest

CHIEF JOSEPH SURRENDERS, 1877

I am tired of fighting. The old men are all dead. [My brother] who led the young men is dead. It is cold, and we have no blankets. The little children are freezing to death. My people, some of them, have run away to the hills. No one knows where they are. I want to have some time to look for my children. Maybe I shall find them among the dead.

Hear me, my chiefs. From where the sun now stands, I will fight no more forever.

SITTING BULL DESCRIBES LIFE ON THE SIOUX RESERVATION, 1883

Whatever you wanted of me I have obeyed. The Great Father sent me word that whatever he had against me in the past had been forgiven and thrown aside, and I accepted his promises and came in [the reservation]. And he told me not to step aside from the white man's path, and I am doing my best to travel in that path. I sit here and look around me now, and I see my people starving. We want cattle to butcher. That is the way you live, and we want to live the same way. When the Great Father told me to live like his people, I told him to send me six teams of mules, because that is the way the white people make a living. I asked for a horse and buggy for my children; I was advised to follow the ways of the white man, and that is why I asked for those things.

them up and force them back onto the reservation. With the expedition, as colonel of the famous Seventh Cavalry, was the dashing and reckless George A. Custer. At the Battle of the Little Bighorn in 1876—perhaps the most famous of all conflicts between whites and Indians—an unprecedented gathering of tribal warriors, estimated at more than 4,000, surprised Custer and part of his regiment in southern Montana, surrounded them, and killed them all.

But the Indians could not keep their troops united. The warriors soon drifted off in bands to elude pursuit or search for food, and the army ran them down singly and returned them to Dakota. The power of the Sioux was soon broken, and the proud leaders, Crazy Horse and Sitting Bull, finally gave up the fight and settled on reservations. Both were later killed by reservation police after being tricked or taunted into last shows of resistance.

Another dramatic example of Indian resistance occurred in Idaho in 1877. The Nez Percé, a small and relatively peaceful tribe, refused to accept white demands that they move to a smaller reservation. When United States troops converged on them, their able leader, Chief Joseph, attempted to lead the band into Canada. Most Nez Percé did not follow Joseph and instead moved west to Washington state. But those who did became a part of a remarkable chase. Pursued by four columns, Joseph and more than 500 men, women, and children, covered 1,321 miles in seventy-five days, repelling or evading the army time and again. Finally, however, the troops trapped the Indian band just short of the Canadian border. Chief Joseph surrendered. Like so many other defeated tribes, the Nez Percé were finally transported to Indian Territory in Oklahoma, where most of them soon died of disease and malnutrition (although Joseph himself lived until 1908).

The last Indians to sustain organized resistance against the whites were the Chiricahua Apaches, who fought intermittently from the 1860s to the late 1880s. The two ablest chiefs of this fierce tribe were Mangas Colorados and Cochise. Mangas was murdered during the Civil War by white soldiers who tricked him into surrendering, and in 1872 Cochise agreed to peace in exchange for a reservation that included some of the tribe's traditional land. But Cochise died in 1874, and his successor, Geronimo—unwilling to bow to white pressures to assimilate—fought on for more than a decade longer, establishing bases in the mountains of Arizona and Mexico and leading warriors in intermittent raids against white outposts. With each raid, however, the number of warring Apaches dwindled, as some warriors died and others drifted away to the reservation. By 1886, Geronimo's plight was hopeless. His band consisted of only about 30 people, including women and

THE SURRENDER OF GERONIMO The great Apache warrior Geronimo
(front row, third from right) sits with members of his diminished band
after surrendering to United States troops in 1886. The two men at
front row, left, are Geronimo's half brothers. The young boy at
front row, right, is his son.

children, while his white pursuers numbered perhaps 10,000. Geronimo
recognized the odds and surrendered, an event that marked the end of
formal warfare between Indians and whites.

But the end of the Apache wars was not the end of the violence. Another
tragic conflict between Indians and whites occurred in 1890 as a result of a
religious revival among the tribes. The Western Indians sensed that their
culture and their glories were irrevocably fading; some were also near
starvation because corrupt government agents had reduced their food
rations. As other tribes had done in trying times in the past, many of these
Indians turned to a prophet and joined a religious revival. This time the
prophet was Wovoka, a Paiute who inspired an ecstatic spiritual awakening
that began in Nevada and spread quickly to the plains. The new revival
emphasized the coming of a messiah, but its most conspicuous feature was
a mass, emotional "Ghost Dance," which apparently inspired mystical

visions among its participants. Among those visions were a retreat by white people from Indian lands and the restoration of the decimated buffalo herds. White agents on the Sioux reservation watched the dances in bewilderment and fear; some believed they might be the preliminary to hostilities and called for troops to stop the ceremonies.

Some of the Indian revivalists fled to the Badlands. When white troops caught up with them at Wounded Knee, South Dakota, fighting broke out in which about 40 white soldiers and more than 200 of the Indians, including women and children, died. What precipitated the conflict is a matter of dispute. But the battle soon turned into a one-sided massacre, as the white soldiers turned their new machine guns on the Indians and mowed them down in the snow.

The Dawes Act

Even before the Ghost Dance and the Wounded Knee tragedy, the federal government had launched new efforts to destroy the tribal structure of Indian life and culture. For nearly fifty years, its policy had been to create reservations in which the tribes would be isolated from white society. Now Congress—through the Dawes Severalty Act of 1887—abolished the practice by which tribes owned reservation lands communally. The reversal was an effort to force Indians to become landowners and farmers, abandon their traditional culture, and become part of white civilization.

The Bureau of Indian Affairs moved quickly and relentlessly to promote assimilation. Not only did they try to move Indian families onto their own plots of land; they also took Indian children away from their families and sent them to boarding schools run by whites, where they believed the young people could be educated to abandon tribal ways. Few Indians were prepared for this wrenching change from their traditional collective society to Western individualism. In any case, white administration of the program was so corrupt and inept, and Indian resistance so strong and enduring, that decades later the government simply abandoned it.

THE RISE AND DECLINE
OF THE WESTERN FARMER

Farmers had begun moving into the plains region in the 1850s, challenging the ranchers and the Indians and occasionally coming into conflict with both. By the 1870s, farmers were pouring into the plains and beyond in great numbers, enclosing land that had once been hunting territory for Indians and grazing territory for open-range cattle, and establishing a new agricultural region.

Farming on the Plains

Many factors combined to produce this surge of Western settlement, but the most important was the railroads. Before the Civil War, the Great Plains had been accessible only through a difficult journey by wagon. But beginning in the 1860s, a great new network of railroad lines developed, spearheaded by the transcontinental routes Congress had authorized and subsidized in 1862. They made huge new areas of settlement accessible.

COMPLETING THE TRANSCONTINENTAL RAILROAD Officials of the Union Pacific and Central Pacific companies shake hands and exchange bottles of champagne at Promontory Point, Utah, on May 10, 1869, after the last spike has been driven to join the two lines and complete the nation's first transcontinental railroad.

The building of the transcontinental line was a dramatic and monumental achievement. Thousands of immigrant workers—mostly Irish on the Eastern route, Chinese on the Western—labored, in what were at times unimaginably difficult conditions, to penetrate mountain ranges, cross deserts, protect themselves against Indians, and—finally—connect the two lines at Promontory Point in northern Utah in the spring of 1869. But while this first transcontinental line captured the public imagination, the construction of subsidiary lines in the following years proved of greater importance to the West. State governments, imitating Washington, induced railroad development by offering direct financial aid, favorable loans, and more than 50 million acres of land (on top of the 130 million acres the federal government had already offered). Although operated by private corporations, the railroads were essentially government projects.

It was not only by making access to the Great Plains easier that the railroads helped spur agricultural settlement there. The railroad companies themselves actively promoted settlement—both to provide themselves with customers for their services and to increase the value of their vast landholdings. In addition, the companies set rates so low for settlers that almost anyone could afford the trip west. And they sold much of their land at very low prices and provided liberal credit to prospective settlers. Contributing further to the great surge of white agricultural expansion was a temporary change in the climate of the Great Plains. For several years in succession, beginning in the 1870s, rainfall in the plains states was well above average. White Americans now rejected the old idea that the region was the Great American Desert. Some even claimed that cultivation of the plains actually encouraged rainfall.

Even under the most favorable conditions, farming on the plains presented special problems. First was the problem of fencing. Farmers had to enclose their land, if for no other reason than to protect it from the herds of the open-range cattlemen. But traditional wood or stone fences were too expensive and were ineffective as barriers to cattle. In the mid-1870s, however, two Illinois farmers, Joseph H. Glidden and I. L. Ellwood, solved this problem by developing and marketing barbed wire, which became standard equipment on the plains and revolutionized fencing practices all over the country.

The second problem was water. Water was scarce even when rainfall was above average. After 1887, a series of dry seasons began. Lands that had been fertile now turned back into semidesert. Some farmers dealt with the problem by using deep wells pumped by steel windmills, or by turning to what was called dry-land farming (a system of tillage designed to conserve moisture in the soil by covering it with a dust blanket), or by planting drought-resistant crops. In many areas of the plains, however, only large-scale irrigation could save the endangered farms. But irrigation projects of the magnitude necessary required government assistance. And neither the state nor the federal government was prepared to fund the projects.

Most of the people who moved into the region had previously been farmers in the Midwest, the East, and Europe. In the booming years of the early 1880s, with land values rising, the new farmers had no problem obtaining extensive and easy credit and had every reason to believe they would soon be able to retire their debts. But the arid years of the late 1880s—during which crop prices were falling while production was becoming more expensive—changed that prospect. Tens of thousands of farmers could not pay their debts and were forced to abandon their farms. There was, in effect, a reverse migration: white settlers moving back to the East, sometimes turning once-flourishing communities into desolate ghost towns. Those who remained continued to suffer from falling prices (wheat, which had sold for $1.60 a bushel at the end of the Civil War, dropped to 49 cents in the 1890s) and persistent indebtedness.

Changes in Agriculture

American farming by the late nineteenth century no longer bore very much relation to the comforting image many Americans continued to embrace. The sturdy, independent farmer of popular myth was being replaced by the commercial farmer—a person attempting to do in the agricultural economy what industrialists were doing in the manufacturing economy.

Commercial farmers were not self-sufficient and made no effort to become so. They specialized in cash crops and sold them in national or world markets. They did not make their own household supplies or grow their own food but bought them instead at town or village stores. This kind of farming, when it was successful, raised the farmers' living standards. But it also made them dependent on bankers and interest rates, railroads and freight rates, national and European markets, world supply and demand. And unlike the capitalists of the industrial order, the farmers could not regulate their production or influence the prices of what they sold.

Between 1865 and 1900, agriculture became an international business. Farm output increased dramatically, not only in the United States but in Brazil, Argentina, Canada, Australia, New Zealand, Russia, and elsewhere.

At the same time, modern forms of communication and transportation—the telephone, the telegraph, steam navigation, railroads—were creating new markets around the world for agricultural goods. American commercial farmers, constantly opening new lands, produced much more than the domestic market could absorb; they relied on the world market to absorb their surplus, but in that market they faced major competition. Cotton farmers depended on export sales for 70 percent of their annual income, and wheat farmers for 30 to 40 percent; but the volatility of the international market put them at great risk.

Beginning in the 1880s, worldwide overproduction led to a drop in prices for most agricultural goods and hence to great economic distress for many of the more than 6 million American farm families. By the 1890s, 27 percent of the farms in the country were mortgaged; by 1910, 33 percent. In 1880, 25 percent of all farms were operated by tenants; by 1910, the proportion had grown to 37 percent. Commercial farming made some people fabulously wealthy. But the farm economy as a whole was suffering a significant decline relative to the rest of the nation.

The Farmers' Grievances

American farmers were painfully aware that something was wrong. But few yet understood the implications of national and world overproduction. Instead, they concentrated their attention and anger on more immediate, more comprehensible—and no less real—problems: inequitable freight rates, high interest charges, and an inadequate currency.

The farmers' first and most burning grievance was against the railroads. In many cases, the railroads charged higher rates for farm goods than for other kinds and higher rates in the South and West than in the Northeast. Railroads also controlled elevator and warehouse facilities in buying centers and charged arbitrary storage rates.

Farmers also resented the institutions controlling credit—banks, loan companies, insurance corporations. Since sources of credit in the West and South were few, farmers had to take loans on whatever terms they could get, often at interest rates of 10 to 25 percent. Many farmers had to pay these loans back in years when prices were dropping and currency was becoming scarce.

A third grievance concerned prices: both the prices farmers received for their products and the prices they paid for goods they bought. Farmers disposed of their products in a competitive world market over which they had no control and of which they had no advance knowledge. A farmer could plant a large crop at a moment when prices were high and find that by the time of the harvest the price had declined. Fortunes rose and fell in response to unpredictable forces. But many farmers became convinced (often with some reason) that "middlemen"—speculators, bankers, regional and local agents—were combining to fix prices so as to benefit themselves at the expense of the growers. Many farmers also came to believe (again, not entirely without reason) that manufacturers in the East were conspiring to keep the prices of farm goods low and the prices of industrial goods high. Farmers sold their crops in a competitive world market, but they bought manufactured goods in a domestic market protected by tariffs and dominated by trusts and corporations.

The Agrarian Malaise

These economic difficulties produced social, cultural, and ultimately political resentments. In part, this was a result of the isolation of farm life. Farm families in some parts of the country—particularly in the prairie and plains regions, where large farms were scattered over vast areas—were virtually cut off from the outside world and human companionship. During the winter months and spells of bad weather, the loneliness and boredom could become nearly unbearable. Many farmers lacked access to adequate education for their children, to proper medical facilities, to recreational or cultural activities, to virtually anything that might give them a sense of being members of a community. Older farmers felt the sting of watching their children leave the farm for the city. They felt the humiliation of being ridiculed as "hayseeds" by the new urban culture that was coming to dominate American life.

The result of this sense of isolation and obsolescence was a growing malaise among many farmers, a discontent that would help to create a great national political movement in the 1890s. The agrarian malaise also found reflection in the literature that emerged from rural America. Writers in the late nineteenth century might romanticize the rugged life of the cowboy and the Western miner. For the farmer, however, the image was different. Hamlin Garland, for example, reflected the growing disillusionment in a series of novels and short stories. In the past, Garland wrote in the introduction to his novel *Jason Edwards* (1891), the agrarian frontier had seemed to be "the Golden West, the land of wealth and freedom and happiness. All of the associations called up by the spoken word, the West, were fabulous, mythic, hopeful." Now, however, the bright promise had faded. The trials of rural life were crushing the human spirit. "So this is the reality of the dream!" a character in Jason Edwards exclaims. "A shanty on a barren plain, hot and lone as a desert. My God!" Once, sturdy yeoman farmers had viewed themselves as the backbone of American life. Now, they were becoming painfully aware that their position was declining in relation to the rising urban-industrial society to the east.

CHAPTER SEVENTEEN

Industrial Supremacy

Sources of Industrial Growth ~ *Capitalism and Its Critics*
The Ordeal of the Worker

W ITH A STRIDE that astonished statisticians, the conquering hosts of business enterprise swept over the continent; twenty-five years after the death of Lincoln, America had become, in the quantity and value of her products, the first manufacturing nation of the world. What England had accomplished in a hundred years, the United States had achieved in half the time." So wrote the historians Charles and Mary Beard in the 1920s, expressing the amazement many Americans felt when they considered the remarkable expansion of their industrial economy in the late nineteenth century.

In fact, America's rise to industrial supremacy was not as sudden as such observers suggested. The nation had been building a manufacturing economy since early in the nineteenth century; industry was well established before the Civil War. But Americans were clearly correct in observing that the accomplishments of the last three decades of the nineteenth century overshadowed all the earlier progress. Those years witnessed nothing less than the transformation of the nation.

The remarkable growth did much to increase the wealth and improve the lives of many Americans. But such benefits were far from equally shared. While industrial titans and a growing middle class were enjoying a prosperity without precedent in the nation's history, workers, farmers, and others were experiencing an often painful ordeal that slowly edged the United States toward a great economic and political crisis.

SOURCES OF INDUSTRIAL GROWTH

Many factors contributed to the growth of American industry: abundant raw materials; a large and growing labor supply; a surge in technological innovation; the emergence of a talented, ambitious, and often ruthless group of entrepreneurs; a federal government eager to assist the growth of business; and a great and expanding domestic market for the products of manufacturing.

Industrial Technology

The rapid emergence of new technologies and the discovery of new materials and productive processes was one of the prerequisites to late-nineteenth-century industrial growth. In the entire history of the United States up to 1860, only 36,000 patents had been granted. For the period from 1860 to 1890, the figure was 440,000. Americans also benefited from comparable technological advances in Europe.

Some of the most important innovations were in communications. In 1866, Cyrus W. Field laid a transatlantic telegraph cable to Europe. During the next decade, Alexander Graham Bell developed the first commercially useful telephone; and by the 1890s, the American Telephone and Telegraph Company, which handled his interests, had installed nearly half a million telephones in American cities. Other inventions that speeded the pace of business organization were the typewriter (by Christopher L. Sholes in 1868), the cash register (by James Ritty in 1879), and the calculating or adding machine (by William S. Burroughs in 1891).

Among the most revolutionary innovations was the introduction in the 1870s of electricity as a source of light and power. Among the pioneers of electric lighting were Charles F. Brush, who devised the arc lamp for street illumination, and Thomas A. Edison, who invented the incandescent lamp (or light bulb), which could be used for both street and home lighting. Edison and others designed improved generators and built large power plants to furnish electricity to whole cities. By the turn of the century, electric power was becoming commonplace in street railway systems, in the elevators of urban skyscrapers, in factories, and increasingly in offices and homes.

A process by which iron could be transformed into steel—a much more durable and versatile material—had been discovered simultaneously in the 1850s by an Englishman, Henry Bessemer, and an American, William Kelly.

(The process consisted of blowing air through molten iron to burn out the impurities.) After the Civil War, the new process transformed the metal industry; and in 1868, the New Jersey ironmaster Abram S. Hewitt introduced from Europe another method of making steel—the open-hearth process. These techniques made possible the production of steel in great quantities and large dimensions, for use in the production of locomotives, steel rails, and girders for the construction of tall buildings.

The steel industry emerged first in western Pennsylvania and eastern Ohio, a region where iron ore and coal were abundant and where there was already a flourishing iron industry. Pittsburgh quickly became the center of the steel world. But the industry was growing so fast that new sources of ore were soon necessary. The upper peninsula of Michigan, the Mesabi range in Minnesota, and the area around Birmingham, Alabama, became important ore-producing centers by the end of the century, and new centers of steel production emerged near them: Cleveland, Detroit, Chicago, and Birmingham, among others. Most steel centers also had access to major waterways, permitting cheap transportation of goods to distant markets.

The oil industry emerged in the late nineteenth century largely in response to the steel industry's need for lubrication for its machines. (Not until later did oil become important primarily for its potential as a fuel.) The existence of petroleum reserves in western Pennsylvania, where oil often seeped to the surface of streams and springs, had been common knowledge for some time. At first, no one was quite sure what it was or what to do with it. In the 1850s, however, experiments commissioned by the Pennsylvania businessman George Bissell showed that the substance could be burned in lamps and that it could also yield such products as paraffin, naphtha, and lubricating oil. Bissell then raised money to begin drilling; and in 1859, Edwin L. Drake, one of Bissell's employees, established the first oil well near Titusville, Pennsylvania, which was soon producing 500 barrels of oil a month. Demand for petroleum grew quickly, and promoters soon developed other fields in Pennsylvania, Ohio, and West Virginia. By the 1870s, oil had advanced to fourth place among the nation's exports.

Other great innovations were emerging by the beginning of the twentieth century. The Italian inventor Guglielmo Marconi was taking the first steps toward the development of radio in the 1890s. The Wright brothers launched the first airplane flight at Kitty Hawk, North Carolina, in 1903. Perhaps most important, the automobile was in development. In the 1870s, designers in France, Germany, and Austria—inspired by the success of railroad engines—were already beginning to develop engines that might drive independently controlled vehicles. They achieved early successes with an "internal combustion engine," which used the expanding power of burning gas to drive pistons; and with this new engine, they created the first automobiles.

In the United States, the automobile industry developed rapidly. Charles and Frank Duryea built the first gasoline-driven motor vehicle in America in 1903. Three years later, Henry Ford produced the first of the famous cars that would bear his name. By 1910, the industry had become a major force in the economy, and the automobile was beginning to reshape American social and cultural life. In 1895, there were only four automobiles on the American highways. By 1917, there were nearly 5 million.

The Science of Production

Central to the growth of the automobile and other industries were changes in the techniques of production. By the turn of the century, many industrialists were embracing the new principles of "scientific management," often known as "Taylorism" because its leading theoretician was Frederick Winslow Taylor. Taylor's ideas were controversial during his lifetime, and they have remained controversial since. Taylor himself, and his many admirers, argued that scientific management was a way to manage human labor to make it compatible with the demands of the machine age. But scientific management was also a way to increase the employer's control of the workplace, to make working people less independent. Taylor urged employers to reorganize the production process by subdividing tasks. This would speed up production; it would also make workers more interchangeable (less skilled, less in need of training) and thus diminish a manager's dependence on any particular employee. If properly managed by trained experts, he claimed, workers using modern machines could perform simple tasks at much greater speed, greatly increasing productive efficiency.

The most important change in production technology in the industrial era was the emergence of mass production and, above all, of the moving assembly line, which Henry Ford introduced in his automobile plants in 1914. This revolutionary technique cut the time for assembling a chassis from twelve and a half hours to one and a half hours. It enabled Ford to raise the wages and reduce the hours of his workers while cutting the base price of his Model T from $950 in 1914 to $290 in 1929. It became a standard for many other industries.

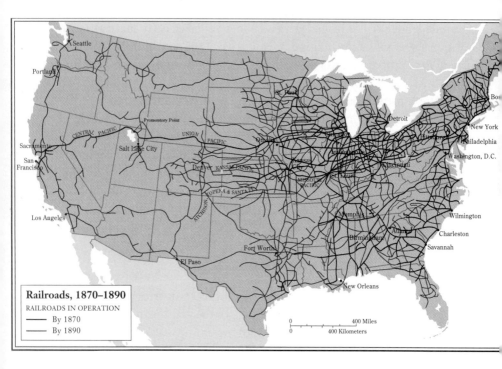

Railroads, 1870–1890
RAILROADS IN OPERATION
——— By 1870
——— By 1890

Railroad Expansion

The principal agent of industrial development in the late nineteenth century was the expansion of the railroads. Railroads promoted economic growth in many ways. They were the nation's principal method of transportation and gave industrialists access to distant markets and distant sources of raw materials. They were the nation's largest businesses and created new forms of corporate organization that served as models for other industries. And they were America's biggest investors, stimulating economic growth through their own enormous expenditures on construction and equipment.

In every decade in the late nineteenth century, total railroad trackage increased dramatically: from 30,000 miles in 1860, to 52,000 miles in 1870, to 93,000 in 1880, to 163,000 in 1890, and to 193,000 in 1900. Subsidies from federal, state, and local governments were (along with foreign loans and investments) vital to this expansion, which required far more capital than private entrepreneurs could raise by themselves. Equally important was the emergence of great railroad combinations that brought most of the nation's rails under the control of a few men. Through the last decades of the century, many railroad combinations continued to be dominated by one or two individuals. The achievements (and excesses) of these tycoons—Cornelius Vanderbilt, James J. Hill, Collis P. Huntington, and others—became symbols to much of the nation of great economic power concentrated in individual hands. But railroad development was less significant for the individual barons it created than for its contribution to the growth of a new institution: the modern corporation.

The Corporation

There had been various forms of corporations in America since colonial times, but the modern corporation emerged as a major force only after the Civil War. By then, railroad magnates and other industrialists realized that their great ventures could not be financed by any single person, no matter how wealthy, or even by any single group of partners.

Under the laws of incorporation passed in many states in the 1830s and 1840s, business organizations could raise money by selling stock to members of the public; after the Civil War, one industry after another began doing so. At the same time, affluent Americans began to consider the purchase of stock a good investment even if they were not themselves involved in the business whose stock they were purchasing. What made the practice appealing was that investors had only "limited liability"—that is, they risked only the amount of their investments; they were not liable for any debts the corporation might accumulate beyond that point. The ability to sell stock to a broad public made it possible for entrepreneurs to gather vast sums of capital and undertake great projects.

The Pennsylvania and other railroads were among the first to adopt the new corporate form of organization. But incorporation quickly spread beyond the railroad industry. In steel, the central figure was Andrew Carnegie, a Scottish immigrant who had worked his way up from modest beginnings and in 1873 opened his own steelworks in Pittsburgh. Soon he dominated the industry. His methods were much like those of other industrial titans. He cut costs and prices by striking deals with the railroads and then bought out rivals who could not compete with him. With his associate Henry Clay Frick, he bought up coal mines and leased part of the Mesabi iron range in Minnesota, operated a fleet of ore ships on the Great Lakes, and acquired railroads. Ultimately, he controlled the processing of his steel from mine to market. He financed his vast undertakings not only out of his own profits but out of the sale of stock. Then, in 1901, he sold out for $450 million to the banker J. Pierpont Morgan, who merged the Carnegie interests with others to create the giant United States Steel Corporation—a $1.4 billion enterprise that controlled almost two-thirds of the nation's steel production.

There were similar developments in other industries. Gustavus Swift developed a relatively small meat-packing company into a great national corporation. Isaac Singer patented a sewing machine in 1851 and created—in I. M. Singer and Company—one of the first modern manufacturing corporations.

Many of the corporate organizations developed a new approach to management. Large, national business enterprises needed more systematic administrative structures than the limited, local ventures of the past. As a

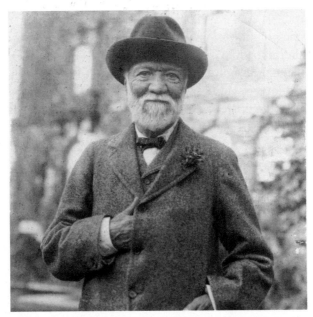

ANDREW CARNEGIE Carnegie was one of relatively small number of the great industrialists of the late nineteenth century who genuinely rose "from rags to riches." Born in Scotland, he came to the United States in 1848 and soon found work as a messenger in a Pittsburgh telegraph office. In 1873 he invested all his assets in the development of the first American steel mills. In 1901 he abruptly resigned from the industrial world and spent the remaining years of his life as a philanthropist. By the time of his death in 1919, he had given away some $350 million.

result, corporate leaders introduced a set of managerial techniques—the genesis of modern business administration—that relied on the division of responsibilities, a carefully designed hierarchy of control, modern cost-accounting procedures, and perhaps above all a new breed of business executive: the "middle manager," who formed a layer of command between workers and owners. Beginning in the railroad corporations, these new management techniques moved quickly into virtually every area of large-scale industry. Efficient administrative capabilities helped make possible another major feature of the modern corporation: consolidation.

Businessmen created large, consolidated organizations primarily through two methods. One was "horizontal integration"—the combining of a number of firms engaged in the same enterprise into a single corporation. The consolidation of many different railroad lines into one company was an example. Another method, which became popular in the 1890s, was "vertical integration"—the taking over of all the different businesses on which a company relied for its primary function. Carnegie Steel, which came to control not only steel mills but mines, railroads, and other enterprises, was an example of vertical integration.

The most celebrated corporate empire of the late nineteenth century was John D. Rockefeller's Standard Oil, a great combination created through both horizontal and vertical integration. Shortly after the Civil War, Rockefeller launched a refining company in Cleveland and immediately began trying to eliminate his competition. Allying himself with other wealthy capitalists, he proceeded methodically to buy out competing refineries. In 1870, he formed the Standard Oil Company of Ohio, which in a few years had acquired twenty of the twenty-five refineries in Cleveland, as well as plants in Pittsburgh, Philadelphia, New York, and Baltimore.

So far, Rockefeller had expanded only horizontally. But soon he began expanding vertically as well. He built his own barrel factories, terminal warehouses, and pipelines. Standard Oil owned its own freight cars and developed its own marketing organization. By the 1880s, Rockefeller had established such dominance within the petroleum industry that to much of the nation he served as the leading symbol of monopoly. He controlled access to 90 percent of the nation's refined oil.

Rockefeller and other industrialists saw consolidation as a way to cope with what they believed was the greatest curse of the modern economy: "cutthroat competition." Most businessmen claimed to believe in free enterprise and a competitive marketplace, but in fact they feared the existence of too many competing firms. They were convinced that substantial competition could spell instability and ruin for all. A successful enterprise, many capitalists believed (but did not say), was one that could eliminate or absorb its competitors.

As the movement toward combination accelerated, new vehicles emerged to facilitate it. The railroads began with so-called pool arrangements—informal agreements among various companies to stabilize rates and divide markets (arrangements that would, in later years, be known as cartels). But the pools did not work very well. If even a few firms in an industry were unwilling to cooperate (as was almost always the case), the pool arrangements collapsed.

The failure of the pools led to new techniques of consolidation resting less on cooperation than on centralized control. At first, the most successful such technique was the creation of the "trust"—pioneered by Standard Oil in the early 1880s and perfected by the banker J. P. Morgan. Over time, the word "trust" became a term for any great economic combination, but the trust was in fact a particular kind of organization. Under a trust agreement, stockholders in individual corporations transferred their stocks to a small group of trustees in exchange for shares in the trust itself. Owners of trust certificates often had no direct control over the decisions of the trustees; they simply received a share of the profits of the combination. The trustees themselves, on the other hand, might literally own only a few companies but could exercise effective control over many.

In 1889, the state of New Jersey helped produce a third form of consolidation by changing its laws of incorporation to permit companies to buy up other companies. Other states soon followed. That made the trust unnecessary and permitted actual corporate mergers. Rockefeller, for example, quickly relocated Standard Oil in New Jersey and created there what became known as a "holding company"—a central corporate body that would buy up the stock of various members of the Standard Oil trust and establish direct, formal ownership of the corporations in the trust.

By the end of the nineteenth century, as a result of corporate consolidation, 1 percent of the corporations in America were able to control more than 33 percent of the manufacturing. A system of economic organization was emerging that lodged enormous power in the hands of very few men—the great bankers of New York such as J. P. Morgan, industrial titans such as Rockefeller (who himself gained control of a major bank), and others.

Whether or not this ruthless concentration of economic power was the only way (or the best way) to promote industrial expansion, the industrial giants of the era were clearly reponsible for substantial economic growth.

They were integrating operations, cutting costs, creating a great industrial infrastructure, stimulating new markets, creating jobs for millions of un-skilled workers, and opening the way to large-scale mass production. They were also creating the basis for some of the greatest public controversies of their era: a raging debate over concentrated economic and political power that continued well into the twentieth century.

CAPITALISM AND ITS CRITICS

The rise of big business was not without its critics. Farmers and workers saw in the growth of the new corporate power centers a threat to notions of a republican society in which wealth and authority were widely distributed. Middle-class critics pointed to the corruption that the new industrial titans seemed to produce in their own enterprises and in local, state, and national politics. The growing criticisms challenged the captains of industry to create a defense of the new corporate economy, one that would convince the public (and themselves) that such an economy was compatible with the ideology of individualism and equal opportunity that was so central to American life.

Survival of the Fittest

The new rationale for capitalism rested squarely on the older ideology of individualism. The new industrial economy, its defenders argued, was not shrinking opportunities for individual advancement. It was expanding those opportunities. It was providing every individual with a chance to succeed and attain great wealth.

There was an element of truth in such claims, but only a small element. Before the Civil War there had been few millionaires in America; by 1892 there were more than 4,000 of them. Some of them—Carnegie, Rockefeller, and a few others—were in fact what almost all millionaires claimed to be: "self-made men." But most of the new business tycoons had begun their careers from positions of comfort, privilege, and wealth. Nor was their rise to power and prominence always a result simply of hard work and ingenuity, as they liked to claim. It was also a result of ruthlessness and, at times, rampant corruption. Industrialists made large financial contributions to politicians, political parties, and government officials in exchange for assis-tance and support.

Nevertheless, most tycoons continued to claim that they had attained their wealth and power through hard work, acquisitiveness, and thrift—the traditional virtues of Protestant America. Those who succeeded, they argued, deserved their success, and those who failed had earned their failure— through their own laziness, stupidity, or carelessness. Such assumptions became the basis of a popular social theory of the late nineteenth century: Social Darwinism, the application to human society of Charles Darwin's laws of evolution and natural selection among species. Just as only the fittest survived in the process of evolution, the Social Darwinists argued, so in human society only the fittest individuals survived and flourished in the marketplace.

The English philosopher Herbert Spencer was the first and most important proponent of this theory. Society, he argued, benefited from the elimination of the unfit and the survival of the strong and talented. Spencer's books were popular in America in the 1870s and 1880s. And his teachings found prominent supporters among American intellectuals, most notably William Graham Sumner of Yale, who promoted similar ideas in lectures, articles, and a famous 1906 book, *Folkways*. Sumner did not agree with everything Spencer wrote, but he did share Spencer's belief that individuals must have absolute freedom to struggle, to compete, to succeed, or to fail.

Social Darwinism appealed to corporate leaders because it seemed to legitimize their success and confirm their virtues. It placed their activities within the context of traditional American ideas of freedom and individualism, and it justified their tactics. It was not, however, an ideology that had very much to do with the realities of the corporate economy. At the same time that businessmen were celebrating the virtues of competition and the free market, they were making active efforts to protect themselves from competition and to replace the natural workings of the marketplace with control by great combinations. Vicious competitive battle—the thing that Spencer and Sumner celebrated and called a source of healthy progress— was in fact the very thing that American businessmen most feared and tried to eliminate.

The Gospel of Wealth

Some businessmen attempted to temper the harsh philosophy of Social Darwinism with a gentler, if in some ways equally self-serving, idea: the "gospel of wealth." People of great wealth, advocates of this idea argued, had not only great power but great responsibilities. It was their duty to use their riches to advance social progress. Andrew Carnegie elaborated on the creed in his 1901 book, *The Gospel of Wealth*, in which he wrote that people of wealth should consider all revenues in excess of their own needs as "trust funds" to be used for the good of the community. Carnegie was only one of many great industrialists who devoted large parts of their fortunes to philanthropic works.

The notion of private wealth as a public blessing existed alongside another popular concept: the notion of great wealth as something available to all. Russell H. Conwell, a Baptist minister, became the most prominent spokesman for the idea by delivering one lecture, "Acres of Diamonds," more than 6,000 times between 1880 and 1900. Conwell told a series of stories, which he claimed were true, of individuals who had found opportunities for extraordinary wealth in their own back yards. (One such story involved a modest farmer who discovered a vast diamond mine in his own fields in the course of working his land.) Most of the millionaires in the country, Conwell claimed (inaccurately), had begun on the lowest rung of the economic ladder and had worked their way to success. Every industrious individual had the chance to do likewise.

Horatio Alger was the most famous promoter of the success story. Alger was originally a minister in a small town in Massachusetts but was driven from his pulpit as a result of a sexual scandal. He moved to New York, where he wrote his celebrated novels—*Ragged Dick*, *Tom the Bootblack*, *Sink or Swim*, and many others, more than 100 in all, which together sold more than 20 million copies. The titles and characters varied, but the story and message were invariably the same: a poor boy from a small town went to the big city to seek his fortune. By work, perseverance, and luck, he became rich.

Alternative Visions

Alongside the celebrations of competition, the justifications for great wealth, and the legitimation of the existing order stood a group of alternative philosophies, challenging the corporate ethos and at times capitalism itself.

One such philosophy emerged in the work of the sociologist Lester Frank Ward. Ward was a Darwinist, but he rejected the application of Darwinian laws to human society. In *Dynamic Sociology* (1883) and other books, he argued that civilization was not governed by natural selection but by human intelligence, which was capable of shaping society as it wished. In contrast to Sumner, who believed that state intervention to remodel the environment was futile, Ward thought that an active government engaged in positive planning was society's best hope. The people, through their government, could intervene in the economy and adjust it to serve their needs.

Other Americans skeptical of the laissez-faire ideas of the Social Darwinists adopted more drastic approaches to reform. Some dissenters found a home in the Socialist Labor party, founded in the 1870s and led for many years by Daniel De Leon, an immigrant from the West Indies. Although De Leon attracted a modest following in the industrial cities, the party never became a major political force and never polled more than 82,000 votes. De Leon's theoretical and dogmatic approach appealed to intellectuals more than to workers; and a dissident faction of his party, eager to forge ties with organized labor, broke away and in 1901 formed the more enduring American Socialist party.

Other radicals gained a wider following. One of the most influential was the California writer and activist Henry George. His angrily eloquent *Progress and Poverty*, published in 1879, became one of the best-selling nonfiction works in American publishing history. George tried to explain why poverty existed amidst the wealth created by modern industry. He blamed social problems on the ability of a few monopolists to grow wealthy as a result of rising land values. An increase in the value of land, he claimed, was a result not of any effort by the owner but of the growth of society around the land. It was an "unearned increment," and it was rightfully the property of the community. And so George proposed a "single tax," to replace all other taxes, which would return the increment to the people. The tax, he argued, would destroy monopolies, distribute wealth more equally, and eliminate poverty. Single-tax societies sprang up in many cities; and in 1886, George, with the support of labor and the socialists, narrowly missed being elected mayor of New York.

Rivaling George in popularity was Edward Bellamy, whose utopian novel *Looking Backward*, published in 1888, sold more than 1 million copies. It described the experiences of a young Bostonian who went into a hypnotic sleep in 1887 and awoke in the year 2000 to find a new social order in which want, politics, and vice were unknown. The new society had emerged from a peaceful, evolutionary process. The large trusts of the late nineteenth century had continued to grow in size and to combine with one another until ultimately they formed a single, great trust, controlled by the government, which distributed the abundance of the industrial economy equally among all the people. "Fraternal cooperation" had replaced competition. Class divisions had disappeared. Bellamy labeled the philosophy behind this vision "nationalism," and his work inspired the formation of more than 160 Nationalist Clubs to propagate his ideas.

The Problems of Monopoly

Relatively few Americans shared the views of those who questioned capitalism itself. But as time went on, a growing number of people were becoming deeply concerned about a particular, glaring aspect of capitalism: the growth of monopoly.

By the end of the century, a wide range of groups had begun to assail monopoly and economic concentration. Laborers, farmers, consumers, small manufacturers, conservative bankers and financiers, advocates of radical change—all joined the attack. They blamed monopoly for creating artificially high prices and for producing a highly unstable economy. Beginning in 1873, the economy fluctuated erratically, with severe recessions creating havoc every five or six years, each recession worse than the previous one, until finally, in 1893, the system seemed on the verge of total collapse.

Adding to the resentment of monopoly was the emergence of a new class of enormously and conspicuously wealthy people, whose life styles

"THE BOSSES OF THE SENATE" The magazine *Puck* conveyed through its savage cartoons the growing popular belief in the 1880s that the United States government had fallen under the control of corrupt "trusts." As bloated, reptilian plutocrats crowd the back of the U.S. Senate chamber, a sign in the gallery notes that the "People's Entrance" is "closed."

became an affront to those struggling to stay afloat in the erratic economy. According to one estimate early in the century, 1 percent of the families in the United States controlled nearly 88 percent of the nation's assets. Some of the wealthy—Andrew Carnegie, for example—lived relatively modestly and donated large sums to philanthropic causes. Others, however, lived in almost grotesque luxury. Observing their flagrant displays of wealth were the four-fifths of the American people who lived modestly, and at least 10 million people who lived below the commonly accepted poverty line. The standard of living was rising for everyone, but the gap between rich and poor was increasing dramatically. To those in difficult economic circumstances, the sense of relative deprivation could be as frustrating and embittering as poverty itself.

THE ORDEAL OF THE WORKER

The American working class was both a beneficiary and a victim of the growth of industrial capitalism. Most workers in the late nineteenth century experienced a real rise in their standard of living. But they did so at the cost of arduous and often dangerous working conditions, diminishing control over their own work, and a growing sense of powerlessness.

The Immigrant Work Force

The industrial work force expanded dramatically in the late nineteenth century as demand for factory labor grew. The source of that expansion was a massive migration into industrial cities—immigration of two sorts. The first was the continuing flow of rural Americans into factory towns and cities—people disillusioned with or bankrupted by life on the farm and eager for new economic and social opportunities. The second was the great wave of immigration from abroad (primarily from Europe, but also from Asia, Canada, and other areas) in the decades following the Civil War—an influx greater than that of any previous era. The 25 million immigrants who arrived in the United States between 1865 and 1915 were more than four times the number who had arrived in the fifty years before.

In the 1870s and 1880s, most of the immigrants came from the nation's traditional sources: England, Ireland, and northern Europe. By the end of the century, however, the major sources of immigrants had shifted, with large numbers of southern and eastern Europeans (Italians, Poles, Russians,

Greeks, Slavs, and others) moving into the country and into the industrial work force.

The new immigrants were coming to America in part to escape poverty and oppression in their homelands. But they were also lured to the United States by expectations of new opportunities. Some such expectations were realistic, but others were the result of false promises. Railroads tried to lure immigrants into their Western landholdings by distributing misleading advertisements overseas. Industrial employers actively recruited immigrant workers under the Labor Contract Law, which—until its repeal in 1885—permitted them to pay for the passage of workers in advance and deduct the amount later from their wages. Even after the repeal of the law, employers continued to encourage the immigration of unskilled laborers, often with the assistance of foreign-born labor brokers, such as the Greek and Italian *padrones* who recruited work gangs of their fellow nationals.

The arrival of these new groups introduced heightened ethnic tensions into the dynamics of the working class. Low-paid Poles, Greeks, and French Canadians began to displace higher-paid British and Irish workers in the textile factories of New England. Italians, Slavs, and Poles emerged as a major source of labor for the mining industry, traditionally dominated by native workers or northern European immigrants. Within industries, more-over, workers tended to cluster in particular occupations (and thus, often, at particular income levels) by ethnic group.

Wages and Working Conditions

The average standard of living for workers may have been rising in the years after the Civil War; but for many laborers, the return for their labor remained very small. At the turn of the century, the average income of the American worker was $400 to $500 a year—below the $600 figure that many believed was the minimum required to maintain a reasonable level of comfort. Nor did workers have much job security. All were vulnerable to the boom-and-bust cycle of the industrial economy, and some lost their jobs because of technological advances or because of the cyclical or seasonal nature of their work. Even those who kept their jobs could find their wages suddenly and substantially cut in hard times. Few workers, in other words, were ever very far from poverty.

American laborers faced a wide array of other hardships as well. For first-generation workers accustomed to the patterns of agrarian life, there was a difficult adjustment to the nature of modern industrial labor: the

CHILD LABOR Many working-class children of the early twentieth century found employment as "breaker boys," picking pieces of slate out of piles of coal. The coal dust was often so thick that they could hardly see one another, as this Lewis Hine photograph suggests.

performance of routine, repetitive tasks, often requiring little skill, on a strict and monotonous schedule. To skilled artisans whose once-valued tasks were now performed by machines, the new system was impersonal and demeaning. Factory laborers worked ten-hour days, six days a week; in the steel industry they worked twelve hours a day. Many worked in appallingly unsafe or unhealthy factories. Industrial accidents were frequent and severe. Compensation to the victims, either from their employers or from the government, was limited.

Women and Children at Work

The decreasing need for skilled work in factories induced many employers to increase the use of women and children, whom they could hire for lower wages than adult males. By 1900, 20 percent of all manufacturing workers were women; and 20 percent of all women (well over 5 million) were wage earners. Women worked in all areas of industry, even in some of the most arduous jobs. Most women, however, worked in a few industries where unskilled and semiskilled machine labor (as opposed to heavy manual labor) prevailed. The textile industry remained the largest single industrial employer of women. (Domestic service remained the most common female occupation overall.) Women worked for wages as low as $6 to $8 a week, well below the minimum necessary for survival (and well below the wages paid to men working the same jobs).

At least 1.7 million children under sixteen years of age were employed in factories and fields, more than twice the number of thirty years before; 10 percent of all girls aged ten to fifteen, and 20 percent of all boys, held jobs. Under the pressure of outraged public opinion, thirty-eight state legislatures passed child labor laws in the late nineteenth century; but these laws were of limited impact. Sixty percent of child workers were employed in agriculture, which was typically exempt from the laws. And even for children employed in factories, the laws merely set a minimum age of twelve years and a maximum workday of ten hours, standards that employers often ignored in any case.

Emerging Unionization

Laborers attempted to fight back against such conditions by adopting some of the same tactics their employers had used so effectively: creating large combinations—national unions. By the end of the century, however, their efforts had met with little success.

There had been craft unions in America, representing small groups of skilled workers, since well before the Civil War. Alone, however, individual unions could not hope to exert significant power in the economy. And during the recession years of the 1870s, unions faced the additional problem of widespread public hostility. When labor disputes with employers turned bitter and violent, as they occasionally did, much of the public instinctively blamed the workers (or the "radicals" and "anarchists" they believed were influencing the workers) for the trouble, rarely the employers. Particularly alarming to middle-class Americans was the emergence of the "Molly Maguires," in the anthracite coal region of western Pennsylvania. This militant labor organization occasionally used violence and even murder in its battle with coal operators. Much of the violence attributed to the Molly Maguires, however, was deliberately instigated by informers and agents employed by the mine owners, who wanted a pretext for ruthless measures suppressing unionization.

Excitement over the Molly Maguires paled beside the near hysteria that gripped the country during the railroad strike of 1877, which began when the Eastern railroads announced a 10 percent wage cut and which soon expanded into something approaching a class war. Strikers disrupted rail service from Baltimore to St. Louis, destroyed equipment, and rioted in the streets of Pittsburgh and other cities. State militias were called out, and in July President Hayes ordered federal troops to suppress the disorders in West Virginia. In Baltimore, eleven demonstrators died and forty were wounded in a conflict between workers and militiamen. In Philadelphia, the state militia killed twenty people when the troops opened fire on thousands of workers and their families who were attempting to block the railroad crossings. In all, over 100 people died before the strike finally collapsed several weeks after it had begun.

The great railroad strike was America's first major, national labor conflict, and it illustrated that disputes between labor and capital could no longer be localized in the increasingly national economy. It illustrated as well the depth of resentment among many American workers and the lengths to which they were prepared to go to express that resentment. And, finally, it indicated the serious problems afflicting the labor movement. The failure of the strike severely weakened the railroad unions and damaged the reputation of labor organizations in other industries as well.

The Knights of Labor

The first major effort to create a genuinely national labor organization was the founding in 1869 of the Noble Order of the Knights of Labor, under the leadership of Uriah S. Stephens. Membership was open to all who "toiled," a definition that included all workers, most business and professional people, and virtually all women—whether they worked in factories, as domestic servants, or in their own homes. The only excluded groups were lawyers, bankers, liquor dealers, and professional gamblers. The Knights of Labor was loosely organized, without much central direction. Its program was similarly vague. Although its leaders championed an eight-hour day and the abolition of child labor, they were more interested in long-range reform of the economy. The Knights hoped to replace the "wage system" with a new "cooperative system," in which workers would themselves control a large part of the economy.

For several years, the Knights remained a secret fraternal organization. But in the late 1870s, under the leadership of Terence V. Powderly, the order moved into the open and entered a spectacular period of expansion. By 1886, it claimed a total membership of over 700,000, including some militant elements that the moderate leadership could not always control. Local unions or assemblies associated with the Knights launched a series of railroad and other strikes in the 1880s in defiance of Powderly's wishes. Their failure helped discredit the organization. By 1890, the membership of the Knights had shrunk to 100,000. A few years later, the organization disappeared altogether.

The AFL

Even before the Knights began to decline, a rival association based on a very different organizational concept appeared. In 1881, representatives of a number of craft unions formed the Federation of Organized Trade and Labor Unions of the United States and Canada. Five years later, this body took the name it has borne ever since, the American Federation of Labor (AFL), and soon became the most important labor group in the country.

Rejecting the Knights' idea of one big union for everybody, the Federation was an association of essentially autonomous craft unions and represented mainly skilled workers. Samuel Gompers, the powerful leader of the AFL, accepted the basic premises of capitalism; his goal was simply to secure for the workers he represented a greater share of capitalism's material rewards. The AFL concentrated on labor's immediate objectives: wages, hours, and working conditions. While it hoped to attain its ends by collective bargaining, it was ready to use strikes if necessary. As one of its first objectives, the AFL demanded a national eight-hour day and called for a general strike if the goal was not achieved by May 1, 1886. On that day, strikes and demonstrations for a shorter workday took place all over the country, most of them staged by AFL unions but a few by more radical groups.

In Chicago, a center of labor and radical strength, a strike was already in progress at the McCormick Harvester Company. City police had been harassing the strikers, and labor and radical leaders called a protest meeting at Haymarket Square. When the police ordered the crowd to disperse, someone threw a bomb that killed seven policemen and injured sixty-seven others. The police, who had killed four strikers the day before, fired into the crowd and killed four more people. Conservative, property-conscious

Americans—frightened and outraged—demanded retribution, even though no one knew who had thrown the bomb. Chicago officials finally rounded up eight anarchists and charged them with murder, on the grounds that their statements had incited whoever had hurled the bomb. All eight scapegoats were found guilty after a remarkably injudicious trial. Seven were sentenced to death. One of them committed suicide, four were executed, and two had their sentences commuted to life imprisonment.

To most middle-class Americans, the Haymarket bombing was an alarming symbol of social chaos and radicalism. "Anarchism" now became in the public mind a code word for terrorism and violence, even though most anarchists were relatively peaceful visionaries dreaming of a new social order. For the next thirty years, the specter of anarchism remained one of the most frightening concepts in the American imagination. It was a constant obstacle to the goals of the AFL and other labor organizations, and it did particular damage to the Knights of Labor. However much they tried to distance themselves from radicals, labor leaders were always vulnerable to accusations of anarchism, as the violent strikes of the 1890s occasionally illustrated.

The Homestead Strike

The Amalgamated Association of Iron and Steel Workers, which was affiliated with the American Federation of Labor, was the most powerful trade union in the country. Its members were skilled workers, in great demand by employers and had thus long been able to exercise significant power in the workplace. In the mid-1880s, however, demand for skilled workers was in decline as new production methods and new, large-scale corporate organizations streamlined the steelmaking process. In the Carnegie system, which was coming to dominate the steel industry, the union was able to win a foothold in only one of the corporation's three major factories—the Homestead plant near Pittsburgh.

By 1890, Carnegie and his chief lieutenant, Henry Clay Frick, had decided that the Amalgamated "had to go" even at Homestead. Over the next two years, they repeatedly cut wages at Homestead. At first, the union acquiesced, aware that it was not strong enough to wage a successful strike. In 1892, however, the company stopped even discussing its decisions with the Amalgamated, in effect denying the union's right to negotiate at all. Finally, when Frick announced another wage cut at Homestead and gave the union two days to accept it, the Amalgamated called for a strike.

BREAKING THE HOMESTEAD STRIKE, 1892 State militiamen enter Homestead, Pennsylvania, to put an end to the Amalgamated union's violent strike by opening the Carnegie-owned steel plant to strikebreaking workers. This double photograph forms a "stereograph," which when viewed through a special lens (a "stereoscope") gave the impression of a three-dimensional scene.

Frick abruptly shut down the plant and called in 300 guards from the Pinkerton Detective Agency to enable the company to hire nonunion workers. The hated Pinkertons were well-known strikebreakers, and their mere presence was often enough to incite workers to violence. They approached the plant by river on barges on July 6, 1892. The strikers poured gasoline on the water, set it on fire, and then met the Pinkertons at the docks with guns and dynamite. A pitched battle broke out. After several hours of fighting, which brought death to three guards and ten strikers and injuries to many others, the Pinkertons surrendered and were escorted roughly out of town.

But the workers' victory was temporary. The governor of Pennsylvania, at the company's request, sent the state's entire National Guard contingent, some 8,000 troops, to Homestead. Production resumed, with strikebreakers now protected by troops. And public opinion turned against the strikers when a radical made an attempt to assassinate Frick. Slowly, workers drifted back to their jobs; and finally—four months after the strike began—the Amalgamated surrendered. By 1900, every major steel plant in the Northeast had broken with the Amalgamated, which now had virtually no power to resist. Its membership shrank from a high of 24,000 in 1891 (two-thirds of all eligible steelworkers) to fewer than 7,000 a decade later.

The Pullman Strike

A dispute of greater magnitude and equal bitterness, if less violence, was the Pullman strike in 1894. The Pullman Palace Car Company manufactured sleeping and parlor cars for railroads, which it built and repaired at a plant near Chicago. There the company built a 600-acre town, Pullman, and rented its trim, orderly houses to the employees. George M. Pullman, owner of the company, saw the town as a model solution of the industrial problem; he referred to the workers as his "children." But many residents chafed at the regimentation (and the high rents).

In the winter of 1893–1894, the Pullman Company slashed wages by about 25 percent, citing its own declining revenues in the depression. At the same time, Pullman refused to reduce rents in its model town, which were 20 to 25 percent higher than those for comparable accommodations in surrounding areas. Workers went on strike and persuaded the militant American Railway Union, led by Eugene V. Debs, to support them by refusing to handle Pullman cars and equipment. Within a few days thousands of railroad workers in twenty-seven states and territories were on strike, and transportation from Chicago to the Pacific coast was paralyzed.

Most state governors responded readily to appeals from strike-threatened businesses; but the governor of Illinois, John Peter Altgeld, was a man with demonstrated sympathies for workers and their grievances. Altgeld had criticized the trials of the Haymarket anarchists and had pardoned the convicted men who were still in prison when he took office. He refused to call out the militia to protect employers now. Bypassing Altgeld, railroad operators asked the federal government to send regular army troops to Illinois, using the pretext that the strike was preventing the movement of mail on the trains. President Grover Cleveland and Attorney General Richard Olney, a former railroad lawyer and a bitter foe of unions, complied. In July 1894, the president, over Altgeld's objections, ordered 2,000 troops to the Chicago area. A federal court issued an injunction forbidding the union to continue the strike. When Debs and his associates defied it, they were arrested and imprisoned. With federal troops protecting the hiring of new workers and with the union leaders in a federal jail, the strike quickly collapsed.

Sources of Labor Weakness

The last decades of the nineteenth century were years in which labor, despite its organizing efforts, made few real gains. Industrial wages rose hardly at all. Labor leaders won a few legislative victories—the abolition by Congress in 1885 of the Contract Labor Law; the establishment by Congress in 1868 of an eight-hour day on public works projects and in 1892 of the same workday for government employees; and state laws governing hours of labor and safety standards. But most such laws were not enforced. There were strikes and protests, but few real gains. The end of the century found most workers with less political power and less control of the workplace than they had had forty years before.

Workers failed to make greater gains for many reasons. The principal labor organizations represented only a small percentage of the industrial work force; the AFL, the most important, excluded unskilled workers, who were emerging as the core of the industrial work force, and along with them most women, blacks, and recent immigrants. Divisions within the work force contributed further to union weakness. Tensions among different ethnic and racial groups kept laborers divided.

Another source of labor weakness was the shifting nature of the work force. Many immigrant workers came to America intending to remain only briefly, to earn some money and return home. The assumption that they had no long-range future in the country eroded their willingness to organize. Other workers—natives and immigrants alike—were in constant motion, moving from one job to another, one town to another, seldom in one place long enough to establish any sort of institutional ties or exert any real power.

Above all, perhaps, workers made few gains in the late nineteenth century because of the strength of the forces arrayed against them. They faced corporate organizations of vast wealth and power, which were generally determined to crush any efforts by workers to challenge their prerogatives. And as the Homestead and Pullman strikes suggest, the corporations had the support of local, state, and federal authorities, who were willing to send in troops to "preserve order" and crush labor uprisings on demand.

Despite the creation of new labor unions, despite a wave of strikes and protests that in the 1880s and 1890s reached startling proportions, workers in the late nineteenth century failed on the whole to create successful organizations or to protect their interests in the way the large corporations managed to do. In the battle for power within the emerging industrial economy, almost all the advantages seemed to lie with capital.

CHAPTER EIGHTEEN

The Age of the City

The New Urban Growth ~ Society and Culture in Urbanizing America
High Culture in the Urban Age

THE INDUSTRIALIZATION AND commercialization of America changed the face of society in countless ways. Nowhere, however, were the changes more profound than in the growth of cities and the creation of an urban society and culture. Having begun its life as a primarily agrarian republic, the United States in the late nineteenth century was becoming an urban nation.

THE NEW URBAN GROWTH

The great folk movement from the countryside to the city was not unique to the United States. It was occurring simultaneously throughout much of the Western world in response to industrialization and the factory system. But America, a society with little experience of great cities, found urbanization particularly jarring. The city attracted people because it offered conveniences, entertainments, and cultural experiences unavailable in rural communities. But it attracted people most of all because it offered more and better-paying jobs than were available in the countryside. Whatever the reasons, the urban population of America increased sevenfold in the half-century after the Civil War. And in 1920, the census revealed that for the first time, a majority of the American people lived in "urban" areas—defined as communities of 2,500 people or more.

Natural increase accounted for only a small part of the urban growth. Urban families experienced a high rate of infant mortality, a declining fertility rate, and a high death rate from disease. Without immigration, cities would have grown relatively slowly.

The Migrations

The late nineteenth century was an age of unprecedented geographical mobility, as Americans left the declining agricultural regions of the East at a dramatic rate. Some of those who left were moving to the newly developing farmlands of the West. But almost as many were moving to the cities of the East and the Midwest.

Among those leaving rural America for industrial cities in the 1880s were Southern blacks. That was a testament to the poverty, debt, violence, and oppression African-Americans encountered in the late-nineteenth-century South. The opportunities they found in cities were limited, but an improvement nevertheless over what they left behind. Factory jobs for blacks were rare and professional opportunities almost nonexistent. Urban blacks tended to work as cooks, janitors, and domestic servants, as well as in other service occupations. Since many such jobs were considered women's work, black women often outnumbered black men in the cities. By the end of the nineteenth century, there were substantial black communities (10,000 people or more) in over thirty cities.

The most important source of urban population growth in the late nineteenth century, however, was the arrival of great numbers of new immigrants from abroad. Some came from Canada, Latin America, and—particularly on the West Coast—China and Japan. But by far the greatest number came from Europe. After 1880, the flow of new arrivals began for the first time to include large numbers of people from southern and eastern Europe. By the 1890s, more than half of all immigrants came from these new regions, as opposed to fewer than 2 percent in the 1860s.

In earlier stages of immigration, most new immigrants from Europe (particularly Germans and Scandinavians) were at least modestly prosperous and educated. They had generally headed west—either to be farmers or to work as businessmen, professionals, or skilled laborers in Midwestern cities such as St. Louis, Cincinnati, and Milwaukee. Most of the new immigrants of the late nineteenth century lacked the capital to buy farmland and lacked the education to establish themselves in professions. So, like similarly poor Irish immigrants before the Civil War, they settled overwhelmingly in industrial cities, where they occupied largely unskilled jobs.

The Ethnic City

By 1890, most of the population of the major urban areas consisted of immigrants: 87 percent of the population in Chicago, 80 percent in New

York, 84 percent in Milwaukee and Detroit. (London, the largest industrial city in Europe, had by contrast a population that was 94 percent native.)

Equally striking was the diversity of the new immigrant populations. In other countries experiencing heavy immigration in this period, most of the new arrivals were coming from one or two sources. But in the United States, no single national group dominated. In the last four decades of the nineteenth century, substantial groups arrived from Italy, Germany, Scandinavia, Austria, Hungary, Russia, Great Britain, Ireland, Poland, Greece, Canada, Japan, China, Holland, Mexico, and other nations. In some towns, a dozen different ethnic groups might find themselves living in close proximity to one another.

Most of the new immigrants were rural people, and their adjustment to city life was often a painful one. To help ease the transition, many national groups formed close-knit ethnic communities within the cities: Italian, Polish, Jewish, Slavic, Chinese, French Canadian, Mexican, and other neighborhoods (often called "immigrant ghettoes") that attempted to re-create in the New World many of the features of the Old. Some ethnic neighborhoods consisted of people who had migrated to America from the same province, town, or village. Even when the population was more diverse, however, the community offered newcomers much that was familiar. They could find newspapers and theaters in their native languages, stores selling their native foods, church and fraternal organizations that provided links with their national pasts. Many immigrants also maintained close ties with their native countries. They stayed in touch with relatives who had remained behind. Some (perhaps as many as a third in the early years) returned to Europe after a relatively short time; others helped bring the rest of their families to America.

The cultural cohesiveness of the ethnic communities clearly eased the pain of separation from the immigrants' native lands. What role it played in helping immigrants become absorbed into the economic life of America is a more difficult question to answer. It is clear that some ethnic groups (Jews and Germans in particular) advanced economically more rapidly than others (for example, the Irish). One explanation is that, by huddling together in ethnic neighborhoods, immigrant groups tended to reinforce the cultural values of their previous societies. When those values were particularly well suited to economic advancement—as was, for example, the high value Jews placed on education—ethnic identification may have helped members of a group to improve their lots. When other values predominated—maintaining community solidarity, strengthening family ties, preserving order—progress could be less rapid.

Assimilation and Exclusion

Yet it would be easy to overstate the differences among the various immigrant communities, because virtually all groups had certain things in common. Most immigrants, of course, shared the experience of living in cities (and of adapting from a rural past to an urban present). Most were young; the majority of newcomers were between fifteen and forty-five years old. And in virtually all immigrant communities, the strength of ethnic ties had to compete against another powerful force: the desire for assimilation.

Many of the new arrivals had come to America with romantic visions of the New World. And however disillusioning they might find their first contact with the United States, they usually retained the dream of becoming true "Americans." Even some first-generation immigrants worked hard to rid themselves of all vestiges of their old cultures, to become thoroughly Americanized. Second-generation immigrants were even more likely to attempt to break with the old ways, to assimilate themselves completely into what they considered the real American culture. Some even looked with contempt on parents and grandparents who continued to defend traditional ethnic habits and values or who tried to maintain control of adult children. Young women, in particular, sometimes rebelled against parents who tried to arrange (or prevent) marriages, or who disapproved of women entering the workplace.

Assimilation was not, of course, entirely a matter of choice. Native-born Americans encouraged it, both deliberately and inadvertently, in countless ways. Public schools taught children in English, and employers often insisted that workers speak English on the job. Most stores sold mainly American products, forcing immigrants to adapt their diets, clothing, and life styles to American norms. Church leaders were often native-born Americans or more assimilated immigrants who encouraged their parishioners to adopt American ways. Some even reformed their theology and liturgy to make it more compatible with the norms of the new country. Reform Judaism, for example, was an effort by American Jewish leaders to make their faith less "foreign" to the dominant culture of a largely Christian nation.

The arrival of these vast numbers of new immigrants, and the way many of them clung to old ways and created culturally distinctive communities, provoked fear and resentment among some native-born Americans in much the same way earlier arrivals had done. Some people reacted against the immigrants out of generalized fears and prejudices, seeing in their "foreignness" the source of all the disorder and corruption of the urban world.

A M E R I C A N V O I C E S

ANZIA YEZIERSKA

A Jewish Immigrant Strains Against the Past

FOR SEVENTEEN YEARS I had stood [my father's] preaching and his bullying. But now all the hammering hell that I had to listen to since I was born cracked my brain. His heartlessness to Mother, his pitiless driving away Bessie's only chance to love, bargaining away Fania to a gambler and Mashah to a diamond-faker—when they each had the luck to win lovers of their own—all these tyrannies crashed over me. Should I let him crush me as he crushed them? No. This is America, where children are people. . . .

Blindly, I grabbed my things together into a bundle. I didn't care where I was going or what was to become of me. Only to break away from my black life. Only not to hear Father's preaching voice again. . . .

As I came through the door with my bundle, Father caught sight of me. "What's this?" he asked. "Where are you going?"

"I'm going back to work, in New York. . . . I've got to live my own life. It's enough that Mother and the others lived for you. . . . Thank God, I'm not living in olden times. Thank God I'm living in America! You made the lives of the other children. I'm going to make my own life!"

"You blasphemer!" His hand flung out and struck my cheek. "Denier of God! I'll teach you respect for the law!"

I leaped back and dashed for the door. The Old World had struck its last on me.

SOURCE: From the novel *Bread Givers* by Anzia Yezierska. Copyright © 1925 by Doubleday, copyright © 1952 by Anzia Yezierska, transferred to Louise Levitas Henriksen in 1970. Reprinted by permission of Persea Books, Inc.

Others had economic concerns. Native laborers were often incensed by the willingness of the immigrants to accept lower wages and to take over the jobs of strikers.

The rising nativism provoked political responses. In 1887, Henry Bowers, a self-educated lawyer obsessed with a hatred of Catholics and foreigners, founded the American Protective Association, a group committed to stopping immigration. By 1894, membership in the organization reportedly reached 500,000, with chapters throughout the Northeast and Midwest. That same year, a more genteel organization—the Immigration Restriction League—was founded in Boston by five Harvard alumni. It was dedicated to the belief that immigrants should be screened, through literacy tests and other standards designed to separate the "desirable" from the "undesirable."

Even before the rise of these new organizations, politicians were struggling to find answers to the "immigration question." In 1882 Congress responded to strong anti-Asian sentiment in California and elsewhere and excluded the Chinese, who had been arriving in large numbers on the West Coast and who, among other things, made up a significant portion of the work force building the Western railroads. In the same year, Congress denied entry to "undesirables"—convicts, paupers, the mentally incompetent—and placed a tax of 50 cents on each person admitted. Later legislation of the 1890s enlarged the list of those barred from immigrating and increased the tax.

But these laws kept out only a small number of aliens, and more ambitious restriction proposals made little progress in Congress. That was because many native-born Americans, far from fearing immigration, welcomed it and exerted strong political pressure against the restrictionists. Immigration was providing a cheap and plentiful labor supply to the rapidly growing economy; and many argued that America's industrial (and indeed agricultural) development would be impossible without it.

The Urban Landscape

The city was a place of remarkable contrasts. It had homes of almost unimaginable size and grandeur and hovels of indescribable squalor. It had conveniences unknown to earlier generations, and problems that seemed beyond the capacity of society to solve. Both the attractions and the problems were a result of the stunning pace with which cities were growing. The expansion of the urban population helped spur important new technological and industrial developments. But the rapid growth also produced mis-government, poverty, congestion, filth, epidemics, and great fires. The rate of growth was simply too fast for planning and building to keep pace.

One of the greatest problems was providing housing for the thousands of new residents who were pouring into the cities every day. For the prosperous, housing was seldom a worry. The availability of cheap labor and the increasing accessibility of tools and materials reduced the cost of building in the late nineteenth century and permitted anyone with even a moderate income to afford a house. Some of the richest urban residents lived in palatial mansions in the heart of the city. Many of the moderately well-to-do took advantage of less expensive land on the edges of the city and settled in new suburbs, linked to the downtowns by trains or streetcars.

Most urban residents, however, could not afford either to own a house in the city or to move to the suburbs. Instead, they stayed in the city centers and rented. And because demand was so high and space so scarce, they had little bargaining power. Landlords tried to squeeze as many rent-paying residents as possible into the smallest available space. In Manhattan, for example, the average population density in 1894 was 143 people per acre—a rate higher than that of the most crowded cities of Europe (Paris had 127 per acre, Berlin 101) and far higher than that of any other American city then or since. Landlords were also reluctant to invest much in immigrant housing; they were confident they could rent the dwellings they owned regardless of the conditions. In the cities of the South—Charleston, New Orleans, Richmond—poor blacks lived in crumbling former slave quarters. In Boston, immigrants moved into cheap three-story wooden houses ("triple deckers"), many of them decaying fire hazards. In Baltimore and Philadelphia, the new arrivals crowded into narrow brick row houses. And in New York and many other cities, they lived in tenements.

The word "tenement" had originally referred simply to a multiple-family rental building, but by the late nineteenth century it was used to describe slum dwellings only. The first tenements, built in 1850, had been hailed as a great improvement in housing for the poor. But most were, in fact, miserable places, with many windowless rooms, little or no plumbing or central heating, and perhaps a row of privies in the basement. Jacob Riis, a Danish immigrant and New York newspaper reporter and photographer, shocked many middle-class Americans with his sensational (and some would say sensationalized) descriptions and pictures of tenement life in his 1890 book, *How the Other Half Lives*. But the solution reformers often adopted was simply to raze slum dwellings without building any new housing to replace them.

A NEW YORK TENEMENT, 1910 This photograph of a woman and her children in a rear tenement bedroom was meant to illustrate the crowding and squalor of urban immigrant life. The photographer was Lewis Hine, who from 1907 to 1914 worked for a government committee investigating child labor and whose efforts to expose social conditions helped spur legislative action.

Urban growth posed monumental transportation challenges. Old downtown streets were often too narrow for the heavy traffic that was beginning to move over them. Most were without a hard, paved surface and resembled either a sea of mud or a cloud of dust, depending on the weather. But it was not simply the conditions of the streets that impeded urban transportation. It was the numbers of people who needed to move everyday from one part of the city to another, numbers that mandated the development of mass transportation. Streetcars drawn on tracks by horses had been introduced into some cities even before the Civil War. But the horsecars were not fast enough, so many communities developed new forms of mass transit. In 1870, New York opened its first elevated railway, whose noisy, filthy steam-powered trains moved rapidly above the city streets on massive iron structures. New York, Chicago, San Francisco, and other cities also experimented with cable cars, towed by continuously moving underground cables. Richmond, Virginia, introduced the first electric trolley line in 1888, and by 1895 such systems were operating in 850 towns and cities. Boston in 1897 opened the first American subway when it put some of its trolley lines underground. At the same time, cities were developing new techniques of road and bridge building. One of the great technological marvels of the 1880s was the completion of the Brooklyn Bridge in New York—a dramatic steel-cable suspension span designed by John A. Roebling.

Cities were growing upward as well as outward. In Chicago, the construction of the first modern "skyscraper"—by later standards a relatively modest building, ten stories high—launched a new era in urban architecture. Once builders perfected the technique of constructing tall buildings with cast iron and then steel beams, and once other inventors produced the electric elevator, no obstacle remained to even higher buildings.

Strains of Urban Life

The increasing congestion of the city and the absence of adequate public services produced serious hazards. One was fire. In one major city after another, fires destroyed large downtown areas. Chicago and Boston suffered "great fires" in 1871. Other cities—among them Baltimore and San Francisco, where a tremendous earthquake produced a catastrophic fire in 1906—experienced similar disasters. The great fires were terrible experiences, but they were also important events in the development of the cities involved. They encouraged the construction of fireproof buildings and the development of professional fire departments. They also forced cities to rebuild at a time when new technological and architectural innovations were available. Some of the modern, high-rise downtowns of American cities arose out of the rubble of great fires.

An even greater hazard than fire was disease, especially in poor neighborhoods with inadequate sanitation facilities. But an epidemic that began in a poor neighborhood could (and often did) spread easily into other neighborhoods as well. Few municipal officials recognized the relationship of improper sewage disposal and water contamination to such epidemic diseases as typhoid fever and cholera; and many cities lacked adequate systems for disposing of human waste until well into the twentieth century.

Above all, perhaps, the expansion of the city spawned widespread and often desperate poverty. Despite the rapid growth of urban economies, the sheer number of new residents ensured that many people would be unable to earn enough for a decent subsistence. Public agencies and private philanthropic organizations offered very limited relief. And they were generally dominated by middle-class people, who tended to believe that too much assistance would breed dependency and that poverty was the fault of the poor themselves. Some charitable societies—for example, the Salvation Army, which began operating in America in 1879, one year after it was founded in London—concentrated more on religious revivalism than on the relief of the homeless and hungry.

Poverty and crowding naturally bred crime and violence. Much of it was relatively petty, the work of pickpockets, con artists, swindlers, and petty thieves. But some was more dangerous. The American murder rate rose rapidly in the late nineteenth century (even as such rates were declining in Europe), from 25 murders for every million people in 1880 to over 100 by the end of the century. The rising crime rates encouraged many cities to develop larger and more professional police forces. But police forces themselves could spawn corruption and brutality, particularly since jobs on them were often filled through political patronage.

Americans and Europeans alike reacted to the city with marked ambivalence. It was a place of strong allure and great excitement. Yet it was also a place of alienating impersonality, of a new feeling of anonymity, of a different kind of work with which the individual could feel only limited identification. To some, it was also a place of degradation and exploitation. Theodore Dreiser's novel *Sister Carrie* (1900) exposed one troubling aspect of urban life: the plight of single women (like Dreiser's heroine, Carrie) who moved from the countryside into the city and found themselves without any means of support. Carrie first took an exhausting and ill-paying job in a Chicago shoe factory; then she drifted into a life of "sin," exploited by predatory men. Many women were experiencing in reality the dilemmas Carrie experienced in fiction. Living in conditions of extreme poverty and hardship, some moved into prostitution—which, degrading and dangerous as it was, produced a livelihood and a sense of community for desperate people.

The Machine and the Boss

Newly arrived immigrants, many of whom could not speak English, were much in need of institutions to help them adjust to American urban life. But they could expect little assistance from government or from middle-class philanthropic institutions. Some ethnic communities created their own self-help organizations. But for many residents of the inner cities, the principal source of assistance was the political "machine."

The urban machine was one of America's most distinctive political institutions. It owed its existence to the power vacuum that the chaotic growth of cities (and the very limited growth of governments) had created. It was also a product of the potential voting power of large immigrant communities. Any politician who could mobilize that power stood to gain enormous influence or public office. And so there emerged a group of "urban" bosses, themselves often of foreign birth or parentage. Many were Irish, because they spoke English and because some had previous political experience from the long Irish struggle against the English at home.

The principal function of the political boss was simple: to win votes for his organization. That meant winning the loyalty of his constituents. To do so, a boss might provide them with occasional relief—a basket of groceries or a bag of coal. He might step in to save those arrested for petty crimes from jail. When he could, he found work for the unemployed. Above all, he rewarded many of his followers with patronage: with jobs in city government or in such city agencies as the police (which the machine's elected officials often controlled); with jobs building or operating the new transit systems; and with opportunities to rise in the political organization itself.

Machines were also vehicles for making money. Politicians enriched themselves and their allies through various forms of graft and corruption. Some of it might be fairly open—what George Washington Plunkitt of New York's Tammany Hall called "honest graft." For example, a politician might discover in advance where a new road or streetcar line was to be built, buy an interest in the land near it, and profit when the city had to buy the land from him or when property values rose as a result of the construction. But there was also covert graft. Officials received kickbacks from contractors in exchange for contracts to build streets, sewers, public buildings, and other projects; and they sold franchises for the operation of such public utilities as street railways, waterworks, and electric light and power systems. The most famously corrupt city boss was William M. Tweed, boss of New York City's Tammany Hall in the 1860s and 1870s, whose extravagant use of public funds on projects that paid kickbacks to the organization finally landed him in jail in 1872. Middle-class critics cited corruption as the principal characteristic of the machine, but other things were at least as important. Political organizations were responsible for modernizing city infrastructures, for expanding the role of government, and for creating stability in a political and social climate that otherwise would have lacked a center.

Several factors made boss rule possible. One was the power of immigrant voters, who were less concerned with middle-class ideas of political morality than with obtaining the services that machines provided and reformers did not. Another was the link between the political organizations and many wealthy, prominent citizens who profited from their dealings with bosses and resisted efforts to overthrow them. Still others were the rising tax revenues in fast-growing cities and the enormous public expenditures on infrastructure projects, combined with the structural weakness of city governments, which had few established procedures for controlling the expenditures. Within the municipal government, no single official usually had decisive power or responsibility. Instead, authority was generally divided among many officeholders and was limited by the state legislature. The boss, by virtue of his control over his machine, formed an "invisible government" that provided an alternative to the inadequacy of the regular government.

The urban machine was not without competition. Reform groups frequently mobilized public outrage at the corruption of the bosses and often succeeded in driving machine politicians from office. Tammany, for example, saw its candidates for mayor and other high city offices lose almost as often as they won in the last decades of the nineteenth century. But the reform organizations typically lacked the permanence of the machine; and more often than not, their power faded after a few years. Thus, many critics of machines began to argue for more basic reforms: for structural changes in the nature of city government.

SOCIETY AND CULTURE IN URBANIZING AMERICA

For urban middle-class Americans, the last decades of the nineteenth century were a time of dramatic advances. Indeed, it was in those years that a distinctive middle-class culture began to exert a powerful influence over the whole of American life. Other groups in society advanced less rapidly, or not at all; but almost no one was unaffected by the rise of the new urban, consumer culture.

The Rise of Mass Consumption

The growth of American industry could not have occurred without the expansion of markets for the goods being produced. Much of the emerging mass market for industrial goods consisted of the increasingly wealthy middle class. But much of it also consisted of less affluent people who consumed more because mass production and mass distribution were making consumer goods less expensive.

Incomes were rising for almost everyone in the industrial era, although at highly uneven rates. The most conspicuous result of the new economy was the creation of vast fortunes, but perhaps the most important result for society as a whole was the growth and increasing prosperity of the middle class. The salaries of clerks, accountants, middle managers, and other "white-collar" workers rose by an average of a third between 1890 and 1910—and in some parts of the middle class, much higher. Doctors, lawyers, and other professionals, for example, experienced a particularly dramatic increase in both the prestige and the profitability of their professions. Working-class incomes rose too in those years, although from a much lower base and often more slowly. The iron and steel industries saw workers' hourly wages increase by a third between 1890 and 1910; but industries with large female work forces—shoes, textiles, and paper—saw more modest increases, as did almost all industries in the South.

Also important to the new mass market was the development of affordable products and the creation of new merchandising techniques, which made many consumer goods available to a mass market for the first time. A good example of such changes was the emergence of ready-made clothing. In the early nineteenth century, most Americans had made their own clothing—usually from cloth they bought from merchants, at times from fabrics they spun and wove themselves. The invention of the sewing machine and the spur that the Civil War (and its demand for uniforms) gave to the manufacture of clothing created an enormous industry devoted to producing ready-made garments. By the end of the century, virtually all Americans bought their clothing from stores. Partly as a result, much larger numbers of people became concerned with personal style. Interest in women's fashion, for example, had once been a luxury reserved for the relatively affluent. Now middle-class and even working-class women could strive to develop a distinctive style of dress.

Another example was the way Americans bought and prepared food. The development and mass production of tin cans in the 1880s created a large new industry devoted to packaging and selling canned food and

THE DEPARTMENT STORE, C. 1892 This detail from an advertisement shows an interior cross section of the Abraham and Straus department store in Brooklyn, New York. Early department stores boasted not just of the variety of their merchandise but also of the magical qualities of the consumer world they created.

condensed milk. Refrigerated railroad cars made it possible for perishables—meats, vegetables, dairy products, and other foodstuffs—to be transported over long distances without spoiling. The growth of artificially frozen ice made it possible for many more households to afford iceboxes. Among other things, the changes meant improved diets and better health. Life expectancy rose six years in the first two decades of the twentieth century.

Changes in marketing also altered the way Americans bought goods. Small local stores faced competition from new "chain stores." The Atlantic and Pacific Tea Company (the A & P) began a national network of grocery stores in the 1870s. F. W. Woolworth's built a chain of dry goods stores. Sears and Roebuck established a large market for its mail-order merchandise by distributing an enormous catalogue each year. Even people in remote rural areas could order its products.

In larger cities, the emergence of great department stores helped transform buying habits and turn shopping into a more alluring and glamorous activity. Marshall Field in Chicago created one of the first American department stores—a place deliberately designed to create a sense of wonder and excitement. Similar stores emerged in New York, Brooklyn, Boston, Philadelphia, and other cities.

The rise of mass consumption had particularly dramatic effects on American women, who were generally the primary consumers within families. Women's clothing styles changed much more rapidly and dramatically than those of men. Women generally bought and prepared food for their families, so the availability of new food products changed not only the way everyone ate but the way women shopped and cooked. Canning and refrigeration meant greater variety in the diet. It also meant that food did not always have to be purchased on the day it was eaten. The consumer economy also produced new employment opportunities for women as salesclerks in department stores and as waitresses in rapidly proliferating restaurants. And it spawned the creation of a new movement in which women were to play a vital role: the consumer protection movement. The National Consumers League, formed in the 1890s under the leadership of Florence Kelley, attempted to mobilize the power of women as consumers to force retailers and manufacturers to improve wages and working conditions.

Leisure and Sport

Closely related to the growth of consumption was a growing interest in leisure time, which for many people was increasing rapidly. Members of the urban middle and professional classes had large blocks of time in which they were not at work—evenings, weekends, even vacations. Working hours in many factories declined, from an average of nearly seventy hours a week in 1860 to under sixty in 1900. Even farmers found that the mechanization of agriculture gave them more free time. The lives of many Americans were becoming more compartmentalized, with clear distinctions between work and leisure that had not existed in the past. The change produced a search for new forms of recreation and entertainment.

Among the most important responses to this search was the rise of organized spectator sports, and especially baseball, which by the end of the century was well on its way to becoming the "national pastime." A game much like baseball—known as "rounders" and derived from cricket—had enjoyed limited popularity in Great Britain in the early nineteenth century. Versions of the game began to appear in America in the early 1830s, well before Abner Doubleday (who is erroneously believed to have invented baseball) laid out a diamond-shaped field in West Point, New York, in 1839 and attempted to standardize the rules.

By the end of the Civil War, interest in the game had grown rapidly. More than 200 amateur or semiprofessional teams or clubs existed, many of which joined a national association and proclaimed a set of standard rules. As the game grew in popularity, it offered opportunities for profit. The first salaried team, the Cincinnati Red Stockings, was formed in 1869. Other cities soon fielded professional teams, and in 1876 they banded together in the National League. A rival league, the American Association, soon appeared. It eventually collapsed, but in 1901 the American League emerged to replace it. And in 1903, the first modern World Series was played, in which the American League Boston Red Sox beat the National League Pittsburgh Pirates. By then, baseball had become an important business and a great national preoccupation (at least among men), attracting paying crowds at times as large as 50,000.

Baseball had great appeal to working-class males. The second most popular game, football, appealed at first to a more elite segment of the male population, in part because it originated in colleges and universities. The first intercollegiate football game in America occurred between Princeton and Rutgers in 1869, and soon the game began to become entrenched as part of collegiate life. Early intercollegiate football bore only an indirect relation to the modern game; it was more similar to what is now known as rugby. By the late 1870s, however, the game was becoming standardized and was taking on the outlines of its modern form. Basketball was invented in 1891 at Springfield, Massachusetts, by Dr. James A. Naismith, a Canadian working as athletic director for a local college. Boxing, which had long been a disreputable activity concentrated primarily among the urban lower classes, became by the 1880s a more popular and in some places more reputable sport.

The major spectator sports of the era were activities open almost exclusively to men. But a number of other sports were emerging in which women became important participants. Golf and tennis seldom attracted crowds in the late nineteenth century, but both experienced a rapid increase in participation among relatively wealthy men and women. Bicycling and croquet also enjoyed widespread popularity in the 1890s among women as well as men. Women's colleges were beginning to introduce their students to more strenuous sports as well—track, crew, swimming, and (beginning in the late 1890s) basketball—challenging the once-prevalent notion that vigorous exercise was dangerous to women.

Leisure and Popular Culture

Other forms of popular entertainment developed in the cities in response to the large potential markets there. Many ethnic communities maintained their own theaters, in which immigrants heard the music of their homelands and listened to comedians making light of their experiences in the New

World. Urban theaters also introduced some of the most distinctively American entertainment forms: the musical comedy, which evolved gradually from the comic operettas of European theater; and vaudeville, a form of theater adapted from French models, which remained the most popular urban entertainment in the first decades of the twentieth century. Even saloons and small community theaters could afford to offer their customers vaudeville, which consisted of a variety of acts (musicians, comedians, magicians, jugglers, and others) and was, at least in the beginning, inexpensive to produce. As the economic potential of vaudeville grew, some promoters—most prominently Florenz Ziegfeld of New York—staged much more elaborate spectacles.

Vaudeville was also one of the few entertainment media open to black performers. They brought to it elements of the minstrel shows they had earlier developed for black audiences in the late nineteenth century. Some minstrel singers (including the most famous, Al Jolson) were whites wearing heavy makeup (or "blackface"), but most were black. Entertainers of both races performed music based on the gospel and folk tunes of the plantation and on the jazz and ragtime of black urban communities. Performers of both

A NICKELODEON An early movie theater, with musicians providing a live accompaniment to a silent film. The first feature-length sound picture (or "talkie"), *The Jazz Singer*, appeared in 1927.

races also tailored their acts to prevailing white prejudices, ridiculing blacks by acting out demeaning stereotypes.

The most important form of mass entertainment (until the invention of radio and television), and the one that reached most widely across the nation, was the movies. Thomas Edison and others had created the technology of the motion picture in the 1880s. Soon after that, short films became available to individual viewers watching peepshows in pool halls, penny arcades, and amusement parks. Soon, larger projectors made it possible to project the images onto big screens, which permitted substantial audiences to see films in theaters. By 1900, Americans were becoming attracted in large numbers to these early movies—usually plotless films of trains or waterfalls or other spectacles designed mainly to show off the technology. The great D. W. Griffith carried the motion picture into a new era with his silent epics—*The Birth of a Nation* (1915), *Intolerance* (1916), and others—which introduced serious (if notoriously racist) plots and elaborate productions to filmmaking. Motion pictures were the first truly mass-entertainment medium—one that reached all areas of the country and almost all groups in the population.

Not all popular entertainment, however, involved public events. Many Americans amused themselves privately by reading novels and poetry. The so-called dime novels, cheaply bound and widely circulated, became popular after the Civil War, with tales of the Wild West, detective stories, sagas of scientific adventure (such as the Tom Swift stories), and novels of "moral uplift" (among them those of Horatio Alger). Publishers also distributed sentimental novels of romance, which developed a large audience among women, as did books about animals and about young children growing up. Louisa May Alcott's *Little Women*, most of whose readers were women, sold more than 2 million copies.

Mass Communications

Urban-industrial society required new vehicles for transmitting news and information. And so American publishing and journalism experienced an important change in the decades following the Civil War. Between 1870 and 1910, the circulation of daily newspapers increased nearly ninefold (from under 3 million to more than 24 million), a rate three times as great as the rate of population increase. And while standards varied widely from one paper to another, American journalism began to develop the beginnings of a professional identity. Salaries of reporters increased; many newspapers began separating the reporting of news from the expression of opinion; and newspapers themselves became important businesses.

One striking change was the emergence of national press services, which made use of the telegraph to supply papers throughout the country with news and features and which contributed, as a result, to the standardization of the product. By the turn of the century important newspaper chains had emerged as well. The most powerful was owned by William Randolph Hearst, who by 1914 controlled nine newspapers and two magazines. Hearst and rival publisher Joseph Pulitzer helped popularize what became known as "yellow journalism"—a deliberately sensational, even lurid, style of reporting presented in bold graphics, designed to reach a mass audience uninterested in the sober, detailed reporting of more traditional newspapers. Another major change occurred in the nature of American magazines. Beginning in the 1880s, a new kind of magazine appeared, designed to achieve a mass circulation. One of the pioneers in this field was Edward W. Bok, who took over the *Ladies' Home Journal* in 1899 and, by targeting a mass female audience, built the circulation of the journal to over 700,000.

HIGH CULTURE IN THE URBAN AGE

In addition to the important changes in popular culture that accompanied the rise of cities and industry, there were profound changes in the realm of "high culture"—in the ideas and activities of intellectuals and elites. Even the idea of a distinction between "highbrow" and "lowbrow" culture was new to the industrial era. In the early nineteenth century, most cultural activities attracted people of widely varying backgrounds and targeted people of all classes. By the late nineteenth century, however, elites were developing a cultural and intellectual life quite separate from the popular amusements of the urban masses.

The Literature of Urban America

Many foreign observers and even some Americans in the late nineteenth century viewed the culture of the United States with contempt. Critics claimed that American life, despite its glittering surface, was essentially acquisitive and corrupt, with little cultural depth. But whatever the quality of culture and society in late-nineteenth-century America, the growth of industry and the rise of the city were having profound effects on them. Some writers and artists—the local-color writers of the South, for example, and Mark Twain, in such novels as *Huckleberry Finn* and *Tom Sawyer*—responded to the new civilization by evoking an older, more natural world. But others grappled directly with the modern order.

One of the strongest impulses in late-nineteenth- and early-twentieth-century American literature was the effort to re-create urban social reality. This trend toward realism found an early voice in Stephen Crane, who—although best known for his novel of the Civil War, *The Red Badge of Courage* (1895)—was the author of an earlier, powerful indictment of the plight of the working class. Crane created a sensation in 1893 when he published *Maggie: A Girl of the Streets*, a grim picture of urban poverty and slum life. Theodore Dreiser, Frank Norris, and Upton Sinclair—whose 1906 novel, *The Jungle*, inspired federal legislation with its exposure of abuses in the meat-packing industry—were similarly drawn to social issues as themes. Kate Chopin, a Southern writer who explored the oppressive features of traditional marriage, encountered widespread public abuse (and in some places formal bans) after publication of her shocking novel *The Awakening* in 1899. It described a young wife and mother who abandoned her family in search of personal fulfillment. William Dean Howells, in *The Rise of Silas Lapham* and other works, described what he considered the shallowness and corruption in ordinary American life styles.

Other critics of American society responded to the new civilization not by attacking it but by withdrawing from it. The historian Henry Adams published an autobiography in 1906, *The Education of Henry Adams*, which portrayed a man disillusioned with and unable to relate to his society, even though he continued to live in it. The novelist Henry James lived the major part of his adult life in England and Europe and produced a series of coldly realistic novels—*The American* (1877), *Portrait of a Lady* (1881), *The Ambassadors* (1903), and others—that showed his ambivalence about the merits of both American and European civilization.

Art in the Age of the City

American art through most of the nineteenth century had been overshadowed by the art of Europe. By 1900, however, a number of American artists, although some continued to study and even live in Europe, broke from the Old World traditions and experimented with new styles. Winslow Homer was vigorously American in his paintings of New England maritime life and other native subjects. James McNeil Whistler was one of the first Western artists to appreciate the beauty of Japanese color prints and to introduce Oriental concepts into American and European art.

By the first years of the new century, some American artists were turning decisively away from the traditional academic style (a style perhaps best exemplified in America by the brilliant portraitist John Singer Sargent). Instead, many younger painters were exploring the same grim aspects of modern life that were becoming the subject of American literature. Members of the so-called Ashcan School produced work startling in its naturalism and stark in its portrayal of the social realities of the era. John Sloan portrayed the dreariness of American urban slums; George Bellows caught the vigor and violence of his time in paintings and drawings of prizefights; Edward Hopper explored the starkness and loneliness of the modern city. The Ashcan artists were also among the first Americans to appreciate expressionism and abstraction; and they showed their interest in new forms in 1913 when they helped stage the famous "Armory Show" in New York City, which displayed works of the French postimpressionists and of some American moderns.

The Impact of Darwinism

The single most profound intellectual development in the late nineteenth century was the widespread acceptance of the theory of evolution, associated most prominently with the English naturalist Charles Darwin. Darwinism argued that the human species had evolved from earlier forms of life (and most immediately from simian creatures similar to apes) through a process of "natural selection." It challenged almost every tenet of traditional religious faith. History, Darwinism suggested, was not the working out of a divine plan, as most Americans had always believed. It was a random process dominated by the fiercest or luckiest competitors.

The theory of evolution met widespread resistance at first from educators, theologians, and even many scientists. By the end of the century, however, the evolutionists had converted most members of the urban professional and educated classes. Even many middle-class Protestant religious leaders had accepted the doctrine, making significant alterations in theology to accommodate it. Evolution had become enshrined in schools and universities; virtually no serious scientist any longer questioned its basic validity. Unseen by most urban Americans at the time, however, the rise of Darwinism was contributing to a deep schism between the new, cosmopolitan culture of the city—which was receptive to new ideas such as evolution—and the more traditional, provincial culture of some rural areas—which remained wedded to fundamentalist religious beliefs and older values. Thus the late nineteenth century saw not only the rise of a liberal Protestantism in tune with new scientific discoveries. It also saw the beginning of an organized Protestant fundamentalism, which would make its presence felt politically in the 1920s and again in the 1980s.

Darwinism helped spawn other new intellectual currents. There was the Social Darwinism of William Graham Sumner and others, which industrialists used so enthusiastically to justify their favored position in American life. But there were also more sophisticated philosophies, among them a doctrine that became known as "pragmatism," which seemed peculiarly a product of America's changing material civilization. William James, a Harvard psychologist (and brother of the novelist Henry James), was the most prominent publicist of the new theory, although earlier intellectuals such as Charles S. Peirce and later ones such as John Dewey were also important to its development and dissemination. According to the pragmatists, modern society should rely for guidance not on inherited ideals and moral principles but on the test of scientific inquiry. No idea or institution (not even religious faith) was valid, they claimed, unless it worked, unless it stood the test of experience.

A similar concern for scientific inquiry was intruding into the social sciences and challenging traditional orthodoxies. Economists such as Richard T. Ely and Simon Patten argued for a more active and pragmatic use of the discipline. Sociologists such as Edward A. Ross and Lester Frank Ward urged applying the scientific method to the solution of social and political problems. Historians such as Frederick Jackson Turner and Charles Beard argued that economic factors more than spiritual ideals had been the governing force in historical development. John Dewey proposed a new approach to education that placed less emphasis on the rote learning of traditional knowledge and more on a flexible, democratic approach to schooling, one that enabled students to acquire knowledge that would help them deal with the realities of their society. The relativistic implications of Darwinism also promoted the growth of anthropology and encouraged some scholars to begin examining other cultures—most significantly, perhaps, the culture of American Indians—in new ways. Some white Americans began to look at Indian society as a coherent culture with its own norms and values that were worthy of respect and preservation, even though they were different from those of white society.

Toward Universal Schooling

A society that was coming to depend increasingly on specialized skills and scientific knowledge was, of course, a society with a high demand for education. The late nineteenth century, therefore, was a time of rapid expansion and reform of American schools and universities.

One example was the spread of free public primary and secondary education. In 1860, there were only 100 public high schools in the entire United States. By 1900, the number had reached 6,000 and by 1914 over 12,000. By 1900, compulsory school attendance laws were in effect in thirty-one states and territories. But education was still far from universal. Rural areas lagged far behind urban-industrial ones in funding public education. And in the South, blacks had very limited access to any schools at all.

Educational reformers sought to provide educational opportunities to the Indian tribes as well, in an effort to "civilize" them and help them adapt to white society. In the 1870s, reformers recruited small groups of Indians to attend Hampton Institute (a primarily black college). In 1879 they organized the Carlisle Indian Industrial School in Pennsylvania. Like many black colleges, Carlisle emphasized the kind of practical "industrial" education that Booker T. Washington had urged on blacks. Ultimately, however, these reform efforts failed, partly because of inadequate funding and commitment and partly because the venture itself—the effort to remove Indians from their traditional surroundings and transform them into members of white society—was unpopular with its intended beneficiaries.

Colleges and universities were also proliferating rapidly in the late nineteenth century. They benefited particularly from the Morrill Land Grant Act of the Civil War era, by which the federal government had donated land to states for the establishment of colleges. After 1865, states in the South and West took particular advantage of the law. In all, sixty-nine "land-grant" institutions were established in the last decades of the century—among them the state university systems of California, Illinois, Minnesota, and Wisconsin. Other universities benefited from millions of dollars contributed by business and financial tycoons. Rockefeller, Carnegie, and others gave generously to such schools as Columbia, Chicago, Harvard, Northwestern, Princeton, Syracuse, and Yale. Other philanthropists founded new universities or reorganized older ones and perpetuated their family names—Vanderbilt, Johns Hopkins, Cornell, Duke, Tulane, and Stanford.

Education for Women

The post–Civil War era saw, too, an important expansion of educational opportunities for women, although such opportunities continued to lag far behind those available to men and were almost without exception denied to black women.

Most public high schools accepted women readily, but opportunities for higher education were fewer. At the end of the Civil War, only three American colleges were coeducational. In the years after the war, many of the land-grant colleges and universities in the Midwest and such private universities as Cornell and Wesleyan began to admit women along with men. But coeducation was less crucial to women's education in this period than was the creation of a network of women's colleges. Mount Holyoke in central Massachusetts had begun its life in 1836 as a "seminary" for women;

WELLESLEY COLLEGE STUDENTS IN PHYSICS CLASS Wellesley College, founded in 1870, was the first women's college in America to have scientific laboratories, including the physics lab shown here. Wellesley was one of a number of institutions founded shortly after the Civil War to give young women access to advanced education.

it became a full-fledged college in the 1880s, at about the same time that entirely new female institutions were emerging: Vassar, Wellesley, Smith, Bryn Mawr, Wells, and Goucher. A few of the larger private universities created separate colleges for women on their campuses (Barnard at Columbia and Radcliffe at Harvard, for example). Proponents of women's colleges saw the institutions as places where female students would not be treated as "second-class citizens" by predominantly male student bodies and faculties.

The female college was among the first examples of an important phenomenon in the history of modern American women: the emergence of a distinctive women's community. Most faculty members and many administrators were women (usually unmarried). And the life of the college produced a spirit of sorority and commitment among educated women that had important effects in later years, as women became the leaders of many reform activities. Most female college graduates ultimately married, but they married at a more advanced age than their noncollege counterparts. A significant minority, perhaps over 25 percent, did not marry at all, but devoted themselves to careers. The growth of female higher education clearly became for some women a liberating experience, persuading them that they had roles to perform in society other than as wives and mothers.

CHAPTER NINETEEN

From Stalemate to Crisis

The Politics of Equilibrium ~ *The Agrarian Revolt*
The Crisis of the 1890s

T HE ENORMOUS CHANGES America was experiencing in the late nineteenth century strained not only the nation's traditional social arrangements but its political institutions as well. Economic growth brought both progress and disorder. And it was to government, gradually, that Americans began to look for leadership in their search for stability.

Yet American government during much of this period was ill equipped to deal with the new challenges confronting it. In the face of unprecedented dilemmas, it responded with apparent passivity and confusion. Its leaders, for the most part, seemed political mediocrities. The issues with which it was concerned generally had little to do with the nation's most important problems. Rather than taking active leadership of America's dramatic transformation, the American political system for nearly two decades after the end of Reconstruction (a period often called "the Gilded Age," a phrase used by Mark Twain) was locked in a rigid stalemate—watching the remarkable changes that were occurring in the nation and doing little to affect them. The result was a set of problems and grievances that festered and grew without any natural outlet. It was not surprising, under the circumstances, that in the 1890s the United States entered a period of national crisis.

THE POLITICS OF EQUILIBRIUM

To modern eyes, the nature of the American political system in the late nineteenth century appears in many ways paradoxical. The two political parties enjoyed a strength and stability during those years that neither was ever to know again. And yet the federal government, which the two parties were struggling to control, was doing little of importance. In fact, most Americans in those years engaged in political activity not because of an interest in particular issues but because of broad regional, ethnic, or religious sentiments. Party loyalty had less to do with positions on public policy than with the way Americans defined themselves culturally.

The Party System

The most striking feature of the late-nineteenth-century party system was its remarkable stability. From the end of Reconstruction until the late 1890s, the electorate was divided almost precisely evenly between the Republicans and the Democrats. Loyalties fluctuated almost not at all. Sixteen states were solidly and consistently Republican, and fourteen states (most of them in the South) were solidly and consistently Democratic. Only five states (the most important of them New York and Ohio) were usually in doubt; and it was in them that national elections were commonly decided, often on the basis of voter turnout. The Republican party captured the presidency in all but two of the elections of the era, but the party was not really as dominant as those victories suggest. In the five presidential elections beginning in 1876, the average popular-vote margin separating the Democratic and Republican candidates was 1.5 percent. The congressional balance was similarly stable. Between 1875 and 1895, the Republicans generally controlled the Senate and the Democrats generally controlled the House; in any given election, the number of seats that shifted from one party to the other was very small.

As striking as the balance between the parties was the intensity of public loyalty to them. In most of the country, Americans viewed their party affiliations with a passion and enthusiasm that is difficult for later generations to understand. Voter turnout in presidential elections between 1860 and 1900 averaged over 78 percent of all eligible voters (as compared with only slightly over 50 percent in the 1970s and 1980s). Even in nonpresidential years, from 60 to 80 percent of the voters turned out to cast ballots for congressional candidates. Large groups of potential voters were disfranchised in these years: women in most states; almost all blacks and many poor whites in the South. But for adult white males outside the South, there were few franchise restrictions. The remarkable turnout represented a genuinely mass-based politics.

Party politics in the late nineteenth century occupied a central position in American culture, comparable in some ways to the role that spectator sports and mass popular entertainment play today. Political campaigns were often the most important public events in the lives of communities. Political organizations served important social and cultural functions. Political identification was almost as important to most individuals as identification with a church or an ethnic group. Partisanship was an intense, emotional force, widely admired and often identified with patriotism.

What explains this remarkable loyalty to the two political parties? It was not, certainly, because the parties took distinct positions on important public issues. Party loyalties reflected other factors. Region was perhaps the most important. To white Southerners, loyalty to the Democratic party was a matter of unquestioned faith. It was the vehicle by which they had triumphed over Reconstruction, the vehicle by which they preserved white supremacy. To many old-stock Northerners, white and black, Republican loyalties were equally intense for the opposite reason. The party of Lincoln had freed the slaves and preserved the Union; it was a bulwark against slavery and treason.

Religious and ethnic differences also shaped party loyalties. The Democratic party attracted most of the Catholic voters, most of the recent immigrants, and most of the poorer workers; those three groups, of course, often overlapped. The Republican party appealed to Northern Protestants and citizens of old stock. Among the few substantive issues on which the parties took clearly different stands were matters concerning immigrants. The Republicans tended to be more nativist and to support measures restricting immigration. Republicans tended as well to favor temperance legislation. Catholics and immigrants viewed such proposals as an assault on their cultures and life styles and opposed them, and the Democratic party followed their lead.

Party identification, then, was usually more a reflection of cultural inclinations than a calculation of economic interest. Individuals might affiliate with a party because their parents had done so; or because it was the party of their region, their church, or their ethnic group. Most clung to their party loyalties with great persistence and passion.

Presidents and Patronage

One reason the two parties managed to avoid major conflicts over substantive issues was that the federal government (and for the most part state and local governments as well) did very little. There were few concrete policy issues over which to disagree. The leaders of both parties, therefore, were primarily concerned not with policy but with office—with winning elections and controlling patronage. Both parties were dominated by powerful bosses and machines chiefly concerned with controlling and dispensing jobs. The Democrats relied on the big city organizations (such as New York's Tammany Hall), which enabled them to mobilize the voting power of immigrants. The Republicans tended to depend on strong statewide organizations such as those of Roscoe Conkling in New York or Matt Quay of Pennsylvania.

The power of party bosses had an important effect on the power of the presidency. The office had great symbolic importance, but its occupants were unable to do very much except distribute government appointments. A new president had to make almost 100,000 appointments (most of them

PRESIDENT AND MRS. RUTHERFORD B. HAYES Hayes was one of a series of generally undistinguished late-nineteenth-century presidents whose subordination to the fiercely competitive party system left them with little room for independent leadership. This photograph captures the dignity and sobriety that Hayes and his wife sought to convey to the public.

in the post office, the only really large government agency); and to do that, he had to rely on a tiny staff working in a few rooms in the White House. Even in making appointments, presidents had limited latitude, since they had to avoid offending the various factions within their own parties.

Sometimes that proved impossible, as the presidency of Rutherford B. Hayes (1877–1881) demonstrated. By the end of his term, two groups—the Stalwarts, led by Roscoe Conkling of New York, and the Half-Breeds, captained by James G. Blaine of Maine—were competing for control of the Republican party and threatening to split it. The dispute between the Stalwarts and the Half-Breeds was characteristic of the political battles of the era. It had virtually no substantive foundation. Rhetorically, the Stalwarts favored traditional, professional machine politics, while the Half-Breeds favored reform. In fact, neither group was much interested in political change; each simply wanted a larger share of the patronage pie. Hayes tried to satisfy both and ended up satisfying neither.

The battle over patronage overshadowed all else during Hayes's unhappy presidency. His one important substantive initiative—an effort to create a civil-service system—attracted no support from either party. And his early announcement that he would not seek reelection only weakened him further. He had virtually no power in Congress. The Democrats controlled the House throughout his presidency and the Senate during the last two years of his term. And Senate Republicans, led by Roscoe Conkling, opposed his efforts to defy the machines in making appointments. (His popularity with politicians in Washington was not enhanced by the unwillingness of his wife, a temperance advocate widely known as "Lemonade Lucy," to permit alcoholic beverages to be served in the White House.) Hayes's presidency was a study in frustration.

The Republicans managed to retain the presidency in 1880 in part because of rising prosperity and in part because they managed to agree on a ticket that made it possible for the Stalwarts and the Half-Breeds briefly to paper over their differences. After a long convention deadlock, they nominated a "dark horse," James A. Garfield, a veteran congressman from Ohio and a Half-Breed; to conciliate the Stalwarts, the convention gave the vice presidential nomination to Chester A. Arthur of New York, a Conkling henchman. To oppose Garfield, the Democrats nominated General Winfield Scott Hancock, a minor Civil War commander with no national following. Benefiting from the end of the recession of 1879, Garfield won a decisive electoral victory, although his popular-vote margin was very thin. The Republicans also captured both houses of Congress.

Garfield began his presidency by trying to defy Conkling and the Stalwarts in his appointments and by showing support for civil-service reform. He soon found himself embroiled in an ugly public quarrel with both Conkling and Thomas Platt, the other senator from New York and another important Stalwart leader. But before it could be resolved, Garfield was victimized by the spoils system in a more terrible sense. On July 2, 1881, only four months after his inauguration, Garfield was shot twice while standing in the Washington railroad station by an apparently deranged gunman (and unsuccessful office seeker) who shouted, "I am a Stalwart and Arthur is president now!" Garfield lingered for nearly three months but finally died, a victim as much of bungled medical treatment as of the wounds themselves.

Chester A. Arthur, who succeeded Garfield, had spent a political lifetime as a devoted, skilled, and open spoilsman and a close ally of Roscoe Conkling. But on becoming president, he tried—like Hayes and Garfield before him—to follow an independent course and even to promote reform. He was undoubtedly influenced by the horrible circumstances that had brought him to the presidency and by his realization that the Garfield assassination had to some degree discredited the traditional spoils system.

The revelation of the "new" Arthur dismayed the party bosses. He kept most of Garfield's appointees in office. He also supported civil-service reform, aware that the legislation was likely to pass whether he supported it or not. In 1883, finally, Congress passed the first national civil-service measure, the Pendleton Act, which identified some federal jobs to be filled by competitive written examinations rather than by patronage. Relatively few offices fell under civil service at first, but its reach extended steadily so that by the mid-twentieth century most federal employees were civil servants.

The Return of the Democrats

The unsavory election of 1884 was typical of national political contests in the late nineteenth century for its emphasis on personalities rather than policies. The Republicans repudiated Arthur and chose instead their most popular and controversial figure, Senator James G. Blaine of Maine— known to his adoring admirers as "the Plumed Knight" but to thousands of other Americans as a symbol of seamy party politics. An independent reform faction, known derisively by their critics as the "mugwumps," announced they would bolt the party and support an honest Democrat.

Rising to the bait, the Democrats nominated Grover Cleveland, the "reform" governor of New York. He differed from Blaine on no substantive issues but had acquired a reputation as an enemy of corruption.

In a campaign filled with personal invective, what may have decided the election was the last-minute introduction of a religious controversy. Shortly before the election, a delegation of Protestant ministers called on Blaine in New York City; their spokesman, Dr. Samuel Burchard, referred to the Democrats as the party of "rum, Romanism, and rebellion." Blaine was slow to repudiate Burchard's indiscretion, and Democrats quickly spread the news that Blaine had tolerated a slander on the Catholic church. Cleveland's narrow victory was probably a result of an unusually heavy Catholic vote for the Democrats in New York. Cleveland won 219 electoral votes to Blaine's 182; his popular margin was only 23,000.

Grover Cleveland was respected, if not often liked, for his stern and righteous opposition to politicians, grafters, pressure groups, and Tammany Hall. He had become famous as the "veto governor," as an official who was not afraid to say no. He was the embodiment of an era in which few Americans believed the federal government could, or should, do very much. His administration was characterized from beginning to end by an unwavering commitment to economy in government.

Cleveland did grapple with one major economic issue. He had always doubted the wisdom of protective tariffs (taxes on imported goods designed to protect domestic producers). And he concluded finally that the existing high rates were responsible for the annual surplus in federal revenues, which was tempting Congress to pass the "reckless" and "extravagant" legislation he so frequently vetoed. In December 1887, therefore, he asked Congress to reduce the tariff rates. Democrats in the House approved a tariff reduction; but Senate Republicans defiantly passed a bill of their own actually raising the rates. The resulting deadlock made the tariff an issue in the election of 1888.

The Democrats renominated Cleveland and supported tariff reductions. The Republicans settled on former Senator Benjamin Harrison of Indiana, who was obscure but respectable (and the grandson of President William Henry Harrison); and they endorsed protection. The campaign was the first since the Civil War to involve a clear question of economic difference between the parties. It was also one of the most corrupt (and one of the closest) elections in American history. Harrison won an electoral majority of 233 to 168, but Cleveland's popular vote exceeded Harrison's by 100,000, making him, with Samuel Tilden, one of only two presidential candidates since the Civil War to win the popular vote and lose the election.

Emerging Issues

Benjamin Harrison's record as president was little more substantial than that of his grandfather, who had died a month after taking office. One reason for Harrison's failure was the intellectual drabness of the members of his administration—beginning with the president himself and extending through his cabinet. Another was Harrison's unwillingness to make any effort to influence Congress. And yet during Harrison's dreary administration, public opinion was beginning to force the government to confront some of the pressing social and economic issues of the day. Most notably, perhaps, sentiment was rising in favor of legislation to curb the power of trusts.

By the mid-1880s, fifteen Western and Southern states had adopted laws prohibiting combinations that restrained competition. But corporations found it easy to escape limitations by incorporating in states such as New Jersey and Delaware that offered them special privileges. If antitrust legislation was to be effective, it would have to come from the national government. Responding to growing popular demands, both houses of Congress passed the Sherman Antitrust Act in July 1890, almost without dissent. Most members of Congress saw the act as a largely symbolic measure, one that would help deflect public criticism but was not likely to have any real effect on corporate power.

For over a decade after its passage, the Sherman Act had virtually no impact. As of 1901, the Justice Department had instituted many antitrust suits against unions, but only fourteen against business combinations; there had been few convictions. The courts, meanwhile, weakened the bill considerably. In *United States* v. *E. C. Knight Co.* (1895), in which the government charged that a single trust controlled 98 percent of refined-sugar manufacturing in the country, the Supreme Court rejected the government's case. The sugar trust was engaged in manufacturing, not in interstate commerce, the Court declared; and so, despite its obviously monopolistic characteristics, it was not illegal—since the Sherman Act's only legal basis was the clause of the Constitution giving Congress the right to regulate interstate commerce.

The Republicans were more interested, however, in the issue they believed had won them the 1888 election: the tariff. Representative William McKinley of Ohio and Senator Nelson W. Aldrich of Rhode Island drafted the highest protective measure ever proposed to Congress. Known as the McKinley Act, it became law in October 1890. But Republican leaders apparently misinterpreted public sentiment, for the party suffered a stunning reversal in the 1890 congressional election. The Republicans' substantial Senate majority was slashed to 8; in the House, the party retained only 88 of the 323 seats. McKinley himself was among those who went down to defeat. Nor were the Republicans able to recover in the course of the next two years. In the presidential election of 1892, Benjamin Harrison once again supported protection; Grover Cleveland, renominated by the Democrats, once again opposed it. Only a new third party, the People's party, with James B. Weaver as its candidate, advocated any serious economic reform. Cleveland won 277 electoral votes to Harrison's 145 and had a popular margin of 380,000. Weaver ran far behind. For the first time since 1878, the Democrats won a majority of both houses of Congress.

The policies of Cleveland's second term were much like those of his first—devoted to minimal government and hostile to active state measures to deal with social or economic problems. But this time, a major economic crisis created popular demands for a more active government. For the most part, Cleveland resisted those pressures.

Again, he supported a tariff reduction, which the House approved but the Senate gutted. Cleveland denounced the result but allowed it to become law as the Wilson-Gorman Tariff. The bill threw one small crumb to agrarian interests: a small federal income tax (2 percent of incomes over $4,000). But the Supreme Court declared the new tax unconstitutional. Only after approval of the Sixteenth Amendment in 1913 was the federal government able to tax incomes. Public pressure was also growing in the 1880s for regulation of the railroads. Farm organizations in the Midwest (most notably the Grangers) had persuaded several state legislatures to pass regulatory legislation in the early 1870s. But in 1886, the Supreme Court—in *Wabash, St. Louis, and Pacific Railway Co.* v. *Illinois*, known as the *Wabash* case—ruled one of the Granger Laws in Illinois unconstitutional, holding that it was an attempt to control interstate commerce that infringed on the exclusive power of Congress. Later, the courts limited the powers of the states to regulate commerce even within their own boundaries.

Railroad regulation, it was now clear, could come only from the federal government. Congress grudgingly responded to public pressure in 1887 with the Interstate Commerce Act, which banned discrimination in rates between long and short hauls, required that railroads publish their rate schedules and file them with the government, and declared that all interstate rail rates must be "reasonable and just"—although the act did not define what that meant. A five-person agency, the Interstate Commerce Commission (ICC), was to administer the act. But it had to rely on the courts to enforce its rulings. For almost twenty years after its passage, the Interstate Commerce Act—haphazardly enforced and narrowly interpreted by the courts—was without practical effect.

The agitation over the tariff, the trusts, and the railroads was a sign that the dramatic changes in the American economy were creating problems that much of the public considered too important and dangerous to ignore. But the federal government's response to that agitation reflected the continuing weakness of the American state. The government still lacked institutions adequate to perform any significant role in American economic life. And American politics still lacked an ideology sufficient to justify any major expansion of government responsibilities. The effort to create such institutions and to produce such an ideology would occupy much of American public life in the coming decades. And it became visible first in a dramatic dissident movement that shattered the political equilibrium that the nation had experienced for the previous twenty years.

THE AGRARIAN REVOLT

No group watched the performance of the federal government in the 1880s with more dismay than American farmers. Isolated from the urban-industrial society that was beginning to dominate national life, suffering from a long, painful economic decline, afflicted with a sense of obsolescence, rural Americans were keenly aware of the problems of the modern economy and particularly eager for government assistance in dealing with them. The result was the emergence of one of the most powerful movements of political protest in American history: what became known as Populism.

The Grangers

Farmers had been making efforts to organize politically for several decades before the 1880s. The first major farm organization had its origins shortly after the Civil War in a tour through the South by a minor Agriculture Department official, Oliver H. Kelley, who became appalled by what he considered the isolation and drabness of rural life. In 1867 he left the government and helped found the National Grange of the Patrons of Husbandry, from which emerged a network of local organizations. At first, the Granges simply tried to teach new scientific agricultural techniques and attempted to create a feeling of community, to relieve the loneliness of rural life. But when the depression of 1873 caused a sharp decline in farm prices, membership rapidly increased and the direction of the organization changed. Granges in the Midwest began to organize marketing cooperatives, which would allow farmers to circumvent the hated middlemen. And they promoted political action to curb the monopolistic practices of the railroads and warehouses.

The Grangers succeeded for a time both in creating an impressive network of farm cooperatives and in putting effective pressure on state legislatures. At their peak, their supporters controlled the legislatures in most of the Midwestern states. The result was the Granger Laws of the early 1870s, by which many states imposed strict regulations on railroad rates and practices. But the destruction of the new regulations by the courts, combined with the political inexperience of many Grange leaders and the return

"THE GRANGE AWAKENING THE SLEEPERS" This 1873 cartoon suggests the way the Grange embraced many of the same concerns that the Farmers' Alliances and their People's party later expressed. A farmer is attempting to arouse passive citizens (lying in place of the "sleepers," or cross ties on railroad tracks).

of prosperity in the late 1870s, produced a dramatic decline in the power of the association by the end of the decade.

The Alliances

The successor to the Granges as the leading vehicle of agrarian protest began to emerge even before the Granger movement had faded. As early as 1875, farmers in parts of the South (most notably in Texas) were banding together in so-called Farmers' Alliances. By 1880, the Southern Alliance had more than 4 million members; and a comparable Northwestern Alliance was taking root in the plains states and the Midwest and developing ties with its Southern counterpart.

Like the Granges, the Alliances formed cooperatives and other marketing mechanisms. They established stores, banks, processing plants, and other facilities for their members—to free them from dependence on the hated "furnishing merchants" who kept so many farmers in debt. Some Alliance leaders, however, saw the movement in larger terms: as an effort to build a new society in which economic competition might give way to cooperation—not a rigid collectivism but a sense of mutual, neighborly responsibility that would enable farmers to resist oppressive outside forces. Alliance lecturers traveled throughout rural areas lambasting the concentration of power in the hands of a few great corporations and financial institutions.

Although the Alliances quickly became far more widespread than the Granges had ever been, they suffered from similar problems. Their cooperatives did not always work well, partly because the market forces operating against them were sometimes too strong to be overcome and partly because the cooperatives themselves were often mismanaged. These economic frustrations helped push the movement into a new phase at the end of the 1880s: the creation of a national political organization.

In 1889, the Southern and Northwestern Alliances, despite continuing differences between them, agreed to a loose merger. The next year the Alliances held a national convention at Ocala, Florida, and issued the so-called Ocala Demands, which were, in effect, a party platform. In the 1890 off-year elections, candidates supported by the Alliances won partial or complete control of the legislatures in twelve states. They also won six governorships, three seats in the Senate, and approximately fifty in the House of Representatives. Many of the successful Alliance candidates were simply Democrats who had benefited—often passively—from Alliance endorsements. But dissident farmers drew enough encouragement from the results to contemplate further political action, including forming a party of their own.

Plans for a third party were discussed at meetings in Cincinnati in May 1891 and St. Louis in February 1892—meetings attended by many Northern Alliance members, a smaller but still significant number of Southern Alliance leaders, and representatives of the fading Knights of Labor, whom some farm leaders hoped to bring into the coalition. Then, in July 1892, 1,300 exultant delegates poured into Omaha, Nebraska, to proclaim the creation of the new party, approve an official set of principles, and nominate candidates for the presidency and vice presidency. The new organization's official name was the People's party, but the movement was more commonly referred to as Populism.

The election of 1892 demonstrated the potential power of the new movement. The Populist presidential candidate—James B. Weaver of Iowa, a former Greenbacker—polled more than 1 million votes, 8.5 percent of the total, and carried six mountain and plains states for 22 electoral votes. Nearly 1,500 Populist candidates won election to state legislatures and local offices. The party elected three governors, five senators, and ten congressmen. It could also claim the support of many Republicans and Democrats in Congress who had been elected by appealing to Populist sentiment.

The Populist Constituency

Already, however, there were signs of the limits of Populist strength. Populism had great appeal to farmers, and particularly to small farmers with little long-range economic security—people whose operations were only minimally mechanized, if at all, who relied on one crop, and who had access only to limited and unsatisfactory mechanisms of credit. But Populism failed to move much beyond that group. There were energetic efforts to include labor within the coalition. Representatives of the Knights of Labor attended early organizational meetings; the new party added a labor plank to its platform—calling for shorter hours for workers and restrictions on immigration and denouncing the use of private detective agencies as strikebreakers in labor disputes. But Populism never attracted any substantial labor support, in part because the economic interests of labor and the interests of farmers were often at odds.

In the South in particular, white Populists struggled with the question of accepting African-Americans in the party, since their numbers and their poverty made them possibly valuable allies. And indeed there was an important black component to the movement—a network of "Colored Alliances" that by 1890 numbered over 1.25 million members. But most white Populists were willing to accept the assistance of blacks only as long as it was clear that whites would remain indisputably in control. When Southern conservatives began to attack the Populists for undermining white supremacy, the interracial character of the movement quickly faded.

Populist Ideas

The reform program of the Populists was spelled out first in the Ocala Demands of 1890 and then, even more clearly, in the Omaha platform of 1892. It proposed a system of "subtreasuries," which would replace and strengthen the cooperatives with which the Granges and Alliances had been experimenting for years. The government would establish a network of warehouses, where farmers could deposit their crops. Using those crops as collateral, growers could then borrow money from the government at low rates of interest and wait for the price of their goods to go up before selling them. In addition, the Populists called for the abolition of national banks, which they believed were dangerous institutions of concentrated power; the end of absentee ownership of land; the direct election of United States senators (which would weaken the power of conservative state legislatures); and other devices to improve the ability of the people to influence the political process. They called as well for regulation and (after 1892) government ownership of railroads, telephones, and telegraphs. And they demanded a system of government-operated postal savings banks, a graduated income tax, the inflation of the currency, and, later, the remonetization of silver.

Some Populists were openly anti-Semitic. Others were anti-intellectual, anti-Eastern, and antiurban. Yet the occasional bigotry of some Populists should not be allowed to dominate the image of Populism as a whole, which was a serious and usually responsible effort to find solutions to real problems. Populists emphatically rejected the laissez-faire orthodoxies of their time, the idea that the rights of ownership are absolute. They raised one of the most overt and powerful challenges of the era to the direction in which American industrial capitalism was moving. Populism was less a challenge to industrialization or to capitalism itself than a response to what the Populists considered the brutal and chaotic way in which the economy was developing. Progress and growth should continue, they urged, but it should be strictly defined by the needs of individuals and communities.

THE CRISIS OF THE 1890s

The agrarian protest was only one of many indications of the national political crisis emerging in the 1890s. There was a severe depression, which began in 1893. There was widespread labor unrest and violence, culminating in the tumultuous strikes of 1894. There was the continuing failure of either major party to respond to the growing distress. And there was the rigid conservatism of Grover Cleveland, who took office for the second time just at the moment that the economy collapsed. Out of this growing sense of crisis came some of the most heated political battles in American history, culminating in the dramatic campaign of 1896, on which, many Americans came to believe, the future of the nation hung.

The Panic of 1893

The Panic of 1893 precipitated the most severe depression the nation had ever experienced. It began in March 1893, when the Philadelphia and Reading Railroads declared bankruptcy, unable to meet demands for payment by British banks from whom they had borrowed large sums. Two months later, the National Cordage Company failed as well. Together, the two corporate failures triggered a collapse of the stock market. And since many of the major New York banks were heavy investors in the market, a wave of bank failures soon began. That caused a contraction of credit, which meant that many of the new, aggressive businesses that had recently begun operations soon went bankrupt because they were unable to secure the loans they needed. There were other, longer-range causes of the financial collapse. Depressed prices in agriculture since 1887 had weakened the purchasing power of farmers, the largest group in the population. Depression conditions that had begun earlier in Europe were resulting in a loss of American markets abroad and a withdrawal by foreign investors of gold invested in the United States. Railroads and other major industries had expanded far too rapidly, well beyond market demand.

The depression reflected, too, the degree to which all parts of the American economy were now interconnected, the degree to which failures in one area affected all other areas. And the depression showed how dependent the economy was on the health of the railroads, which remained the nation's most powerful corporate and financial institutions. When the railroads suffered, as they did beginning in 1893, everything suffered.

Once the panic began, its effects spread with startling speed. Within six months, more than 8,000 businesses, 156 railroads, and 400 banks failed. Already low agricultural prices tumbled further. Up to 1 million workers, 20 percent of the labor force, lost their jobs—the highest level of unemployment in American history to that point, a level comparable to that of the Great Depression of the 1930s. The depression was unprecedented not only in its severity but also in its persistence. Although there was slight improvement beginning in 1895, prosperity did not fully return until after 1898.

The suffering the depression caused naturally produced social unrest, not least among the enormous numbers of unemployed workers. In 1894, Jacob S. Coxey, an Ohio businessman and Populist, began advocating an inflation of the currency and a massive public works program to create jobs for the unemployed. When it became clear that his proposals were making no progress in Congress, Coxey organized a march of the unemployed (known as "Coxey's Army") to Washington to present his demands to the government. Congress took no action on the demands.

COXEY'S ARMY Jacob S. Coxey's "army" of the unemployed marches toward Washington in 1894 to demand relief from the federal government. Although several thousand people started out from various parts of the country to join the army, only about 400 actually reached the Capitol. The protest disbanded after Coxey and several others were arrested for "trespassing" on the grounds of the United States Capitol.

There were major labor upheavals as well during the decade—of which the Homestead and Pullman strikes were only the most prominent examples. (See pp. 482–485.) To many middle-class Americans, the worker unrest was a sign of a dangerous social instability, even perhaps a revolution. Labor radicalism—some of it real, much of it imagined by the frightened middle class—was seldom far from the public mind, heightening the general sense of crisis.

The Silver Question

The financial panic weakened the nation's monetary system, and in the minds of many conservatives, among them President Cleveland, the instability of the currency was the primary cause of the depression. The "money question" became the basis for some of the most dramatic political conflicts of the era.

The currency issue is a complicated and confusing one, and it has often been difficult for later generations to understand the enormous passions the controversy aroused. The heart of the debate was over what would form the basis of the dollar, what would lie behind it and give it value. Today, the value of the dollar rests on little more than public confidence in the government. But in the nineteenth century, currency was assumed to be worthless if there was not something concrete behind it—precious metal (specie), which holders of paper money could collect if they presented their currency to a bank or to the Treasury.

During most of its existence as a nation, the United States had recognized two metals—gold and silver—as a basis for the dollar, a formula known as "bimetallism." In the 1870s, however, that had changed. The official ratio of the value of silver to the value of gold for purposes of creating currency (the "mint ratio") was 16 to 1: sixteen ounces of silver equaled one ounce of gold. But the actual commercial value of silver (the "market ratio") was much higher than that. Owners of silver could get more by selling it for manufacture into jewelry and other objects than they could by taking it to the mint for conversion to coins. So they stopped taking it to the mint, and the mint stopped coining silver.

In 1873, Congress passed a law that seemed simply to recognize the existing situation by officially discontinuing silver coinage. Few objected at the time. But later in the 1870s, the market value of silver fell well below the official mint ratio of 16 to 1. (Sixteen ounces of silver, in other words, were now worth *less*, not more, than one ounce of gold.) Silver was suddenly available for coinage again, and it soon became clear that Congress had foreclosed a potential method of expanding the currency. Before long, many Americans concluded that a conspiracy of big bankers had been responsible for the "demonetization" of silver and referred to the law as the "Crime of '73."

Two groups of Americans were especially determined to undo the "Crime of '73." One consisted of the silver-mine owners, now understandably eager to have the government take their surplus silver and pay them much more than the market price. The other group consisted of discontented farmers, who wanted an increase in the quantity of money—an inflation of the currency—as a means of raising the prices of farm products and easing payment of the farmers' debts. The inflationists demanded that the government return at once to "free silver"—that is, to the "free and unlimited coinage of silver" at the old ratio of 16 to 1. But by the time the depression began in 1893, Congress had made no more than a token response to their demands.

At the same time, the nation's gold reserves were steadily dropping. And the Panic of 1893 intensified the demands on those reserves. President Cleveland believed that the chief cause of the weakening gold reserves was the Sherman Silver Purchase Act of 1893, which had required that the government purchase (but not coin) silver and pay for it in gold. Early in his second administration, therefore, a special session responded to his request and repealed the Sherman Act—although only after a bitter and divisive battle that helped create a permanent split in the Democratic party. The president's gold policy had aligned the Southern and Western Democrats in a solid phalanx against him and his Eastern followers.

By now, both sides had invested the currency question with great symbolic and emotional importance. Supporters of the gold standard considered its survival essential to the honor and stability of the nation. Because the supply of gold was limited, a gold-based currency would be assured of stable, long-term value. Supporters of free silver considered the gold standard an instrument of tyranny and silver an instrument of liberation. The issue aroused widespread passions rarely seen in American politics, culminating in the tumultuous presidential election of 1896.

"A Cross of Gold"

Republicans, watching the failure of Cleveland and the Democrats to deal effectively with the depression, were confident of success in 1896. Party leaders, led by the Ohio boss Marcus A. Hanna, settled on former Senator

William McKinley, author of the 1890 tariff act and now governor of Ohio, as the party's presidential candidate. The Republican platform opposed the free coinage of silver except by agreement with the leading commercial nations (which everyone realized was unlikely). Thirty-four delegates from the mountain and plains states walked out in protest and joined the Democratic party.

The Democratic convention of 1896 was the scene of unusual drama. Southern and Western delegates, eager to fight off the challenge of the People's party, were determined to seize control of the party from conservative Easterners and incorporate some Populist demands—among them free silver—into the Democratic platform. They wanted as well to nominate a prosilver candidate. The divided platform committee presented two reports to the convention. The majority report, the work of Westerners and Southerners, called for tariff reduction, an income tax, "stricter control" of trusts and railroads, and—most prominently—free silver. The minority report, the product of the party's Eastern wing, echoed the Republican platform by opposing the free coinage of silver except by international agreement. The debate over the two competing platforms dominated the convention.

Defenders of the gold standard seemed to prevail in the debate, until the final speech. Then William Jennings Bryan, a handsome, thirty-six-year-old congressman from Nebraska, already well known as an effective orator, mounted the podium to address the convention. His great voice echoed through the hall as he delivered a defense of free silver that became one of the most famous political speeches in American history. The closing passage sent his audience into something close to a frenzy: "If they dare to come out in the open and defend the gold standard as a good thing, we will fight them to the uttermost. Having behind us the producing masses of this nation and the world, supported by the commercial interests, the laboring interests and the toilers everywhere, we will answer their demand for a gold standard by saying to them: 'You shall not press down upon the brow of labor this crown of thorns; you shall not crucify mankind upon a cross of gold.' " It became known as the "Cross of Gold" speech.

The convention voted to adopt the prosilver platform. Perhaps more important, the agrarians had found a leader. The following day, Bryan (as he had eagerly, and not entirely secretly, hoped) was nominated for president on the fifth ballot. He remains the youngest man ever nominated for president by a major party.

The choice of Bryan and the nature of the Democratic platform created a quandary for the Populists. They had expected both major parties to adopt

WILLIAM JENNINGS BRYAN Bryan addresses a crowd late in his career, displaying the flamboyant oratorical style that characterized his public life from the beginning. The poster at the lower left of the platform shows him as he appeared in the 1890s, when, as a young congressman from Nebraska, he became known as the "Boy Orator of the Platte" and the leader of the national free-silver movement.

conservative programs and nominate conservative candidates, leaving the Populists to represent the growing forces of protest. But now the Democrats had stolen much of their thunder. The Populists faced the choice of naming their own candidate and splitting the protest vote or endorsing Bryan and losing their identity as a party. The Populists had embraced the free-silver cause, but they supported it somewhat reluctantly, convinced that other issues remained more important. Many Populists argued that "fusion" with the Democrats—who had endorsed free silver but ignored the other, more important Populist demands—would destroy their party. But the majority concluded that there was no viable alternative. Amid considerable acrimony, the convention voted to support Bryan. In a feeble effort to maintain their independence, the Populists repudiated the Democratic nominee for vice president and chose their own, Tom Watson of Georgia.

The Conservative Victory

The campaign of 1896 produced desperation among conservatives. The business and financial community, frightened beyond reason at the prospect of a Bryan victory, contributed lavishly to the Republican campaign, which may have spent as much as $7 million, as compared with the Democrats' $300,000. From his home at Canton, Ohio, McKinley conducted a dignified "front-porch" campaign before pilgrimages of the Republican faithful, customary behavior in an age when many Americans considered it undignified to campaign too openly for the presidency.

Bryan showed no such restraint. He became the first presidential candidate in American history to stump the country systematically, to appear in villages and hamlets—indeed, the first to say frankly to the voters that he wanted to be president. He traveled 18,000 miles (mostly in the West and South) and addressed an estimated 5 million people. But Bryan may have done himself more harm than good. His revivalistic, camp-meeting style pleased old-stock Protestants, but it alienated many of the immigrant Catholics and other ethnics who normally voted Democratic. Employers, meanwhile, warned workers that a Bryan victory would cost them their jobs, thus intimidating many traditional Democrats into supporting McKinley or not voting at all.

On election day, McKinley polled 271 electoral votes to Bryan's 176 and received 51.1 percent of the popular vote to Bryan's 47.7. Bryan carried only those areas of the South and West where miners or struggling staple farmers predominated. The Democratic program, like that of the Populists, had been too narrow to win a national election.

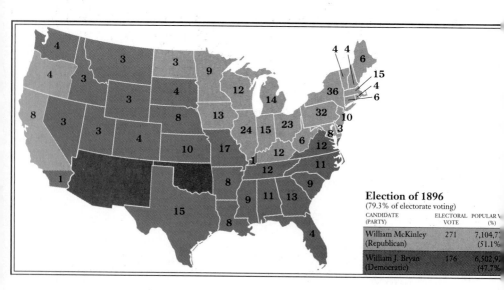

Election of 1896
(79.3% of electorate voting)

CANDIDATE (PARTY)	ELECTORAL VOTE	POPULAR VOTE (%)
William McKinley (Republican)	271	7,104,7 (51.1%)
William J. Bryan (Democratic)	176	6,502,9 (47.7%)

For the Populists and their allies, the election results were a disaster. They had gambled everything on their "fusion" with the Democratic party and lost. Within months of the election, the People's party began to dissolve. Never again would American farmers unite so militantly to demand economic reform. And never again would so large a group of Americans raise so forceful a protest against the nature of the industrial economy.

McKinley and Prosperity

The administration of William McKinley, which began in the aftermath of turmoil, saw a return to relative calm. One reason was the exhaustion of dissent. By 1897, when McKinley took office, the labor unrest that had so frightened many middle-class Americans and so excited working-class people had subsided. With the simultaneous decline of agrarian protest, two of the greatest destabilizing forces in the nation's politics were—temporarily at least—removed. Another reason was the character of the McKinley administration itself, which was politically shrewd and committed to a reassuring stability. Most important, however, was the gradual easing of the economic crisis, a change that undercut the appeal of many of those who were agitating for change.

McKinley and his allies committed themselves fully to only one issue, one on which they knew virtually all Republicans were agreed: the need for higher tariff rates. Within weeks of McKinley's inauguration, the administration won approval of the Dingley Tariff, raising duties to the highest point in American history. The administration dealt more gingerly with the explosive silver question (an issue McKinley himself had never considered very important in any case). McKinley sent a commission to Europe to explore the possibility of a silver agreement with Great Britain and France. As he and everyone else anticipated, the effort produced no agreement. The Republicans then enacted the Currency, or Gold Standard, Act of 1900, which confirmed the nation's commitment to the gold standard.

And so the "battle of the standards" ended in victory for the forces of conservatism. Economic developments at the time seemed to vindicate them. Prosperity returned beginning in 1898. Foreign crop failures sent U.S. farm prices surging upward, and American business entered another cycle of booming expansion. Prosperity and the gold standard, it seemed, were closely allied.

But while the free-silver movement had failed, it had raised an important question for the American economy. In the quarter-century before

1900, the countries of the Western world had experienced a spectacular growth in productive facilities and population. Yet the supply of money had not kept pace with economic progress, because the supply was tied to gold and the amount of gold had remained practically constant. Had it not been for a dramatic increase in the gold supply in the late 1890s (a result of new techniques for extracting gold from low-content ores and the discovery of huge new gold deposits in Alaska, South Africa, and Australia), Populist predictions of financial disaster might in fact have proved correct. In 1898, two and a half times as much gold was produced as in 1890, and the currency supply was soon inflated far beyond anything Bryan and the free-silver forces had proposed.

By then, however, Bryan—like many other Americans—was becoming engaged with another major issue: a growing United States presence in world affairs and the possibility of America becoming an imperialist nation.

D E B A T I N G   T H E   P A S T

Populism

T HE SCHOLARLY DEBATES over the nature of Populism have tended to reflect a larger debate over the nature of popular mass movements. To some historians, mass uprisings seem dangerous and potentially antidemocratic; and to them, the Populist movement has usually appeared ominous. To others, such insurgency is evidence of a healthy democratic resistance to oppression; and to them, Populism has generally seemed more appealing.

The latter view shaped the first, and for many years the only, general history of Populism: John D. Hicks's *The Populist Revolt* (1931). Reflecting the influence of Frederick Jackson Turner, Hicks portrayed Populism as an expression of the healthy, democratic sentiments of the West. Populists were reacting rationally and constructively to the harsh impact of Eastern industrial growth on agrarian society, and they were proposing potentially valuable reforms to restrict the power of the new financial titans. Populism was, he wrote, "the last phase of a long and perhaps a losing struggle—the struggle to save agricultural America from the devouring jaws of industrial America."

In the early 1950s, scholars sensitive to the nature of European fascism and contemporary communism took a more suspicious view of mass popular politics and a more hostile view of Populism. The leading figure in this reinterpretation was Richard Hofstadter. In *The Age of Reform* (1955), he conceded that the Populists had genuine grievances and advanced some sensible reforms. But he concentrated on revealing what he called the "soft" and "dark" sides of the movement. Populism, Hofstadter claimed, rested on a romanticized and obsolete vision of the role of farmers in American society. And it was permeated with bigotry and ignorance.

Hofstadter's harsh portrait inspired a series of spirited challenges. Norman Pollack, beginning in 1962, argued that the agrarian revolt rested

(continued on next page)

not on nostalgic and romantic concepts but on a sophisticated and even radical vision of reform. A year later, Walter T. K. Nugent attempted to show that Populists were not bigoted, that they not only tolerated but welcomed Jews and other minorities into their party. And in 1976, Lawrence Goodwyn published *Democratic Promise*, the first full-scale history of the Populist movement since Hicks's study forty-five years earlier. Goodwyn described Populism as a "cooperative crusade," battling against the "coercive potential of the emerging corporate state." It was offering a genuine alternative to the inequities of modern, corporate capitalism; and it was promoting that alternative by developing an intensely democratic popular movement.

At the same time that historians were debating the meaning of Populism, they were also arguing over who the Populists were. Hicks, Hofstadter, and Goodwyn, for all their many disagreements, shared a belief that Populists were victims of economic distress—usually one-crop farmers in economically marginal regions victimized by drought and debt. Others, however, have suggested that this description is, if not wrong, at least inadequate. Sheldon Hackney maintained in 1969 that Populists in Alabama were not only economically troubled but socially rootless, "only tenuously connected to society by economic function, by personal relationships, by stable community membership, by political participation, or by psychological identification with the South's distinctive myths." Peter Argersinger, Stanley Parsons, James Turner, and others have similarly suggested that Populists tended to be people who were socially and even geographically isolated. Steven Hahn's 1983 study *The Roots of Southern Populism* described the poor farmers of "upcountry" Georgia who became Populists as people almost entirely unconnected to the modern capitalist economy. They were reacting not simply to the distress of being "left behind," but also to a real economic threat to their way of life from the intrusion into their world of a new commercial order of which they were not a part and from which they were unlikely to benefit.

There has, finally, been continuing disagreement over whether Populism has survived into the twentieth century—whether it is part of an enduring political language used by such later popular leaders as Huey Long, George Wallace, or even Ross Perot, or whether the idea of Populism has meaning only in reference to the insurgents of the 1890s.

CHAPTER TWENTY

The Imperial Republic

Stirrings of Imperialism ∼ *War with Spain*
The Republic As Empire

T HE AMERICAN REPUBLIC had been an expansionist nation since the earliest days of its existence. Throughout the first half of the nineteenth century, as the population of the United States grew and pressed westward, the government, through purchase or conquest, had continually acquired new lands: the trans-Appalachian West, the Louisiana Territory, Florida, Texas, Oregon, California, New Mexico, Alaska. It was the nation's "Manifest Destiny," many Americans believed, to expand into new realms.

In the last years of the nineteenth century, with little room left for territorial growth on the North American continent, expansionism moved into a new phase. In the past, the nation had generally annexed land adjacent to its existing boundaries; American citizens could move there relatively easily, and the new lands could ultimately become states of the Union. But the expansionism of the 1890s, the new Manifest Destiny, involved acquiring possessions separate from the continental United States: distant island territories, many thickly populated, most of which were unlikely to attract massive settlement from America, few of which were expected to become states of the Union. The United States was joining England, France, Germany, and others in the great imperial drive that was, by the end of the century, to bring much of the non-industrial world under the control of the industrial powers of the West.

STIRRINGS OF IMPERIALISM

For over two decades after the Civil War, the United States expanded geographically hardly at all. By the 1890s, however, some Americans were ready—indeed, eager—to resume the course of Manifest Destiny that had inspired their ancestors to wrest an empire from Mexico in the expansionist 1840s.

The New Manifest Destiny

Several developments helped shift American attention to lands across the seas. The experience of subjugating the Indian tribes had established a precedent for exerting colonial control over dependent peoples. The supposed "closing of the frontier," widely heralded by Frederick Jackson Turner and others in the 1890s, produced fears that natural resources would soon dwindle and that alternative sources must be found abroad. The depression that began in 1893 encouraged some businessmen to look for new markets abroad. The bitter social protests of the time—the Populist movement, the free-silver crusade, the bloody labor disputes—led some politicians to urge a more aggressive foreign policy as an outlet for frustrations that would otherwise destabilize domestic life.

Foreign trade was becoming increasingly important to the American economy in the late nineteenth century. The nation's exports had totaled about $392 million in 1870; by 1900, the figure had reached $1.4 billion. Many Americans began to consider the possibility of acquiring colonies that might expand overseas markets further. "Today," Senator Albert J. Beveridge of Indiana cried in 1899, "we are raising more than we can consume. Today, we are making more than we can use. Therefore, we must find new markets for our produce, new occupation for our capital, new work for our labor."

Americans were, moreover, well aware of the imperialist fever that was raging through Europe. It was leading the major powers to partition most of Africa among themselves and to turn covetous eyes on the Far East and the feeble Chinese Empire. Some Americans feared that their nation would soon be left out, that no territory would remain to be acquired.

Scholars and others found a philosophic justification for expansionism in Charles Darwin's theories. They contended that nations or "races," like biological species, struggled constantly for existence and that only the fittest could survive. For strong nations to dominate weak ones was, therefore, in accordance with the laws of nature. (This was an application to world affairs of the same strained reinterpretation of Darwinism that industrialists and others had long been applying to domestic economic affairs in the form of Social Darwinism.)

The ablest and most effective apostle of imperialism was Alfred Thayer Mahan, a captain and later admiral in the navy. Mahan's thesis—presented in *The Influence of Sea Power upon History* (1890) and other works—was simple: Countries with sea power were the great nations of history; the greatness of the United States, bounded by two oceans, would rest on naval power. Among other things, effective sea power required colonies. Mahan believed America should, at the least, acquire defensive bases in the Caribbean and the Pacific and take possession of Hawaii and other Pacific islands.

Mahan feared that the United States did not have a large enough navy to play the great role he envisioned. But during the 1870s and 1880s, the government launched a shipbuilding program that by 1898 had moved the United States to fifth place among the world's naval powers, and by 1900 to third.

Hemispheric Hegemony

James G. Blaine, who served as secretary of state in two Republican administrations in the 1880s, led the early efforts to expand American influence into Latin America, where, Blaine believed, the United States must look for markets for its surplus goods. In October 1889, he helped organize the first Pan-American Congress, which attracted delegates from nineteen nations. The delegates agreed to create the Pan-American Union, a weak international organization located in Washington that served as a clearinghouse for distributing information to the member nations. But they rejected Blaine's more substantive proposals: an inter-American customs union and arbitration procedures for hemispheric disputes.

The second Cleveland administration took a similarly lively interest in Latin America. In 1895, it supported Venezuela in a dispute with Great Britain over the boundary between Venezuela and British Guiana. When the British ignored American demands that the matter be submitted to arbitration, Secretary of State Richard Olney charged that Britain was violating the Monroe Doctrine. When Britain still did not act, Cleveland created a special commission to determine the boundary line; if Britain resisted the commission's decision, he insisted, the United States should be willing to go to war to enforce it. As war talk raged throughout the country, the British government finally realized that it had stumbled into a genuine diplomatic crisis and agreed to arbitration.

Hawaii and Samoa

The islands of Hawaii in the mid-Pacific had been an important way station for American ships in the China trade since the early nineteenth century. By the 1880s, officers of the expanding United States Navy were looking covetously at Pearl Harbor on the island of Oahu as a possible permanent base for American ships. Pressure for an increased American presence in

Hawaii was emerging from another source as well: the growing number of Americans who had settled on the islands and who had gradually come to dominate their economic and political life.

Commercial relations were inexorably pushing Hawaii into the orbit of the United States. An 1875 treaty permitted Hawaiian sugar to enter the United States duty-free and obliged the Hawaiian kingdom to make no territorial or economic concessions to other powers. In 1887, a new treaty granted the United States exclusive use of Pearl Harbor as a naval station. The McKinley Tariff of 1890 strengthened sentiment among Americans in Hawaii for union with the United States. The tariff gave domestic producers of sugar a bounty and deprived Hawaii of its privileged position in the American sugar market. Annexation would give Hawaiian planters the same bounty that American planters were receiving. It seemed the only alternative to economic disaster.

In 1891, in the midst of growing sentiment among white Hawaiians for union with the United States, the passive native king, Kalakaua, died and was succeeded by Queen Liliuokalani, a nationalist determined to eliminate American influence in the government. The American residents resisted. In 1893 they staged a revolution and called on the United States for protection. After the American minister ordered marines from a warship in Honolulu harbor to go ashore to aid the rebels, the queen yielded her authority. A provisional government, dominated by Americans, immediately sent a delegation to Washington to negotiate a treaty of annexation. President Harrison happily signed an annexation agreement in February 1893. But the Senate refused to ratify the treaty, and Grover Cleveland, the new president, refused to support it. Debate over the annexation of Hawaii continued until 1898, when the Republicans returned to power and approved the agreement.

The Samoan islands, 3,000 miles south of Hawaii, had also long served as a way station for American ships in the Pacific trade. As American commerce with Asia increased, business groups in the United States regarded Samoa with new interest, and the American navy began eyeing the Samoan harbor at Pago Pago. In 1878, the Hayes administration extracted a treaty from Samoan leaders that provided for an American naval station at Pago Pago. The treaty bound the United States to arbitrate any differences between Samoa and other nations. Clearly, the United States now expected to have a voice in Samoan affairs.

But Great Britain and Germany were also interested in the islands, and they too secured treaty rights from the native princes. For the next ten years the three powers jockeyed for dominance in Samoa, playing off one native ruler against another and coming dangerously close to war. Finally, the three powers agreed to create a tripartite protectorate over Samoa, with the native chiefs exercising only nominal authority. The three-way arrangement failed to halt the intrigues and rivalries of its members; and in 1899, the United States and Germany divided the islands between them, compensating Britain with territories elsewhere in the Pacific. The United States retained the harbor at Pago Pago.

WAR WITH SPAIN

Imperial ambitions had thus begun to stir within the United States well before the late 1890s. But a war with Spain in 1898 turned those stirrings into overt expansionism. The war transformed America's relationship to the rest of the world, and it left the nation with a far-flung overseas empire.

Controversy over Cuba

The Spanish-American War emerged out of events in Cuba, which along with Puerto Rico represented virtually all that remained of Spain's once-extensive American empire. Cubans had been resisting Spanish rule since at least 1868, when they began a long but ultimately unsuccessful fight for independence. Many Americans had sympathized with the Cubans during that ten-year struggle, but the United States did not intervene.

In 1895, the Cubans rose up again. (Although their goal was an end to Spanish misrule, the island's problems were now in part a result of the Wilson-Gorman Tariff of 1894, whose high duties on sugar had prostrated Cuba's important sugar economy by cutting off exports to the United States, the island's principal market.) This rebellion produced a ferocity on both sides that horrified Americans. The Cubans deliberately devastated the island to force the Spaniards to leave. The Spanish, commanded by General Valeriano Weyler (known in the American press as "Butcher" Weyler), confined civilians in certain areas to hastily prepared concentration camps, where they died by the thousands, victims of disease and malnutrition. The Spanish had used some of these same savage methods during the earlier struggle in Cuba without shocking American sensibilities. But the revolt of 1895 was reported more fully and floridly by American newspapers, and particularly by the new "yellow press" of William Randolph Hearst and Joseph Pulitzer, who were engaged in a ruthless circulation war with each other in New York City and elsewhere. In their effort to play to popular sentiment, they gave the impression that all the cruelties were being perpe-trated by the Spaniards.

A growing population of Cuban émigrés in the United States—cen-tered in Florida, New York, Philadelphia, and Trenton, New Jersey—gave extensive support to the Cuban Revolutionary party (whose headquarters was in New York) and helped publicize its leader, José Martí, who was killed in Cuba in 1895. Later, Cuban-Americans formed other clubs and associa-tions to support the cause of *Cuba Libre* (Free Cuba). In some areas of the country, their efforts were as important as those of the yellow journalists in generating popular support for the revolution.

The mounting storm of indignation against Spain did not persuade President Cleveland to intervene in the conflict. He proclaimed American neutrality and tried to stop the agitation by Cuban refugees in New York City. But when McKinley became president in 1897, he took a stronger stand. He formally protested Spain's "uncivilized and inhuman" conduct, causing the Spanish government (fearful of American intervention) to recall Weyler, modify the concentration policy, and grant the island a qualified autonomy. At the end of 1897, with the insurrection losing ground, it seemed that American involvement in the war might be averted.

But whatever chances there were for a peaceful settlement vanished as a result of two dramatic incidents in February 1898. The first occurred when a Cuban agent in Havana stole a private letter written by Dupuy de Lôme, the Spanish minister in Washington, and turned it over to the American press. It described McKinley as a weak man and "a bidder for the admiration of the crowd." This was no more than what many Americans, including some Republicans, were saying about their president (Assistant Secretary of the Navy Theodore Roosevelt described McKinley as having "no more backbone than a chocolate eclair"). But coming from a foreigner, it created intense popular anger. Dupuy de Lôme promptly resigned.

While excitement over the de Lôme letter was still high, the American battleship *Maine* blew up in Havana harbor with a loss of more than 260 people. The ship had been ordered to Cuba in January to protect American lives and property against possible attacks by Spanish loyalists. Many Ameri-cans assumed that the Spanish had sunk the ship, particularly when a naval court of inquiry reported that an external explosion by a submarine mine had caused the disaster. (Later evidence suggested that the disaster was actually the result of an accidental explosion inside one of the engine rooms.) War hysteria swept the country, and Congress unanimously appropriated $50 million for military preparations. "Remember the *Maine*!" became a national chant for revenge.

THE YELLOW PRESS AND THE WRECK OF THE *MAINE* No evidence
was ever found tying the Spanish to the explosion in Havana
harbor that destroyed the American battleship *Maine* in
February 1898. Nevertheless, newspapers in the United States
ran sensational stories designed to arouse public sentiment in
support of a war against the Spanish. This front page from
Joseph Pulitzer's *New York World* is an example of the lurid
coverage the event received.

McKinley still hoped to avoid a conflict. But others in his administration (including Theodore Roosevelt) were clamoring for war. In March
1898, the president asked Spain to agree to an armistice, negotiations for a
permanent peace, and an end to the concentration camps. Spain agreed to
stop the fighting and eliminate the concentration camps, but it refused to
negotiate with the rebels and reserved the right to resume hostilities at its
discretion. That satisfied neither public opinion nor Congress. A few days
later, McKinley asked for and, on April 25, received a congressional declaration of war.

"A Splendid Little War"

Secretary of State John Hay called the Spanish-American conflict "a splendid little war," an opinion that most Americans—with the exception of
many of the enlisted men who fought in it—seemed to share. Declared in

April, it was over in August. That was in part because Cuban rebels had already greatly weakened the Spanish resistance, which made the American intervention in many respects little more than a "mopping up" exercise. Only 460 Americans were killed in battle or died of wounds, although some 5,200 perished of disease: malaria, dysentery, and typhoid, among others. Casualties among Cuban insurgents, who continued to bear the brunt of the struggle, were much higher.

Yet the American war effort was not without difficulties. United States soldiers faced serious supply problems: a shortage of modern rifles and ammunition, uniforms too heavy for the warm Caribbean weather, inadequate medical services, and skimpy, almost indigestible food. The regular army numbered only 28,000 troops and officers, most of whom had experience in quelling Indian outbreaks but none in larger-scale warfare. That meant that, as in the Civil War, the United States had to rely heavily on National Guard units, organized by local communities and commanded for the most part by local leaders without military experience. The entire mobilization process was conducted with remarkable inefficiency.

There were also racial conflicts. A significant proportion of the American invasion force consisted of black soldiers. Some were volunteer troops

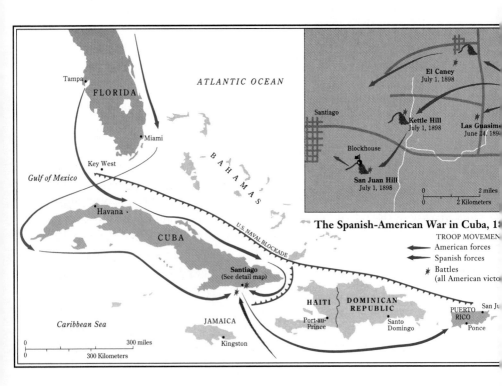

The Spanish-American War in Cuba, 1898

TROOP MOVEMENTS
→ American forces
→ Spanish forces
✳ Battles (all American victories)

put together by black communities (although some governors refused to allow the formation of such units). Others were members of the four black regiments in the regular army, who had been stationed on the frontier to defend white settlements against Indians and were now transferred east to fight in Cuba. As the black soldiers traveled through the South toward the training camps, they chafed at the rigid segregation to which they were subjected and occasionally openly resisted the restrictions. Black soldiers in Georgia deliberately made use of a "whites only" park; in Florida, they beat a soda-fountain operator for refusing to serve them; in Tampa, white provocations and black retaliation led to a night-long riot that left thirty wounded.

Racial tensions continued in Cuba itself, where American blacks played crucial roles in some of the important battles of the war (including the famous charge at San Juan Hill) and won many medals. Nearly half the Cuban insurgents fighting with the Americans were black, and unlike their American counterparts they were fully integrated into the rebel army. (Indeed, two of the leading insurgent commanders, Antonio Maceo and Quintin Bandera, were black men.) The sight of black Cuban soldiers fighting alongside whites as equals gave African-Americans a stronger sense of the injustice of their own position.

Seizing the Philippines

No agency in the American military had clear authority over strategic planning. Only the navy had worked out an objective, but its objective had little to do with freeing Cuba. Assistant Secretary of the Navy Theodore Roosevelt was an ardent imperialist, an active proponent of war, and a man uninhibited by the fact that he was a relatively lowly figure in the military chain of command. Roosevelt unilaterally strengthened the navy's Pacific squadron and instructed its commander, Commodore George Dewey, to attack Spanish naval forces in the Philippines, a colony of Spain, in the event of war.

Immediately after war was declared, Dewey sailed for the Philippines. On May 1, 1898, he steamed into Manila Bay and completely destroyed the aging Spanish fleet there. Only one American sailor had died in the battle (of heatstroke), and George Dewey, immediately promoted to admiral, became the first hero of the war. Several months later, after the arrival of an American expeditionary force, the Spanish surrendered the city of Manila itself. In the rejoicing over Dewey's victory, few Americans paused to note that the character of the war was changing. What had begun as a war to free Cuba was becoming a war to strip Spain of its colonies.

The Battle for Cuba

Cuba, however, remained the principal focus of American military efforts. At first, the American commanders planned a long period of training before actually sending troops into combat. But when a Spanish fleet under Admiral Pascual Cervera slipped past the American navy into Santiago harbor, on the southern coast of Cuba, plans changed quickly. The American Atlantic fleet quickly bottled Cervera up in the harbor. And the army's commanding general, Nelson A. Miles, hastily altered his strategy. He ordered General William R. Shafter to leave Tampa in June with a force of 17,000 to attack Santiago. Both the departure from Florida and the landing in Cuba were scenes of fantastic incompetence. It took five days for the relatively small army to get ashore, and that was with the enemy offering no opposition.

Shafter moved toward Santiago, which he planned to surround and capture. On the way he met and defeated Spanish forces at Las Guasimas and, a week later, in two simultaneous battles, El Caney and San Juan Hill. At the center of the fighting (and on the front pages of the newspapers) during all these engagements was a cavalry unit known as the Rough Riders. Nominally commanded by General Leonard Wood, its real leader was Colonel Theodore Roosevelt, who had resigned from the Navy Department to get into the war and who had struggled with an almost desperate fury to ensure that his regiment made it to the front before the fighting ended. Roosevelt rapidly emerged as a hero of the conflict. His fame rested in large part on his role in leading a bold, if perhaps reckless, charge up Kettle Hill (a charge that was a minor part of the larger battle for the adjacent San Juan Hill) directly into the face of Spanish guns. Roosevelt himself emerged unscathed, but nearly a hundred of his soldiers were killed or wounded. He remembered the battle as "the great day of my life."

Although Shafter was now in position to assault Santiago, his army was so weakened by sickness that he feared he might have to abandon his position, particularly as the commander of the American naval force blockading Santiago refused to enter the harbor because of mines. Disaster seemed imminent. But unknown to the Americans, the Spanish government had by now decided that Santiago was lost and had ordered Cervera to evacuate. On July 3, even though he knew the effort was hopeless, Cervera

THE ROUGH RIDERS Theodore Roosevelt, center, poses with some of the Rough Riders after their famous charge in the Battle of San Juan Hill. The brigade had an unofficial anthem: "Rough, rough, we're the stuff. We want to fight, and we can't get enough."

tried to escape the harbor. The waiting American squadron destroyed his entire fleet. On July 16, the commander of the Spanish ground forces in Santiago surrendered. At about the same time, an American army landed in Puerto Rico and occupied it against virtually no opposition. On August 12, an armistice ended the war.

Decision for Imperialism

Under the terms of the armistice, Spain recognized the independence of Cuba. It ceded Puerto Rico (now occupied by American troops) and the Pacific island of Guam to the United States. And it accepted continued American occupation of Manila pending the final disposition of the Philippines.

The vagueness of the agreement on the Philippines reflected the American confusion over what to do with the islands. Although few Americans objected to annexing nearby Puerto Rico or the distant and seemingly insignificant Guam, annexation of the Philippines was intensely controversial. Supporters and opponents alike realized that acquiring so large and important a territory would mean a major change in America's position in the world.

McKinley claimed to be reluctant to support annexation. But, according to his own accounts, he emerged from an agonizing night of prayer convinced that there were no acceptable alternatives. Returning the Philippines to Spain would be "cowardly and dishonorable," he claimed. Turning the islands over to another imperialist power (France, Germany, or Britain) would be "bad business and discreditable." Granting them independence would be irresponsible; the Filipinos were "unfit for self government." The only solution was "to take them all and to educate the Filipinos, and uplift and Christianize them, and by God's grace do the very best we could by them." Growing popular support for annexation and the pressure of the imperialist leaders of his party undoubtedly helped him reach this decision of conscience.

The Treaty of Paris, signed in December 1898, brought a formal end to the war. It confirmed the terms of the armistice concerning Cuba, Puerto Rico, and Guam. But American negotiators startled the Spanish by demanding that they cede the Philippines to the United States. The Spanish objected briefly, but an American offer of $20 million for the islands softened their resistance. They accepted all the American terms.

In the United States Senate, however, resistance was fierce. During debate over ratification of the treaty, a powerful anti-imperialist movement arose throughout the country to oppose acquisition of the Philippines. Among the anti-imperialists were some of the nation's wealthiest and most powerful figures: Andrew Carnegie, Mark Twain, Samuel Gompers, Senator John Sherman, and others. Their motives were various. Some believed simply that imperialism was immoral, a repudiation of America's commitment to human freedom. Some feared "polluting" the American population by introducing "inferior" Asian races into it. Industrial workers feared being undercut by a flood of cheap laborers from the new colonies. Conservatives feared the large standing army and entangling foreign alliances that they thought imperialism would require and that they believed would threaten American liberties. Sugar growers and others feared unwelcome competition from the new territories. The Anti-Imperialist League, established by upper-class Bostonians, New Yorkers, and others late in 1898 to fight against annexation, attracted a widespread following in the Northeast and waged a vigorous campaign against ratification of the Paris treaty.

Favoring ratification was an equally varied group. There were the exuberant imperialists such as Theodore Roosevelt, who saw the acquisition of empire as a way to reinvigorate the nation, to keep alive what they considered the healthy, restorative influence of the war. Some businessmen saw opportunities in the Philippines and believed annexation would position the United States to dominate the Oriental trade. And most Republicans saw partisan advantages in acquiring valuable new territories through a war fought and won by a Republican administration. Perhaps the strongest argument in favor of annexation, however, was the apparent ease with which it could be accomplished. The United States, after all, already possessed the islands.

When anti-imperialists warned of the danger of acquiring heavily populated territories whose people might have to become citizens, the imperialists had a ready answer: The nation's longstanding policies toward Indians—treating them as dependents rather than as citizens—had created a precedent for annexing land without absorbing people. Senator Henry Cabot Lodge of Massachusetts, one of the leading imperialists in Congress, made the point explicitly:

> The other day . . . a great Democratic thinker announced that a Republic can have no subjects. He seems to have forgotten that this Republic not only has held subjects from the beginning, . . . but [that we have] acquired them by purchase. . . . [We] denied to the Indian tribes even the right to choose their allegiance, or to become citizens.

The fate of the treaty remained in doubt for weeks, until it received the unexpected support of William Jennings Bryan. Bryan was a fervent anti-imperialist who hoped to move the issue out of the Senate and make annexation the subject of a national referendum in 1900, when he expected to be the Democratic presidential candidate again. Bryan persuaded a number of anti-imperialist Democrats to support the treaty so as to set up the 1900 debate. The Senate ratified it finally on February 6, 1899.

But Bryan miscalculated. If the election of 1900 was in fact a referendum on the Philippines, as Bryan tried to make it, it proved beyond doubt that the nation had decided in favor of imperialism. Once again, Bryan ran against McKinley; and once again, McKinley won—even more decisively than in 1896. It was not only the issue of the colonies, however, that ensured McKinley's victory. The Republicans were the beneficiaries of growing national prosperity—and also of the colorful personality of their vice presidential candidate, Colonel Theodore Roosevelt, the hero of San Juan hill.

THE REPUBLIC AS EMPIRE

The new American empire was a small one by the standards of the great imperial powers of Europe. But it created large problems. It embroiled the United States in the politics of both Europe and the Far East in ways the nation had always tried to avoid in the past. It also drew Americans into a brutal war in the Philippines.

Governing the Colonies

Three of the new American dependencies—Hawaii, Alaska, and Puerto Rico—presented relatively few problems. They received territorial status (and their residents American citizenship) relatively quickly: Hawaii in 1900, Alaska in 1912, and Puerto Rico (in stages) by 1917. The navy took control of Guam and Tutuila. And some of the smallest, least populated Pacific islands the United States had acquired it simply left alone.

Cuba was a thornier problem. American military forces, commanded by General Leonard Wood, remained there until 1902 to prepare the island

"MEASURING UNCLE SAM FOR A NEW SUIT," BY J. S. PUGHE, IN *PUCK* MAGA-
ZINE, 1900 President William McKinley is approvingly depicted here as a tailor, measuring his client for a suit large enough to accommodate the new possessions the United States obtained in the aftermath of the Spanish-American War. The cartoon tries to link this expansion with earlier, less controversial ones such as the Louisiana Purchase.

for independence. They built roads, schools, and hospitals; reorganized the legal, financial, and administrative systems; and introduced medical and sanitation reforms. But the United States was also laying the basis for years of American economic domination of the island. When Cuba drew up a constitution that made no reference to the United States, Congress responded by passing the Platt Amendment in 1901 and pressuring Cuba into incorporating the amendment's terms into its constitution. The Platt Amendment barred Cuba from making treaties with other nations (thus, in effect, giving the United States effective control of Cuban foreign policy); it gave the United States the right to intervene in Cuba to preserve independence, life, and property; and it required Cuba to permit American naval stations on its territory. The amendment left Cuba only nominally independent politically. And American capital, which quickly took over the island's economy, made the new nation an American economic appendage as well.

The Philippine War

Americans did not like to think of themselves as imperial rulers in the European mold. Yet like other imperial powers, the United States soon discovered—as it had discovered at home in its relations with the Indians—that subjugating another people required more than ideals; it also required strength and brutality. That, at least, was the lesson of the American experience in the Philippines, where American forces soon became engaged in a long and bloody war with insurgent forces fighting for independence.

The conflict in the Philippines is the least remembered of all American wars. It was also one of the longest (it lasted from 1898 to 1902) and one of the most vicious. It involved 200,000 American troops and resulted in 4,300 American deaths, nearly ten times the number who had died in combat in the Spanish-American War. The number of Filipinos killed in the conflict is still in dispute, but it seems likely that at least 50,000 natives (and perhaps many more) died. The American occupiers faced guerrilla tactics in the Philippines very similar to those the Spanish occupiers had faced prior to 1898 in Cuba. And they soon found themselves drawn into the same pattern of brutality that had outraged so many Americans when Weyler had used them in the Caribbean.

The Filipinos had been rebelling against Spanish rule even before 1898. And as soon as they realized the Americans had come to stay, they rebelled against them as well. Ably led by Emilio Aguinaldo, who claimed to head the legitimate government of the nation, Filipinos harried the American army of occupation from island to island for more than three years. At first,

American commanders believed the rebels had only a small popular follow-ing. But by early 1900, General Arthur MacArthur, an American com-mander in the islands (and the father of General Douglas MacArthur), was writing: "I have been reluctantly compelled to believe that the Filipino masses are loyal to Aguinaldo and the government which he heads."

To MacArthur and others, that realization was not a reason to moderate American tactics or conciliate the rebels. It was a reason to adopt more severe measures. Gradually, the American military effort became more systemati-cally vicious and brutal. Captured Filipino guerrillas were treated not as prisoners of war but as murderers. Most were summarily executed. On some islands, entire communities were evacuated—the residents forced into con-centration camps while American troops destroyed their villages, farms, crops, and livestock. A spirit of savagery grew among American soldiers, who came to view the Filipinos as almost subhuman and at times seemed to take pleasure in killing almost arbitrarily.

By 1902, reports of the brutality and of the American casualties had soured the American public on the war. But by then, the rebellion had largely exhausted itself and the occupiers had established control over most of the islands. The key to their victory was the March 1901 capture of Aguinaldo, who later signed a document in which he urged his followers to stop fighting and declared his own allegiance to the United States. (Aguinaldo then retired from public life and lived quietly until 1964.) Fighting continued in some places for another year, and the war revived intermittently until as late as 1906; but American possession of the Philippines was now secure.

In the summer of 1901, the military transferred authority over the islands to William Howard Taft, who became the first civilian governor. Taft announced that the American mission in the Philippines was to prepare the islands for independence, and he gave the Filipinos broad local autonomy. The Americans also built roads, schools, bridges, and sewers; instituted major administrative and financial reforms; and established a public health system. Filipino self-rule slowly increased. But not until July 4, 1946, did the islands finally gain their independence.

The Open Door

The acquisition of the Philippines greatly increased the already strong American interest in Asia. Americans were particularly concerned about the future of China, with which the United States already had an important trade and which was now so enfeebled that it provided a tempting target for exploitation by stronger countries. By 1900, England, France, Germany,

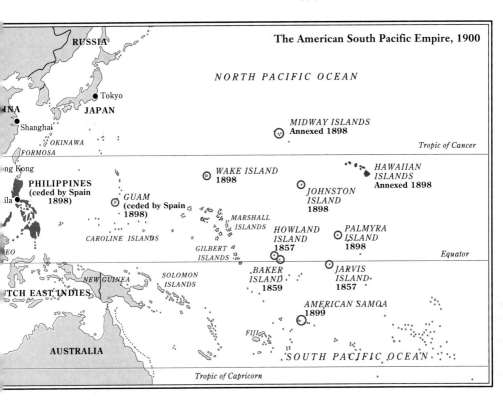

The American South Pacific Empire, 1900

Russia, and Japan were beginning to carve up China among themselves, pressuring the Chinese government for "concessions" that gave them effective economic control over various regions or, in some cases, simply seizing Chinese territory and claiming it as their own "spheres of influence." Many Americans feared the process would soon cut them out of the China trade altogether.

Eager for a way to protect American interests in China without risking war, McKinley issued a statement in September 1898 saying the United States wanted access to China, but no special advantages there: "Asking only the open door for ourselves, we are ready to accord the open door to others." Later, Secretary of State John Hay translated the president's words into policy when he addressed identical messages—which became known as the "Open Door notes"—to England, Germany, Russia, France, Japan, and Italy. He asked them to approve three principles: Each nation with a "sphere of influence" in China was to respect the rights and privileges of other nations in its sphere; Chinese officials were to continue to collect tariff duties in all spheres (the existing tariff favored the United States); and nations were not to discriminate against other nations in levying port dues and railroad rates within their own spheres. Together, these principles would allow the United States to trade freely with the Chinese without fear of interference and without having to become militarily involved in the region.

But the Open Door proposals were coolly received in Europe and Japan. Russia openly rejected them; each of the other powers claimed to accept them in principle but to be unable to act unless all the other powers agreed. Hay refused to consider this a rebuff. He announced that all the powers had accepted the principles of the Open Door and that the United States expected them to observe those principles. But unless the United States was willing to resort to war, it could not prevent any nation that wanted to violate the Open Door from doing so.

THE BOXER REBELLION American troops march through the grounds of the Temple of Agriculture in Beijing's Imperial City during the Boxer Rebellion in 1900. They were among 5,000 American soldiers summoned to China. In mid-August, they joined British, Russian, Japanese and French soldiers to rescue diplomats, foreigners, and Christians who had barricaded themselves in the city's diplomatic quarter in June to protect themselves from the Boxers.

No sooner had the diplomatic maneuvering over the Open Door ended than the Boxers, a secret Chinese martial-arts society, launched a revolt against foreigners in China. The climax of the Boxer Rebellion was a siege of the entire foreign diplomatic corps in the British embassy in Peking. The imperial powers (including the United States) sent an international expeditionary force into China to rescue the diplomats. In August 1900, it fought its way into Peking and broke the siege.

McKinley and Hay had agreed to American participation so as to secure a voice in the settlement of the uprising and to prevent the partition of China. Hay now won support for his Open Door approach from England and Germany and then induced the other participating powers to accept compensation from the Chinese for the damages the Boxer Rebellion had caused. Chinese territorial integrity survived at least in name, and the United States retained access to its lucrative trade.

A Modern Military System

The war with Spain had revealed glaring deficiencies in the American military system. The army had exhibited the greatest weaknesses, but the entire military organization had failed to coordinate its efforts. Had the United States been fighting a more powerful nation, disaster might have resulted. After the war, McKinley appointed Elihu Root, an able New York corporate lawyer, as secretary of war to supervise a major overhaul of the armed forces. (Root was one of the first of several generations of attorney-statesmen who moved easily between public and private roles and constituted what has often been called the American "foreign policy establishment.") Between 1900 and 1903, Root created a new military system.

The Root reforms enlarged the regular army from 25,000 to a maximum of 100,000. They established federal command of the National Guard, ensuring that never again would the nation fight a war with volunteer regiments over which the federal government had only limited control. They sparked the creation of a system of officer training schools, including the Army Staff College (later the Command and General Staff School) at Fort Leavenworth, Kansas, and the Army War College in Washington, D.C. And in 1903, they established a general staff (now known as the Joint Chiefs of Staff) to act as military advisers to the secretary of war. As a result of the new reforms, the United States entered the twentieth century with something resembling a modern military system. The country would make substantial use of it in the turbulent century to come.

CHAPTER TWENTY-ONE

The Rise
of Progressivism

The Progressive Impulse ∼ *The Assault on the Parties*
Crusades for Order and Reform

ELL BEFORE THE turn of the century, many Americans had become convinced that the rapid industrialization and urbanization of their society had created intolerable problems—that the nation's most pressing need was to impose order on the growing chaos and to curb industrial society's most glaring injustices. In the early years of the new century, that outlook acquired a name: progressivism.

Not even those who called themselves progressives could always agree on what the word "progressive" really meant. Indeed, more than one historian has suggested that the word ultimately came to mean so many different things to so many different people that it ceased to mean anything at all. Yet if progressivism was a phenomenon of great scope and diversity, it was also one that rested on an identifiable set of central assumptions. It was, first, an optimistic vision. Progressives believed, as their name implies, in the idea of progress. They believed that society was capable of improvement, even of perfection, and that continued growth and advancement were the nation's destiny. But progressives believed, too, that growth and progress could not continue to occur recklessly, as they had in the late nineteenth century. The "natural laws" of the marketplace, and the doctrines of laissez faire and Social Darwinism that celebrated those laws, were not sufficient to create the order and stability that the growing society required. Purposeful human intervention was necessary to solve the nation's problems. Progressives did not always agree on the form that intervention should take, but most believed that government could play an important role in the process.

THE PROGRESSIVE IMPULSE

Beyond these central premises, progressivism flowed outward in a number of different directions. One powerful impulse was the spirit of "antimonopoly," the fear of concentrated power and the urge to limit and disperse authority and wealth. A second progressive impulse was a belief in the importance of social cohesion: the belief that individuals are not autonomous but part of a great web of social relationships, that the welfare of any single person is dependent on the welfare of society as a whole. And a third progressive impulse was a belief in organization and efficiency: the belief that social order was a result of intelligent social organization and rational procedures for guiding social and economic life. These varied reform impulses were not entirely incompatible with one another. Many progressives made use of all these ideas at times as they tried to restore order and stability to their turbulent society.

The Muckrakers and the Social Gospel

Among the first to articulate the new spirit of reform was a group of crusading journalists who began in the late nineteenth and early twentieth centuries to direct public attention toward social, economic, and political injustices. They became known as the "muckrakers" after Theodore Roosevelt accused one of them of raking up muck through his writings. They were committed to exposing scandal, corruption, and injustice to public view.

At first, their major targets were the trusts and particularly the railroads, which the muckrakers considered dangerously powerful and deeply corrupt. Exposés of the great corporate organizations began to appear as early as the 1860s, when Charles Francis Adams, Jr., and others uncovered corruption among the railroad barons. By the turn of the century, many muckrakers were turning their attention to government and particularly to the urban political machines. The most influential, perhaps, was Lincoln Steffens, a reporter for *McClure's* magazine. His portraits of "machine government" and "boss rule"; his exposures of "boodlers" in cities as diverse as St. Louis, Minneapolis, Cleveland, Cincinnati, Chicago, Philadelphia, and New York; his tone of studied moral outrage (as reflected in the title of his series and of the book that emerged from it, *The Shame of the Cities*)—all helped arouse sentiment for urban political reform. The muckrakers reached the peak of their influence in the first decade of the twentieth century. They investigated governments, labor unions, and corporations. They explored the problems of child labor, immigrant ghettoes, prostitution, and family disorganization. They denounced waste and destruction of natural resources, the subjugation of women, even occasionally the oppression of blacks.

The moralistic tone of the muckrakers' exposés reflected one important aspect of emerging progressive sentiment: a sense of outrage at social and economic injustice. That outrage, combined with a humanitarian sense of social responsibility, helped produce one of the central missions of many reformers: the pursuit of "social justice." A clear expression of that concern was the rise of what became known as the "Social Gospel." By the early twentieth century, it had become a powerful movement within American Protestantism (and, to a lesser extent, within American Catholicism and

MCCLURE'S MAGAZINE, MAY 1903 *McClure's* was the leading outlet for a form of journalism known as "muckraking," which exposed social and economic scandals in the hope of promoting reform. This issue contains articles by two of the leading muckrakers, Lincoln Steffens and Ida Tarbell.

Judaism) to redeem the nation's cities. The Salvation Army, which began in England but soon spread to the United States, was a Christian social welfare organization with a vaguely military structure. By 1900, it had recruited 3,000 "officers" and 20,000 "privates" and was offering both material aid and spiritual service to the urban poor. In addition, many ministers, priests, and rabbis left traditional parish work to serve in the troubled cities. Charles Sheldon's *In His Steps* (1898), the story of a young minister who abandoned a comfortable post to work among the needy, sold more than 15 million copies and established itself as the most successful novel of the era. The engagement of religion with reform helped bring to progressivism a powerful moral impulse and a concern for the plight of some of society's most impoverished and degraded people.

The Settlement House Movement

One of the strongest elements of progressive thought was the belief that the environment shaped individual development. Social Darwinists such as William Graham Sumner had argued that people's fortunes reflected their inherent "fitness" for survival. Most progressive theorists disagreed. Ignorance, poverty, even criminality, they argued, were not the result of inherent moral or genetic failings or of the workings of providence. They were, rather, the effects of an unhealthy environment. To elevate the distressed, therefore, required an improvement of the conditions in which the distressed lived.

Nothing produced more distress, many reformers believed, than the crowded immigrant neighborhoods of American cities. One response to the problems of such communities, borrowed from England, was the settlement house. The most famous, and one of the first, was Hull House, which opened in 1889 in Chicago as a result of the efforts of Jane Addams. It became a model for more than 400 similar institutions throughout the nation. Staffed by members of the educated middle class, settlement houses sought to help immigrant families adapt to the language and customs of their new country. Settlement houses avoided the condescension and moral disapproval of earlier philanthropic efforts. But they generally embodied a belief that middle-class Americans had a responsibility to impart their own values to immigrants and to teach them how to live middle-class life styles. Even the word "settlement" suggested as much: middle-class people "settling" in the inner city and bringing civilization to the urban frontier.

A M E R I C A N   V O I C E S

JANE ADDAMS

First Days at Hull House

FROM THE FIRST it seemed understood that we were ready to perform the humblest neighborhood services. We were asked to wash the newborn babies, and to prepare the dead for burial, to nurse the sick, and to "mind the children." Occasionally these neighborly offices unexpectedly uncovered ugly human traits. . . . a little Italian bride of fifteen sought shelter with us one November evening, to escape her husband who had beaten her every night for a week when he returned home from work, because she had lost her wedding ring; two of us officiated quite alone at the birth of an illegitimate child because the doctor was late in arriving, and none of the honest Irish matrons would "touch the likes of her." . . .

We were . . . early impressed with the curious isolation of many of the immigrants; an Italian woman once expressed her pleasure in the red roses that she saw at one of our receptions in surprise that they had been "brought so fresh all the way from Italy." She would not believe for an instant that they had been grown in America. . . . Her conception of America had been the untidy street in which she lived and had made her long struggle to adapt herself to American ways.

But in spite of some untoward experiences, we were constantly impressed with the uniform kindness and courtesy we received. Perhaps these first days laid the simple human foundations which are certainly essential for continuous living among the poor: . . . the conviction . . . that the things which make men alike are finer and better than the things that keep them apart, and that these basic likenesses, if they are properly accentuated, easily transcend the less essential differences of race, language, creed, and tradition.

SOURCE: Jane Addams, *Twenty Years at Hull House* (New York: The Macmillan Company, 1910), pp. 88–89.

Central to the settlement houses were the efforts of college women. Indeed, the movement became a training ground for many important female leaders of the twentieth century, including Eleanor Roosevelt. The settlement houses also helped spawn another important institution of reform: the profession of social work—a profession in which women were to play an important role. The professional social worker combined a compassion for the poor with a commitment to the values of bureaucratic progressivism: scientific study, efficient organization, reliance on experts.

The Allure of Expertise

As the emergence of the social work profession suggests, progressives involved in humanitarian efforts often placed high value on knowledge and expertise. Even nonscientific problems, they believed, could be analyzed and solved scientifically. Many reformers came to believe that only enlightened experts and well-designed bureaucracies could create the stability and order America needed.

This belief found expression in many ways, among them the writings of a new group of scholars and intellectuals. Unlike the Social Darwinists of the nineteenth century, these theorists were no longer content with merely justifying the existing industrial system. They spoke instead of the creation of a new civilization, one in which the expertise of scientists and engineers could be brought to bear on the problems of the economy and society. Among the most influential was the social scientist Thorstein Veblen. Harshly critical of the industrial tycoons of the late nineteenth century—the "leisure class," as he satirically described them in his first major work, *A Theory of the Leisure Class* (1899)—Veblen proposed instead a new economic system in which power would reside in the hands of highly trained engineers. Only they, he argued, could fully understand the "machine process" by which modern society must be governed.

In practical terms, the impulse toward expertise and organization helped produce the idea of scientific management, or "Taylorism." It encouraged the development of modern mass-production techniques and, above all, the assembly line. It inspired a revolution in American education and the creation of a new area of inquiry—social science, the use of scientific techniques in the study of society and its institutions. It produced a generation of bureaucratic reformers concerned with the structure of organizations and committed to building new political and economic institutions capable of managing a modern society. It also helped create a movement toward organization among the expanding new group of middle-class professionals.

The Professions

The late nineteenth century saw a dramatic expansion in the number of Americans engaged in administrative and professional tasks. Industries needed managers, technicians, and accountants as well as workers. Cities required commercial, medical, legal, and educational services. The new technology required scientists and engineers who, in turn, required institutions and instructors to train them. By the turn of the century, the people performing these services had come to constitute a distinct social group—what some have called a new middle class.

The new middle class placed a high value on education and individual accomplishment. By the early twentieth century, its millions of members were building organizations and establishing standards to secure their position in society. As their principal vehicle, they created the modern, organized professions. The idea of professionalism had been a frail one in America even as late as 1880. But as the demand for professional services increased, so did the pressures for reform.

Among the first to respond was the medical profession. Throughout the 1890s, doctors who considered themselves trained professionals began forming local associations and societies. In 1901, they reorganized the American Medical Association (AMA) into a national professional society. By 1920, nearly two-thirds of all American doctors were members. The AMA quickly called for strict, scientific standards for admission to the practice of medicine, with doctors themselves serving as protectors of the standards. State and local governments responded by passing new laws that required the licensing of all physicians and that restricted licenses to those practitioners approved by the profession.

There was similar movement in other professions. By 1916, lawyers in all forty-eight states had established professional bar associations, virtually all of which had succeeded in creating central examining boards, composed of lawyers, to regulate admission to the profession. Increasingly, aspiring lawyers found it necessary to enroll in graduate programs, and the nation's law schools accordingly expanded greatly, both in numbers and in the rigor of their curricula. Businessmen supported the creation of schools of business administration and created their own national organizations: the National Association of Manufacturers in 1895 and the United States Chamber of

Commerce in 1912. Even farmers, long the symbol of the romantic spirit of individualism, responded to the new order by forming, through the National Farm Bureau Federation, a network of agricultural organizations designed to spread scientific farming methods, teach sound marketing techniques, and lobby for the interests of their members.

Among the chief purposes of the new professionalism was guarding entry into the professions. This was only partly an effort to defend the professions from the untrained and incompetent. The admission requirements also protected those already in the professions from excessive competition and lent prestige and status to the professional label. Some professions used their entrance requirements to exclude blacks, women, immigrants, and other "undesirables" from their ranks. Others used them simply to keep the numbers down, to ensure that demand for the services of existing members would remain high.

Women and the Professions

American women found themselves excluded—both by custom and by active barriers of law and prejudice—from most of the emerging professions. But a substantial number of middle-class women—particularly those emerging from the new women's colleges and from the coeducational state universities—nevertheless entered professional careers.

A few women managed to establish themselves as physicians, lawyers, engineers, scientists, and corporate managers. Several leading medical schools admitted women, and about 5 percent of all American physicians were female in 1900 (a proportion that remained unchanged until the 1960s). Most, however, turned by necessity to those professions that society considered "suitable" for women. Settlement houses and social work provided two "appropriate" professional outlets for women. The most important, however, was teaching. Indeed, in the late nineteenth century, more than two-thirds of all grammar-school teachers were women, and perhaps 90 percent of all professional women were teachers. For educated black women, in particular, teaching was often the only professional opportunity they could hope to find. The existence of segregated black schools in the South created a substantial market for African-American teachers.

Women also dominated other professional activities. Nursing had become primarily a women's field when it was still considered a menial occupation, akin to domestic service. But by the early twentieth century, it too was adopting professional standards. Prospective nurses generally

SETTLEMENT HOUSE WORKERS Nurses from the Henry
Street settlement in New York leave their headquarters to
begin their visits to the homes of poor immigrants in lower
Manhattan. This photograph dates from the early 1900s.

needed certification from schools of nursing and could not simply learn on
the job. Women also found opportunities as librarians, another field beginning to define itself in professional terms. And many women entered
academia—often receiving advanced degrees at such predominantly male
institutions as the University of Chicago, MIT, and Columbia, and finding
professional opportunities in the new and expanding women's colleges.

The "women's professions" had much in common with other professions: the value they placed on training and expertise, the creation of
professional organizations and a professional "identity," the monitoring of
admission to professional work. But they also had distinctive qualities.
Careers such as teaching, nursing, and library work were "helping" professions. They involved working primarily with other women or with children.

Their activities occurred in places that seemed different from the offices that dominated the predominantly male business and professional worlds; such places as schools, hospitals, and libraries had a vaguely "domestic" or "feminine" image.

The Clubwomen

Many middle-class women who did not enter professional careers neverthe-less played an important role in the effort to remake society. In the vanguard of progressive social reforms was a large network of women's associations that proliferated rapidly beginning in the 1880s and 1890s. Large numbers of women gravitated to the growing temperance movement. Others turned to women's clubs.

The women's clubs began largely as cultural organizations to provide middle- and upper-class women with an outlet for their intellectual energies. In 1892, when women formed the General Federation of Womens Club's to coordinate the activities of local organizations, there were more than 100,000 members in nearly 500 clubs. Eight years later, there were 160,000 members; and by 1917, over 1 million.

By the early twentieth century, the clubs were becoming less concerned with cultural activities and more concerned with making a contribution to social betterment. Much of what they did was uncontroversial: planting trees; supporting schools, libraries, and settlement houses; building hospitals and parks. But clubwomen also supported such controversial measures as child labor laws, worker compensation, pure food and drug legislation, occupational safety, reforms in Indian policy, and—beginning in 1914—woman suffrage. Because many club members were from wealthy families, some organizations had substantial funds at their disposal to make their influence felt.

Black women occasionally joined clubs dominated by whites. But African-Americans also formed clubs of their own, some of which affiliated with the General Federation, but more of which became part of the independent National Association of Colored Women. They modeled themselves primarily on their white counterparts, but some black clubs also took positions on issues of particular concern to blacks. Some crusaded against lynching and called for congressional legislation to make lynching a federal crime. Others protested aspects of segregation.

The women's club movement raised few overt challenges to prevailing assumptions about the proper role of women in society. But it did represent an important effort by women to extend their influence beyond the traditional female sphere within the home and the family. Few clubwomen were willing to accept the arguments of such committed feminists as Charlotte Perkins Gilman, who in her 1898 book, *Women and Economics*, argued that the traditional definition of sexual roles was exploitive and obsolete. The club movement, rather, allowed women to define a space for themselves in the public world without openly challenging the existing, male-dominated order.

But the importance of the club movement did not lie simply in what it did for middle-class women. It lay also in what those women did for the working-class people they attempted to help. The women's club movement was an important force in winning passage of state (and ultimately federal) laws that regulated the conditions of woman and child labor, that established government inspection of workplaces, that regulated the food and drug industries, and that applied new standards to urban housing. In many of these efforts, the clubwomen formed alliances with such other women's groups as the Women's Trade Union League, founded in 1903 by female union members and upper-class reformers and committed to persuading women to join unions.

THE ASSAULT ON THE PARTIES

Sooner or later, most progressive goals required the involvement of government. Only government, reformers agreed, could effectively counter the powerful private interests that threatened the nation. But American government at the dawn of the new century was, progressives believed, poorly adapted to perform their ambitious tasks. At every level, political institutions were outmoded, inefficient, and corrupt. Before society could be effectively reformed, it would be necessary to reform government itself. In the beginning, at least, many progressives believed that such reform should start with an assault on the domination of government and politics by the political parties, which they thought had become corrupt, undemocratic, and reactionary.

Early Attacks

Attacks on party dominance had been frequent in the late nineteenth century. Greenbackism and Populism, for example, had been efforts to break the hammerlock with which the Republicans and Democrats controlled public life. The Independent Republicans (or mugwumps; see p. 517) had attempted to challenge the grip of partisanship; and former mugwumps became important supporters of progressive political reform activity in the 1890s and later.

The early assaults enjoyed some success. In the 1880s and 1890s, for example, most states adopted the secret ballot. Prior to that, the political parties themselves had printed ballots (or "tickets"), which they distributed to their supporters, who then simply went to the polls to deposit the tickets in the ballot box. The old system had made it possible for bosses to monitor the voting behavior of their constituents; it had also made it difficult for voters to "split" their tickets—to vote for candidates of different parties for different offices. The new secret ballot—printed by the government and distributed at the polls, where it was filled out and deposited in secret—helped chip away at the power of the parties over the voters. (It also excluded many illiterate and non-English speaking voters.)

By the late 1890s, critics of the parties were expanding their goals. Party rule could be broken, they believed, in one of two ways. It could be broken by increasing the power of the people, by permitting them to circumvent partisan institutions and express their will directly at the polls. Or it could be broken by placing more power in the hands of nonpartisan, nonelective officials, insulated from political life. Reformers promoted measures that moved along both those paths.

Municipal Reform

Many progressives believed the impact of party rule was most damaging in the cities. Municipal government, therefore, became the first target of those working for political reform. Muckraking journalists such as Lincoln Steffens were especially successful in arousing public outrage at corruption and incompetence in city politics.

The muckrakers struck a responsive chord among a powerful group of urban middle-class progressives. For several decades after the Civil War, "respectable" citizens of the nation's large cities had avoided participation in municipal government. Viewing politics as a debased and demeaning activity, they shrank from contact with the "vulgar" elements who were coming to dominate public life. By the end of the century, however, a new generation of activists—some of them members of old aristocratic families, others a part of the new middle class—were taking a renewed interest in government.

They faced a formidable array of opponents. In addition to challenging the powerful city bosses and their entrenched political organizations, they were attacking a large group of special interests: saloon owners, brothel keepers, and, perhaps most significantly, those businessmen who had established lucrative relationships with the urban machines and viewed reform as a threat to their profits. Allied with these interests were many influential newspapers, which ridiculed the reformers as naïve do-gooders. Finally, there was the great constituency of urban working people, many of them recent immigrants, for whom the machines were a source of needed jobs and services. Gradually, however, the reformers gained in political strength—in part because of their own growing numbers, in part because of the failures of the existing political leadership. And in the first years of the twentieth century, they began to score some important victories.

One of the first major successes came in Galveston, Texas, where the old city government proved completely unable to deal with the effects of a destructive tidal wave in 1900. Capitalizing on public dismay, reformers (many of them local businessmen) won approval of a new city charter. The mayor and council were replaced by an elected, nonpartisan commission. In 1907, Des Moines, Iowa, adopted its own version of the commission plan, and other cities soon followed.

Another approach to reform, similarly motivated by the desire to remove city government from the hands of the parties, was the city-manager plan (first adopted in Staunton, Virginia, in 1908), by which elected officials hired an outside expert—often a professionally trained business manager or engineer—to take charge of the government. The city manager would presumably remain untainted by the corrupting influence of politics. By the end of the progressive era, almost 400 cities were operating under commissions, and another 45 employed city managers.

In most urban areas, and in the larger cities in particular, the enemies of party had to settle for less absolute victories. Some cities made the election of mayors nonpartisan (so that the parties could not choose the candidates) or moved them to years when no presidential or congressional races were in progress (to reduce the influence of the large turnouts that party organizations produced on such occasions). Reformers tried to make city council members run at large so as to limit the influence of ward leaders and district bosses. They tried to strengthen the power of the mayor at the expense of the city council, on the assumption that reformers were more likely to get a sympathetic mayor elected than win control of the entire council.

Statehouse Progressivism

But the assault on boss rule in the cities often did not produce results satisfying to reformers. As a result, many progressives turned to state government as an agent for reform. These state-level progressives, like their municipal counterparts, considered existing state governments unfit to provide reform. They looked with particular scorn on state legislatures, whose ill-paid, relatively undistinguished members were, they believed, generally incompetent, often corrupt, and always controlled by party bosses. Many reformers began looking for ways to circumvent the legislatures (and the party bosses that controlled them) by increasing the power of the electorate.

Two of the most important changes were innovations first proposed by Populists in the 1890s: the initiative and the referendum. The initiative allowed reformers to circumvent state legislatures altogether by submitting legislation directly to the voters in general elections. The referendum provided a method by which actions of the legislature could be returned to the electorate for approval. By 1918, more than twenty states had enacted one or both of these reforms.

The direct primary and the recall were, similarly, efforts to limit the power of parties and improve the quality of elected officials. The primary election was an attempt to take the selection of candidates away from the bosses and give it to the people. (In the South, it was also a device for excluding African-Americans from voting.) The recall gave voters the right to remove a public official from office at a special election, which could be called after a sufficient number of citizens had signed a petition. By 1915 every state in the nation had instituted primary elections for at least some offices. The recall encountered more strenuous opposition, but some states adopted it as well.

Reform efforts proved most effective in states that elevated vigorous and committed politicians to positions of leadership. In New York, Governor Charles Evans Hughes exploited progressive sentiment to create a commission to regulate public utilities. In California, Governor Hiram Johnson promoted reforms to limit the political power of the Southern Pacific Railroad. In New Jersey, Woodrow Wilson, the Princeton University president who was elected governor in 1910, used executive leadership to win reforms designed to end New Jersey's widely denounced position as the "mother of trusts."

But the most celebrated state-level reformer was Robert M. La Follette of Wisconsin. Elected governor in 1900, he helped turn his state into what reformers across the nation described as a "laboratory of progressivism." The Wisconsin progressives won approval of direct primaries, initiatives, and referendums. They regulated railroads and utilities. They passed laws to regulate the workplace and provide compensation for laborers injured on the job. They instituted graduated taxes on inherited fortunes, and they nearly doubled state levies on railroads and other corporate interests. Ultimately, La Follette would find himself overshadowed by other national progressive leaders. In the early years of the century, however, few men were as effective in publicizing the message of reform. None was as successful in bending state government to that goal.

Parties and Interest Groups

The reformers did not, of course, eliminate party from American political life. But they did diminish the parties' centrality. Evidence of that came from, among other things, the decline in voter turnout. In the late nine-

ROBERT LA FOLLETTE CAMPAIGNING IN WISCONSIN After three terms as governor of Wisconsin, La Follette began a long career in the United States Senate in 1906 during which he worked uncompromisingly for advanced progressive reforms—so uncompromisingly, in fact, that he was often almost completely isolated.

teenth century, up to 81 percent of eligible voters routinely turned out for national elections. In the early twentieth century, while turnout remained very high by today's dismal standards, the figure declined markedly. In the presidential election of 1900, 73 percent of the electorate voted. By 1912, the figure had dropped to about 59 percent. Never again did voter turnout reach as high as 70 percent.

At the same time that parties were declining, another kind of power center was beginning to replace them: what have become known as "interest groups." Beginning late in the nineteenth century and accelerating rapidly in the twentieth, new organizations emerged, outside the party system, that were designed to pressure government to do the bidding of their members: professional organizations; trade associations, representing particular businesses and industries; labor organizations; farm lobbies; and many others. Social workers, the settlement house movement, women's clubs, and others learned to operate as interest groups to advance their demands. A new pattern of politics, in which many individual interests organized to influence government directly rather than operating through party structures, was emerging. It would become the characteristic form of American politics in the twentieth century.

Reform by Machine

One result of the assault on the parties was a change in the party organizations themselves, which attempted to adapt to the new realities so as to preserve their influence. Such efforts achieved considerable success. Some party machines emerged from the progressive era almost as powerful as they had entered it. In large part, this was because bosses themselves recognized that they must change in order to survive. Thus they sometimes allowed their machines to become vehicles of social reform. One example was New York's Tammany Hall, the nation's oldest and most notorious city machine. Its astute leader, Charles Francis Murphy, began in the early years of the century to fuse the techniques of boss rule with some of the concerns of social reformers. Murphy did nothing to challenge the fundamental workings of Tammany Hall. At the same time, however, Tammany began to take an increased interest in state and national politics, which it had traditionally scorned; and it used its political power on behalf of legislation to improve working conditions, protect child laborers, and eliminate the worst abuses of the industrial economy.

In 1911, a terrible fire swept through the factory of the Triangle Shirtwaist Company in New York; 146 workers, most of them women, died. Many of them had been trapped inside the burning building because management had locked the emergency exits to prevent malingering. For the next three years, a state commission studied not only the background of the fire but the general condition of the industrial workplace; and by 1914, it had issued a series of reports calling for major reforms in the conditions of modern labor.

The report itself was a classic progressive document, based on the testimony of experts, filled with statistics and technical data. Yet when its recommendations reached the New York legislature, its most effective supporters were not middle-class progressives but two Tammany Democrats: Senator Robert F. Wagner and Assemblyman Alfred E. Smith. With the support of Murphy and the backing of other Tammany legislators, they steered through a series of pioneering labor laws that imposed strict regulations on factory owners and established effective mechanisms for enforcement.

CRUSADES FOR ORDER AND REFORM

Reformers directed many of their energies at the political process. But they also crusaded on behalf of what they considered moral issues. There were campaigns to eliminate alcohol from national life, to curb prostitution, to regulate divorce. There were efforts to restrict immigration or curb the power of monopoly in the industrial economy. There were crusades to resolve what many considered longstanding injustices, of which the most prominent was the campaign for woman suffrage. Proponents of each of those reforms believed that success would help regenerate society as a whole.

The Temperance Crusade

Many progressives considered the elimination of alcohol from American life a necessary step in restoring order to society. Workers in settlement houses and social agencies abhorred the effects of drinking on working-class families: Scarce wages vanished as workers spent hours in saloons; drunkenness spawned violence, and occasionally murder, within urban families. Women, in particular, saw alcohol as a source of some of the greatest problems of working-class wives and mothers, and hoped through temperance to reform abusive or irresponsible male behavior and thus improve women's lives. Employers, too, regarded alcohol as an impediment to industrial efficiency; workers often missed time on the job because of drunkenness or, worse, came to the factory intoxicated and performed their tasks sloppily and dangerously. Critics of economic privilege denounced the liquor industry as one of the nation's most sinister trusts. And political reformers, who looked on the saloon (correctly) as one of the central institutions of the machine, saw an attack on drinking as part of an attack on the bosses. Out of such sentiments emerged the temperance movement.

Temperance had been a major reform movement before the Civil War, mobilizing large numbers of people (and particularly large numbers of women) in a crusade with strong evangelical overtones. Beginning in the 1870s, it experienced a major resurgence. As in the antebellum years, it was a movement led and supported primarily by women. In 1873, temperance advocates formed the Women's Christian Temperance Union (WCTU), led after 1879 by Frances Willard. By 1911, it had 245,000 members and had become the largest single women's organization in American history to that point. The WCTU publicized the evils of alcohol and the connection between drunkenness and family violence, unemployment, poverty, and disease. In 1893, the Anti-Saloon League joined the temperance movement and, along with the WCTU, began to press for a specific legislative solution: the legal abolition of saloons. Gradually, that demand grew to include the complete prohibition of the sale and manufacture of alcoholic beverages.

Despite substantial opposition from immigrant and working-class voters, pressure for prohibition grew steadily through the first decades of the new century. By 1916, nineteen states had passed prohibition laws. But since the consumption of alcohol was actually increasing in many unregulated areas, temperance supporters were beginning to advocate a national prohibition law. America's entry into World War I, and the moral fervor it unleashed, provided the last push to the advocates of prohibition. In 1917, with the support of rural fundamentalists who opposed alcohol on moral and religious grounds, progressive advocates of prohibition steered through Congress a constitutional amendment embodying their demands. Two years later, after ratification by every state in the nation except Connecticut and Rhode Island (bastions of Catholic immigrants), the Eighteenth Amendment became law, to take effect in January 1920.

Immigration Restriction

Virtually all reformers agreed that the growing immigrant population had created social problems, but there was wide disagreement on how best to respond. Some progressives believed that helping the new residents adapt to American society was the proper approach. Others argued that efforts at assimilation had failed and that the only solution was to limit the flow of new arrivals.

In the first decades of the century, therefore, pressure grew to close the nation's gates. New scholarly theories, appealing to the progressive respect for expertise, argued that the introduction of immigrants into American society was diluting the purity of the nation's racial stock. The spurious "science" of eugenics spread the belief that human inequalities were hereditary and that immigration was contributing to the multiplication of the unfit. A special federal commission of "experts," chaired by Senator William P. Dillingham of Vermont, issued an elaborate report filled with statistics and scholarly testimony. It argued that the newer immigrant groups—largely southern and eastern Europeans—had proved themselves less assimilable than earlier immigrants. Immigration, the report implied, should be restricted by nationality. Even many people who rejected racial arguments supported limiting immigration as a way to solve such urban problems as overcrowding, unemployment, strained social services, and social unrest.

The combination of these concerns gradually won for the nativists the support of some of the nation's leading progressives: Theodore Roosevelt, Senator Henry Cabot Lodge, and others. Powerful opponents—employers who saw immigration as a source of cheap labor, immigrants themselves, and the immigrants' political representatives—managed to block the restriction movement for a time. But by the beginning of World War I (which itself effectively blocked immigration temporarily), the nativist tide was clearly gaining strength.

Suffrage for Women

Perhaps the largest single reform movement of the progressive era, indeed one of the largest in American history, was the fight for woman suffrage—a movement that attracted support from both women and men.

It is sometimes difficult for today's Americans to understand why the suffrage (or right-to-vote) issue could have become the source of such enormous controversy in the early twentieth century. But at the time, suffrage seemed to many of its critics a very radical demand—in part because of the rationale some of its supporters used to advance it. Throughout the late nineteenth century, many suffrage advocates presented their views in terms of "natural rights," arguing that women deserved the same rights as men—including, first and foremost, the right to vote. Elizabeth Cady Stanton, for example, wrote in 1892 of woman as "the arbiter of her own destiny. . . . if we are to consider her as a citizen, as a member of a great nation, she must have the same rights as all other members." A woman's role as "mother, wife, sister, daughter" was "incidental" to her larger role as a part of society.

This was an argument that boldly challenged the views of many men (and even many women) who believed that society required a distinctive female "sphere" in which women would serve first and foremost as wives and mothers. And so a powerful antisuffrage movement emerged, which challenged this apparent threat to the existing social order.

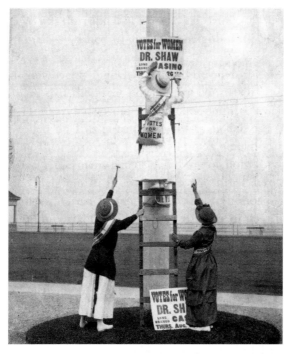

SUFFRAGISTS Suffrage activists hang posters along the boardwalk in the beachfront town of Long Branch, New Jersey. Twenty-nine states had permitted women at least some access to the ballot before ratification of the Nineteenth Amendment in 1920. New Jersey was not one of them.

The suffrage movement began to overcome this opposition and to win some substantial victories in the first years of the twentieth century. That was in part because suffragists were becoming better organized and more politically sophisticated than their opponents. Under the leadership of Anna Howard Shaw, a Boston social worker, and Carrie Chapman Catt, a journalist from Iowa, the National American Woman Suffrage Association grew from a membership of about 13,000 in 1893 to over 2 million in 1917. The involvement of such well-known and widely admired women as Jane Addams gave added respectability to the cause.

But the movement also gained strength because many of its most prominent leaders began to justify suffrage in "safer," less threatening ways. Suffrage, some supporters began to argue, would not challenge the "separate sphere" in which women resided. It would allow women to bring their special and distinct virtues more widely to bear on society's problems. It was, they claimed, precisely because women occupied a distinct sphere—because as mothers and wives and homemakers they had special experiences and special sensitivities to bring to public life—that woman suffrage could make such an important contribution to politics. In particular, many suffragists argued that enfranchising women would help the temperance movement, by giving its largest group of supporters a political voice. Some suffrage advocates claimed that once women had the vote, war would become a thing of the past, since women would—by their calming, peaceful influence—help curb the belligerence of men. That was one reason why World War I gave the final, decisive push to the movement for suffrage.

Not all suffragists narrowed their arguments. Among working-class, immigrant, and black women in particular, suffrage continued to generate substantial support precisely because it seemed so radical, because it promised to reshape the role of women and reform the social order. But among members of the middle class, the separation of the suffrage movement from more radical feminist goals, and its association with other reform causes of concern to many Americans, helped it gain widespread support.

The principal triumphs of the suffrage movement began in 1910. That year, Washington became the first state in fourteen years to extend suffrage to women. California joined it a year later, and in 1912 four other Western states did the same. In 1913, Illinois became the first state east of the Mississippi to embrace woman suffrage. And in 1917 and 1918, New York and Michigan—two of the most populous states in the Union—gave women the vote. By 1919, thirty-nine states had granted women the right to vote in at least some elections; fifteen had allowed them full participation. In

1920, finally, suffragists won ratification of the Nineteenth Amendment, which guaranteed political rights to women throughout the nation.

To some feminists, however, the victory seemed less than complete. Alice Paul, the head of the militant National Woman's party (founded in 1916), never accepted the relatively conservative "separate sphere" justification for suffrage. She argued that the Nineteenth Amendment alone would not be sufficient to protect women's rights. Women needed more: a constitutional amendment that would provide clear, legal protection for their rights and would prohibit all discrimination on the basis of sex. But Alice Paul's argument found limited favor even among many of the most important leaders of the recently triumphant suffrage crusade.

The Dream of Socialism

At no time in the history of the United States to that point, and in few times after it, did radical critiques of the capitalist system attract more support than in the period between 1900 and 1914. Although never a force to rival, or even seriously threaten, the two major parties, the Socialist party of America grew during the progressive era into a force of considerable strength. In the election of 1900, it had attracted the support of fewer than 100,000 voters; in 1912, its durable leader and perennial presidential candidate, Eugene V. Debs, received nearly 1 million ballots. Strongest in urban immigrant communities (particularly among Germans and Jews), it attracted the loyalties, too, of a substantial number of Protestant farmers in the South and Midwest. Socialists won election to over 1,000 state and local offices. And they had the support at times of such intellectuals as Lincoln Steffens, the crusader against municipal corruption, and Walter Lippmann, the brilliant young journalist and social critic. Florence Kelley, Frances Willard, and other women reformers were attracted to socialism because of its support for pacifism and labor militancy.

Virtually all socialists agreed on the need for basic structural changes in the economy, but they differed widely on the extent of those changes and the tactics necessary to achieve them. Some endorsed the radical goals of European Marxists; others envisioned a more moderate reform that would allow small-scale private enterprise to survive but would nationalize the major industries. Militant groups within the party favored militant direct action. Most conspicuous was the radical labor union the Industrial Workers of the World (IWW), whose members were known to their opponents as the "Wobblies." Under the leadership of William ("Big Bill") Haywood, the IWW advocated a single union for all workers, making it one of the few labor organizations of its time committed to organizing the unskilled, and abolition of the "wage slave" system; it rejected political action in favor of strikes—especially the general strike. The Wobblies were widely believed to have been responsible for the dynamiting of railroad lines and power stations and other acts of terror, although evidence of their actual participation in such activities is slim.

More moderate socialists advocated peaceful change through political struggle, and it was they who dominated the party. They emphasized a gradual education of the public to the need for change and patient efforts within the system to enact it. But by the end of World War I, because the party had refused to support the war effort and because of a growing wave of antiradicalism that subjected the socialists to enormous harassment and persecution, socialism was in decline as a significant political force.

Decentralization and Regulation

Many reformers agreed with the socialists that the greatest threat to the nation's economy was excessive centralization and consolidation but retained a faith in the possibilities of reform within a capitalist system. Rather than nationalize basic industries, they hoped to restore the economy to a more human scale. Few envisioned a return to a society of small, local enterprises; some consolidation, they recognized, was inevitable. They did, however, argue that the federal government should work to break up the largest combinations and enforce a balance between the need for bigness and the need for competition. This viewpoint came to be identified particularly closely with Louis D. Brandeis, a brilliant lawyer and later justice of the Supreme Court, who spoke and wrote widely (most notably in his 1913 book, *Other People's Money*) about the "curse of bigness."

Other progressives were less enthusiastic about the virtues of competition. More important to them was efficiency, which they believed economic concentration encouraged. What government should do, they argued, was not fight "bigness" but guard against abuses of power by large institutions. It should distinguish between "good trusts" and "bad trusts," encouraging the good while disciplining the bad. Since economic consolidation was destined to remain a permanent feature of American society, continuing oversight by a strong, modernized government, led by a strong president, was essential. One of the most influential spokesmen for this emerging "nationalist" position was Herbert Croly, whose 1909 book, *The Promise of American Life*, became one of the most influential progressive documents.

Opinions varied widely on how that unity should be achieved. But increasingly, attention focused on some form of coordination of the industrial economy. To some, that meant businesses themselves should learn new ways of cooperation and self-regulation; some of the most energetic "progressive" reformers of the period, in fact, were businessmen searching for ways to bring order to their own troubled world. To others, the solution was for government to play a more active role in regulating and planning economic life. One of those who came to endorse that position (although not fully until after 1910) was Theodore Roosevelt, who became for a time the most powerful symbol of the reform impulse at the national level.

D E B A T I N G   T H E   P A S T

Progressivism

NTIL THE EARLY 1950S, most historians seemed to agree on the central characteristics of early twentieth-century progressivism. It was just what the progressives themselves said it was: a movement by the "people" to curb the power of "special interests." More specifically, it was a protest by an aroused citizenry against the excessive power of urban bosses, corporate moguls, and corrupt elected officials.

In 1951, George Mowry began the process of challenging these assumptions by examining progressives in California and describing them as a small, privileged elite of business and professional figures: people who considered themselves the natural leaders of society and who were trying to recover their fading influence from the new capitalist institutions that had displaced them. Progressivism was not, in other words, a popular, democratic movement; it was the effort of a displaced elite to restore its authority. Richard Hofstadter expanded on this idea in *The Age of Reform* (1955) by describing reformers as people afflicted by "status anxiety," fading elites suffering not from economic but from psychological discontent.

The Mowry-Hofstadter argument soon encountered a range of challenges. In 1963, Gabriel Kolko published his influential study *The Triumph of Conservatism*, in which he rejected both the older "democratic" view of progressivism and the newer "status-anxiety" view. Progressive reform, he argued, was not an effort to protect the people from the corporations; it was, rather, a vehicle through which corporate leaders used the government to protect themselves from competition. Regulation, Kolko argued, was "invariably controlled by the leaders of the regulated industry and directed towards ends they deemed acceptable or desirable."

A more moderate reinterpretation came from historians embracing what would later be called the "organizational" approach to twentieth-century American history. First Samuel Hays, in *The Response to Industrial-*

ism (1957), and then Robert Wiebe, in *The Search for Order* (1967), portrayed progressivism as a broad effort by businessmen, professionals, and other middle-class people to bring order and efficiency to political and economic life. In the new industrial society, economic power was increasingly concentrated in large, national organizations, while social and political life remained centered primarily in local communities. Progressivism, Wiebe argued, was the effort of a "new middle class"—a class tied to the emerging national economy—to stabilize and enhance its position in society by bringing those two worlds together.

In the 1970s and 1980s, scholarship on progressivism moved in so many different directions that some historians came to despair of finding any consistent meaning in the term. Much of the new scholarship focused on discovering new groups among whom "progressive" ideas and efforts flourished. Historians found evidence of progressivism in the rising movement by consumers to define their interests; in the growth of reform movements among African-Americans; in the changing nature of urban political machines. Particularly influential was the effort to reveal the crucial role of women in promoting reform as a way of protecting their interests within a rapidly changing domestic sphere or of expanding their role in the public world.

Other scholars attempted to identify progressivism with broad changes in the structure and culture of politics. Richard McCormick, writing in 1981, argued that the crucial change in the "progressive era" was the decline of political parties and the corresponding rise of interest groups working for particular social and economic goals. Progressivism, he and others have suggested, was not so much a coherent "movement" as part of the broader process by which Americans adapted their political and social systems to the realities of the modern industrial age. At the same time, many historians were arguing that the role of women in progressive efforts helped determine the nature of early-twentieth-century reform, that women not only dominated many reform activities but shaped them to serve what they perceived to be the interests of their gender.

The search for the "essence" of progressivism will undoubtedly continue. But the scholarship of recent decades suggests that the real answer to the nature of progressive reform may be a recognition of its enormous diversity.

CHAPTER TWENTY-TWO

The Battle
for National Reform

Theodore Roosevelt and the Progressive Presidency
The Troubled Succession ~ Woodrow Wilson and the New Freedom
The "Big Stick": America and the World, 1901–1917

E fforts to reform the industrial economy encountered repeated frustrations at the state and local level. The great combinations were national in scope, and reformers gradually concluded that only national action could effectively control their power. Beginning early in the twentieth century, they began to look to the federal government.

But just as at the state and local levels, the national government—mired in partisan politics—seemed poorly suited to serve as an agent of reform. Progressives attempted to make it more responsive to their demands. Some reformers, for example, urged an end to the system by which state legislatures elected the members of the United States Senate; they proposed instead a direct popular election, which they believed would force the Senate to react more directly to public demands. The Seventeenth Amendment, passed by Congress in 1912 and ratified by the states in 1913, provided for that change.

But even a reformed Congress, progressives believed, could not be expected to provide the kind of coherent leadership their agenda required. Congress was too clumsy, too divided, too tied to local, parochial interests. If the federal government was truly to fulfill its mission, most reformers agreed, it would require leadership from one office capable of providing "modern," "efficient" leadership: the presidency.

THEODORE ROOSEVELT AND
THE PROGRESSIVE PRESIDENCY

To a generation of progressive reformers, Theodore Roosevelt was more than an admired public figure; he was an idol. No president before and few after attracted such attention and devotion. Yet for all his popularity among reformers, Roosevelt was in many respects decidedly conservative. He earned his extraordinary popularity less because of the extent of his reforms than because of his ebullient public personality and because he brought to his office a broad conception of its powers and invested the presidency with something of its modern status as the center of national political life.

The Accidental President

When President William McKinley suddenly died in September 1901, the victim of an assassination, Roosevelt (who had been elected vice president less than a year before) was only forty-two years old, the youngest man ever to assume the presidency. Already, however, he had achieved a reputation within the Republican party as something of a wild man. Party leaders sensed his independence and despaired of controlling him. Mark Hanna, who had warned McKinley against selecting Roosevelt as his running mate, exclaimed, "Now look, that damned cowboy is president of the United States!" But Roosevelt as president never openly rebelled against the leaders of his party. He became, rather, a champion of cautious, moderate change.

Roosevelt envisioned the federal government not as the agent of any particular interest but as a mediator of the public good, with the president at its center. This attitude found expression in Roosevelt's policies toward the great industrial combinations. He was not opposed to the principle of economic concentration, but he acknowledged that consolidation produced dangerous abuses of power. He allied himself, therefore, with those progressives who urged regulation (but not destruction) of the trusts.

At the heart of Roosevelt's policy was his desire to win for government the power to investigate the activities of corporations and publicize the results. The pressure of educated public opinion, he believed, would alone eliminate most corporate abuses. Government could legislate solutions for those that remained. Although Roosevelt was not a trust buster at heart, he engaged in a few highly publicized efforts to break up combinations. In 1902, he ordered the Justice Department to invoke the Sherman Antitrust Act against a great new railroad monopoly in the Northwest, the Northern

Securities Company. At the same time, however, he assured financial leaders that the suit did not signal a general campaign to dissolve trusts. Although he filed more than forty additional antitrust suits during the remainder of his presidency, Roosevelt made no serious effort to reverse the prevailing trend toward economic concentration.

A similar commitment to establishing the government as an impartial regulatory mechanism shaped Roosevelt's policy toward labor. In the past, federal intervention in industrial disputes had almost always meant action on behalf of employers. Roosevelt was willing to consider labor's position as well. When a bitter 1902 strike by the United Mine Workers against the anthracite coal industry dragged on long enough to endanger coal supplies for the coming winter, Roosevelt asked both the operators and the miners to accept impartial federal arbitration. When the mine owners balked, Roosevelt threatened to send federal troops to seize the mines and resume coal production. The operators finally relented. Arbitrators awarded the strikers a 10 percent wage increase and a nine-hour day but no recognition of their union—less than they had wanted but more than they would likely have won without Roosevelt's intervention. Despite such episodes, Roosevelt viewed himself as no more the champion of labor than of management. On several occasions, he ordered federal troops to intervene in strikes on behalf of employers.

Reform was not Roosevelt's main priority during his first years as president. He was principally concerned with winning the election in his own right, which meant not antagonizing the conservative Republican Old Guard. By early 1904, Roosevelt had all but neutralized his opposition within the party. He won its presidential nomination with ease. And in the general election, where he faced a pallid conservative Democrat, Alton B. Parker, he captured over 57 percent of the popular vote and lost no states outside the South. Now, relieved of immediate political concerns, he was free to display the extent (and the limits) of his commitment to reform.

The Square Deal

During the 1904 campaign, Roosevelt boasted that he had worked in the anthracite coal strike to provide everyone with a "square deal." In his second term, he tried to extend his square deal further. One of his first targets was the powerful railroad industry. The Interstate Commerce Act of 1887, establishing the Interstate Commerce Commission (ICC), had been an early effort to regulate the industry; but over the years, the courts had sharply limited its influence. The Hepburn Railroad Regulation Act of 1906 sought to restore some regulatory authority to the government by giving the ICC authority to inspect the books of railroad companies. But it was too cautious a bill to satisfy progressives.

Roosevelt also pressured Congress to enact the Pure Food and Drug Act, which, despite weaknesses in its enforcement mechanisms, restricted the sale of dangerous or ineffective medicines. When Upton Sinclair's powerful novel *The Jungle* appeared in 1906, featuring appalling descriptions of conditions in the meat-packing industry, Roosevelt insisted on passage of the Meat Inspection Act, which ultimately helped eliminate many diseases once transmitted in impure meat. Starting in 1907, he proposed even more stringent measures: an eight-hour day for workers, broader compensation for victims of industrial accidents, inheritance and income taxes, regulation of the stock market, and others. He also started openly to

MAKING SAUSAGES The shockingly unsanitary conditions by which meatpackers (such as those shown here in the Chicago stockyards) made sausages inspired Upton Sinclair's novel *The Jungle*, which in turn precipitated federal legislation, the Meat Inspection Act of 1906, establishing government inspection of meat products.

criticize conservatives in Congress and the judiciary, who were obstructing these programs. The result was not only a general stalemate in Roosevelt's reform agenda but a widening gulf between the president and the conservative wing of his party.

Roosevelt's aggressive policies on behalf of conservation contributed to that gulf. A lifelong sportsman and naturalist, he had long been concerned about the unchecked exploitation of America's natural resources and its remaining wilderness. Using executive powers, he limited private development on millions of acres of undeveloped government land by adding them to the previously modest national forest system. When conservatives in Congress restricted his authority over public lands in 1907, Roosevelt and his chief forester, Gifford Pinchot, worked furiously before the bill became law to seize all the forests and many of the water power sites still in the public domain.

Roosevelt was the first president to take an active interest in the new and struggling American conservation movement, and his policies had a lasting effect on national environmental policies. More than most public figures, he was sympathetic to the concerns of the naturalists—those within the movement committed to protecting the natural beauty of the land. But

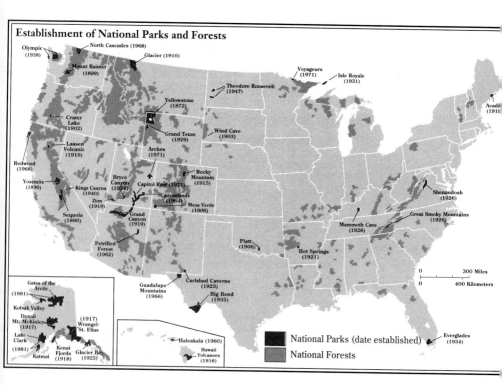

Establishment of National Parks and Forests

Olympic (1938)
North Cascades (1968)
Glacier (1910)
Mount Rainier (1899)
Voyageurs (1971)
Isle Royale (1931)
Theodore Roosevelt (1947)
Yellowstone (1872)
Acadia (1919)
Crater Lake (1902)
Grand Teton (1929)
Wind Cave (1903)
Lassen Volcanic (1916)
Arches (1971)
Redwood (1968)
Yosemite (1890)
Bryce Canyon (1924)
Capitol Reef (1971)
Rocky Mountain (1915)
Kings Canyon (1940)
Zion (1919)
Canyonlands (1964)
Mesa Verde (1906)
Shenandoah (1926)
Sequoia (1890)
Grand Canyon (1919)
Great Smoky Mountains (1926)
Petrified Forest (1962)
Platt (1906)
Mammoth Cave (1926)
Hot Springs (1921)
Gates of the Arctic (1981)
Guadalupe Mountains (1966)
Carlsbad Caverns (1923)
Big Bend (1935)
Kobuk Valley
Denali
Mt. McKinley (1917)
(1917)
Wrangel-St. Elias
Lake Clark (1981)
Kenai Fjords (1918)
Glacier Bay (1925)
Katmai
Haleakala (1960)
Hawaii Volcanoes (1916)
Everglades (1934)

300 Miles
400 Kilometers

■ National Parks (date established)
▨ National Forests

Roosevelt's policies tended to favor another faction within the conservation movement—those who believed in carefully managed development. That was in part a result of the influence of Pinchot, the first director of the National Forest Service, who supported rational and efficient human use of the wilderness.

The Old Guard may have opposed Roosevelt's efforts to extend government control over vast new lands. But they eagerly supported another important aspect of Roosevelt's natural resource policy: public reclamation and irrigation projects. In 1902, the president backed the Newlands Reclamation Act, which provided federal funds for the construction of dams, reservoirs, and canals in the West—projects to open new lands for cultivation and, years later, to provide cheap electric power. It was the beginning of many years of federal aid for irrigation and power development in the Western states.

Despite the flurry of reforms Roosevelt was able to enact, the government still had relatively little control over the industrial economy. That became clear in 1907, when a serious panic and recession began. Conservatives blamed Roosevelt's "mad" economic policies for the disaster. And while the president, naturally (and correctly), disagreed, he nevertheless acted quickly to reassure business leaders that he would not interfere with their private recovery efforts.

The great financier J. P. Morgan helped construct a pool of the assets of several important New York banks to prop up shaky financial institutions. The key to the arrangement, Morgan told the president, was the purchase by U.S. Steel of the shares of the Tennessee Coal and Iron Company, currently held by a threatened New York bank. He would, he insisted, need assurances that the purchase would not prompt antitrust action. Roosevelt tacitly agreed, and the Morgan plan proceeded. Whether or not as a result, the panic soon subsided.

Roosevelt loved being president, and many people assumed he would run for the office again in 1908 despite the longstanding tradition of presidents' serving no more than two terms. But the panic of 1907, combined with Roosevelt's growing "radicalism" during his second term, so alienated conservatives in his own party that he might have had difficulty winning the Republican nomination for another term despite his great popularity. In 1904, moreover, he had made a public promise to step down four years later. And so, after nearly eight energetic years in the White House, during which he had transformed the role of the presidency in American government, Theodore Roosevelt, fifty years old, retired from public life—briefly.

THE TROUBLED SUCCESSION

William Howard Taft, who assumed the presidency in 1909, had been Theodore Roosevelt's most trusted lieutenant and his hand-picked successor; progressive reformers believed him to be one of their own. But Taft had also been a restrained and moderate jurist, a man with a punctilious regard for legal process; conservatives expected him to abandon Roosevelt's aggressive use of presidential powers. By seeming acceptable to almost everyone, Taft won election to the White House in 1908 with almost ridiculous ease. He received his party's nomination virtually uncontested. His victory in the general election in November—over William Jennings Bryan, running forlornly for the Democrats for the third time—was a foregone conclusion. Taft entered the White House on a wave of good feeling.

Four years later, however, Taft would leave office the most decisively defeated president of the twentieth century, with his party deeply divided and the government in the hands of a Democratic administration for the first time in twenty years. Taft's failure was a result in part of his own character and style: his cautious, limited use of presidential powers; his failure to match Roosevelt's personal dynamism. (Contributing to Taft's image as a not very vigorous man was his enormous weight, which at times rose to 350 pounds.) More significant, however, was that having come into office as the darling of progressives and conservatives alike, he soon found that he could not please both groups. Gradually he found himself, without really intending it, pleasing the conservatives and alienating the progressives.

Taft and the Progressives

Taft's first problem arose in the opening months of the new administration, when he called Congress into special session to lower protective tariff rates, an old progressive demand. But the president made no effort to overcome the opposition of the congressional Old Guard, arguing that it would violate the constitutional doctrine of separation of powers if he were to intervene in legislative matters. The result was the feeble Payne-Aldrich Tariff, which reduced tariff rates scarcely at all and in some areas actually raised them. Progressives resented the president's passivity and were suspicious of his motives.

With Taft's standing among Republican progressives deteriorating and with the party growing more and more deeply divided, a sensational controversy broke out late in 1909 that helped destroy Taft's popularity with reformers for good. Many progressives had been unhappy when Taft replaced Roosevelt's secretary of the interior, James R. Garfield, an aggressive conservationist, with Richard A. Ballinger, a more conservative corporate lawyer. Suspicion of Ballinger grew when he attempted to invalidate Roosevelt's removal of nearly 1 million acres of forests and mineral reserves from the public lands available for private development.

In the midst of this mounting concern, Louis Glavis, an Interior Department investigator, charged the new secretary with having once connived to turn over valuable public coal lands in Alaska to a private syndicate for personal profit. Glavis took the evidence to Gifford Pinchot, still head of the Forest Service and a critic of Ballinger's policies. Pinchot took the charges to the president. Taft investigated them and decided they were groundless. But Pinchot was not satisfied, particularly after Taft fired Glavis for his part in the episode. He leaked the story to the press and asked Congress to investigate the scandal. The president discharged him for insubordination, and the congressional committee appointed to study the controversy, dominated by the Old Guard, exonerated Ballinger. But progressives throughout the country supported Pinchot. The controversy aroused as much public passion as any dispute of its time; and when it was over, Taft had alienated the supporters of Roosevelt completely and, it seemed, irrevocably.

The Return of Roosevelt

During most of these controversies, Theodore Roosevelt was far away: on a long hunting safari in Africa and an extended tour of Europe. To the American public, however, Roosevelt remained a formidable presence. And his return to New York in the spring of 1910 was a major public event.

Roosevelt insisted that he had no plans to return to active politics, but his resolve lasted less than a week. Politicians began flocking immediately to his home at Oyster Bay, Long Island, for conferences. Roosevelt took an active role in several New York political controversies; and within a month, he announced that he would embark on a national speaking tour before the end of the summer. Furious with Taft, he was becoming convinced that he alone was capable of reuniting the Republican party.

The real signal of Roosevelt's decision to assume leadership of Republican reformers came in a speech he gave on September 1, 1910, in Osawatomie, Kansas. In the speech, he outlined a set of principles, which he labeled the "New Nationalism," that made clear he had moved a consider-

ROOSEVELT AT OSAWATOMIE Roosevelt's famous speech at Osawatomie, Kansas, in 1910 was the most radical of his career and openly marked his break with the Taft administration and the Republican leadership.

able way from the cautious conservatism of the first years of his presidency. Influenced by Herbert Croly's writings, he argued that social justice was possible only through the vigorous efforts of a strong federal government whose executive acted as the "steward of the public welfare." Those who thought primarily of property rights and personal profit "must now give way to the advocate of human welfare, who rightly maintains that every man holds his property subject to the general right of the community to regulate its use to whatever degree the public welfare may require it." He supported graduated income and inheritance taxes, workers' compensation for industrial accidents, regulation of the labor of women and children, tariff revision, and firmer regulation of corporations.

Spreading Insurgency

The congressional elections of 1910 provided further evidence of how far the progressive revolt had spread. In primary elections, conservative Republicans suffered defeat after defeat while almost all the progressive incumbents were reelected. In the general election, the Democrats, who were now offering progressive candidates of their own, won control of the House of Representatives for the first time in sixteen years and gained strength in the Senate. Reform sentiment seemed clearly on the rise. But Roosevelt still denied any presidential ambitions and claimed that his real purpose was to pressure Taft to return to progressive policies. Two events, however, changed his mind.

The first was a 1911 antitrust decision by the Taft administration. Taft had been more active than Roosevelt in enforcing the provisions of the Sherman Antitrust Act and had launched dozens of suits against corporate combinations. On October 27, 1911, the administration announced a suit against U.S. Steel, charging, among other things, that the 1907 acquisition of the Tennessee Coal and Iron Company had been illegal. Roosevelt had approved that acquisition in the midst of the 1907 panic, and he was enraged by the implication that he had acted improperly.

But Roosevelt was reluctant at first to become a candidate for president, largely because Senator Robert La Follette had been working since 1911 to secure the presidential nomination for himself. But La Follette's candidacy stumbled in February 1912, when, exhausted and distraught over his daughter's illness, he appeared to suffer a nervous breakdown during a speech in Philadelphia. Roosevelt announced his candidacy on February 22.

TR Versus Taft

La Follette retained some diehard support. But for all practical purposes, the campaign for the Republican nomination had now become a battle between Roosevelt, the champion of the progressives, and Taft, the candidate of the conservatives. Roosevelt scored overwhelming victories in all thirteen presidential primaries and arrived at the convention convinced that he was the choice of the party rank and file. Taft, however, remained the choice of most party leaders, whose preference was decisive.

The battle for the nomination at the Chicago convention revolved around an unusually large number of contested delegates: 254 in all. Roosevelt needed fewer than half the disputed seats to clinch the nomination. But the Republican National Committee, controlled by the Old Guard, awarded all but 19 of them to Taft. At a rally the night before the convention opened, Roosevelt addressed 5,000 cheering supporters and announced that if the party refused to seat his delegates, he would continue his own candidacy outside the party. "We stand at Armageddon," he told the roaring crowd, "and we battle for the Lord." The next day, he led his supporters out of the convention, and out of the party. Taft was then quietly nominated on the first ballot.

Roosevelt summoned his supporters back to Chicago in August for another convention, this one to launch the new Progressive party and nominate himself as its presidential candidate. Roosevelt approached the battle feeling, as he put it, "fit as a bull moose" (thus giving his new party an enduring nickname). But by then, he was aware that his cause was virtually hopeless. That was partly because many of the insurgents who had supported him during the primaries refused to follow him out of the Republican party. It was also because of the man the Democrats had nominated for president.

WOODROW WILSON AND THE NEW FREEDOM

The 1912 presidential contest was not simply one between conservatives and reformers. It was also one between two brands of progressivism, that reflected two different views of America's future. And it was one that matched the two most important national leaders of the early twentieth century in unequal contest.

Woodrow Wilson

Reform sentiment had been gaining strength within the Democratic as well as the Republican party in the first years of the century. At the 1912 Democratic convention in Baltimore in June, Champ Clark, the conservative Speaker of the House, was unable to assemble the necessary two-thirds majority because of progressive opposition. Finally, on the forty-sixth ballot, Woodrow Wilson, the governor of New Jersey and the only genuinely progressive candidate in the race, emerged as the party's nominee.

Wilson had risen to political prominence by an unusual path. He had been a professor of political science at Princeton until 1902, when he was named president of the university. Elected governor of New Jersey in 1910, he demonstrated a commitment to reform that he had already displayed as a university president; and during his two years in the statehouse, he earned a national reputation for winning passage of progressive legislation.

As a presidential candidate in 1912, Wilson presented a progressive program that came to be called the "New Freedom." Wilson's New Freedom differed from Roosevelt's New Nationalism, most clearly in its approach to economic policy and the trusts. Roosevelt believed in accepting economic concentration and using government to regulate and control it. Wilson seemed to side with those who (like Brandeis) believed that bigness was both unjust and inefficient, that the proper response to monopoly was not to regulate it but to destroy it.

The 1912 presidential campaign was something of an anticlimax. William Howard Taft, resigned to defeat, delivered a few desultory, conservative speeches and then lapsed into silence. Roosevelt campaigned energetically (until a gunshot wound from a would-be assassin forced him to the sidelines during the last weeks before the election), but he failed to draw any significant numbers of Democratic progressives away from Wilson. In November, Roosevelt and Taft split the Republicans; Wilson held onto the Democrats and won. He polled only a plurality of the popular vote: 42 percent, compared with 27 percent for Roosevelt, 23 percent for Taft, and 6 percent for the socialist Eugene Debs. But in the electoral college, Wilson won 435 of the 531 votes. Roosevelt had carried only six states, Taft two, Debs none.

The Scholar as President

Wilson was a bold and forceful president. More than William Howard Taft, more even than Theodore Roosevelt, Wilson concentrated the powers of the executive branch in his own hands. He exerted firm control over his

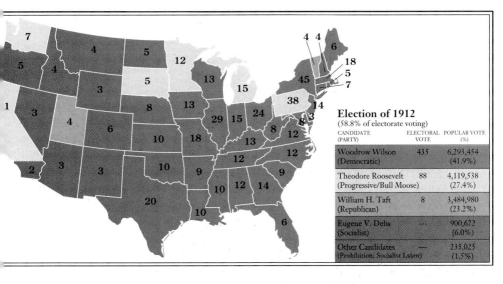

Election of 1912
(58.8% of electorate voting)

CANDIDATE (PARTY)	ELECTORAL VOTE	POPULAR VOTE (%)
Woodrow Wilson (Democratic)	435	6,293,454 (41.9%)
Theodore Roosevelt (Progressive/Bull Moose)	88	4,119,538 (27.4%)
William H. Taft (Republican)	8	3,484,980 (23.2%)
Eugene V. Debs (Socialist)	---	900,672 (6.0%)
Other Candidates (Prohibition; Socialist Labor)	---	235,025 (1.5%)

cabinet, and he delegated real authority only to those whose loyalty to him was beyond question. Perhaps the clearest indication of his style of leadership was the identity of the most powerful figure in his administration: Colonel Edward M. House, an intelligent and ambitious Texan who held no office and whose only claim to authority was his personal intimacy with the president.

In legislative matters, Wilson skillfully used his position as party leader and his appointive powers to weld together a coalition of Southern conservatives and Northern and Western progressives who would, he believed, support his program. Democratic majorities in both houses of Congress made his task easier, as did the realization of many Democrats that the party must enact a progressive program in order to maintain those majorities.

Wilson's first triumph as president was a substantial lowering of the protective tariff. The Underwood-Simmons Tariff, passed in a special session of Congress that Wilson summoned shortly after his inauguration, provided cuts substantial enough, progressives believed, to introduce real competition into American markets and thus to help break the power of trusts. It passed easily in the House; and despite Senate efforts to weaken its provisions, the bill survived more or less intact. Wilson had succeeded where Roosevelt and Taft had not. To make up for the loss of revenue under the new tariff, Congress approved a graduated income tax, which the recently adopted Sixteenth Amendment to the Constitution now permitted. This first modern income tax imposed a 1 percent tax on individuals and corporations earning over $4,000, with rates ranging up to 6 percent on incomes over $500,000.

Wilson held Congress in session through the summer to work on a major reform of the American banking system. Few argued that change was unnecessary, but there were many different opinions about how best to attack the problem. Some legislators, among them Representative Carter Glass of Virginia, wanted to decentralize control of the banking system so as to limit the power of the great Wall Street financiers without substantially increasing the power of government. Others, including William Jennings Bryan and fellow agrarians, wanted firm government control. Wilson endorsed a plan that divided power in the system. The government would have substantial control at the national level; the bankers would retain control at the local level. The Federal Reserve Act passed both houses of Congress and was signed by the president on December 23, 1913. It was the most important piece of domestic legislation of Wilson's administration.

The Federal Reserve Act created twelve regional banks, each to be owned and controlled by the individual banks of its district. The regional Federal Reserve banks would hold a certain percentage of the assets of their member banks in reserve; they would use those reserves to support loans to private banks at an interest (or "discount") rate that the Federal Reserve system would set; they would issue a new type of paper currency—Federal Reserve notes—which would become the nation's basic medium of trade and would be backed by the government. Most important, perhaps, they would serve as central institutions able to shift funds quickly to troubled areas—to meet increased demands for credit or to protect imperiled banks. Supervising and regulating the entire system was a national Federal Reserve Board, whose members were appointed by the president. All "national" banks were required to join the system; smaller banks were encouraged to do the same. Nearly half the nation's banking resources were represented in the system within a year, and 80 percent by the late 1920s.

The cornerstone of Wilson's campaign for the presidency had been his promise to attack economic concentration, most notably to destroy monopolistic trusts. By the beginning of his second year in office, however, his approach to the trusts appeared to have changed. He was moving away from his earlier insistence that government dismantle the combinations and toward a commitment to regulating them. On this issue, at least, the New Freedom was beginning to resemble the New Nationalism.

In 1914, he proposed two measures to deal with the problem of monopoly. There was a proposal to create a federal agency through which the government would help business police itself—in other words, a regulatory commission of the type Roosevelt had advocated in 1912. There were, in addition, proposals to strengthen the government's power to prosecute and dismantle the trusts—a decentralizing approach more characteristic of Wilson's campaign. The two measures took shape, ultimately, as the Federal Trade Commission Act and the Clayton Antitrust Act.

The Federal Trade Commission Act created a regulatory agency of the same name that would help businesses determine in advance whether their actions would be acceptable to the government. The agency would also have authority to launch prosecutions against "unfair trade practices," which the law did not define, and it would have wide power to investigate corporate behavior. The act, in short, increased the government's regulatory authority significantly. Wilson signed it happily. But he seemed to lose interest in the Clayton Antitrust Bill and did little to protect it from conservative assaults, which greatly weakened it. The vigorous legal pursuit of monopoly that Wilson had promised in 1912 never materialized. The future, he had apparently decided, lay with government supervision.

Retreat and Advance

By the fall of 1914, Wilson believed that the program of the New Freedom was essentially complete and that agitation for reform would now subside. He refused to support the movement for national woman suffrage. Deferring to Southern Democrats, and reflecting his own Southern background, he condoned the reimposition of segregation in the agencies of the federal government (in contrast to Theodore Roosevelt, who had ordered the elimination of many such barriers). When congressional progressives attempted to enlist his support for new reform legislation, he dismissed their proposals as unconstitutional or unnecessary.

The congressional elections of 1914, however, shattered the president's complacency. Democrats suffered major losses in the House of Representatives, and voters who in 1912 had supported the Progressive party began returning to the Republicans. Wilson would not be able to rely on a divided opposition when he ran for reelection in 1916. By the end of 1915, Wilson had begun to support a second flurry of reforms. In January 1916, he appointed Louis Brandeis to the Supreme Court, making him not only the first Jew but the most advanced progressive to serve there. Later, he supported a measure to make it easier for farmers to receive credit and one creating a system of workers' compensation for federal employees.

Much of this renewed effort at reform suggested that Wilson had moved even closer to the New Nationalism. He was sponsoring measures that expanded the role of the national government in important ways, giving it new instruments by which it could regulate the economy and help shape the nation's economic and social structure. In 1916, for example, Wilson supported the Keating-Owen Act, the first federal law regulating child labor. The measure prohibited the shipment of goods produced by underage children across state lines, thus giving an expanded importance to the constitutional clause assigning Congress the task of regulating interstate commerce. (It would be some years before the Supreme Court would uphold this interpretation of the clause; the Court invalidated the Keating-Owen Act in 1918.) The president similarly supported measures that used federal taxing authority as a vehicle for legislating social change. After the Court struck down Keating-Owen, a new law attempted to achieve the same goal by imposing a heavy tax on the products of child labor. (The Court later struck it down too.) And the Smith-Lever Act of 1914 demonstrated another way in which the federal government could influence local behavior; it used federal spending to change public behavior by offering matching federal grants to states that agreed to support agricultural extension education.

THE "BIG STICK": AMERICA AND THE WORLD, 1901–1917

American foreign policy during the progressive years reflected many of the same impulses that were motivating domestic reform. But more than that, it reflected the nation's new sense of itself as a world power with far-flung economic and political interests.

Roosevelt and "Civilization"

Theodore Roosevelt was well suited, both by temperament and by ideology, for an activist foreign policy. He believed in the value and importance of using American power in the world (a conviction he once described by citing the proverb, "Speak softly, but carry a big stick"). And he believed that an important distinction existed between the "civilized" and "uncivilized" nations of the world. "Civilized" nations, as he defined them, were predominantly white and Anglo-Saxon or Teutonic; "uncivilized" nations were generally non-white, Latin, or Slavic. But racism was only partly the basis of the distinction. At least as important was economic development. He believed, therefore, that Japan, a rapidly industrializing society, had earned admission to the ranks of the civilized.

Civilized nations were, by Roosevelt's definition, producers of industrial goods; uncivilized nations were suppliers of raw materials and markets. There was, he believed, an economic relationship between the two parts that was vital to both of them. A civilized society, therefore, had the right and duty to intervene in the affairs of a "backward" nation to preserve order and stability—for the sake of both nations. Accordingly, Roosevelt became an early champion of the development of American sea power. By 1906, Roosevelt's support had enabled the American navy to attain a size and strength surpassed only by that of Great Britain (although Germany was fast gaining ground).

Protecting the Open Door in Asia

Roosevelt considered the "Open Door" vital for maintaining American trade in the Pacific and for preventing any single nation from establishing dominance there. He looked with alarm, therefore, at the military rivalries involving Japan, Russia, Germany, and France in Asia.

In 1904 the Japanese staged a surprise attack on the Russian fleet at Port Arthur in southern Manchuria, a province of China that both Russia and Japan hoped to control. Roosevelt, hoping to prevent either nation from becoming dominant there, agreed to a Japanese request to mediate an end to the conflict. Russia, faring badly in the war, had no choice but to agree. At a peace conference in Portsmouth, New Hampshire, in 1905, Roosevelt extracted from the embattled Russians a recognition of Japan's territorial gains and from the Japanese an agreement to cease the fighting and expand no further. At the same time, he negotiated a secret agreement with the Japanese to ensure that the United States could continue to trade freely in the region. Roosevelt won the Nobel Peace Prize in 1906 for his work in ending the Russo-Japanese War. But in the years that followed, relations between the United States and Japan steadily deteriorated. Having destroyed the Russian fleet at Port Arthur, Japan now emerged as the preeminent naval power in the Pacific and soon began to exclude American trade from many of the territories it controlled.

It did not help matters that in 1906 the school board of San Francisco voted to segregate the city's Asian schoolchildren in separate schools; or that a year later, the California legislature attempted to pass legislation limiting the immigration of Japanese laborers into the state. Anti-Asian riots in California and inflammatory stories in the Hearst papers about the "Yellow Peril" further fanned resentment in Japan. The president persuaded the San Francisco school board to rescind its edict in return for a Japanese agreement to stop the flow of agricultural immigrants into California. Then, lest the Japanese government construe his actions as a sign of weakness, Roosevelt sent sixteen battleships of the new American navy (known as the "Great White Fleet") on an unprecedented voyage around the world that included a call on Japan—to remind the Japanese of the potential might of the United States.

The Iron-Fisted Neighbor

Roosevelt took a particular interest in events in what he (and most other Americans) considered the nation's special sphere of interest: Latin America. Unwilling to share trading rights, let alone military control, with any other nation, Roosevelt embarked on a series of ventures in the Caribbean and South America that established a pattern of American intervention in the region that would long survive his presidency.

Crucial to Roosevelt's thinking was an incident early in his administration. When the government of Venezuela began in 1902 to renege on debts to European bankers, naval forces of Britain, Italy, and Germany blockaded the Venezuelan coast. Then German ships began to bombard a Venezuelan port amid rumors that Germany planned to establish a permanent base in the region. Roosevelt used the threat of American naval power to pressure the German navy to withdraw.

The incident helped persuade Roosevelt that European intrusions into Latin America could result not only from aggression but from instability or irresponsibility (such as defaulting on debts) within the Latin American nations themselves. As a result, in 1904 he added a "Roosevelt Corollary" to the Monroe Doctrine. The United States, he claimed, had the right not only to oppose European intervention in the Western Hemisphere but to intervene itself in the domestic affairs of its neighbors if those neighbors proved unable to maintain order on their own.

The immediate motivation for the Roosevelt Corollary, and the first

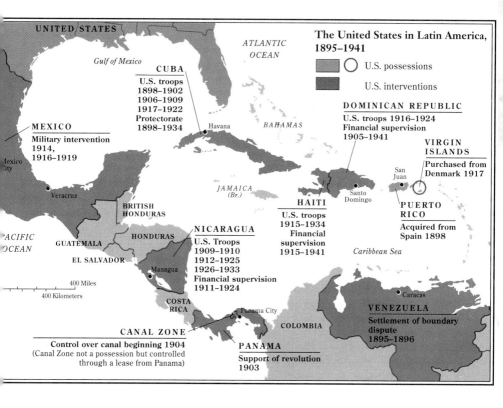

The United States in Latin America, 1895–1941

○ U.S. possessions

U.S. interventions

UNITED STATES

ATLANTIC OCEAN

Gulf of Mexico

CUBA
U.S. troops
1898–1902
1906–1909
1917–1922
Protectorate
1898–1934

Havana

BAHAMAS

DOMINICAN REPUBLIC
U.S. troops 1916–1924
Financial supervision
1905–1941

VIRGIN ISLANDS
Purchased from Denmark 1917

MEXICO
Military intervention
1914,
1916–1919

Mexico City

Veracruz

JAMAICA (Br.)

HAITI
U.S. troops
1915–1934
Financial
supervision
1915–1941

San Juan

Santo Domingo

PUERTO RICO
Acquired from Spain 1898

BRITISH HONDURAS

PACIFIC OCEAN

GUATEMALA

HONDURAS

NICARAGUA
U.S. Troops
1909–1910
1912–1925
1926–1933
Financial supervision
1911–1924

Caribbean Sea

EL SALVADOR

Managua

400 Miles
400 Kilometers

COSTA RICA

Panama City

Caracas

VENEZUELA
Settlement of boundary
dispute
1895–1896

CANAL ZONE
Control over canal beginning 1904
(Canal Zone not a possession but controlled
through a lease from Panama)

COLOMBIA

PANAMA
Support of revolution
1903

opportunity for using it, was a crisis in the Dominican Republic. A revolution had toppled its corrupt and bankrupt government in 1903, but the new regime proved no better able than the old to make good on the country's $22 million in debts to European nations. Using the Roosevelt Corollary rationale, Roosevelt established, in effect, an American receivership, assuming control of Dominican customs and distributing 45 percent of the revenues to the Dominicans and the rest to foreign creditors. This arrangement lasted, in one form or another, for more than three decades.

In 1902, the United States had granted political independence to Cuba, but only after the new government had agreed to the so-called Platt Amendment to its constitution, giving the United States the right to prevent any foreign power from intruding into the new nation. In 1906, when domestic uprisings seemed to threaten the internal stability of the island, Roosevelt reasoned that America must intervene to "protect" Cuba from disorder. American troops landed in Cuba, quelled the fighting, and remained there for three years.

The Panama Canal

The most celebrated accomplishment of Roosevelt's presidency was the construction of the Panama Canal. Linking the Atlantic and the Pacific by creating a channel through Central America had been an unfulfilled dream of many nations since the mid-nineteenth century. Roosevelt was determined to achieve it.

The first step was the 1901 Hay-Pauncefote Treaty between America and Britain, canceling an 1850 pact in which the two nations had agreed to construct any such canal together. The United States was now free to act alone. The next step was to choose a site for the canal. At first, Roosevelt and many others favored a route across Nicaragua, which would permit a sea-level canal requiring no locks. But they soon turned instead to the narrow Isthmus of Panama in Colombia, the site of an earlier, failed effort by a French company to construct a channel. Although the Panama route was not at sea level (and would thus require locks), it was shorter than the one in Nicaragua. And construction was already about 40 percent complete. When the French company lowered the price for its holdings from $109 million to $40 million, the United States chose Panama.

BUILDING THE PANAMA CANAL Construction proceeds at the Gatun Middle Locks, November 1910. Whatever its political implications, the Panama Canal was one of the great engineering feats of the early twentieth century.

Roosevelt dispatched John Hay, his secretary of state, to negotiate an agreement with Colombian diplomats in Washington that would allow construction to begin without delay. Under heavy American pressure, the Colombian chargé d'affaires, Tomas Herrán, unwisely signed an agreement giving the United States perpetual rights to a six-mile-wide "canal zone" across Colombia; in return, the United States would pay Colombia $10 million and an annual rental of $250,000. The treaty produced outrage in the Colombian senate, which refused to ratify it. Colombia then sent a new representative to Washington with instructions to demand at least $20 million from the Americans plus a share of the payment to the French.

Roosevelt was furious and began to look for ways to circumvent the Colombian government. Philippe Bunau-Varilla, chief engineer of the French canal project, was a ready ally. In November 1903, he helped organize and finance a revolution in Panama. There had been many previous revolts, all of them failures. But this one had the support of the United States. Roosevelt landed troops from the U.S.S. *Nashville* in Panama to "maintain order." Their presence prevented Colombian forces from suppressing the rebellion, and three days later Roosevelt recognized Panama as an independent nation. The new Panamanian government quickly agreed to the terms the Colombian senate had rejected. Work on the canal proceeded rapidly, and it opened in 1914.

Taft and "Dollar Diplomacy"

Like his predecessor, William Howard Taft worked to advance the nation's economic interests overseas. But he showed little interest in Roosevelt's larger vision of world stability. Taft's secretary of state, the corporate attorney Philander C. Knox, worked aggressively to extend American investments into less developed regions. Critics called his policies "Dollar Diplomacy."

The Taft-Knox foreign policy faced its severest test, and encountered its greatest failure, in the Far East. Ignoring Roosevelt's tacit 1905 agreement with Japan to limit American involvement in Manchuria, the new administration responded to pressure from American bankers and moved aggressively to increase America's economic influence in the region. In particular, Knox worked to include the United States in a consortium of Western powers formed to build railroads in China; and when the Europeans agreed, he went further and tried to exclude the Japanese from any role in Manchuria's railroads. When Japan responded by forming a loose alliance with Russia, the entire railroad project quickly collapsed.

In the Caribbean, the new administration continued and even expanded upon Roosevelt's policies of limiting European and expanding American influence in the region. That meant, Taft and Knox believed, not only preventing disorder but establishing a significant American economic presence there—replacing the investments of European nations with investments from the United States. But Dollar Diplomacy also had a more violent side. When a revolution broke out in Nicaragua in 1909, the administration quickly sided with the insurgents (who had been inspired to revolt by an American mining company) and sent American troops into the country to seize the customs houses. As soon as peace was restored, Knox encouraged American bankers to offer substantial loans to the new government, thus increasing Washington's financial leverage over the country. When the new pro-American government faced an insurrection less than two years later, Taft again landed American troops in Nicaragua, this time to protect the existing regime. The troops remained there for more than a decade.

Diplomacy and Morality

Woodrow Wilson entered the presidency with relatively little interest or experience in international affairs. Yet he faced international challenges of a scope and gravity unmatched by those of any president before him. Although the greatest test of Wilsonian diplomacy did not occur until after World War I, many of the qualities that he would bring to that ordeal were evident in his foreign policy from his first moments in office, and particularly in his dealings with Latin America.

Having already seized control of the finances of the Dominican Republic in 1905, the United States established a military government there in 1916 when the Dominicans refused to accept a treaty that would have made the country a virtual American protectorate. The military occupation lasted eight years. In Haiti, which shares the island of Hispaniola with the Dominican Republic, Wilson landed the marines in 1915 to quell a revolution in the course of which a mob had murdered an unpopular president. American military forces remained in the country until 1934, and American officers drafted the new Haitian constitution adopted in 1918. When Wilson began to fear that the Danish West Indies might be about to fall into the hands of Germany, he bought the colony from Denmark and renamed it the Virgin Islands. Concerned about the possibility of European influence in Nicaragua, he signed a treaty with that country's government ensuring that no other nation would build a canal there and winning for the United States the right to intervene in Nicaragua's internal affairs to protect American interests.

Wilson's view of America's role in the Western Hemisphere became clearest in his dealings with Mexico. For many years, under the friendly auspices of the corrupt dictator Porfirio Díaz, American businessmen had been establishing an enormous economic presence in Mexico. In 1910, however, Díaz had been overthrown by the popular leader Francisco Madero, who promised democratic reform but who also seemed hostile to American businesses in Mexico. With American approval, Madero was himself deposed early in 1913 by a reactionary general, Victoriano Huerta. The Taft administration, in its last weeks in office, prepared to recognize the new Huerta regime and welcome back a receptive environment for American investments in Mexico. Before it could do so, however, the new government murdered Madero, and Woodrow Wilson took office in Washington. The new president instantly announced that he would never recognize Huerta's "government of butchers."

The problem dragged on for years. At first, Wilson hoped that simply by refusing to recognize Huerta he could help topple the regime and bring to power the opposing Constitutionalists, led by Venustiano Carranza. But when Huerta, with the support of American business interests, established a full military dictatorship in October 1913, the president became more assertive. He pressured the British to stop supporting Huerta. Then he offered to send American troops to assist Carranza. Carranza, aware that such an open alliance with the United States would undermine his popular support in Mexico, declined the offer; but he did secure the right to buy arms in the United States.

In April 1914, a minor naval incident provided the president with an excuse for more open intervention. An officer in Huerta's army briefly arrested several American sailors from the U.S.S. *Dolphin* who had gone ashore in Tampico. The men were immediately released, but the American admiral—unsatisfied with the apology he received—demanded that the Huerta forces fire a twenty-one-gun salute to the American flag as a public display of penance. The Mexicans refused. Wilson used the trivial incident as a pretext for seizing the Mexican port of Veracruz.

Wilson had envisioned a bloodless action, but in a clash with Mexican troops in Veracruz, the Americans killed 126 of the defenders and suffered 19 casualties of their own. Now at the brink of war, Wilson began to look for a way out. His show of force, however, had helped strengthen the position of the Carranza faction, which captured Mexico City in August and forced Huerta to flee the country. At last, it seemed, the crisis might be over.

But Wilson was not yet satisfied. He reacted angrily when Carranza refused to accept American guidelines for the creation of a new government, and he briefly considered throwing his support to still another aspirant to leadership: Carranza's erstwhile lieutenant Pancho Villa, who was now leading a rebel army of his own. When Villa's military position deteriorated, however, Wilson abandoned him and finally, in October 1915, granted preliminary recognition to the Carranza government. But by now he had created yet another crisis. Villa, angry at what he considered an American betrayal, retaliated in January 1916 by taking sixteen American mining engineers from a train in northern Mexico and shooting them. Two months later, he led his soldiers (or "bandits," as the United States preferred to call them) across the border into Columbus, New Mexico, where they killed seventeen more Americans. His goal, apparently, was to destabilize relations

PANCHO VILLA AND HIS SOLDIERS In 1913, when this photograph was taken, Pancho Villa (second from left) was still on good terms with the government of Woodrow Wilson, which viewed him as a fighter for democracy in Mexico. Three years later, Wilson declared Villa a "bandit" and sent American troops into Mexico in a futile effort to capture him.

between Wilson and Carranza and provoke a war between them, which might provide him with an opportunity to improve his own declining fortunes.

With the permission of the Carranza government, Wilson ordered General John J. Pershing to lead an American expeditionary force across the Mexican border in pursuit of Villa. The American troops never found Villa, but they did engage in two ugly skirmishes with Carranza's army, in which forty Mexicans and twelve Americans died. Again, the United States and Mexico stood at the brink of war. But at the last minute, Wilson drew back. He quietly withdrew American troops from Mexico; and in March 1917, he at last granted formal recognition to the Carranza regime. By now, however, Wilson's attention was turning elsewhere—to the far greater international crisis engulfing the European continent and ultimately much of the world.

CHAPTER TWENTY-THREE

America and the Great War

The Road to War ~ *"War Without Stint"*
The Search for a New World Order ~ *A Society in Turmoil*

T HE GREAT WAR, as it was known to a generation unaware that another, greater war would soon follow, began quietly in August 1914 when Austria-Hungary invaded the tiny Balkan nation of Serbia. Within weeks, however, it had grown into a widespread conflagration, engaging the armies of most of the major nations of Europe and shattering forever the delicate balance of power that had maintained a general peace on the Continent since the early nineteenth century. Americans looked on with horror as the war became the most savage in history, and as it dragged on, murderously and inconclusively, for two and a half years. But Americans also believed at first that the conflict had little to do with them. They were wrong. After nearly three years of attempting to affect the outcome of the conflict without becoming embroiled in it, the United States formally entered the war in April 1917.

THE ROAD TO WAR

The causes of the war in Europe have been the subject of continued debate for nearly eighty years. What is clear is that the European nations had by 1914 created an unusually precarious international system that careened into war very quickly on the basis of what most historians agree was a minor series of provocations.

The Collapse of the European Peace

The major powers of Europe were organized by 1914 in two great, competing alliances. The "Triple Entente" linked Britain, France, and Russia. The "Triple Alliance" united Germany, the Austro-Hungarian Empire, and Italy. The chief rivalry, however, was not between the two alliances but between the great powers that dominated them: Great Britain and Germany—the former long established as the world's most powerful colonial and commercial nation, the latter ambitious to expand its own empire and become at least Britian's equal.

The Anglo-German rivalry may have been the most important underlying source of the tensions that led to World War I, but it was not the immediate cause of its outbreak. The conflict emerged most directly out of a controversy involving nationalist movements within the Austro-Hungarian Empire. On June 28, 1914, the Archduke Franz Ferdinand, heir to the throne of the tottering empire, was assassinated while paying a state visit to Sarajevo. Sarajevo was the capital of Bosnia, a province of Austria-Hungary that Slavic nationalists wished to annex to neighboring Serbia; the archduke's assassin was a Serbian nationalist.

This local controversy quickly escalated through the workings of the system of alliances that the great powers had constructed. Germany supported Austria-Hungary's decision to launch a punitive assault on Serbia. The Serbians called on Russia to help with their defense. The Russians began mobilizing their army on July 30. Things quickly careened out of control. By August 3, Germany had declared war on both Russia and France and had invaded Belgium in preparation for a thrust across the French border. On August 4, Great Britain—ostensibly to honor its alliance with France, but more importantly to blunt the advance of its principal rival—declared war on Germany. Russia and the Austro-Hungarian Empire formally began hostilities on August 6. Italy, the Ottoman Empire (Turkey) and other, smaller nations all joined the fighting later in 1914 or 1915. By the end of the year, virtually the entire European continent (and part of Asia) was embroiled in a major war.

Wilson's Neutrality

Wilson called on his fellow citizens in 1914 to remain "impartial in thought as well as deed." But that was impossible, for several reasons. For one thing, many Americans were not, in fact, genuinely impartial. Some sympathized with the German cause (German-Americans, because of affection for Germany; Irish-Americans, because of hatred of Britain). Many more (including Wilson himself) sympathized with Britain. Lurid reports of German atrocities in Belgium and France, skillfully exaggerated by British propagandists, strengthened the hostility of many Americans toward Germany.

Economic realities also made it impossible for the United States to deal with the belligerents on equal terms. The British had imposed a naval blockade on Germany to prevent munitions and supplies from reaching the enemy. As a neutral, the United States had the right, in theory, to trade with Germany. A truly neutral response to the blockade would be either to defy it or to stop trading with Britain as well. But while the United States could survive an interruption of its relatively modest trade with the Central Powers (Germany, the Austro-Hungarian Empire, and the Ottoman Empire), it could not easily weather an embargo on its much more extensive trade with the Allies (Britain, France, Italy, and Russia), particularly when war orders from Britain and France soared after 1914, helping produce one of the greatest economic booms in the nation's history. So America tacitly ignored the blockade of Germany and continued trading with Britain. By 1915, the United States had gradually transformed itself from a neutral power into the arsenal of the Allies.

The Germans, in the meantime, were resorting to a new and, in American eyes, barbaric tactic: submarine warfare. Unable to challenge British domination on the ocean's surface, Germany began early in 1915 to use the newly improved submarine to try to stem the flow of supplies to England. Enemy vessels, the Germans announced, would be sunk on sight. Months later, on May 7, 1915, a German submarine sank the British passenger liner *Lusitania* without warning, causing the deaths of 1,198 people, 128 of them Americans. The ship was, it later became clear, carrying not only passengers but munitions; but most Americans considered the attack an unprovoked act.

Wilson angrily demanded that Germany promise not to repeat such outrages and that the Central Powers affirm their commitment to neutral rights (among which, he implausibly insisted, was the right of American citizens to travel on the nonmilitary vessels of belligerents). The Germans finally agreed to Wilson's demands, but tensions between the nations continued to grow. Early in 1916, in response to an announcement that the Allies were now arming merchant ships to sink submarines, Germany proclaimed that it would fire on such vessels without warning. A few weeks later, it attacked the unarmed French steamer *Sussex*, injuring several American passengers. Again, Wilson demanded that Germany abandon its "unlawful" tactics; again, the German government relented.

Preparedness Versus Pacifism

Despite the president's increasing bellicosity in 1916, he was still far from ready to commit the United States to war. One obstacle was American domestic politics. Facing a difficult battle for reelection, Wilson could not ignore the powerful factions that continued to oppose intervention.

The question of whether America should make military and economic preparations for war provided a preliminary issue over which pacifists and interventionists could debate. Wilson at first sided with the antipreparedness forces, denouncing the idea of an American military build-up as needless and provocative. As tensions between the United States and Germany grew, however, he changed his mind. In the fall of 1915, he endorsed an ambitious proposal by American military leaders for a large and rapid increase in the nation's armed forces. By midsummer 1916, armament for a possible conflict was well under way.

Still, the peace faction wielded considerable political strength, as became clear at the Democratic Convention in the summer of 1916. The convention became almost hysterically enthusiastic when the keynote speaker, enumerating Wilson's accomplishments, punctuated his list of the president's diplomatic achievements with the chant, "What did we do? What did we do? . . . We didn't go to war! We didn't go to war!" That speech helped produce one of the most prominent slogans of Wilson's reelection campaign: "He kept us out of war." During the campaign, Wilson did nothing to discourage those who argued that the Republican candidate, the progressive New York governor Charles Evans Hughes, was more likely than he to lead the nation into war. Wilson ultimately won reelection by one of the smallest margins for an incumbent in American history: fewer than 600,000 popular votes and only 23 electoral votes. The Democrats retained a precarious control over Congress.

A War for Democracy

The election was behind him, and tensions between the United States and Germany were unabated. But Wilson still required a justification for American intervention that would unite public opinion and satisfy his own sense of morality. In the end, he created that rationale himself. The United States, Wilson insisted, had no material aims in the conflict. The nation was, rather, committed to using the war as a vehicle for constructing a new world order, one based on the same progressive ideals that had motivated a generation of reform efforts in America. In a speech before a joint session of Congress in January 1917, he presented a plan for a postwar order in which the United States would help maintain peace through a permanent league of nations—a peace that would ensure self-determination for all nations, a "peace without victory." These were, Wilson believed, goals worth fighting for if there was sufficient provocation. That provocation came quickly.

In January, after months of bloody but inconclusive warfare in the trenches of France, the military leaders of Germany decided on one last dramatic gamble to achieve victory. They would launch a series of major assaults on the enemy's lines in France. At the same time, they would begin unrestricted submarine warfare (against American as well as Allied ships) to cut Britain off from vital supplies. Then, on February 25, the British gave Wilson an intercepted telegram from the German foreign minister, Arthur Zimmermann, to the government of Mexico, which was still awash in anti-American sentiment in the wake of Wilson's interventions there. It proposed that in the event of war between Germany and the United States, the Mexicans should join with Germany against the Americans. In return, they would regain their "lost provinces" in the north (Texas and much of the rest of the American Southwest) when the war was over. Widely publicized by British propagandists and in the American press, the Zimmermann telegram inflamed public opinion and helped build up popular sentiment for war. Wilson drew additional comfort from another event, in March 1917. A revolution in Russia toppled the reactionary czarist regime and replaced it with a new, republican government. The United States would now be spared the embarrassment of allying itself with a despotic monarchy. The war for a progressive world order could proceed untainted.

On the rainy evening of April 2, two weeks after German submarines had torpedoed three American ships, Wilson appeared before a joint session of Congress and asked for a declaration of war. Even then, opposition remained. For four days, pacifists in Congress carried on their futile struggle. When the declaration of war finally passed on April 6, fifty representatives and six senators had voted against it.

"WAR WITHOUT STINT"

Armies on both sides in Europe were decimated and exhausted by the time of Woodrow Wilson's declaration of war. The German offensives of early 1917 had failed to produce an end to the struggle, and French and British counteroffensives had accomplished little beyond adding to the appalling number of casualties. The Allies looked desperately to the United States for help. Wilson, who had called on the nation to wage war "without stint or limit," was eager to oblige.

The Military Struggle

American intervention had its most immediate effect on the conflict at sea. By the spring of 1917, Great Britain was suffering such vast losses from attacks by German submarines—one of every four ships setting sail from British ports never returned—that its ability to continue receiving vital supplies from across the Atlantic was in question. Within weeks of joining the war, the United States had begun to alter the balance. A fleet of American destroyers aided the British navy in its assault on the U-boats. Other American warships escorted merchant vessels across the Atlantic. Americans also helped plant antisubmarine mines in the North Sea. The results were dramatic. Sinkings of Allied ships had totaled nearly 900,000 tons in the month of April 1917; by December, the figure had dropped to 350,000; by October 1918, it had declined to 112,000.

Many Americans had hoped that providing naval assistance alone would be enough to turn the tide in the war, but it quickly became clear that a major commitment of American ground forces would be necessary as well to shore up the tottering Allies. Britain and France had few remaining reserves. By early 1918, Russia had withdrawn from the war altogether. After the Bolshevik Revolution in November 1917, the new communist government, led by V. I. Lenin, negotiated a hasty and costly peace with the Central Powers, thus freeing German troops to fight on the western front.

But the United States did not have a large enough standing army to provide the necessary ground forces in 1917. Some (including Theodore Roosevelt, who hoped to raise and lead a regiment himself, much as he had done in the Spanish-American War) urged a voluntary recruitment process. The president, however, decided that only a national draft could provide the needed men; and despite protests, he won passage of the Selective Service

America in World War I:
The Western Front, 1918

Act in mid-May. The draft brought nearly 3 million men into the army; another 2 million joined various branches of the armed services voluntarily.

The engagement of these forces in combat was intense but brief. Not until the spring of 1918 were significant numbers of American troops available for battle. Eight months later, the war was over. Under the command of General John J. Pershing, the American troops joined the existing Allied forces in turning back a series of new German assaults. In early June, they assisted the French in repelling a bitter German offensive at Château-Thierry, near Paris. Six weeks later, the American Expeditionary Force (AEF) helped turn away another assault, at Rheims, farther south. By July 18, the German advance had been halted, and the Allies were beginning a successful offensive of their own. On September 26, an American fighting force of over 1 million soldiers advanced against the Germans in the Argonne Forest as part of a 200-mile attack that lasted nearly seven weeks. By the end of October, the force had helped push the Germans back toward their own border and had cut the enemy's major supply lines to the front.

Faced with an invasion of their own country, German military leaders now began to seek an armistice—an immediate cease-fire that would, they hoped, serve as a prelude to negotiations among the belligerents. Pershing wanted to drive on into Germany itself; but other Allied leaders, after first insisting on terms that made the agreement (in their eyes at least) little

LONGPONT, FRANCE, 1918 American soldiers lead German prisoners-of-war through the streets of a French town shortly before the end of World War I. The devastation was typical of many areas of France where heavy fighting occurred.

different from a surrender, accepted the German proposal. On November 11, 1918, the Great War shuddered to a close.

Organizing the Economy for War

By the time the war ended, the federal government had appropriated $32 billion for expenses directly related to the conflict. This was a staggering sum by the standards of the time. The entire federal budget had seldom exceeded $1 billion before 1915, and the nation's entire gross national product had been only $35 billion as recently as 1910. To raise the money, the government relied on two devices. First, it launched a major drive to solicit loans from the American people by selling "Liberty Bonds" to the public. By 1920, the sale of bonds, accompanied by elaborate patriotic appeals, had produced $23 billion. At the same time, new taxes were bringing in an additional sum of nearly $10 billion—some from levies on the "excess profits" of corporations, much from new, steeply graduated income and inheritance taxes that ultimately rose as high as 70 percent in some brackets.

An even greater challenge was organizing the economy to meet war needs. The administration tried two very different approaches. In 1916, Wilson established a Council of National Defense, composed of members of his cabinet, and a Civilian Advisory Commission, which set up local defense councils in every state and locality. Economic mobilization, according to this first plan, was to rest on a large-scale dispersal of power to local communities.

But this early administrative structure soon proved completely unworkable. Some members of the Council of National Defense, many of them disciples of the engineering gospel of Thorstein Veblen and the "scientific management" principles of Frederick Winslow Taylor, urged a more centralized approach. Instead of dividing the economy geographically, they proposed dividing it functionally by organizing a series of planning bodies, each to supervise a specific sector of the economy. Thus one agency would control transportation, another agriculture, another manufacturing. The administrative structure that slowly emerged from such proposals was dominated by a series of "war boards," one to oversee the railroads (led by Secretary of the Treasury William McAdoo), one to supervise fuel supplies (largely coal), another to handle food (a board that helped elevate to prominence the brilliant young engineer and business executive Herbert Hoover). The boards were not without weaknesses, but they generally succeeded in meeting essential war needs without paralyzing the domestic economy.

At the center of the effort to rationalize the economy was the War Industries Board (WIB), an agency created in July 1917 to coordinate government purchases of military supplies. Casually organized at first, it stumbled badly until March 1918, when Wilson restructured it and placed it under the control of the Wall Street financier Bernard Baruch. From then on, the board wielded powers greater (in theory at least) than any government agency had ever possessed. Baruch decided which factories would convert to the production of which war materials and set prices for the goods they produced. When materials were scarce, Baruch decided to whom they should go. When corporations were competing for government contracts, he chose among them. He was, it seemed, providing the centralized regulation of the economy that some progressives had long urged.

In reality, the vaunted efficiency of the WIB was something of a myth. The agency was, in fact, plagued by mismanagement and inefficiency and was less responsible for the nation's ability to meet its war needs than the

WOMEN WAR WORKERS With much of the male work force fighting overseas, women moved into occupations that in other times would have been considered "unsuitable" for them. One such occupation, pictured here, was delivering huge blocks of ice daily to households to be used (in this age before electric refrigeration) in wooden iceboxes.

sheer extent of American resources and productive capacities. Nor was the WIB in any real sense an example of state control of the economy. Baruch viewed himself, openly and explicitly, as a partner of business; and within the WIB, businessmen themselves—the so-called "dollar-a-year men," who took paid leave from their corporate jobs and worked for the government for a token salary—supervised the affairs of the private economy. Baruch ensured that manufacturers coordinating their efforts in accord with his goals would be exempt from antitrust laws. He helped major industries earn enormous profits from their efforts. Rather than working to restrict private power and limit corporate profits, as many progressives had urged, the government was working to enhance the private sector through a mutually beneficial alliance.

This growing link between the public and the private sectors extended, although in greatly different form, to labor. The National War Labor Board, established in April 1918, served as the final mediator of labor disputes. It pressured industry to grant important concessions to workers: an eight-hour day, the maintenance of minimal living standards, equal pay for women doing equal work, recognition of the right of unions to organize and bargain collectively. In return, it insisted that workers forgo all strikes and that employers not engage in lockouts. To the delight of Samuel Gompers, membership in labor unions increased by more than 1.5 million between 1917 and 1919.

The effort to organize the economy for war produced some spectacular accomplishments: Hoover's efficient organization of food supplies, McAdoo's success in establishing state control of the railroads, and others. In other areas, however, progress was so slow that the war was over before many of the supplies ordered for it were ready. Even so, many leaders of both government and industry emerged from the experience convinced of the advantages of a close, cooperative relationship between the public and the private sectors. Some hoped to continue and extend the wartime experiments in the peacetime world.

The Search for Social Unity

The idea of unity—not only in the direction of the economy but in the nation's social purpose—had been the dream of many progressives for decades. To them, the war seemed to offer an unmatched opportunity for the United States to close ranks behind a great common cause. In the process, they hoped, society could achieve a lasting sense of collective purpose. In fact, however, the search for unity produced considerable repression.

Government leaders were painfully aware that public sentiment about American involvement in the war had been divided before April 1917 and remained so even after the declaration of war. Many believed that a crucial prerequisite for victory was the uniting of public opinion behind the war effort. The government approached that task in several ways.

The most conspicuous of its efforts was a vast propaganda campaign aimed at drumming up enthusiasm for the conflict. It was orchestrated by the Committee on Public Information (CPI), under the direction of the Denver journalist George Creel. The CPI supervised the distribution of over 75 million pieces of printed material and controlled much of the information that was available for newspapers and magazines. Creel encouraged journalists to exercise "self-censorship" when reporting war news, and most journalists—fearful of more coercive measures—complied by covering the war largely as the government wished. The CPI attempted at first to distribute only the "facts," believing that the truth would speak for itself. As the war continued, however, the committee's tactics became increasingly crude. Government-promoted posters and films were by 1918 becoming lurid portrayals of the savagery of the Germans.

The government also soon began efforts to suppress dissent. CPI-financed advertisements in magazines appealed to citizens to report to the authorities any evidence among their neighbors of disloyalty, pessimism, or yearning for peace. The Espionage Act of 1917 gave the government new tools with which to combat spying, sabotage, or obstruction of the war effort (crimes that were often broadly defined). More repressive were two measures of 1918: the Sabotage Act of April 20 and the Sedition Act of May 16. These bills expanded the meaning of the Espionage Act to make illegal any public expression of opposition to the war; in practice, they allowed officials to prosecute anyone who criticized the president or the government.

The most frequent target of the new legislation (and one of the reasons for its enactment in the first place) were such anticapitalist groups as the Socialist party and the Industrial Workers of the World (IWW). Unlike their counterparts in Europe, American socialists had not dropped their opposition to the war after their country had decided to join it. Many Americans had favored the repression of socialists and radicals even before the war; the wartime policies now made it possible to move against them with full legal sanction. Eugene V. Debs, the humane leader of the Socialist party and an opponent of the war, was sentenced to ten years in prison in 1918. A pardon by President Warren G. Harding ultimately won his release in 1921. Big Bill Haywood and members of the IWW were especially energetically prosecuted. Only by fleeing to the Soviet Union did Haywood avoid a long imprisonment. In all, more than 1,500 people were arrested in 1918 for the crime of criticizing the government.

State and local governments, corporations, universities, and private citizens contributed as well to the climate of repression. Vigilante mobs sprang up to "discipline" those who dared challenge the war. A cluster of citizens' groups emerged to mobilize "respectable" members of their communities to root out disloyalty. The American Protective League, probably the largest of such groups, enlisted the services of 250,000 people, who served as "agents"—prying into the activities and thoughts of their neighbors, opening mail, tapping telephones, and in general attempting to impose unity of opinion on their communities. The most frequent victims of such activities were immigrants: Irish-Americans, because of their historic animosity toward the British and because some had, before 1917, expressed hopes for a German victory; Jews, because many had expressed opposition to the anti-Semitic policies of the Russian government, until 1917 one of the Allies; and others. Immigrant ghettoes were strictly policed by "loyalist" citizens' groups. Even some settlement house workers, many of whom had once championed ethnic diversity, contributed to such efforts.

The greatest target of abuse was the German-American community. Its members had unwittingly contributed to their plight. In the first years of the war in Europe, some had openly advocated American assistance to the Central Powers, and many had opposed United States intervention on behalf of the Allies. But while most German-Americans supported the American war effort once it began, public opinion turned bitterly hostile. A campaign to purge society of all things German quickly gathered speed, at times assuming ludicrous forms. Sauerkraut was renamed "liberty cabbage." Hamburger became "liberty sausage." Performances of German music were frequently banned. German books were removed from the shelves of libraries. Courses in the German language were removed from school curricula. Germans were routinely fired from jobs in war industries, lest they "sabotage" important tasks. Some were fired from positions entirely unrelated to the war, among them Karl Muck, the German-born conductor of the Boston Symphony Orchestra. Vigilante groups subjected Germans to harassment and beatings, including a lynching in southern Illinois in 1918. Relatively few Americans favored such extremes, but many came to agree with the belief of the eminent psychologist G. Stanley Hall that "there is something fundamentally wrong with the Teutonic soul."

THE SEARCH FOR A NEW WORLD ORDER

Woodrow Wilson had led the nation into war promising a more just and stable peace at its conclusion. Even before the armistice, he was preparing to lead the fight for what he considered a democratic postwar settlement—for a set of war aims resting on a vision of a new world order that became known as Wilsonian internationalism.

The Fourteen Points

On January 8, 1918, Wilson appeared before Congress to present the principles for which he claimed the nation was fighting. The war aims were listed under fourteen headings, widely known as the Fourteen Points; but they fell into three broad categories. First, Wilson's proposals contained a series of eight specific recommendations for adjusting postwar boundaries and for establishing new nations to replace the defunct Austro-Hungarian and Ottoman empires. Those recommendations reflected his belief in the right of all peoples to self-determination. Second, there was a set of five general principles to govern international conduct in the future: freedom of the seas, open covenants instead of secret treaties, reductions in armaments, free trade, and impartial mediation of colonial claims. Finally, there was a proposal for a "League of Nations" that would help implement these new principles and territorial adjustments and resolve future controversies.

There were serious flaws in Wilson's proposals. He provided no formula for deciding how to implement the "national self-determination" he promised for subjugated peoples. He made no mention of the new Soviet leadership in Russia, even though its existence had frightened the Western governments (and had helped spur Wilson to announce his own war aims in an effort to undercut Lenin's appeal). He said little about economic rivalries and their effect on international relations, even though such economic tensions had been in large part responsible for the war. Nevertheless, Wilson's international vision quickly came to enchant not only much of his own generation (in both America and Europe) but members of generations to come. It reflected his belief, strongly rooted in the ideas of progressivism, that the world was as capable of just and efficient government as were individual nations—that once the international community accepted certain basic principles of conduct, and once it constructed modern institutions to implement them, the human race could live in peace.

Wilson was confident, as the war neared its end, that popular support would enable him to win Allied approval of his peace plan. There were, however, ominous signs both at home and abroad that his path might be more difficult than he expected. In Europe, leaders of the Allied powers were preparing to resist him even before the armistice was signed. Britain and France in particular, having suffered terrible losses and having developed great bitterness toward Germany as a result, were in no mood for a benign and generous peace. David Lloyd George, the British prime minister, had campaigned for reelection in 1918 by calling for the execution of Kaiser Wilhelm II.

At the same time, Wilson was encountering problems at home. In 1918, with the war almost over, Wilson unwisely appealed to the American voters to support his peace plans by electing Democrats to Congress in the November elections. Days later, the Republicans captured majorities in both houses. Domestic economic troubles, more than international issues, had been the most important factor in the voting; but because of the president's ill-timed appeal, the results damaged his ability to claim broad popular support for his peace plans.

The leaders of the Republican party, in the meantime, were developing their own reasons for opposing Wilson. Many were angry that he had tried to make the 1918 balloting a referendum on his war aims, especially since many Republicans had been supporting the Fourteen Points. Wilson further antagonized them when he refused to appoint any important Republicans to the negotiating team that would represent the United States at the peace conference in Paris.

But the president considered such matters unimportant. There would be only one member of the American negotiating team with any real authority: Wilson himself. And once he had produced a just and moral treaty, he believed, the weight of world and American opinion would compel his enemies to support him.

The Paris Peace Conference

Wilson arrived in Europe to a welcome such as few men in history have experienced. To the war-weary people of the Continent, he was nothing less than a savior, the man who would create a new and better world. When he entered Paris on December 13, 1918, he was greeted, some claimed, by the largest crowd in the history of France. The negotiations themselves, however, proved less satisfying.

The principal figures in the negotiations were the leaders of the victorious Allied nations: David Lloyd George, the prime minister of Great Britain; Georges Clemenceau, the president of France; Vittorio Orlando, the prime minister of Italy; and Wilson, who hoped to dominate them all. Some of Wilson's advisers had warned him that if agreement could not be reached at the "summit," there would be nowhere else to go and that it would be better to begin negotiations at a lower level. Wilson, however, was adamant; he alone would represent the United States.

From the beginning, the atmosphere of idealism Wilson had sought to create was competing with a spirit of national aggrandizement. There was, moreover, a pervasive sense of unease about the unstable situation in eastern Europe and the threat of communism. Russia, whose new Bolshevik government was still fighting "White" counterrevolutionaries, was unrepresented in Paris; but the radical threat it seemed to pose to Western governments was never far from the minds of the delegates. Wilson himself had sent American troops into Russia in 1918, allegedly to protect trapped Czech forces but really, many believed, to support the anti-Bolshevik forces in the civil war there.

In this tense and often vindictive atmosphere, Wilson was unable to win approval of many of the broad principles he had espoused: freedom of the seas, which the British refused even to discuss; free trade; "open covenants openly arrived at" (the Paris negotiations themselves were often conducted in secret). Despite his support for "impartial mediation" of colonial claims, he was forced to accept a transfer of German colonies in the Pacific to Japan, to which the British had promised them in exchange for Japanese assistance in the war. His pledge of "national self-determination" for all peoples suffered numerous assaults. Economic and strategic demands were constantly coming into conflict with the principle of cultural nationalism.

Where the treaty departed most conspicuously from Wilson's ideals was on the question of reparations. When the conference began, the president opposed demanding reparations from the defeated Central Powers. The other Allied leaders, however, were intransigent, and slowly Wilson gave way and accepted the principle of reparations, the specific sum to be set later by a commission. The final amount, established in 1921, was less than some earlier demands but far more than the crippled German economy could absorb.

Wilson did manage to win some important victories in Paris in setting boundaries and dealing with former colonies. But his most visible triumph, and the one of most importance to him, was the creation of a permanent international organization to oversee world affairs and prevent future wars. On January 25, 1919, the Allies voted to accept the "covenant" of the League of Nations; and with that, Wilson believed, the peace treaty was transformed from a disappointment into a success. Any mistakes and inequities that had emerged from the peace conference, he was convinced, could be corrected later by the League.

The covenant provided for an assembly of nations that would meet regularly to debate means of resolving disputes and protecting the peace. Authority to implement League decisions would rest with a nine-member Executive Council; the United States would be one of five permanent members of the council, along with Britain, France, Italy, and Japan. The covenant left many questions unanswered, most notably how the League would enforce its decisions. Wilson, however, was confident that once established, the new organization would find suitable answers.

The Ratification Battle

Wilson was well aware of the political obstacles awaiting him at home. Many Americans, accustomed to their nation's isolation from Europe, questioned the wisdom of this major new commitment to internationalism. Others had serious reservations about the specific features of the treaty and the covenant. After a brief trip to Washington in February 1919, during which he listened to harsh objections to the treaty from members of the Senate and others, he returned to Europe and insisted on certain modifications in the covenant (limiting America's obligations to the League) to satisfy his critics. The changes were not enough to mollify his opponents, but Wilson refused to go further.

Wilson presented the Treaty of Versailles (which took its name from the former royal palace outside Paris where the final negotiating sessions had taken place) to the Senate on July 10, 1919. In the weeks that followed, he refused to consider even the most innocuous compromise. But members of the Senate had many objections to the treaty. Some—the so-called "Irreconcilables," many of them Western isolationists—opposed the agreement on principle. But many other opponents, with less fervent convictions, were principally concerned with constructing a winning issue for the Republicans in 1920. Most notable of these was Senator Henry Cabot Lodge

THE BIG FOUR The principal negotiators of the Versailles Treaty—Vittorio Orlando, prime minister of Italy; Lloyd George, prime minister of Great Britain; Georges Clemenceau, president of France; and Woodrow Wilson—pose for a group portrait in the library of the Ritz Hotel in Paris.

of Massachusetts, the powerful chairman of the Foreign Relations Committee. Lodge loathed President Wilson. ("I never thought I could hate a man as I hate Wilson," Lodge once said.) He used every possible tactic to obstruct, delay, and amend the treaty.

Public sentiment clearly favored ratification, so at first Lodge could do little more than play for time. Gradually, however, Lodge's general opposition to the treaty crystallized into a series of "reservations"—amendments to the League covenant further limiting American obligations to the organization. Wilson might still have won approval at this point if he had agreed to some relatively minor changes in the language of the treaty. But the president refused to yield. The United States had a moral obligation, he claimed, to respect the terms of the agreement precisely as they stood. When he realized the Senate would not budge, he decided to appeal to the public.

What followed was a political disaster and a personal tragedy. Wilson embarked on a grueling, cross-country speaking tour to arouse public support for the treaty. For more than three weeks, he traveled over 8,000 miles by train, speaking as often as four times a day, resting hardly at all.

Finally, he reached the end of his strength. After speaking at Pueblo, Colorado, on September 25, 1919, he collapsed with severe headaches. Canceling the rest of his itinerary, he rushed back to Washington, where, a few days later, he suffered a major stroke. For two weeks, he was close to death; for six weeks more, he was so seriously ill that he could conduct virtually no public business. His wife and his doctor formed an almost impenetrable barrier around him, shielding the president from any official pressures that might impede his recovery and preventing the public from receiving any accurate information about the gravity of his condition.

Wilson ultimately recovered enough to resume a limited official schedule, but he was essentially an invalid for the remaining eighteen months of his presidency. His left side was partially paralyzed; more important, his mental and emotional state was unstable. His condition only intensified what had already been his strong tendency to view public issues in moral terms and to resist any attempts at compromise. When the Foreign Relations Committee finally sent the treaty to the Senate, recommending nearly fifty amendments and reservations, Wilson refused to consider any of them. When the full Senate voted in November to accept fourteen of the reservations, Wilson gave stern directions to his Democratic allies: they must vote only for a treaty with no changes whatsoever; any other version must be defeated. On November 19, 1919, forty-two Democrats, following the president's instructions, joined thirteen Republican "irreconcilables" to reject the amended treaty. When the Senate voted on the original version without any reservations, thirty-eight senators, all but one a Democrat, voted to approve it; fifty-five voted no.

There were sporadic efforts to revive the treaty over the next few months. But Wilson's opposition to anything but the precise settlement he had negotiated in Paris remained too formidable an obstacle to surmount. He was, moreover, becoming convinced that the 1920 national election would serve as a "solemn referendum" on the League. By now, however, public interest in the peace process had begun to fade—partly as a reaction against the tragic bitterness of the ratification fight, but more in response to a series of other crises.

A SOCIETY IN TURMOIL

Even during the Paris Peace Conference, many Americans were concerned less about international matters than about turbulent events at home. Some of this unease was a legacy of the almost hysterical social atmosphere of the war years; some of it was a response to issues that surfaced after the armistice.

The Troubled Economy

The war ended sooner than almost anyone had anticipated; and without warning, without planning, the nation was launched into the difficult task of economic reconversion. At first, the wartime boom continued. But the postwar prosperity rested largely on the lingering effects of the war (government deficit spending continued for some months after the armistice) and on sudden, temporary demands (a booming market for scarce consumer goods at home and a strong market for American products in the war-ravaged nations of Europe). The postwar boom was accompanied, moreover, by raging inflation, a result in part of the precipitous abandonment of wartime price controls. Through most of 1919 and 1920, prices rose at an average of more than 15 percent a year.

Finally, late in 1920, the economic bubble burst as many of the temporary forces that had created it disappeared and as inflation began killing the market for consumer goods. Between 1920 and 1921, the gross national product declined nearly 10 percent; 100,000 businesses went bankrupt; 453,000 farmers lost their land; and nearly 5 million Americans lost their jobs.

Well before the recession began, there was a dramatic increase in labor unrest. The raging inflation of 1919 wiped out the modest wage gains workers had achieved during the war; many laborers were worried about job security, as hundreds of thousands of veterans returned to the work force; arduous working conditions—such as the twelve-hour day in the steel industry—continued to be a source of discontent. Employers aggravated the resentment by using the end of the war (and the end of government controls) to rescind benefits they had been forced to concede to workers in 1917 and 1918—most notably recognition of unions. The year 1919, therefore, saw an unprecedented wave of strikes—more than 3,600 in all, involving over 4 million workers. In January, a walkout by shipyard workers in Seattle, Washington, evolved into a general strike that brought the entire city to a virtual standstill. In September, there was a strike by the Boston police force, which was demanding recognition of its union in the wake of substantial layoffs and wage cuts. Seattle had remained generally calm; but with its police off the job, Boston erupted in violence and looting.

THE GREAT STEEL STRIKE Striking steelworkers stand around uneasily as mounted
police patrol the streets of a steel town near Pittsburgh, during the
Great Steel Strike of 1919.

These and other strikes aroused widespread middle-class hostility to
the unions, a hostility that played a part in defeating the greatest strike of
1919: a steel strike that began in September, when 350,000 steelworkers in
several Midwestern cities demanded an eight-hour day and recognition of
their union. The steel strike was long and bitter and climaxed in a riot in
Gary, Indiana, in which eighteen strikers were killed. Steel executives
managed to keep most plants running with nonunion labor, and public
opinion was so hostile to the strikers that the AFL timidly repudiated them.
By January, the strike had collapsed. It was a setback from which organized
labor would not recover for more than a decade.

The Red Scare

To much of the public at the time, the industrial warfare appeared to be a
frightening omen of instability and radicalism. This was in part because
other evidence emerging at the same time seemed likewise to suggest the
existence of a radical menace. The Russian Revolution of November 1917
indicated that communism was no longer simply a theory but now an
important regime. Concerns about the communist threat grew in 1919

when the Soviet government announced the formation of the Communist International (or Comintern), whose purpose was to export revolution around the world.

In America, meanwhile, there was, in addition to the great number of imagined radicals, a modest number of real ones. These small groups of radicals were presumably responsible for a series of bombings in the spring of 1919 that produced great national alarm. In April, the post office intercepted several dozen parcels addressed to leading businessmen and politicians that were triggered to explode when opened. Two months later, eight bombs exploded in eight cities within minutes of one another, suggesting a nationwide conspiracy. One of them damaged the façade of United States Attorney General A. Mitchell Palmer's home in Washington.

In response to these and other provocations, what became known as the Red Scare began. Nearly thirty states enacted new peacetime sedition laws imposing harsh penalties on those who promoted revolution; some 300 people went to jail as a result. There were spontaneous acts of violence against supposed radicals in some communities, and more calculated efforts by universities and other institutions to expel radicals from their midst.

Perhaps the greatest contribution to the Red Scare came from the federal government. On New Year's Day, 1920, Attorney General A. Mitchell Palmer and his ambitious young assistant, J. Edgar Hoover, orchestrated a series of raids on alleged radical centers throughout the country and arrested more than 6,000 people. The Palmer Raids had been intended to uncover huge caches of weapons and explosives; they netted a total of three pistols and no dynamite. Most of those arrested were ultimately released, but about 500 who were not American citizens were summarily deported.

The ferocity of the Red Scare soon abated, but its effects lingered well into the 1920s, most notably in the celebrated case of Sacco and Vanzetti. In May of 1920, two Italian immigrants, Nicola Sacco and Bartolomeo Vanzetti, were charged with the murder of a paymaster in Braintree, Massachusetts. The case against them was questionable and suffused with nativist prejudices and fears; but because both men were confessed anarchists, they faced a widespread public presumption of guilt. They were convicted and sentenced to death. Over the next several years, public support for Sacco and Vanzetti grew to formidable proportions. But all requests for a new trial or a pardon were denied. On August 23, 1927, amid widespread protests around the world, Sacco and Vanzetti, still proclaiming their innocence, died in the electric chair.

Racial Unrest

No group suffered more from the inflamed climate of the postwar years than American blacks. Over 400,000 blacks served in the army, half of them in Europe and more than 40,000 of them in combat. They had endured numerous indignities during the conflict. They had been placed in segregated units, under the command of white officers who often held them in contempt. They had put up with these humiliations, however, in the belief that their service would earn them the gratitude of the nation when they returned.

For many other American blacks, the war raised expectations in other ways. Nearly half a million migrated from the rural South to industrial cities (often enticed by Northern "labor agents," who offered them free transportation) in search of the factory jobs the war was rapidly generating. This was the beginning of what became known as the "Great Migration." Within a few years, the nation's racial demographics were transformed; suddenly there were large black communities crowding into Northern cities, in some of which very few African-Americans had lived in the past. Just as black soldiers expected their military service to enhance their social status, so black factory workers regarded their move north as an escape from racial prejudice and an opportunity for economic gain.

By 1919, the racial climate had become savage and murderous. In the South, there was a sudden increase in lynchings: more than seventy blacks, some of them war veterans, died at the hands of white mobs in 1919 alone. In the North, black factory workers faced widespread layoffs as returning white veterans displaced them from their jobs. Black veterans were disillusioned when they returned to find a society still unwilling to grant them any significant opportunities for advancement. Rural black migrants to Northern cities encountered white communities unfamiliar with and generally hostile to them; and as whites became convinced that African-American workers with lower wage demands were hurting them economically, animosity grew. The result was a rash of urban disorders. As early as 1917, serious race riots had flared in Houston, Philadelphia, and East St. Louis (where forty-nine people, thirty-nine of them African-Americans, were killed). In Chicago in 1919, a black teen-ager swimming in Lake Michigan on a hot July day happened to drift toward a white beach. Whites on shore allegedly stoned him unconscious; he sank and drowned. The incident inflamed already severe racial tensions in the city, and for more than a week Chicago was virtually at war. In the end, 38 people died—15 whites and 23 blacks—and 537 were injured; over 1,000 people were left homeless. The

Chicago riot was the worst but not the only racial violence during the so-called "Red Summer" of 1919; in all, 120 people died in such racial outbreaks in the space of little more than three months.

The NAACP urged blacks to fight back, to defend themselves and demand government protection. At the same time, a black Jamaican, Marcus Garvey, began to attract a wide following in the United States with an ideology of black nationalism. Garvey encouraged American blacks to take pride in their own achievements and to develop an awareness of their African heritage—to reject assimilation into white society and develop pride in their own race. Garvey even urged supporters to leave America and return to Africa, where they could create a new society of their own. At the peak of his popularity, Garvey claimed a following of 4 million. In the end, however, most African-Americans had little choice but to acquiesce in the social and economic subjugation being forced on them.

The Retreat from Idealism

On August 26, 1920, the Nineteenth Amendment, guaranteeing women the right to vote, became part of the Constitution. To the woman suffrage movement, this was the culmination of nearly a century of struggle. To many progressives, who had seen the inclusion of women in the electorate as a way of bolstering their political strength, it seemed to promise new support for reform. Yet the passage of the Nineteenth Amendment marked not the beginning of an era of reform but the end of one.

The economic problems, the labor unrest, the fear of radicalism, the racial tensions—all combined in the years immediately following the war to produce a general sense of disillusionment. That became particularly apparent in the election of 1920. Woodrow Wilson wanted the campaign to be a referendum on the League of Nations, and the Democratic candidates, Governor James M. Cox of Ohio and Assistant Secretary of the Navy Franklin D. Roosevelt, dutifully tried to keep Wilson's ideals alive. The Republican presidential nominee, however, offered a different vision. He was Warren Gamaliel Harding, an obscure Ohio senator whom party leaders had chosen as their nominee confident that he would do their bidding once in office. Harding offered no ideals, only a vague promise of a return, as he later phrased it, to "normalcy." He won in a landslide. The Republican ticket received 61 percent of the popular vote and carried every state outside the South. The party made major gains in Congress as well. To many Americans it seemed that, for better or worse, a new era had begun.

CHAPTER TWENTY-FOUR

The New Era

The New Economy ~ *The New Culture*
A Conflict of Cultures ~ *Republican Government*

T HE 1920S ARE often remembered as an era of affluence, conservatism, and cultural frivolity: the Roaring Twenties, the age of what Warren G. Harding once called "normalcy." In reality, however, the decade was a time of significant, even dramatic social, economic, and political change. It was an era in which the American economy not only enjoyed spectacular growth but developed new forms of organization. It was a time in which American popular culture reshaped itself to reflect the increasingly urban, industrial, consumer-oriented society of the United States. And it was a decade in which American government, for all its conservatism, experimented with new approaches to public policy that helped pave the way for the important period of reform that was to follow. That was why contemporaries liked to refer to the 1920s as the "New Era"—an age in which America was becoming a modern nation.

At the same time, however, the decade saw the rise of a series of spirited and at times effective rebellions against the modern developments that were transforming American life. The intense cultural conflicts that characterized the 1920s were evidence of how much of American society remained unreconciled to the modernizing currents of the New Era.

THE NEW ECONOMY

After the recession of 1921–1922, the United States began a long period of almost uninterrupted prosperity and economic expansion. Less visible at the time, but equally significant, was the survival (and even the growth) of severe inequalities and imbalances.

Economic Growth and Organization

No one could deny the remarkable, some believed miraculous, feats of the American economy in the 1920s. The nation's manufacturing output rose by more than 60 percent during the decade. Per capita income grew by a third. Inflation was negligible. A mild recession in 1923 interrupted the pattern of growth; but when it subsided early in 1924, the economy expanded with even greater vigor than before.

The economic boom was a result of many things, but one of the most important causes was technology, and the great industrial expansion it made possible. The automobile industry, as a result of the development of the assembly line and other innovations, now became one of the most important industries in the nation. It stimulated growth in other, related industries as well. Auto manufacturers purchased the products of steel, rubber, glass, and tool companies. Auto owners bought gasoline from the oil corporations. Road construction in response to the proliferation of motor vehicles itself became an important industry. The increased mobility that the automobile made possible increased the demand for suburban housing, fueling a boom in the construction industry.

Other new industries benefiting from technological innovations contributed as well to the economic growth. Radio became a booming concern within a few years of its commercial debut in 1920. The motion picture industry expanded dramatically, especially after the introduction of sound in 1927. Aviation, electronics, home appliances, plastics, synthetic fibers, aluminum, magnesium, oil, electric power, and other industries fueled by technological advances—all grew dramatically and spurred the economic boom.

Large sectors of American business were accelerating their drive toward national organization and consolidation. Certain industries—notably those such as steel and automobiles, dependent on large-scale mass production—seemed naturally to move toward concentrating production in a few large firms. Others—industries less dependent on technology and less susceptible to great economies of scale—proved resistant to consolidation, despite the efforts of many businessmen to promote it.

Some industries less prone to domination by a few great corporations attempted to stabilize themselves not through consolidation but through cooperation. An important vehicle was the trade association—a national organization created by various members of an industry to encourage coordination in production and marketing techniques. But trade associations worked best in the mass-production industries that had already succeeded in limiting competition through consolidation. In more decentralized industries, such as cotton textiles, their effectiveness was limited.

The strenuous efforts by industrialists throughout the economy to find ways to curb competition through consolidation or cooperation reflected a strong fear of overcapacity. Even in the booming 1920s, industrialists remembered how too-rapid expansion and overproduction had helped produce recessions in 1893, 1907, and 1920. The great, unrealized dream of the New Era was to find a way to stabilize the economy so that such collapses would never occur again.

Workers in the Era of Capital

The remarkable economic growth was accompanied by a continuing, and in some areas even increasing, maldistribution of wealth and purchasing

THE STEAMFITTER Lewis Hine was among the first American photographers to recognize his craft as an art. In this carefully posed photograph from the mid-1920s, Hine made a point that many other artists were making in other media: The rise of the machine could serve human beings, but might also bend them to its own needs.

power. More than two-thirds of the American people in 1929 lived at no better than what one major study described as the "minimum comfort level." Half of those languished at or below the level of "subsistence and poverty." Large segments of society, unable to organize, were without power to protect their economic interests.

American labor experienced both the successes and the failures of the 1920s as much as any other group. On the one hand, most workers saw their standard of living rise during the decade; many enjoyed greatly improved working conditions and other benefits. Some employers in the 1920s, eager to avoid disruptive labor unrest and forestall the growth of unions, adopted paternalistic techniques that came to be known as "welfare capitalism." Henry Ford, for example, shortened the workweek, raised wages, and instituted paid vacations. By 1926, nearly 3 million industrial workers were eligible for pensions on retirement. When labor grievances surfaced despite these efforts, workers could voice them through the so-called company unions that were emerging in many industries—workers' councils and shop committees, organized by the corporations themselves. But welfare capitalism, in the end, gave workers no real control over their own fates. Company unions were feeble vehicles. And welfare capitalism survived only as long as industry prospered. After 1929, with the economy in crisis, the entire system collapsed.

Welfare capitalism affected only a relatively small number of workers in any case. Most laborers worked for employers interested primarily in keeping their labor costs to a minimum. Workers as a whole, therefore, received wage increases that were proportionately far below the increases in corporate profits. Unskilled workers, in particular, saw their wages increase very slowly—by only a little over 2 percent between 1920 and 1926. In the end, American workers remained in the 1920s a relatively impoverished and powerless group. Their wages rose; but the average annual income of a worker remained below $1,500 a year when $1,800 was considered necessary to maintain a minimally decent standard of living. Only by relying on the earnings of several family members at once could many working-class families make ends meet.

Some laborers continued to consider effective independent union movement their best hope. But the New Era was a bleak time for labor organization, in part because many unions themselves were relatively conservative and failed to adapt to the realities of the modern economy. The American Federation of Labor remained wedded to the concept of the craft union, in which workers were organized on the basis of particular skills. In the meantime, a huge new segment of the work force was emerging:

unskilled industrial workers, many of them recent immigrants from southern or eastern Europe. They received little attention from the craft unions and found themselves, as a result, with no organizations to join. William Green, who became president of the AFL in 1924, was committed to peaceful cooperation with employers and strident opposition to communism and socialism. He frowned on strikes.

A growing proportion of the work force consisted of women, who were concentrated in what have since become known as "pink-collar" jobs—low-paying service occupations with many of the same problems as manufacturing employment. Large numbers of women worked as secretaries, sales-clerks, and telephone operators and in other nonmanual service capacities. Because such positions were not technically industrial jobs, the AFL and other labor organizations were uninterested in organizing these workers. Similarly, the half-million African-Americans who had migrated from the rural South into the cities during the Great Migration after 1914 had few opportunities for union representation. The skilled crafts represented in the AFL often worked actively to exclude blacks from their trades and organizations. Most blacks worked in jobs in which the AFL took no interest at all—as janitors, dishwashers, garbage collectors, domestics, and other service jobs. A. Philip Randolph's Brotherhood of Sleeping Car Porters was one of the few important unions dominated and led by African-Americans.

But whatever the weaknesses of the unions, the strength of the corporations was the principal reason for the absence of effective labor organization. After the turmoil of 1919, corporate leaders worked hard to spread the doctrine that unionism was somehow subversive, that a crucial element of democratic capitalism was the protection of the "open shop" (a shop in which no worker could be required to join a union). The crusade for the open shop, euphemistically titled the "American Plan," received the endorsement of the National Association of Manufacturers in 1920 and became a pretext for a harsh campaign of union busting across the country. As a result, union membership fell from more than 5 million in 1920 to under 3 million in 1929.

The Plight of the Farmer

Like industry, American agriculture in the 1920s was embracing new technologies for increasing production. The number of tractors on American farms, for example, quadrupled during the 1920s, helping to open 35 million new acres to cultivation. Agricultural production was increasing in other parts of the world as well. But unlike increased industrial production, increased agricultural production did not stimulate an increase in demand. The result was overproduction, a disastrous decline in food prices, and a severe drop in farmers' income beginning early in the 1920s. Farm income in 1920, had been 15 percent of the national total; by 1929, it was 9 percent. The average farmer made only about a quarter as much money each year in the 1920s as the average nonfarmer. More than 3 million people left agriculture altogether in the course of the decade. Of those who remained, many were forced into tenancy—losing ownership of their lands and having to rent instead from banks or other landlords.

In response, some farmers began to demand relief in the form of government price supports. Through organizations such as the Farm Bureau Federation, they put increasing pressure on Congress (where farmers continued to enjoy disproportionately high representation). One price-raising scheme in particular came to dominate agrarian demands: the idea of "parity." Parity referred to a price for an agricultural commodity based on the average price of the crop during the years 1909–1913 (a good time for farmers) as compared with the general average of all prices during the same period. Its purpose was to ensure that farmers would earn back at least their production costs no matter how the national or world agricultural market might fluctuate. Champions of parity urged high tariffs against foreign agricultural goods and a government commitment to buy surplus domestic crops at parity and sell them abroad at whatever the market would bring.

The legislative expression of the demand for parity was the McNary-Haugen Bill, named after its two principal sponsors in Congress and introduced repeatedly between 1924 and 1928. In 1926, Congress approved a bill requiring parity for grain, cotton, tobacco, and rice, but President Coolidge vetoed it. In 1928, it won congressional approval again, only to succumb to another presidential veto.

THE NEW CULTURE

The increasingly urban and consumer-oriented culture of the 1920s helped Americans in all regions live their lives and perceive their world in increasingly similar ways. That same culture exposed them to a new set of values that reflected the prosperity and complexity of the modern economy.

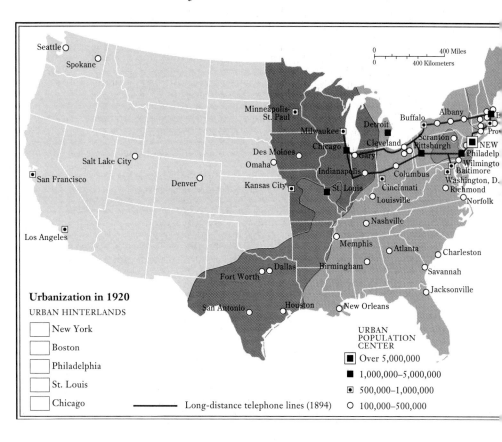

Urbanization in 1920

URBAN HINTERLANDS

[ ] New York
[ ] Boston
[ ] Philadelphia
[ ] St. Louis
[ ] Chicago

URBAN
POPULATION
CENTER

■ Over 5,000,000
■ 1,000,000–5,000,000
◨ 500,000–1,000,000
○ 100,000–500,000

———— Long-distance telephone lines (1894)

Consumerism and Communications

The United States of the 1920s was becoming a consumer society—a society in which many men and women (although not, of course, all) could afford not merely the means of subsistence but a considerable measure of additional, discretionary goods and services; a society in which many people could buy items not just because of need but for pleasure. Middle-class families purchased new appliances such as electric refrigerators, washing machines, and vacuum cleaners. Men and women wore wristwatches and smoked cigarettes. Women purchased cosmetics and mass-produced fashions. Above all, Americans bought automobiles. By the end of the decade, there were more than 30 million cars on American roads.

No group was more aware of the emergence of consumerism (or more responsible for creating it) than the advertising industry. The first advertising and public relations firms (N. W. Ayer and J. Walter Thompson) had appeared well before World War I; but in the 1920s, partly as a result of techniques pioneered by wartime propaganda, advertising came of age. Publicists no longer simply conveyed information; they sought to identify products with a particular life style. They also encouraged the public to absorb the values of promotion and salesmanship and to admire those who were effective "boosters" and publicists. One of the most successful books of the 1920s was *The Man Nobody Knows*, by advertising executive Bruce Barton. It portrayed Jesus Christ as not only a religious prophet but also a "super salesman." Barton's message, a message apparently in tune with the new spirit of the consumer culture, was that Jesus had been a man concerned with living a full and rewarding life in this world; twentieth-century men and women should be concerned with doing the same.

The advertising industry could never have had the impact it did without the emergence of new vehicles of communication that made it possible to reach large audiences quickly and easily. Newspapers were being absorbed into national chains. Mass-circulation magazines—*Collier's, Ladies' Home Journal*, the *Saturday Evening Post*, and others—attracted broad, national audiences. The movies were becoming an ever more popular and powerful form of mass communication; over 100 million people saw films in 1930, as compared with 40 million in 1922.

The most important communications vehicle, however, was the only one truly new to the 1920s: radio. The first commercial radio station in America, KDKA in Pittsburgh, began broadcasting in 1920; and the first national radio network, the National Broadcasting Company, was formed in 1927. By 1923, there were more than 500 radio stations, covering virtually every area of the country; by 1929, more than 12 million families owned radio sets.

The influence of the consumer culture, and its increasing emphasis on immediate, personal fulfillment, was even visible in religion. Theological modernists—among them Harry Emerson Fosdick and A. C. McGiffert— taught their followers to abandon some of the traditional tenets of evangelical Christianity (literal interpretation of the Bible, belief in the Trinity, attribution of human traits to the deity) and to accept a faith that would help individuals to live more fulfilling lives in the present world.

The New Woman

College-educated women were no longer pioneers in the 1920s. There were now two and even three generations of graduates of women's or coeducational colleges and universities; and some were making their presence felt in professional areas that in the past women had rarely penetrated.

Still, professional opportunities for women remained limited by society's assumptions about what were suitable occupations for them. Although there were notable success stories about female business executives, journalists, doctors, and lawyers, most professional women remained confined to such traditionally "feminine" fields as fashion, education, social work, and nursing or to the lower levels of business management. The "new professional woman" was a vivid and widely publicized image in the 1920s. In reality, however, most employed women were nonprofessional, lower-class workers. Middle-class women, in the meantime, remained largely in the home.

Yet the 1920s constituted a new era for middle-class women nonetheless. In particular, the decade saw a redefinition of motherhood. Shortly after World War I, an influential group of psychologists—the "behaviorists," led by John B. Watson—began to challenge the long-held assumption that women had an instinctive capacity for motherhood. Maternal affection was not, they claimed, sufficient preparation for child rearing. Instead, mothers should rely on the advice and assistance of experts and professionals: doctors, nurses, and trained educators in nursery schools and kindergartens.

For many middle-class women, these changes devalued what had been an important and consuming activity. Many attempted to compensate by devoting new attention to their roles as wives and companions. A woman's relationship with her husband assumed a greatly enhanced importance. And many women now openly considered their sexual relationships with their husbands not simply a means of procreation, as earlier generations had been taught to do, but an important and pleasurable experience in its own right, as the culmination of romantic love.

One result was progress in birth control. The pioneer of the American birth-control movement, Margaret Sanger, began her career as a promoter of the diaphragm and other birth-control devices out of a concern for working-class women; she believed that large families were among the major causes of poverty and distress in poor communities. By the 1920s (partly because she had limited success in persuading working-class women to accept her teachings), she was becoming more concerned with persuading middle-class women of the benefits of birth control. Birth-control devices began to find a large market among middle-class women, even though some techniques remained illegal in many states (and abortion remained illegal nearly everywhere).

The new, more secular view of womanhood had effects on women beyond the middle class as well. Some women concluded that in the New Era it was no longer necessary to maintain a rigid, Victorian female "respectability." They could smoke, drink, dance, wear seductive clothes and makeup, and attend lively parties. Those assumptions became the basis of the "flapper"—the modern woman whose liberated life style found expression in dress, hair style, speech, and behavior. The flapper life style had a particular impact on lower-middle-class and working-class single women, who were flocking to new jobs in industry and the service sector. (The young, middle-class, "Bohemian" women most often associated with the flapper image were, in fact, imitating a style that emerged among this larger group.) At night, such women flocked to clubs and dance halls in search of excitement and companionship.

Despite all the changes, most women remained highly dependent on men—both in the workplace and in the home—and relatively powerless when men exploited that dependence. The realization that the "new woman" was as much myth as reality inspired some American feminists to continue their crusade for reform. The National Woman's party, under the leadership of Alice Paul, pressed on with its campaign for the Equal Rights Amendment, although it found little support in Congress (and met continued resistance from other feminist groups). Nevertheless, women's organizations and female political activities grew in many ways in the 1920s. Responding to the suffrage victory, women organized the League of Women Voters and the women's auxiliaries of both the Democratic and Republican parties. Female-dominated consumer groups grew rapidly and increased the range and energy of their efforts.

Women activists won an apparent triumph in 1921 when they helped secure passage of a measure in keeping with the traditional feminist goal of securing "protective" legislation for women: the Sheppard-Towner Act. It provided federal funds to states to establish prenatal and child health-care programs. From the start, however, it produced controversy. Alice Paul and her supporters opposed the measure, complaining that it classified all women as mothers. Margaret Sanger complained that the new programs would discourage birth-control efforts. More important, the American Medical Association fought Sheppard-Towner, warning that it would introduce untrained outsiders into the health-care field. In 1929, Congress terminated the program.

The Disenchanted

Many artists and intellectuals coming of age in the 1920s were experiencing a disenchantment with modern America so fundamental that they were often able to view it only with contempt. As a result, they adopted a role different from that of most intellectuals of earlier eras. Rather than trying to influence and reform their society, they isolated themselves from it and embarked on a restless search for personal fulfillment.

At the heart of their critique of modern society was a sense of personal alienation, a belief that contemporary America no longer provided the individual with avenues by which he or she could achieve personal fulfillment. This disillusionment had its roots in many things, but in nothing so deeply as the experience of World War I. To those who had fought in the conflict, and even to many who had not, the aftermath of the war was shattering. The repudiation of Wilsonian idealism, the restoration of "business as usual," and the growing emphasis on materialism and consumerism suggested that nothing had been gained. The war had been a fraud; the suffering and the dying had been in vain.

One result of this alienation was a series of savage critiques of modern society by a wide range of writers, some of whom were known as the "debunkers." Among them was the Baltimore journalist H. L. Mencken, who delighted in ridiculing everything Americans held dear: religion, politics, the arts, even democracy itself. When someone asked Mencken why he continued to live in a society he found so loathsome, he replied: "Why do people go to the zoo?" Echoing Mencken's contempt was the novelist Sinclair Lewis, the first American to win a Nobel Prize in literature. In a series of savage novels—*Main Street* (1920), *Babbitt* (1922), *Arrowsmith* (1925), and others—he lashed out at one aspect of modern bourgeois society after another. Intellectuals of the 1920s claimed to reject the "success ethic" that they believed dominated American life (even though many of them hoped for—and a few achieved—commercial and critical success on their own terms). The novelist F. Scott Fitzgerald, for example, ridiculed the American obsession with material success in *The Great Gatsby* (1925).

Some artists and intellectuals expressed their disillusionment by leaving America to live in France, making Paris for a time a center of American artistic life. Others moved to the Southwestern United States—to the art colonies at Taos and Santa Fe, New Mexico—attracted by the cultural and geographical distinctiveness of the region. Some adopted hedonistic life styles, involving alcohol, drugs, casual sex, and wild parties. Most of these young men and women, however, believed the only real refuge from the travails of modern society was art. Only art, they argued, could allow them full individual expression; only the act of creation could offer them fulfillment.

The result of this quest for fulfillment through art was not, for the most part, real personal satisfaction for the writers and artists themselves; many continued to lead restless, unhappy lives. They did, however, produce a body of work that made the decade one of the great eras of American literature. The roster of important American writers who did significant work in the 1920s may have no equal in any other period: Ernest Hemingway, Fitzgerald, Lewis, Thomas Wolfe, John Dos Passos, Ezra Pound, T. S. Eliot, Gertrude Stein, Edna Ferber, William Faulkner, and Eugene O'Neill.

Not all intellectuals of the 1920s, however, expressed alienation and despair. Some expressed reservations about their society not by withdrawing from it but by advocating reform. John Dewey, for example, kept alive the philosophical tradition of pragmatism and appealed for "practical" education and experimentation in social policy. Charles and Mary Beard, perhaps the most influential historians of their day, stressed economic factors, and the clash of competing economic interests, in tracing the development of modern society.

To another group of intellectuals, the solution to contemporary problems lay neither in escapism nor in progressivism but in an exploration of their own cultural or regional origins. In New York City, a new generation of black intellectuals created a flourishing African-American culture widely described as the "Harlem Renaissance." The Harlem poets, novelists, and artists drew heavily from their African roots in an effort to prove the richness of their own racial heritage (and not incidentally to demonstrate to whites that their race was worthy of respect). The poet Langston Hughes captured much of the spirit of the movement in a single sentence: "I am a Negro—and beautiful." Other black writers in Harlem and elsewhere—James Weldon Johnson, Countee Cullen, Zora Neale Hurston, Claude McKay, Alain Locke—as well as black artists and musicians helped to establish a thriving culture rooted in the historical legacy of their race.

A strangely similar effort was under way among an influential group of white Southern intellectuals. Known first as the "Fugitives" and later as the "Agrarians," these young poets, novelists, and critics sought to counter the depersonalization of industrial society by evoking the strong rural and, they argued, communitarian traditions of their own region. In their controversial manifesto *I'll Take My Stand* (1930), a collection of essays by twelve Southern intellectuals, they issued a simultaneously radical and conservative appeal for a rejection of the doctrine of "economic progress" and the spiritual debilitation that had accompanied it. The supposedly "backward" South, they argued, could serve as a model for a nation drunk with visions of limitless growth and modernization.

A M E R I C A N   V O I C E S

LANGSTON HUGHES

I, Too (1926)

I, too, sing America.

I am the darker brother.
They send me to eat in the kitchen
When company comes,
But I laugh,
And eat well,
And grow strong.

Tomorrow,
I'll be at the table
When company comes.
Nobody'll dare
Say to me,
'Eat in the kitchen,'
Then.

Besides,
They'll see how beautiful I am
And be ashamed—

I, too, am America.

A CONFLICT OF CULTURES

The modern, secular culture of the 1920s was not unchallenged. It grew up alongside an older, more traditional culture, with which it continually and often bitterly competed. The older culture expressed the outlook of generally less affluent, less urban, more provincial Americans—men and women who continued to revere traditional values and customs and who feared and resented modernist threats to their way of life. The result of their fears was a series of harsh cultural controversies.

Prohibition

When the prohibition of the sale and manufacture of alcohol went into effect in January 1920, it had the support of most members of the middle class and most of those who considered themselves progressives. Within a year, however, it had become clear that the "noble experiment," as its defenders called it, was not working well. Prohibition did substantially reduce drinking, at least in some regions of the country. But it also produced conspicuous and growing violations that made the law an almost immediate source of disillusionment and controversy.

The government hired only 1,500 agents to enforce prohibition, and in many places they received little help from local law enforcement agencies. Before long, it was almost as easy to acquire illegal alcohol in much of the country as it had once been to acquire legal alcohol. And since an enormous, lucrative industry was now barred to legitimate businessmen, organized-crime figures took it over.

Many middle-class progressives who had originally supported prohibition soon soured on the experiment. But an enormous constituency of provincial, largely rural, Protestant Americans continued vehemently to defend it. To them, prohibition had always meant more than drinking. It represented the effort of an older America to maintain its dominance in a society in which they were becoming relatively less powerful. Drinking, which they associated with the modern city and with Catholic immigrants, became a symbol of the new culture they believed was displacing them.

As the decade proceeded, opponents of prohibition (or "wets," as they came to be known) gained steadily in influence. Not until 1933, however, when the Great Depression added weight to their appeals, were they finally able effectively to challenge the "drys" and win repeal of the Eighteenth Amendment.

Nativism and the Klan

As with prohibition (itself in part a result of old-stock Americans trying to discipline the new immigrant population), agitation for a curb on foreign immigration to the United States had begun in the nineteenth century; and as with prohibition, it had gathered strength in the years before the war largely because of the support of middle-class progressives. Such concerns had not been sufficient in the first years of the century to win passage of curbs on immigration; but in the years immediately following the war, when immigration began to be associated with radicalism, popular sentiment on behalf of restriction grew rapidly.

In 1921, Congress passed an emergency immigration act, establishing a quota system by which annual immigration from any country could not exceed 3 percent of the number of persons of that nationality who had been in the United States in 1910. The new law cut immigration from 800,000 to 300,000 in any single year, but the nativists remained unsatisfied. The National Origins Act of 1924 banned immigration from east Asia entirely and reduced the quota for Europeans from 3 to 2 percent. The quota would be based, moreover, not on the 1910 census, but on the census of 1890, a

THE KU KLUX KLAN IN WASHINGTON, 1926 So powerful was the Ku Klux Klan in the mid-1920s that its members felt emboldened to march openly and defiantly down the streets of major cities—even down Pennsylvania Avenue in Washington, in the shadow of the Capitol of the United States.

year in which there had been far fewer southern and eastern Europeans in the country. What immigration there was, in other words, would heavily favor northwestern Europeans—people of "Nordic" or "Teutonic" stock. Five years later, a further restriction set a rigid limit of 150,000 immigrants a year. In the years that followed, immigration officials seldom permitted even half that number actually to enter the country.

But the nativism of the 1920s extended well beyond restricting immigration. To defenders of an older, more provincial America, the growth of large communities of foreign peoples, alien in their speech, their habits, and their values, came to seem a direct threat to their own embattled way of life. Among other things, this provincial nativism helped instigate the rebirth of the Ku Klux Klan as a major force in American society. The first Klan, founded during Reconstruction, had died in the 1870s. But in 1915, shortly after the premiere of the film *The Birth of a Nation*, which celebrated the early Klan, a new group of Southerners established a modern version of the society. At first the new Klan, like the old, was largely concerned with intimidating blacks. After World War I, however, concern about blacks gradually became secondary to concern about Catholics, Jews, and foreigners. At that point, membership in the Klan expanded rapidly and dramatically, not just in the small towns and rural areas of the South but in industrial cities in the North and Midwest. By 1924, there were reportedly 4 million members, and the largest state Klan was not in the South but in Indiana. Beginning in 1925, a series of scandals involving the organization's leaders precipitated a slow but steady decline in the Klan's influence.

Most Klan units (or "klaverns") tried to present their members as patriots and defenders of morality; and some did nothing more menacing than stage occasional parades and rallies. Often, however, the Klan also operated as a brutal, even violent, opponent of "alien" groups and as a defender of traditional, fundamentalist morality. Klansmen systematically terrorized blacks, Jews, Catholics, and foreigners. At times, they did so violently, through public whipping, tarring and feathering, arson, and lynching. What the Klan feared, however, was not simply "foreign" or "racially impure" groups; it was anyone who posed a challenge to traditional values. Klansmen persecuted not only immigrants and blacks but those white Protestants they considered guilty of irreligion, sexual promiscuity, or drunkenness. The Ku Klux Klan, in short, was fighting not just to preserve racial homogeneity but to defend its definition of traditional culture against the values and morals of modernity.

Religious Fundamentalism

Another cultural controversy of the 1920s was the result of a bitter conflict over the place of religion in contemporary society. By 1921, American Protestantism was already divided into two warring camps. On one side stood the modernists: mostly urban, middle-class people who had attempted to adapt religion to the teachings of modern science and to the realities of their modern, secular society. On the other side stood the fundamentalists: provincial, largely (although not exclusively) rural men and women fighting to preserve traditional faith and to maintain the centrality of religion in American life. The fundamentalists were outraged at the abandonment of traditional beliefs in the face of scientific discoveries. They insisted the Bible was to be interpreted literally. Above all, they opposed the teachings of Charles Darwin, who had openly challenged the biblical story of the Creation. Human beings had not evolved from lower orders of animals, the fundamentalists insisted. They had been created by God, as described in the Book of Genesis.

Fundamentalism was a highly evangelical movement, interested in spreading the doctrine to new groups. Evangelists, among them the celebrated former professional baseball player Billy Sunday, traveled from state to state (particularly in the South and parts of the West) attracting huge crowds to their revival meetings. Protestant modernists looked on much of this activity with condescension and amusement. But by the mid-1920s, to the great alarm of modernists, evangelical fundamentalism was gaining political strength in some states with its demands for legislation to forbid the teaching of evolution in the public schools. In Tennessee in March 1925, the legislature actually adopted a measure making it illegal for any public school teacher "to teach any theory that denies the story of the divine creation of man as taught in the Bible."

When the fledgling American Civil Liberties Union (ACLU) offered free counsel to any Tennessee educator willing to defy the law and become the defendant in a test case, a twenty-four-year-old biology teacher in the town of Dayton, John T. Scopes, agreed to have himself arrested. And when the ACLU decided to send the famous attorney Clarence Darrow to defend Scopes, the aging William Jennings Bryan (now an important fundamentalist spokesman) announced that he would travel to Dayton to assist the prosecution. Journalists from across the country, among them H. L. Mencken, flocked to Tennessee to cover the trial, which opened in an almost circus atmosphere. Scopes had, of course, clearly violated the law; and a verdict of guilty was a foregone conclusion, especially when the judge refused to permit "expert" testimony by evolution scholars. Scopes was fined $100, and the case was ultimately dismissed in a higher court because of a technicality. Nevertheless, Darrow scored an important victory for the modernists by calling Bryan himself to the stand to testify as an "expert on the Bible." In the course of the cross-examination, which was broadcast by radio to much of the nation, Darrow made Bryan's stubborn defense of biblical truths appear foolish and finally tricked him into admitting the possibility that not all religious dogma was subject to only one interpretation.

The Scopes trial did not resolve the conflict between fundamentalists and modernists. Four other states soon proceeded to pass antievolution laws of their own, and the issue continued to smolder for decades.

The Democrats' Ordeal

The anguish of provincial Americans attempting to defend an embattled way of life proved particularly troubling to the Democratic party, which was seriously debilitated during the 1920s as a result of tensions between its urban and rural factions. More than the Republicans, the Democrats consisted of a diverse coalition of interest groups, linked to the party more by local tradition than common commitment. Among those interest groups were prohibitionists, Klansmen, and fundamentalists on one side and Catholics, urban workers, and immigrants on the other.

In 1924, the tensions between them proved devastating. At the Democratic National Convention in New York that summer, a bitter conflict broke out over the platform when the party's urban wing attempted to win approval of planks calling for the repeal of prohibition and a denunciation of the Klan. Both planks narrowly failed. More serious was a deadlock in the balloting for a presidential candidate. Urban Democrats supported Alfred E. Smith, the Irish Catholic Tammanyite who had risen to become a progressive governor of New York; rural Democrats backed William McAdoo, Woodrow Wilson's Treasury secretary (and son-in-law), later to become a senator from California, who had skillfully positioned himself to win the support of Southern and Western delegates suspicious of Tammany Hall and modern urban life. For 103 ballots, the convention dragged on, until finally both Smith and McAdoo withdrew and the party settled on a compromise: the corporate lawyer John W. Davis.

A similar schism plagued the Democrats again in 1928, when Al Smith finally secured his party's nomination for president after another acrimonious but less prolonged battle. He was not, however, able to unite his divided party—in part because of widespread anti-Catholic sentiment, especially in the South; and in part because of Smith's own conspicuous New York provincialism. He was the first Democrat since the Civil War not to carry the entire South. Elsewhere, although he did well in large cities, he carried no states at all except Massachusetts and Rhode Island. Smith's opponent, and the victor in the presidential election, was a man who perhaps more than any other personified the modern, prosperous, middle-class society of the New Era: Herbert Hoover. The business civilization of the 1920s, with its new institutions, fashions, and values, continued to arouse the animosity of large portions of the population; but the majority of the American people appeared to have accepted and approved it. In 1928, at least, the New Era seemed to be permanently enshrined—as the success of the Republican party, its political embodiment, suggested.

REPUBLICAN GOVERNMENT

For twelve years, beginning in 1921, both the presidency and the Congress rested in the hands of the Republican party—a party in which the power of reformers had greatly dwindled. For most of those years, the federal government enjoyed a warm and supportive relationship with the American business community. Yet the government of the New Era was also more

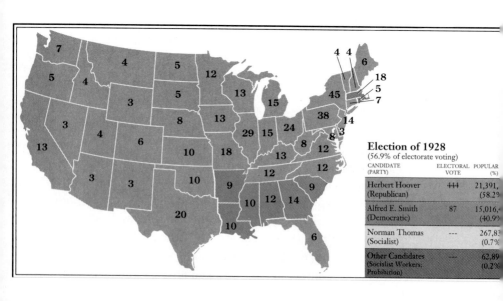

Election of 1928
(56.9% of electorate voting)

CANDIDATE (PARTY)	ELECTORAL VOTE	POPULAR (%)
Herbert Hoover (Republican)	444	21,391, (58.2%
Alfred E. Smith (Democratic)	87	15,016, (40.9%
Norman Thomas (Socialist)	---	267,83 (0.7%
Other Candidates (Socialist Workers; Prohibition)	---	62,89 (0.2%

than the passive, pliant instrument that critics often described. It attempted to serve in many respects as an active agent of economic change.

Harding and Coolidge

Nothing seemed more clearly to illustrate the unadventurous character of 1920s' politics than the characters of the two men who served as president during most of the decade: Warren G. Harding and Calvin Coolidge.

Harding was elected to the presidency in 1920, having spent many years in public life doing little of note. An undistinguished senator from Ohio, he had received the Republican presidential nomination as a result of an agreement among leaders of his party, who considered him, as one noted, a "good second-rater." Harding appointed capable men to the most important cabinet offices; he attempted to stabilize the nation's troubled foreign policy; and he displayed on occasion a vigorous humanity, as when he pardoned socialist Eugene V. Debs in 1921. But even as he attempted to rise to his office, he seemed baffled by his responsibilities, as if he recognized his own unfitness. "I am a man of limited talents from a small town," he reportedly told friends on one occasion. "I don't seem to grasp that I am President." Harding's intellectual limits were compounded by personal weaknesses: his penchant for gambling, illegal alcohol, and attractive women. Unsurprisingly, perhaps, Harding soon found himself delegating much of his authority to others: to members of his cabinet, to political cronies, to Congress, to party leaders.

Harding realized the importance of capable subordinates in an administration in which the president himself was reluctant to act. But he lacked the strength to abandon the party hacks who had helped create his political success. One of them, Harry Daugherty, the Ohio party boss principally responsible for his meteoric political ascent, he appointed attorney general. Another, New Mexico Senator Albert B. Fall, he made secretary of the interior. Members of the so-called Ohio Gang filled important offices throughout the administration.

Unknown to the public (and perhaps also to Harding), Daugherty, Fall, and others were engaged in fraud and corruption. The most spectacular scandal involved the rich naval oil reserves at Teapot Dome, Wyoming, and Elk Hills, California. At the urging of Fall, Harding transferred control of those reserves from the Navy Department to the Interior Department. Fall then secretly leased them to two wealthy businessmen and received in return nearly half a million dollars in "loans" to ease his private financial troubles.

Fall was ultimately convicted of bribery and sentenced to a year in prison; Harry Daugherty barely avoided a similar fate for his part in another scandal.

In the summer of 1923, only months before Senate investigations and press revelations brought the scandals to light, a tired and depressed Harding left Washington for a speaking tour in the West and a visit to Alaska. In Seattle late in July, he suffered severe pain, which his doctors wrongly diagnosed as food poisoning. A few days later, in San Francisco, he died. He had suffered two major heart attacks.

In many ways, Calvin Coolidge, who succeeded Harding in the presidency, was utterly different from his predecessor. Where Harding was genial, garrulous, and debauched, Coolidge was dour, silent, even puritanical. And while Harding was, if not perhaps personally corrupt, then at least tolerant of corruption in others, Coolidge seemed honest beyond reproach. In other ways, however, Harding and Coolidge were similar figures. Both took an essentially passive approach to their office.

Like Harding, Coolidge had risen to the presidency on the basis of few substantive accomplishments. Elected governor of Massachusetts in 1919,

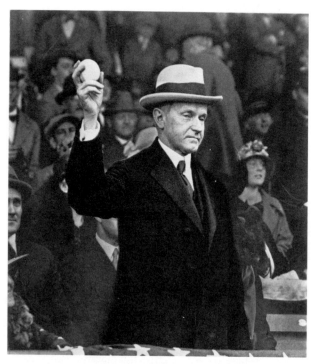

CALVIN COOLIDGE President Coolidge opens the 1924 professional baseball season in characteristically dour form.

he had won national attention with his laconic response to the Boston police strike that year: "There is no right to strike against the public safety." That was enough to make him his party's vice presidential nominee in 1920. Three years later, after Harding's death, he took the oath of office by the light of a kerosene lamp, from his father, a justice of the peace.

If anything, Coolidge was even less active as president than Harding, partly as a result of his conviction that government should interfere as little as possible in the life of the nation and partly as a result of his own personal lassitude. ("No president of my time ever slept so much," the journalist William Allen White once said of Coolidge, whose penchant for long naps was well known.) He proposed no significant legislation and took little part in the running of the nation's foreign policy. In 1924, he received his party's presidential nomination virtually unopposed. Running against John W. Davis, he won a comfortable victory: 54 percent of the popular vote and 382 of the 531 electoral votes. Robert La Follette, the candidate of the reincarnated Progressive party, received 16 percent of the popular vote but carried only his home state of Wisconsin. Coolidge probably could have won renomination and reelection in 1928. Instead, in characteristically laconic fashion, he walked into a press room one day and handed each reporter a slip of paper containing a single sentence: "I do not choose to run for president in 1928."

Government and Business

The story of Harding and Coolidge themselves, however, is only a part—and by no means the most important part—of the story of their administrations. However inert the New Era presidents may have been, much of the federal government was working effectively and efficiently during the 1920s to adapt public policy to the widely accepted goal of the time: helping business and industry operate with maximum efficiency and productivity. The close relationship between the private sector and the federal government that had been forged during World War I continued.

Secretary of the Treasury Andrew Mellon, a wealthy steel and aluminum tycoon, devoted himself to working for substantial reductions in taxes on corporate profits and personal incomes and inheritances. Largely because of his efforts, Congress cut them all by more than half. Mellon also worked closely with President Coolidge after 1924 on a series of measures to trim dramatically the already modest federal budget. The administration even managed to retire half the nation's World War I debt.

The most prominent member of the cabinet was Commerce Secretary Herbert Hoover, who considered himself, and was considered by others, a notable progressive. During his eight years in the Commerce Department, Hoover constantly encouraged voluntary cooperation in the private sector as the best avenue to stability. But the idea of voluntarism did not require that the government remain passive; on the contrary, public institutions, Hoover believed, had a duty to play an active role in creating the new, cooperative order. Above all, Hoover became the champion of the concept of business "associationalism"—a concept that envisioned the creation of national organizations of businessmen in particular industries. Through these trade associations, private entrepreneurs could, Hoover believed, stabilize their industries and promote efficiency in production and marketing. Hoover resisted those who urged that the government sanction collusion among manufacturers to fix prices. He did, however, believe that shared information and limited cooperation would keep competition from becoming destructive and thus improve the strength of the economy as a whole.

The probusiness policies of the Republican administrations were not without their critics. In Congress, progressive reformers of the old school continued to criticize the monopolistic practices of big business, to attack government's alliance with the corporate community, and to decry social injustices. Occasionally, they were able to mobilize enough support to win congressional approval of progressive legislation, most notably the McNary-Haugen plan for farmers and an ambitious proposal to use federal funds to develop public electric power projects on the Tennessee River at Muscle Shoals. But the progressive reformers lacked the power to override the presidential vetoes that their bills almost always received.

Some progressives derived encouragement from the election of Herbert Hoover—widely regarded as the most progressive member of the Harding and Coolidge administrations—to the presidency in 1928. Hoover easily defeated Al Smith, the Democratic candidate. And he entered office promising bold new efforts to solve the nation's remaining economic problems. But Hoover had few opportunities to prove himself. Less than a year after his inauguration, the nation plunged into the severest and most prolonged economic crisis in its history—a crisis that brought many of the optimistic assumptions of the New Era crashing down and launched the nation into a period of unprecedented social innovation and reform.

CHAPTER TWENTY-FIVE

The Great Depression

The Coming of the Depression ~ *The American People in Hard Times*
The Ordeal of Herbert Hoover

W E IN AMERICA today," Herbert Hoover had proclaimed in August 1928, not long before his election to the presidency, "are nearer to the final triumph over poverty than ever before in the history of any land. The poorhouse is vanishing from among us." Only fifteen months later, those words would return to haunt him, as the nation plunged into the severest and most prolonged economic depression in its history—a depression that continued in one form or another for a full decade, not only in the United States but throughout much of the rest of the world. The Depression was a traumatic experience for individual Americans, who faced unemployment, the loss of land and other property, and in some cases homelessness and starvation. It also placed great strains on the political and social fabric of the nation.

THE COMING OF THE DEPRESSION

The sudden financial collapse in 1929 came as an especially severe shock because it followed so closely a period in which the New Era seemed to be performing another series of economic miracles.

In February 1928, stock prices began a steady ascent that continued, with only a few temporary lapses, for a year and a half. Between May 1928 and September 1929, the average price of stocks rose over 40 percent. The stocks of the major industrials—the stocks that are used to determine the Dow Jones Industrial Average—doubled in value in that same period. Trading mushroomed from 2 or 3 million shares a day to over 5 million, and at times to as many as 10 or 12 million. There was, in short, a widespread speculative fever that grew steadily more intense, particularly once brokerage firms began encouraging the mania by offering absurdly easy credit to those buying stocks.

The Great Crash

In the autumn of 1929, the market began to fall apart. On October 21 and again on October 24, there were alarming declines in stock prices, in both cases followed by a temporary recovery. (The second recovery was engineered by J. P. Morgan and Company and other big bankers, who conspicuously bought up stocks to restore public confidence.) But on October 29, "Black Tuesday," all efforts to save the market failed. Sixteen million shares of stock were traded; the industrial index dropped 43 points, wiping out all the gains of the previous year; stocks in many companies became virtually worthless. Within a month stocks had lost half their September value, and they continued to decline for years after that. In July 1932, the industrial index—which had stood at 452 in September 1929—bottomed out at 58. The market remained deeply depressed for more than four years and did not fully recover for over a decade.

Popular folklore has established the stock market crash as the beginning, and even the cause, of the Great Depression. But although October 1929 might have been the first visible sign of the crisis, the Depression had earlier beginnings and more important causes.

Causes of the Depression

Economists, historians, and others have argued for decades about the causes of the Great Depression. But most agree on several things. They agree, first, that what is remarkable about the crisis is not that it occurred; periodic recessions are a normal feature of capitalist economies. What is remarkable is that it was so severe and that it lasted so long. The important question, therefore, is not so much why there was a depression but why it was such a bad one. Most observers agree, too, that a number of different factors account for the severity of the crisis, even if there is considerable disagreement about which was the most important.

One of those factors was a lack of diversification in the American economy in the 1920s. Prosperity had depended excessively on a few basic industries, notably construction and automobiles. In the late 1920s, those industries began to decline. Expenditures on construction fell from $11 billion to under $9 billion between 1926 and 1929. Automobile sales fell by more than a third in the first nine months of 1929. Newer industries were emerging to take up the slack—among them petroleum, chemicals, and plastics—but had not yet developed enough strength to compensate for the decline in other sectors.

A second important factor was the maldistribution of purchasing power and, as a result, a weakness in consumer demand. As industrial and agricultural production increased, the proportion of the profits going to farmers, workers, and other potential consumers was too small to create an adequate market for the goods the economy was producing. Even in 1929, after nearly a decade of economic growth, more than half the families in America lived on the edge of or below the minimum subsistence level—too poor to buy the goods the industrial economy was producing.

A third major problem was the credit structure of the economy. Farmers were deeply in debt—their land was mortgaged, and crop prices were too low to allow them to pay off what they owed. Small banks, especially those tied to the agricultural economy, were in constant trouble in the 1920s as their customers defaulted on loans; many of them failed. Large banks were in trouble too. Although most American bankers were very conservative, some of the nation's biggest banks were investing recklessly in the stock market or making unwise loans.

A fourth factor contributing to the coming of the Depression was America's position in international trade. Late in the 1920s, European demand for American goods began to decline. That was partly because European industry and agriculture were becoming more productive and partly because some European nations were having financial difficulties and could not afford to buy goods from overseas. But it was also because the European economy was being destabilized by the international debt structure that had emerged in the aftermath of World War I.

The international debt structure, therefore, was a fifth factor contributing to the Depression. When the war came to an end in 1918, all the European nations that had been allied with the United States owed large sums of money to American banks, sums much too large to be repaid out of their shattered economies. That was one reason why the Allies had insisted (over Woodrow Wilson's objections) on reparation payments from Germany and Austria. Reparations, they believed, would provide them with a way to pay off their own debts. But Germany and Austria were themselves in economic trouble after the war; they were no more able to pay the reparations than the Allies were able to pay their debts.

The American government refused to forgive or reduce the debts. Instead, American banks began making large loans to European governments with which they paid off their earlier loans. Thus debts (and reparations) were being paid only by piling up new and greater debts. In the late 1920s, and particularly after the American economy began to weaken in 1929, the European nations found it much more difficult to borrow money from the United States. At the same time, high American protective tariffs were making it difficult for them to sell their goods in American markets. Without any source of foreign exchange with which to repay their loans, they began to default. The collapse of the international credit structure was one of the reasons the Depression spread to Europe (and grew much worse in America) after 1931.

Progress of the Depression

The stock market crash of 1929 did not so much cause the Depression, then, as help trigger a chain of events that exposed longstanding weaknesses in the American economy. During the next three years, the crisis grew steadily worse.

The most serious problem was the collapse of much of the banking system. Over 9,000 American banks either went bankrupt or closed their doors to avoid bankruptcy between 1930 and 1933. Depositors lost over $2.5 billion in deposits. Partly as a result of these banking closures, the nation's money supply greatly decreased. The total money supply, according to some measurements, fell by more than a third between 1930 and 1933. The declining money supply meant a decline in purchasing power, and thus deflation. Manufacturers and merchants began reducing prices, cutting back on production, and laying off workers. Some economists argue that a severe depression could have been avoided if the Federal Reserve system had acted more responsibly. Late in 1931, in a misguided effort to build international confidence in the dollar, it raised interest rates, which contracted the money supply even further and hastened the demise of many banks and corporations.

The collapse was so rapid and so devastating that at the time it created only bewilderment among many of those who attempted to explain it. The American gross national product plummeted from over $104 billion in 1929 to $76.4 billion in 1932—a 25 percent decline in three years. In 1929, Americans had spent $16.2 billion to promote capital growth; in 1933, they invested only a third of a billion. The consumer price index declined 25 percent between 1929 and 1933; the wholesale price index, 32 percent.

SELLING APPLES, NEW YORK CITY In the fall of 1931 and again in the fall of 1932, large numbers of unemployed took to selling apples on the streets of major cities and became in the process a popular symbol of economic despair.

Gross farm income dropped from $12 billion to $5 billion in four years. By 1932, according to the relatively crude estimates of the time, 25 percent of the American work force was unemployed. (Some believe the figure was even higher.) For the rest of the decade, unemployment averaged nearly 20 percent, never dropping below 15 percent. Up to another one-third of the work force was "underemployed"—experiencing major reductions in wages, hours, or both.

THE AMERICAN PEOPLE IN HARD TIMES

Someone asked the British economist John Maynard Keynes in the 1930s whether he was aware of any historical era comparable to the Great Depression. "Yes," Keynes replied. "It was called the Dark Ages, and it lasted 400 years." The Depression did not last 400 years. It did, however, bring unprecedented despair to the economies of the United States and much of the Western world. And it had far-reaching effects on American society and culture.

Unemployment and Relief

The suffering extended into every area of society. In the industrial North-east and Midwest, cities were becoming virtually paralyzed by unemployment. Cleveland, Ohio, for example, had an unemployment rate of 50 percent in 1932; Akron, 60 percent; Toledo, 80 percent. Unemployed workers walked through the streets day after day looking for jobs that did not exist. An increasing number of families were turning to state and local public relief systems, just to be able to eat. But those systems, which in the 1920s had served only a small number of indigents, were totally unequipped to handle the new demands being placed on them. In many cities, therefore, relief simply collapsed. Private charities attempted to supplement the public relief efforts, but the problem was far beyond their capabilities as well. State governments felt pressure to expand their own assistance to the unemployed; but tax revenues were declining along with everything else, and state leaders balked at placing additional strains on already tight budgets.

In rural areas conditions were in many ways worse. Farm income declined by 60 percent between 1929 and 1932. A third of all American farmers lost their land. In addition, a large area of agricultural settlement in the Great Plains was suffering from a catastrophic natural disaster: one of

DOWN AND OUT, 1930 A "bread line" forms outside a rescue society. Evangelical missions such as this one, which was originally established to encourage Chinese immigrants to convert to Christianity, shifted their energies to offering assistance to the unemployed as the crisis of the Great Depression grew.

the worst droughts in the history of the nation. Beginning in 1930, the region, which came to be known as the "Dust Bowl" and which stretched north from Texas into the Dakotas, experienced a steady decline in rainfall and an accompanying increase in heat. The drought continued for a decade, turning what had once been fertile farm regions into virtual deserts. It is a measure of how productive American farmers were and how depressed the market for agricultural goods had become that even with these disastrous conditions, the farm economy continued through the 1930s to produce far more than American consumers could afford to buy.

Many farmers, like many urban unemployed, left their homes in search of work. In the South, in particular, many dispossessed farmers—black and white—simply wandered from town to town, hoping to find jobs or hand-outs. Hundreds of thousands of families from the Dust Bowl (often known as "Okies," since many came from Oklahoma) traveled to California and other states, where they found conditions little better than those they had left. Owning no land of their own, many worked as agricultural migrants, traveling from farm to farm picking fruit and other crops at starvation wages.

African-Americans and the Depression

Most African-Americans had not shared very much in the prosperity of the previous decade; they now experienced more unemployment, homeless-ness, malnutrition, and disease than they had in the past, and more than most whites experienced.

As the Depression began, over half of all black Americans still lived in the South. Most were farmers. The collapse of prices for cotton and other staple crops left some with no income at all. Many left the land altogether—either by choice or because they had been evicted by landlords who no longer found the sharecropping system profitable. Some migrated to South-ern cities. But there, unemployed whites believed they had first claim to what work there was, and some now began to take positions as janitors, street cleaners, and domestic servants, displacing the blacks who formerly occu-pied them. By 1932, over half the blacks in the South were without employ-ment. And what limited relief there was went almost invariably to whites first.

Unsurprisingly, therefore, many black Southerners—perhaps 400,000 in all—left the South in the 1930s and journeyed to the cities of the North. There they generally found less blatant discrimination. But conditions were in most respects little better than those in the South. In New York, black unemployment was nearly 50 percent. In other cities, it was higher. Two million African-Americans were on some form of relief by 1932.

Traditional patterns of segregation and disfranchisement in the South survived the Depression largely unchallenged. But a few particularly notorious examples of racism did attract the attention of the nation. The most celebrated was the Scottsboro case. In March 1931, nine black teen-agers were taken off a freight train in northern Alabama (in a small town near Scottsboro) and arrested for vagrancy and disorder. Later, two white women who had also been riding the train accused them of rape. In fact, there was overwhelming evidence, medical and otherwise, that the women had not been raped at all; they may have made their accusations out of fear of being arrested themselves. Nevertheless, an all-white jury in Alabama quickly convicted all nine of the "Scottsboro boys" (as they were known to both friends and foes) and sentenced eight of them to death.

The Supreme Court overturned the convictions in 1932, and a series of new trials began that gradually attracted national attention. The International Labor Defense, an organization associated with the Communist party, came to the aid of the accused youths and began to publicize the case. The trials continued throughout the 1930s. Although the white Southern juries who sat on the case never acquitted any of the defendants, all of them eventually gained their freedom—four because the charges were dropped, four because of early paroles, and one because he escaped. The last of the Scottsboro defendants did not leave prison until 1950.

The Depression was a time of important changes in the role and behavior of leading black organizations. The NAACP, for example, began to work diligently to win a position for blacks within the emerging labor movement, supporting the formation of the Congress of Industrial Organizations and helping break down racial barriers within labor unions. Partly as a result of such efforts, more than half a million blacks were able to join the labor movement. In the steelworkers union, for example, African-Americans constituted about 20 percent of the membership.

Hispanics in Depression America

Similar patterns of discrimination confronted many Mexicans and Mexican-Americans. The Hispanic population of the United States had been growing steadily since early in the century, largely in California and other areas of the Southwest through massive immigration from Mexico (which was specifically excluded from the immigration restriction laws of the

1920s). Chicanos (as Mexican-Americans are sometimes known) filled many of the same menial jobs there that blacks had traditionally filled in other regions. Some farmed small, marginal tracts. Some became agricultural migrants, traveling from region to region harvesting fruit, lettuce, and other crops. Even during the prosperous 1920s, it had been a precarious existence. The Depression made things significantly worse. As in the South, unemployed whites in the Southwest demanded jobs held by Hispanics, jobs that whites had previously considered beneath them. Thus Mexican unemployment rose quickly to levels far higher than those for whites. Some Mexicans were, in effect, forced to leave the country by officials who arbitrarily removed them from relief rolls or simply rounded them up and transported them across the border. Perhaps half a million Chicanos left the United States for Mexico, many involuntarily, in the first years of the Depression.

Those who remained faced persistent discrimination. Most relief programs excluded Mexicans from their rolls or offered them benefits far below those available to whites. Hispanics generally had limited access to American schools. Many hospitals refused them admission. Unlike American blacks, who had established certain educational and social facilities of their own in response to discrimination, Hispanics generally had nowhere to turn. Even many who possessed American citizenship found themselves treated like foreigners.

There were, occasionally, signs of organized resistance by Mexican-Americans themselves, most notably in California, where some formed a union of migrant farm workers. But harsh repression by local growers and the public authorities allied with them prevented such organizations from having much impact. Like African-American farm workers, many Hispanics began as a result to migrate to cities such as Los Angeles, where they lived in a poverty comparable to that of urban blacks in the South and Northeast.

Women and Families in the Great Depression

The economic crisis served in many ways to strengthen the widespread belief that a woman's proper place was in the home. Most men and many women believed that with employment so scarce, what work there was should go to men. There was a particularly strong belief that no woman whose husband was employed should accept a job. Indeed, from 1932 until 1937, it was illegal for more than one member of a family to hold a federal civil-service job.

But the widespread assumption that married women, at least, should not work outside the home did not stop them from doing so. Both single and married women worked in the 1930s, despite public condemnation of the practice, because they or their families needed the money. In fact, the largest new group of female workers consisted of precisely those people who, according to popular attitudes, were supposed to be leaving the labor market: wives and mothers. By the end of the Depression, 25 percent more women were working than had been doing so at the beginning.

This occurred despite considerable obstacles. Professional opportunities for women declined because unemployed men began moving into professions such as teaching and social work that had previously been considered women's fields. Female industrial workers were more likely to be laid off or to experience wage reductions than their male counterparts. But white women also had certain advantages in the workplace. The nonprofessional jobs that women traditionally held—as salesclerks and stenographers, and in other service positions—were less likely to disappear than the predominantly male jobs in heavy industry.

Black women, however, enjoyed few such advantages. In the South, in particular, they suffered massive unemployment because of a great reduction of domestic service jobs. As many as half of all black working women lost their jobs in the 1930s. Even so, at the end of the 1930s, 38 percent of black women were employed, as compared with 24 percent of white women. That was because black women—both married and unmarried—had always been more likely to work than white women, less out of preference than out of economic necessity.

For American feminists, the Depression years were, on the whole, a time of frustration. Although economic pressures pushed more women into the work force, those same pressures helped to erode the frail support feminists had won in the 1920s for the idea of women becoming economically and professionally independent. In the difficult years of the 1930s, such aspirations seemed to many to be less important than dealing with economic hardship. By the end of the 1930s, American feminism had reached its lowest ebb in nearly a century.

The economic hardships of the Depression years placed great strains on American families. Middle-class families that had become accustomed in the 1920s to a steadily rising standard of living now found themselves plunged suddenly into uncertainty, because of unemployment or the reduction of incomes among those who remained employed. Some working-class families too had achieved a precarious prosperity in the 1920s and saw their gains disappear in the 1930s.

A M E R I C A N   V O I C E S

A Pennsylvania Mother Responds to the Depression, December 1930

NOW THAT OUR income is but $15.60 a week (their are five of us My husband Three little children and myself). My husband who is a world war Veteran . . . became desperate and applied for Compensation or a pension from the Government and was turned down and that started me thinking. [The government should provide] enough to pay all world war veterans a pension, dysabeled or not dysabeled and there by relieve a lot of suffering, and banish resentment that causes Rebellions and Bolshevism. Oh why is it that it is allways a bunch of overley rich, selfish, dumb, ignorant money hogs that persist in being Senitors, legislatures, representitives. Where would they and their possessions be if it were not for the Common Soldier, the common laborer that is compelled to work for a starvation wage. for I tell you again the hog of a Landlord gets his there is not enough left for the necessaries if a man has three or more children. . . . In the Public Schools our little children stand at salute and recite a "rig ma role" in which is mentioned "Justice to all" What a lie, what a naked lie, when honest, law abiding citizens, decendents of Revilutionary heros, Civil War heros, and World war heros are denied the priviledge of owning their own homes, that foundation of good citizenship, good morals, and the very foundation of good government the world over. . . . Oh for a few Statesmen, oh for but one statesman, as fearless as Abraham Lincoln, the amancipator who died for us.

SOURCE: Robert S. McElvaine, ed., *Down & Out in the Great Depression* (Chapel Hill: University of North Carolina Press, 1983), pp. 47–48.

Such circumstances forced many families to retreat from the consumer patterns they had developed in the 1920s. Women often returned to sewing clothes for themselves and their families and to preserving their own food rather than buying such products in stores. Others engaged in home businesses—taking in laundry, selling baked goods, accepting boarders. Many households expanded to include more distant relatives. Parents often moved in with their children and grandparents with their grandchildren, or vice versa.

But the Depression also worked to erode the strength of many family units. There was a decline in the divorce rate, but largely because divorce was now too expensive for some. More common was the informal breakup of families, particularly the desertion of families by unemployed men trying to escape the humiliation of being unable to earn a living. The marriage rate and the birth rate both declined for the first time since the early nineteenth century.

Values and Culture

Prosperity and industrial growth had done much to shape American values in the 1920s. Mainstream culture, at least, had celebrated affluence and consumerism and had stressed the importance of personal gratification through both. Many Americans assumed, therefore, that the experience of hard times would have profound effects on the nation's social values.

In general, however, American social values seemed to change relatively little in response to the Depression. Rather, many people responded to hard times by redoubling their commitment to familiar ideas and goals.

No assumption would seem to have been more vulnerable to erosion during the Depression than the belief that the individual was in control of his or her own fate, that anyone displaying sufficient talent and industry could become a success. And in some respects, the economic crisis did work to undermine the traditional "success ethic" in America. Many people began to look to government for assistance; many learned to blame corporate moguls, international bankers, "economic royalists," and others for their distress. Yet the Depression did not destroy the success ethic.

The survival of the ideals of work and individual advancement was evident in many ways, not least in the reactions of those most traumatized by the Depression: conscientious working people who suddenly found themselves without employment. Some expressed anger and struck out at the economic system. Many, however, seemed to blame themselves. That was one reason why the effects of the Depression were sometimes hard to see, because the unemployed tended to hide themselves, unwilling to display to the world what many of them considered their own personal failure.

At the same time, millions responded eagerly to reassurances that they could, through their own efforts, restore themselves to prosperity and success. Dale Carnegie's *How to Win Friends and Influence People* (1936), a self-help manual preaching individual initiative, was one of the best-selling books of the decade. Harry Emerson Fosdick, a Protestant theologian who similarly preached the virtues of positive thinking and individual initiative, attracted large audiences with his radio addresses.

Not all Americans, of course, responded to the crisis of the Depression so passively. Many men and women believed that the economic problems of their time were the fault of society, not of individuals, and that some collective social response was necessary. Such beliefs found expression in, among other places, American artistic and intellectual life.

Just as many progressives had become alarmed when, early in the twentieth century, they "discovered" the existence of widespread poverty in the cities, so many Americans were shocked during the 1930s at their discovery of debilitating rural poverty. Perhaps most effective in conveying the dimensions of rural poverty was a group of documentary photographers, many of them employed by the federal Farm Security Administration in the late 1930s, who traveled through the South recording the nature of agricultural life. Men such as Roy Stryker, Walker Evans, Arthur Rothstein, and Ben Shahn and women such as Margaret Bourke-White and Dorothea Lange produced memorable studies of farm families and their surroundings, studies designed to show the savage impact of a hostile environment on its victims.

Many writers, similarly, turned away from the personal concerns of the 1920s and devoted themselves to exposés of social injustice. Erskine Caldwell's *Tobacco Road* (1932), which later became a long-running play, was an exposé of poverty in the rural South. James Agee's *Let Us Now Praise Famous Men* (1941), with photographs by Walker Evans, was a careful, nonjudgmental description of the lives of three poor rural families in the South. Richard Wright, a major African-American novelist, exposed the plight of residents of the urban ghetto in *Native Son* (1940). John Steinbeck's *The Grapes of Wrath* (1939) portrayed the trials of a migrant family in California, concluding with an open call for collective social action against injustice. John Dos Passos's *U.S.A.* trilogy (1930) openly attacked modern capitalism. Playwright Clifford Odets provided an explicit demonstration of the appeal of political radicalism in *Waiting for Lefty* (1935).

But the cultural products of the 1930s that attracted the widest popular audiences were those that diverted attention away from the Depression. The two most powerful instruments of popular culture in the 1930s—radio and the movies—provided mostly light and diverting entertainment. Although radio stations occasionally carried socially and politically provocative programs, the staple of broadcasting was escapism: comedies such as *Amos 'n Andy*, adventures such as *Superman*, *Dick Tracy*, and *The Lone Ranger*, and other entertainment programs. Hollywood continued to exercise tight control over its products through its resilient censor Will Hays, who ensured that most movies carried only safe, conventional messages. A few films, such as the adaptation of *The Grapes of Wrath* (1940), did explore political themes. Director Frank Capra provided a muted social message in several of his comedies—*Mr. Deeds Goes to Town* (1936), *Mr. Smith Goes to Washington* (1939), and *Meet John Doe* (1941)—which celebrated the virtues of the small town and the decency of the common people in contrast to the selfish, corrupt values of the city and the urban rich. Gangster films and westerns celebrated violence and implicitly glamorized resistance to authority. Often, however, the commercial films of the 1930s were deliberately and explicitly escapist: lavish musicals and "wacky" comedies designed to divert audiences from their troubles and, very often, satisfy their fantasies about quick and easy wealth.

Popular literature, similarly, offered Americans an escape from the Depression. Two of the best-selling novels of the decade were romantic sagas set in bygone eras: Margaret Mitchell's *Gone with the Wind* (1936) and Hervey Allen's *Anthony Adverse* (1933). Leading magazines, and particularly such popular new photographic journals as *Life*, focused on fashions, stunts, and eye-catching scenery. Even the newsreels distributed to movie theaters across the country tended to give more attention to beauty contests and ship launchings than to the Depression itself.

The Allure of the Left

For a relatively small but important group of Americans—intellectuals, artists, workers, African-Americans, and others who became disenchanted for various reasons with the prevailing values of American life—the Depression produced a commitment, for a time at least, to radical politics.

The importance of the 1936 Spanish Civil War to many American intellectuals was a good example of how the left produced a sense of commitment and purpose in individual lives. The battle against the Spanish fascists of Francisco Franco (who was receiving support from Hitler and Mussolini) attracted a substantial group of young Americans, more than 3,000 in all, who formed the "Abraham Lincoln Brigade" and traveled to Spain to join in the fight. About a third of its members died in combat; but those who survived remembered the experience with pride, as one of the great moments of their lives.

Instrumental in creating the Lincoln brigade, and directing many of its activities, was the American Communist party. Its membership reached perhaps 100,000 at its peak in the mid-1930s. For several years beginning in 1935, the party dropped its insistence on working completely apart from other organizations and began to advocate a democratic alliance of all antifascist groups in the United States, a "Popular Front." It began to praise Franklin Roosevelt and John L. Lewis, a powerful (and strongly anticommunist) labor leader. It adopted the slogan "Communism is twentieth-century Americanism."

The party was active in organizing the unemployed in the early 1930s and staged a hunger march in Washington, D.C., in 1931. Party members were among the most effective union organizers in some industries. And the party was one of the few political organizations to take a firm stand in favor of racial justice; its active defense of the Scottsboro defendants was but one example of its efforts to ally itself with the aspirations of African-Americans. It also helped organize a union of black sharecroppers in Alabama, which resisted—in several instances violently—efforts of white landowners and authorities to displace them from their farms.

But despite its efforts to appear a patriotic organization, the American Communist party was always under the close and rigid supervision of the Soviet Union. Its leaders took their orders from the Comintern in Moscow. Most members obediently followed the "party line." The subordination of the party leadership to the Soviet Union was most clearly demonstrated in 1939, when Stalin signed a nonaggression pact with Nazi Germany. Moscow then sent orders to the American Communist party to abandon the Popular Front idea and return to its old stance of harsh criticism of American liberals; and the leaders in the United States immediately obeyed—although thousands of disillusioned members left the party as a result.

The Socialist party of America, now under the leadership of Norman Thomas, also cited the economic crisis as evidence of the failure of capitalism and sought vigorously to win public support for its own political program. Among other things, it attempted to mobilize support among the rural poor. The Southern Tenant Farmers Union (STFU), supported by the party, attempted to create a biracial coalition of sharecroppers, tenant farmers, and others to demand economic reform. Neither the STFU nor the party itself, however, made any real progress toward establishing socialism as a major force in American politics. By 1936, in fact, membership in the Socialist party had fallen below 20,000.

THE ORDEAL OF HERBERT HOOVER

Herbert Hoover began his presidency in March 1929 believing, like most Americans, that the nation faced a bright and prosperous future. For the first six months of his administration, he attempted to expand the policies he had advocated during his eight years as secretary of commerce, policies that would, he believed, complete a stable system of cooperative individualism and sustain a successful economy. The economic crisis that began before the year was out forced the president to deal with a new set of problems; but for most of the rest of his term, he continued to rely on the principles that had always governed his public life.

The Hoover Program

Hoover's first response to the Depression was to attempt to restore public confidence in the economy. "The fundamental business of this country, that is, production and distribution of commodities," he said in 1930, "is on a sound and prosperous basis." Subsequently, he summoned leaders of business, labor, and agriculture to the White House and urged upon them a program of voluntary cooperation for recovery. He implored businessmen not to cut production or lay off workers; he talked labor leaders into forgoing demands for higher wages or better hours. But by mid-1931, economic conditions had deteriorated so much that the structure of voluntary cooperation he had erected collapsed. Frightened industrialists soon began cutting production, laying off workers, and slashing wages.

Hoover also attempted to use government spending as a tool for fighting the Depression. The president proposed to Congress an increase of $423 million—a substantial sum by the standards of the time—in federal public works programs; and he exhorted state and local governments to fund public construction. But Hoover was not willing to spend enough money,

HERBERT HOOVER RECEIVING A LOAD OF POTATOES The Maine Potato Growers Association sent a team of oxen to Washington with a load of Maine potatoes in 1931. They presented them as a gift to President Hoover on the White House lawn on November 23, to remind him of the difficulties that faced the agricultural economy as the Great Depression worsened.

or to spend it for a long enough time, to do very much good. And when economic conditions worsened, he became less willing to increase government spending, worrying instead about maintaining federal solvency. In 1932, at the depth of the Depression, he proposed a tax increase to help the government avoid a deficit.

Even before the stock market crash, Hoover had begun to construct a program to assist the troubled agricultural economy. In April 1929, he proposed the Agricultural Marketing Act, which established for the first time a major government bureaucracy to help farmers maintain prices. A federally sponsored Farm Board would administer a budget of $500 million, from which it could make loans to national marketing cooperatives or establish corporations to buy surpluses and thus raise prices. At the same time, Hoover attempted to protect American farmers from international competition by raising agricultural tariffs. The Smoot-Hawley Tariff of 1930 contained protective increases on seventy-five farm products.

Neither the Agricultural Marketing Act nor the Smoot-Hawley Tariff ultimately helped American farmers significantly. The Marketing Act relied on voluntary cooperation among farmers and gave the government no authority to effect what the agricultural economy most badly needed: a limit on production. Prices continued to fall despite its efforts. The Smoot-Hawley Tariff provoked foreign governments to enact trade restrictions of their own in reprisal, further diminishing the market for American agricultural goods.

By the spring of 1931, Herbert Hoover's political position had deteriorated considerably. In the 1930 congressional elections, Democrats won control of the House and made substantial inroads in the Senate by promising increased government assistance to the economy. Many Americans held the president personally to blame for the crisis. Shantytowns established on the outskirts of cities were labeled "Hoovervilles." Democrats urged the president to support more vigorous programs of relief and public spending. Hoover, instead, seized on a slight improvement in economic conditions early in 1931 as proof that his policies were working.

The international financial panic of the spring of 1931 destroyed the illusion that the economic crisis was coming to an end. Throughout the 1920s, European nations had depended on loans from American banks to allow them to make payments on their debts. After 1929, when they could no longer get such loans, the financial fabric of several European nations began to unravel. In May 1931, the largest bank in Austria collapsed. Over the next several months, panic gripped the financial institutions of neighboring countries. The American economy rapidly declined to new lows.

By the time Congress convened in December 1931, conditions had grown so desperate that Hoover supported a series of measures designed to keep endangered banks afloat and protect homeowners from foreclosure on their mortgages. More important was a bill passed in January 1932 establishing the Reconstruction Finance Corporation (RFC), a government agency whose purpose was to provide federal loans to troubled banks, railroads, and other businesses. It even made funds available to local governments to support public works projects and assist relief efforts. Unlike some earlier Hoover programs, it operated on a large scale. In 1932, the RFC had a budget of $1.5 billion for public works alone.

Nevertheless, the new agency failed to deal directly or forcefully enough with the real problems of the economy to produce any significant recovery. Because the RFC was permitted to lend funds only to those financial institutions with sufficient collateral, much of its money went to large banks and corporations. And at Hoover's insistence, it helped finance only those public works projects that promised ultimately to pay for themselves (toll bridges, public housing, and others). Above all, the RFC did not have enough money to make any real impact on the Depression; and it did not even spend all the money it had. Of the $300 million available to support local relief efforts, the RFC lent out only $30 million in 1932. Of the $1.5 billion public works budget, it released only about 20 percent.

The Rise of Popular Protest

For the first several years of the Depression, most Americans were either too stunned or too confused to raise any effective protest. By the middle of 1932, however, dissident voices began to be heard.

In the Midwest, farmers called for legislation similar to the McNary-Haugen Bill of the 1920s by which the government would guarantee them a return on their crops at least equal to the cost of production. Lobbyists from the larger farm organizations pressured members of Congress to act, and some disgruntled farmers staged public protests in the capital. But neither the president nor Congress showed any signs of movement.

In the summer of 1932, a group of unhappy farm owners gathered in Des Moines, Iowa, to establish a new organization: the Farmers' Holiday Association, which endorsed the withholding of farm products from the market—in effect a farmers' strike. The strike began in August in western Iowa, spread briefly to a few neighboring areas, and succeeded in blockading several markets; but in the end it dissolved in faiiure. The scope of the effort was too modest to affect farm prices, and many farmers in the region refused to cooperate in any case. Nevertheless, the uprising created considerable consternation in state governments in the farm belt and even more in Washington, where the president and much of Congress were facing a national election.

A more celebrated protest movement emerged from a less likely quarter: American veterans. In 1924, Congress had approved the payment of a $1,000 bonus to all those who had served in World War I, the money to be paid beginning in 1945. By 1932, however, many veterans were demanding that the bonus be paid immediately. Hoover, concerned about balancing the budget, refused to comply. In June, more than 20,000 veterans, members of the self-proclaimed Bonus Expeditionary Force, or "Bonus Army," marched into Washington, built crude camps around the city, and promised to stay until Congress approved legislation to pay the bonus. A few of the veterans departed in July, after Congress had voted down their proposal. Most, however, remained where they were.

Their continued presence in Washington was an embarrassment to Herbert Hoover. Finally, in mid-July, he ordered police to clear the marchers out of several abandoned federal buildings in which they had been staying. A few marchers threw rocks at the police, and someone opened fire; two veterans fell dead. Hoover considered the incident evidence of dangerous radicalism. He ordered the United States Army to assist the police in clearing out the buildings.

General Douglas MacArthur, the army chief of staff, carried out the mission himself (with the assistance of his aide, Dwight D. Eisenhower) and greatly exceeded the president's orders. He led the Third Cavalry (under the command of George S. Patton), two infantry regiments, a machine-gun detachment, and six tanks down Pennsylvania Avenue in pursuit of the Bonus Army. The veterans fled in terror. MacArthur followed them across the Anacostia River, where he ordered the soldiers to burn their tent city to the ground. More than 100 marchers were injured. One baby died.

The incident served as perhaps the final blow to Hoover's already battered political standing. Hoover's own cold and gloomy personality did nothing to change the public image of him as aloof and unsympathetic to distressed people. The Great Engineer, the personification of the optimistic days of the 1920s, had become a symbol of the nation's failure to deal effectively with its startling reversal of fortune.

The Election of 1932

As the 1932 presidential election approached, few people doubted the outcome. The Republican party dutifully renominated Herbert Hoover for a second term in office, but the lugubrious atmosphere of their convention made it clear that few delegates believed he could win. The Democrats, in the meantime, gathered jubilantly in Chicago to nominate the governor of New York, Franklin Delano Roosevelt.

Roosevelt had been a well-known figure in the party for many years already. A Hudson Valley aristocrat, a distant cousin of Theodore Roosevelt (a connection strengthened by his marriage in 1904 to the president's niece,

Eleanor), and a handsome, charming young man, he progressed rapidly: from a seat in the New York State legislature to a position as assistant secretary of the navy under Woodrow Wilson during World War I to his party's vice presidential nomination in 1920 on the ill-fated ticket with James M. Cox. Less than a year later, he was stricken with polio. Although he was never again able to walk without the use of crutches and braces, he built up sufficient physical strength to return to politics in 1928. When Al Smith received the Democratic nomination for president that year, Roosevelt was elected to succeed him as governor. In 1930, he easily won reelection.

Roosevelt worked no miracles in New York, but he did initiate enough positive programs of government assistance to be able to present himself as a more energetic and imaginative leader than Hoover. Equally important, he avoided such divisive cultural issues as religion and prohibition; and by emphasizing the economic grievances that most Democrats shared, he assembled a coalition within the party that enabled him to win his party's nomination. In a dramatic break with tradition, he flew to Chicago to address the convention in person and accept the nomination.

In the course of his acceptance speech, Roosevelt aroused the delegates with his ringing promise: "I pledge you, I pledge myself, to a new deal for the American people," giving his program a name that would long endure. Neither then nor in the subsequent campaign, however, did Roosevelt give much indication of what that program would be. But Herbert Hoover's unpopularity virtually ensured Roosevelt's election.

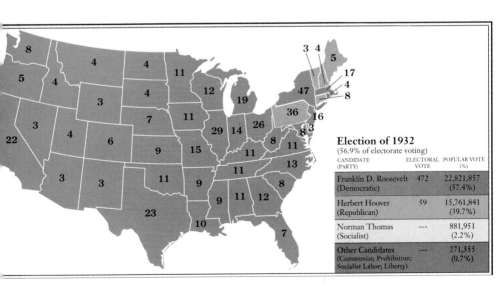

Election of 1932
(56.9% of electorate voting)

CANDIDATE (PARTY)	ELECTORAL VOTE	POPULAR VOTE (%)
Franklin D. Roosevelt (Democratic)	472	22,821,857 (57.4%)
Herbert Hoover (Republican)	59	15,761,841 (39.7%)
Norman Thomas (Socialist)	---	881,951 (2.2%)
Other Candidates (Communist; Prohibition; Socialist Labor; Liberty)	---	271,355 (0.7%)

In November, to the surprise of no one, Roosevelt won by a landslide. He received 57.4 percent of the popular vote to Hoover's 39.7. In the electoral college, the result was even more overwhelming. Hoover carried Pennsylvania, Connecticut, Vermont, New Hampshire, and Maine. Roosevelt won everything else. Democrats won majorities in both houses of Congress. It was a broad and convincing mandate, but it was not yet clear what Roosevelt intended to do with it.

THE CHANGING OF THE GUARD Well before the event actually occurred, Peter Arno of the *New Yorker* magazine drew this image of Franklin D. Roosevelt and Herbert Hoover traveling together to the Capitol for Roosevelt's inauguration. It predicted with remarkable accuracy the mood of the uncomfortable ride—Hoover glum and uncommunicative, Roosevelt buoyant and smiling. This was to have been the magazine's cover for the week of the inauguration; but after an attempted assassination of the president-elect several weeks earlier in Florida (in which the mayor of Chicago was killed), the editors decided to substitute a more subdued drawing.

The Interregnum

The period between the election and the inauguration (which in the early 1930s lasted more than four months) was a season of growing economic crisis. Presidents-elect traditionally do not involve themselves directly in government. But in a series of brittle exchanges with Roosevelt in the months following the election, Hoover tried to exact from the president-elect a pledge to maintain policies of economic orthodoxy. Roosevelt genially refused.

In February, only a month before the inauguration, a new crisis developed when the American banking system began to collapse. Public confidence in the banks was ebbing; depositors were withdrawing their money in panic; and one bank after another was closing its doors and declaring bankruptcy. In mid-February, the governor of Michigan, one of the states hardest hit by the panic, ordered all banks temporarily closed. Other states soon followed, and by the end of the month banking activity was restricted drastically in every state but one. Hoover again asked Roosevelt to give prompt public assurances that there would be no tinkering with the currency, no heavy borrowing, no unbalancing of the budget. Roosevelt again refused.

March 4, 1933, was, therefore, a day of both economic crisis and considerable personal bitterness. On that morning, Herbert Hoover, convinced that the United States was headed for disaster, rode glumly down Pennsylvania Avenue with a beaming, buoyant Franklin Roosevelt, who would shortly be sworn in as the thirty-second president of the United States.

CHAPTER TWENTY-SIX

The New Deal

Launching the New Deal ~ *The New Deal in Transition*
The New Deal in Disarray ~ *Limits of the New Deal*

RANKLIN ROOSEVELT SERVED longer as president than anyone else before or since, and during his twelve years in office he became more central to the life of the nation than any chief executive had ever been. Most important, his administration constructed a series of programs that permanently altered the federal government and its relationship to society.

By the end of the 1930s, the New Deal (as the Roosevelt administration was called) had created many of the broad outlines of the political world we know today. It had constructed the beginnings of a modern welfare system. It had extended federal regulation over new areas of the economy. It had presided over the birth of the modern labor movement. It had made the government a major force in the agricultural economy. It had created a powerful coalition within the Democratic party that would dominate American politics for most of the next thirty years. And it had produced the beginnings of a new liberal ideology that would govern reform efforts for several decades after the war. One thing the New Deal had not done, however, was end the Great Depression. It had helped stabilize the economy in 1933, and there had been a limited, if erratic, recovery after that. But by the end of 1939, many of the basic problems of the Depression remained unsolved.

LAUNCHING THE NEW DEAL

Roosevelt's first task upon taking office was to alleviate the panic that was threatening to create chaos in the financial system. He did so in part by force of personality and in part by constructing very rapidly an ambitious and diverse program of legislation.

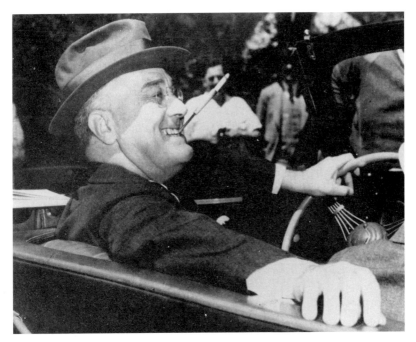

THE ROOSEVELT SMILE The battered hat, the uptilted cigarette holder, the jaunty smile—all were hallmarks of Franklin Roosevelt's ebullient public personality. In part, at least, the president's hearty optimism was a deliberate pose, adopted to distract attention from the paralysis that had denied him the use of his legs since 1921.

Restoring Confidence

Much of Roosevelt's early success was a result of his ebullient personality. He was the first president to make regular use of the radio; and his friendly "fireside chats," during which he explained his programs and plans to the people, helped build public confidence in the administration. Roosevelt held frequent informal press conferences and won both the respect and the friendship of most reporters.

But Roosevelt could not rely on image alone. On March 6, two days after taking office, he issued a proclamation closing all American banks for four days until Congress could meet in special session to consider banking reform legislation. So great was the panic about bank failures that the "bank holiday," as the president euphemistically described it, created a general sense of relief and hope.

Three days later, Roosevelt sent to Congress the Emergency Banking Act, a generally conservative bill (much of it drafted by holdovers from the Hoover administration) designed primarily to protect the larger banks from being dragged down by the weakness of smaller ones. The bill provided for Treasury Department inspection of all banks before they would be allowed to reopen, for federal assistance to some troubled institutions, and for a thorough reorganization of those banks in the greatest difficulty. A confused and frightened Congress passed the bill within a few hours of its introduction. Whatever else the new law accomplished, it helped dispel the panic. Three-quarters of the banks in the Federal Reserve system reopened within the next three days, and $1 billion in hoarded currency and gold flowed back into them within a month. The immediate banking crisis was over.

On the morning after passage of the Emergency Banking Act, Roosevelt sent to Congress another measure—the Economy Act—designed to convince the public (and especially the business community) that the federal government was in safe, responsible hands. The act proposed to balance the federal budget by cutting the salaries of government employees and reducing pensions to veterans by as much as 15 percent. Otherwise, the president warned, the nation faced a $1 billion deficit. Like the banking bill, this one passed through Congress almost instantly—despite heated protests from some congressional progressives.

Roosevelt also moved in his first days in office to put to rest one of the divisive issues of the 1920s. He supported and then signed a bill to legalize the manufacture and sale of beer with a 3.2 percent alcohol content—an interim measure pending the repeal of prohibition, for which a constitutional amendment (the Twenty-first) was already in process. The amendment was ratified later in 1933.

Agricultural Adjustment

These initial actions were largely stopgaps, to buy time for more comprehensive programs. The first such program was the Agricultural Adjustment Act, which Congress passed in May 1933. Its most important feature was its provision for reducing crop production to end agricultural surpluses and halt the downward spiral of farm prices.

Under the "domestic allotment" system of the act, producers of seven basic commodities (wheat, cotton, corn, hogs, rice, tobacco, and dairy products) would decide on production limits for their crops. The government, through the Agricultural Adjustment Administration (AAA), would then tell individual farmers how much they should produce and would pay them subsidies for leaving some of their land idle. A tax on food processing (for example, the milling of wheat) would provide the funds for the new payments. Farm prices were to be subsidized up to the point of parity.

The results of the AAA efforts were in many ways heartening. Prices for farm commodities did indeed rise in the years after 1933, and gross farm income increased by half in the first three years of the New Deal. The agricultural economy as a whole emerged from the 1930s much more stable and prosperous than it had been in many years. The AAA did, however, tend to favor larger farmers over smaller ones, particularly since local administration of its programs often fell into the hands of the most powerful producers in a community. New Deal farm programs actually contributed to dispossessing some struggling farmers, even if unintentionally. By distributing payments to landowners, not those who worked the land, the government did little to discourage planters who were reducing their acreage from evicting tenants and sharecroppers and firing field hands.

In January 1936, the Supreme Court struck down the crucial provisions of the Agricultural Adjustment Act, arguing that the government had no constitutional authority to require that farmers limit production. But within a few weeks the administration had secured passage of new legislation (the Soil Conservation and Domestic Allotment Act), which permitted the government to pay farmers to reduce production so as to "conserve soil," prevent erosion, and accomplish other secondary goals. The new law apparently met the Court's objections.

It also attempted to correct one of the injustices of the original act: its failure to protect sharecroppers and tenant farmers. Now landlords were required to share the payments they received for cutting back production with those who worked their land. (The new requirements were, however, largely evaded.) The administration launched other efforts to assist poor farmers as well. The Resettlement Administration, established in 1935, and its successor, the Farm Security Administration, created in 1937, provided loans to help farmers cultivating submarginal soil to relocate on better lands. But the programs never moved more than a few thousand farmers. More effective was the Rural Electrification Administration, created in 1935, which worked to make electric power available for the first time to thousands of farmers through utility cooperatives.

Industrial Recovery

The challenge of rescuing the industrial economy from the spiraling deflation of the early 1930s was even more important to the administration. Ever since 1931, leaders of the United States Chamber of Commerce and many others had been urging the government to adopt an antideflation scheme that would permit trade associations to cooperate in stabilizing prices within their industries. Existing antitrust laws clearly forbade such practices, but businesspeople argued that the economic emergency justified a suspension of the restrictions. Herbert Hoover had refused to endorse suspension of the antitrust laws. But the Roosevelt administration was more receptive.

In exchange for relaxing antitrust provisions, however, New Dealers insisted on additional provisions that would deal with other economic problems. Businesspeople would have to make important concessions to labor—recognize the workers' right to bargain collectively through unions—to ensure that the incomes of workers would rise along with prices. And to ensure that consumer buying power would not lag behind, the administration added a major program of public works spending designed to pump needed funds into the economy. The result of these many impulses was the National Industrial Recovery Act, which Congress passed in June 1933.

At first, the new program appeared to work miracles. At its center was a new federal agency, the National Recovery Administration (NRA), under the direction of the flamboyant and energetic Hugh S. Johnson. Johnson approached the task of fighting deflation in two ways. First, he called on every business establishment in the nation to accept a temporary "blanket code": a minimum wage of between thirty and forty cents an hour, a maximum workweek of thirty-five to forty hours, and the abolition of child labor. The result, he claimed, would be to raise consumer purchasing power, increase employment, and eliminate the sweatshop. At the same time, Johnson was busy negotiating another, more specific set of codes with leaders of the nation's major industries. These industrial codes set floors below which no company would lower prices or wages in its search for a competitive advantage, and they included agreements on maintaining employment and production. He quickly won agreements from almost every major industry in the country.

From the beginning, however, the NRA encountered serious difficulties, and the entire effort ultimately dissolved in failure. The codes themselves were hastily and often poorly written. Administering them was beyond the capacities of federal officials with no prior experience in running so vast a program. Large producers consistently dominated the code-writing process and ensured that the new regulations would work to their advantage and to the disadvantage of smaller firms. And the codes at times did more than simply set floors under prices; they actively and artificially raised them—at times to levels higher than was necessary to ensure a profit and far higher than market forces would have dictated.

Attempts to increase consumer purchasing power did not progress as quickly as the efforts to raise prices. Section 7(a) of the National Industrial Recovery Act promised workers the right to form unions and engage in collective bargaining and encouraged many workers to join unions for the first time. But Section 7(a) contained no enforcement mechanisms. Hence recognition of unions by employers (and thus the significant wage increases the unions were committed to winning) did not follow. The Public Works Administration (PWA), established to administer the NIRA's spending programs, only gradually allowed the $3.3 billion in public works funds to trickle out. Not until 1938 was the PWA budget pumping an appreciable amount of money into the economy.

Perhaps the clearest evidence of the NRA's failure was that industrial production actually declined in the months after the agency's establishment—from an index of 101 in July 1933 to 71 in November—despite the rise in prices the codes had helped to create. By the spring of 1934, therefore, the NRA was besieged by criticism; and businessmen were flaunting its provisions. That fall, Roosevelt pressured Johnson to resign and established a new board of directors to oversee the NRA. Then in 1935, the Supreme Court intervened.

The constitutional basis for the NRA had been Congress's power to regulate commerce among the states, a power the administration had interpreted very broadly. In 1935, a case came before the Court involving alleged NRA code violations by the Schechter brothers, who operated a wholesale poultry business confined to Brooklyn, New York. The Court ruled unanimously that the Schechters were not engaged in interstate commerce and, further, that Congress had unconstitutionally delegated legislative power to the president to draft the NRA codes. The legislation establishing the agency, therefore, was declared void. Roosevelt denounced the justices for their "horse-and-buggy" interpretation of the interstate commerce clause. He was rightly concerned, for the reasoning in the *Schechter* case threatened many other New Deal programs as well. But the destruction of the NRA itself may have been a blessing for the New Deal, providing it with a convenient way to abolish the failed experiment.

Regional Planning

The AAA and the NRA largely reflected the beliefs of New Dealers who favored economic planning but wanted private interests (farmers or business leaders) to dominate the planning process. In some areas, however, other reformers—those who believed that the government itself should be the chief planning agent in the economy—managed to establish dominance. Their most conspicuous success, and one of the most celebrated accomplishments of the New Deal, was an unprecedented experiment in regional planning: the Tennessee Valley Authority (TVA).

The TVA had its roots in a political controversy of the 1920s. Progressive reformers had agitated for years for public development of the nation's water resources as a source of cheap electric power. In particular, they had urged completion of a great dam at Muscle Shoals on the Tennessee River in Alabama—a dam begun during World War I but left unfinished when the war ended. But opposition from the utilities companies had been too powerful to overcome.

In 1932, however, one of the great utility empires—that of the electricity magnate Samuel Insull—collapsed spectacularly, amid widely publicized exposés of corruption. Hostility to the utilities soon grew so intense that the companies were no longer able to block the public power movement. The result was legislation supported by the president and enacted by Congress in May 1933 creating the Tennessee Valley Authority. The TVA was intended not only to complete the dam at Muscle Shoals and build others in the region, and not only to generate and sell electricity from them to the public at reasonable rates. It was also to be the agent for a comprehensive redevelopment of the entire region: for stopping the disastrous flooding that had plagued the Tennessee Valley for centuries, for encouraging the development of local industries, for supervising a substantial program of reforestation, and for helping farmers improve productivity.

Opposition by conservatives within the administration ultimately blocked some of the ambitious social planning projects proposed by the more visionary TVA administrators, but the Authority revitalized the region in numerous ways. It built dams and waterways. It virtually eliminated flooding in the region. It provided electricity to thousands who had never before had it. Throughout the country, largely because of the "yardstick" provided by the TVA's cheap production of electricity, private power rates declined. Still, the Authority worked no miracles. The Tennessee Valley remained a generally impoverished region despite its efforts. And like many other New Deal programs, it made no serious effort to challenge local customs and racial prejudices.

Financial Reforms

A belief that the health of the economy rested above all on the nature of the currency had been a staple of American political thought for more than half a century. For a time, the New Deal too attempted to deal with the nation's problems with monetary reform.

Roosevelt was not an inflationist at heart, but he soon came to consider the gold standard a major obstacle to the restoration of adequate prices. On April 18, 1933, the president issued an executive order that officially ended the country's already weakened adherence to the gold standard. A few weeks later, Congress passed legislation confirming his decision. By itself, the repudiation of the gold standard meant relatively little. But both before and after the April decision, the administration experimented in various ways with manipulating the value of the dollar—by making substantial purchases of gold and silver and later by establishing a new, fixed standard for the dollar (reducing its gold content substantially from the 1932 amount). The resort to government-managed currency—that is, to a dollar whose value could be raised or lowered by government policy according to economic circumstances—created an important precedent for future federal policies and permanently altered the relationship between the public and the private sectors. It did not, however, have any immediate impact on the depressed American economy.

Through other legislation, the early New Deal increased federal authority over previously unregulated or weakly regulated areas of the economy. The Glass-Steagall Act of June 1933 gave the government authority to curb irresponsible speculation by banks. More important, perhaps, it established the Federal Deposit Insurance Corporation, which guaranteed all bank deposits up to $2,500. In other words, even should a bank fail, small depositors would be able to recover their money. Finally, in 1935, Congress passed a major banking act that transferred much of the authority once wielded by the regional Federal Reserve banks to the Federal Reserve Board in Washington.

To protect investors in the stock market, Congress passed the so-called Truth in Securities Act of 1933, requiring corporations issuing new securities to provide full and accurate information about them to the public. Another act, of June 1934, established the Securities and Exchange Commission (SEC) to police the stock market.

The Growth of Federal Relief

Millions of Americans were unemployed and in desperate need of assistance in 1933, and the relief efforts of private organizations and state and local governments were unable to meet the demand. The Roosevelt administration did not consider relief its most important task, but it recognized the necessity of doing something to help impoverished Americans survive until the government could revive the economy to the point where relief might not be necessary.

Among Roosevelt's first acts as president was the establishment of the Federal Emergency Relief Administration (FERA), which provided cash grants to states to prop up bankrupt relief agencies. To administer the program, he chose the director of the New York State relief agency, Harry Hopkins, who disbursed the FERA grants widely and rapidly. But both Hopkins and Roosevelt had misgivings about establishing a government "dole."

They felt somewhat more comfortable with another form of government assistance: work relief. Thus when it became clear that the FERA grants would not be sufficient to pull the country through the winter, the administration established a second program: the Civil Works Administration (CWA). Between November 1933 and April 1934, it put more than 4 million people to work on temporary projects. Some of them were of lasting value, such as the construction of roads, schools, and parks; others were little more than make-work. To Hopkins, however, the important thing was pumping money into an economy badly in need of it and providing assistance to people with nowhere else to turn.

Most of these early relief programs had short lives. Like the FERA, the CWA was intended to be only a temporary expedient. In the spring of 1934, the president began to dismantle the agency, and he ultimately disbanded it altogether. Most economists now agree that massive and sustained government spending would have been the quickest and most effective way to end the Depression. But few policymakers in the 1930s shared that belief.

Roosevelt's favorite relief project was the Civilian Conservation Corps (CCC). Established in the first weeks of the new administration, the CCC was designed to provide employment to the millions of urban young men who could find no jobs in the cities and who many feared might become a source of urban crime and violence. At the same time, it was intended to advance the work of conservation and reforestation—goals Roosevelt had long cherished. The CCC created a series of camps in national parks and forests and in other rural and wilderness settings. There young men (women

THE CIVILIAN CONSERVATION CORPS CCC workers in Wind River, Washington, in 1933 uproot two-year-old fir trees, which they will then ship to other locations for transplanting. The CCC's many defenders, among them Franklin Roosevelt, believed that exposing young urban men to work in the "great outdoors" was at least as valuable to them as providing them with a salary.

were excluded from the program) worked in a semimilitary environment on such projects as planting trees, building reservoirs, developing parks, and improving agricultural irrigation. CCC camps were segregated by race, with the vast majority restricted to whites and a few open to blacks, Mexicans, and Indians.

Mortgage relief was a pressing need for millions of farm owners and homeowners. The Farm Credit Administration, which within two years refinanced one-fifth of all farm mortgages in the United States, was one response to that problem. The Frazier-Lemke Farm Bankruptcy Act of 1933 was another. It enabled some farmers to regain their land even after the foreclosure of their mortgages. Despite such efforts, however, 25 percent of all American farm owners had lost their land by 1934. Homeowners were similarly troubled, and in June 1933 the administration established the Home Owners' Loan Corporation, which by 1936 had refinanced the mortgages of more than 1 million householders. A year later, Congress established the Federal Housing Administration to insure mortgages for new construction and home repairs—a measure that combined an effort to provide relief with a program to stimulate lasting recovery of the construction industry.

The relief efforts of the first two years of the New Deal were intended to be limited and temporary. But they helped stimulate interest in other forms of social protection. Ultimately, the creation of a permanent welfare system would be one of the New Deal's most important and lasting accomplishments.

THE NEW DEAL IN TRANSITION

Seldom has an American president enjoyed such remarkable popularity as Franklin Roosevelt did during his first two years in office. But by early 1935, with no end to the Depression yet in sight, the New Deal was beginning to find itself the target of fierce public criticism. In the spring of 1935, partly in response to these growing attacks, Roosevelt launched an ambitious new program of legislation that has often been called the "Second New Deal."

Critics of the New Deal

Some of the most strident attacks on the New Deal came from critics on the right. Roosevelt had tried for a time to conciliate conservatives and business leaders. By the end of 1934, however, it was clear that the American right in general, and much of the corporate world in particular, had become irreconcilably hostile to the New Deal. In August 1934, a group of the most fervent (and wealthiest) Roosevelt opponents, led by members of the Du Pont family, formed the American Liberty League, designed specifically to arouse public opposition to the New Deal's "dictatorial" policies and its supposed attacks on free enterprise. The new organization generated wide publicity and caused some concern within the administration. In fact, however, it was never able to expand its constituency much beyond the Northern industrialists who had founded it. At its peak, membership in the organization numbered only about 125,000.

The real impact of the Liberty League and other conservative attacks on Roosevelt was not to undermine the president's political strength. It was, rather, to convince Roosevelt that his efforts to conciliate the business community had failed. By 1936, he no longer harbored any illusions about cooperation with conservatives. The forces of "organized money," he said near the end of his campaign for reelection, "are unanimous in their hate for me—and I welcome their hatred."

Roosevelt's critics on the far left also managed to produce alarm among some supporters of the administration; but like the conservatives, they proved to have only limited strength. The Communist party, the Socialist party, and other radical and semiradical organizations were at times harshly critical of the New Deal. But they too failed ever to attract genuine mass support.

More menacing to the New Deal than either the far right or the far left was a group of dissident political movements that defied easy ideological classification. Some were marginal "crackpot" organizations with little popular following. Others gained substantial public support within particular states and regions. Three men, however, succeeded in mobilizing genuinely national followings.

Dr. Francis E. Townsend, an elderly California physician, rose from obscurity to lead a movement of more than 5 million members with his plan for federal pensions for the elderly. According to the Townsend Plan, all Americans over the age of sixty would receive monthly government pensions of $200, provided they retired (thus freeing jobs for younger, unemployed Americans) and spent the money in full each month (which would pump needed funds into the economy). By 1935, the Townsend Plan had attracted the support of many older men and women. And while the plan itself made little progress in Congress, the public sentiment behind it helped build support for the Social Security system, which Congress did approve in 1935.

Father Charles E. Coughlin, a Catholic priest in the Detroit suburb of Royal Oak, Michigan, achieved even greater renown through his weekly sermons broadcast nationally over the radio. He proposed a series of monetary reforms—remonetization of silver, issuing of greenbacks, and nationalization of the banking system—that he insisted would restore prosperity and ensure economic justice. At first a warm supporter of Franklin Roosevelt, by late 1934 he had become disheartened by what he claimed was the president's failure to deal harshly enough with the "money powers." In the spring of 1935, he established his own political organization, the National Union for Social Justice. He was attracting public support throughout much of the nation—primarily from Catholics, but from others as well. He was widely believed to have one of the largest regular radio audiences of anyone in America.

HUEY LONG Few public speakers could arouse a crowd
more effectively than Huey Long of Louisiana, known to
many as "the Kingfish" (a nickname borrowed from the
popular radio show *Amos 'n Andy*). It was Long's effective
use of radio, however, that contributed most directly to his
spreading national popularity in the early 1930s.

Most alarming of all to the administration was the growing national
popularity of Senator Huey P. Long of Louisiana. Long had risen to power
in his home state through his strident attacks on the banks, oil companies,
and utilities and on the conservative political oligarchy allied with them.
Elected governor in 1928, he launched an assault on his opponents so
thorough and forceful that they were soon left with virtually no political
power whatever. Many claimed that he had, in effect, become a dictator.
(Friends and enemies alike called him the "Kingfish," a nickname borrowed
from the popular *Amos 'n Andy* radio show.) But he also maintained the
overwhelming support of the Louisiana electorate, in part because of his

flamboyant personality and in part because of his solid record of conventional progressive accomplishment: building roads, schools, and hospitals; revising the tax codes; distributing free textbooks; lowering utility rates. Barred by law from succeeding himself as governor, he ran in 1930 for a seat in the United States Senate, won easily, and left the state government in the hands of loyal, docile allies.

Long, like Coughlin, supported Franklin Roosevelt for president in 1932. But within six months of Roosevelt's inauguration he had broken with the president. As an alternative to the New Deal, he advocated a drastic program of wealth redistribution, a program he ultimately named the Share-Our-Wealth Plan. The government, he claimed, could end the Depression easily by using the tax system to confiscate the surplus riches of the wealthiest men and women in America, whose fortunes were, he claimed, so bloated that not enough wealth remained to satisfy the needs of the great mass of citizens. That surplus wealth would allow the government to guarantee every family a minimum "homestead" of $5,000 and an annual wage of $2,500.

Long made little effort to disguise his interest in running for president. In 1934, he established his own national organization: the Share-Our-Wealth Society, which soon attracted a large following—not only in Long's native South but in New York, Pennsylvania, parts of the Midwest, and above all California. A poll by the Democratic National Committee in the spring of 1935 disclosed that Long might attract more than 10 percent of the vote if he ran as a third-party candidate, enough to tip a close election to the Republicans.

Long, Coughlin, Townsend, and other dissidents had certain concerns in common. They spoke harshly of the "plutocrats," "international bankers," and other remote financial powers who were, they claimed, not only impoverishing the nation but exercising tyrannical power over individuals and communities. They spoke equally harshly, however, of the dangers of excessive government bureaucracy, attacking the New Deal for establishing a menacing, "dictatorial" state. They envisioned a society in which government would, through a series of simple economic reforms, guarantee prosperity to every American without exercising intrusive control over private and community activities.

To members of the Roosevelt administration, the dissident politics appeared in 1935 to have become a genuine threat to the president. An increasing number of advisers were warning Roosevelt that he would have to do something dramatic to counter their strength.

The "Second New Deal"

Roosevelt launched the so-called Second New Deal in the spring of 1935 in response both to the growing political pressures and to the continuing economic crisis. The new proposals represented, if not a new direction, at least a change in the emphasis of New Deal policy. Perhaps the most conspicuous change was in the administration's attitude toward big business. Symbolically at least, the president was now willing to attack corporate interests openly. In March, for example, he proposed to Congress an act designed to break up the great utility holding companies, and he spoke harshly of monopolistic control of their industry. Congress did indeed pass the Holding Company Act of 1935 (often known as the "death sentence" bill), but furious lobbying by the utilities resulted in amendments that sharply limited its effects.

Equally alarming to affluent Americans was a series of tax reforms proposed by the president in 1935, a program conservatives quickly labeled a "soak-the-rich" scheme. Apparently designed to undercut the appeal of Huey Long's Share-Our-Wealth Plan, the Roosevelt proposals called for establishing the highest and most progressive peacetime tax rates in history. Rates in the highest brackets reached 75 percent on income, 70 percent on inheritance, and 15 percent on corporate income. In fact, however, the actual impact of these taxes was far less radical than the president liked to claim (as Huey Long quickly pointed out).

The Supreme Court decision in 1935 to invalidate the National Industrial Recovery Act solved some problems for the administration, but it also created others. Section 7(a) of the now-defunct act had guaranteed workers the right to organize and bargain collectively. Supporters of labor, both in the administration and in Congress, advocated quick action to restore that protection. With the president himself slow to respond, a group of progressives in Congress led by Senator Robert F. Wagner of New York introduced what became the National Labor Relations Act of 1935. The new law, popularly known as the Wagner Act, provided workers with more federal protection than Section 7(a) of the National Industrial Recovery Act had offered. It created a crucial enforcement mechanism, the National Labor Relations Board (NLRB), which would have power to compel employers to recognize and bargain with legitimate unions. The president was not entirely happy with the bill, but he signed it anyway. That was in large part because American workers themselves had by 1935 become so important and vigorous a force that Roosevelt realized his own political future would depend in part on responding to their demands.

Labor Militancy

The emergence of a powerful trade union movement in the 1930s was one of the most important social and political developments of the decade. It occurred partly in response to government efforts to enhance the power of unions; but it was also a result of the increased militancy of American workers and their leaders.

During the 1920s, most workers had displayed relatively little militancy in challenging employers or demanding recognition of their unions. In the 1930s, however, many of the factors that had impeded militancy vanished or grew weaker. Business leaders and industrialists lost (at least temporarily) the ability to control government policies. Both Section 7(a) of the National Industrial Recovery Act of 1933 and the Wagner Act of 1935 were passed over the strong objections of most (although not all) corporate leaders. Equally important, new and more militant labor organizations emerged to challenge the established, conservative unions.

The growing militancy first became obvious in 1934, when newly organized workers (many of them inspired by the collective bargaining provisions of the National Industrial Recovery Act) demonstrated an assertiveness and at times radicalism seldom seen in recent years. Some became involved in violent confrontations with employers and local authorities. Despite the new militancy, however, it was clear that without stronger legal protection, most organizing drives would end in frustration. Once the Wagner Act became law, the search for more effective forms of organization rapidly gained strength in labor ranks.

The American Federation of Labor, under the leadership now of William Green, remained committed to the idea of the craft union: organizing workers on the basis of their skills. But that concept had little to offer unskilled laborers, who now constituted the bulk of the industrial work force. During the 1930s, therefore, a new concept of labor organization challenged the craft union ideal: industrial unionism. Advocates of this approach argued that all the workers in a particular industry should be organized in a single union, regardless of what functions the workers performed. All autoworkers should be in a single automobile union; all steelworkers should be in a single steel union. United in this way, workers would greatly increase their power.

Leaders of the AFL craft unions for the most part opposed the new concept. But industrial unionism found a number of important advocates, most prominent among them John L. Lewis, the talented, flamboyant, and eloquent leader of the United Mine Workers. At first, Lewis and his allies

attempted to work within the AFL, but friction between the new industrial organizations Lewis was promoting and the older craft unions grew
rapidly.

At the 1935 AFL convention, Lewis became embroiled in a series of
angry confrontations (and one celebrated fistfight) with craft union leaders
before finally walking out. A few weeks later, he created the Committee on
Industrial Organization—a body officially within the AFL but unsanctioned
by its leadership. After a series of bitter jurisdictional conflicts, the AFL
finally expelled the new committee from its ranks, and along with it all
the industrial unions it represented. In response, Lewis renamed the
committee the Congress of Industrial Organizations (CIO), established
it in 1936 as an organization directly rivaling the AFL, and became its
first president. The schism clearly weakened the labor movement in many
ways. But by freeing the advocates of industrial unionism from the restrictive
rules of the AFL, it gave impetus to the creation of powerful new organizations.

The CIO also expanded the constituency of the labor movement. It was
more receptive to women and to blacks than the AFL had been, in part
because women and blacks were more likely to be relegated to unskilled jobs
and in part because CIO organizing drives targeted previously unorganized
industries (textiles, laundries, tobacco factories, and others) where women
and minorities constituted much of the work force. The CIO was also a
more militant organization than the AFL. By the time of the 1936 schism,
it was already engaged in major organizing battles in the automobile and
steel industries.

Organizing Battles

Out of several competing auto unions, the United Auto Workers (UAW)
was gradually emerging preeminent in the early and mid-1930s. But although it was gaining recruits, it was making little progress in winning
recognition from the corporations.

In December 1936, however, autoworkers employed a controversial
and effective new technique for challenging corporate opposition: the
sit-down strike. Employees in several General Motors plants in Detroit
simply sat down inside the plants, refusing either to work or to leave, thus
preventing the company from using strikebreakers. The tactic spread to
other locations, and by February 1937 strikers had occupied seventeen GM
plants. The strikers ignored court orders and local police efforts to force

them to vacate the buildings. When Michigan's governor, Frank Murphy, a liberal Democrat, refused to call up the National Guard to clear out the strikers, and when the federal government also refused to intervene on behalf of employers, General Motors relented. In February 1937, it became the first major manufacturer to recognize the UAW; other automobile companies soon did the same. The sit-down strike proved effective for rubber workers and others as well, but it survived only briefly as a labor technique. Its apparent illegality aroused so much public opposition that labor leaders soon abandoned it.

In the steel industry, the battle for unionization was less easily won. In 1936, the Steel Workers' Organizing Committee (SWOC; later the United Steelworkers of America) began a major organizing drive involving thousands of workers and frequent, at times bitter strikes. These conflicts were notable not only for the militancy of the (predominantly male) steelworkers themselves but for the involvement of thousands of women (many of them wives or relatives of workers), who provided important logistical support for

THE MEMORIAL DAY MASSACRE A newsreel photographer captured the moment, May 30, 1937, when Chicago police using guns, tear gas, and clubs charged striking workers near the Republic Steel plant in South Chicago. Ten strikers died as a result of the melee, and many more were injured.

the strikers and who at times took direct action by creating a buffer between strikers and the police.

In March 1937, to the surprise of almost everyone, United States Steel, the giant of the industry, recognized the union rather than risk a costly strike at a time when it sensed itself on the verge of recovery from the Depression. But the smaller companies (known collectively as "Little Steel") were less accommodating. On Memorial Day 1937, a group of striking workers from Republic Steel gathered with their families for a picnic and demonstration in South Chicago. When they attempted to march peacefully (and legally) toward the steel plant, police opened fire on them. Ten demonstrators were killed; another ninety were wounded. Despite a public outcry against the "Memorial Day Massacre," the harsh tactics of Little Steel were successful. The 1937 strike failed.

But the victory of Little Steel was one of the last gasps of the kind of brutal strikebreaking that had proved so effective in the past. In 1937 alone, there were 4,720 strikes—over 80 percent of them settled in favor of the unions. By the end of the year, more than 8 million workers were members of unions recognized as official bargaining units by employers (as compared with 3 million in 1932). By 1941, that number had expanded to 10 million and included the workers of Little Steel, whose employers had finally recognized the SWOC.

Social Security

From the first moments of the New Deal, important members of the administration, most notably Secretary of Labor Frances Perkins, had been lobbying for a system of federally sponsored social insurance for the elderly and the unemployed. In 1935, Roosevelt gave public support to what became the Social Security Act, which Congress passed the same year. It established several distinct programs. For the elderly, there were two types of assistance. Those who were presently destitute could receive up to $15 a month in federal assistance. More important for the future, many Americans presently working were incorporated into a pension system, to which they and their employers would contribute by paying a payroll tax; it would provide them with an income on retirement. Pension payments would not begin until 1942 and even then would provide only $10 to $85 a month to recipients. And broad categories of workers (including domestic servants and agricultural laborers, among them blacks and women) were excluded from the program. But the act was a crucial first step in building the nation's most important social program for the elderly.

In addition, the Social Security Act created a system of unemployment insurance, which employers alone would finance and which made it possible for workers laid off from their jobs to receive government assistance for a limited period of time. It also established a system of federal aid to disabled people and a program of aid to dependent children.

The framers of the Social Security Act wanted to create a system of "insurance," not "welfare." And the largest programs (old-age pensions and unemployment insurance) were in many ways similar to private insurance programs, with contributions from participants and benefits available to all. But the act also provided considerable direct assistance based on need—to the elderly poor, to the disabled, to dependent children. These groups were widely perceived to be small and genuinely unable to support themselves. But in later generations those programs would expand until they assumed dimensions that the planners of Social Security had neither foreseen nor desired. Whatever one thinks of Social Security, however, it is clear that the 1935 act was the most important single piece of social welfare legislation in American history.

New Directions in Relief

Social Security was designed primarily to fulfill long-range goals. But millions of unemployed Americans had immediate needs. To help meet them, the administration established in 1935 the Works Progress Administration (WPA). Like the Civil Works Administration and other earlier efforts, the WPA established a system of work relief for the unemployed. But it was much bigger than the earlier agencies, both in the size of its budget ($5 billion at first) and in the energy and imagination of its operations.

Under the direction of Harry Hopkins, the WPA was responsible for building or renovating 110,000 public buildings (schools, post offices, government office buildings) and for constructing almost 600 airports, more than 500,000 miles of roads, and over 100,000 bridges. In the process, the WPA kept an average of 2.1 million workers employed and pumped needed money into the economy.

The WPA also displayed remarkable flexibility and imagination in offering assistance to those whose occupations did not fit into any traditional category of relief. The Federal Writers Project of the WPA, for example, gave unemployed writers a chance to do their work and receive a government salary. The Federal Arts Project, similarly, helped painters, sculptors, and others to continue their careers. The Federal Music Project and the Federal Theater Project oversaw the production of concerts and plays, creating work for unemployed musicians, actors, and directors.

Other relief agencies emerged alongside the WPA. The National Youth Administration (NYA) provided work and scholarship assistance to high-school and college-age men and women. The Emergency Housing Division of the Public Works Administration began federal sponsorship of public housing.

The hiring practices of the WPA, the NYA, and other work-relief programs revealed another important, if at the time largely unrecognized, feature of the New Deal welfare system. Men and women alike were in distress in the 1930s (as in all difficult times). But the new welfare system dealt with members of the two sexes in very different ways. For men, the government concentrated mainly on work relief—on such programs as the CCC, the CWA, and the WPA, all of which were overwhelmingly male. The principal government aid to women was not work relief but cash assistance—most notably through the Aid to Dependent Children program of Social Security, which was designed largely to assist single mothers. This disparity in treatment reflected a widespread assumption that men consti-tuted the bulk of the paid work force and that women needed to be treated within the context of the family. In fact, millions of women were already employed by the 1930s.

The 1936 "Referendum"

The presidential election of 1936, it was clear from the start, was to be a national referendum on Franklin Roosevelt and the New Deal. And while in 1935 there had been reason to question the president's political prospects, by the middle of 1936—with the economy visibly reviving—there could be little doubt that he would win a second term. The Republican party nominated the moderate governor of Kansas, Alf M. Landon, and produced a program that promised, in effect, to continue the programs of the New Deal—but "constitutionally," and without running a deficit. Republican conservatives seemed impotent even within their own party.

Roosevelt's dissident challengers now appeared similarly powerless. One reason was the violent death of their most effective leader, Huey Long, who was assassinated in Louisiana in September 1935. Another reason was the ill-fated alliance among several of the remaining dissident leaders in 1936. Father Coughlin, Dr. Townsend, and Gerald L. K. Smith (an intemperate henchman of Huey Long) joined forces that summer to establish a new political movement—the Union party, which nominated an undistinguished North Dakota congressman, William Lemke, for president.

The result was the greatest landslide in American history to that point. Roosevelt polled just under 61 percent of the vote to Landon's 36 percent. The Republican candidate carried only Maine and Vermont. The Democrats increased their already large majorities in both houses of Congress. The Union party received fewer than 900,000 votes.

The election results demonstrated the party realignment that the New Deal had produced. The Democrats now controlled a broad coalition of Western and Southern farmers, the urban working classes, the poor and unemployed, and the black communities of Northern cities, as well as traditional progressives and committed new liberals—a coalition that constituted a substantial majority of the electorate. It would be decades before the Republican party could again muster anything approaching a true majority coalition of its own.

THE NEW DEAL IN DISARRAY

Roosevelt emerged from the 1936 election at the zenith of his popularity. Within months, however, the New Deal was mired in serious new difficulties—a result of continuing opposition, of the president's own political errors, and of major economic setbacks.

The Court Fight and the "Purge"

The 1936 mandate, Franklin Roosevelt believed, made it possible for him to do something about the problem of the Supreme Court. No program of reform, he had become convinced, could long survive the obstructionist justices, who had already struck down the NRA and the AAA and threatened to invalidate even more legislation.

In February 1937, Roosevelt offered a solution. Without informing congressional leaders in advance, he sent a surprise message to Capitol Hill proposing a general overhaul of the federal court system; included among the many provisions was one to add up to six new justices to the Supreme Court. The courts were "overworked," he claimed, and needed additional manpower and younger blood to enable them to cope with their increasing burdens. But Roosevelt's real purpose was to give himself the opportunity to appoint new, liberal justices and change the ideological balance of the Court.

Conservatives were outraged at the "court-packing plan," and even many Roosevelt supporters were disturbed by what they considered evidence of the president's hunger for power. Still, Roosevelt might well have persuaded Congress to approve at least a compromise measure had not the Supreme Court itself intervened. Even before the court-packing fight began, the ideological balance of the Court had been precarious. Four justices consistently opposed the New Deal, and three generally supported it. Of the remaining two, Chief Justice Charles Evans Hughes often sided with the progressives and Associate Justice Owen J. Roberts usually voted with the conservatives.

On March 29, 1937, Roberts, Hughes, and the three progressive justices voted together to uphold a state minimum-wage law—in the case of *West Coast Hotel* v. *Parrish*—thus reversing a 5-to-4 decision of the previous year invalidating a similar law. Two weeks later, again by a 5-to-4 margin, the Court upheld the Wagner Act; and in May, it validated the Social Security Act. The Court had prudently moderated its position to make the court-packing bill unnecessary. Congress ultimately defeated it.

On one level, the affair was a significant victory for Franklin Roosevelt. The Court was no longer an obstacle to New Deal reforms, particularly after the older justices began to retire, to be replaced by Roosevelt appointees. But the court-packing episode did lasting damage to the administration. By giving members of his own party an excuse to oppose him, he had helped destroy his congressional coalition. From 1937 on, Southern Democrats and other conservatives voted against his measures much more often than in the past.

A year later, the president's political situation deteriorated further. Roosevelt was determined to regain the initiative in his legislative battles, and in several primary campaigns in spring 1938 he openly spoke against members of his own party who had opposed his programs. Not only was he unable to unseat any of the five Democratic senators against whom he campaigned, but his "purge" efforts drove an even deeper wedge between the administration and its conservative opponents.

Retrenchment and Recession

By the summer of 1937, the national income, which had dropped from $82 billion in 1929 to $40 billion in 1932, had risen to nearly $72 billion. Other economic indices showed similar advances. Roosevelt seized on these improvements as an excuse to try to balance the federal budget, convinced by Treasury secretary Henry Morgenthau and many economists that the real danger now was no longer depression but inflation. Between January and August 1937, for example, he cut the WPA in half, laying off 1.5 million relief workers. A few weeks later, the fragile boom collapsed. The index of industrial production dropped from 117 in August 1937 to 76 in May 1938. Four million additional workers lost their jobs. Economic conditions were soon almost as bad as the bleak days of 1932–1933.

The recession of 1937 was a result of many factors. But to many observers at the time (including, apparently, Roosevelt), it seemed to be a direct result of the administration's unwise decision to reduce spending. And so the new crisis forced a reevaluation of policies. The advocates of government spending as an antidote to the Depression stood vindicated, it seemed; and the notion of using government deficits to stimulate the economy established a timid foothold in American public policy. In April 1938, the president asked Congress for an emergency appropriation of $5 billion for public works and relief programs, and government funds soon began pouring into the economy once again. Within a few months, another tentative recovery seemed to be under way, and the advocates of spending pointed to it as proof of the validity of their approach.

At the same time, a group of younger liberals in the administration who saw the recession as the result of excessively concentrated corporate power were urging the president to launch a new assault on monopoly. In April 1938, Roosevelt sent a stinging message to Congress, vehemently denouncing what he called an "unjustifiable concentration of economic power" and asking for the creation of a commission to examine that concentration with an eye to major reforms in the antitrust laws. In response, Congress established the Temporary National Economic Committee (TNEC), whose members included representatives of both houses of Congress and officials from several executive agencies. At about the same time, Roosevelt appointed a new head of the antitrust division of the Justice Department: Thurman Arnold, a Yale Law School professor who soon proved to be the most vigorous director ever to serve in that office.

By the end of 1938, however, it was becoming clear that these ambitious new goals faced an uncertain future. For the New Deal had by then essentially come to an end. Congressional opposition now made it difficult for the president to enact any major new programs. But more important, perhaps, the threat of world crisis hung heavy in the political atmosphere, and Roosevelt was gradually growing more concerned with persuading a reluctant nation to prepare for war than with pursuing new avenues of reform.

LIMITS OF THE NEW DEAL

In the 1930s, Roosevelt's principal critics were conservatives, who accused him of abandoning the Constitution and establishing a menacing, even tyrannical state. In more recent years, the New Deal's most vocal critics have attacked it from the left, pointing to the major problems it did not solve and the important groups it failed to represent. A full understanding of the New Deal requires examining not just its achievements but also its limits.

African-Americans and the New Deal

One group the New Deal did relatively little to assist was African-Americans. The administration was not hostile to black aspirations. On the contrary, the New Deal was probably more sympathetic to them than any previous government of the twentieth century had been. Eleanor Roosevelt spoke throughout the 1930s on behalf of racial justice and put continuing pressure on her husband and others in the federal government to ease discrimination against blacks. The president himself appointed a number of blacks to significant second-level positions in his administration, creating an informal network of officeholders that became known as the "Black Cabinet." Eleanor Roosevelt, Interior Secretary Harold Ickes, and WPA director Harry Hopkins all made efforts to ensure that New Deal relief programs did not exclude blacks; and by 1935, an estimated 30 percent of all African-Americans were receiving some form of government assistance. One result was a historic change in black electoral behavior. As late as 1932,

ELEANOR ROOSEVELT AND MARY McLEOD BETHUNE Mrs. Roosevelt was a leading champion of racial equality within her husband's administration, and her commitment had an important impact on the behavior of the government even though she held no official post. She is seen here meeting in 1937 with Aubrey Williams, executive director of the National Youth Administration, and Mary McLeod Bethune, the agency's Director of Negro Affairs.

most American blacks were voting Republican, as they had been doing since the Civil War. By 1936, more than 90 percent of them were voting Democratic—the beginnings of a political alliance that would endure for many decades.

Blacks supported Franklin Roosevelt because they knew he was not their enemy. But they had few illusions that the New Deal represented a millennium in American race relations. The president was, for example, never willing to risk losing the support of Southern Democrats by supporting legislation to make lynching a federal crime or to ban the poll tax, one of the most potent tools by which white Southerners kept blacks from voting.

New Deal relief agencies did not challenge, and indeed reinforced, existing patterns of discrimination. The Civilian Conservation Corps established separate black camps. The NRA codes tolerated paying blacks less than whites doing the same jobs. African-Americans were largely excluded from employment in the TVA. The Federal Housing Administration refused to provide mortgages to blacks moving into white neighborhoods, and the first public housing projects financed by the federal government were racially segregated. The WPA routinely relegated black and Hispanic workers to the least skilled and lowest-paying jobs; when funding ebbed, African-Americans, like women, were among the first to be dismissed.

The New Deal was not hostile to black Americans, and it did much to help them advance. But it refused to make the issue of race a significant part of its agenda.

The New Deal and the "Indian Problem"

New Deal policy toward the Indian tribes marked a significant break from the approach in the years before Roosevelt, largely because of the efforts of the extraordinary commissioner of Indian affairs in the 1930s, John Collier. Collier was greatly influenced by the work of twentieth-century anthropologists who advanced the idea of cultural relativism—the theory that every culture should be accepted and respected on its own terms and that no culture is inherently superior to another. Cultural relativism was a challenge to the three-centuries-old assumption among white Americans that Indians were "savages" and that white society was inherently superior and more "civilized."

Collier favored legislation that would, he hoped, reverse the pressures on Native Americans to assimilate and allow them to remain Indians. Not all tribal leaders agreed with Collier. Indeed, his belief in the importance of preserving Indian culture would not find its greatest support among the tribes until the 1960s. Nevertheless, Collier effectively promoted legislation—which became the Indian Reorganization Act of 1934—to advance his goals. Among other things it restored to the tribes the right to own land collectively (reversing the allotment policy adopted in 1887, which encouraged the breaking up of tribal lands into individually owned plots) and to elect tribal governments. In the thirteen years after passage of the 1934 bill, tribal land increased by nearly 4 million acres, and Indian agricultural income increased dramatically (from under $2 million in 1934 to over $49 million in 1947).

Even with the redistribution of lands under the 1934 act, however, Indians continued to possess, for the most part, only territory whites did not want—much of it arid, some of it desert. And as a group, they continued to constitute the poorest segment of the population. The efforts of the 1930s did not solve, or even greatly alleviate, what some called the "Indian problem." They did, however, provide Indians with some tools for rebuilding the viability of the tribes.

Women and the New Deal

Symbolically, at least, the New Deal marked a breakthrough in the role of women in public life. Roosevelt appointed the first female member of the cabinet in the nation's history, Secretary of Labor Frances Perkins. He also named more than 100 other women to positions at lower levels of the federal bureaucracy. But New Deal support for women operated within limits. Even many of the women in the administration were concerned not so much about achieving gender equality as about obtaining special protections for women.

The New Deal generally supported the belief (not always matched by practice) that in hard times women should withdraw from the workplace to open up more jobs for men. Frances Perkins, for example, spoke out against what she called the "pin-money worker"—the married woman working to earn extra money for the household. New Deal relief agencies offered relatively little employment for women. The NRA sanctioned sexually discriminatory wage practices. The Social Security program excluded domestic servants, waitresses, and other predominantly female occupations.

As with African-Americans, so also with women: The New Deal was not actively hostile; in many ways, it was unprecedentedly supportive. It did, however, accept prevailing cultural norms. There was not yet sufficient political pressure from women themselves to persuade the administration to do otherwise.

The New Deal and the Economy

The most frequent criticisms of the New Deal involve its failure genuinely to revive or reform the American economy. New Dealers never fully recognized the value of government spending as a vehicle for recovery, and their efforts along other lines never succeeded in ending the Depression. The economic boom sparked by World War II, not the New Deal, finally ended the crisis. Nor did the New Deal substantially alter the distribution of power within American capitalism; and it had only a small impact on the distribution of wealth among the American people.

Nevertheless, the New Deal did have a number of important and lasting effects on both the behavior and the structure of the American economy. It helped elevate new groups—workers, farmers, and others—to positions from which they could at times effectively challenge the power of the corporations. It increased the regulatory functions of the federal government in ways that helped stabilize previously troubled areas of the economy: the stock market, the banking system, and others. And the administration helped establish the basis for new forms of federal fiscal policy, which in the postwar years would give the government tools for promoting and regulating economic growth.

The New Deal also created the rudiments of the American welfare state, through its many relief programs and above all through the Social Security system. The conservative inhibitions New Dealers brought to this task ensured that the welfare system that ultimately emerged would be limited in its impact (at least in comparison with those of other industrial nations), would reinforce some traditional patterns of gender and racial discrimination, and would be expensive and cumbersome to administer. But for all its limits, the new system marked a historic break with the nation's traditional reluctance to offer any public assistance whatever to its neediest citizens.

D E B A T I N G   T H E   P A S T

The New Deal

C ONTEMPORARIES OF FRANKLIN ROOSEVELT debated the impact of the New Deal with ferocious intensity: conservatives complaining of a menacing tyranny of the state, liberals celebrating the New Deal's progressive achievements, people on the left charging that the reforms of the 1930s were largely cosmetic and left the nation's fundamental problems unsolved. Although the conservative critique of the New Deal has found relatively little scholarly expression since Roosevelt's death, the liberal and left positions continued for many years to shape the way historians described the Roosevelt administration.

The dominant view from the beginning was an approving liberal interpretation, and its most important early voice was that of Arthur M. Schlesinger, Jr. He argued in the three volumes of *The Age of Roosevelt* (1957–1960) that the New Deal marked a continuation of the long struggle between public power and private interests, a struggle Roosevelt had moved to a new level as the unconstrained influence of business elites finally encountered an effective challenge. What emerged from the New Deal was a system of reformed capitalism, with far more protection for workers, farmers, consumers, and others than they had enjoyed in the past.

At almost the same time, however, other historians were offering more qualified assessments of the New Deal, even if ones that remained securely within the liberal framework Schlesinger had used. Richard Hofstadter argued in 1955 that the New Deal was a "drastic new departure . . . different from anything that had yet happened in the United States"; that it gave American liberalism a "social-democratic tinge that had never before been present in American reform movements"; but that its highly pragmatic approach lacked a central, guiding philosophy. James MacGregor Burns argued in 1956 that Roosevelt's wily political methods often led him away from the proper goals of reform, that he had failed to make full use of his

(continued on next page)

potential as a leader and had accommodated himself unnecessarily to existing patterns of power.

William Leuchtenburg's *Franklin D. Roosevelt and the New Deal* (1963) was the first systematic "revisionist" interpretation. Leuchtenburg was a sympathetic critic, arguing that most of the limitations of the New Deal were the result of political and ideological constraints over which Roosevelt had little control. But he challenged the views of earlier scholars who had proclaimed the New Deal a "revolution" in social policy. Leuchtenburg could muster only enough enthusiasm to call it a "halfway revolution," one that helped some previously disadvantaged groups (most notably farmers and workers) but that did little or nothing for many others (blacks, sharecroppers, the urban poor).

Harsher criticisms soon emerged. Barton Bernstein in a 1968 essay compiled a dreary chronicle of missed opportunities and inadequate responses to problems and concluded that the New Deal had saved capitalism, but at the expense of the least powerful and least favored members of society. Ronald Radosh, Allen Matusow, Paul Conkin, Thomas Ferguson, and other scholars writing in a climate shaped by the New Left's attack on liberalism expanded on these criticisms; the New Deal, they contended, was part of the twentieth-century tradition of "corporate liberalism"—a tradition in which reform is closely wedded to the needs and interests of capitalism.

But the attack from the left did not develop very far beyond its preliminary statements. Instead, by the early 1980s, most scholars seemed to have accepted a revised liberal view: that the New Deal was a significant (and, most agree, valuable) reform effort, even if one that worked within rigid, occasionally crippling limits. The scholarship of the last decade, therefore, has paid less attention to arguing over whether or not the New Deal was a good thing, and more attention to the nature of the constraints it faced and to the way it fits into larger patterns of political development.

The phrase "New Deal liberalism" came in the postwar era to seem synonymous with a broad range of reform ideas, many of which had very little connection to the New Deal itself. In fact, the liberal accomplishments of the 1930s can be understood only in the context of their own time; later liberal efforts have drawn from that legacy but also altered it to fit the needs and assumptions of different eras.

CHAPTER TWENTY-SEVEN

The Global Crisis, 1921–1941

The Diplomacy of the New Era ~ *Isolationism and Internationalism*

ENRY CABOT LODGE of Massachusetts, chairman of the Senate Foreign Relations Committee and one of the most powerful figures in the Republican party, led the fight against ratification of the Treaty of Versailles in 1918 and 1919. In part because of his efforts, the treaty was defeated. The United States failed to join the League of Nations; and American foreign policy embarked on an independent course that for the next two decades would attempt, but ultimately fail, to expand American influence and maintain international stability without committing the United States to any lasting relationships with other nations.

Lodge was not an isolationist. He recognized that America had emerged from World War I the most powerful nation in the world. He believed the United States should exert its influence internationally. But he believed, too, that America's expanded role in the world should reflect the nation's own interests and its own special virtues; it should leave the United States unfettered with obligations to anyone else. He said in 1919:

> We are a great moral asset of Christian civilization. . . . How did we get there? By our own efforts. Nobody led us, nobody guided us, nobody controlled us. . . . I would keep America as she has been—not isolated, not prevent her from joining other nations for . . . great purposes—but I wish her to be master of her own fate.

In the end, the limited American internationalism of the interwar years proved insufficient to protect the interests of the United States, to create global stability, or to keep the nation from becoming involved in the most catastrophic war in human history.

THE DIPLOMACY OF THE NEW ERA

Critics of American foreign policy in the 1920s often described it with a single word: isolationism. But in reality, the United States played a more active role in world affairs in the 1920s than it had at almost any previous time in its history.

Replacing the League

By the time the Harding administration took office in 1921, American membership in the League of Nations was no longer a realistic possibility. But Secretary of State Charles Evans Hughes wanted to find something with which to replace the League as a guarantor of world peace and stability. He embarked on a series of efforts to build safeguards against future wars—safeguards, however, that would not hamper American freedom of action in the world.

The most important of such efforts was the Washington Conference of 1921—an attempt to prevent a destabilizing naval armaments race among the United States, Britain, and Japan. Hughes proposed a plan for dramatic reductions in the fleets of all three nations and a ten-year moratorium on the construction of large warships. To the surprise of almost everyone, the conference ultimately agreed to accept most of Hughes's terms. The Five-Power Pact of February 1922 established limits for total naval tonnage and a ratio of armaments among the signatories. For every 5 tons of American and British warships, Japan would maintain 3 and France and Italy 1.75 each.

The Washington Conference began the New Era effort to protect world peace (and the international economic interests of the United States) without accepting international obligations. The Kellogg-Briand Pact of 1928 concluded it. When the French foreign minister, Aristide Briand, asked the United States in 1927 to join an alliance against Germany, Secretary of State Frank Kellogg (who had replaced Hughes in 1925) proposed instead a multilateral treaty outlawing war as an instrument of national policy. Fourteen nations signed the agreement in Paris on August 27, 1928, amid great solemnity and wide international acclaim. Forty-eight other nations later joined the pact. It contained no instruments of enforcement.

Debts and Diplomacy

The first responsibility of diplomacy, Hughes, Kellogg, and others agreed, was to ensure that American overseas trade faced no obstacles. Preventing a dangerous and expensive armaments race and reducing the possibility of war were two steps to that end. So were new financial arrangements to deal with international debts. The Allied powers of Europe were struggling to repay $11 billion in loans they had contracted with the United States during and shortly after the war. At the same time, Germany was attempting to pay the reparations levied by the Allies. With the financial structure of Europe on the brink of collapse as a result, the United States stepped in with a solution.

Charles G. Dawes, an American banker, negotiated an agreement in 1924 among France, Britain, Germany, and the United States under which American banks would provide enormous loans to the Germans, enabling them to meet their reparations payments; in return, Britain and France would agree to reduce the amount of those payments. The Dawes Plan became the source of a troubling circular pattern in international finance. The United States would lend money to Germany, which would use that money to pay reparations to France and England, which would in turn use those funds (as well as large loans they themselves were receiving from American banks) to repay war debts to the United States. The flow was able to continue only by virtue of the enormous debts Germany and the other European nations were acquiring to American banks and corporations. Some in the American government warned that the reckless expansion of overseas loans and investments threatened disaster—that the United States was becoming too dependent on unstable European economies. Such warnings fell, for the most part, on deaf ears; and the American economic involvement in Europe continued to expand until the worldwide depression shattered the system in 1931.

The government felt even fewer reservations about assisting American economic expansion in Latin America. During the 1920s, American military forces maintained a presence in Nicaragua, Panama, and several other countries in the region, while United States investments in Latin America more than doubled. American banks were offering large loans to Latin American governments, just as they were in Europe; and just as in Europe, the Latin Americans were having difficulty earning the money to repay them in the face of the formidable United States tariff barrier.

Hoover and the World Crisis

After the relatively placid international climate of the 1920s, the diplomatic challenges facing the Hoover administration must have seemed bewilder-

ing. The world financial crisis that had begun in 1929 and greatly intensified after 1931 was producing a dangerous nationalism in Europe, toppling
some existing political leaders and replacing them with powerful, belligerent governments committed to expansion as a solution to their economic
problems. Hoover was confronted with the beginning of a process that
would ultimately lead to war.

In Latin America, Hoover tried to repair some of the damage created
by earlier American policies. He made a ten-week good-will tour through
the region before his inauguration. Once in office, he generally abstained
from intervening in the internal affairs of neighboring nations and moved
to withdraw American troops from Nicaragua and Haiti. When economic
distress led to the collapse of several Latin American regimes, Hoover

HITLER AND MUSSOLINI   The German and Italian dictators, shown here
reviewing troops together in Berlin in the mid-1930s, acted publicly as
if they were equals. Privately, however, Hitler viewed Mussolini with
contempt, and the Italian dictator complained frequently of being
treated as a junior partner by his ally.

announced a new policy: America would grant diplomatic recognition to any sitting government in the region without questioning the means it had used to obtain power. He even repudiated the Roosevelt Corollary to the Monroe Doctrine by refusing to permit American intervention when several Latin American countries defaulted on debt obligations to the United States in October 1931.

In Europe, the administration enjoyed few successes in its efforts to promote economic stability. When Hoover's proposed moratorium on debts in 1931 failed to attract broad support or produce financial stability, he refused to cancel all war debts to the United States as many economists advised him to do. Several European nations promptly went into default. American efforts to extend the disarmament agreements of the 1920s met with similar frustration. Efforts to extend the 1921 limits on naval construction fell victim to French and British fears of German and Japanese militarism. And the World Disarmament Conference in Geneva in 1932 similarly ended in frustration.

The ineffectiveness of American diplomacy in Europe was particularly troubling in light of the new governments on the Continent. Benito Mussolini's Fascist party had been in control of Italy since the early 1920s and had become increasingly nationalistic and militaristic. Still more ominous was the growing power of the National Socialist (or Nazi) party in Germany. By the late 1920s, the Weimar Republic, the nation's government since the end of World War I, had been largely discredited by, among other things, a ruinous inflation. Adolf Hitler, the leader of the Nazis, was growing rapidly in popular favor and would take power in 1933. Hitler believed in the genetic superiority of the Aryan (German) people and in extending German territory to provide *Lebensraum* (living space) for the German "master race." He also displayed a pathological anti-Semitism and a passionate militarism.

More immediately alarming to the Hoover administration was a major crisis in Asia—another early step toward World War II. The Japanese, suffering from an economic depression of their own, were concerned about the increasing power of the Soviet Union and of Chiang Kai-shek's nationalist China. In particular, they were alarmed at Chiang's insistence on expanding his government's power in Manchuria, which remained officially a part of China but over which the Japanese had maintained effective economic control since 1905. In 1931, Japan's military leaders staged what was, in effect, a coup and took control of the government in Tokyo. Weeks later, they launched an invasion of northern Manchuria. They had conquered the region by the end of the year. Hoover permitted Secretary of State Henry Stimson to issue stern warnings to the Japanese but barred him from cooperating with the League of Nations to impose economic sanctions against them. Early in 1932, Japan expanded its aggression farther into China, attacking the city of Shanghai and killing thousands of civilians.

By the time Hoover left office, early in 1933, the international system the United States had attempted to create in the 1920s—a system based on voluntary cooperation among nations and on an American refusal to commit itself to any collective obligations—had collapsed. The United States faced a choice. It could adopt a more energetic form of internationalism and enter into firmer and more meaningful associations with other nations. It could resort to nationalism and try to deal with international problems alone. Or it could ignore global problems altogether. For the next six years, it experimented with elements of all three approaches.

ISOLATIONISM AND INTERNATIONALISM

The administration of Franklin Roosevelt faced a dual challenge as it entered office in 1933. It had to deal with the worst economic crisis in the nation's history, and it had to deal as well with the effects of a decaying international structure.

Depression Diplomacy

Perhaps Roosevelt's sharpest break with the policies of his predecessor was on the question of American economic relations with Europe. Hoover had argued that only by resolving the question of war debts and reinforcing the gold standard could the American economy hope to recover. He had, therefore, agreed to participate in the World Economic Conference, to be held in London in June 1933, to attempt to resolve these issues. By the time the conference assembled, however, Roosevelt had already become convinced that the gold value of the dollar had to be allowed to fall in order for American goods to be able to compete in world markets. Shortly after the conference convened, he released what became known as the "bombshell message," repudiating the orthodox views of most of the delegates and rejecting any agreement on currency stabilization. The conference quickly dissolved without reaching agreement.

At the same time, Roosevelt abandoned the commitments of the Hoover administration to settle the issue of war debts through international agreement. In April 1934 he signed a bill that prohibited American banks from making loans to any nation in default on its debts. The result was to stop the old, circular system by which debt payments continued only by virtue of increasing American loans; within months, war-debt payments from every nation except Finland stopped for good.

The United States and Russia had viewed each other with mistrust and even hostility since the Bolshevik Revolution of 1917, and the American government still had not officially recognized the Soviet regime in 1933. But a growing number of influential Americans were urging a change in policy—largely because the Soviet Union appeared to be a possible source of trade. The Russians, for their part, were hoping for American cooperation in containing Japan. In November 1933, the United States and the Soviet Union agreed to open formal diplomatic relations.

Despite this promising beginning, however, relations with the Soviet Union soon soured once again. American trade failed to establish a foothold in Russia, disappointing hopes in the United States; and the American government did little to reassure the Soviets that it was interested in stopping Japanese expansion in Asia, dousing expectations in Russia. By the end of 1934, the Soviet Union and the United States were once again viewing each other with considerable mistrust. And the Soviet leader, Josef Stalin, was beginning to consider making agreements of his own with the fascist governments of Japan and Germany.

The Good Neighbor Policy

The United States succeeded during the 1930s in increasing both its exports to and its imports from Latin America by over 100 percent. At the same time, the Roosevelt administration was taking a new approach toward Latin America, an approach which became known as the "Good Neighbor Policy" and which expanded on the changes the Hoover administration had made. At an Inter-American Conference in Montevideo, Uruguay, in December 1933, Secretary of State Cordell Hull signed a formal convention declaring: "No state has the right to intervene in the internal or external affairs of another." By repudiating military intervention, Roosevelt, like Hoover, eased tensions between the United States and its neighbors considerably. But the Good Neighbor Policy did little to stem the growing American domination of the Latin American economy.

The Rise of Isolationism

With the international system of the 1920s now decayed beyond repair, the United States faced a choice between more active efforts to stabilize the world and more energetic attempts to isolate the nation from it. Most Americans unhesitatingly chose the latter. Support for isolationism emerged from many quarters. Some Wilsonian internationalists had grown disillusioned with the League of Nations and its inability to stop Japanese aggression in Asia. Other Americans were listening to the argument that powerful business interests—Wall Street, munitions makers, and others— had tricked the United States into participating in World War I. An investigation by a Senate committee chaired by Senator Gerald Nye of North Dakota claimed to reveal exorbitant profiteering and tax evasion by many corporations during the war, and it suggested that bankers had pressured Wilson to intervene in the war so as to protect their loans abroad. (Few historians now lend much credence to these charges.)

Roosevelt himself was sympathetic to some of the isolationist arguments. But he continued to hope for at least a modest American role in maintaining world peace. In 1935, he proposed to the Senate a treaty to make the United States a member of the World Court—a largely symbolic gesture. Nevertheless, isolationists such as Father Coughlin and William Randolph Hearst aroused popular opposition to the agreement, and the Senate voted it down. The president would not soon again attempt to challenge the isolationist tide.

In the summer of 1935, it became clear that Mussolini's Italy was preparing to invade Ethiopia. Fearing the invasion would provoke a new European war, American legislators began to design legal safeguards to prevent the United States from being dragged into the conflict. The result was the Neutrality Act of 1935, followed by additional acts in 1936 and 1937. The 1935 law established a mandatory arms embargo against both sides in any military conflict and directed the president to warn American citizens against traveling on the ships of warring nations. Thus, isolationists believed, the "protection of neutral rights" could not again become an excuse for American intervention in war. The 1936 Neutrality Act renewed these provisions, and the 1937 law added new ones, establishing the so-called "cash-and-carry" policy, by which belligerents could purchase only nonmilitary goods from the United States and could do so only by paying cash and shipping their purchases themselves.

Isolationist sentiment showed its strength again in 1936–1937 in response to the civil war in Spain. The Falangists of General Francisco Franco, a group much like the Italian fascists, revolted in July 1936 against the existing republican government. Hitler and Mussolini supported Franco, both vocally and with weapons and supplies. Some individual Americans traveled to Spain to assist the republican cause, but the United States government joined with Britain and France in an agreement to offer no assistance to either side.

Roosevelt, however, was slowly becoming convinced that the course of international events required some more forceful American response. Particularly disturbing was the deteriorating situation in Asia. In the summer of 1937, Japan intensified its six-year-old assault on Manchuria and attacked China's five northern provinces. Roosevelt responded in a speech in Chicago in October 1937. He warned of the dangers of the Japanese actions and argued that aggressors should be "quarantined" by the international community to prevent the contagion of war from spreading. He was deliberately vague about what such a "quarantine" would mean. Even so, public response to the speech was disturbingly hostile, and Roosevelt drew back. On December 12, 1937, Japanese aviators bombed and sank the United States gunboat *Panay*, almost certainly deliberately, as it sailed the Yangtze River in China. But so reluctant was the Roosevelt administration to antagonize the isolationists that the United States eagerly seized on Japanese claims that the bombing had been an accident, accepted Japan's apologies, and overlooked the attack.

The Failure of Munich

In 1936, Hitler had moved the revived German army into the Rhineland, rearming an area that France had, in effect, controlled since World War I. In March 1938, German forces marched into Austria; and Hitler proclaimed a union (or *Anschluss*) between Austria, his native land, and Germany, his adopted one. Neither in America nor in most of Europe was there much more than a murmur of opposition.

The Austrian invasion, however, soon created another crisis, for Germany had by now occupied territory surrounding three sides of western Czechoslovakia, a region Hitler dreamed of annexing. In September 1938, he demanded that Czechoslovakia cede him part of that region, the Sudetenland, an area in which many ethnic Germans lived. Although Czechoslovakia was prepared to fight to stop Hitler, it needed assistance from other nations. But most Western governments, including the United States, were willing to pay almost any price to settle the crisis peacefully. On September

29, Hitler met with the leaders of France and Great Britain at Munich in an effort to resolve the crisis. The French and British agreed to accept the German demands in Czechoslovakia in return for Hitler's promise to expand no farther.

The Munich accords, which Roosevelt applauded at the time, were the most prominent element of a policy that came to be known as "appeasement" and that came to be identified (not altogether fairly) largely with British Prime Minister Neville Chamberlain. Whoever was to blame, the policy was a failure. In March 1939, Hitler occupied the remaining areas of Czechoslovakia, violating the Munich agreement unashamedly. And in April, he began issuing threats against Poland.

At that point, both Britain and France gave assurances to the Polish government that they would come to its assistance in case of an invasion;

THE BLITZ, LONDON The German Luftwaffe terrorized London and other British cities in 1940–1941 and again late in the war by bombing civilian areas indiscriminately in an effort to break the spirit of the English people. The effort failed, and the fortitude of the British did much to arouse support for their cause in the United States.

they even tried, too late, to draw the Soviet Union into a mutual defense agreement. But Stalin, who had not even been invited to the Munich Conference, had already decided he could expect no protection from the West. He signed a nonaggression pact with Hitler in August 1939, freeing the Germans for the moment from the danger of a two-front war.

Shortly after that, Hitler staged an incident on the Polish border to allow him to claim that Germany had been attacked; and on September 1, 1939, he launched a full-scale invasion of Poland. Britain and France, true to their pledges, declared war on Germany two days later. World War II had begun.

Neutrality Tested

"This nation will remain a neutral nation," the president declared shortly after the hostilities began in Europe, "but I cannot ask that every American remain neutral in thought as well." There was never any question that both he and the majority of the American people favored Britain, France, and the other Allied nations in the contest. The question was how much the United States was prepared to do to assist them.

At the very least, Roosevelt believed, the United States should make armaments available to the Allied armies to help them counteract the German munitions industry. In September 1939, he asked Congress to revise the Neutrality Acts and lift the arms embargo against any nation engaged in war. Powerful isolationist opposition forced Congress to maintain the prohibition on American ships entering war zones. But the 1939 law did permit belligerents to purchase arms on the same cash-and-carry basis that the earlier Neutrality Acts had established for the sale of nonmilitary materials.

For a time, it was possible to believe that little more would be necessary. After the German armies quickly subdued Poland, the war in Europe settled into a long, quiet lull that lasted through the winter and spring—a "phony war," some called it. (In the meantime, the Soviet Union overran first the small Baltic republics of Latvia, Estonia, and Lithuania and then, in late November, established effective control over Finland. The United States responded with nothing more than an ineffective "moral embargo" on the shipment of armaments to Russia.)

Whatever illusions Americans had harbored about the war in western Europe were shattered in the spring of 1940 when Germany launched a massive invasion to the west—first attacking Denmark and Norway, sweeping next across the Netherlands and Belgium, and driving finally deep into the heart of France. Allied efforts proved futile against the Nazi *blitzkrieg*. One western European stronghold after another fell into German hands. On June 10, Mussolini invaded France from the south as Hitler was attacking from the north. On June 22, finally, France fell, and Nazi troops marched into Paris. A new collaborationist French regime assembled in Vichy; and in all Europe, only the shattered remnants of the British and French armies, rescued from the beaches of Dunkirk, remained to oppose the Axis forces.

On May 16, in the midst of the offensive, Roosevelt asked Congress for an additional $1 billion for defense and received it quickly. That was one day after Winston Churchill, the new British prime minister, had sent Roosevelt the first of many long lists of requests for armaments, without which, he insisted, England could not long survive. Some Americans (including the United States ambassador to London, Joseph P. Kennedy) argued that the British plight was already hopeless, that any aid to the English was a wasted effort. But the president was determined to make war materials available to Britain. He even circumvented the cash-and-carry provisions of the Neutrality Acts by giving England fifty American destroyers (most of them left over from World War I) in return for the right to build American bases on British territory in the Western Hemisphere; and he returned to the factories a number of new airplanes purchased by the American government so that the British could buy them instead.

Roosevelt was able to take such steps in part because of a major shift in American public opinion. By July 1940, more than 66 percent of the public (according to opinion polls) believed that Germany posed a direct threat to the United States. Congress was, therefore, more willing to permit expanded American assistance to the Allies. It was also becoming more concerned about the need for internal preparations for war, and in September it approved the Burke-Wadsworth Act, inaugurating the first peacetime military draft in American history.

But the isolationists were far from finished. A powerful new isolationist lobby entitled the America First Committee, whose members included such prominent Americans as Charles Lindbergh and Senators Gerald Nye and Burton Wheeler, joined the debate over American policy toward the war. The lobby had at least the indirect support of a large proportion of the Republican party. The debate was a bitter one. Through the summer and fall of 1940, moreover, it was complicated by a presidential campaign.

The biggest political question of 1940 was whether Franklin Roosevelt would break with tradition and run for an unprecedented third term. The president himself did not reveal his own wishes. But by refusing to withdraw from the contest, he made it impossible for any rival Democrat to establish a claim to the nomination. And when, just before the Democratic Convention in July, he let it be known that he would accept a "draft" from his party, the issue was virtually settled. The Democrats quickly renominated him and even reluctantly swallowed his choice for vice president: Agriculture Secretary Henry A. Wallace, a man too liberal and too controversial for the taste of many party leaders.

The Republicans, again uncertain how to oppose Roosevelt effectively, nominated for president a politically inexperienced Indiana businessman, Wendell Willkie, who benefited from a powerful grass-roots movement. Both the candidate and the party platform took positions little different from Roosevelt's: they would keep the country out of war but would extend generous assistance to the Allies. Willkie was an appealing figure and a vigorous campaigner, and he managed to evoke more public enthusiasm than any Republican candidate in decades. The election was closer than in either 1932 or 1936, but Roosevelt still won decisively. He received 55 percent of the popular vote to Willkie's 45 percent, and he won 449 electoral votes to Willkie's 82.

Neutrality Abandoned

In the last months of 1940, with the election behind him and with the situation in Europe deteriorating, Roosevelt began to make subtle but profound changes in the American role in the war. Great Britain was virtually bankrupt and could no longer meet the cash-and-carry requirements imposed by the Neutrality Acts. The president, therefore, proposed a new system for supplying Britain: "lend-lease." It would allow the government not only to sell but to lend or lease armaments to any nation deemed "vital to the defense of the United States." In other words, America could funnel weapons to England on the basis of no more than Britain's promise to return them when the war was over. Isolationists attacked the measure bitterly, but Congress enacted the bill by wide margins.

With lend-lease established, Roosevelt soon faced another serious problem. Attacks by German submarines had made shipping lanes in the Atlantic extremely dangerous. The British navy was losing ships more rapidly than it could replace them and was finding it difficult to transport materials across the Atlantic from America. Secretary of War Henry Stimson (who had been Hoover's secretary of state and who returned to the cabinet at Roosevelt's request in 1940) argued that the United States should itself convoy vessels to England; but Roosevelt took a more limited approach. He argued that the western Atlantic was a neutral zone and the responsibility of the American nations. By July 1941, therefore, American ships were patrolling the ocean as far east as Iceland.

At first, Germany did little to challenge these obviously hostile American actions. By September 1941, however, the situation had changed. Nazi forces had invaded the Soviet Union in June of that year. When the Soviets did not surrender, as many had predicted, Roosevelt persuaded Congress to extend lend-lease privileges to them. Now American industry was providing vital assistance to Hitler's foes on two fronts, and the American navy was protecting the flow of those goods to Europe. In September, Nazi submarines began a concerted campaign against American vessels. Roosevelt ordered American ships to fire on German submarines "on sight." In October, Nazi submarines hit two American destroyers and sank one of them, the *Reuben James*, killing many American sailors. Congress now voted to allow the United States to arm its merchant vessels and to sail all the way into belligerent ports. The United States had, in effect, launched a naval war against Germany.

In August 1941, Roosevelt met with Churchill aboard a British vessel off the coast of Newfoundland. The president made no military commitments, but he did join with the prime minister in releasing a document that became known as the Atlantic Charter, in which the two nations set out "certain common principles" on which to base "a better future for the world." It called openly for "the final destruction of the Nazi tyranny" and for a new world order in which every nation controlled its own destiny. It was, in effect, a statement of war aims.

The Road to Pearl Harbor

Japan, in the meantime, was taking advantage of events in Europe to extend its empire in the Pacific. In September 1940, the Japanese signed the Tripartite Pact, a loose defensive alliance with Germany and Italy (although in reality, the European Axis powers never developed a very strong relationship with Japan). In July 1941, imperial troops moved into Indochina and seized the capital of Vietnam, a colony of France. The United States, having broken Japanese codes, knew their next target would be the Dutch East Indies; and when Tokyo failed to respond to Roosevelt's stern warnings, the president froze all Japanese assets in the United States, severely limiting Japan's ability to purchase needed American supplies.

Tokyo now faced a choice. Either it would have to repair relations with the United States to restore the flow of supplies or it would have to find those supplies elsewhere, most notably by seizing British and Dutch possessions in the Pacific. At first, the Tokyo government seemed willing to negotiate. But in October, militants in Tokyo forced the moderate prime minister out of office and replaced him with the leader of the war party, General Hideki Tojo. There seemed little alternative now to war.

For several weeks, the Tojo government maintained a pretense of wanting to continue negotiations. But Tokyo had already decided it would not yield on the question of China, and Washington had made clear that it would accept nothing less than a reversal of that policy. By late November, the State Department had given up on the possibility of a peaceful settle-

THE JAPANESE ATTACK PEARL HARBOR, DECEMBER 7, 1941 The destroyer U.S.S. *Shaw*, immobilized in a floating drydock in Pearl Harbor in December 1941, survived the first wave of Japanese bombers unscathed. But in the second attack, the Japanese scored a direct hit, which blew off the ship's bow.

ment. American intelligence, meanwhile, had decoded Japanese messages that made clear a Japanese attack was imminent. But Washington did not know where the attack would take place. Most officials continued to believe that the Japanese would move first not against American territory but against British or Dutch possessions to the south. A combination of confusion and miscalculation caused the government to overlook indications that Japan intended a direct attack on American forces.

At 7:55 A.M. on Sunday, December 7, 1941, a wave of Japanese bombers attacked the United States naval base at Pearl Harbor in Hawaii. A second wave came an hour later. Within two hours, the United States lost 8 battleships, 3 cruisers, 4 other vessels, 188 airplanes, and several vital shore installations. More than 2,400 soldiers and sailors died, and another 1,000 were injured. The Japanese suffered only light losses.

American forces were now greatly diminished in the Pacific (although by a fortunate accident, no American aircraft carriers—the heart of the Pacific fleet—had been at Pearl Harbor on December 7). Nevertheless, the raid on Hawaii unified the American people behind war. On December 8, after a stirring speech by the president, the Senate voted unanimously and the House voted 388 to 1 to approve a declaration of war against Japan. Three days later, Germany and Italy, Japan's European allies, declared war on the United States; on the same day, December 11, Congress reciprocated without a dissenting vote.

CHAPTER TWENTY-EIGHT

America in a World at War

War on Two Fronts ~ *The American People in Wartime*
The Defeat of the Axis

T HE ATTACK ON Pearl Harbor had thrust the United States into the greatest and most terrible war in the history of humanity. World War I had destroyed centuries-old European social and political institutions. But World War II created unprecedented carnage and horror, not only in Europe but around much of the rest of the globe. And in the end, it changed the world as profoundly as any event of the twentieth century, perhaps any century.

Less readily apparent is how profoundly the war changed America—its society, its politics, and its image of itself. Except for the combatants themselves, most Americans experienced the war at a remove of several thousand miles. They endured no bombing, no invasion, no massive dislocations, no serious material privations. Veterans returning home in 1945 and 1946 found a country that looked very much like the one they had left—something that clearly could not be said of veterans returning home to Britain, France, Germany, Russia, or Japan.

But World War II did transform the United States in profound, if not always readily visible, ways. As the poet Archibald MacLeish said in 1943, "The great majority of the American people understand very well that this war is not a war only, but an end and a beginning—an end to things known and a beginning of things unknown. We have smelled the wind in the streets that changes weather. We know that whatever the world will be when the war ends, the world will be different." The story of American involvement in the war, therefore, is not just the story of how the military forces and the industrial might of the United States contributed to the defeat of Germany, Italy, and Japan. It is also the story of the creation of a new world, both abroad and at home.

WAR ON TWO FRONTS

Whatever political disagreements and social tensions there may have been among the American people during World War II, there was striking unity of opinion about the conflict itself. But both unity and confidence were severely tested in the first, troubled months of 1942.

Containing the Japanese

Ten hours after the strike at Pearl Harbor, Japanese airplanes attacked the American airfields at Manila in the Philippines, destroying much of America's remaining air power in the Pacific. Three days later Guam, an American possession, fell to Japan; Wake Island and Hong Kong followed. The great British fortress of Singapore in Malaya surrendered in February 1942, the Dutch East Indies in March, Burma in April. In the Philippines, exhausted Filipino and American troops gave up their defense of the islands on May 6.

American strategists planned two broad offensives to turn the tide against the Japanese. One, under the command of General Douglas MacArthur, would move north from Australia, through New Guinea, and eventually to the Philippines. The other, under Admiral Chester Nimitz, would move west from Hawaii toward major Japanese island outposts in the central Pacific. Ultimately, the two offensives would come together to invade Japan itself.

The Allies achieved their first important victory in the Battle of the Coral Sea, just northwest of Australia, on May 7–8, 1942, when American forces turned back the previously unstoppable Japanese. A month later, there was an even more important turning point northwest of Hawaii. An enormous battle raged for four days, June 3–6, 1942, near the small American outpost at Midway Island, at the end of which the United States, despite great losses, was clearly victorious. The American navy destroyed four Japanese aircraft carriers and lost only one of its own; the action regained control of the central Pacific for the United States.

The Americans took the offensive for the first time several months later in the southern Solomon Islands, to the east of New Guinea. In August 1942, American forces assaulted three of the islands: Gavutu, Tulagi, and Guadalcanal. A struggle of terrible ferocity developed at Guadalcanal and continued for six months, inflicting heavy losses on both sides. In the end, however, the Japanese were forced to abandon the island—and with it their last chance of launching an effective offensive to the south.

World War II in the Pacific

Farthest extent of Japanese expansion (to August 1942)	NAVAL AND TROOP MOVEMENTS ← Japanese forces ← Allied forces	BATTLES ✶ Japanese victories ✶ Allied victories	▼ Atomic bombings — Supply route

In both the southern and the central Pacific, therefore, the initiative had shifted to the United States by mid-1943. The Japanese advance had been halted. The Americans, with aid from the Australians and the New Zealanders, now began the slow, arduous process of moving toward the Philippines and Japan itself.

Holding Off the Germans

In the European war, the United States was fighting in cooperation with Britain and with the exiled "Free French" forces in the west; and it was trying also to conciliate its new ally, the Soviet Union, which was now fighting Hitler in the east. The army chief of staff, General George C. Marshall, supported a plan for a major Allied invasion of France across the English Channel in the spring of 1943; and he placed a hitherto little known general, Dwight D. Eisenhower, in charge of planning the operation. But the American plan faced challenges from the other Allies. The Soviet Union, which was absorbing the brunt of the German war effort (as it would throughout the conflict), wanted the Allied invasion to begin at the earliest possible moment. The British, on the other hand, wanted first to launch a series of Allied offensives around the edges of the Nazi empire—in northern Africa and southern Europe—before undertaking the major invasion of France.

Roosevelt was torn, but he ultimately decided to support the British plan—in part because he was eager to get American forces into combat quickly and feared that a cross-Channel invasion would take a long time to prepare. At the end of October 1942, the British opened a counteroffensive

World War II in North Africa and Italy: The Allied Counteroffensive, 1942–1943

against Nazi forces in North Africa under General Erwin Rommel, who was threatening the Suez Canal. In a major battle at El Alamein, they forced the Germans to retreat from Egypt. On November 8, Anglo-American forces landed at Oran and Algiers in Algeria and at Casablanca in Morocco—areas under the Nazi-controlled French government at Vichy—and began moving east toward Rommel. The Germans threw the full weight of their forces in Africa against the inexperienced Americans and inflicted a serious defeat on them at the Kasserine Pass in Tunisia. General George S. Patton, however, regrouped the American troops and began an effective counteroffensive. With the help of Allied air and naval power and of British forces attacking from the east under Field Marshall Bernard Montgomery (the hero of El Alamein), the American offensive finally drove the last Germans from Africa in May 1943.

The North African campaign had tied up so large a proportion of the Allied resources that the planned May 1943 cross-Channel invasion of France had to be postponed, despite angry complaints from the Soviet Union. By now, however, the threat of a Soviet collapse seemed much diminished, for during the winter of 1942–1943, the Red Army had successfully held off a major German assault at Stalingrad in southern Russia. Hitler had committed such enormous forces to the battle, and had suffered such appalling losses, that he could not continue his eastern offensive.

The Soviet successes persuaded Roosevelt to agree, in a January 1943 meeting with Churchill in Casablanca, to a British plan for an Allied invasion of Sicily. Churchill argued that the operation in Sicily might knock Italy out of the war and tie up German divisions that might otherwise be stationed in France. On the night of July 9, 1943, American and British armies landed in southeast Sicily; thirty-eight days later, they had conquered the island and were moving onto the Italian mainland. In the face of these setbacks, Mussolini's government collapsed and the dictator himself fled north toward Germany. Although Mussolini's successor, Pietro Badoglio, quickly committed Italy to the Allies, Germany moved eight divisions into the country and established a powerful defensive line south of Rome. The Allied offensive on the Italian peninsula, which began on September 3, 1943, soon bogged down. Not until May 1944 did the Allies resume their northward advance. On June 4, 1944, they captured Rome.

The invasion of Italy contributed to the Allied war effort in several important ways. But it postponed the invasion of France by as much as a year, deeply embittering the Soviet Union and giving the Soviets time to begin moving toward the countries of eastern Europe.

America and the Holocaust

In the midst of this intensive fighting, the leaders of the American government found themselves confronted with one of history's great tragedies: the Nazi campaign to exterminate the Jews of Europe—the Holocaust. As early as 1942, high officials in Washington had incontrovertible evidence that Hitler's forces were rounding up Jews and others (including Poles, homosexuals, and communists) from all over Europe, transporting them to concentration camps in eastern Germany and Poland, and systematically murdering them. (The death toll would ultimately reach 6 million Jews and at least 4 million others.) News of the atrocities was reaching the public as well, and pressure began to build for an Allied effort to end the killing or at least to rescue some of the surviving Jews.

The American government consistently resisted almost all such entreaties. Although Allied bombers were flying missions within a few miles of the most notorious death camp, at Auschwitz in Poland, pleas that the planes try to destroy the crematoria at the camp were rejected as militarily unfeasible. So were similar requests that the Allies try to destroy railroad lines leading to the camp. The United States also resisted pleas that it admit large numbers of the Jewish refugees attempting to escape Europe.

In fairness to American leaders, there was probably little they could have done to save most of Hitler's victims. But more forceful action by the United States (and Britain, which was even less amenable to Jewish requests for assistance) might well have saved at least some lives. Policymakers found it possible to justify abandoning the Jews to their fate by concentrating their attention solely on the larger goal of winning the war. Any diversion of energy and attention to other purposes, they apparently believed, would distract them from the overriding goal of victory.

THE AMERICAN PEOPLE IN WARTIME

Not since the Civil War had the United States been involved in so prolonged and consuming a military experience as World War II. American armed forces engaged in combat around the globe for nearly four years. American society, in the meantime, experienced changes that reached into virtually every corner of the nation.

Prosperity and the Rights of Labor

World War II had its most profound impact on American domestic life by ending the Great Depression at last. By the middle of 1941, the economic problems of the 1930s—unemployment, deflation, industrial sluggishness—had virtually vanished before the great wave of wartime industrial expansion.

The most important agent of the new prosperity was government spending, which after 1939 was pumping more money into the economy each year than all the New Deal relief agencies combined had done. In 1939, the federal budget had been $9 billion; by 1945, it had risen to $100 billion. Largely as a result, the gross national product soared: from $91 billion in 1939 to $166 billion in 1945. Personal incomes in some regions grew by as much as 100 percent or more. The demands of wartime production created a shortage of consumer goods, so many wage earners diverted much of their new affluence into savings, which would later help keep the economic boom alive in the postwar years.

Instead of the prolonged and debilitating unemployment that had been the most troubling feature of the Depression economy, the war created a serious labor shortage. The armed forces took over 15 million men and women out of the civilian work force at the same time that the demand for labor was rising rapidly. Nevertheless, the civilian work force increased by almost 20 percent during the war. The 7 million who had previously been unemployed accounted for some of the increase; the employment of many people previously considered inappropriate for the work force—the very young, the elderly, minorities, and, most important, several million women—accounted for the rest of it.

The war gave an enormous boost to union membership, which rose from about 10.5 million in 1941 to over 13 million in 1945. But it also created important new restrictions on the ability of unions to fight for their members' demands. The government was principally interested in keeping production moving without disruption and preventing inflation. It managed to win two important concessions from union leaders toward those ends. One was the "no-strike" pledge, by which unions agreed not to stop production in wartime. Another was the so-called Little Steel formula, which set a 15 percent limit on wage increases. In return, the government provided labor with a "maintenance-of-membership" agreement, which ensured that the thousands of new workers pouring into unionized defense plants would be automatically enrolled in the unions. The agreement guaranteed the continued health of the union organizations, but in return workers had to give up the right to demand major gains during the war.

Despite the no-strike pledge, there were nearly 15,000 work stoppages during the war, mostly wildcat strikes (strikes unauthorized by the union leadership), many protesting harsh working conditions and high levels of stress. When the United Mine Workers defied the government by striking in May 1943, Congress reacted by passing, over Roosevelt's veto, the Smith-Connally Act (War Labor Disputes Act), which required that unions wait thirty days before striking and which empowered the president to seize a struck war plant. In the meantime, public animosity toward labor rose rapidly, and many states passed laws to limit union power.

Stabilizing the Boom and Mobilizing Production

The fear of deflation, the central concern of the 1930s, gave way during the war to a fear of inflation, particularly after prices rose 25 percent in the two years before Pearl Harbor. In October 1942, Congress grudgingly responded to the president's request and passed the Anti-Inflation Act, which gave the administration authority to freeze agricultural prices, wages, salaries, and rents throughout the country. Enforcement of these provisions was the task of the Office of Price Administration (OPA), led first by Leon Henderson and then by Chester Bowles. In part because of its success, inflation was a much less serious problem during World War II than it had been during World War I.

Even so, the OPA was never popular. There was widespread resentment of its controls over wages and prices. And there was only grudging acquiescence to its complicated system of rationing scarce consumer goods: coffee, sugar, meat, butter, canned goods, shoes, tires, gasoline, and fuel oil. Black-marketing and overcharging grew in proportions far beyond OPA policing capacity.

From 1941 to 1945, the federal government spent a total of $321 billion—twice as much as it had spent in the entire 150 years of its existence to that point, and ten times as much as the cost of World War I. The national debt rose from $49 billion in 1941 to $259 billion in 1945. The government borrowed about half the revenues it needed by selling $100 billion worth of bonds. Much of the rest it raised by radically increasing income tax rates, through the Revenue Act of 1942. To simplify collection, Congress enacted a withholding system of payroll deductions in 1943.

The search for an effective mechanism to mobilize the economy for war began as early as 1939 and continued for nearly four years. One failed agency after another attempted to bring order to the mobilization effort. Finally, in January 1942, the president responded to widespread criticism by creating the War Production Board (WPB), under the direction of former Sears Roebuck executive Donald Nelson. In theory, the WPB was to be a "superagency," with broad powers over the economy. In fact, it never had as much authority as its World War I equivalent, the War Industries Board.

Throughout its troubled history, therefore, the WPB found itself constantly outmaneuvered and frustrated. It was never able to win complete control over military purchases; the army and navy often circumvented the board entirely in negotiating contracts with producers. It was never able to satisfy the complaints of small business, which charged (correctly) that most contracts were going to large corporations. Gradually, the president transferred much of the WPB's authority to a new office located within the White House: the Office of War Mobilization (OWM). But the OWM was only slightly more successful than the WPB.

Despite the administrative problems, however, the war economy managed to meet almost all of the nation's critical war needs. By the beginning of 1944, American factories were, in fact, producing more than the government needed. Their output was twice that of all the Axis countries combined.

African-Americans and the War

During World War I, many African-Americans had eagerly seized the chance to serve in the armed forces, believing that their patriotic efforts would win them an enhanced position in postwar society. They had been cruelly disappointed. As World War II approached, blacks were again determined to use the conflict to improve the position of their race—this time, however, not by currying favor but by making demands.

In the summer of 1941, A. Philip Randolph, president of the Brotherhood of Sleeping Car Porters, an important black union, began to insist that the government require companies receiving defense contracts to integrate their work forces. To mobilize support for the demand, Randolph planned a massive march on Washington. Roosevelt finally persuaded Randolph to cancel the march in return for a promise to establish the Fair Employment Practices Commission (FEPC) to investigate discrimination against blacks in war industries. The FEPC's enforcement powers, and thus its effectiveness, were limited, but its creation was a rare symbolic victory for African-American demands of the government.

TRAINING AFRICAN-AMERICAN FIGHTER PILOTS Black air corps cadets receive advanced training in Tuskegee, Alabama, during World War II. African-American pilots were generally restricted to flying supply and support missions, but many fought for—and some won—the right to fly in combat as well.

The need for labor in war plants greatly increased the migration of blacks from the rural areas of the South into industrial cities. The migration bettered the economic condition of many African-Americans, but it also created urban tensions and occasionally violence. The most serious conflict occurred in Detroit in 1943, when racial friction in the city produced a major riot in which thirty-four people died, twenty-five of them blacks.

Despite such tensions, the leading black organizations redoubled their efforts during the war to challenge the system of segregation. The Congress of Racial Equality (CORE), organized in 1942, mobilized mass popular resistance to discrimination in a way that the older, more conservative organizations had never done. Randolph, Bayard Rustin, James Farmer, and other, younger black leaders helped organize sit-ins and demonstrations in segregated theaters and restaurants. Their defiant public spirit would survive into the 1950s and help produce the civil-rights movement.

Pressure for change was also growing within the military. At first, the armed forces maintained their traditional practice of limiting blacks to the most menial assignments, keeping them in segregated training camps and units, and barring them entirely from the Marine Corps and the army air forces. Gradually, however, military leaders were forced to make adjustments—in part because of public and political pressures, but also because they recognized that these forms of segregation were wasting manpower. By the end of the war, the number of black servicemen had increased sevenfold, to 700,000; some training camps were being at least partially integrated; blacks were being allowed to serve on ships with white sailors; and more black units were being sent into combat. But tensions remained. In some of the partially integrated army bases—Fort Dix, New Jersey, for example—riots occasionally broke out when blacks protested having to serve in segregated divisions. Substantial discrimination survived in all the services until well after the war. But within the military, as within society at large, the traditional pattern of race relations was slowly eroding.

Indians and the War

Approximately 25,000 Indians performed military service during World War II. Many Native Americans served in combat. Others (mostly Navajos) became "code-talkers," working in military communications and speaking their own language (which enemy forces would be unlikely to understand) over the radio and the telephones. The war had important effects on the Indians who served in the military. It brought them into intimate contact (often for the first time) with white society, and it awakened among some of them a taste for the material benefits of life in capitalist America that they would retain after the war. Some never returned to the reservations, but chose to remain in the non-Indian world and assimilate to its ways.

The war had important effects, too, on those Native Americans who stayed on the reservations. Little war work reached the tribes. Government subsidies dwindled. Talented young people left the reservations to serve in the military or work in war production, creating manpower shortages in some tribes. The wartime emphasis on national unity undermined support for the revitalization of tribal autonomy that the Indian Reorganization Act of 1934 had launched. New pressures emerged to eliminate the reservation system and require the tribes to assimilate into white society—pressures so severe that John Collier, the energetic director of the Bureau of Indian Affairs who had done so much to promote the reinvigoration of the reservations, resigned in 1945.

Mexican-American War Workers

Large numbers of Mexican workers entered the United States during the war in response to labor shortages on the Pacific coast and in the Southwest. The American and Mexican governments agreed in 1942 to a program by which *braceros* (contract laborers) would be admitted to the United States for a limited time to work at specific jobs, and American employers in some parts of the Southwest began actively recruiting Hispanic workers. During the Depression, many Mexican farm workers had been deported to make room for desperate white workers. The wartime labor shortage caused farm owners to begin hiring them again. More important, however, Mexicans were able for the first time to find significant numbers of factory jobs. They formed the second-largest group of migrants (after blacks) to American cities in the 1940s. They were concentrated mainly in the West, but there were significant Mexican communities in Chicago, Detroit, and other industrial cities in the Midwest and East.

The sudden expansion of Mexican-American neighborhoods created tensions and occasionally conflict in some American cities. White residents of Los Angeles became alarmed at the activities of Mexican-American teen-agers, many of whom were joining street gangs (*pachucos*). They were particularly distinctive because of their style of dress, which whites considered outrageous. They wore long, loose jackets with padded shoulders, baggy pants tied at the ankles, long watch chains, broad-brimmed hats, and greased, ducktail hair styles. The outfit was known as a "zoot suit."

In June 1943, animosity toward the "zoot-suiters" produced a four-day riot in Los Angeles, during which white sailors stationed at a base in Long Beach invaded Mexican-American communities and attacked "zoot-suiters" (in response to alleged attacks by them on servicemen). The police did little to restrain the sailors, who grabbed Hispanic teen-agers, tore off and burned their clothes, cut off their ducktails, and beat them. When Hispanics tried to fight back, the police moved in and arrested them. In the aftermath of the "zoot suit riots," Los Angeles passed a law prohibiting the wearing of zoot suits.

Women and Children in Wartime

The war drew increasing numbers of women into roles from which they had previously been largely barred, either by custom or law. The number of women in the work force increased by nearly 60 percent, as many women took industrial jobs to replace male workers serving in the military. And these wage-earning women were more likely to be married and were on the whole older than most of those who had entered the work force in the past.

But while economic and military necessity eroded some of the popular objections to women in the workplace, obstacles remained. Many factory owners continued to categorize jobs by gender, reserving the most lucrative positions for men. (Female work, like male work, was also categorized by race: black women were usually assigned more menial tasks, and paid at a lower rate, than their white counterparts.) Still, women did make important inroads in industrial employment during the war. Women had been working in industry for over a century, but some began now to take on heavy industrial jobs that had long been considered "men's work." The famous wartime image of "Rosie the Riveter" symbolized the new importance of the female industrial worker. Women joined unions in substantial numbers, and they helped erode at least some of the prejudice, including the prejudice against mothers working, that had previously kept many of them from paid employment.

In the end, however, most women workers during the war were employed not in factories but in service-sector jobs. Above all, they worked for the government, whose bureaucratic needs expanded dramatically alongside its military and industrial needs. Even within the military, which enlisted substantial numbers of women as WAACs (army) and WAVEs (navy), most female work was clerical.

The new opportunities produced new problems. Many mothers whose husbands were in the military had to combine working with caring for their children. The scarcity of child-care facilities or other community services meant that some women had no choice but to leave young children—often known as "latch-key children" or "eight-hour orphans"—at home alone (or sometimes locked in cars in factory parking lots) while they worked.

Perhaps in part because of the family dislocations the war produced, juvenile crime rose markedly in the war years. Young boys were arrested at rapidly increasing rates for car theft and other burglary, vandalism, and vagrancy. The arrest rate for prostitutes, many of whom were teen-age girls, rose too, as did the incidence of venereal disease. For many children, however, the distinctive experience of the war years was not crime but work. More than a third of all teen-agers between the ages of fourteen and eighteen were employed late in the war, causing some reduction in high-school enrollments.

The return of prosperity helped increase the marriage rate and lower the age at which people married, but many marriages were unable to survive the pressures of wartime separation. The divorce rate rose rapidly. The rise

A M E R I C A N   V O I C E S

SARAH KILLINGSWORTH

An African-American Woman Encounters the Wartime Industrial Boom

THE WAR STARTED and jobs kinda opened up for women that the men had. . . . They started takin' applications at Douglas, to work in a defense plant. I was hired.

I didn't want a job on the production line. I heard so many things about accidents. . . . I was frightened. All I wanted to do was get in the factory, because they were payin' more than what I'd been makin'. . . . I got the job workin' nights in the ladies' rest room, which wasn't hard. . . .

I do know one thing, this place was very segregated when I first come here. Oh, Los Angeles, you just couldn't go and sit down like you do now. You had certain places you went. You had to more or less stick to the restaurants and hotels where black people were. It wasn't until the war that it really opened up. 'Cause when I come out here it was awful, just like bein' in the South. . . .

For a person that grew up and knew nothin' but hard times to get out on my own at eighteen years old and make a decent livin' and still make a decent person outa myself, I really am proud of me. . . .

In ways it was too bad that so many lives were lost. But I think it was for a worthy cause, because it did make a way for us. And we were able to really get out.

SOURCE: Studs Terkel, *The Good War*, pp. 113–116. Copyright ©1984 by Studs Terkel. Reprinted by permission of Pantheon Books.

in the birth rate that accompanied the increase in marriages was the first sign of what would become the great postwar "baby boom."

The Internment of the Japanese-Americans

During World War I, popular prejudice against the German people—and against German-Americans—had run high. No such passions emerged against Germans, Italians, or Americans of German and Italian descent during World War II. The same could not be said, however, about the Japanese. After the attack on Pearl Harbor, government propaganda and popular culture combined to create an image of the Japanese as a devious, malign, and savage people.

Predictably, this racial animosity soon extended to Americans of Japanese descent. There were not many Japanese-Americans in the United States—only about 127,000, most of them concentrated in a few areas in

REGISTERING FOR INTERNMENT, 1942 Japanese-Americans, forcibly removed from their homes by military authorities on the West Coast, wait in line to sign up for an internment that would continue until the last days of World War II. Many were American citizens.

California. About a third of them were unnaturalized, first-generation immigrants (Issei); two-thirds were naturalized or native-born citizens of the United States (Nisei). Because they generally kept to themselves and preserved traditional Japanese cultural patterns, it was possible for others to imagine that the Japanese-Americans were engaged in conspiracies on behalf of their ancestral homeland. (There is no evidence to suggest that they actually were.) Public pressure to remove the "threat" grew steadily.

Finally, in February 1942, in response to pressure from military officials and political leaders on the West Coast and recommendations from the War Department, the president authorized the army to "intern" the Japanese-Americans. More than 100,000 people (Issei and Nisei alike) were rounded up, told to dispose of their property however they could (which often meant simply abandoning it), and taken to what the government euphemistically termed "relocation centers" in the "interior." In fact, they were facilities little different from prisons, many of them located in the Western mountains and desert. Conditions in the internment camps were not brutal, but they were harsh and uncomfortable. More important, loyal, hard-working Americans were forced to spend up to three years in grim, debilitating isolation, barred from lucrative employment, provided with only minimal medical care, and deprived of decent schools for their children. (In Hawaii, by contrast, residents of Japanese descent encountered little harassment, perhaps because they were more numerous and more crucial to the economy of the islands.) The Supreme Court upheld the evacuation in a 1944 decision; and although most of the Japanese-Americans were released later that year, they were largely unable to win any compensation for their losses until Congress finally acted to redress the wrongs in the late 1980s.

The Retreat from Reform

Late in 1943, Franklin Roosevelt publicly suggested that "Dr. New Deal," as he called it, had served its purpose and should now give way to "Dr. Win-the-War." The statement reflected the president's own genuine shift in concern: victory was now more important than reform. But it reflected, too, the political reality that had emerged during the first two years of war. Liberals in government were finding themselves unable to enact new programs. They were even finding it difficult to protect existing ones from conservative assault.

The greatest assault on New Deal reforms came from conservatives in Congress, who seized on the war as an excuse to do what many had wanted to do in peacetime: dismantle many of the achievements of the New Deal. They were assisted by the end of mass unemployment, which decreased the need for such relief programs as the Civilian Conservation Corps and the Works Progress Administration (both of which were abolished). They were assisted, too, by their own increasing numbers. In the congressional elections of 1942, Republicans gained 47 seats in the House and 10 in the Senate.

Republicans approached the 1944 election determined to exploit what they believed was resentment of wartime regimentation and unhappiness with Democratic reform. They nominated as their candidate the young and vigorous governor of New York, Thomas E. Dewey. Roosevelt was unopposed within his party; but Democratic leaders pressured him to abandon Vice President Henry Wallace, an advanced New Dealer and hero of the CIO, and replace him with a more moderate figure. Roosevelt reluctantly acquiesced in the selection of Senator Harry S. Truman of Missouri, who had won acclaim as chairman of the Senate War Investigating Committee (known as the Truman Committee), which had compiled an impressive record uncovering waste and corruption in wartime production.

The conduct of the war was not an issue in the campaign. Instead, the election revolved around domestic economic issues and, indirectly, the president's health. The president was, in fact, gravely ill, suffering from, among other things, arteriosclerosis. It is not too much to say that he was dying. But the campaign seemed momentarily to revive him. He made several strenuous public appearances late in October, which dispelled popular doubts about his health and ensured his reelection. He captured 53.5 percent of the popular vote to Dewey's 46 percent (the lowest percentage of his four campaigns); and he won 432 electoral votes to Dewey's 99. Democrats lost 1 seat in the Senate, gained 20 in the House, and maintained control of both.

THE DEFEAT OF THE AXIS

By the middle of 1943, America and its allies had succeeded in stopping the Axis advance both in Europe and in the Pacific. In the next two years, the Allies themselves seized the offensive and launched a series of powerful drives that rapidly led the way to victory.

The Liberation of France

By early 1944, American and British bombers were attacking German industrial installations and other targets almost around the clock, drastically cutting production and impeding transportation. Especially devastating was the massive bombing of such German cities as Leipzig, Dresden, and Berlin. A February 1945 incendiary raid on Dresden created a great

World War II in Eur
The Allied Counter-
offensive, 1943–1945

Axis countries
and colonies

Axis conquests
to Dec. 1941

Vichy France
(nominally neutral,
controlled by Axis)

Allied countries and
territories occupied
by Allies

Neutral countries

NAVAL AND TROOP
MOVEMENTS

Allied forces

Allied convoy rout

Battles

SUMMER ROUTE
WINTER ROUTE

ICELAND

Murmansk

Archangel

ATLANTIC
OCEAN

NORWAY

FINLAND

Leningrad
Jan. 15–19, 1944

SWEDEN

Baltic
Sea

North
Sea

ESTONIA

Moscow

IRELAND

GREAT
BRITAIN

Battle of
the Bulge
Dec. 16, 1944–
Jan. 16, 1945

DENMARK

LATVIA

LITHUANIA

London

GERMANY

German
surrender May 8, 1945

EAST
PRUSSIA

Allied landings at
Normandy
June 6, 1944

NETH.

BEL.

Remagen
Mar. 7, 1945

Berlin

Warsaw

SOVIET UNION

Stalingrad
Aug. 1942–Feb.

Paris liberated
Aug. 23, 1944

FRANCE

Vichy

SWITZ.

CZECHOSLOVAKIA

Vienna

AUSTRIA

POLAND

Kiev

Budapest

Marseilles

ITALY

Corsica

Rome

RUMANIA

YUGOSLAVIA

Black Sea

Cas
S

SPAIN

Sardinia

ALB.

BULGARIA

TURKEY

Sicily

GREECE

ALGERIA

TUNISIA

Mediterranean Sea

Crete

Cyprus

SYRIA

IRAQ

D-DAY, 1944 American infantry troops wade ashore along the beaches of Normandy, June 6, 1944, to begin the great Allied invasion of France— one of the principal turning points of the war in Europe.

firestorm that destroyed three-fourths of the previously undamaged city and killed approximately 135,000 people, almost all civilians. The morality of such attacks has been much debated in the years since the war; but at the time, few Americans questioned the claims of military leaders that the bombing cleared the way for the great Allied invasion of France in the late spring.

An enormous offensive force had been gathering in England for two years: almost 3 million troops, and perhaps the greatest array of naval vessels and armaments ever assembled in one place. On the morning of June 6, 1944, this vast invasion force moved into action. The landing came not at the narrowest part of the English Channel, where the Germans had expected and prepared for it, but along sixty miles of the Cotentin Peninsula on the coast of Normandy. While airplanes and battleships offshore bombarded the Nazi defenses, 4,000 vessels landed troops and supplies on the beaches. (Three divisions of paratroopers had been dropped behind the German lines the night before.) Fighting was intense along the beach, but the superior manpower and equipment of the Allied forces gradually prevailed. Within a week, the German forces had been dislodged from virtually the entire Normandy coast.

For the next month, further progress remained slow. But in late July in the Battle of Saint-Lô, General Omar Bradley's First Army smashed through the German lines. George S. Patton's Third Army, spearheaded by heavy tank attacks, then moved through the hole Bradley had created and began a drive into the heart of France. On August 25, Free French forces arrived in Paris and liberated the city from four years of German occupation. By mid-September the Allied armies had driven the Germans almost entirely out of France and Belgium.

The great Allied drive came to a halt, however, at the Rhine River against a firm line of Nazi defenses. In mid-December, German forces struck in desperation along fifty miles of front in the Ardennes Forest. In the Battle of the Bulge (named for a large bulge that appeared in the American lines as the Germans pressed forward), they drove fifty-five miles toward Antwerp before they were finally stopped at Bastogne. It was the last major battle on the western front.

While the Allies were fighting their way through France, Soviet forces were sweeping westward into central Europe and the Balkans. In late January 1945, the Russians launched a great offensive toward the Oder River inside Germany. By early spring, they were ready to launch a final assault against Berlin. General Omar Bradley, in the meantime, was pushing toward the Rhine from the west. Early in March, his forces captured the city of Cologne, on the river's west bank. The next day, he discovered and seized an undamaged bridge over the river at Remagen; Allied troops were soon pouring across the Rhine. In the following weeks the British commander, Montgomery, with a million troops, pushed into Germany in the north while Bradley's army, sweeping through central Germany, completed the encirclement of 300,000 German soldiers in the Ruhr.

The German resistance was now broken on both fronts. American forces were moving eastward faster than they had anticipated and could have beaten the Russians to Berlin and Prague. The American and British high commands decided, instead, to halt the advance along the Elbe River in central Germany to await the Russians. That decision enabled the Soviets to occupy eastern Germany and Czechoslovakia.

On April 30, with Soviet forces on the outskirts of Berlin, Adolf Hitler killed himself in his bunker in the capital. And on May 8, 1945, the remaining German forces surrendered unconditionally. V-E (Victory in Europe) Day prompted great celebrations in western Europe and in the United States, tempered by the knowledge of the continuing war against Japan.

The Pacific Offensive

In February 1944, American naval forces under Admiral Chester Nimitz won a series of victories in the Marshall Islands and cracked the outer perimeter of the Japanese Empire. Within a month, the navy had destroyed other vital Japanese bastions. American submarines, in the meantime, were decimating Japanese shipping and crippling Japan's domestic economy.

A more frustrating struggle was in progress in the meantime on the Asian mainland. In 1942, the Japanese had forced General Joseph H. Stilwell of the United States out of Burma and had moved their own troops as far west as the mountains bordering on India. For a time, Stilwell supplied the isolated Chinese forces still fighting Japan with an aerial ferry over the Himalayas. In 1943, finally, he led Chinese, Indian, and a few American troops back through northern Burma, constructing a road and pipeline across the mountains into China (the Burma Road, also known as the Ledo Road or Stilwell Road); the road opened in the fall of 1944.

By then, however, the Japanese had launched a major counteroffensive and had driven so deep into the Chinese interior that they threatened the terminus of the Burma Road and the center of Chinese government at Chungking. The Japanese offensive precipitated a long-simmering feud between General Stilwell and Premier Chiang Kai-shek of China. Stilwell was indignant because Chiang was using many of his troops to maintain an armed frontier against the Chinese communists and would not deploy those troops against the Japanese.

The decisive battles of the war against Japan, however, occurred in the Pacific. In mid-June 1944, an enormous American armada struck the heavily fortified Mariana Islands and, after some of the bloodiest operations of the war, captured Tinian, Guam, and Saipan, 1,350 miles from Tokyo. In September, American forces landed on the western Carolines. And on October 20, General MacArthur's troops landed on Leyte Island in the Philippines. The Japanese now employed virtually their entire fleet against the Allied invaders in three major encounters—which together constituted the decisive Battle of Leyte Gulf, the largest naval engagement in history. American forces held off the Japanese onslaught and sank four Japanese carriers, all but destroying Japan's capacity to continue a serious naval war.

Nevertheless, as American forces advanced closer to the Japanese mainland early in 1945, the imperial forces seemed only to increase their resistance. In February 1945, American marines seized the tiny volcanic island of Iwo Jima, only 750 miles from Tokyo, but only after the costliest battle in the history of the Marine Corps.

The battle for Okinawa, an island only 370 miles south of Japan, was further evidence of the strength of the Japanese resistance in these last desperate days. Week after week, the Japanese sent *Kamikaze* (suicide) planes against American and British ships, sacrificing 3,500 of them while inflicting great damage. Japanese troops on shore launched desperate nighttime attacks on the American lines. The United States and its allies suffered nearly 50,000 casualties before finally capturing Okinawa in late June 1945. Over 100,000 Japanese died in the siege.

It seemed that the same kind of bitter fighting would await the Americans when they invaded Japan. But there were signs early in 1945 that such an invasion might not be necessary. The Japanese had almost no ships or planes left with which to fight. The firebombing of Tokyo in May, in which American bombers dropped napalm on the city and created a firestorm in which over 80,000 people died, further weakened the Japanese will to resist. Moderate Japanese leaders, who had long since concluded the war was lost, were increasing their power within the government and were looking for ways to bring the fighting to an end, although they continued to face powerful opposition from military leaders. Whether the moderates could ultimately have prevailed is a question about which historians and others continue to disagree. In any case, their efforts became superfluous in mid-July 1945, when American scientists successfully tested the world's first atomic weapon.

The Manhattan Project and Atomic Warfare

Reports had reached the United States in 1939 that Nazi scientists had taken the first step toward the creation of an atomic bomb, a weapon more powerful than any ever previously devised. The United States and Britain immediately began a race to develop the weapon before the Germans did.

Over the next three years, the government secretly poured nearly $2 billion into the so-called Manhattan Project—a massive scientific effort conducted at hidden laboratories in Oak Ridge, Tennessee; Los Alamos, New Mexico; and other sites. (Its name had emerged earlier, when many of the atomic physicists had been working at Columbia University in New York.) The scientists pushed ahead much faster than anyone had predicted. Even so, the war in Europe ended before they were ready to test the first bomb. Just before dawn on July 16, 1945, in the desert near Alamogordo,

New Mexico, the scientists gathered to witness the first atomic explosion in history: a blinding flash of light brighter than any ever seen on earth, and a huge, billowing mushroom cloud.

News of the explosion reached President Harry S. Truman (who had taken office in April on the death of Roosevelt) in Potsdam, Germany, where he was attending a conference of Allied leaders. He issued an ultimatum to the Japanese (signed jointly by the British) demanding that they surrender by August 3 or face utter devastation. When the Japanese failed to meet the deadline, Truman ordered the air force to use the new atomic weapons against Japan.

Controversy has continued for decades over whether Truman's decision to use the bomb was justified and what his motives were. Some have argued that the atomic attack was unnecessary—that had the United States agreed to the survival of the emperor (which it ultimately did agree to in any case), or had it waited only a few more weeks, the Japanese would have surrendered. Others argue that nothing less than the atomic bombs could have persuaded the Japanese to surrender without a costly American invasion. Some critics of the decision, including some of the scientists involved in the

HIROSHIMA AFTER THE BOMB Where once a bustling city stood, only rubble remains. This photograph shows the center of Hiroshima shortly after it was devastated by the first of two atomic bombs the United States dropped on Japan in the last days of World War II.

Manhattan Project, have argued that whatever the Japanese intentions, the United States, as a matter of morality, should not have used the terrible new weapon.

The nation's military and political leaders, however, showed little concern about such matters. Truman, who had not even known of the existence of the Manhattan Project until he became president, was, apparently, making what he believed to be a simple military decision. A weapon was available that would end the war quickly; he could see no reason not to use it.

On August 6, 1945, an American B-29, the *Enola Gay*, dropped an atomic weapon on the Japanese industrial center at Hiroshima. With a single bomb, the United States completely incinerated a four-square-mile area at the center of the previously undamaged city. More than 80,000 civilians died, according to later American estimates. Many more survived to suffer the crippling effects of radioactive fallout or to pass those effects on to their children in the form of birth defects.

The Japanese government, stunned by the attack, was at first unable to agree on a response. Two days later, on August 8, the Soviet Union declared war on Japan. And the following day, another American plane dropped another atomic weapon—this time on the city of Nagasaki—inflicting 100,000 deaths and horrible damage on yet another unfortunate community. Finally, the emperor intervened to break the stalemate in the cabinet; and on August 14, the government announced that it was ready to give up. On September 2, 1945, on board the American battleship *Missouri*, anchored in Tokyo Bay, Japanese officials signed the articles of surrender.

The greatest war in the history of mankind had come to an end, and the United States had emerged from it not only victorious but in a position of unprecedented power, influence, and prestige. It was a victory, however, that few could greet with unambiguous joy. Fourteen million combatants had died in the struggle. Many more civilians had perished. The United States had suffered only light casualties in comparison with some other nations, but the cost had still been high: 322,000 dead, another 800,000 injured. And despite the sacrifices, the world continued to face an uncertain future, menaced by the threat of nuclear warfare and by an emerging antagonism between the world's two strongest nations—the United States and the Soviet Union—that would darken the peace for many decades to come.

CHAPTER TWENTY-NINE

America and the Cold War

Origins of the Cold War ~ The Collapse of the Peace
America After the War ~ The Korean War
The Crusade Against Subversion

VEN BEFORE World War II ended, there were signs of tension between the United States and the Soviet Union. Once the hostilities were over, those tensions quickly grew to create what became known as a "Cold War" between the two former allies that would cast its shadow over international affairs for decades. The Cold War also had profound effects on American domestic life, ultimately producing the most corrosive outbreak of antiradical hysteria of the century. America in the postwar years was both powerful and prosperous, but it was also for a time troubled and uncertain about its future.

ORIGINS OF THE COLD WAR

No issue in twentieth-century American history has aroused more debate than the question of the origins of the Cold War. Some have claimed that Soviet duplicity and expansionism created the international tensions, others that American provocations and imperial ambitions were at least equally to blame. Most historians agree, however, that wherever the preponderance of blame may lie, both the United States and the Soviet Union contributed to the atmosphere of hostility and suspicion that quickly clouded the peace.

Sources of Soviet-American Tension

The wartime alliance between the United States and the Soviet Union was an aberration from the normal tenor of Soviet-American relations, for the two nations had long viewed each other with deep mutual mistrust. At the heart of their differences in the 1940s, however, was a fundamental difference in the ways the great powers envisioned the postwar world. One vision was that of many people in the United States. First openly outlined in the Atlantic Charter in 1941, it was a vision of a world in which nations abandoned their traditional belief in military alliances and spheres of influence and governed their relations with one another through democratic processes, with an international organization serving as the arbiter of disputes and the protector of every nation's right of self-determination.

The other vision was that of the Soviet Union and to some extent, it gradually became clear, of Great Britain. Both Stalin and Churchill had signed the Atlantic Charter. But Britain had always been uneasy about the implications of the self-determination ideal for its own enormous empire. And the Soviet Union was determined to create a secure sphere for itself in Central and Eastern Europe as protection against possible future aggression from the West. Both Churchill and Stalin, therefore, tended to envision a postwar structure in which the great powers would control areas of strategic interest to them, in which something vaguely similar to the traditional European balance of power would reemerge.

By the end of the war Roosevelt was able to win at least the partial consent of Winston Churchill to his principles; but although he believed at times that Stalin would similarly relent, he never managed to steer the Soviets from their determination to control Central and Eastern Europe and from their vision of a postwar order in which each of the great powers would dominate its own sphere. Gradually, the differences between these two positions would turn the peacemaking process into a form of warfare.

Wartime Diplomacy

Serious strains began to develop in the alliance with the Soviet Union as early as 1942, a result of Stalin's irritation at delays in opening the second front and his resentment of the Anglo-American decision to invade North Africa before Europe. In this deteriorating atmosphere, Roosevelt and Churchill met in Casablanca, Morocco, in January 1943 to discuss Allied strategy. (Stalin had declined Roosevelt's invitation to attend.) The two leaders could not accept Stalin's most important demand—the immediate opening of a second front. But they tried to reassure Stalin by announcing that they would accept nothing less than the unconditional surrender of the Axis powers. It was a signal that the Americans and British would not negotiate a separate peace with Hitler and leave the Soviets to fight on alone.

In November 1943, Roosevelt and Churchill traveled to Teheran, Iran, for their first meeting with Stalin. By now, however, Roosevelt's most effective bargaining tool—Stalin's need for American assistance in his struggle against Germany—had been largely removed. The German advance against Russia had been halted; Soviet forces were now launching their own westward offensive. Meanwhile, new tensions had emerged in the alliance as a result of the refusal by the British and Americans to allow any Soviet participation in the creation of a new Italian government following the fall of Mussolini. To Stalin, at least, the American vision of an "open world" already seemed to be a double standard: America and Britain expected to have a voice in the future of Eastern Europe, but the Soviet Union was to have no voice in the future of the West.

Nevertheless, the Teheran Conference seemed in most respects a success. Roosevelt and Stalin established a cordial personal relationship. Stalin agreed to an American request that the Soviet Union enter the war in the Pacific soon after the end of hostilities in Europe. Roosevelt, in turn, promised that an Anglo-American second front would be established within six months. All three leaders agreed in principle to a postwar international organization and to efforts to prevent a resurgence of German expansionism.

On other matters, however, the origins of future disagreements were already visible. Most important was the question of the future of Poland. Roosevelt and Churchill were willing to agree to a movement of the Soviet border westward, allowing Stalin to annex some historically Polish territory. But on the nature of the postwar government in the portion of Poland that would remain independent, there were sharp differences. Roosevelt and Churchill supported the claims of the Polish government-in-exile that had been functioning in London since 1940; Stalin wished to install another, procommunist exiled government that had spent the war in Lublin, in the Soviet Union. The three leaders avoided a bitter conclusion to the Teheran Conference only by leaving the issue unresolved.

Yalta

For more than a year after Teheran, the Grand Alliance among the United States, Britain, and the Soviet Union alternated between high tension and warm amicability. In the fall of 1944, Churchill flew by himself to Moscow for a meeting with Stalin to resolve issues arising from a civil war in Greece. In return for a Soviet agreement to cease assisting Greek communists, who were challenging the British-supported monarchical government, Churchill consented to a proposal whereby control of Eastern Europe would be divided between Britain and the Soviet Union. To Roosevelt, however, the Moscow agreement was evidence of how little the Atlantic Charter principles seemed to mean to his two most important allies.

In February 1945, Roosevelt joined Churchill and Stalin for a great peace conference in the Soviet city of Yalta. On a number of issues, the Big Three reached mutually satisfactory agreements. In return for Stalin's renewed promise to enter the Pacific war, Roosevelt agreed that the Soviet Union should receive the Kurile Islands north of Japan; should regain southern Sakhalin Island and Port Arthur, both of which Russia had lost in the 1904 Russo-Japanese War; and could exercise some influence (along with the government of China) in Manchuria. The negotiators also agreed to accept a plan for a new international organization, a plan that had been hammered out the previous summer at a conference in Washington, D.C., at the Dumbarton Oaks estate. The new United Nations would contain a General Assembly, in which every member would be represented, and a Security Council, with permanent representatives of the five major powers (the United States, Britain, France, the Soviet Union, and China), each of which would have veto power, and temporary delegates from several other nations. These agreements became the basis of the United Nations charter, drafted at a conference of fifty nations beginning April 25, 1945, in San Francisco. The United States Senate ratified the charter in July by a vote of 80 to 2 (a striking contrast to the slow and painful defeat it had administered to the charter of the League of Nations twenty-five years before).

On other issues, however, the Yalta Conference either left fundamental differences unresolved or papered them over with weak and unstable compromises. Basic disagreement remained about the postwar Polish government. Stalin, whose armies now occupied Poland, had already installed a government composed of the procommunist "Lublin" Poles. Roosevelt and Churchill insisted that the pro-Western "London" Poles must be allowed a place in the Warsaw regime. Roosevelt envisioned a government based on free, democratic elections—which both he and Stalin recognized the pro-Western forces would win. Stalin agreed only to a vague compromise by which an unspecified number of pro-Western Poles would be granted a place in the government. He reluctantly consented to hold "free and unfettered elections" in Poland, but he made no commitment to a date for them. They did not take place for more than forty years.

Nor was there agreement about the future of Germany. Stalin wanted to impose $20 billion in reparations on the Germans, of which Russia would receive half. Roosevelt and Churchill agreed only to leave final settlement of the issue to a future reparations commission. A more important difference was in the way the leaders envisioned postwar German politics and society. Roosevelt seemed to want a reconstructed and reunited Germany—one that would be permitted to develop a prosperous, modern economy while remaining under the careful supervision of the Allies. Stalin wanted a permanent dismemberment of Germany. The final agreement was, like the Polish accord, vague and unstable. The United States, Great Britain, France, and the Soviet Union would each control its own "zone of occupation" in Germany—the zones to be determined by the position of troops at the end of the war. Berlin, the German capital, was already well inside the Soviet zone, but because of its symbolic importance it would itself be divided into four sectors, one for each nation to occupy. At an unspecified date, the nation would be reunited; but there was no agreement on how the reunification would occur. As for the rest of Europe, the conference produced a murky accord on the establishment of interim governments "broadly representative of all democratic elements." They would be replaced ultimately by permanent governments "responsible to the will of the people" and created through free elections. Once again, no specific provisions or timetables accompanied the agreements.

The Yalta accords, in other words, were less a settlement of postwar issues than a set of loose principles that sidestepped the most divisive issues. Roosevelt, Churchill, and Stalin returned home from the conference each apparently convinced that he had signed an important agreement. But the Soviet interpretation of the accords differed so sharply from the Anglo-American interpretation that the illusion endured only briefly. In the weeks following the Yalta Conference, Roosevelt watched with growing alarm as the Soviet Union moved systematically to establish procommunist governments in one Central and Eastern European nation after another and as Stalin refused to make the changes in Poland that the president believed he had promised.

But Roosevelt did not abandon hope. Still believing the differences could be settled, he left Washington early in the spring for a vacation at his retreat in Warm Springs, Georgia. There, on April 12, 1945, he suffered a sudden, massive stroke and died.

THE COLLAPSE OF THE PEACE

Harry S. Truman, who succeeded Roosevelt in the presidency, had almost no familiarity with international issues. Nor did he share Roosevelt's faith in the flexibility of the Soviet Union. Roosevelt had believed that Stalin was, essentially, a reasonable man with whom an ultimate accord could be reached. Truman, in contrast, sided with those in the government (and there were many) who considered the Soviet Union fundamentally untrustworthy and viewed Stalin himself with suspicion and even loathing.

The Failure of Potsdam

Truman had been in office only a few days before he decided to "get tough" with the Soviet Union. Stalin had made what the new president considered solemn agreements with the United States at Yalta. The United States would insist that he honor them. Dismissing the advice of Secretary of War Stimson that the Polish question was a lost cause and not worth a world crisis, Truman met on April 23 with Soviet Foreign Minister Molotov and sharply chastised him for violations of the Yalta accords.

In fact, Truman had only limited leverage by which to compel the Soviet Union to carry out its agreements. Russian forces already occupied Poland and much of the rest of Central and Eastern Europe. Germany was already divided among the conquering nations. The United States was still engaged in a war in the Pacific and was neither able nor willing to enter in a second conflict in Europe. Truman insisted that the United States should be able to get "85 percent" of what it wanted, but he was ultimately forced to settle for much less.

He conceded first on Poland. When Stalin made a few minor concessions to the pro-Western exiles, Truman recognized the Warsaw government, hoping that noncommunist forces might gradually expand their influence there. Until the 1980s, they did not. Other questions remained, above all the question of Germany. To settle them, Truman met in July at Potsdam, in Russian-occupied Germany, with Churchill (who was replaced as prime minister by Clement Attlee in the midst of the negotiations) and Stalin. Truman reluctantly accepted adjustments of the Polish-German border that Stalin had long demanded; he refused, however, to permit the Russians to claim any reparations from the American, French, and British zones of Germany. The result, in effect, was to confirm that

Germany would remain divided, with the western zones united into one nation, friendly to the United States, and the Russian zone surviving as another nation, with a pro-Soviet, communist government. Soon, the Soviet Union was siphoning between $1.5 and $3 billion a year out of its zone of occupation.

The China Problem

Central to American hopes for an open, peaceful world "policed" by the great powers was a strong, independent China. But even before the war ended, the American government was aware that those hopes faced a major, perhaps insurmountable obstacle: the Chinese government of Chiang Kai-shek. Chiang was generally friendly to the United States, but he had few other virtues. His government was corrupt and incompetent. His popular legitimacy was feeble. And Chiang himself lived in a world of almost surreal isolation, unable or unwilling to face the problems that were threatening to engulf him. Ever since 1927, the nationalist government he headed had been engaged in a prolonged and bitter rivalry with the communist armies of Mao Zedong. So successful had the communist challenge grown that Mao was in control of one-fourth of the population by 1945.

At Potsdam, Truman had managed to persuade Stalin to recognize Chiang as the legitimate ruler of China; but Chiang was rapidly losing his grip on his country. Some Americans urged the government to try to find a "third force" to support as an alternative to either Chiang or Mao. A few argued that America should try to reach some accommodation with Mao. Truman, however, decided reluctantly that he had no choice but to continue supporting Chiang. For the next several years, as the long struggle between the nationalists and the communists erupted into a full-scale civil war, the United States continued to pump money and weapons to Chiang, even as it was becoming clear his cause was lost. But Truman was not prepared to intervene militarily to save the nationalist regime.

Instead, the American government was beginning to consider an alternative to China as the strong, pro-Western force in Asia: a revived Japan. Abandoning the restrictive occupation policies of the first years after the war (when General Douglas MacArthur had governed the nation), the United States lifted all restrictions on industrial development and encouraged rapid economic growth in Japan. The vision of an open, united Asia had been replaced, as in Europe, with an acceptance of the necessity of developing a strong, pro-American sphere of influence.

The Containment Doctrine

By the end of 1945, the Grand Alliance was a shambles, and with it any realistic hope of a postwar world constructed according to the Atlantic Charter ideals Roosevelt and others had supported. Instead, a new American policy was slowly emerging. Rather than attempting to create a unified, "open" world, the West would work to "contain" the threat of further Soviet expansion. The United States would be the leading force in that effort.

The new doctrine emerged in part as a response to events in Europe in 1946. In Turkey, Stalin was trying to win some control over the vital sea lanes to the Mediterranean. In Greece, communist forces were again threatening the pro-Western government; the British had announced they could no longer provide assistance. Faced with these challenges, Truman decided to enunciate a firm new policy. In doing so, he drew from the ideas of the influential American diplomat George F. Kennan, who warned that in the Soviet Union the United States faced "a political force committed fanatically to the belief that with the U.S. there can be no permanent *modus vivendi*," and that the only answer was "a long-term, patient but firm and vigilant containment of Russian expansive tendencies." On March 12, 1947, Truman appeared before Congress and used Kennan's warnings as the basis of what became known as the Truman Doctrine. "I believe," he argued, "that it must be the policy of the United States to support free peoples who are resisting attempted subjugation by armed minorities or by outside pressures." In the same speech he requested $400 million—part of it to bolster the armed forces of Greece and Turkey, another part to provide economic assistance to Greece. Congress quickly approved the measure.

The American commitment ultimately helped ease Soviet pressure on Turkey and helped the Greek government defeat the communist insurgents. More important, it established a basis for American foreign policy that would survive for more than thirty years. On the one hand, the Truman Doctrine was a way of accommodating the status quo: it accepted that there was no immediate likelihood of overturning the communist governments Stalin had established in Eastern Europe. On the other hand, it was a strategy for the future: communism was an innately expansionist force, and it must be contained within its present boundaries.

The Marshall Plan

An integral part of the containment policy was a proposal to aid in the economic reconstruction of Western Europe. There were many motives:

humanitarian concern for the European people; a fear that Europe would remain an economic drain on the United States if it could not quickly rebuild and begin to feed itself; a desire for a strong European market for American goods. But above all, American policymakers believed that unless something could be done to strengthen the shaky pro-American governments in Western Europe, those governments might fall under the control of rapidly growing domestic communist parties.

In June 1947, therefore, Secretary of State George C. Marshall announced a plan to provide economic assistance to all European nations (including the Soviet Union) that would join in drafting a program for recovery. Although Russia and its Eastern satellites quickly and predictably rejected the plan, sixteen Western European nations eagerly participated. Whatever domestic opposition there was in the United States largely vanished after a sudden coup in Czechoslovakia in February 1948 that established a Soviet-dominated communist government there. In April, Congress approved the creation of the Economic Cooperation Administration, the agency that would administer the Marshall Plan, as it became known. And over the next three years, the Marshall Plan channeled over $12 billion of American aid into Europe, helping to spark a substantial economic revival. By the end of 1950, European industrial production had risen 64 percent, communist strength in the member nations was declining, and opportunities for American trade had revived.

Mobilization at Home

That the United States had fully accepted a continuing commitment to the containment policy became clear in 1947 and 1948 through a series of measures designed to maintain American military power at near wartime levels. In 1948, at the president's request, Congress approved a new military draft and revived the Selective Service System. In the meantime, the United States, having failed to reach agreement with the Soviet Union on international control of nuclear weapons, redoubled its own efforts in atomic research, elevating nuclear weaponry to a central place in its military arsenal. The Atomic Energy Commission, established in 1946, became the supervisory body charged with overseeing all nuclear research, civilian and military alike.

Particularly important was the National Security Act of 1947, which created several instruments of foreign policy. A new Department of Defense would oversee all branches of the armed services, combining functions previously performed by the War and Navy departments. A National Security Council (NSC), operating out of the White House, would govern foreign and military policy. A Central Intelligence Agency (CIA) would be responsible for collecting information through both open and covert methods and, as the Cold War continued, for engaging secretly in political and military operations on behalf of American goals. The National Security Act, in other words, gave the president expanded powers with which to pursue the nation's international goals. It centralized in the White House control that had once been widely dispersed; it enabled the president to take

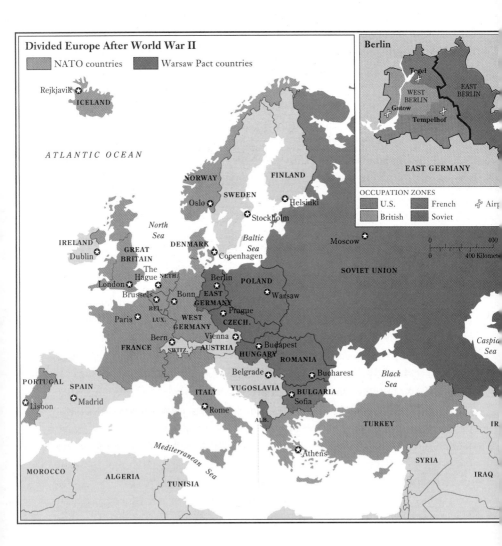

Divided Europe After World War II

- NATO countries
- Warsaw Pact countries

Berlin

EAST GERMANY

OCCUPATION ZONES
- U.S.
- British
- French
- Soviet
- Airport

warlike actions without an open declaration of war; and it created vehicles by which the government could at times act politically and militarily overseas behind a veil of secrecy.

The Road to NATO

At about the same time, the United States was moving to strengthen the military capabilities of Western Europe. Convinced that a reconstructed Germany was essential to the hopes of the West, Truman reached an agreement with England and France to merge the three western zones of occupation into a new West German republic (which would include the American, British, and French sectors of Berlin, even though that city lay well within the Soviet zone). Stalin responded quickly. On June 24, 1948, he imposed a tight blockade around the western sectors of Berlin. If Germany was to be officially divided, he was implying, then the country's Western government would have to abandon its outpost in the heart of the Soviet-controlled eastern zone. Truman refused to do so. Unwilling to risk war through a military response to the blockade, he ordered a massive airlift to supply the city with food, fuel, and supplies. The airlift continued for more than ten months, transporting nearly 2.5 million tons of material, keeping a city of 2 million people alive, and transforming West Berlin into a symbol of the West's resolve to resist communist expansion. In the spring of 1949, Stalin lifted the now ineffective blockade. And in October, the division of Germany into two nations—the Federal Republic in the west and the Democratic Republic in the East—became official.

The crisis in Berlin accelerated the consolidation of what was already in effect an alliance among the United States and the countries of Western Europe. On April 4, 1949, twelve nations signed an agreement establishing the North Atlantic Treaty Organization (NATO) and declaring that an armed attack against one member would be considered an attack against all. The NATO countries would, moreover, maintain a standing military force in Europe to defend against what many believed was the threat of a Soviet invasion. The American Senate quickly ratified the treaty, which fused European nations that had been fighting one another for centuries into a strong and enduring alliance. The formation of NATO spurred the Soviet Union to create an alliance of its own with the communist governments in Eastern Europe—an alliance formalized in 1955 by the Warsaw Pact.

Survival Secrets for Atomic Attacks

ALWAYS PUT FIRST THINGS FIRST

Try to Get Shielded

If you have time, get down in a basement or subway. Should you unexpectedly be caught out-of-doors, seek shelter alongside a building, or jump in any handy ditch or gutter.

Drop Flat on Ground or Floor

To keep from being tossed about and to lessen the chances of being struck by falling and flying objects, flatten out at the base of a wall, or at the bottom of a bank.

Bury Your Face in Your Arms

When you drop flat, hide your eyes in the crook of your elbow. That will protect your face from flash burns, prevent temporary blindness and keep flying objects out of your eyes.

NEVER LOSE YOUR HEAD

SURVIVING NUCLEAR WAR Preoccupation with the possibility of a nuclear war reached a fever pitch in the early years of the atomic era. The Federal Civil Defense Agency, which in 1950 issued these simple rules for civilians to follow in dealing with an atomic attack, was one of many organizations attempting to convince the American public that a nuclear war was survivable.

The Enduring Crisis

For a time, Americans believed that these initial achievements had turned the tide of the battle against communism. But a series of events in 1949 eroded that confidence and propelled the Cold War in new directions. An announcement in September that the Soviet Union had successfully exploded its first atomic weapon, years earlier than predicted, shocked and frightened many Americans. So did the collapse of Chiang Kai-shek's nationalist government in China, which occurred with startling speed in the last months of 1949. Chiang fled with his political allies and the remnants of his army to the offshore island of Formosa (Taiwan), and the entire Chinese mainland came under the control of a communist government that many Americans believed to be an extension of the Soviet Union. Few policymakers shared the belief of the so-called China lobby that the United States should now commit itself to the rearming of Chiang Kai-shek. But neither would the United States recognize the new communist regime. The Chinese mainland would remain almost entirely closed to the West for a generation. The United States, in the meantime, would devote increased attention to the revitalization of Japan as a buffer against Asian communism, ending the American occupation in 1952.

In response to these and other setbacks, Truman called for a thorough review of American foreign policy. The result was a National Security Council report, commonly known as NSC-68, which outlined a shift in the American position. The first statements of the containment doctrine—the writings of George Kennan, the Truman Doctrine speech—made at least some distinctions between areas of vital interest to the United States and areas of less importance to the nation's foreign policy. They also had viewed containment as a commitment shared among the United States and its allies. But the April 1950 document argued that the United States could no longer rely on other nations to take the initiative in resisting communism. It must itself establish firm and active leadership of the noncommunist world. And it must move to stop communist expansion anywhere it occurred, regardless of the intrinsic strategic or economic value of the lands in question. Among other things, the report called for a major expansion of American military power, with a defense budget almost four times the previously projected figure.

AMERICA AFTER THE WAR

The crises overseas were not the only frustrations the American people encountered after the war. The nation also faced serious economic difficulties in adapting to the peace. The instability that resulted contributed to an increasingly heated political climate.

The Problems of Reconversion

Despite predictions that the end of the war would return America to Depression conditions, economic growth continued after 1945. Pent-up consumer demand from workers who had accumulated substantial savings during the war helped spur the boom. So did a $6 billion tax cut. The Servicemen's Readjustment Act of 1944, better known as the GI Bill of Rights, provided housing, education, and job training subsidies to veterans and increased spending even further.

This flood of consumer demand ensured that there would be no new depression, but it contributed to more than two years of serious inflation, during which prices rose at rates of 14 to 15 percent annually. In the summer of 1946, the president vetoed an extension of the authority of the wartime Office of Price Administration, thus eliminating price controls. (He was opposed not to the controls but to congressional amendments that had weakened the OPA.) Inflation soared to 25 percent before he relented a month later and signed a bill little different from the one he had rejected.

Compounding the economic difficulties was a sharp rise in labor unrest, driven in part by the impact of inflation. By the end of 1945, there had already been major strikes in the automobile, electrical, and steel industries. In April 1946, John L. Lewis led the United Mine Workers out on strike, shutting down the coal fields for forty days. Fears grew rapidly that without vital coal supplies, the entire nation might virtually grind to a halt. Truman finally forced coal production to resume by ordering government seizure of the mines. But in the process, he pressured mine owners to grant the union most of its demands, which he had earlier denounced as inflationary. Almost simultaneously, the nation's railroads suffered a total shutdown—the first in the nation's history—as two major unions walked out on strike. By threatening to use the army to run the trains, Truman pressured the strikers back to work after only a few days.

Reconversion was particularly difficult for the millions of women and minorities who had entered the work force during the war. With veterans returning home and looking for jobs in the industrial economy, employers tended to push women, blacks, Hispanics, and others out of the plants to make room for white males. Some of the war workers, particularly women, left the work force voluntarily, out of a desire to return to their former domestic lives. But as many as 80 percent of women workers, and virtually all black and Hispanic males, wanted to continue working. The postwar inflation, the pressure to meet the growing expectations of a high-consumption society, the rising divorce rate (which left many women responsible for their own economic well-being)—all combined to create a high demand for paid employment among women. As they found themselves excluded from industrial jobs, therefore, women workers moved increasingly into other areas of the economy (above all, the service sector).

The Fair Deal Rejected

Days after the Japanese surrender, Truman submitted to Congress a twenty-one-point domestic program outlining what he later termed the "Fair Deal." It called for expansion of Social Security benefits, the raising of the legal minimum wage from 40 to 65 cents an hour, a program to ensure full employment through aggressive use of federal spending and investment, a permanent Fair Employment Practices Act, public housing and slum clear-

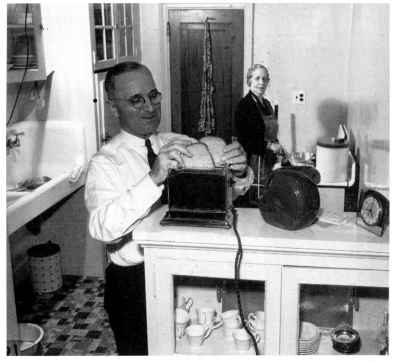

HARRY AND BESS TRUMAN AT HOME Shortly before the 1944 Democratic National Convention, Senator Truman and his wife posed for photographers in the kitchen of their Washington apartment and conveyed the "common man" image that Truman retained throughout his public life. A few weeks later, Truman was a candidate for vice president; and less than a year after that, he and Mrs. Truman were living in the White House.

ance, long-range environmental and public works planning, and government promotion of scientific research. Weeks later he added other proposals: federal aid to education, government health insurance, prepaid medical care, funding for the St. Lawrence Seaway, and nationalization of atomic energy. The president was declaring an end to the wartime moratorium on liberal reform.

But the Fair Deal programs fell victim to the same public and congressional conservatism that had crippled the last years of the New Deal. Indeed, that conservatism seemed to be intensifying, as the November 1946 congressional elections suggested. Using the simple but devastating slogan "Had Enough?" the Republican party won control of both houses of Congress.

The new Republican Congress quickly moved to reduce government spending and chip away at New Deal reforms. Its most notable action, perhaps, was its assault on the Wagner Act of 1935. Conservatives had always resented the new powers the legislation had granted unions; and in response to the labor difficulties during and after the war, such resentments intensified sharply. The result was the Labor-Management Relations Act of 1947, better known as the Taft-Hartley Act. It made illegal the closed shop (a workplace in which no one can be hired without first being a member of a union). And although it continued to permit the creation of union shops (in which workers must join a union after being hired), it permitted states to pass "right-to-work" laws prohibiting even that. This provision, the controversial Section 14(b), remained a target of the labor movement for decades. The Taft-Hartley Act also empowered the president to call for a ten-week "cooling-off" period before a strike by issuing an injunction against any work stoppage that endangered national safety or health. Outraged workers and union leaders denounced the measure as a "slave labor bill." Truman vetoed it. But both houses easily overruled him the same day.

The Taft-Hartley Act did not destroy the labor movement, as many union leaders had predicted. But it did damage weaker unions in relatively lightly organized industries such as chemicals and textiles; and it made far more difficult the organizing of workers who had never been union members at all, especially in the South and West.

The Election of 1948

Truman and his advisers believed that the American public was not ready to abandon the achievements of the New Deal, despite the 1946 election results. As they planned strategy for the 1948 campaign, therefore, they placed their hopes in an appeal to enduring Democratic loyalties. Throughout 1948, Truman proposed one reform measure after another (including, on February 2, the first major civil-rights bill of the century). Congress ignored or defeated them all, but the president was building campaign issues for the fall.

There remained, however, the problem of Truman's personal unpopularity—the assumption among much of the electorate that he lacked stature and that his administration was weak and inept—and the deep divisions within the Democratic party. At the Democratic Convention that summer, two factions abandoned the party altogether. Southern conservatives were angered by Truman's proposed civil-rights bill and by the approval at the convention of a civil-rights plank in the platform (engineered by Hubert Humphrey, the reform mayor of Minneapolis). They walked out and formed the States' Rights (or "Dixiecrat") party, with Governor Strom Thurmond of South Carolina as its nominee. At the same time, some members of the party's left wing joined the new Progressive party, whose candidate was Henry A. Wallace. Wallace supporters objected to what they considered the slow and ineffective domestic policies of the Truman administration, but they resented even more the president's confrontational stance toward the Soviet Union.

In addition, many Democratic liberals unwilling to leave the party attempted to dump the president in 1948. The Americans for Democratic Action (ADA), a coalition of liberals, tried to entice Dwight D. Eisenhower, the popular war hero, to contest the nomination. Only after Eisenhower had refused did liberals bow to the inevitable and concede the nomination to Truman. The Republicans, in the meantime, had once again nominated Governor Thomas E. Dewey of New York, whose substantial reelection victory in 1946 had made him one of the nation's leading political figures. Austere, dignified, and competent, he seemed to offer an unbeatable alternative to the president.

Only Truman, it seemed, believed he could win. As the campaign gathered momentum, he became ever more aggressive, turning the fire away from himself and toward Dewey and the "do-nothing, good-for-nothing" Republican Congress, which was, he told the voters, responsible for fueling inflation and abandoning workers and common people. To dramatize his point, he called Congress into special session in July to give it a chance, he said, to enact the liberal measures the Republicans had recently written into their platform. Congress met for two weeks and, predictably, did almost nothing.

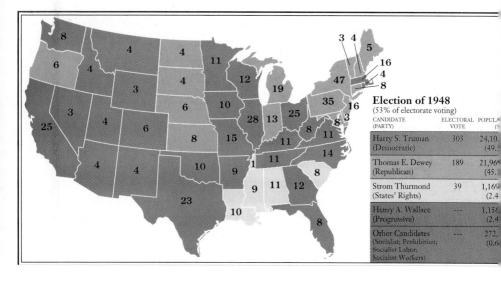

Election of 1948
(53% of electorate voting)

CANDIDATE (PARTY)	ELECTORAL VOTE	POPULA (%
Harry S. Truman (Democratic)	303	24,10. (49.
Thomas E. Dewey (Republican)	189	21,96' (45.
Strom Thurmond (States' Rights)	39	1,169 (2.4
Henry A. Wallace (Progressive)	---	1,156 (2.4
Other Candidates (Socialist; Prohibition; Socialist Labor; Socialist Workers)	---	272. (0.6

The president traveled nearly 32,000 miles and made 356 speeches, delivering blunt, extemporaneous attacks. He had told Alben Barkley, his running mate, "I'm going to fight hard. I'm going to give them hell." He called for repeal of the Taft-Hartley Act, increased price supports for farmers, and strong civil-rights protection for African-Americans. (He was the first president to campaign in Harlem since it had become a predominantly black community.) He sought, in short, to re-create much of Franklin Roosevelt's New Deal coalition. To the surprise of virtually everyone, he succeeded. On election night, he won a narrow but decisive victory: 49.5 percent of the popular vote to Dewey's 45.1 percent (with the two splinter parties dividing the small remainder evenly between them), and an electoral margin of 303 to 189. Democrats, in the meantime, had regained both houses of Congress by substantial margins. It was perhaps the most dramatic comeback in the history of presidential elections.

The Fair Deal Revived

Despite the Democratic victories, the Eighty-first Congress was no more hospitable to Truman's Fair Deal reform than its Republican predecessor had been. Truman did win some important victories, to be sure. Congress raised the legal minimum wage from 40 cents to 75 cents an hour. It approved an important expansion of the Social Security system, increasing benefits by 75 percent and extending them to 10 million additional people. And it passed the National Housing Act of 1949, which provided for the construction of 810,000 units of low-income housing accompanied by long-term rent subsidies. (Inadequate funding plagued the program for years, and the initial goal was reached only in 1972.)

But on other issues—national health insurance and aid to education among them—Truman made little progress. Nor was he able to persuade Congress to accept the civil-rights legislation he proposed in 1949, legislation that would have made lynching a federal crime, provided federal protection of black voting rights, abolished the poll tax, and established a new Fair Employment Practices Commission to curb discrimination in hiring. Southern Democrats filibustered to kill the bill.

Truman did proceed on his own to battle several forms of racial discrimination. He ordered an end to discrimination in the hiring of government employees. He began to dismantle segregation within the armed forces. And he allowed the Justice Department to become actively involved in court battles against discriminatory statutes. The Supreme Court, in the meantime, signaled its own growing awareness of the issue by ruling, in *Shelley* v. *Kraemer* (1948), that the courts could not be used to

KOREA, AUGUST 1950 American troops stand watch at a bridge they had demolished to slow down North Korean troop movements. Until MacArthur's surprise landing at Inchon on September 15, the United Nations forces (most of them American) played a largely defensive role, defending a small area in southeast Korea.

enforce private "covenants" meant to bar blacks from residential neighborhoods. The achievements of the Truman years made only minor dents in the structure of segregation, but they were the tentative beginnings of a federal commitment to confront the problem of race.

THE KOREAN WAR

On June 24, 1950, the armies of communist North Korea swept across their southern border in an invasion of the pro-Western half of the Korean peninsula to the south. Within days, they had occupied much of South Korea, including Seoul, its capital. Almost immediately, the United States committed itself to the conflict. It was the first American military engagement of the Cold War.

The Divided Peninsula

Both the United States and the Soviet Union sent troops into Korea at the end of World War II to fill the power vacuum left by the collapse of the Japanese. Once there, neither was willing to leave. Instead, they divided the nation, supposedly temporarily, along the 38th parallel. The Russians finally departed in 1949, leaving behind a communist government in the north with a strong, Soviet-equipped army. The Americans left a few months later, handing control to the pro-Western government of Syngman Rhee, anticommunist but only nominally democratic. He had a relatively small military, which he used primarily to suppress internal opposition.

The relative weakness of the south offered a strong temptation to nationalists in the North Korean government who wanted to reunite the country. The temptation grew stronger when the American government implied that it did not consider South Korea within its own "defense perimeter." The role of the Soviet Union remains unclear; there is some reason to believe that the North Koreans acted without Stalin's approval. But the Soviets supported the offensive once it began.

The Truman administration responded quickly. On June 27, 1950, the president ordered limited American military assistance to South Korea, and on the same day he appealed to the United Nations to intervene. The Soviet Union was boycotting the Security Council at the time (to protest the council's refusal to recognize the new communist government of China) and was thus unable to exercise its veto power. As a result, American delegates

Korean War, 1950–1953

North Korean attack
(June 25, 1950–Sept. 10, 1950)
U.N. counterattack
(Sept. 15, 1950–Nov. 24, 1950)

Chinese and North Korean counterattack
(Nov. 26, 1950–Jan. 24, 1951)
Final U.N. counterattack
(Jan. 25, 1951–April 21, 1951)

CHINA

100 Miles

100 Kilometers

Tumen River

Furthest extent
of U.N. counter-offensive
Nov. 24, 1950

NORTH
KOREA

Sea of
Japan

38th Parallel

hon landing
t. 15, 1950

Seoul

Inchon

MACARTHUR

SOUTH
KOREA

U.N. defensive
line Sept. 10, 1950

ow Sea

Pusan

JAPAN

CHINA

0   100 Miles

0   100 Kilometers

Tumen River

Yalu River

NORTH
KOREA

Pyongyang

Armistice Line
Nov. 1951–July 1953

38th Parallel

Panmunjom Seoul

Inchon

Sea of
Japan

Extent of
Communist
counterattack
Jan. 12, 1951

SOUTH
KOREA

Yellow Sea

Pusan

JAPAN

were able to win UN agreement to a resolution calling for international assistance to the Rhee government. On June 30, the United States ordered its own ground forces into Korea, and Truman appointed General Douglas MacArthur to command the UN operations there. (Several other nations provided assistance and troops, but the "UN" armies were, in fact, over-whelmingly American.)

The intervention in Korea was the first expression of the newly expan-sive American foreign policy outlined in NSC-68. But the administration quickly went beyond NSC-68. It decided that the war would be an effort not simply at containment but also at "liberation." After a surprise American invasion at Inchon in September had routed the North Korean forces from the south and sent them fleeing back across the 38th parallel, Truman gave MacArthur permission to pursue the communists into their own territory. His aim, as an American-sponsored UN resolution proclaimed in October, was to create "a unified, independent and democratic Korea."

From Invasion to Stalemate

For several weeks, MacArthur's invasion of North Korea proceeded smoothly. On October 19, the capital, Pyongyang, fell to the UN forces. Victory seemed near. By November 4, however, eight divisions of the Chinese army had entered the war. The UN offensive stalled and then collapsed. Through December 1950, outnumbered American forces fought a bitter, losing battle against the Chinese divisions, retreating at almost every juncture. Within weeks, communist forces had pushed the Americans back below the 38th parallel once again and had recaptured the South Korean capital of Seoul. By mid-January 1951 the rout had ceased; and by March the UN armies had managed to regain much of the territory they had recently lost, taking back Seoul and pushing the communists north of the 38th parallel for the second time. But with that, the war degenerated into a protracted stalemate.

From the start, Truman had been determined to avoid a direct conflict with China, which he feared might lead to a new world war. Once China entered the war, he began seeking a negotiated solution to the struggle; and for the next two years, he insisted that there be no wider war. But he faced a formidable opponent in General MacArthur, who resisted any limits on his military discretion. The United States was really fighting the Chinese, MacArthur argued. It should, therefore, attack China itself, if not through an actual invasion, then at least by bombing communist forces massing north of the Chinese border. In March 1951, he indicated his unhappiness in a public letter to House Republican leader Joseph W. Martin that concluded: "There is no substitute for victory." His position had wide popular support.

The Martin letter came after nine months during which MacArthur had resisted Truman's decisions. More than once, the president had warned the general to keep his objections to himself. The release of the Martin letter, therefore, struck the president as intolerable insubordination. On April 11, 1951, he relieved MacArthur of his command.

There was a storm of public outrage. Sixty-nine percent of the American people supported MacArthur, a Gallup poll reported. When the general returned to the United States later in 1951, he was greeted with wild enthusiasm. Public criticism of Truman finally abated somewhat when a number of prominent military figures, including General Omar Bradley, publicly supported the president's decision. But substantial hostility toward Truman remained.

In the meantime, the Korean stalemate continued. Negotiations between the opposing forces began at Panmunjom in July 1951, but the talks—and the war—dragged on until 1953.

Limited Mobilization

Just as the war in Korea produced only a limited American military commitment abroad, so it created only a limited economic mobilization at home. Still, the government did try to control the wartime economy in several important ways.

First, Truman set up the Office of Defense Mobilization to fight inflation by holding down prices and discouraging high union wage demands. When these cautious regulatory efforts failed, the president took more drastic action. Railroad workers walked off the job in 1951, and Truman, who considered the workers' demands inflationary, ordered the government to seize control of the railroads. That helped keep the trains running, but it had no effect on union demands. Workers ultimately got most of what they had demanded. In 1952, during a nationwide steel strike, Truman seized the steel mills, citing his powers as commander in chief. But in a 6-to-3 decision, the Supreme Court ruled that the president had exceeded his authority, and Truman was forced to relent. A long and costly strike followed, and the president's drastic actions appeared to many to have been both rash and ineffective.

The Korean War gave a significant boost to economic growth by pumping new government funds into the economy at a point when many believed it was about to decline. But the war had other, less welcome effects. It came at a time of rising insecurity about America's position in the world and intensified anxiety about communism. As the long stalemate continued, producing 140,000 American dead and wounded, frustration turned to anger. The United States, which had recently won the greatest war in history, seemed unable to conclude what many Americans considered a minor border skirmish in a small country. Many began to believe that

A M E R I C A N V O I C E S

WHITTAKER CHAMBERS

The Hiss Case

 I BELIEVED THAT I was not meant to be spared from testifying [against Alger Hiss]. I sensed, with a force greater than any fear or revulsion, that it was for this that my whole life had been lived. For this I had been a Communist, for this I had ceased to be a Communist. . . . This challenge was the terrible meaning of my whole life, of all that I had done that was evil, of all that I had sought that was good, of my weakness and my strength. . . .

For the moment had arrived when some man must be a witness. . . . The danger to the nation from Communism had now grown acute, both within its own house and abroad. Its existence was threatened. And the nation did not know it. For the first time, the [House Unamerican Activities] Committee's subpoena gave me an opportunity to tell what I knew about that danger. . . .

I did not wish to harm, more than was unavoidable, those whom I must testify against. . . . But I must testify that they had been concealed Communists and that an underground had existed in the Government. . . . They and I must stand up in face of the nation and confess what we had been that it might take alarm, throw off its apathy and skepticism, see that the enemy really was embedded in its midst, and be given time to act and save itself. That was the least that we could do in atonement.

SOURCE: Whittaker Chambers, *Witness*, pp. 533–534. Copyright ©1952 by Whittaker Chambers. Reprinted by permission of Random House.

something must be deeply wrong—not only in Korea but within the United States as well. Such fears contributed to the rise of the second major campaign of the century against domestic communism.

THE CRUSADE AGAINST SUBVERSION

Why did the American people develop a growing fear of internal communist subversion that by the early 1950s had reached the point of near hysteria? There are many possible answers, but no single definitive explanation.

One factor was obvious. Communism was not an imagined enemy in the 1950s. It had tangible shape, in Josef Stalin and the Soviet Union. Adding to the concern were the setbacks America had encountered in its battle against communism: the Korean stalemate, the "loss" of China, the Soviet development of an atomic bomb. Searching for someone to blame, many were attracted to the idea of a communist conspiracy within American borders. But there were other factors as well, rooted in events in American domestic politics.

HUAC and Alger Hiss

Much of the anticommunist furor emerged out of the search by the Republican party for an issue with which to attack the Democrats, and out of the efforts of the Democrats to take that issue away. Beginning in 1947, the House Un-American Activities Committee (HUAC) held widely publicized investigations to prove that, under Democratic rule, the government had tolerated (if not actually encouraged) communist subversion. The committee turned first to the movie industry, arguing that communists had infiltrated Hollywood and tainted American films with propaganda. Writers and producers, some of them former communists, were called to testify; and when some of them ("the Hollywood Ten") refused to answer questions about their own political beliefs and those of their colleagues, they were sent to jail for contempt. Others were barred from employment in the industry when Hollywood, attempting to protect its public image, adopted a "blacklist" of those of "suspicious loyalty."

More alarming to the public was HUAC's investigation into charges of disloyalty leveled against a former high-ranking member of the State Department: Alger Hiss. In 1948, Whittaker Chambers, a self-avowed former communist agent, now a conservative editor at *Time* magazine, told the committee that Hiss had passed classified State Department documents to him in 1937 and 1938. When Hiss sued him for slander, Chambers produced microfilms of the documents (called the "pumpkin papers," because Chambers had kept them hidden in a pumpkin in his vegetable garden). Hiss could not be tried for espionage because of the statute of limitations (a law that protects individuals from prosecution for most crimes after seven years have passed). But largely because of the relentless efforts of Richard M. Nixon, a freshman Republican congressman from California and a member of HUAC, Hiss was convicted of perjury and served several years in prison. The Hiss case not only discredited a prominent young diplomat; it cast suspicion on a generation of liberal Democrats and made it possible for the public to believe that communists had actually infiltrated the government. It also transformed Nixon into a national figure and helped him win a seat in the U.S. Senate in 1950.

The Federal Loyalty Program and the Rosenberg Case

Partly to protect itself against Republican attacks, partly to encourage support for the president's foreign policy initiatives, the Truman administration in 1947 initiated a widely publicized program to review the "loyalty" of federal employees. In August 1950, the president authorized sensitive agencies to fire people deemed no more than "bad security risks." By 1951, more than 2,000 government employees had resigned under pressure and 212 had been dismissed.

The employee loyalty program became a signal throughout the executive branch to launch a major assault on subversion. The attorney general established a widely cited list of supposedly subversive organizations. The director of the Federal Bureau of Investigation (FBI), J. Edgar Hoover, investigated and harassed alleged radicals. The anticommunist frenzy quickly grew so intense that even a Democratic Congress felt obliged to bow to it. In 1950, Congress passed the McCarran Internal Security Act, which, among other restrictions on "subversive" activity, required that all communist organizations register with the government and publish their records. Truman vetoed the bill. Congress easily overrode his veto.

The successful Soviet detonation of an atomic bomb in 1949, earlier than generally expected, suggested to some people that there had been a conspiracy to pass American atomic secrets to the Russians. In 1950, Klaus

Fuchs, a young British scientist, seemed to confirm those fears when he testified that he had delivered to the Russians details of the manufacture of the bomb. The case ultimately settled on an obscure New York couple, Julius and Ethel Rosenberg, members of the Communist party. The government claimed the Rosenbergs had received secret information from Ethel's brother, a machinist who had worked on the Manhattan Project in New Mexico, and had passed it on to the Soviet Union through other agents (including Fuchs). The Rosenbergs were convicted and, on April 5, 1951, sentenced to death. After two years of appeals and public protests, they died in the electric chair on June 19, 1953, proclaiming their innocence to the end.

All these factors—the HUAC investigations, the Hiss trial, the loyalty investigations, the McCarran Act, the Rosenberg case—combined with other concerns by the early 1950s to create a fear of communist subversion that seemed to grip the entire country. State and local governments, the judiciary, schools and universities, labor unions—all sought to purge themselves of real or imagined subversives. A pervasive fear settled on the country—not only the fear of communist infiltration but the fear of being suspected of communism. It was a climate that made possible the rise of an extraordinary public figure, whose behavior at any other time might have been dismissed as preposterous.

THE ROSENBERGS Julius and Ethel Rosenberg leave federal court in a police van after being convicted in March 1951 of transmitting atomic secrets to the Soviet Union. A week later, Judge Irving Kaufman sentenced them to death.

McCarthyism

Joseph McCarthy was an undistinguished, first-term Republican senator from Wisconsin when, in February 1950, he suddenly burst into national prominence. In the midst of a speech in Wheeling, West Virginia, he lifted a sheet of paper and claimed to "hold in my hand" a list of 205 known communists currently working in the American State Department. No person of comparable stature had ever made so bold a charge against the federal government; and in the weeks to come, as McCarthy repeated and expanded on his accusations, he emerged as the nation's most prominent leader of the crusade against domestic subversion.

Within weeks of his charges against the State Department, McCarthy was leveling accusations at other agencies. After 1952, with the Republicans in control of the Senate and McCarthy the chairman of a special subcommittee, he conducted highly publicized investigations of subversion in many areas of the government. McCarthy never produced conclusive evidence that any federal employee had communist ties. But a growing constituency adored him nevertheless for his coarse, "fearless" assaults on a government establishment that many considered arrogant, effete, even traitorous. Republicans, in particular, rallied to his claims that the Democrats had been responsible for "twenty years of treason" and that only a change of parties could rid the country of subversion. McCarthy, in short, provided his followers with an issue into which they could channel a wide range of resentments: fear of communism, animosity toward the country's "Eastern establishment," and frustrated partisan ambitions.

For a time, McCarthy intimidated all but a few people from opposing him. Even the highly popular Dwight D. Eisenhower, running for president in 1952, did not speak out against him, although he disliked McCarthy's tactics and was outraged at, among other things, McCarthy's attacks on General George Marshall.

The Republican Revival

Public frustration over the stalemate in Korea and popular fears of internal subversion combined to make 1952 a bad year for the Democratic party. Truman, whose own popularity had diminished almost to the vanishing point, wisely withdrew from the presidential contest. The party united instead behind Governor Adlai E. Stevenson of Illinois. Stevenson's dignity, wit, and eloquence made him a beloved figure to many liberals and intellectuals. But those same qualities seemed only to fuel Republican charges that

Stevenson lacked the strength or the will to combat communism sufficiently.

Stevenson's greatest problem, however, was the Republican candidate opposing him. Rejecting the efforts of conservatives to nominate Robert Taft or Douglas MacArthur, the Republicans turned to a man who had no previous identification with the party: General Dwight D. Eisenhower—military hero, commander of NATO, president of Columbia University in New York—who won nomination on the first ballot. He chose as his running mate the young California senator who had gained national prominence through his crusade against Alger Hiss: Richard M. Nixon.

In the fall campaign, Eisenhower attracted support through his geniality and his statesmanlike pledges to settle the Korean conflict. Nixon (after surviving early accusations of financial improprieties, which he effectively neutralized in a famous television address, the "Checkers speech") effectively exploited the issue of domestic anticommunism by attacking the Democrats for "cowardice" and "appeasement." The response at the polls was overwhelming. Eisenhower won both a popular and an electoral landslide: 55 percent of the popular vote to Stevenson's 44 percent, 442 electoral votes to Stevenson's 89. Republicans gained control of both houses of Congress for the first time since 1946. The election of 1952 ended twenty years of Democratic government. And while it might not have seemed so at the time, it also signaled the end of some of the worst turbulence of the postwar era.

D E B A T I N G   T H E   P A S T

The Cold War

F OR MORE THAN a decade after the beginning of the Cold War, few historians saw any reason to challenge the official American interpretation of its origins. The breakdown of relations between the United States and the Soviet Union was, most agreed, a direct result of Soviet expansionism and of Stalin's violation of the wartime agreements forged at Yalta and Potsdam. The Soviet imposition of communist regimes in Eastern Europe was part of a larger ideological design to spread communism throughout the world. American policy was the logical and necessary response.

Disillusionment with the official justifications for the Cold War began to find expression even in the late 1950s, when anticommunist sentiment in America remained strong and pervasive. William Appleman Williams's *The Tragedy of American Diplomacy* (1959) insisted that the Cold War was simply the most recent version of a consistent American effort in the twentieth century to preserve an "open door" for American trade in world markets. The confrontation with the Soviet Union, he argued, was less a response to Soviet aggressive designs than an expression of the American belief in the necessity of capitalist expansion.

As the Vietnam War grew larger and more unpopular in the 1960s, the scholarly critique of the Cold War quickly gained intensity. Walter LaFeber's *America, Russia, and the Cold War,* first published in 1967, maintained that America's supposedly idealistic internationalism at the close of the war was in reality an effort to ensure a postwar order shaped in the American image—with every nation open to American influence (and to American trade). That was why the United States was so eager to misinterpret Soviet policy, much of which reflected a perfectly reasonable concern to ensure the security of the Soviet Union itself, as part of a larger aggressive design. Important to many revisionist arguments has been the American decision to use atomic weapons against Japan in 1945. Gar Alperovitz's *Atomic Diplomacy* (1965) expanded on arguments that had begun to appear as early as 1948 and claimed that American decision makers used the bombs not to win the war (for Japan was already effectively defeated) but to impress and intimidate the Soviet Union so as to make it more "manageable" after the war.

The revisionist interpretations of the Cold War ultimately produced a reaction of their own: what has come to be known as "postrevisionist" scholarship. Some postrevisionists have done little more than revive the traditional, orthodox interpretations of the 1950s. But the most important works in this school have attempted to strike a balance between orthodoxy and revisionism and to identify areas of blame and patterns of misconception on both sides of the conflict. Thomas G. Patterson, John Lewis Gaddis, Melvin Leffler, and others have presented a picture of two nations—each with a highly inadequate understanding of the other—struggling to preserve a wartime alliance that had in fact temporarily disguised a basic difference in outlook and interests. "The United States and the Soviet Union were doomed to be antagonists," Ernest May wrote in 1984. "There probably was never any real possibility that the post-1945 relationship could be anything but hostility verging on conflict."

The collapse of Soviet communism and the dissolution of the Soviet empire will undoubtedly stimulate new interpretations of the Cold War and will (by facilitating the opening of Soviet archives) cast new light on many contested issues. For the moment, however, the dominant scholarly view is one that de-emphasizes the question of who is to blame and emphasizes the ways in which both sides learned to manage a conflict that neither could easily have avoided.

CHAPTER THIRTY

The Affluent Society

Abundance and Society ~ The Rise of the Civil-Rights Movement
Eisenhower Republicanism ~ Eisenhower, Dulles, and the Cold War

I F AMERICA EXPERIENCED a golden age in the 1950s and early 1960s, as many Americans believed at the time and many continue to believe today, it was largely a result of two developments. One was a booming national prosperity, which profoundly altered the social, economic, and even physical landscape of the United States, as well as the way many Americans thought about their lives and their world. The other was the continuing struggle against communism, a struggle that created considerable anxiety but that also encouraged Americans to look even more approvingly at their own society.

But if these powerful forces created a widespread sense of national purpose and self-satisfaction, they also helped blind many Americans to serious problems plaguing large groups of the population. More than 30 million Americans, according to some estimates, continued to live in poverty in the 1950s. And significant minorities—most prominently the 10 percent of the American people who were black—continued to suffer social, political, and economic discrimination. Ironically, perhaps, the very things that made America seem so successful in the 1950s also contributed, in the end, to making the nation's social problems more difficult to avoid.

ABUNDANCE AND SOCIETY

Perhaps the most striking feature of American society in the 1950s and early 1960s was the booming, almost miraculous economic growth that made even the heady 1920s seem pale by comparison. It was a better-balanced and more widely distributed prosperity than that of thirty years earlier. It was not, however, as universal as some Americans liked to believe.

Economic Growth

By 1949, despite the continuing problems of postwar reconversion, an economic expansion had begun that would continue with only brief interruptions for almost twenty years. Between 1945 and 1960, the gross national product grew by 250 percent, from $200 billion to over $500 billion. Unemployment, which during the Depression had averaged between 15 and 25 percent, remained at about 5 percent or lower throughout the 1950s and early 1960s. Inflation, in the meantime, hovered around 3 percent a year or less.

The causes of this growth were varied. Government spending, which had ended the Depression in the 1940s, continued to stimulate growth through public funding of schools, housing, veterans' benefits, welfare, and interstate highways. Above all, there was military spending. Economic growth was at its peak during the first half of the 1950s, when military spending was highest because of the Korean War. In the late 1950s, with spending on armaments in decline, the rate of growth declined by half.

The national birth rate reversed a long pattern of decline with the so-called baby boom, which had begun during the war and peaked in 1957. The nation's population rose almost 20 percent in the decade, from 150 million in 1950 to 179 million in 1960. The baby boom meant increased consumer demand and expanding economic growth.

The rapid expansion of suburbs—whose population grew 47 percent in the 1950s—helped stimulate growth in several important sectors of the economy. The number of privately owned cars (more essential for suburban than for urban living) more than doubled in a decade, sparking a great boom in the automobile industry. Demand for new homes helped sustain a vigorous housing industry. The construction of roads, which was both a cause and a result of the growth of suburbs, stimulated the economy as well.

Because of this unprecedented growth, the economy grew nearly ten times as fast as the population in the thirty years after the war. And while that growth was far from equally distributed, it affected most of society. The average American in 1960 had over 20 percent more purchasing power than in 1945, and more than twice as much as during the prosperous 1920s. The American people had achieved the highest standard of living of any society in the history of the world.

Capital and Labor

There were more than 4,000 corporate mergers in the 1950s; and more than ever before, a relatively small number of large-scale organizations controlled an enormous proportion of the nation's economic activity. By the end of the decade, half of the net corporate income in the nation was going to only slightly more than 500 firms, or one-tenth of 1 percent of the total number of corporations.

A similar consolidation was occurring in the agricultural economy. Increasing mechanization reduced the need for farm labor, and the agricultural work force declined by more than half in the two decades after the war. Mechanization also endangered one of the most cherished American institutions: the family farm. By the 1960s, relatively few individuals could any longer afford to buy and equip a modern farm; and much of the nation's most productive land had been purchased by financial institutions and corporations.

Corporations enjoying booming growth were reluctant to allow strikes to interfere with their operations; and since the most important labor unions were now so large and entrenched that they could not easily be suppressed or intimidated, business leaders made important concessions to them. As early as 1948, Walter Reuther, president of the United Automobile Workers, obtained a contract from General Motors that included a built-in "escalator clause"—an automatic cost-of-living increase pegged to the consumer price index. In 1955, Reuther received a guarantee from Ford Motor Company of continuing wages to autoworkers even during layoffs. A few months later, steelworkers in several corporations won a guaranteed annual salary. By the mid-1950s, factory wages in all industries had risen substantially, to an average of $80 per week.

The labor movement enjoyed significant success in winning better wages and benefits for workers already organized in strong unions. For the majority of laborers who were as yet unorganized, however, there were fewer advances. Total union membership remained relatively stable, at about 16 million, throughout the 1950s; and while this was in part a result of a shift in the work force from blue-collar to white-collar jobs, it was also a result of new obstacles to organization. The Taft-Hartley Act and the state right-to-work laws that the act spawned made it more difficult to create new unions powerful enough to demand recognition from employers.

The economic successes of the 1950s helped pave the way for a reunification of the labor movement. In December 1955, the American Federation of Labor and the Congress of Industrial Organizations ended their twenty-year rivalry and merged to create the AFL-CIO, under the leadership of George Meany.

But success also bred stagnation and corruption in some union bureaucracies. In 1957, the powerful Teamsters Union became the subject of a congressional investigation; and its president, David Beck, was charged with the misappropriation of union funds. Beck ultimately stepped down to be replaced by Jimmy Hoffa, whom government investigators pursued for nearly a decade before finally winning a conviction against him (for tax evasion) in 1967. The United Mine Workers, similarly, became tainted by violence and charges of corruption.

Consumerism and Suburbanization

Among the most striking social developments of the immediate postwar era was the rapid extension of a middle-class life style and outlook to an expanding portion of the population. The American middle class was becoming a larger, more powerful, and more self-conscious force than it had ever been before.

LEVITTOWN BEFORE THE TREES A section of the Levittown on Long Island in New York, photographed in July 1948 a few months after the first families moved in. The Levitt family pioneered techniques in constructing mass-produced housing that made possible the proliferation of similar inexpensive suburbs in many areas of the country.

At the center of middle-class culture in the 1950s was a growing absorption with consumer goods. That was a result of increased prosperity, of the increasing variety and availability of products, and of the adeptness of advertisers in creating a demand for those products. It was also a result of the growth of consumer credit, which increased by 800 percent between 1945 and 1957 through the development of credit cards, revolving charge accounts, and easy-payment plans. Prosperity fueled such longtime consumer crazes as the automobile, and Detroit responded to the boom with ever-flashier styling and accessories. Consumers also responded eagerly to the development of such new products as dishwashers, garbage disposals, television, and high-fidelity and stereo record players.

A third of the nation's population lived in suburbs by 1960. The growth of suburbs was a result not only of increased affluence but of important innovations in home building, which made single-family houses affordable to millions of new people. The most famous of the suburban developers, William Levitt, came to symbolize the new suburban growth with his use of mass-production techniques to construct a large housing development on Long Island, near New York City. The houses sold for under $10,000. Young couples—often newly married war veterans eager to start a family—rushed to purchase the inexpensive homes, not only in the Levittowns but in similar developments that soon began appearing throughout the country.

Why did so many Americans want to move to the suburbs? One reason was the enormous importance postwar Americans placed on family life after five years of war during which families had often been separated or otherwise disrupted. Suburbs provided families with larger homes than they could find (or afford) in the cities, and thus made it easier to raise larger numbers of children. They provided privacy. They also provided security from the noise and dangers of urban living. They offered space for the new consumer goods—the appliances, cars, boats, outdoor furniture, and other products—that middle-class Americans craved.

For many Americans, suburban life also helped provide a sense of community that was sometimes difficult to develop in large, crowded, impersonal urban areas. In later years, the suburbs would come under attack for their supposed conformity, homogeneity, and isolation. But in the 1950s, many people were attracted by the idea of living in a community populated largely by people of similar age and background, and they found it easier to form friendships and social circles there than in the city. Women in particular often valued the presence of other nonworking mothers living nearby to share the tasks of child raising.

Another factor motivating white Americans to move to the suburbs was race. Most suburbs were restricted to white inhabitants—both because relatively few blacks could afford to live in them and because of formal and informal barriers that kept even prosperous blacks out. In an era when the black population of most cities was rapidly growing, many white families fled to the suburbs to escape the integration of urban neighborhoods and schools.

Suburban neighborhoods were often very much alike. But they were not uniform. The Levittowns and inexpensive developments like them ultimately became the homes of mainly lower-middle-class people one step removed from the inner city. Other, more affluent suburbs became enclaves of wealthy families. Around virtually every city, a clear hierarchy emerged of upper-class suburban neighborhoods and more modest ones, just as such gradations had emerged years earlier among urban neighborhoods.

The Suburban Family

For professional men (who tended to work in the city, at some distance from their homes), suburban life generally meant a rigid division between their working and personal worlds. For many middle-class women, it meant an increased isolation from the workplace. The enormous cultural emphasis on family life in the 1950s strengthened popular prejudices against women entering the professions or occupying any paid job at all. Many middle-class husbands considered it demeaning for their wives to be employed. And many women themselves shied away from the workplace when they could afford to, in part because of prevailing ideas about motherhood (popularized by such widely consulted books as Dr. Benjamin Spock's *Baby and Child Care*, first published in 1946) that instructed women to stay at home with their children.

Affluent women, then, faced heavy pressures—both externally and internally imposed—to remain in the home and concentrate on raising their children. Some women, however, had to balance these pressures against other, contradictory ones. As expectations of material comfort rose, many middle-class families needed a second income to maintain the standard of living they desired. As a result, the number of married women working outside the home increased in the postwar years—even as the social pressure for them to stay out of the workplace grew. By 1960, nearly a third of all married women were part of the paid work force.

The Birth of Television

Television, perhaps the most powerful medium of mass communication in history, was central to the culture of the postwar era. Experiments in broadcasting pictures (along with sound) had begun as early as the 1920s, but commercial television began only shortly after World War II. It experienced a phenomenally rapid growth. In 1946, there were only 17,000 television sets in the country; by 1957, there were 40 million sets in use—almost as many sets as there were families. More people had television sets, according to one report, than had refrigerators.

The impact of television on American life was rapid, pervasive, and profound. By the late 1950s, television news had replaced newspapers, magazines, and radios as the nation's most important vehicle of information. Television advertising helped create a vast market for new fashions and products. Televised athletic events gradually made professional and college sports one of the important sources of entertainment (and one of the biggest businesses) in America. Television entertainment programming, almost all of it controlled by the three national networks (and their corporate sponsors), replaced movies and radio as the principal source of diversion for American families.

EISENHOWER AND DULLES Although President Eisenhower himself was a somewhat colorless television personality, his was the first administration to make extensive use of the new medium to promote its policies and dramatize its actions. The president's press conferences were frequently televised, and on several occasions Secretary of State John Foster Dulles reported to the president in front of the cameras.

Much of the programming of the 1950s and early 1960s created a relatively uniform image of American life—an image that was predominantly white, middle-class, and suburban, an image epitomized by such popular situation comedies as *Ozzie and Harriet* and *Leave It to Beaver*. But television also conveyed other images: the gritty, urban working-class families in Jackie Gleason's *The Honeymooners*; the childless show-business family of the early *I Love Lucy*; the unmarried professional women in *Our Miss Brooks* and *My Little Margie*. Television not only sought to create an idealized image of a homogeneous suburban America. It also sought to convey experiences at odds with that image, but to convey them in warm, unthreatening terms—taking social diversity and cultural conflict and domesticating them, turning them into something benign and even comic.

Yet television also, inadvertently, created conditions that could accentuate social conflict. Even those unable to share in the affluence of the era could, through television, acquire a vivid picture of how the rest of their society lived. At the same time that television was reinforcing the homogeneity of the white middle class, therefore, it was also contributing to the sense of alienation and powerlessness among groups excluded from the world it portrayed.

Science and Space

In 1961, *Time* magazine chose as its "man of the year" not a specific person but "the American Scientist." The choice was an indication of the widespread fascination with which Americans in the age of atomic weapons viewed science and technology. Major medical advances accounted for much of that fascination. Jonas Salk's vaccine to prevent polio was provided to the public free by the federal government beginning in 1955, and within a few years it had virtually eliminated the much feared polio from American life. Other dread diseases such as diphtheria and tuberculosis also all but vanished from society as new drugs and treatments were discovered. Infant mortality and the death rate among young children both declined significantly in the first twenty-five years after the war (although less than in Western Europe). Average life expectancy in that same period rose by five years, to seventy-one.

But Americans were at least equally attracted to other scientific and technological innovations: the jet plane, the computer, synthetics, new types of commercially prepared foods. And nothing better illustrated the nation's veneration of scientific expertise than the popular enthusiasm for the American space program.

The program began in large part because of the Cold War. When the Soviet Union announced in 1957 that it had launched a satellite—*Sputnik*—into outer space, the American government (and much of society) reacted with alarm, as if the Soviet achievement was also a massive American failure. Strenuous efforts began to improve scientific education in the schools, to develop more research laboratories, and, above all, to speed the development of America's own exploration of outer space. The centerpiece of that exploration was the manned space program, established in 1958 with the selection of the first American space pilots, or "astronauts," who quickly became the nation's most revered heroes. On May 5, 1961, Alan Shepard became the first American launched into space (several months after a Soviet "cosmonaut," Yuri Gagarin, had made a similar, if longer, flight). On February 2, 1962, John Glenn (later a United States senator) became the first American to orbit the globe (again, only after Gagarin had already done so).

Interest in the space program remained high in the summer of 1969, when Neil Armstrong and Edwin Aldrin became the first men to walk on the surface of the moon. Not long after that, however, the government began to cut the funding for future missions; and popular enthusiasm for the program began to wane.

Organized Society and Its Detractors

Large-scale organizations and bureaucracies increased their influence over American life in the postwar era, as they had been doing for many decades before. White-collar workers came to outnumber blue-collar laborers for the first time, and an increasing proportion of them worked in corporate settings with rigid hierarchical structures. Industrial workers also confronted large bureaucracies both in the workplace and in their own unions.

As in earlier eras, Americans reacted to these developments with ambivalence, often hostility. The debilitating impact of bureaucratic life on the individual slowly became one of the central themes of popular and scholarly debate. William H. Whyte, Jr., produced one of the most widely discussed books of the decade: *The Organization Man* (1956), which attempted to describe the special mentality of the worker in a large, bureaucratic setting. Self-reliance, Whyte claimed, was losing place to the ability to "get along" and "work as a team" as the most valuable trait in the modern character. Sociologist David Riesman made similar observations in *The Lonely Crowd* (1950), in which he argued that the traditional "inner-directed" man, who judged himself on the basis of his own values and the esteem of his family, was giving way to a new "other-directed" man, more concerned with winning the approval of the larger organization or community.

The most derisive critics of bureaucracy, and of middle-class society generally, were a group of young poets, writers, and artists generally known as the "beats" (or, by derisive critics, as "beatniks"). They wrote harsh critiques of what they considered the sterility and conformity of American life, the meaninglessness of American politics, and the banality of popular culture. Allen Ginsberg's dark, bitter poem *Howl* (1955) decried the "Robot apartments! invincible suburbs! skeleton treasuries! blind capitals! demonic industries!" of modern life. Jack Kerouac produced what may have been the central document of the Beat Generation in his novel *On the Road* (1957)— an account of a cross-country automobile trip that depicted the rootless, iconoclastic life style of Kerouac and his friends.

Other, less starkly alienated writers also used their work to express misgivings about the enormity and impersonality of modern society. Saul Bellow produced a series of novels—*The Adventures of Augie March* (1953), *Seize the Day* (1956), *Herzog* (1964), and others—that chronicled the difficulties of urban American Jews in finding fulfillment in modern urban America. J. D. Salinger wrote in *The Catcher in the Rye* (1951) of a prep-school student, Holden Caulfield, who was unable to find any area of society—school, family, friends, city—in which he could feel secure or committed.

The Other America

Despite the growing general prosperity of America in the 1950s and 1960s, much of the population continued to struggle on the fringes of the economic boom. In 1948, farmers had received 8.9 percent of the national income; in 1956, they received only 4.1 percent. In part, this decline reflected the steadily shrinking farm population. But it also reflected declining farm prices, which affected even those farmers who managed to survive.

Farmers, at least, were able to attract some public attention to their plight. Other, poorer groups languished in virtual obscurity. Inner-city ghettoes were expanding rapidly in the 1950s. In most places, that was a result of African-American farmers moving from country to city and of a significant growth in the black population as a whole. In New York, Los

Angeles, and many smaller cities in the Southwest, immigrants from Puerto Rico, Mexico, and other Spanish-speaking areas created significant poor Hispanic neighborhoods (or *barrios*) as well. Historic patterns of racial discrimination doomed large proportions of these communities to continuing, and in some cases increasing, poverty.

A similar predicament faced residents of several particularly destitute rural regions—most notably the Appalachian areas of the Southern and border states, where the decline of the coal industry was eroding the only significant economic support many communities had known. Lacking adequate schools, health care, and services, the residents of Appalachia, like the residents of the urban ghettoes, were almost entirely shut off from the mainstream of American economic life. Not until the 1960s, when such exposés as Michael Harrington's *The Other America* (1962) began drawing attention to the continuing existence of poverty in the nation, did the middle class begin to recognize the seriousness of the problem.

THE RISE OF THE CIVIL-RIGHTS MOVEMENT

After decades of skirmishes, an open battle began in the 1950s against racial segregation and discrimination, a battle that would prove to be one of the longest and most difficult of the century. White Americans played an important role in the civil-rights movement. But pressure from African-Americans themselves was the crucial element in raising the issue of race to prominence.

The Brown *Decision and "Massive Resistance"*

On May 17, 1954, the Supreme Court announced one of the most important decisions in its history in the case of *Brown* v. *Board of Education of Topeka*. In considering the legal segregation of a Kansas public school system, the Court rejected its own 1896 *Plessy* v. *Ferguson* decision, which had ruled that communities could provide blacks with separate facilities as long as the facilities were equal to those of whites. The Brown decision unequivocally declared the segregation of public schools on the basis of race unconstitutional.

The *Brown* decision was the culmination of many decades of effort by black opponents of segregation, and particularly by a group of talented NAACP lawyers, many of them trained at Howard University in Washington by the great legal educator Charles Houston. Thurgood Marshall, William Hastie, James Nabrit, and others spent years filing legal challenges to segregation in one state after another, nibbling at the edges of the system, and accumulating precedents to support their assault on the "separate but equal" doctrine itself. The same lawyers filed the suits against the school boards of Topeka, Kansas, and several other cities that became the basis for the *Brown* decision.

The Topeka suit involved the case of a black girl who had to travel several miles to a segregated public school every day even though she lived virtually next door to a white elementary school. When the case arrived before the Supreme Court, the justices concluded that school segregation inflicted unacceptable damage on those it affected, regardless of the relative quality of the separate schools. Chief Justice Earl Warren explained the unanimous opinion of his colleagues: "We conclude that in the field of public education the doctrine of 'separate but equal' has no place. Separate educational facilities are inherently unequal." The following year, the Court issued another decision (known as *"Brown* II") to provide rules for implementing the 1954 order. It ruled that communities must work to desegregate their schools "with all deliberate speed," but it set no timetable and left specific decisions up to lower courts.

In some communities, for example Washington, D.C., compliance came relatively quickly and quietly. More often, however, strong local opposition (what came to be known in the South as "massive resistance") produced long delays and bitter conflicts. Some school districts ignored the ruling altogether. Others attempted to circumvent it with purely token efforts to integrate. More than 100 Southern members of Congress signed a "manifesto" in 1956 denouncing the *Brown* decision and urging their constituents to defy it. Southern governors, mayors, local school boards, and nongovernmental pressure groups (including hundreds of White Citizens' Councils) all worked to obstruct desegregation. By the fall of 1957, only 684 of 3,000 affected school districts in the South had even begun to desegregate their schools. The *Brown* decision, far from ending segregation, had launched a prolonged battle between federal authority and state and local governments.

The Eisenhower administration was not eager to commit itself to that battle. But in September 1957, it faced a case of direct state defiance of federal authority and felt compelled to act. Federal courts had ordered the desegregation of Central High School in Little Rock, Arkansas. An angry white mob tried to block implementation of the order by blockading the entrances to the school, and Governor Orval Faubus refused to do anything to stop the obstruction. President Eisenhower finally responded by sending federal troops to Little Rock to keep the peace and ensure that the court orders would be obeyed. Only then did Central High School admit its first black students.

The Expanding Movement

The *Brown* decision helped spark a growing number of popular challenges to segregation in the South. On December 1, 1955, Rosa Parks, an African-American woman, was arrested in Montgomery, Alabama, when she refused to give up her seat on a Montgomery bus to a white passenger (as required by the Jim Crow laws that regulated race relations in the city and through-

ROSA PARKS IN THE FRONT OF THE BUS In December 1955 Rosa Parks was arrested in Montgomery, Alabama, for refusing to obey a law that required her to give up her seat to a white passenger and move to the back of the bus. Her defiance sparked an almost total boycott of Montgomery's transit system by black citizens. Just over a year later, the U.S. Supreme Court ruled that racial segregation of public transit systems was unconstitutional.

out most of the South). Parks, an active civil-rights leader in the community, had apparently decided spontaneously to resist the order to move. Her feet were tired, she later explained. The arrest of this admired woman produced outrage in the city's African-American community, which organized a successful boycott of the bus system to demand an end to segregated seating.

The bus boycott owed much of its success to the prior existence of well-organized black citizens' groups. A black women's political caucus had, in fact, been developing plans for some time for a boycott of the segregated buses. Local leaders seized on Rosa Parks as the vehicle for their plans, because she was so well suited to serve as a symbol of the movement. Once launched, the boycott was almost completely effective. It put economic pressure not only on the bus company (a private concern) but on many Montgomery merchants, because the bus boycotters found it difficult to get to downtown stores and tended to shop instead in their own neighborhoods. Even so, the boycott might well have failed had it not been for a Supreme Court decision late in 1956, inspired in part by the protest, that declared segregation in public transportation to be illegal. The buses in Montgomery abandoned their discriminatory seating policies, and the boycott came to a close.

The most important accomplishments of the Montgomery boycott were less its immediate victories than its success in establishing a new form of racial protest and in elevating to prominence a new figure in the movement for civil rights. The man chosen to lead the boycott movement once it was launched was a local Baptist pastor, Martin Luther King, Jr., son of a prominent Atlanta minister, a powerful orator, and a gifted leader. King was reluctant at first to assume the leadership of the movement. But once he accepted the role, he became consumed by it.

King's approach to black protest was based on the doctrine of nonviolence—that is, of passive resistance even in the face of direct attack. He drew from the teachings of Mahatma Gandhi, the Indian nationalist leader; from Henry David Thoreau and his doctrine of civil disobedience; and from Christian dogma. And he produced an approach to racial struggle that captured the moral high ground for his supporters. He urged African-Americans to engage in peaceful demonstrations; to allow themselves to be arrested, even beaten, if necessary; and to respond to hate with love. For the next thirteen years—as leader of the Southern Christian Leadership Conference (SCLC), an interracial group he founded shortly after the bus boycott—he was the most influential and most widely admired black leader in the country. The popular movement he came to represent soon spread throughout the South and throughout the country.

EISENHOWER REPUBLICANISM

Dwight D. Eisenhower was the least experienced politician to serve in the White House in the twentieth century. He was also among the most popular and politically successful presidents of the postwar era. At home, he pursued essentially moderate policies, avoiding most new initiatives but accepting the work of earlier reformers. Abroad, he continued and even intensified American commitments to oppose communism but brought to some of those commitments a measure of restraint that his successors did not always match.

"What's Good for General Motors . . ."

The first Republican administration in twenty years staffed itself with men drawn from the same quarter as those who had staffed Republican administrations in the 1920s: the business community. But many in the American business community had acquired a very different social and political outlook by the 1950s from that of their predecessors of earlier decades. Above all, many of the nation's leading businessmen and financiers had reconciled themselves to at least the broad outlines of the Keynesian welfare state the New Deal had launched. Indeed, many corporate leaders had come to see it as something that actually benefited them—by helping maintain social order, by increasing mass purchasing power, and by stabilizing labor relations.

To his cabinet, Eisenhower appointed wealthy corporate lawyers and business executives who were not apologetic about their backgrounds. Charles Wilson, president of General Motors, assured senators considering his nomination for secretary of defense that he foresaw no conflict of interest because he was certain that "What was good for our country was good for General Motors, and vice versa." But missing from most members of this business-oriented administration was the deep hostility to "government interference" that had so dominated corporate attitudes three decades before.

Eisenhower's leadership style, which stressed delegation of authority to subordinates, helped enhance the power of his cabinet officers and others. Secretary of State John Foster Dulles was widely believed to be running American foreign policy almost single-handedly (although it has since become clear that the president was far more deeply involved in international decisions than was often apparent at the time). The president's White House chief of staff, former New Hampshire governor Sherman Adams, exercised broad authority over relations with Congress and strictly controlled access to the president—until he left office in disgrace, near the end of Eisenhower's presidency, after he was discovered to have accepted gifts from a wealthy businessman.

Eisenhower's consistent inclination was to limit federal activities and encourage private enterprise. He supported the private rather than public development of natural resources (and once talked about selling the Tennessee Valley Authority to a private company). To the chagrin of farmers, he lowered federal support for farm prices. He also removed the last limited wage and price controls maintained by the Truman administration. He opposed the creation of new social service programs such as national health insurance. He strove constantly to reduce federal expenditures (even during the recession of 1958) and balance the budget. He ended 1960, his last full year in office, with a $1 billion surplus.

The president took few new initiatives in domestic policy, but he resisted pressure from the right wing of his party to dismantle those welfare policies of the New Deal that had survived the conservative assaults of the war years and after. Indeed, during his term, he agreed to extend the Social Security system to an additional 10 million people and unemployment compensation to an additional 4 million people; and he agreed to increase the minimum hourly wage from 75 cents to $1. Perhaps the most significant legislative accomplishment of the Eisenhower administration was the Federal Highway Act of 1956, which authorized $25 billion for a ten-year effort to construct over 40,000 miles of interstate highways. The program was to be funded through a highway "trust fund," whose revenues would come from new taxes on the purchase of fuel, automobiles, trucks, and tires.

In 1956, Eisenhower ran for a second term, even though he had suffered a serious heart attack the previous year. With Adlai Stevenson opposing him once again, he won by another, even greater landslide, receiving nearly 57 percent of the popular vote and 442 electoral votes to Stevenson's 89. Still, Democrats retained the control of both houses of Congress they had won back in 1954. And in 1958—during a serious recession—they increased that control by substantial margins.

The Decline of McCarthyism

The Eisenhower administration did little in its first years in office to discourage the anticommunist furor that had gripped the nation. Indeed, in many ways it helped sustain it. The president intensified the search for subversives in the government, which Truman had begun several years earlier. More than 2,220 federal employees resigned or were dismissed as a result of security investigations.

By 1954, such policies were beginning to produce significant popular opposition—an indication that the anticommunist passion of several years earlier was beginning to abate. The clearest signal of that change was the political demise of Senator Joseph McCarthy.

During the first year of the Eisenhower administration, McCarthy continued to operate with impunity. The president, who privately loathed him, nevertheless refused to speak out against him in public. Relatively few others—in the political world or in the press—were any more courageous. But McCarthy finally overreached himself in January 1954 when he attacked Secretary of the Army Robert Stevens and the armed services in general. At that point, the administration and influential members of Congress organized a special investigation of the charges, which became known as the Army-McCarthy hearings. They were among the first congressional hearings to be nationally televised.

The result was devastating to McCarthy. Watching McCarthy in action—bullying witnesses, hurling groundless (and often cruel) accusations, evading issues—much of the public began to see him as a villain, and even

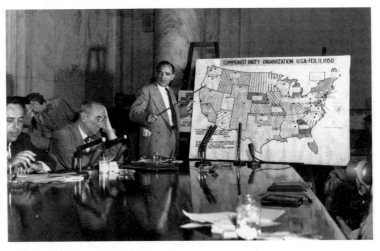

THE ARMY-McCARTHY HEARINGS Senator Joseph McCarthy uses a map to show the supposed distribution of communists throughout the United States during the televised 1954 Senate hearings to mediate the dispute between McCarthy and the U.S. Army. Joseph Welch, chief counsel for the army, remains conspicuously unimpressed.

a buffoon. In December 1954, the Senate voted 67 to 22 to condemn him for "conduct unbecoming a senator." Three years later, with little public support left, he died—a victim, apparently, of complications arising from alcoholism.

EISENHOWER, DULLES, AND THE COLD WAR

The threat of nuclear war with the Soviet Union created a sense of high anxiety in international relations in the 1950s. But the nuclear threat had another effect as well. With the potential devastation of an atomic war so enormous, both superpowers began to edge away from direct confrontations. The attention of both the United States and the Soviet Union began to turn to the rapidly escalating instability in the nations of the Third World.

Dulles and "Massive Retaliation"

Eisenhower's secretary of state, and (except for the president himself) the dominant figure in the nation's foreign policy in the 1950s, was John Foster Dulles, an aristocratic corporate lawyer with a stern moral revulsion to communism. He entered office denouncing the containment policies of the Truman years as excessively passive, arguing that the United States should pursue an active program of "liberation," which would lead to a "rollback" of communist expansion. Once in power, however, he had to defer to the far more moderate views of the president himself, and he began to develop a new set of doctrines that reflected the impact of nuclear weapons on the world.

The most prominent of those doctrines was the policy of "massive retaliation," which Dulles announced early in 1954. The United States would, he explained, respond to communist threats to its allies not by using conventional forces in local conflicts (a policy that had led to so much frustration in Korea) but by relying on "the deterrent of massive retaliatory power" (by which he clearly meant nuclear weapons).

In part, the new doctrine reflected Dulles's inclination for tense confrontations, an approach he once defined as "brinksmanship"—pushing the Soviet Union to the brink of war in order to exact concessions. But the real force behind the massive retaliation policy was economics. With pressure growing both in and out of government for a reduction in American military expenditures, an increasing reliance on atomic weapons seemed to promise, as some advocates put it, "more bang for the buck."

At the same time, Dulles intensified the efforts of Truman and Acheson to "integrate" the entire noncommunist world into a system of mutual defense pacts modeled on NATO—although the new alliances were far weaker than the European pact. By the end of the decade, the United States had become a party to almost a dozen such treaties in all areas of the world.

France, America, and Vietnam

What had been the most troubling foreign policy concern of the Truman years—the war in Korea—plagued the Eisenhower administration only briefly. On July 27, 1953, negotiators at Panmunjom finally signed an agreement ending the hostilities. Each antagonist was to withdraw its troops a mile and a half from the existing battle line, which ran roughly along the 38th parallel, the prewar border between North and South Korea. A conference in Geneva was to consider means by which to reunite the nation peacefully—although in fact the 1954 meeting produced no agreement and left the cease-fire line as the apparently permanent border between the two countries.

Almost simultaneously, however, the United States was becoming drawn into a long, bitter struggle in Southeast Asia. Ever since the end of World War II, France had been attempting to restore its authority over Vietnam, its one-time colony, which it had had to abandon to the Japanese during World War II. Opposing the French, however, were the powerful nationalist forces of Ho Chi Minh, determined to win independence for their nation. Ho had hoped for American support in 1945, on the basis of the anticolonial rhetoric of the Atlantic Charter and Franklin Roosevelt's speeches, and also because he had received support from American intelligence forces during World War II while he was fighting the Japanese. But he was then, as he had been for many years, not only a committed nationalist but a committed communist. The Truman administration ignored him and supported the French, one of America's most important Cold War allies.

By 1954, Ho was receiving aid from communist China and the Soviet Union. America, in the meantime, was paying most of the costs of France's ineffective military campaign in Vietnam since 1950. Early in 1954, 12,000 French troops became surrounded in a disastrous siege at the city of Dienbienphu. Only American intervention, it was clear, could prevent the total collapse of the French military effort. Yet despite the urgings of Secretary of State Dulles, Vice President Nixon, and others, Eisenhower refused to permit direct American military intervention in Vietnam, claiming that neither Congress nor America's other allies would support such action.

Without American aid, the French defense of Dienbienphu finally collapsed on May 7, 1954; and France quickly agreed to a settlement of the conflict at the same conference in Geneva that summer that was considering the Korean settlement. The Geneva accords on Vietnam of July 1954, to which the United States was not a direct party, established a supposedly temporary division of Vietnam along the 17th parallel. The north would be governed by Ho Chi Minh, the south by a pro-Western regime. Democratic elections would be the basis for uniting the nation in 1956.

The agreement marked the end of the French commitment to Vietnam and the beginning of an expanded American presence there. The United States helped establish a pro-American government in the south, headed by Ngo Dinh Diem, a member of his country's Roman Catholic minority. Diem, it was clear, would not permit the 1956 elections, which he knew he would lose. He felt secure in his refusal because the United States had promised to provide him with ample military assistance against any attack from the north. (There is some evidence that the Soviet Union, eager to avoid a confrontation with the United States at this point, was at the same time pressuring Ho and his regime not to press for an election.)

Israel and the Crises of the Middle East

The establishment of a Jewish state in Palestine had been the dream of a powerful international Zionist movement for more than half a century before World War II. The plight of homeless Jews uprooted by the war, and the international horror at revelations of the Holocaust, gave new strength to Zionist demands in the late 1940s. So did the enormous immigration of European Jews into Palestine after 1945, despite the efforts of Britain (which had governed the region since World War I) to limit them.

Finally, Britain brought the problem to the United Nations, which responded by recommending the partition of Palestine into a Jewish and an Arab state. On May 14, 1948, British rule ended, and Jews proclaimed the existence of the nation of Israel. President Truman recognized the new government the following day. But the creation of Israel, while it resolved some conflicts, created others. Palestinian Arabs, unwilling to accept being displaced from what they considered their own country, fought determinedly against the new state in 1948—the first of several Arab-Israeli wars.

Committed as the American government was to Israel, it was also concerned about the stability and friendliness of the Arab regimes in the area. The reason was simple: The region contained the richest oil reserves in the world, reserves in which American companies had already invested heavily, reserves on which the health of the American (and world) economy would ultimately come to depend. Thus the United States reacted with alarm as it watched Mohammed Mossadegh, the nationalist prime minister of Iran, begin to resist the presence of Western corporations in his nation in the early 1950s. In 1953, the American CIA joined forces with conservative Iranian military leaders to engineer a coup that drove Mossadegh from office. To replace him, the CIA helped elevate the young Shah of Iran, Mohammed Reza Pahlevi, from his position as a token constitutional monarch to that of a virtually absolute ruler. The Shah remained closely tied to the United States for the next twenty-five years.

American policy was less effective in dealing with the nationalist government of Egypt, under the leadership of General Gamal Abdel Nasser, which began to develop a trade relationship with the Soviet Union in the early 1950s. In 1956, to punish Nasser for his friendliness toward the communists, Dulles withdrew American offers to assist in building the great Aswan Dam across the Nile. A week later, Nasser retaliated by seizing control of the Suez Canal from the British, saying that he would use the income from it to build the dam himself. The repercussions of that seizure were quick and profound.

On October 29, 1956, Israeli forces struck a preemptive blow against Egypt. The next day the British and French landed troops in the Suez to drive the Egyptians from the canal. Dulles and Eisenhower feared that the Suez crisis would drive the Arab states toward the Soviet Union and precipitate a new world war. By refusing to support the invasion, and by joining in a United Nations denunciation of it, the United States helped pressure the French and British to withdraw and helped persuade Israel to agree to a truce with Egypt.

Nasser's continuing flirtation with the Soviet Union strengthened American resolve to resist the growth of communist influence (which the United States increasingly associated with Arab nationalism) in the Middle East. In 1958, as pan-Arab forces loyal to Nasser challenged the government of Lebanon, Eisenhower ordered 5,000 American marines to land on the beaches of Beirut to protect the existing regime; British troops entered Jordan at about the same time to resist a similar threat there. The effect of the interventions was negligible. The governments of both countries managed to stabilize their positions on their own, and within months both the American and the British forces withdrew.

Latin America and "Yankee Imperialism"

World War II and the Cold War had eroded the limited initiatives of the Good Neighbor Policy toward Latin America, as American economic aid now flowed increasingly to Europe. Latin American animosity toward the United States grew steadily during the 1950s, as many people in the region began to regard the influence of American corporations in their countries as a form of imperialism. Such concerns deepened in 1954, when the Eisenhower administration ordered the CIA to help topple the new, leftist government of Jacobo Arbenz Guzmán in Guatemala, a regime that Dulles (responding to the entreaties of the United Fruit Company, a major investor in Guatemala fearful of Arbenz) argued was potentially communist. Four years later, the depths of anti-American sentiment became clear when Vice President Richard Nixon visited the region, to be greeted in city after city by angry, hostile, occasionally dangerous mobs.

No nation in the region had been more closely tied to America than Cuba. Its leader, Fulgencio Batista, had ruled as a military dictator since 1952, when with American assistance he had toppled a more moderate government. Cuba's relatively prosperous economy had become a virtual fiefdom of American corporations, which controlled almost all the island's natural resources and had cornered over half the vital sugar crop. American-organized crime syndicates controlled much of Havana's lucrative hotel and night-life business. Beginning in 1957, a popular movement of resistance to the Batista regime began to gather power under the leadership of Fidel Castro. By late 1958, the Batista forces were in almost total disarray. And on January 1, 1959, with Batista now in exile in Spain, Castro marched into Havana and established a new government.

At first, many Americans reacted warmly to Castro. But once Castro began implementing drastic policies of land reform and expropriating foreign-owned businesses and resources, Cuban-American relations rapidly deteriorated. Of particular concern to Eisenhower and Dulles was the Cuban regime's growing interest in communist ideas and tactics. When Castro began accepting assistance from the Soviet Union in 1960, the United States cut back the "quota" by which Cuba could export sugar to America at a favored price. Early in 1961, as one of its last acts, the

Eisenhower administration severed diplomatic relations with Castro. The American CIA had already begun secretly training Cuban expatriates for an invasion of the island to topple the new regime. Isolated by the United States, Castro soon cemented an alliance with the Soviet Union.

Europe and the Soviet Union

Although the problems of the Third World were moving slowly toward the center of American foreign policy, the direct relationship with the Soviet Union and the effort to resist communist expansion in Europe remained the principal concerns of the Eisenhower administration.

Even as the United States was strengthening NATO and rearming West Germany, however, many Americans continued to hope for negotiated solutions to some of the remaining problems dividing the superpowers. Such hopes grew after the death of Stalin in 1953, especially when the Soviet Union extended a peace overture to the rebellious Tito government in Yugoslavia, returned a military base to Finland, signed a peace treaty with Japan, and ended its long military occupation of Austria by allowing that nation to become an independent, neutral state. In 1955, Eisenhower and other NATO leaders met with the Soviet premier, Nikolai Bulganin, at a cordial summit conference in Geneva. But when a subsequent conference of foreign ministers met to try to resolve specific issues, they could find no basis for agreement.

Relations between the Soviet Union and the West soured further in 1956 in response to the Hungarian Revolution. Inspired by riots in Poland a year earlier, Hungarian dissidents had launched a popular uprising in November 1956 to demand democratic reforms. For several days, they had control of the Hungarian government. But before the month was out, Soviet tanks and troops entered Budapest to crush the uprising and restore an orthodox, pro-Soviet regime. The Eisenhower administration refused to intervene. But the suppression of the uprising convinced many American leaders that Soviet policies had not softened as much as the events of the previous two years had suggested.

The failure of conciliation brought renewed vigor to the Cold War and, among other things, greatly intensified the Soviet-American arms race. Both nations engaged in extensive nuclear testing. Both nations redoubled efforts to develop effective intercontinental ballistic missiles, which could deliver atomic warheads directly from one continent to another. The American military, in the meantime, developed a new breed of atomic-powered submarines, capable of launching missiles from under water anywhere in the world.

The arms race not only increased tensions between the United States and Russia; it increased tensions within each nation as well. In America, public concern about nuclear war was becoming a pervasive national nightmare, a preoccupation never far from popular thought. Movies, television programs, books, popular songs—all expressed the concern. Fear of communism, therefore, combined with fear of atomic war to create a persistent national anxiety.

The U-2 Crisis

In this tense and fearful atmosphere, the Soviet Union raised new challenges to the West in Berlin in 1958. The continuing existence of an anticommunist West Berlin inside communist East Germany remained an irritant and embarrassment to the Soviets. In November 1958, Nikita Khrushchev, who had succeeded Bulganin as Soviet premier and Communist party chief earlier that year, renewed the demands of his predecessors that the NATO powers abandon the city. The United States and its allies refused.

Khrushchev declined to force the issue. Instead, he suggested that he and Eisenhower discuss the issue personally, both in visits to each other's countries and at a summit meeting in Paris in 1960. The United States agreed. Khrushchev's 1959 visit to America produced a cool but polite public response. Plans proceeded for the summit conference and for Eisenhower's visit to Moscow shortly thereafter. Only days before the scheduled beginning of the Paris meeting, however, the Soviet Union announced that it had shot down an American U-2, a high-altitude spy plane, over Russian territory. Its pilot, Francis Gary Powers, was in captivity. The Eisenhower administration responded clumsily, at first denying the allegations and then, when confronted with proof of them, awkwardly admitting that they were true. Khrushchev lashed back angrily, breaking up the Paris summit almost before it could begin and withdrawing his invitation to Eisenhower to visit the Soviet Union. But the U-2 incident was probably only a pretext. By the spring of 1960, Khrushchev was under pressure from hard-liners in the Kremlin to toughen his stance toward the West, and he knew that no agreement was possible on the Berlin issue. The U-2 incident may simply have been an excuse to avoid what he believed would be fruitless negotiations.

The events of 1960 provided a somber backdrop for the end of the Eisenhower administration. After eight years in office, Eisenhower had failed to eliminate the tensions between the United States and the Soviet Union. He had failed to end the costly and dangerous armaments race. And he had presided over a transformation of the Cold War from a relatively limited confrontation with the Soviet Union in Europe to a global effort to resist communist subversion. Yet Eisenhower had brought to these matters his own sense of the limits of American power. He had resisted military intervention in Vietnam. And he had placed a measure of restraint on those who urged the creation of an enormous American military establishment. In his farewell address in January 1961, he warned of the "unwarranted influence" of a vast "military-industrial complex." His caution, in both domestic and international affairs, stood in marked contrast to the attitudes of his successors, who argued that the United States must act more boldly and aggressively on behalf of its goals at home and abroad.

CHAPTER THIRTY-ONE

The Ordeal of Liberalism

Expanding the Liberal State ~ *The Battle for Racial Equality*
From "Flexible Response" to Vietnam ~ *The Traumas of 1968*

B Y THE LATE 1950s, a growing restlessness was becoming visible beneath the apparently placid surface of American society. Anxiety about America's position in the world, growing pressures from African-Americans and other minorities, the increasing visibility of poverty, the rising frustrations of women, and other long-suppressed discontents were beginning to make themselves felt in the nation's public life. Ultimately, that restlessness would make the 1960s one of the most turbulent eras of the twentieth century. But at first, it contributed to a bold and confident effort by political leaders to attack social and international problems within the framework of conventional liberal politics.

EXPANDING THE LIBERAL STATE

Those who yearned for a more active government in the late 1950s and who accused the Eisenhower administration of allowing the nation to "drift" looked above all to the presidency for leadership. The two men who served in the White House through most of the 1960s—John Kennedy and Lyndon Johnson—seemed for a time to be the embodiment of these liberal hopes.

John Kennedy

The campaign of 1960 produced two young candidates who claimed to offer the nation active leadership. The Republican nomination went almost uncontested to Vice President Richard Nixon, who promised moderate reform. The Democrats, in the meantime, emerged from a spirited primary campaign united, somewhat uneasily, behind John Fitzgerald Kennedy, an attractive and articulate senator from Massachusetts who had narrowly missed being the party's vice presidential candidate in 1956.

John Kennedy grew up in a world of ease and privilege. He was the son of the wealthy, powerful, and highly controversial Joseph P. Kennedy, former American ambassador to Britain. Decorated for bravery during World War II, he returned to Massachusetts in 1946 and, making liberal use of both his own war record and his family's money, won a seat in Congress. Six years later, he was elected to the United States Senate, and in 1958 reelected by a record margin. Within days of his triumph, he was planning his campaign for the White House. He premised his campaign, he said, "on the single assumption that the American people are uneasy at the present drift in our national course." But his appealing public image was at least as important as his political positions in attracting popular support.

A vigorous effort on behalf of Nixon by President Eisenhower in the closing days of the campaign, combined with continuing doubts about Kennedy's youth (he turned forty-three in 1960) and religion (he was a Catholic), almost enabled the Republicans to close what had at one time been a substantial Democratic lead. But in the end, Kennedy held on to win a tiny plurality of the popular vote—49.9 percent to Nixon's 49.6 percent—and only a slightly more comfortable electoral majority—303 to 219.

Kennedy had campaigned promising a program of domestic legislation more ambitious than any since the New Deal, a program he described as

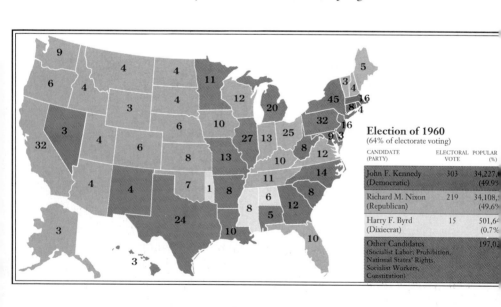

Election of 1960
(64% of electorate voting)

CANDIDATE (PARTY)	ELECTORAL VOTE	POPULAR (%)
John F. Kennedy (Democratic)	303	34,227,0 (49.9%
Richard M. Nixon (Republican)	219	34,108, (49.6%
Harry F. Byrd (Dixiecrat)	15	501,6 (0.7%
Other Candidates (Socialist Labor; Prohibition, National States' Rights, Socialist Workers, Constitution)		197,0

the "New Frontier." But he had serious problems with Congress. Although Democrats remained in control of both houses, their majority included many conservatives from the South and elsewhere, who were far more likely to vote with the Republicans than with Kennedy. One after another of Kennedy's legislative proposals, therefore, found themselves hopelessly stalled.

As a result, the president had to look elsewhere for opportunities to display positive leadership. One area where he believed he could do that was the economy. Economic growth was sluggish in 1961 when Kennedy entered the White House, with unemployment hovering at about 6 percent of the work force. Kennedy initiated a series of tariff negotiations with foreign governments—the "Kennedy Round"—in an effort to stimulate American exports. He began to consider an expanded use of Keynesian fiscal and monetary tools—culminating in his 1962 proposal for a substantial federal tax cut to stimulate the economy.

He also used his personal prestige to battle inflation. In 1962, several steel companies, led by U.S. Steel, announced that they were raising their prices by $6 a ton, a move certain to trigger similar action by the rest of the industry. Kennedy put heavy pressure on U.S. Steel president Roger Blough and other steel executives to rescind the increase. The companies soon relented. But it was a fleeting victory. Kennedy's relationship with the corporate community was now permanently strained, and a few months later the steel companies quietly raised prices again. The president did not protest.

More than any other president of the century (except perhaps the two Roosevelts and, later, Ronald Reagan), Kennedy made his own personality an integral part of his presidency and a central focus of national attention. Nothing illustrated that more clearly than the popular reaction to the tragedy of November 22, 1963. Kennedy had traveled to Texas with his wife and Vice President Lyndon Johnson for a series of political appearances. While the presidential motorcade rode slowly through the streets of Dallas, shots rang out. Two bullets struck the president—one in the throat, the other in the head. He was sped to a nearby hospital, where minutes later he was pronounced dead. Lee Harvey Oswald, who appeared to be a confused and embittered Marxist, was arrested for the crime later that day, and then mysteriously murdered by a Dallas nightclub owner, Jack Ruby, two days later as he was being moved from one jail to another. (The popular assumption at the time was that both Oswald and Ruby had acted alone, assumptions endorsed by a federal commission, chaired by Chief Justice Earl Warren, that was appointed to investigate the assassination. In

JOHN F. KENNEDY AND HIS ADVISERS Kennedy meets in the
White House with Robert McNamara and General Maxwell
Taylor, two men who would play important roles in the
process that would lead to full-scale American military
intervention in Vietnam.

later years, however, many Americans—and in 1978 a congressional subcommittee—claimed that the Warren Commission report had not revealed
the full story.)

The death of President Kennedy was one of several traumatic public
episodes in national history that have left a permanent mark on all who
experienced it. Millions of Americans suspended their normal activities for
four days to watch the televised events surrounding the presidential funeral.
Images of Kennedy's widow, his small children, his funeral procession, his
grave site at Arlington Cemetery with its symbolic eternal flame—all
became deeply embedded in the public mind. When in later times Americans would look back at the optimistic days of the 1950s and early 1960s and
wonder how everything had subsequently seemed to unravel, many would
think of November 22, 1963, as the beginning of the change.

Lyndon Johnson

At the time, however, much of the nation took comfort in the personality and performance of Kennedy's successor in the White House, Lyndon Baines Johnson. Johnson was a native of the poor "hill country" of west Texas and had risen to eminence by dint of extraordinary, even obsessive effort and ambition. He was elected to Congress in 1937 as a fervent supporter of Franklin Roosevelt, and he rose steadily in influence by cultivating the favor of party leaders. In 1948, he won election to the United States Senate; a few years later he became the Senate majority leader, a job in which he displayed a legendary ability to persuade and cajole his colleagues into following his lead. Having failed to win the Democratic nomination for president in 1960, he surprised many who knew him by agreeing to accept the second position on the ticket with Kennedy. The events in Dallas thrust him into the White House.

Johnson's rough-edged, even crude personality could hardly have been more different from Kennedy's. But like Kennedy, Johnson was a man who believed in the active use of power. And he proved, in the end, more effective than his predecessor in translating his goals into reality. Between 1963 and 1966, he compiled the most impressive legislative record of any president since Franklin Roosevelt. He was aided by the tidal wave of emotion that followed the death of President Kennedy, which helped win support for many New Frontier proposals. But Johnson also constructed a remarkable reform program of his own, one that he ultimately labeled the "Great Society." And he won approval of much of it through the same sort of skillful lobbying in Congress that had made him an effective majority leader.

Johnson envisioned himself, as well, as a great "coalition builder." He wanted the support of everyone, and for a time he very nearly got it. His first year in office was, by necessity, dominated by the campaign for reelection. There was little doubt that he would win—particularly after the Republican party fell under the sway of its right wing and nominated the conservative Senator Barry Goldwater of Arizona. Liberal Republicans abandoned Goldwater and openly supported Johnson. In the November election, the president received a larger plurality, over 61 percent, than any candidate before or since. Goldwater managed to carry only his home state of Arizona and five states in the Deep South. Record Democratic majorities in both houses of Congress, many of whose members had been swept into office only because of the margin of Johnson's victory, ensured that the president would be able to fulfill many of his goals. Johnson seemed well on his way to achieving his cherished aim: becoming the most successful reform president of the century.

The Assault on Poverty

The domestic programs of the Kennedy and Johnson administrations had two basic goals: maintaining the strength of the American economy and expanding the responsibilities of the federal government for social welfare.

For the first time since the 1930s, the federal government took steps in the 1960s to create important new social welfare programs. The most important of these, perhaps, was Medicare: a program to provide federal aid to the elderly for medical expenses. Its enactment in 1965 came at the end of a bitter, twenty-year debate between those who believed in the concept of national health assistance and those who denounced it as "socialized medicine." But the program as it went into effect removed many objections. For one thing, it avoided the stigma of "welfare" by making Medicare benefits available to all elderly Americans, regardless of need (just as Social Security had done with pensions). That created a large middle-class con-stituency for the program. The program also defused the opposition of the medical community by allowing doctors serving Medicare patients to prac-tice privately and to charge their normal fees; Medicare simply shifted responsibility for paying those fees from the patient to the government. In 1966, Johnson steered to passage the Medicaid program, which extended federal medical assistance to welfare recipients of all ages. Criticism of the two programs grew in subsequent years, both from those who thought Medicare and Medicaid were inadequate and from those who thought they were too expensive. But broad public support ensured their survival.

Medicare and Medicaid were the first steps in a much larger assault on poverty—one that Kennedy had been contemplating in the last months of his life and that Johnson launched only weeks after taking office. The centerpiece of this "war on poverty," as Johnson called it, was the Office of Economic Opportunity (OEO), which created an array of new educational, employment, housing, and health-care programs. But the OEO was con-troversial from the start, in part because of its commitment to the idea of "community action."

Community action was an effort to involve members of poor commu-nities themselves in the planning and administration of the programs designed to help them. It was an effort to promote what some of its advocates called "maximum feasible participation." The Community Action programs provided some important benefits. In particular, they provided jobs for many poor people and gave them valuable experience in administrative and political work. Many people who went on to significant careers in politics or community organizing, including many black and Hispanic politicians who would rise to prominence in the 1970s and 1980s, got their start in Community Action programs.

The programs were also important to American Indians. The Community Action approach allowed tribal leaders to design and run programs for themselves and to apply for funds from the federal government on an equal basis with state and municipal authorities. Administering these programs helped produce a new generation of tribal leaders who learned much about political and bureaucratic power from the experience.

But despite its achievements, the Community Action approach proved impossible to sustain. Many programs fell victim to mismanagement or to powerful opposition from the local governments with which they were at times competing. Some activists in Community Action agencies employed tactics that mainstream politicians considered frighteningly radical. The apparent excesses of a few agencies damaged the popular image of the Community Action program, and indeed the war on poverty, as a whole.

The OEO spent nearly $3 billion during its first two years of existence, and it helped reduce poverty significantly in certain areas. But it fell far short of eliminating poverty altogether. That was in part because of the weaknesses of the programs themselves and in part because funding for them, inadequate from the beginning, dwindled as the years passed and a costly war in Southeast Asia became the nation's first priority.

Cities, Schools, and Immigration

Closely tied to the antipoverty program were federal efforts to promote the revitalization of decaying cities and to strengthen the nation's schools. The Housing Act of 1961 offered $4.9 billion in federal grants to cities for the preservation of open spaces, the development of mass-transit systems, and the subsidization of middle-income housing. In 1966, Johnson established a new cabinet agency, the Department of Housing and Urban Development (whose first secretary, Robert Weaver, became the first African-American ever to serve in the cabinet). Johnson also inaugurated the Model Cities program, which offered federal subsidies for urban redevelopment.

Kennedy had long fought for federal aid to public education, but he had failed to overcome two important obstacles: Many Americans feared that aid to education was the first step toward federal control of the schools; and Catholics insisted that federal assistance must extend to parochial as well as public schools, a demand that raised serious constitutional issues and one that Kennedy refused to consider. Johnson managed to circumvent both objections with the Elementary and Secondary Education Act of 1965 and a series of subsequent measures. The bills extended aid to both private and parochial schools and based the aid on the economic conditions of the students, not on the needs of the schools themselves. Total federal expenditures for education and technical training rose from $5 billion to $12 billion between 1964 and 1967.

The Johnson administration also supported the Immigration Act of 1965, one of the most important pieces of legislation of the 1960s, even if largely unnoticed at the time. The law maintained a strict limit on the number of newcomers admitted to the country each year (170,000), but it eliminated the "national origins" system established in the 1920s, which gave preference to immigrants from northern Europe over those from other parts of the world. It continued to restrict immigration from some parts of Latin America, but it allowed people from all parts of Europe, Asia, and Africa to enter the United States on an equal basis. This meant that large new categories of immigrants—and especially large numbers of Asians— would begin entering the United States by the early 1970s and changing the character of the American population.

Legacies of the Great Society

The great surge of reform of the Kennedy-Johnson years reflected a new awareness of social problems in America. It also reflected the confident belief of liberals that America's resources were virtually limitless and that purposeful public effort could surmount any obstacle. By the time Johnson left office, legislation had been either enacted or initiated to deal with a remarkable number of social issues: poverty, health care, education, cities, transportation, the environment, consumer protection, agriculture, science, the arts.

Taken together, the Great Society reforms meant a significant increase in federal spending. For a time, rising tax revenues from the growing economy nearly compensated for the new expenditures. In 1964, Johnson managed to win passage of the $11.5 billion tax cut that Kennedy had first proposed in 1962. The cut increased the federal deficit, but it helped produce substantial economic growth over the next several years that made up for much of the revenue initially lost. As Great Society programs began to multiply, however, and particularly as they began to compete with the escalating costs of America's military ventures, the federal budget rapidly outpaced increases in revenues. In 1961, the federal government had spent $94.4 billion. By 1970, that sum had risen to $196.6 billion.

The high costs of the Great Society programs and the inability of the government to find the revenues to pay for them contributed to a growing disillusionment in later years with the idea of federal efforts to solve social problems. By the 1980s, many Americans had become convinced that the Great Society efforts had not worked and that, indeed, government programs to solve social problems could not work. Others, however, argued equally fervently that social programs had made important contributions both to the welfare of the groups they were designed to help and to the health of the economy as a whole. They pointed, in particular, to the reduction of hunger in America, the inclusion of poor people in health-care programs, and the increased services available to young children.

Whether because of economic growth or because of government anti-poverty efforts—or, as seems most likely, because of both—the decade of the 1960s saw the most substantial decrease in poverty in the United States of any period in the nation's history. In 1959, according to the most widely accepted estimates, 21 percent of the American people lived below the officially established poverty line. By 1969, only 12 percent remained below that line. The improvements affected blacks and whites in about the same proportion: 56 percent of the black population had lived in poverty in 1959, while only 32 percent did so ten years later—a 42 percent reduction; 18 percent of all whites had been poor in 1959, but only 10 percent were poor a decade later—a 44 percent reduction.

THE BATTLE FOR RACIAL EQUALITY

The nation's most important domestic initiative in the 1960s was the effort to provide justice and equality to African-Americans. It was the most difficult commitment, the one that produced the severest strains on American society. But it was one that could not be avoided. African-Americans were themselves ensuring that the nation would have to deal with the problem of race.

A M E R I C A N   V O I C E S

MALCOLM X

The Angriest Negro in America

THEY CALLED ME "the angriest Negro in America." I wouldn't deny that charge. I spoke exactly as I felt. "I *believe* in anger. The Bible says there is a *time* for anger." They called me "a teacher, a fomentor of violence." I would say point blank, "That is a lie. I'm not for wanton violence, I'm for justice. I feel that if white people were attacked by Negroes—if the forces of law prove unable, or inadequate, or reluctant to protect those whites from those Negroes—then those white people should protect and defend themselves from those Negroes, using arms if necessary. And I feel that when the law fails to protect Negroes from whites' attack, then those Negroes should use arms, if necessary, to defend themselves." . . .

What was wrong with that? I'll tell you what was wrong. I was a black man talking about physical defense against the white man. The white man can lynch and burn and bomb and beat Negroes—that's all right: "Have patience" . . . "The customs are entrenched" . . . "Things are getting better."

Well, I believe it's a crime for anyone who is being brutalized to continue to accept that brutality without doing something to defend himself. . . . I don't go for non-violence if it also means a delayed solution. To me a delayed solution is a non-solution.

SOURCE: *The Autobiography of Malcolm X,* pp. 366–367. © 1964 by Alex Haley and Malcolm X, © 1965 by Malcolm X and Betty Shabazz. Reprinted by permission of Ballantine Books.

Expanding Protests

John Kennedy had long been sympathetic to the cause of racial justice, but he was hardly a committed crusader. Like many presidents before him, he feared alienating Southern Democratic voters and powerful Southern Democrats in Congress. His administration hoped to contain the racial problem by expanding enforcement of existing laws and supporting litigation to overturn existing segregation statutes.

But the pressure for change could not long be contained. In February 1960, black college students in Greensboro, North Carolina, staged a sit-in at a segregated Woolworth's lunch counter; and in the following months, such demonstrations spread throughout the South, forcing many merchants to integrate their facilities. In the fall of 1960, some of those who had participated in the sit-ins formed the Student Nonviolent Coordinating Committee (SNCC), which worked to keep the spirit of resistance alive.

In 1961, an interracial group of students, working with the Congress of Racial Equality (CORE), began what they called "freedom rides." Traveling by bus throughout the South, they tried to force the desegregation of bus stations. They were met in some places with such savage violence on the part of whites that the president finally dispatched federal marshals to help keep the peace and ordered the integration of all bus and train stations. In the meantime, SNCC workers began fanning out through black communities and even into remote rural areas to encourage blacks to challenge the obstacles to voting that white society had created. The SCLC created citizen education and other programs—many of them organized by the remarkable Ella Baker, one of the great grass-roots leaders of the movement—to mobilize black workers, farmers, housewives, and others to challenge segregation and discrimination.

Events in Alabama in 1963 helped bring the growing movement to something of a climax. In April, Martin Luther King, Jr., helped launch a series of nonviolent demonstrations in Birmingham, Alabama, a city unsurpassed in the strength of its commitment to segregation. Police Commissioner Eugene "Bull" Connor personally supervised a brutal effort to break up the peaceful marches, arresting hundreds of demonstrators and using attack dogs, tear gas, electric cattle prods, and fire hoses—at times even against small children—as much of the nation watched televised reports in horror. Two months later, Governor George Wallace stood in the doorway of a building at the University of Alabama to prevent the court-ordered enrollment of several black students. Only after the arrival of federal marshals did he give way. The same night, NAACP official Medgar Evers was murdered in Mississippi.

A National Commitment

The events in Alabama and Mississippi were a warning to the president that he could not any longer contain or avoid the issue of race. In an important television address the night of the University of Alabama confrontation, Kennedy spoke eloquently of the "moral issue" facing the nation. Days later, he introduced a series of new legislative proposals prohibiting segregation in "public accommodations" (stores, restaurants, theaters, hotels), barring discrimination in employment, and increasing the power of the government to file suits on behalf of school integration.

To generate support for the legislation, and to dramatize the power of the growing movement, more than 200,000 demonstrators marched down the Mall in Washington, D.C., in August 1963 and gathered before the Lincoln Memorial for the largest civil-rights demonstration in the nation's history. Martin Luther King, Jr., in one of the greatest speeches of his distinguished oratorical career, aroused the crowd with a litany of images prefaced again and again by the phrase "I have a dream." The march was the high-water mark of the peaceful, interracial civil-rights movement—and one of the last moments of real harmony within it.

The assassination of President Kennedy three months later gave new impetus to the battle for civil-rights legislation. The ambitious measure that Kennedy had proposed in June 1963 was stalled in the Senate after having passed through the House of Representatives with relative ease. Early in 1964, after Johnson had applied both public and private pressure, supporters of the measure finally mustered the two-thirds majority necessary to close debate and end a filibuster by Southern senators; and the Senate passed the most comprehensive civil-rights bill in the history of the nation.

The Battle for Voting Rights

Having won a significant victory in one area, the civil-rights movement shifted its focus to another: voting rights. During the summer of 1964, thousands of civil-rights workers, black and white, Northern and Southern, spread out through the South, but primarily in Mississippi, to work on behalf of black voter registration and participation. The campaign was known as "Freedom Summer," and it produced a violent response from some Southern whites. Three of the first freedom workers to arrive in the South—two whites, Andrew Goodman and Michael Schwerner, and one black, James Chaney—were murdered. Local law enforcement officials were involved in the crime.

The "Freedom Summer" also produced the Mississippi Freedom Democratic party (MFDP), an integrated alternative to the regular state party organization. Under the leadership of Fannie Lou Hamer and others, the MFDP challenged the regular party's right to its seats at the Democratic National Convention that summer. President Johnson, with King's help, managed to broker a compromise by which members of the MFDP could be seated as observers, with promises of party reforms later on, while the regular party retained its official standing. Both sides grudgingly accepted the agreement, but both were embittered by it.

KING MARCHES THROUGH SELMA Martin Luther King, Jr., and his wife, Coretta (right), lead demonstrators on a march through Selma, Alabama, during his turbulent campaign for black voting rights in 1965. Selma was one of the last of the great interracial crusades on behalf of civil rights.

A year later, in March 1965, King helped organize a major demonstration in Selma, Alabama, to press the demand for the right of blacks to register to vote. Selma sheriff Jim Clark led local police in a brutal attack on the demonstrators—which, as in Birmingham, was televised to a horrified nation. Two Northern whites participating in the Selma march were murdered in the course of the effort there—one, a minister, beaten to death in the streets of the town; the other, a Detroit housewife, shot as she drove along a highway at night. The national outrage that followed the events in Alabama helped push Lyndon Johnson to propose and win passage of the Civil Rights Act of 1965, which provided federal protection to blacks attempting to exercise their right to vote.

But important as such gains were, they failed to satisfy the rapidly rising expectations of American blacks, as the focus of the movement began to move from political to economic issues.

The Changing Movement

For decades, the nation's African-American population had been undergoing a major demographic shift; and by the 1960s, the problem of race was no longer a primarily Southern or rural one, as it had been earlier in the century. By 1966, 69 percent of American blacks were living in metropolitan areas and 45 percent outside the South. Although the economic condition of much of American society was improving, in the poor urban communities in which the black population was concentrated, things were getting significantly worse. More than half of all American nonwhites lived in poverty at the beginning of the 1960s; black unemployment was twice that of whites.

By the mid-1960s, therefore, the issue of race was moving out of the South and into the rest of the nation. The legal battle against school desegregation had moved beyond the initial assault on "de jure" segregation (segregation by law) to an attack on "de facto" segregation (segregation by practice, as through residential patterns), thus carrying the fight into Northern cities. Many African-American leaders (and their white supporters) were demanding, similarly, that the battle against job discrimination move to a new level. Employers should not only abandon negative measures to deny jobs to blacks; they should adopt positive measures to recruit minorities, thus compensating for past injustices. Lyndon Johnson gave his support to the concept of "affirmative action" in 1965. Over the next decade, affirmative action guidelines gradually extended to virtually all institutions doing business with or receiving funds from the federal government (including schools and universities)—and to many others as well.

A symbol of the movement's new direction, and of the problems it would cause, was a major campaign in the summer of 1966 in Chicago, in which King played a prominent role. Organizers of the Chicago campaign hoped to direct national attention to housing and employment discrimination in Northern industrial cities in much the same way similar campaigns had exposed legal racism in the South. But the Chicago campaign not only evoked vicious and at times violent opposition from white residents of that city; it failed to attract wide attention or arouse the national conscience in the way events in the South had done.

Urban Violence

Well before the Chicago campaign, the problem of urban poverty had thrust itself into national prominence when riots broke out in black neighborhoods in major cities, terrifying much of the nation's white population. There were a few scattered disturbances in the summer of 1964, most notably in New York City's Harlem. The first large race riot since the end of World War II occurred the following summer in the Watts section of Los Angeles. In the midst of a traffic arrest, a white police officer struck a protesting black bystander with his club. The incident triggered a storm of anger and a week of violence. Thirty-four people died during the uprising, which was eventually quelled by the National Guard; twenty-eight of them were black. In the summer of 1966, there were forty-three additional outbreaks, the most serious of them in Chicago and Cleveland. And in the summer of 1967, there were eight major riots, including the largest of them all—a racial clash in Detroit in which forty-three people (thirty-three of them black) died.

Televised reports of the violence alarmed millions of Americans and created both a new sense of urgency and a growing sense of doubt among those whites who had embraced the cause of racial justice only a few years before. A special Commission on Civil Disorders, created by the president in response to the riots, issued a celebrated report in the spring of 1968 recommending massive spending to eliminate the abysmal conditions of the ghettoes. To many white Americans, however, the lesson of the riots was the need for stern measures to stop violence and lawlessness.

Black Power

Disillusioned with the ideal of peaceful change in cooperation with whites, an increasing number of African-Americans were turning to a new approach to the racial issue: the philosophy of "black power." Black power could mean many different things. But in all its forms, it suggested a shift away from the goal of assimilation and toward increased awareness of racial distinctiveness.

Perhaps the enduring impact of the black-power ideology was a social and psychological one: instilling racial pride in African-Americans who had been taught by their nation's dominant culture to think of themselves as somehow inferior to whites. But black power had political manifestations as well, most notably in creating a deep schism within the civil-rights movement. Traditional black organizations that had emphasized cooperation with sympathetic whites—groups such as the NAACP, the Urban League, and King's Southern Christian Leadership Conference—now faced competition from more radical groups. The Student Nonviolent Coordinating Commit-

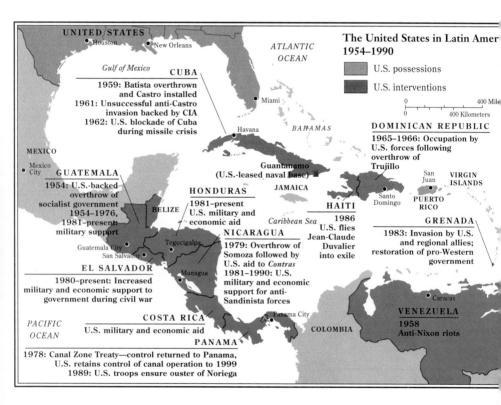

The United States in Latin America 1954–1990

U.S. possessions

U.S. interventions

0 ____ 400 Miles
0 ____ 400 Kilometers

UNITED STATES
Houston · New Orleans
ATLANTIC OCEAN

Gulf of Mexico

CUBA
1959: Batista overthrown and Castro installed
1961: Unsuccessful anti-Castro invasion backed by CIA
1962: U.S. blockade of Cuba during missile crisis

Miami

Havana · *BAHAMAS*

DOMINICAN REPUBLIC
1965–1966: Occupation by U.S. forces following overthrow of Trujillo

MEXICO
Mexico City

GUATEMALA
1954: U.S.-backed overthrow of socialist government 1954–1976, 1981–present: military support

Guantanamo (U.S.-leased naval base)

San Juan

VIRGIN ISLANDS

HONDURAS
1981–present: U.S. military and economic aid

BELIZE

JAMAICA

Santo Domingo

PUERTO RICO

HAITI
1986 U.S. flies Jean-Claude Duvalier into exile

Caribbean Sea

GRENADA
1983: Invasion by U.S. and regional allies; restoration of pro-Western government

Guatemala City
San Salvador
Tegucigalpa

NICARAGUA
1979: Overthrow of Somoza followed by Contras
1981–1990: U.S. military and economic support for anti-Sandinista forces

EL SALVADOR
1980–present: Increased military and economic support to government during civil war

Managua

Caracas

VENEZUELA
1958 Anti-Nixon riots

PACIFIC OCEAN

COSTA RICA
U.S. military and economic aid

Panama City

COLOMBIA

PANAMA
1978: Canal Zone Treaty—control returned to Panama, U.S. retains control of canal operation to 1999
1989: U.S. troops ensure ouster of Noriega

tee and the Congress of Racial Equality had both begun as relatively moderate, interracial organizations. SNCC, in fact, had been a student branch of the SCLC. By the mid-1960s, however, these and other groups were calling for more radical and occasionally even violent action against the racism of white society and were openly rejecting the approaches of older, more established black leaders.

Particularly alarming to whites were such overtly revolutionary organizations as the Black Panthers, based in Oakland, California, and the separatist group, the Nation of Islam, which denounced whites as "devils" and appealed to blacks to embrace the Islamic faith and work for complete racial separation. The most celebrated of the Black Muslims, as whites often termed them, was Malcolm Little, who had adopted the name Malcolm X ("X" to denote his lost African surname). He died in 1965 when black gunmen, presumably under orders from rivals within the Nation of Islam, assassinated him. But he remained a major figure in many black communities long after his death—as important and revered a symbol to many African-Americans as Martin Luther King, Jr.

FROM "FLEXIBLE RESPONSE" TO VIETNAM

In international affairs as much as in domestic reform, the optimistic liberalism of the Kennedy and Johnson administrations dictated a more active and aggressive approach to dealing with the nation's problems than in the past.

Diversifying Foreign Policy

The Kennedy administration entered office convinced that the United States needed to be able to counter communist aggression in more flexible ways than the atomic-weapons-oriented defense strategy of the Eisenhower years permitted. In particular, Kennedy was unsatisfied with the nation's ability to meet communist threats in "emerging areas" of the Third World—the areas in which, Kennedy believed, the real struggle against communism would be waged in the future. He gave enthusiastic support to the development of the Special Forces (or "Green Berets," as they were soon known)—soldiers trained specifically to fight guerrilla conflicts and other limited wars.

Kennedy also favored expanding American influence through peaceful means. To repair the badly deteriorating relationship with Latin America, he proposed an "Alliance for Progress": a series of projects undertaken cooperatively by the United States and Latin American governments for peaceful development and stabilization of the nations of that region. Its purpose was both to spur social and economic development and to inhibit the rise of Castro-like movements in other Central or South American countries. Kennedy also inaugurated the Agency for International Development (AID) to coordinate foreign aid. And he established what became one of his most popular innovations: the Peace Corps, which sent young American volunteers abroad to work in developing areas.

Among the first foreign policy ventures of the Kennedy administration was a disastrous assault on the Castro government in Cuba. The Eisenhower administration had launched the project; and by the time Kennedy took office, the CIA had been working for months to train a small army of anti-Castro Cuban exiles in Central America. On April 17, 1961, with the approval of the new president, 2,000 of the armed exiles landed at the Bay of Pigs in Cuba, expecting first American air support and then a spontaneous uprising by the Cuban people on their behalf. They received neither. At the last minute, as it became clear things were going badly, Kennedy withdrew the air support, fearful of involving the United States too directly in the invasion. The expected uprising did not occur. Instead, well-armed Castro forces easily crushed the invaders, and within two days the entire mission had collapsed.

Confrontations with the Soviet Union

In the grim aftermath of the Bay of Pigs, Kennedy traveled to Vienna in June 1961 for his first meeting with Soviet Premier Nikita Khrushchev. Their frosty exchange of views did little to reduce tensions between the two nations. Nor did Khrushchev's continuing irritation over the existence of a noncommunist West Berlin in the heart of East Germany.

Particularly embarrassing to the communists was the mass exodus of residents of East Germany to the West through the easily traversed border in the center of Berlin. Before dawn on August 13, 1961, the Soviet Union stopped the exodus by directing East Germany to construct a wall between East and West Berlin. Guards fired on those who continued to try to escape. For nearly thirty years, the Berlin Wall served as the most potent physical symbol of the conflict between the communist and noncommunist worlds.

The rising tensions culminated the following October in the most dangerous and dramatic crisis of the Cold War. During the summer of 1962,

American intelligence agencies had become aware of the arrival of a new wave of Soviet technicians and equipment in Cuba and of military construction in progress. On October 14, aerial reconaissance photos produced clear evidence that the Soviets were constructing sites on the island for offensive nuclear weapons. To the Soviets, placing missiles in Cuba probably seemed a reasonable—and relatively inexpensive—way to counter the presence of American missiles in Turkey (and a way to deter any future American invasion of Cuba). But to Kennedy and most other Americans, the missile sites represented an act of aggression by the Soviets toward the United States. Almost immediately, the president decided that the weapons could not be allowed to remain. On October 22, he ordered a naval and air blockade around Cuba, a "quarantine" against all offensive weapons. Preparations were under way for an American air attack on the missile sites when, late in the evening of October 26, Kennedy received a message from Khrushchev implying that the Soviet Union would remove the missile bases in exchange for an American pledge not to invade Cuba. Ignoring other, tougher Soviet messages, the president agreed. The crisis was over.

The Cuban missile crisis brought the world closer to nuclear war than at any time since World War II. And in the following months, both seemed ready to move toward a new accommodation. In June 1963, President Kennedy spoke at American University in Washington, D.C., and seemed for the first time to offer hope for a peaceful rapprochement with the Soviet Union. That same summer, the United States and the Soviet Union concluded years of negotiation by agreeing to a treaty to ban the testing of nuclear weapons in the atmosphere—the first step toward mutual arms reduction since the beginning of the Cold War.

Johnson and the World

Lyndon Johnson entered the presidency lacking even John Kennedy's limited prior experience with international affairs. He was eager, therefore, not only to continue the policies of his predecessor but to prove quickly that he too was a strong and forceful leader.

An internal rebellion in the Dominican Republic gave him an early opportunity to do so. A 1961 assassination had toppled the repressive dictatorship of General Rafael Trujillo, and for the next four years various factions in the country had struggled for dominance. In the spring of 1965, a conservative military regime began to collapse in the face of a revolt by a broad range of groups on behalf of the left-wing nationalist Juan Bosch.

Arguing (without any evidence) that Bosch planned to establish a pro-Castro, communist regime, Johnson dispatched 30,000 American troops to quell the disorder. Only after a conservative candidate defeated Bosch in a 1966 election were the forces withdrawn.

From Johnson's first moments in office, however, his foreign policy was almost totally dominated by the bitter civil war in Vietnam and by the expanding involvement of the United States there. In many respects, Johnson was simply the unfortunate legatee of commitments initiated by his predecessors. But the determination of the new president, and of others within his administration, to prove their resolve in the battle against communism helped produce the final, decisive steps toward a full-scale commitment.

Guns and Advisers

The American involvement in Vietnam had developed so slowly and imperceptibly that when it began spectacularly to expand, in 1964 and 1965, few could remember how it had originated. The first steps toward intervention had seemed at the time to be little more than minor events on the periphery of the larger Cold War. American aid to French forces in Indochina before 1954 had been limited and indirect; the nation's involvement with the Diem regime thereafter, while more substantial, seemed for several years no greater than its involvement with many other Third World governments. But as Diem began to face growing internal opposition, and as the threat from the communist regime to the north appeared to grow, the United States found itself drawn ever deeper into what would ultimately become widely known as the "quagmire."

Ngo Dinh Diem had been an unfortunate choice as the basis of American hopes for a noncommunist South Vietnam. Autocratic, aristocratic, and corrupt, he staunchly resisted any economic reforms that would weaken the position of the Vietnamese upper class and the power of his own family. A fervent Roman Catholic, he invited dissent through his efforts to suppress Buddhism, the religion of the majority of Vietnamese.

Diem's own limitations intensified problems that would have faced any South Vietnamese ruler, for North Vietnam had never accepted the partition of the country in 1954. When Diem began in the late 1950s to try to exterminate the communist cadres that were loyal to Ho Chi Minh but remained in the south, the North Vietnamese ordered a resumption of the war. Communists in the south organized the National Front for the Liberation of South Vietnam (NLF), known to many Americans as the Viet Cong. The communist government in Hanoi sent crucial assistance and, as the war continued, began introducing troops of its own into the south.

His political and military position steadily deteriorating, Diem appealed to the United States for assistance. The Eisenhower administration increased the flow of weapons and ammunition to South Vietnam during its last years in office and introduced the first few American military advisers to the area—about 650 in all. The Kennedy administration expanded that assistance considerably, despite misgivings about Diem, by increasing the flow of munitions into South Vietnam and raising the number of American military personnel to 15,500.

Even so, by 1963, the Diem regime stood on the brink of collapse. The military struggle against the Viet Cong was going badly. Diem's brutal tactics against Buddhist demonstrators in Saigon had produced a religious crisis as well. Several Buddhist monks burned themselves to death in the streets of the capital, arousing further popular resistance to the government and horrifying the American public, which witnessed the immolations on television. Early in November, after receiving tacit assurances of support from the United States, South Vietnamese military leaders staged a coup, during which Diem, his brother, and others were murdered. A few weeks later, John Kennedy too was dead.

From Aid to Intervention

Lyndon Johnson, therefore, inherited what was already a substantial American commitment to the survival of an anticommunist South Vietnam. During his first months in office, he expanded the American involvement in Vietnam only slightly, sending an additional 5,000 military advisers there and preparing to send 5,000 more. Then, early in August 1964, the president announced that American destroyers on patrol in international waters in the Gulf of Tonkin had been attacked by North Vietnamese torpedo boats. Later information raised serious doubts as to whether the administration reported the attacks accurately. At the time, however, virtually no one questioned Johnson's portrayal of the incident as a serious act of aggression or his insistence that the United States must respond. By a vote of 416 to 0 in the House and 88 to 2 in the Senate, Congress hurriedly passed the Gulf of Tonkin Resolution, which authorized the president to "take all necessary measures" to protect American forces and "prevent further aggression" in

The War in Vietnam and
Indochina, 1964–1975

□ U.S. bases

⇐ U.S. and South Viet
invasion of Cambod

➤ Ho Chi Minh Trail ▶
(communist supply ▶

Southeast Asia. The resolution became, in Johnson's view at least, an open-ended legal authorization for escalation of the conflict.

With the South Vietnamese leadership still in disarray and the communist military pressure on the South growing stronger, more and more of the burden of opposition to the Viet Cong fell on the United States. In February 1965, seven marines died when communist forces attacked an American military base at Pleiku. Johnson retaliated by ordering American bombings of the north, in an attempt to destroy the depots and transportation lines responsible for the flow of North Vietnamese soldiers and supplies into South Vietnam. The bombing continued intermittently until 1972. A month later, in March 1965, two battalions of American marines landed at Da Nang in South Vietnam. There were now more than 100,000 American troops in Vietnam.

Four months later, the president finally admitted that the character of the war had changed. American soldiers would now, he announced, begin playing an active combat role in the conflict. By the end of the year, there were more than 180,000 American combat troops in Vietnam; in 1966, that number doubled; and by the end of 1967, there were over 500,000 American soldiers there. In the meantime, the air war had intensified until the tonnage of bombs dropped ultimately exceeded that in all theaters during World War II. And American casualties were mounting. By the spring of 1966, more than 4,000 Americans had been killed.

The Quagmire

For more than seven years, American combat forces remained bogged down in a war that the United States was never able either to win or fully to understand. Combating a foe whose strength lay less in weaponry than in its infiltration of the population, the United States responded with heavy-handed technological warfare designed for conventional battles against conventional armies. American forces succeeded in winning most of the major battles in which they became engaged. There were astounding (if not always reliable) casualty figures showing that far more communists than Americans were dying in combat. But if the war was not actually being lost, neither was it being won.

Central to the American war effort was the heralded "pacification" program, whose purpose was to push the Viet Cong from particular regions and then "pacify" those regions by winning the "hearts and minds" of the people. Routing the Viet Cong was often possible, but the subsequent pacification was more difficult. American forces were not adept at estab-

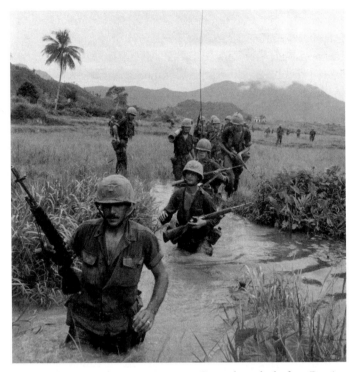

ON PATROL IN VIETNAM, JUNE 1965 Several weeks before President Johnson announced that American ground troops would enter the Vietnam War, United States soldiers were already engaged in combat. These marines, patrolling the area around the American base at Da Nang, were ambushed by communist guerrillas moments after this photograph was taken. One marine was killed and three were wounded.

lishing rapport with provincial Vietnamese; and the American military never gave that part of the program a very high priority in any case. Gradually, the pacification program gave way to the more heavy-handed relocation strategy, through which American troops uprooted villagers from their homes, sent them fleeing to refugee camps or into the cities (producing by 1967 more than 3 million refugees), and then destroyed the vacated villages and surrounding countryside.

As the war dragged on and victory remained elusive, some American officers and officials began to urge the president to expand the military efforts. Some argued for heavier bombing and increased troop strength; others insisted that the United States attack communist enclaves in surrounding countries; a few began to urge the use of nuclear weapons. The Johnson administration, however, resisted. Unwilling to abandon its commitment to South Vietnam for fear of destroying American "credibility" in the world, the government was also unwilling to expand the war too far, for fear of provoking direct intervention by the Chinese, the Soviets, or both. In the meantime, the president began to encounter additional obstacles and frustrations at home.

The War at Home

Few Americans, and even fewer influential ones, had protested the American involvement in Vietnam as late as the end of 1965. But as the war dragged on and its futility began to become apparent, political support for it began to erode. A series of "teach-ins" on university campuses, beginning at the University of Michigan in 1965, sparked a national debate over the war before such debate developed inside the government itself. By the end of 1967, American students opposed to the war had become a significant political force. Enormous peace marches in New York, Washington, D.C., and other cities drew broad public attention to the antiwar movement. In the meantime, a growing number of journalists, particularly reporters who had spent time in Vietnam, helped sustain the movement with their frank revelations about the brutality and apparent futility of the war.

The growing chorus of popular protest soon began to stimulate opposition to the war from within the government. Senator J. William Fulbright of Arkansas, chairman of the powerful Senate Foreign Relations Committee, turned against the war and in January 1966 began to stage highly publicized and occasionally televised congressional hearings to air criticisms of it. Other members of Congress joined Fulbright in opposing Johnson's policies—including, in 1967, Robert F. Kennedy, brother of the slain president, now a senator from New York. Even within the administration, the consensus seemed to be crumbling. Robert McNamara, who had done much to help extend the American involvement in Vietnam, quietly left the government, disillusioned, in 1968. His successor as secretary of defense, Clark Clifford, became a quiet but powerful voice within the administration on behalf of a cautious scaling down of the commitment.

In the meantime, the American economy was beginning to suffer. Johnson's commitment to fighting the war while continuing his Great Society reforms—his promise of "guns and butter"—proved impossible to maintain. The inflation rate, which had remained at 2 percent through most of the early 1960s, rose to 3 percent in 1967, 4 percent in 1968, and 6 percent in 1969. In August 1967, Johnson asked Congress for a tax increase—a 10 percent surcharge that was widely labeled a "war tax"—which he knew was necessary if the nation was to avoid even more ruinous inflation. In return, congressional conservatives demanded and received a $6 billion reduction in the funding for Great Society programs.

THE TRAUMAS OF 1968

By the end of 1967, the twin crises of the war in Vietnam and the deteriorating racial situation at home, crises that fed upon and inflamed each other, had produced profound social and political tensions. In the course of 1968, those tensions seemed suddenly to burst to the surface and threaten national chaos. Not since World War II had the United States experienced so profound a sense of crisis.

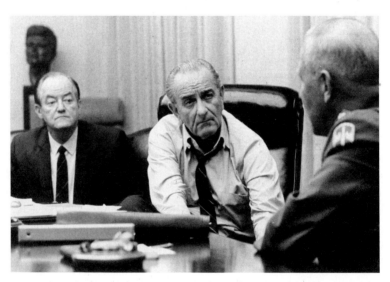

JOHNSON AND HUMPHREY, MARCH 27, 1968 Four days before announcing he would not run for reelection, a grim and tired Lyndon Johnson, accompanied by Vice President Hubert Humphrey, receives a briefing on the military situation in Vietnam.

The Tet Offensive

On January 31, 1968, the first day of the Vietnamese New Year (Tet), communist forces launched an enormous, concerted attack on American strongholds throughout South Vietnam. A few cities, most notably Hue, fell to the communists. Others suffered major disruptions. But what made the Tet offensive so shocking to the American people, who saw vivid reports of it on television, was the sight of communist forces in the heart of Saigon, setting off bombs, shooting down South Vietnamese officials and troops, and holding down fortified areas (including, briefly, the grounds of the American embassy). The Tet offensive also suggested to the American public something of the brutality of the fighting in Vietnam. In the midst of the fighting, television cameras recorded the sight of a South Vietnamese officer shooting a captured Viet Cong soldier in the head in the streets of Saigon.

American forces soon dislodged the Viet Cong from most of the positions they had seized, and the Tet offensive in the end cost the communists such appalling casualties that they were significantly weakened for months to come. Indeed, the Tet defeats permanently depleted the ranks of the NLF and forced North Vietnamese troops to take on a much larger share of the subsequent fighting. But all that had little impact on American opinion. Tet may have been a military victory for the United States; but it was a political defeat for the administration, a defeat from which it would never fully recover.

In the following weeks, opposition to the war grew substantially. Leading newspapers and magazines, television commentators, and mainstream politicians began taking public stands in favor of de-escalation of the conflict. Within weeks of the Tet offensive, public opposition to the war had almost doubled. And Johnson's personal popularity rating had slid to 35 percent, the lowest of any president since Harry Truman.

The Political Challenge

Beginning in the summer of 1967, dissident Democrats tried to mobilize support behind an antiwar candidate who would challenge Lyndon Johnson in the 1968 primaries. When Robert Kennedy turned them down, they recruited Senator Eugene McCarthy of Minnesota. A brilliantly orchestrated campaign by young volunteers in the New Hampshire primary produced a startling showing by McCarthy in March; he nearly defeated the president.

A few days later, Robert Kennedy finally entered the campaign, embittering many McCarthy supporters but bringing his own substantial strength among blacks, poor people, and workers to the antiwar cause. Polls showed the president trailing badly in the next scheduled primary, in Wisconsin. On March 31, Johnson went on television to announce a limited halt in the bombing of North Vietnam—his first major concession to the antiwar forces—and, much more surprising, his withdrawal from the presidential contest.

For a moment, it seemed as though the antiwar forces had won. Robert Kennedy quickly established himself as the champion of the Democratic primaries, winning one election after another. In the meantime, however, Vice President Hubert Humphrey, with the support of President Johnson, entered the contest and began to attract the support of party leaders and of the many delegations that were selected not by popular primaries but by state party organizations. He soon appeared to be the front runner in the race.

The King Assassination

In the midst of this bitter political battle, in which the war had been the dominant issue, the attention of the nation suddenly turned again to race in response to a shocking tragedy. On April 4, Martin Luther King, Jr., who had traveled to Memphis, Tennessee, to lend his support to striking black sanitation workers in the city, was shot and killed while standing on the balcony of his motel. The assassin, James Earl Ray, who was captured days later in London, had no apparent motive. Subsequent evidence suggested that he had been hired by others to do the killing, but he himself never revealed the identity of his employers.

King's tragic death produced an outpouring of grief matched in recent memory only by the reaction to the death of John Kennedy. Among American blacks, it also produced anger. In the days after the assassination, major riots broke out in more than sixty American cities. Forty-three people died; more than 3,000 suffered injuries; as many as 27,000 people were arrested.

The Kennedy Assassination and Chicago

Robert Kennedy continued his campaign for the presidential nomination. Late in the night of June 6, he appeared in the ballroom of a Los Angeles hotel to acknowledge his victory in that day's California primary. As he left the ballroom after his victory statement, Sirhan Sirhan, a young Palestinian apparently enraged by pro-Israeli remarks Kennedy had recently made, emerged from a crowd and shot him in the head. Early the next morning, Kennedy died.

The presidential campaign continued gloomily during the last weeks before the convention. Hubert Humphrey, who had seemed likely to win the nomination even before Robert Kennedy's death, now faced opposition only from McCarthy's weakened campaign. Humphrey's nomination seemed assured, despite the embittered claims of many Democrats that Humphrey would simply continue the policies of the Johnson administration. The approaching Democratic Convention, therefore, began to take on the appearance of an exercise in futility; and antiwar activists, despairing of winning any victories within the convention, began to plan major demonstrations outside it.

When the Democrats finally gathered in Chicago in August, even the most optimistic observers were predicting a turbulent convention. Inside the hall, delegates bitterly debated an antiwar plank in the party platform that both Kennedy and McCarthy supporters favored. Miles away, in a downtown park, thousands of antiwar protesters were staging demonstrations. On the third night of the convention, as the delegates were beginning their balloting on the now virtually inevitable nomination of Hubert Humphrey, demonstrators and police clashed in a bloody riot in the streets of Chicago. Hundreds of protesters were injured as police attempted to disperse them with tear gas and billy clubs. Aware that the violence was being televised to the nation, the demonstrators taunted the authorities with the chant, "The whole world is watching!" And Hubert Humphrey, who had spent years dreaming of becoming his party's candidate for president, received a nomination that night which appeared at the time to be almost worthless.

The Conservative Response

The turbulent events of 1968 persuaded many observers that American society was in the throes of revolutionary change. In fact, however, the prevailing response of the American people to the turmoil was a conservative one.

The most visible sign of the conservative backlash was the surprising success of the campaign of George Wallace for the presidency. Wallace had established himself in 1963 as one of the leading spokesmen for the defense

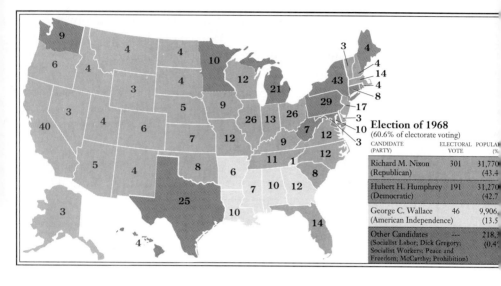

Election of 1968
(60.6% of electorate voting)

CANDIDATE (PARTY)	ELECTORAL VOTE	POPULAR (%)
Richard M. Nixon (Republican)	301	31,770 (43.4
Hubert H. Humphrey (Democratic)	191	31,270 (42.7
George C. Wallace (American Independence)	46	9,906 (13.5
Other Candidates (Socialist Labor; Dick Gregory; Socialist Workers; Peace and Freedom; McCarthy; Prohibition)	---	218,3 (0.4

of segregation when, as governor of Alabama, he had attempted to block the admission of black students to the University of Alabama. In 1968, he became a third-party candidate for president, basing his campaign on a host of conservative grievances. He denounced the forced busing of students, the proliferation of government regulations and social programs, and the permissiveness of authorities toward race riots and antiwar demonstrations. There was never any serious chance that Wallace would win the election; but his standing in the polls rose at times to over 20 percent.

A more effective effort to mobilize the "silent majority" in favor of order and stability was under way within the Republican party. Richard Nixon, whose political career had seemed at an end after his losses in the presidential race of 1960 and a California gubernatorial campaign two years later, reemerged as the preeminent spokesman for what he sometimes called "Middle America." Nixon recognized that many Americans were tired of hearing about their obligations to the poor, tired of hearing about the sacrifices necessary to achieve racial justice, tired of judicial reforms that seemed designed to help criminals. By offering a vision of stability, law and order, government retrenchment, and "peace with honor" in Vietnam, he easily captured the nomination of his party for the presidency. And after the spectacle of the Democratic Convention, he enjoyed a commanding lead in the polls as the November election approached.

That lead diminished greatly in the last weeks before the voting. Old doubts about Nixon's character continued to haunt the Republican candidate. A skillful last-minute surge by Hubert Humphrey, who managed to restore a tenuous unity to the Democratic party, narrowed the gap further. And the Wallace campaign appeared to be hurting the Republicans more than the Democrats. In the end, however, Nixon eked out a victory almost as narrow as his defeat in 1960. He received 43.4 percent of the popular vote to Humphrey's 42.7 percent (a margin of only about 500,000 votes), and 301 electoral votes to Humphrey's 191. George Wallace, who like most third-party candidates faded in the last weeks of the campaign, still managed to poll 13.5 percent of the popular vote and to carry five Southern states with a total of 46 electoral ballots. Nixon had hardly won a decisive personal mandate. But the election made clear that a majority of the American electorate was more interested in restoring stability than in promoting social change.

D E B A T I N G   T H E   P A S T

The Vietnam Commitment

T HE DEBATE OVER why the United States became involved in the conflict in Vietnam (which is only one of many debates about the meaning of the war) has centered on two different, if related, questions. One is an effort to assess the broad objectives Americans believed they were pursuing in Vietnam. The other is an effort to explain how and why policymakers made the specific decisions that led the United States to a military commitment in Indochina.

Scholars and writers such as Norman Podhoretz, Guenter Lewy, and R. B. Smith, reflecting the official government explanation of American intervention in the war, have argued that the communist aggression in Vietnam was part of a Chinese and Soviet design to spread revolution throughout Asia. America, therefore, was not only protecting Vietnam, although that was an important part of its mission; it was also defending the rest of Asia, which would soon be threatened by communism if Vietnam fell. The intervention in Vietnam was a rational and even necessary expression of America's legitimate security interests and its belief in democracy.

Most scholars, however, have been more skeptical. Historians on the left argue that America's intervention in Vietnam was a form of imperialism—part of a larger effort by the United States after World War II to impose a particular political and economic order on the world. "The Vietnam War," Gabriel Kolko wrote in 1985, "was for the United States the culmination of its frustrating postwar effort to merge its arms and politics to halt and reverse the emergence of states and social systems opposed to the international order Washington sought to establish." Others argued that the United States fought in Vietnam to serve the domestic economic interests that had a stake in the region or in the arms production the war stimulated. Other, more moderate critics blame the Vietnam intervention on the myopia of a foreign policy elite unwilling to question its own unreflective commitment to containing communism everywhere and unable to distinguish between international aggression and domestic insurgency.

Those who have looked less at the nation's broad objectives than at the workings of the policymaking process have also produced competing explanations. David Halberstam's *The Best and the Brightest* (1972) argued that policymakers deluded themselves into thinking they could achieve their goals in Vietnam by ignoring, suppressing, or dismissing information that should have suggested that they were wrong; because of arrogance or ideological rigidity, they simply refused to consider that victory was beyond their grasp.

Larry Berman, writing in 1982, offered a rather different view. Neither Johnson nor his advisers were unaware of the obstacles to success in Vietnam. Almost everyone suspected that victory would be difficult, even impossible, to attain. The president was not misled or misinformed. But Johnson committed troops to the war anyway, because he feared that allowing Vietnam to fall would ruin him politically and destroy his hopes for building his "Great Society" at home. Leslie Gelb and Richard Betts made a related argument in 1979. Vietnam, they claimed, was the logical, perhaps inevitable result of a political and bureaucratic order shaped by the ideology of the Cold War. However costly the intervention in Vietnam, policymakers concluded, the costs of not intervening and allowing South Vietnam to fall always seemed higher. The war escalated in the 1960s not because American aims changed but because the situation in Vietnam deteriorated to the point where nothing short of intervention would prevent defeat. Only when the national and international political situation itself shifted in the late 1960s and early 1970s—only when it became clear that the political costs of staying in Vietnam were higher than the political costs of getting out—was it possible for the United States to begin disengaging.

CHAPTER THIRTY-TWO

The Crisis of Authority

The Turbulent Society ～ The Mobilization of Minorities ～ The New Feminism
Nixon, Kissinger, and the War ～ Nixon, Kissinger, and the World
Politics and Economics in the Nixon Years ～ The Watergate Crisis

THE ELECTION OF Richard Nixon in 1968 was the result of more than the unpopularity of Lyndon Johnson and the war. It was the result, too, of a broad public reaction against what many Americans considered a dangerous assault on the foundations of their society and culture. In Richard Nixon they found a man who seemed perfectly to match their mood. Himself a product of a hard-working, middle-class family, he projected an image of stern dedication to traditional values. Yet the presidency of Richard Nixon, far from returning calm and stability to American politics, coincided with, and helped to produce, more years of crisis.

THE TURBULENT SOCIETY

What was perhaps most alarming to conservative Americans in the 1960s and 1970s was a pattern of social and cultural protest by younger Americans, who were giving vent to two related impulses. One was the impulse, emerging from the political left, to create a great new community of "the people," which would rise up to break the power of elites and force the nation to end the war, pursue racial and economic justice, and transform its political life. The other, at least equally powerful impulse was related to, but not entirely compatible with, the first: the vision of personal "liberation." It found expression in part through the efforts of groups—African-Americans, Indians, Hispanics, women, gay people, and others—to define and assert themselves and make demands on the larger society. It also found expression through the efforts of individuals to create a new culture—one that would allow them to escape from what some considered the dehumanizing pressures of the modern "technocracy."

The New Left

Among the products of the racial crisis and the war in Vietnam was a radicalization of many American students, who in the course of the 1960s formed what became known as the New Left. The New Left emerged from many sources, but from nothing so much as the civil-rights movement, in which many idealistic young white Americans had become involved in the early 1960s. Within a few years, some white civil-rights activists were beginning to consider broader political commitments. In 1962, a group of students (most of them white) gathered in Michigan to form an organization to give voice to their demands: Students for a Democratic Society (SDS). Their declaration of beliefs, the Port Huron Statement, expressed their disillusionment with the society they had inherited and their determination to build a new politics. In the following years, SDS became the leading organization of student radicalism.

Since most members of the New Left were students, their radicalism centered for a time on issues related to the modern university. A 1964 dispute at the University of California at Berkeley over the rights of students to engage in political activities on campus—the Free Speech Movement—was the first outburst of what was to be nearly a decade of campus turmoil. Students at Berkeley and elsewhere protested the impersonal character of the modern university, and they denounced the role of educational institutions in sustaining what they considered corrupt or immoral public policies. The antiwar movement greatly inflamed and expanded the challenge to the universities; and beginning in 1968, campus demonstrations, riots, and building seizures became almost commonplace. At Columbia University in New York, students seized the offices of the president and other members of the administration and occupied them for days until local police forcibly ejected them. Over the next several years, hardly any major university was immune to some level of disruption. Small groups of especially dogmatic radicals—among them the "Weathermen," an offshoot of SDS—were responsible for a few cases of arson and bombing that destroyed campus buildings and claimed several lives.

Not many people ever accepted the radical political views that lay at the heart of the New Left. But many supported the position of SDS and other groups on particular issues, and above all on the Vietnam War. Between 1967 and 1969, student activists organized some of the largest political demonstrations in American history—in Washington, D.C., and around the country—to protest the war. They helped thrust the issue of Vietnam into the center of American politics.

Closely related to opposition to the war—and another issue that helped fuel the New Left—was opposition to the military draft. The gradual abolition of many traditional deferments—for graduate students, teachers, husbands, fathers, and others—swelled the ranks of those faced with conscription (and thus likely to oppose it). Draft card burnings became common features of antiwar rallies on college campuses. Many draft-age Americans simply refused induction, accepting what were occasionally long terms in jail as a result. Thousands of others fled to Canada, Sweden, and elsewhere (where they were joined by many deserters from the armed forces) to escape conscription. Not until 1977, when President Jimmy Carter issued a general pardon to draft resisters and a far more limited amnesty for deserters, did the Vietnam exiles begin to return to the country in substantial numbers.

The Counterculture

Closely related to the New Left was a new youth culture openly scornful of the values and conventions of middle-class society. The most visible characteristic of the counterculture, as it became known, was a change in life style. As if to display their contempt for conventional standards, young Americans flaunted long hair, shabby or flamboyant clothing, and a rebellious disdain for traditional speech and decorum. Central to the counterculture were drugs: marijuana smoking—which after 1966 became almost as common a youthful diversion as beer drinking had once been—and the use of other, more potent hallucinogens, such as LSD. There was also a new, more permissive view of sex.

The counterculture's iconoclasm and hedonism sometimes masked its philosophy, which offered a fundamental challenge to the American middle-class mainstream. Like the New Left, with which it in many ways overlapped, the counterculture challenged the structure of modern American society, attacking its banality, its hollowness, its artificiality, its isolation from nature. The most committed adherents of the counterculture—the hippies, who came to dominate the Haight-Ashbury neighborhood of San Francisco and other places, and the social dropouts, many of whom retreated to rural communes—rejected modern society altogether and attempted to find refuge in a simpler, more "natural" existence. But even those whose commitment to the counterculture was less dramatic shared a commitment to the idea of personal fulfillment through rejecting the inhibitions and conventions of middle-class culture. In a corrupt and alienating society, the new creed seemed to suggest, the first responsibility of the individual is cultivation of the self, the unleashing of one's own full potential for pleasure and fulfillment.

The effects of the counterculture reached out to the larger society and helped create a new set of social norms that many young people (and some adults) chose to imitate. Long hair and freakish clothing became the badge not only of hippies and radicals but of an entire generation. The use of marijuana, the freer attitudes toward sex, the iconoclastic (and often obscene) language—all spread far beyond the realm of the true devotees of the counterculture. And perhaps the most pervasive element of the new youth society was one that even the least radical members of the generation embraced: rock music. Rock's driving rhythms, its undisguised sensuality, its often harsh and angry tone—all made it an appropriate vehicle for expressing the themes of the social and political unrest of the late 1960s.

Virtually no Americans could avoid evidence of how rapidly the norms of their society were changing in the late 1960s. Those who attended movies saw a gradual shift away from the banal, conventional messages that had dominated films since the 1920s. Instead, they saw explorations of political issues, of new sexual mores, of violence, of social conflict. Television too began to turn (even if more slowly than the other media) to programming that reflected social and cultural conflict—as exemplified by the enormously popular *All in the Family*, whose protagonist, Archie Bunker, was a lower-middle-class bigot.

THE MOBILIZATION
OF MINORITIES

The growth of black protest, and of a significant white response to it, both preceded the political and cultural upheavals of the 1960s and helped to produce them. It also encouraged other minorities to assert themselves and demand redress of their grievances. For Indians, Hispanic Americans, gay men and women, and others, the late 1960s and 1970s were a time of growing self-expression and political activism.

Seeds of Indian Militancy

Few minorities had deeper or more justifiable grievances against the prevailing culture than American Indians—or Native Americans, as some began defiantly to call themselves in the 1960s. Indians were the least prosperous, least healthy, and least stable group in the nation. Average annual family income for Indians was $1,000 less than that for blacks. The Native American unemployment rate was ten times the national rate. Joblessness was particularly high on the reservations, where nearly half of all Indians lived. But even most Indians living in cities were victims of limited education and training and could find only menial jobs. Life expectancy among Indians was more than twenty years less than the national average. Suicides among Indian youths were a hundred times more frequent than among white youths. And while black Americans attracted the attention (for good or for ill) of many whites, Indians for many years remained largely ignored.

For much of the postwar era, and particularly after the resignation of John Collier as Commissioner of Indian Affairs in 1945, federal policy toward the tribes had been shaped by a determination to incorporate Indians into mainstream American society whether Indians wanted to assimilate or not. Two laws passed in 1953 established the basis of a new policy, which became known as "termination." Through termination, the federal government withdrew all official recognition of the tribes as legal entities, administratively separate from state governments, and made them subject to the same local jurisdictions as white residents. At the same time, the government encouraged Indians to assimilate into the white world and worked to funnel Native Americans into cities, where, presumably, they would adapt themselves to the white world and lose their cultural distinctiveness.

To some degree, the termination and assimilation policies achieved their objectives. The tribes grew weaker as legal and political entities. Many Native Americans adapted to life in the cities, at least to a degree. On the whole, however, the new policies were a disastrous failure. Indians themselves fought so bitterly against them that in 1958 the Eisenhower administration barred further "terminations" without the consent of the affected tribes. In the meantime, the struggle against termination had mobilized a new generation of Indian militants and had breathed life into the principal Native American organization, the National Congress of American Indians (NCAI), which had been created in 1944.

The Democratic administrations of the 1960s did not disavow the termination policy, but neither did they make any effort to revive it. Instead, they made modest efforts to restore at least some degree of tribal autonomy. The funneling of OEO money to tribal organizations through the Community Action program was one prominent example. In the meantime, the tribes themselves were beginning to fight for self-determination—partly in response to the black civil-rights movement and partly in response to other social and cultural changes (among them, the expanding mobility and rising educational levels of younger Indians, who were becoming more aware of the world around them and of their own anomalous place within it). The new militancy also benefited from the rapid increase in the Indian population, which was growing much faster than that of the rest of the nation (nearly doubling between 1950 and 1970 to a total of about 800,000).

The Indian Civil-Rights Movement

In 1961, more than 400 members of 67 tribes gathered in Chicago to discuss ways of bringing all Indians together in an effort to redress common wrongs. The manifesto they issued, the Declaration of Indian Purpose, stressed the "right to choose our own way of life" and the "responsibility of preserving our precious heritage."

The 1961 meeting was only one example of a growing Indian self-consciousness. The National Indian Youth Council, created in the aftermath of the 1961 Chicago meeting, promoted the idea of Indian nationalism and intertribal unity. In 1968, a group of young, militant Indians established the American Indian Movement (AIM), which drew its greatest support from those Indians who lived in urban areas but which soon established a significant presence on the reservations as well.

The new activism had some immediate political results. In 1968, Congress passed the Indian Civil Rights Act, which guaranteed reservation Indians many of the protections accorded other citizens by the Bill of Rights but which also recognized the legitimacy of tribal laws within the reservations. But leaders of AIM and other insurgent groups were not satisfied and turned increasingly to direct action. In 1968, Indian fishermen, citing old treaty rights, clashed with Washington state officials on the Columbia River and in Puget Sound. The following year, members of several tribes occupied the abandoned federal prison on Alcatraz Island in San Francisco Bay, claiming the site "by right of discovery."

In response to the growing pressure, the new Nixon administration appointed Louis Bruce, a Mohawk-Sioux, to the position of Commissioner of Indian Affairs in 1969; and in 1970, the president promised both increased tribal self-determination and an increase in federal aid. But the protests continued. In November 1972, nearly a thousand demonstrators, most of them Lakota (or Sioux) Indians, forcibly occupied the building of the Bureau of Indian Affairs in Washington for six days. A more celebrated protest occurred later that winter at Wounded Knee, South Dakota, the site of the 1890 massacre of Sioux by federal troops.

In the early 1970s, Wounded Knee was part of a large Sioux reservation, two-thirds of which had been leased to white ranchers for generations as an outgrowth of the Dawes Act. Conditions for the Indian residents were desperate, and passions grew quickly in 1972 in response to the murder of a Sioux by a group of whites, who were not, many Indians believed, adequately punished. In February 1973, members of AIM seized and occupied the town of Wounded Knee for two months, demanding radical changes in the administration of the reservation and insisting that the government honor its long-forgotten treaty obligations. A brief clash between the occupiers and federal forces left one Indian dead and another wounded. Shortly thereafter the siege came to an end.

More immediately effective than these militant protests were the victories that various tribes were achieving in the 1970s in the federal courts. In 1985, the United States Supreme Court, in *County of Oneida* v. *Oneida Indian Nation* supported Indian claims to 100,000 acres in upstate New York that the Oneida tribe claimed by virtue of treaty rights long forgotten by whites. In doing so, the Court raised the possibility that some longstanding grievances could be addressed through judicial action.

The Indian civil-rights movement, like other civil-rights movements of the same time, fell far short of winning full justice and equality for Native Americans. But it helped the tribes win a series of new legal rights and protections that, together, gave them a stronger position than they had enjoyed at any previous time in this century. It also helped many Indians gain a renewed awareness of and pride in their identity as Indians and as part of a distinct community within the larger United States.

Hispanic-American Activism

More numerous and more visible than Indians were Hispanic Americans (sometimes known as Latinos), the fastest-growing minority group in the United States. Large numbers of Mexican-Americans (or Chicanos) had entered the country during World War II in response to the wartime labor shortage, and many had remained in the cities of the Southwest and the Pacific coast. After the war, when the legal agreements that had allowed Mexican contract workers to enter the country expired, large numbers of immigrants continued to move to the United States illegally. In 1953, the government launched what it called Operation Wetback to deport the illegals, but the effort failed to stem the flow of new arrivals. By 1960, there were already substantial Chicano neighborhoods (or *barrios*) in American cities from El Paso to Detroit. The largest (with more than 500,000 people, according to census figures) was in Los Angeles, which by then had a bigger Mexican population than anyplace except Mexico City.

But the greatest expansion in the Hispanic population of the United States was yet to come. In 1960, the census reported slightly more than 3 million Hispanics living in the United States. By 1970, that number had grown to 9 million and by 1990 to 20 million. Hispanics constituted more than a third of all legal immigrants to the United States after 1960. Since there was also an uncounted but very large number of illegal immigrants in those years (estimates ranged from 7 million to 12 million), the real percentage of Hispanic immigrants was undoubtedly much larger.

Large numbers of Puerto Ricans (who were entitled to American citizenship by birth) migrated to Eastern urban areas, particularly New York, where they formed one of the poorest communities in the city. South Florida's substantial Cuban population began with a wave of middle-class refugees fleeing the Castro regime in the early 1960s. These first Cuban migrants quickly established themselves as a successful and highly assimilated part of Miami's middle class. In 1980, a second, much poorer wave of Cuban immigrants—the so-called Marielistas, named for the port from which they left Cuba—arrived in Florida when Castro temporarily relaxed exit restrictions. (This group included a large number of criminals, whom Castro had, in effect, expelled from the country.) This second wave was less welcomed by the government (and the existing Cuban community) and less easily assimilated. Later in the 1980s, large numbers of immigrants (both legal and illegal) began to arrive from Central and South America—from Guatemala, Nicaragua, El Salvador, Peru, and others. The most numerous Hispanic group, however, remained the Mexican-Americans, who were concentrated in the Southwest and California but who were also spreading throughout the nation's interior.

Many Hispanic Americans were affluent and successful people. But most newly arrived Chicanos and others were less well educated than either "Anglo" or black Americans and hence less well prepared for high-paying jobs. The fact that many spoke English poorly or not at all further limited their employment prospects. As a result, they found themselves concentrated in poorly paid service jobs.

Like blacks and Indians, many Hispanic Americans responded to the highly charged climate of the 1960s by strengthening their ethnic identification and by organizing for political and economic power. Affluent Hispanics in Miami filled influential positions in the professions and local government; in the Southwest, they elected Mexican-Americans to seats in Congress and to governorships. A Mexican-American political organization, La Raza Unida, exercised influence in southern California and elsewhere in the Southwest in the 1970s and beyond.

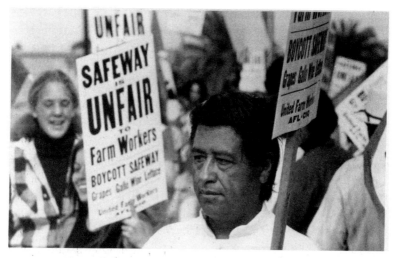

CÉSAR CHÁVEZ As the leader of the United Farm Workers, the first Chicano-dominated labor organization to attract national attention, Chávez became for a time the most visible spokesman for and symbol of the needs of Hispanic-Americans. He is shown here leading a demonstration outside the headquarters of the Safeway supermarket chain in San Diego, California, in 1973, protesting the arrest of other UFW members several days earlier.

One of the most visible efforts to organize Hispanics occurred in California, where an Arizona-born Mexican-American farm worker, César Chávez, created an effective union of itinerant farm workers. His United Farm Workers (UFW), a largely Hispanic organization, launched a prolonged strike in 1965 against growers to demand, first, recognition of the union and, second, increased wages and benefits. When employers resisted, Chávez enlisted the cooperation of college students, churches, and civil-rights groups (including CORE and SNCC) and organized a nationwide boycott, first of table grapes and then of lettuce. In 1968, Chávez campaigned openly for Robert Kennedy. Two years later, he won a substantial victory when the growers of half of California's table grapes signed contracts with his union.

For most Hispanics, however, the path to economic and political power was more difficult. Partly because of language barriers, partly because of ineffective organization, and partly because of discrimination, Mexican-Americans and others were slow to develop political influence in proportion to their numbers. In the meantime, Hispanics formed one of the poorest segments of the United States population.

Challenging the "Melting Pot" Ideal

The efforts of blacks, Hispanics, Indians, and others to forge a clearer group identity seemed to challenge a longstanding premise of American political thought—the idea of the "melting pot." Older, European immigrant groups liked to believe that they had advanced in American society by adopting the values and accepting the rules of the world to which they had moved and advancing within it on its own terms. The newly militant ethnic groups of the 1960s were less willing to accept the standards of the larger society and more likely to demand recognition of their own ethnic identity. African-Americans, Indians, and Hispanics all challenged the assimilationist idea and advocated instead a culturally pluralist society, in which racial and ethnic groups would preserve not only a sense of their own heritage (which older, more "assimilationist" ethnic groups did as well) but also their own social and cultural norms.

To a large degree, the advocates of cultural pluralism succeeded. Recognition of the special character of particular groups was embedded in federal law through a wide range of affirmative action programs, which extended not only to blacks, but to Indians, Hispanics, and others as well. Ethnic studies programs proliferated in schools and universities. Eventually, this impulse led to an even more assertive (and highly controversial) cultural movement that in the 1980s and 1990s became known as "multiculturalism," which challenged the "Eurocentric" basis of American education and culture and demanded that non-European civilizations be accorded equal attention.

Gay Liberation

The last important liberation movement to emerge in the 1960s, and the most unexpected, was the effort by homosexuals and lesbians to win political and economic rights and, more important, social acceptance. Homosexuality had been an unacknowledged reality throughout American history. Nonheterosexual men and women had long been forced either to suppress their sexual preferences, to exercise them surreptitiously, or to live within isolated and often persecuted communities. But by the late 1960s, the liberating impulses that had affected other groups helped mobilize gay men and women (as homosexuals and lesbians had come to term themselves) to fight for their own rights.

On June 27, 1969, police officers raided the Stonewall Inn, a gay nightclub in New York City's Greenwich Village, and began arresting patrons simply for frequenting the place. The raid was not unusual, but the response was. Gay onlookers taunted the police and then attacked them. Someone started a blaze in the Stonewall Inn itself, almost trapping the policemen inside. Rioting continued throughout Greenwich Village (the center of New York's gay community) through much of the night.

The "Stonewall Riot" marked the beginning of the gay liberation movement—one of the most controversial challenges to traditional values and assumptions of its time. New organizations—among them the Gay Liberation Front, founded in New York in 1969—sprang up around the country. Public discussion and media coverage of homosexuality, long subject to an unofficial taboo, quickly and dramatically increased. Gay activists were having some success in challenging the longstanding assumption that homosexuality was aberrant behavior and were arguing that no sexual preference was any more normal than another.

Most of all, however, the gay liberation movement transformed the outlook of gay men and women themselves. It helped them to "come out," to express their preferences openly and unapologetically, and to demand from society a recognition that gay relationships could be as significant and worthy of respect as heterosexual ones. Some gays advocated not only an acceptance of homosexuality as a valid and "normal" preference but a change in the larger society as well: a redefinition of personal identity to give much greater importance to erotic impulses. Those changes did not quickly occur. But by the early 1980s, the gay liberation movement had made remarkable strides. Even the ravages of the AIDS epidemic, which, in the beginning at least, affected the gay community more disastrously than it affected any other group, failed to halt the growth of gay liberation. In many ways, it strengthened it.

By the early 1990s, homosexuals and lesbians were achieving many of the same milestones that other oppressed minorities had attained in earlier decades. Openly gay politicians were winning election to public office. Universities were establishing gay and lesbian studies programs. And laws prohibiting discrimination on the basis of sexual preference were making slow, halting progress at the state and local level.

THE NEW FEMINISM

American women constituted 51 percent of the population in the 1960s. But during the 1960s and 1970s, many women began to identify with minority groups as they renewed demands for a liberation of their own. Sexual discrimination was so deeply embedded in the fabric of society that when feminists first began to denounce it, many men (and even many women) responded with bafflement and anger. By the 1970s, however, public awareness of the issue had increased greatly, and the role of women in American life had changed more dramatically than that of any other group in the nation.

The Rebirth

Feminism had been a weak and often embattled force in American life for more than forty years after the adoption of the woman suffrage amendment in 1920. A few determined women kept feminist political demands alive in the National Woman's Party and other organizations. Many more women expanded the acceptable bounds of female activity by entering new areas of the workplace or engaging in political activities. Nevertheless, through the 1950s and early 1960s, active feminism was often difficult to detect. Yet within a very few years, it evolved from an almost invisible remnant to one of the most powerful social movements in American history.

The 1963 publication of Betty Friedan's *The Feminine Mystique* is often cited as the first event of contemporary women's liberation. Friedan, who had been a writer for women's magazines in the 1950s, traveled around the country interviewing the women who had graduated with her from Smith College in 1947. Most of these women were living out the dream that postwar American society had created for them; they were affluent wives and mothers living in comfortable suburbs. And yet many of them were deeply frustrated and unhappy, with no outlets for their intelligence, talent, and education. By chronicling their unhappiness and frustration, Friedan's book had a powerful impact. But it did not so much cause the revival of feminism as help give voice to a movement that was already stirring.

By the time *The Feminine Mystique* appeared, John Kennedy had established the President's Commission on the Status of Women, which brought national attention to sexual discrimination and helped create important networks of feminist activists who would lobby for legislative redress. Also in 1963, the Kennedy administration helped win passage of the Equal Pay Act, which barred the pervasive practice of paying women less than men for equal work. A year later, Congress incorporated into the Civil Rights Act of 1964 an amendment—Title VII—that extended to women many of the same legal protections against discrimination that were being extended to blacks.

In 1966, Friedan joined with other feminists to create the National Organization for Women (NOW), which was to become the nation's largest and most influential feminist organization. NOW reflected the varying constituencies of the emerging feminist movement. It responded to the complaints of the women Friedan's book had examined—affluent suburbanites with no outlet for their interests—by demanding greater educational opportunities for women and denouncing the domestic ideal and the traditional concept of marriage. But the heart of the movement, at least in the beginning, was directed toward the needs of women in the workplace. NOW denounced the exclusion of women from professions, from politics, and from countless other areas of American life. By the end of the decade, its membership had expanded to 15,000.

Women's Liberation

By the late 1960s, new and more radical feminist demands were also attracting a large following, especially among younger, affluent, white, educated women. Many of them drew inspiration from the New Left and the counterculture. Some were involved in the civil-rights movement, others in the antiwar crusade. Many had found that even within those movements, they faced discrimination and exclusion and were subordinated to male leaders.

In its most radical form, the new feminism rejected the whole notion of marriage, family, and even heterosexual intercourse (a vehicle, some women claimed, of male domination). Not many women, not even many feminists, embraced such extremes. But by the early 1970s large numbers of women were coming to see themselves as an exploited group banding together against oppression and developing a culture of their own. The women's liberation movement inspired the creation of grass-roots organizations and activities through which women not only challenged sexism and discrimination but created communities of their own. In cities and towns across the country, feminists opened women's bookstores, bars, and coffee shops. They founded feminist newspapers and magazines. They created centers to assist victims of rape and abuse, women's health clinics (and, particularly after 1973, abortion clinics), and day-care centers.

Expanding Achievements

By the early 1970s, the public and private achievements of the women's movement were already substantial. In 1971, the government extended its affirmative action guidelines to include women—linking sexism with racism as an officially acknowledged social problem. Women were making rapid progress, in the meantime, in their efforts to move into the economic and political mainstream. The nation's major all-male educational institutions began to open their doors to women. (Princeton and Yale did so in 1969, and most other colleges and universities soon did the same.) Some women's colleges, in the meantime, began accepting male students.

Women were also becoming an important force in business and the professions. Nearly half of all married women held jobs by the mid-1970s, and almost nine-tenths of all women with college degrees worked. The two-career family, in which both the husband and the wife maintained active professional lives, was becoming a widely accepted norm; many women were postponing marriage or motherhood for the sake of their careers. There were also important symbolic changes, such as the refusal of many women to adopt their husbands' names when they married and the use of the term "Ms." in place of "Mrs." or "Miss" to denote the irrelevance of a woman's marital status in the professional world.

In politics, women began to compete effectively with men for both elected and appointive positions in the 1970s. By the mid-1980s, women were serving in both houses of Congress, on the Supreme Court, in numerous federal cabinet positions, as governors of several states, and in many other political positions. And in 1984, the Democratic party chose a woman, Representative Geraldine Ferraro of New York, as its vice presidential candidate. In academia, women were expanding their presence in traditional scholarly fields; they were also creating a field of their own—women's studies, which in the 1980s and early 1990s was the fastest-growing area of American scholarship. Women even joined what had previously been the most celebrated all-male fraternity in American culture: the space program. Sally Ride became the first woman astronaut to travel in space in 1983.

In 1972, Congress approved the Equal Rights Amendment (ERA) to the Constitution, which some feminists had been promoting since the 1920s, and sent it to the states. For a while ratification seemed almost certain. By the late 1970s, however, the momentum behind the amendment had died. The ERA was in trouble not because of indifference but because of a rising chorus of objections to it from people (including many antifeminist women) who feared that it would disrupt traditional social patterns. In 1982, the amendment finally died when the ten years allotted for ratification expired.

The Abortion Controversy

A vital element of American feminism since the 1920s has been the effort by women to win greater control of their own sexual and reproductive lives. In its least controversial form, this impulse helped produce an increasing awareness in the 1960s and 1970s of the problems of rape, sexual abuse, and wife beating. There continued to be some controversy over the dissemination of contraceptives and birth-control information; but that issue, at least, seemed to have lost much of the explosive character it had once possessed. A related issue, however, stimulated as much popular passion as any question of its time: abortion.

Abortion had once been legal in much of the United States, but by the beginning of the twentieth century it was banned by statute in most of the country and remained so into the 1960s (although many abortions continued to be performed quietly, and often dangerously, out of sight of the law). The women's movement created strong new pressures on behalf of the legalization of abortion. Several states had abandoned restrictions on abortion by the end of the 1960s. And in 1973, the Supreme Court's decision in *Roe v. Wade*, based on a new theory of a constitutional "right to privacy" first recognized by the Court only a few years earlier, invalidated all laws prohibiting abortion during the "first trimester"—the first three months of pregnancy. The issue, it seemed, was finally settled. But it soon became clear that it was not.

In many ways, feminism was much like other "liberation" movements of the 1960s and 1970s. But it differed from them in one fundamental respect: its success. The women's movement may not have fulfilled all its goals. But it achieved fundamental and permanent changes in the position of women in American life, and it promised to do much more.

NIXON, KISSINGER, AND THE WAR

Richard Nixon assumed office in 1969 committed not only to restoring stability at home but to creating a new and more stable order in the world. Central to Nixon's hopes for international stability was a resolution of the stalemate in Vietnam. Yet the new president felt no freer than his predecessor to abandon the American commitment there.

Vietnamization

Despite Nixon's own deep interest in international affairs, he brought with him into government a man who ultimately seemed to overshadow the president himself in the conduct of diplomacy: Henry Kissinger, a Harvard professor whom Nixon appointed as his special assistant for national security affairs. Kissinger quickly established dominance over the secretary of state, William Rogers, and the secretary of defense, Melvin Laird, who were both more experienced in public life. That was in part a result of Nixon's passion for concentrating decision making in the White House. But Kissinger's keen intelligence, his bureaucratic skills, and his success in handling the press were at least equally important. Together, Nixon and Kissinger set out to find an acceptable solution to the stalemate in Vietnam.

The new Vietnam policy moved along several fronts. One was an effort to limit domestic opposition to the war so as to permit the administration more political space in which to maneuver. Aware that the military draft was one of the most visible targets of dissent, the administration devised a new "lottery" system, through which only a limited group—those nineteen-year-olds with low lottery numbers—would be subject to conscription. Later, the president urged the creation of an all-volunteer army. By 1973, the Selective Service System was on its way to at least temporary extinction.

More important in stifling dissent, however, was a new policy: the "Vietnamization" of the war—that is, the training and equipping of the South Vietnamese military to assume the burden of combat in place of American forces. In the fall of 1969, Nixon announced the withdrawal of 60,000 American ground troops from Vietnam, the first reduction in United States troop strength since the beginning of the war. The withdrawals continued steadily for more than three years, so that by the fall of 1972 relatively few American soldiers remained in Indochina. From a peak of more than 540,000 in 1969, the number had dwindled to about 60,000.

Vietnamization did help quiet domestic opposition to the war for a time. It did nothing, however, to break the stalemate in the negotiations with the North Vietnamese in Paris. The new administration quickly decided that new military pressures would be necessary to do that.

Escalation

By the end of their first year in office, Nixon and Kissinger had decided that the most effective way to tip the military balance in America's favor was to destroy the bases in Cambodia from which the American military believed the North Vietnamese were launching many of their attacks. Very early in his presidency, Nixon ordered the air force to begin bombing Cambodian territory to destroy the enemy sanctuaries. He kept the raids secret from Congress and the public. In the spring of 1970, whether with American encouragement and support is not clear, conservative military leaders overthrew the neutral government of Cambodia and established a new, pro-American regime under General Lon Nol. Lon Nol quickly gave his approval to American incursions into his territory; and on April 30, Nixon went on television to announce that he was ordering American troops across the border into Cambodia to "clean out" the bases that the enemy had been using for its "increased military aggression."

Literally overnight, the Cambodian invasion restored the dwindling antiwar movement to vigorous life. The first days of May saw the most widespread and vocal antiwar demonstrations ever. A mood of crisis was already mounting when, on May 4, four college students were killed and nine others injured after members of the National Guard opened fire on antiwar demonstrators at Kent State University in Ohio. Ten days later, police killed two black students at Jackson State University in Mississippi during a demonstration there.

The clamor against the war spread into the government and the press. Congress angrily repealed the Gulf of Tonkin Resolution in December, stripping the president of what had long served as the legal basis for the war. Nixon ignored the action. Then, in June 1971, first the *New York Times* and later other newspapers began publishing excerpts from a secret study of the war prepared by the Defense Department during the Johnson administration. The so-called Pentagon Papers, leaked to the press by former Defense official Daniel Ellsberg, provided confirmation of what many had long believed: the government had been dishonest, both in reporting the military progress of the war and in explaining its own motives for American involvement. The administration went to court to suppress the documents, but the Supreme Court finally ruled that the press had the right to publish them.

Particularly troubling, both to the public and to the government itself, were signs of decay within the American military. Morale and discipline among American troops in Vietnam, who had been fighting a savage and inconclusive war for more than five years, was rapidly deteriorating. The

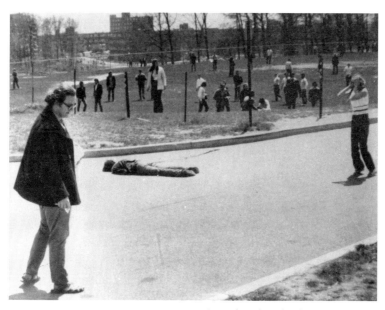

KENT STATE UNIVERSITY, MAY 4, 1970 A student lies dead at Kent State University, one of four who died after National Guardsmen opened fire on a group of protesters.

trial and conviction in 1971 of Lieutenant William Calley, who was charged with overseeing a massacre of more than 100 unarmed South Vietnamese civilians, attracted wide public attention to the dehumanizing impact of the war on those who fought it—and to the terrible consequences for the Vietnamese people of that dehumanization. Less publicized were other, more widespread problems among American troops in Vietnam: desertion, drug addiction, racial bias, refusal to obey orders, even the killing of unpopular officers by enlisted men.

The continuing carnage, the increasing savagery, and the social distress at home had largely destroyed public support for the war. By 1971, nearly two-thirds of those interviewed in public-opinion polls were urging American withdrawal from Vietnam. President Nixon, however, was determined to resist, and if possible destroy, his critics, convinced that a defeat in Vietnam would cause unacceptable damage to the nation's (and his own) credibility. The FBI, the CIA, the White House itself, and other federal agencies increased their efforts to discredit and harass antiwar and radical groups, often through illegal means.

In Indochina, meanwhile, the fighting raged on. In February 1971, the president ordered the air force to assist the South Vietnamese army in an invasion of Laos—a test, as he saw it, of his Vietnamization program. Within weeks, the South Vietnamese scrambled back across the border in defeat. American bombing in Vietnam and Cambodia increased, despite its apparent ineffectiveness. In March 1972, the North Vietnamese mounted their biggest offensive since 1968 (the so-called Easter Offensive). American and South Vietnamese forces managed to halt the communist advance, but it was clear that without American support the South Vietnamese would not have succeeded. At the same time, Nixon ordered American planes to bomb targets near Hanoi, the capital of North Vietnam, and Haiphong, its principal port, and called for the mining of seven North Vietnamese harbors (including Haiphong).

"Peace with Honor"

As the 1972 presidential election approached, the administration stepped up its effort to produce a breakthrough in negotiations with the North Vietnamese. In April 1972, the president dropped his longtime insistence on a removal of North Vietnamese troops from the south before any American withdrawal. Meanwhile, Henry Kissinger was meeting privately in Paris with the North Vietnamese foreign secretary, Le Duc Tho, to work out terms for a cease-fire. On October 26, only days before the presidential election, Kissinger announced that "peace is at hand."

Several weeks later (after the election), negotiations broke down once again. Although both the American and the North Vietnamese governments were ready to accept the Kissinger-Tho plan for a cease-fire, President Nguyen Van Thieu of South Vietnam balked, still insisting on a full withdrawal of North Vietnamese forces from the south. Kissinger tried to win additional concessions from the communists to meet Thieu's objections; but on December 16, talks broke off.

The next day, December 17, American B-52s began the heaviest and most destructive air raids of the entire war on Hanoi, Haiphong, and other North Vietnamese targets. Civilian casualties were high. And fifteen American B-52s were shot down by the North Vietnamese; in the entire war to that point, the United States had lost only one of the giant bombers. On December 30, Nixon terminated the "Christmas bombing." The United States and the North Vietnamese returned to the conference table. And on January 27, 1973, they signed an "agreement on ending the war and restoring peace in Vietnam." Nixon claimed that the Christmas bombing had forced the North Vietnamese to relent. At least equally important, however, was the enormous American pressure on Thieu to accept the cease-fire.

The terms of the Paris accords were little different from those Kissinger and Tho had accepted in principle a few months before. There would be an immediate cease-fire. The North Vietnamese would release several hundred American prisoners of war, whose fate had become an emotional issue of great importance within the United States. The Thieu regime would survive for the moment, but North Vietnamese forces already in the south would remain there. An undefined committee would work out a permanent settlement.

Defeat in Indochina

American forces were hardly out of Indochina before the Paris accords collapsed. In March 1975, finally, the North Vietnamese launched a full-scale offensive against the now greatly weakened forces of the south. Thieu appealed to Washington for assistance; the president (now Gerald Ford) appealed to Congress for additional funding; Congress refused. Late in April 1975, communist forces marched into Saigon, shortly after officials of the Thieu regime and the staff of the American embassy had fled the

THE FALL OF SAIGON The chaotic evacuation of Americans from Saigon in the spring of 1975, only hours before victorious North Vietnamese troops entered the city, was a humiliating spectacle. Desperate South Vietnamese soldiers and officials fought with American soldiers and diplomats for space on the few airplanes and helicopters available.

country in humiliating disarray. Communist forces quickly occupied the capital, renamed it Ho Chi Minh City, and began the process of reuniting Vietnam under the harsh rule of Hanoi. At about the same time, the Lon Nol regime in Cambodia fell to the murderous communists of the Khmer Rouge—whose brutal policies led to the death of more than a third of the country's people over the next several years.

Such were the dismal results of more than a decade of direct American military involvement in Vietnam. More than 1.2 million Vietnamese soldiers had died in combat, along with countless civilians throughout the region. A beautiful land had been ravaged, its agrarian economy left in ruins; even in the early 1990s, Vietnam remained one of the poorest and most politically oppressive nations in the world. The United States had paid a heavy price as well. The war had cost the nation almost $150 billion in direct costs and much more indirectly. It had resulted in the deaths of over 57,000 young Americans and the injury of 300,000 more. And the nation had suffered a blow to its confidence and self-esteem from which it would not soon recover.

NIXON, KISSINGER, AND THE WORLD

The continuing war in Vietnam provided a dismal backdrop to what Nixon considered his larger mission in world affairs: the construction of a new international order. The president had become convinced that the old assumptions of a "bipolar" world—in which the United States and the Soviet Union were the only truly great powers—were now obsolete. America must adapt to the new "multipolar" international structure, in which China, Japan, and Western Europe were becoming major, independent forces. Nixon and Kissinger believed it was possible to construct something like the "balance of power" that had permitted nineteenth-century Europe to enjoy nearly a century of relative stability. To do so, however, required a major change in several longstanding assumptions of American foreign policy.

The China Initiative and Détente

For more than twenty years, ever since the fall of Chiang Kai-shek in 1949, the United States had treated China, the second-largest nation on earth, as if it did not exist. Instead, America recognized the forlorn regime-in-exile on Taiwan as the legitimate government of mainland China. Nixon and Kissinger wanted to forge a new relationship with the Chinese communists—in part to strengthen them as a counterbalance to the Soviet Union. The Chinese, for their part, were eager to forestall the possibility of a Soviet-American alliance against China and to end China's own isolation from the international arena.

In July 1971, Nixon sent Henry Kissinger on a secret mission to Beijing. When Kissinger returned, the president made the startling announcement that he would visit China himself within the next few months. That fall, with American approval, the United Nations admitted the communist government of China and expelled the representatives of the Taiwan regime. Finally, in February 1972, Nixon paid a formal visit to China and, in a single stroke, erased much of the deep American animosity toward the Chinese communists. Nixon did not yet formally recognize the communist regime, but in 1972 the United States and China began low-level diplomatic relations.

The initiatives in China coincided with (and probably assisted) an effort by the Nixon administration to improve relations with the Soviet Union. In 1969, American and Soviet diplomats met in Helsinki, Finland, to begin talks on limiting nuclear weapons. In 1972, they produced the first Strategic

A M E R I C A N V O I C E S

RICHARD NIXON

The China Trip, 1972

ON FEBRUARY 17, 1972, at 10:35 A.M. we left Andrews Air Force Base for Peking. . . . We stopped briefly in Shanghai . . . ; an hour and a half later we prepared to land in Peking. I looked out the window. It was winter, and the countryside was drab and gray. The small towns and villages looked like pictures I had seen of towns in the Middle Ages. . . .

Chou En-lai stood at the foot of the ramp, hatless in the cold. Even a heavy overcoat did not hide the thinness of his frail body. When we were about halfway down the steps, he began to clap. I paused for a moment and then returned the gesture, according to the Chinese custom.

I knew that Chou had been deeply insulted by Foster Dulles's refusal to shake hands with him at the Geneva Conference in 1954. When I reached the bottom step, therefore, I made a point of extending my hand as I walked toward him. When our hands met, one era ended and another began. . . .

I stood on Chou's left while the band played the anthems. "The Star-Spangled Banner" had never sounded so stirring to me as on that windswept runway in the heart of Communist China. . . .

Chou and I rode into the city in a curtained car. As we left the airport, he said, "Your handshake came over the vastest ocean in the world—twenty-five years of no communication." When we came into Tienamen Square at the center of Peking . . . I noticed that the streets were empty.

Arms Limitation Treaty (SALT I), which froze some nuclear missiles (ICBMs) of both sides at present levels. In May of that year, the president traveled to Moscow to sign the agreement. The next year, the Soviet premier, Leonid Brezhnev, visited Washington; and the two leaders pledged renewed efforts to speed the next phase of arms control negotiations.

The Problems of Multipolarity

The policies of rapprochement with communist China and détente with the Soviet Union reflected Nixon's and Kissinger's belief in the importance of stable relationships among the great powers. But great-power relationships could not alone ensure international stability, for the Third World remained the most volatile and dangerous source of international tension.

Central to the Nixon-Kissinger policy toward the Third World was the effort to maintain the status quo without involving the United States too deeply in local disputes. In 1969 and 1970, the president described what became known as the Nixon Doctrine, by which the United States would "participate in the defense and development of allies and friends" but would leave the "basic responsibility" for the future of those "friends" to the nation's themselves. In practice, the Nixon Doctrine meant a declining American interest in contributing to Third World development; a growing contempt for the United Nations, where underdeveloped nations were gaining influence through their sheer numbers; and increasing support to authoritarian regimes attempting to withstand radical challenges from within.

In 1970, for example, the CIA poured substantial funds into Chile to help support the established government against a communist challenge. When the Marxist candidate for president, Salvador Allende, came to power anyway through an honest election, the United States began funneling more money to opposition forces in Chile to help "destabilize" the new government. In 1973, a military junta seized power from Allende, who was subsequently murdered. The United States developed a friendly relationship with the new, repressive military government of General Augusto Pinochet.

In the Middle East, conditions were growing more volatile in the aftermath of the 1967 war, in which Israel had occupied substantial new territories and had increased the number of refugee Palestinians. These Arabs claimed the lands now controlled by Israel; dislodged from their homes, the refugees were a source of considerable instability in Jordan, Lebanon, and the other surrounding countries into which they moved.

In October 1973, on the Jewish high holy day of Yom Kippur, Egyptian and Syrian forces attacked Israel. For ten days, the Israelis struggled to recover from the surprise attack; finally, they launched an effective counteroffensive against Egyptian forces in the Sinai. At that point, the United States intervened, placing heavy pressure on Israel to accept a cease-fire rather than press its advantage.

The imposed settlement of the Yom Kippur War demonstrated the growing dependence of the United States and its allies on Arab oil. Permitting Israel to continue its drive into Egypt might have jeopardized the ability of the United States to purchase needed petroleum from the Arab states. A brief but painful embargo by the Arab governments on the sale of oil to America in 1973 provided an ominous warning of the costs of losing access to the region's resources. The lesson of the Yom Kippur War, therefore, was

DÉTENTE AT HIGH TIDE The visit of Soviet Premier Leonid Brezhnev to Washington in 1973 was a high-water mark in the search for détente between the two nations. Here, Brezhnev and Nixon share friendly words on the White House balcony.

that the United States could not ignore the interests of the Arab nations in its efforts on behalf of Israel.

A larger lesson of 1973 was that the nations of the Third World could no longer be expected to act as passive, cooperative "client states." And the United States could not depend on cheap, easy access to raw materials as it had in the past.

POLITICS AND ECONOMICS IN THE NIXON YEARS

For a time in the late 1960s, it had seemed to many Americans that the forces of chaos and radicalism were taking control of the nation. The domestic policy of the Nixon administration was, the president claimed, an attempt to restore balance: between the needs of the poor and the desires of the middle class, between the power of the federal government and the interests of local communities. In the end, however, economic and political crises sharply limited the administration's ability to fulfill its domestic goals.

Domestic Initiatives

Many of Nixon's domestic policies were a response to what he believed to be the demands of his constituency—conservative, middle-class people, whom he liked to call the "silent majority," who wanted to reduce federal "interference" in local affairs. He tried, unsuccessfully, to persuade Congress to pass legislation prohibiting school desegregation through the use of forced busing. He forbade the Department of Health, Education, and Welfare to cut off federal funds from school districts that had failed to comply with court orders to integrate. At the same time, he began to reduce or dismantle many of the social programs of the Great Society and the New Frontier. In 1973, he abolished the Office of Economic Opportunity, the centerpiece of the antipoverty program of the Johnson years.

Yet Nixon's domestic policies had progressive and creative elements as well. One of the administration's boldest efforts was an attempt to overhaul the nation's enormous welfare system. Nixon proposed replacing the existing system, which almost everyone agreed was cumbersome, expensive, and inefficient, with what he called the Family Assistance Plan (FAP). It would in effect have created a guaranteed annual income for all Americans: $1,600 in federal grants, which could be supplemented by outside earnings up to

$4,000. Even many liberals applauded the proposal as an important step toward expanding federal responsibility for the poor. Nixon, however, presented the plan as something that would reduce the supervisory functions of the federal government and transfer to welfare recipients themselves daily responsibility for their own lives. Although the FAP won approval in the House in 1970, concerted attacks by welfare recipients (who considered the benefits inadequate), members of the welfare bureaucracy (whose own influence stood to be sharply diminished by the bill), and conservatives (who opposed a guaranteed income on principle) helped kill it in the Senate.

From the Warren Court to the Nixon Court

Of all the liberal institutions that aroused the enmity of the "silent majority" in the 1950s and 1960s, none evoked more anger and bitterness than the Supreme Court. Not only did its rulings on racial matters disrupt traditional social patterns in both the North and the South, but its staunch defense of civil liberties directly contributed, in the eyes of many Americans, to the increase in crime, disorder, and moral decay. In *Engel* v. *Vitale* (1962), the Court ruled that prayers in public schools were unconstitutional, sparking outrage among religious fundamentalists and others. In *Roth* v. *United States* (1957), the Court had sharply limited the authority of local governments to curb pornography. In a series of other decisions, the Court greatly strengthened the civil rights of criminal defendants and, many Americans believed, greatly weakened the power of law enforcement officials to do their jobs. For example, in *Gideon* v. *Wainwright* (1963), the Court ruled that every felony defendant was entitled to a lawyer regardless of his or her ability to pay. In *Escobedo* v. *Illinois* (1964), it ruled that a defendant must be allowed access to a lawyer before questioning by police. In *Miranda* v. *Arizona* (1966), the Court confirmed the obligation of authorities to inform a criminal suspect of his or her rights. By 1968, the Warren Court had become the target of Americans of all kinds who felt the balance of power in the United States had shifted too far toward the poor and dispossessed at the expense of the middle class.

Nixon was determined to use his judicial appointments to give the Court a more conservative cast. His first opportunity came almost as soon as he entered office. When Chief Justice Earl Warren resigned early in 1969, Nixon replaced him with a federal appeals court judge of known conservative leanings, Warren Burger. A few months later, Associate Justice Abe Fortas resigned his seat after the disclosure of a series of alleged financial improprieties. To replace him, Nixon named Clement F. Haynsworth, a respected federal circuit court judge from South Carolina. But Haynsworth came under fire from Senate liberals, black organizations, and labor unions for his conservative record on civil rights and for what some claimed was a conflict of interest in several of the cases on which he had sat. The Senate rejected him. Nixon's next choice was G. Harrold Carswell, a judge of the Florida federal appeals court almost entirely lacking in distinction and widely considered unfit for the Supreme Court. The Senate rejected his nomination too.

Nixon angrily denounced the votes, calling them expressions of prejudice against the South. But he was careful thereafter to choose men of standing within the legal community to fill vacancies on the Supreme Court: Harry Blackmun, a moderate jurist from Minnesota; Lewis F. Powell, Jr., a respected judge from Virginia; and William Rehnquist, a member of the Nixon Justice Department. In the process, he transformed the court.

The new Court, however, fell short of what the president and many conservatives had expected. Rather than retreating from its commitment to social reform, the Court in many areas actually moved further toward it. In *Swann* v. *Charlotte-Mecklenburg Board of Education* (1971), it ruled in favor of the use of forced busing to achieve racial balance in schools. Not even the intense and occasionally violent opposition of local communities as diverse as Boston and Louisville, Kentucky, was able to weaken the judicial commitment to integration. In *Furman* v. *Georgia* (1972), the Court overturned existing capital punishment statutes and established strict new guidelines for such laws in the future. In *Roe* v. *Wade* (1973), it struck down laws forbidding abortions.

In other decisions, however, the Burger Court did demonstrate a more conservative temperament than the Warren Court had shown. Although the justices approved busing as a tool for achieving integration, they rejected, in *Milliken* v. *Bradley* (1974), a plan to transfer students across district lines (in this case, between Detroit and its suburbs) to achieve racial balance. While the Court upheld the principle of affirmative action in its celebrated 1978 decision in *Bakke* v. *Board of Regents of California*, it established restrictive new guidelines for such programs in the future. In *Stone* v. *Powell* (1976), the Court agreed to certain limits on the right of a defendant to appeal a state conviction to the federal judiciary.

The Election of 1972

However unsuccessful the Nixon administration may have been in achieving some of its specific goals, Nixon entered the presidential race in 1972 with a substantial reserve of strength. The events of that year improved his position immeasurably. His energetic reelection committee collected enormous sums of money to support the campaign. The president himself used the powers of incumbency, refraining from campaigning and concentrating on highly publicized international decisions and state visits. Agencies of the federal government dispensed funds and favors to strengthen Nixon's political standing in questionable areas.

Nixon was most fortunate in 1972, however, in his opposition. The return of George Wallace to the presidential fray caused some early concern, for Nixon's own reelection strategy rested on the same appeals to the troubled middle class that Wallace was expressing. But the possibility of another third-party campaign in the fall vanished in May, when a would-be assassin shot the Alabama governor during a rally at a Maryland shopping center. Paralyzed from the waist down, Wallace was unable to continue campaigning.

The Democrats, in the meantime, were making the greatest contribution to the Nixon cause by nominating for president a representative of their most liberal wing: Senator George S. McGovern of South Dakota. An outspoken critic of the war, a forceful advocate of advanced liberal positions on virtually every social and economic issue, McGovern seemed to embody those aspects of the turbulent 1960s that middle-class Americans were most eager to reject. McGovern profited greatly from party reforms (which he himself had helped to draft) that gave increased influence to women, blacks, and young people in the selection of the Democratic ticket. But those same reforms helped make the Democratic Convention of 1972 an unappealing spectacle to much of the public. The candidate then disillusioned even some of his own supporters by his indecisive reaction to revelations that his running mate, Senator Thomas Eagleton of Missouri, had undergone treatment for an emotional disturbance. Eagleton finally withdrew from the ticket. The remainder of the Democratic presidential campaign was an exercise in futility.

On election day, Nixon won reelection by one of the largest margins in history: 60.7 percent of the popular vote compared with 37.5 percent for the forlorn McGovern, an electoral margin of 520 to 17. The Democratic candidate had carried only Massachusetts and the District of Columbia. The new commitments that Nixon had so effectively expressed—to restraint in social reform, to decentralization of political power, to the defense of traditional values, and to a new balance in international relations—had clearly won the approval of the American people. But other problems, some beyond the president's control and some of his own making, were already lurking in the wings.

The Troubled Economy

Although it was political scandal that would ultimately destroy the Nixon presidency, the most important national crisis of the early 1970s was the decline of the American economy. For three decades, the American economy had been the envy of the world. It had produced as much as a third of the world's industrial goods and had dominated international trade. The American dollar had been the strongest currency in the world, and the American standard of living had risen steadily from its already substantial heights. Most Americans assumed that this remarkable prosperity was the normal condition of their society. In fact, however, it rested in part on several artificial conditions that were by the late 1960s rapidly disappearing: the absence of significant foreign competition and easy access to raw materials in the Third World.

The most disturbing economic problem of the 1970s was inflation, which had been creeping upward for several years when Richard Nixon took office and which soon began to soar. Its most visible cause was the major increase in federal deficit spending in the 1960s, when the Johnson administration tried to fund the war in Vietnam and its ambitious social programs without raising taxes. But there were other, equally important causes of the inflation and of the economic problems that lay behind it. No more did the United States have exclusive access to cheap raw materials around the globe; not only were other industrial nations now competing for increasingly scarce raw materials, but Third World suppliers of those materials were beginning to realize their value and demand higher prices for them.

The greatest immediate blow to the American economy was the increasing cost of energy. More than any nation on earth, the United States based its economy on the easy availability of cheap and plentiful fuels. No society was more dependent on the automobile; none was more wasteful in its use of oil and gas in its homes, schools, and factories. Domestic petroleum reserves were no longer sufficient to meet this demand, and the nation was growing increasingly dependent on imports from the Middle East and Africa.

For many years, the Organization of Petroleum Exporting Countries (OPEC) had operated as an informal bargaining unit for the sale of oil by Third World nations but had seldom managed to exercise any real strength. But in the early 1970s, OPEC began to assert itself, to use its oil both as an economic tool and as a political weapon. In 1973, in the midst of the Yom Kippur War, Arab members of OPEC announced that they would no longer ship petroleum to nations supporting Israel—that is, to the United States and its allies in Western Europe. At about the same time, the OPEC nations agreed to raise their prices 500 percent (from $3 to $15 a barrel). These twin shocks produced momentary economic chaos in the West. The United States suffered its first fuel shortage since World War II. And although the crisis eased a few months later, the price of energy continued to skyrocket both because of OPEC's new militant policies and because of the weakening competitive position of the dollar in world markets. No single factor did more to produce the soaring inflation of the 1970s.

The Nixon Response

Nixon's initial answer to these mounting economic problems was to reduce spending and raise taxes. But those policies produced both congressional and popular protest, and Nixon turned increasingly to an economic tool more readily available to him: control of the currency. Placing conservative economists at the head of the Federal Reserve Board, he ensured sharply higher interest rates and a contraction of the money supply. But the tight money policy did little to curb inflation. The cost of living rose a cumulative 15 percent during Nixon's first two and a half years in office. Economic growth, in the meantime, declined. The United States was encountering a new and puzzling dilemma: "stagflation," a combination of rising prices and general economic stagnation.

In the summer of 1971, Nixon imposed a ninety-day freeze on all wages and prices at their existing levels. Then, in November, he launched Phase II of his economic plan: mandatory guidelines for wage and price increases, to be administered by a federal agency. Inflation subsided temporarily, but the recession continued. Fearful that the recession would be more damaging than inflation in an election year, the administration reversed itself late in 1971: interest rates were allowed to drop sharply, and government spending increased—producing the largest budget deficit since World War II. The new tactics helped revive the economy in the short term, but inflation rose substantially—particularly after the administration abandoned the strict

Phase II controls and replaced them with a set of voluntary, and almost entirely ineffective, guidelines. In 1973, prices rose 9 percent; in 1974, after the Arab oil embargo and the OPEC price increases, they rose 12 percent—the highest rate since shortly after World War II. The value of the dollar continued to slide, and the nation's international trade continued to decline. The new energy crisis, in the meantime, was quickly becoming a national preoccupation. But while Nixon talked often about the need to achieve "energy independence," he offered few concrete proposals.

The erratic economic programs of the Nixon administration were a sign of a broader national confusion about the prospects for American prosperity. The Nixon pattern—of lurching from a tight money policy to curb inflation at one moment to a spending policy to cure recession at the next—repeated itself during the two administrations that followed. Nowhere was there any serious attempt to address the deeper problems that lay at the heart of the erosion of the American economy.

THE WATERGATE CRISIS

Although economic problems greatly concerned the American people in the 1970s, another stunning development almost entirely preoccupied the nation beginning early in 1973: the fall of Richard Nixon. The president's demise was a result in part of his own personality. Defensive, secretive, resentful of his critics, he brought to his office an element of mean-spiritedness that helped undermine even his most important accomplishments. But the larger explanation for the crisis lay in Nixon's view of American society and the world, and of his own role in both. The president believed the United States faced grave dangers from the radicals and dissidents who were challenging his policies. He came increasingly to consider any challenge to his policies a threat to "national security." By identifying his own political fortunes with those of the nation, Nixon was creating a climate in which he and those who served him could justify almost any tactics to stifle dissent and undermine opposition.

The Scandals

Nixon's approach to his office was in part a culmination of long-term changes in the presidency. Public expectations of the president had increased dramatically in the years since World War II; yet the constraints on the authority of the office had grown as well. In response, a succession of presidents had sought new methods for the exercise of power, often stretching the law, occasionally breaking it.

Nixon not only continued but greatly accelerated these trends. Facing a Democratic Congress hostile to his goals, he attempted to find ways to circumvent the legislature whenever possible. Saddled with a federal bureaucracy unresponsive to his wishes, he constructed a hierarchy of command in which virtually all executive power became concentrated in the White House. Operating within a rigid, even autocratic staff structure, the president became a solitary, brooding figure, whose contempt for his opponents and impatience with obstacles to his policies festered and grew. Unknown to all but a few intimates, he also became mired in a pattern of illegalities and abuses of power that late in 1972 began to break through to the surface.

Early on the morning of June 17, 1972, police arrested five men who had broken into the offices of the Democratic National Committee in the Watergate office building in Washington, D.C. Two others were seized a short time later and charged with supervising the break-in. When reporters for the *Washington Post* began researching the backgrounds of the culprits, they discovered that among those involved in the burglary were former employees of the Committee for the Re-Election of the President (CRP). One of them had worked in the White House itself. They had, moreover, been paid for the break-in from a secret fund of the reelection committee, a fund controlled by members of the White House staff.

Public interest in the disclosures grew slowly in the last months of 1972. Few Americans questioned the president's assurances that neither he nor his staff had any connection with what he called "this very bizarre incident." Early in 1973, however, the Watergate burglars went on trial; and under relentless prodding from federal judge John J. Sirica, one of the defendants, James W. McCord, agreed to cooperate both with the grand jury and with a special Senate investigating committee recently established under Senator Sam J. Ervin of North Carolina. McCord's testimony opened a floodgate of confessions, and for months a parade of White House and campaign officials exposed one illegality after another. Foremost among them was a member of the inner circle of the White House, John Dean, counsel to the president, who leveled allegations against Nixon himself.

Two different sets of scandals were emerging from the investigations. One was a general pattern of abuses of power involving both the White House and the Nixon campaign committee, which included, but was not limited to, the Watergate break-in. The other scandal, and the one that became the major focus of public attention for nearly two years, was the way in which the administration tried to manage the investigations of the Watergate break-in and other abuses—a pattern of behavior that became known as the "cover-up." There was never any conclusive evidence that the president had planned or approved the burglary in advance. But there was mounting evidence that he had been involved in illegal efforts to obstruct investigations of and withhold information about the episode. Testimony before the Ervin Committee provided evidence of the complicity of Dean, Attorney General John Mitchell, top White House assistants H. R. Haldeman and John Ehrlichman, and others. As interest in the case grew to something approaching a national obsession, the investigation focused increasingly on a single question: In the words of Senator Howard Baker of Tennessee, a member of the Ervin Committee, "What did the President know and when did he know it?"

Nixon accepted the departure of those members of his administration implicated in the scandals. But the president himself continued to insist on his own innocence. There the matter might have rested had it not been for the disclosure during the Senate hearings of a White House taping system that had recorded virtually every conversation in the president's office during the period in question. All those investigating the scandals sought access to the tapes; Nixon, pleading "executive privilege," refused to release them. A special prosecutor appointed by the president to handle the Watergate cases, Harvard law professor Archibald Cox, took Nixon to court in October 1973 in an effort to force him to relinquish the recordings. Nixon, now clearly growing desperate, fired Cox and suffered the humiliation of watching both Attorney General Elliot Richardson and his deputy resign in protest. This "Saturday night massacre" made the president's predicament infinitely worse. Not only did public pressure force him to appoint a new special prosecutor, Texas attorney Leon Jaworski, who proved just as determined as Cox to subpoena the tapes; but the episode precipitated an investigation by the House of Representatives into the possibility of impeachment.

The Fall of Richard Nixon

Nixon's situation deteriorated further in the following months. Late in 1973, Vice President Spiro Agnew became embroiled in a scandal of his own when evidence surfaced that he had accepted bribes and kickbacks while serving as governor of Maryland and even as vice president. In return for a

Justice Department agreement not to press the case, Agnew pleaded no contest to a lesser charge of income-tax evasion and resigned from the government. With the controversial Agnew no longer in line to succeed to the presidency, the prospect of removing Nixon from the White House became less worrisome to his opponents. The new vice president (the first appointed under the terms of the Twenty-fifth Amendment, which had been adopted in 1967) was House Minority Leader Gerald Ford, an amiable and popular Michigan congressman.

The impeachment investigation quickly gathered momentum. In April 1974, in an effort to head off further subpoenas of the tapes, the president released transcripts of a number of relevant conversations, claiming that they proved his innocence. Investigators and much of the public felt otherwise. Even these edited tapes seemed to suggest Nixon's complicity in the cover-up. In July, the crisis reached a climax. First the Supreme Court ruled unanimously, in *United States* v. *Richard M. Nixon*, that the president must relinquish the tapes to Special Prosecutor Jaworski. Days later, the House Judiciary Committee voted to recommend three articles of impeachment, charging that Nixon had, first, obstructed justice in the Watergate cover-up; second, misused federal agencies to violate the rights of citizens; and third, defied the authority of Congress by refusing to deliver tapes and other materials subpoenaed by the committee. Even without additional evidence, Nixon might well have been impeached by the full House and convicted by the Senate. Early in August, however, he provided at last the "smoking gun"—the concrete proof of his guilt—that his defenders had long contended was missing from the case against him. Among the tapes that the Supreme Court compelled Nixon to relinquish were several that offered apparently incontrovertible evidence of his involvement in the Watergate cover-up. Only three days after the burglary, the recordings disclosed, the president had ordered the FBI to stop investigating the break-in. Impeachment and conviction now seemed inevitable.

For several days, Nixon brooded in the White House, on the verge, some claimed, of a breakdown. Finally, on August 8, 1974, he announced his resignation—the first president in American history ever to do so. At noon the next day, while Nixon and his family were flying west to their home in California, Gerald Ford took the oath of office as president.

Many Americans expressed relief and exhilaration that, as the new president put it, "our long national nightmare is over." They were relieved to be rid of Richard Nixon, who had lost virtually all of the wide popularity that had won him his landslide reelection victory only two years before. And they were exhilarated that, as some boasted, "the system had worked." But the wave of good feeling could not obscure the deeper and more lasting damage of the Watergate crisis. In a society in which distrust of leaders and institutions of authority was already widespread, the fall of Richard Nixon seemed to confirm the most cynical assumptions about the character of American public life.

CHAPTER THIRTY-THREE

The Unfinished Nation

Politics and Diplomacy After Watergate ∼ The "Reagan Revolution"
George Bush and the Post-Cold War World ∼ Modern Times

HE FRUSTRATIONS OF the 1970s—the defeat in Vietnam, the Watergate crisis, the decay of the American economy—inflicted damaging blows to the confident, optimistic nationalism that had characterized so much of the postwar era. At first, many Americans responded to these problems by announcing the arrival of an "age of limits," in which America would have to learn to live with increasingly constricted expectations. By the end of the decade, however, the contours of another response to the challenges had become visible in both American culture and American politics. It was a response that combined a conservative retreat from some of the heady visions of the 1960s with a reinforced commitment to the idea of economic growth, international power, and American exceptionalism. The election of Ronald Reagan to the presidency in 1980 seemed to mark a repudiation of the doubts and "defeatism" of the previous decade.

But the turbulence that had plagued America in the 1970s could not be so easily banished. By the beginning of the 1990s, the American economy was in the midst of a deep and many believed long-term crisis. The complexity and diversity that had always characterized American society, and the problems associated with them, were straining the nation's social and cultural fabric. And the international system, which had experienced a dismal stability for more than forty years, was in the throes of a genuinely revolutionary transformation. Even for a nation accustomed to rapid change, the events of the 1980s and 1990s seemed at times dizzying and disorienting. The result was an impassioned and at times divisive debate about both the nature of the American past and the prospects for the American future.

POLITICS AND DIPLOMACY AFTER WATERGATE

In the aftermath of Richard Nixon's ignominious departure from office, many wondered whether faith in the presidency, and in the government as a whole, could easily be restored. The administrations of the two presidents who succeeded Nixon did little to answer those questions.

The Ford Custodianship

Gerald Ford inherited the presidency under unenviable circumstances. He had to try to rebuild confidence in government after the Watergate scandals. And he had to try to restore prosperity in the face of domestic and international challenges to the American economy. He enjoyed some success in the first of these efforts but very little in the second.

The new president's effort to establish himself as a symbol of political integrity suffered a setback only a month after he took office, when he granted Richard Nixon "a full, free, and absolute pardon" for any crimes he may have committed during his presidency. Ford explained that he was attempting to spare the nation the ordeal of years of litigation and to spare Nixon himself any further suffering. But much of the public suspected a secret deal with the former president. The pardon caused a decline in Ford's popularity from which he never fully recovered. Nevertheless, most Americans considered Ford a decent man; his honesty and amiability did much to reduce the bitterness and acrimony of the Watergate years.

The Ford administration enjoyed less success in its effort to solve the problems of the American economy. In his attempts to curb inflation, the president rejected the idea of wage and price controls and called instead for largely ineffective voluntary efforts. After supporting high interest rates, opposing increased federal spending (through liberal use of his veto power), and resisting pressures for a tax reduction, Ford had to deal with a serious recession in 1974 and 1975. Central to the economic problems was the continuing energy crisis. In the aftermath of the Arab oil embargo of 1973, the OPEC cartel began to raise the price of oil—by 400 percent in 1974 alone. Even so, American dependence on OPEC supplies continued to grow—one of the principal reasons why inflation reached 11 percent in 1976.

At first it seemed that the foreign policy of the new administration would differ little from that of its predecessor. The new president retained

Henry Kissinger, whom Nixon had appointed secretary of state in 1973, and continued the general policies of the Nixon years. Late in 1974, Ford met with Leonid Brezhnev at Vladivostok in Siberia and signed an arms control accord that was to serve as the basis for SALT II, thus achieving a goal the Nixon administration had long sought. The following summer, after a European security conference in Helsinki, Finland, the Soviet Union and Western nations agreed to ratify the borders that had divided Europe since 1945; and the Soviets pledged to increase respect for human rights within their own country. In the Middle East, in the meantime, Henry Kissinger helped produce a new accord by which Israel agreed to return large portions of the occupied Sinai to Egypt; the two nations pledged not to resolve future differences by force. In China, finally, the death of Mao Zedong in 1976 brought to power a new, apparently more moderate government, eager to expand its ties with the United States.

Nevertheless, as the 1976 presidential election approached, Ford's policies were coming under attack from both the right and the left. In the Republican primary campaign, Ford faced a powerful challenge from former California governor Ronald Reagan, leader of the party's conservative wing, who spoke for many on the right who were unhappy with any conciliation of communists. The president only barely survived the assault to win his party's nomination. The Democrats, in the meantime, were gradually uniting behind a new and, before 1976, almost entirely unknown candidate: Jimmy Carter, a former governor of Georgia who organized a brilliant primary campaign and appealed to the general unhappiness with Washing-

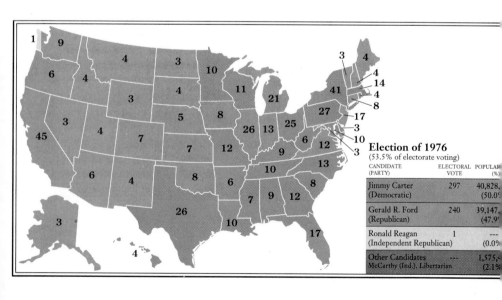

Election of 1976
(53.5% of electorate voting)

CANDIDATE (PARTY)	ELECTORAL VOTE	POPULAR (%)
Jimmy Carter (Democratic)	297	40,828, (50.0%
Gerald R. Ford (Republican)	240	39,147, (47.9%
Ronald Reagan (Independent Republican)	1	--- (0.0%
Other Candidates McCarthy (Ind.), Libertarian	---	1,575, (2.1%

ton by offering honesty, piety, and an outsider's skepticism of the federal government. And while Carter's mammoth lead dwindled to almost nothing by election day, unhappiness with the economy and a general disenchantment with Ford enabled the Democrat to hold on for a narrow victory. Carter emerged with 50 percent of the popular vote to Ford's 47.9 percent and 297 electoral votes to Ford's 240.

The Trials of Jimmy Carter

Jimmy Carter assumed the presidency at a moment when the nation faced problems of staggering complexity and difficulty. Perhaps no leader could have thrived in such inhospitable circumstances. But Carter seemed at times

JIMMY AND ROSALYNN CARTER, JANUARY 20, 1977
Jimmy Carter startled the crowds (and alarmed the Secret Service) on his Inauguration Day by walking down Pennsylvania Avenue from the Capitol to the White House after taking the oath of office. Not since Jefferson, whose effort to identify with the "common man" Carter hoped to emulate, had a president walked in his inaugural parade.

to make his predicament worse by a style of leadership that many considered self-righteous and inflexible. He left office in 1981 as one of the least popular presidents of the century.

Carter had campaigned for the presidency as an "outsider," representing Americans suspicious of entrenched bureaucracies and complacent public officials. He carried much of that suspiciousness with him to Washington. He surrounded himself in the White House with a group of close-knit associates from Georgia; and in the beginning, at least, he seemed deliberately to spurn assistance from more experienced political figures. Carter was among the most intelligent and quick-witted men ever to serve in the White House, but his critics charged that he provided no overall vision or direction to his government.

Carter devoted much of his time to the problems of energy and the economy. Entering office in the midst of a recession, he moved first to reduce unemployment by raising public spending and cutting federal taxes. Unemployment declined, but inflation soared. During Carter's last two years in office, prices rose at well over a 10-percent annual rate. Like Nixon and Ford before him, Carter responded with a combination of tight money and calls for voluntary restraint. He appointed first G. William Miller and then Paul Volcker, conservative economists, to head the Federal Reserve Board, thus ensuring a policy of high interest rates and reduced currency supplies. By 1980, interest rates had risen to the highest levels in American history; at times, they exceeded 20 percent.

The problem of energy also grew steadily more troublesome in the Carter years. In the summer of 1979, instability in the Middle East produced a second major fuel shortage in the United States. In the midst of the crisis, OPEC announced another major price increase, clouding the economic picture still further. Faced with increasing pressure to act (and with public-opinion polls showing his approval rating at a dismal 26 percent), Carter withdrew to Camp David, the presidential retreat in the Maryland mountains. Ten days later, he emerged to deliver a remarkable television address. It included a series of proposals for resolving the energy crisis. But it was most notable for Carter's bleak assessment of the national condition. Speaking with unusual fervor, he complained of a "crisis of confidence" that had struck "at the very heart and soul of our national will." The address became known as the "malaise" speech (although Carter himself had never used that word), and it helped fuel attacks that the president was trying to blame his own problems on the American people. Carter's sudden firing of several members of his cabinet a few days later deepened his political problems.

Human Rights and National Interests

Among Jimmy Carter's most frequent campaign promises was a pledge to build a new basis for American foreign policy, one in which the defense of "human rights" would replace the pursuit of "selfish interests." Carter spoke out sharply and often about violations of human rights in many countries (including, most prominently, the Soviet Union). Beyond that general commitment, the Carter administration focused on several more traditional concerns. Carter completed negotiations begun several years earlier on a pair of treaties to turn over control of the Panama Canal to the government of Panama. Domestic opposition to the treaties was intense, especially among conservatives who viewed the new arrangements as part of a general American retreat from international power. But the administration argued that relinquishing the canal was the best way to improve relations with Latin America and avoid violence in Panama. After an acrimonious debate, the Senate ratified the treaties by 68 to 32, only one vote more than the necessary two-thirds.

Less controversial, within the United States at least, was Carter's success in arranging a peace treaty between Egypt and Israel—the crowning accomplishment of his presidency. Middle East negotiations had seemed hopelessly stalled when a dramatic breakthrough occurred in November 1977. The Egyptian president, Anwar Sadat, accepted an invitation from Prime Minister Menachem Begin to visit Israel. In Tel Aviv, he announced that Egypt was now willing to accept the state of Israel as a legitimate political entity. But translating these good feelings into an actual peace treaty proved more difficult.

When talks between Israeli and Egyptian negotiators stalled, Carter invited Sadat and Begin to a summit conference at Camp David in September 1978, holding them there for two weeks while he and others helped mediate the disputes between them. On September 17, Carter escorted the two leaders into the White House to announce agreement on a framework for an Egyptian-Israeli peace treaty. Carter intervened again several months later, when talks stalled once more, and helped produce a compromise on the most sensitive issue between the two parties: the Palestinian refugee issue. On March 26, 1979, Begin and Sadat returned together to the White House to sign a formal peace treaty between their two nations.

In the meantime, Carter continued trying to improve relations with China and the Soviet Union and to complete a new arms agreement. He responded eagerly to the overtures of Deng Xiaoping, the new Chinese leader who was attempting to open his nation to the outside world. On

December 15, 1978, Washington and Beijing announced the resumption of formal diplomatic relations between the two nations. A few months later, Carter traveled to Vienna to meet with the aging and visibly ailing Brezhnev to finish drafting the new SALT II arms control agreement. The treaty set limits on the number of long-range missiles, bombers, and nuclear war-heads on each side. Almost immediately, however, SALT II met with fierce conservative opposition in the United States. Central to the arguments was a fundamental distrust of the Soviet Union that nearly a decade of détente had failed to destroy. By the fall of 1979, with the Senate scheduled to begin debate over the treaty shortly, ratification was already in jeopardy. Events in the following months would provide a final blow, both to the treaty and to the larger framework of détente.

The Year of the Hostages

Ever since the early 1950s, the United States had provided political support and, more recently, massive military assistance to the government of the Shah of Iran, hoping to make his nation a bulwark against Soviet expansion in the Middle East. By 1979, however, the Shah was in deep trouble with his own people. Iranians resented the repressive, authoritarian tactics through which the Shah had maintained his autocratic rule. At the same time, Islamic clergy (and much of the fiercely religious populace) opposed his efforts to modernize and Westernize a fundamentalist society. The combination of resentments produced a powerful revolutionary movement. In January 1979, the Shah fled the country.

The United States made cautious efforts in the first months after the Shah's abdication to establish cordial relations with the succession of in-creasingly militant regimes that followed. By late 1979, however, revolu-tionary chaos in Iran was making any normal relationships impossible. What power there was resided with a zealous religious leader, the Ayatollah Ruhollah Khomeini, whose hatred of the West in general and the United States in particular was intense.

In late October 1979, the deposed Shah arrived in New York to be treated for cancer. Days later, on November 4, an armed mob invaded the American embassy in Teheran, seized the diplomats and military personnel inside, and demanded the return of the Shah to Iran in exchange for their freedom. Fifty-three Americans remained hostages in the embassy for over a year. Coming after years of what many Americans considered international humiliations and defeats, the hostage seizure released a deep well of anger and emotion.

Only weeks after the hostage seizure, on December 27, 1979, Soviet troops invaded Afghanistan, the mountainous nation lying between the Soviet Union and Iran. The Soviet Union had, in fact, been a power in Afghanistan for years, and the dominant force since April 1978, when a coup had established a Marxist government there with close ties to the Kremlin. But while some observers claimed that the Soviet invasion was a Russian attempt to secure the status quo, others—most notably the president—claimed that the invasion was a Russian "stepping stone to their possible control over much of the world's oil supplies." It was also the "gravest threat to world peace since World War II." Carter angrily imposed a series of economic sanctions on the Russians, canceled American participation in the 1980 summer Olympic Games in Moscow, and announced the withdrawal of SALT II from Senate consideration.

The Campaign of 1980

By the time of the crises in Iran and Afghanistan, Jimmy Carter was in desperate political trouble. His standing in popularity polls was lower than that of any president in history. Senator Edward Kennedy, younger brother of John and Robert Kennedy, was preparing to challenge him in the

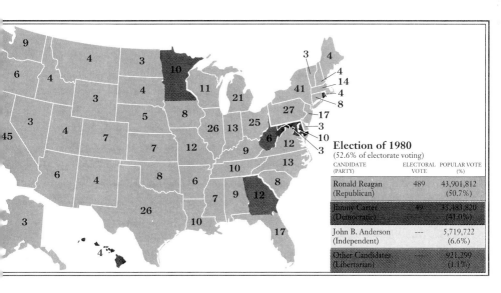

Election of 1980
(52.6% of electorate voting)

CANDIDATE (PARTY)	ELECTORAL VOTE	POPULAR VOTE (%)
Ronald Reagan (Republican)	489	43,901,812 (50.7%)
Jimmy Carter (Democratic)	49	35,483,820 (41.0%)
John B. Anderson (Independent)	---	5,719,722 (6.6%)
Other Candidates (Libertarian)	---	921,299 (1.1%)

primaries. For a short while, the seizure of the hostages and the stern American response to the Soviet invasion revived Carter's candidacy. But as the hostage crisis dragged on, public impatience grew. Kennedy won a series of victories over the president in the later primaries. Carter managed in the end to stave off Kennedy's challenge and win his party's nomination. But it was an unhappy convention that heard the president's listless call to arms, and Carter's campaign aroused little popular enthusiasm as he prepared to face a powerful challenge.

The Republican party, in the meantime, had rallied enthusiastically behind a man whom, not many years before, many Americans had considered a frightening reactionary. Ronald Reagan, a one-time film actor, a former California governor, and a poised and articulate campaigner, was a sharp critic of the size and expense of the federal government. More important, he championed a restoration of American "strength" and "pride" in the world. Although he refrained from discussing the issue of the hostages, Reagan clearly benefited from the continuing popular frustration at Carter's inability to resolve the crisis. In a larger sense, he benefited as well from the accumulated frustrations of more than a decade of domestic and international disappointments.

On election day 1980, the anniversary of the seizure of the hostages in Iran, Reagan swept to victory with 51 percent of the vote to 41 percent for Jimmy Carter and 7 percent for John Anderson—a moderate Republican congressman from Illinois who had mounted an independent campaign. Carter carried only five states and the District of Columbia, for a total of 49 electoral votes to Reagan's 489. The Republican party won control of the Senate for the first time since 1952; and although the Democrats retained a diminished majority in the House, the lower chamber too seemed firmly in the hands of conservatives.

On the day of Reagan's inauguration, the American hostages in Iran were released after their 444-day ordeal. Jimmy Carter, in the last hours of his presidency, had concluded months of negotiations by agreeing to release several billion dollars in Iranian assets that he had frozen in American banks shortly after the seizure of the embassy. The government of Iran, desperate for funds to support its floundering war against neighboring Iraq, ordered the hostages freed in return. Americans welcomed the hostages home with demonstrations of joy and patriotism not seen since the end of World War II. But while the celebration in 1945 had marked a great American triumph, the euphoria in 1981 marked something quite different—a troubled nation grasping for reassurance. Ronald Reagan set out to provide it.

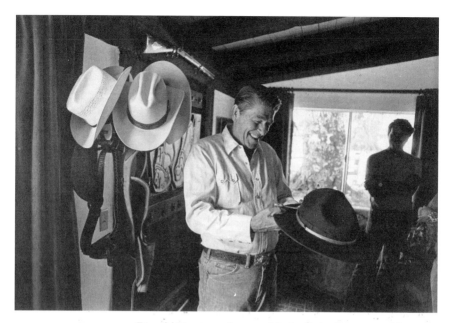

REAGAN AT THE RANCH Ronald Reagan relaxes at his ranch in the mountains near Santa Barbara, California, demonstrating the informal geniality that accounted for much of his remarkable popularity.

THE "REAGAN REVOLUTION"

Ronald Reagan assumed the presidency in January 1981 promising a change in government more profound than any since the New Deal of fifty years before. His eight years in office produced a significant shift in public policy, but they brought nothing so fundamental as many of his supporters had hoped or his opponents had feared. There was, however, no ambiguity about his administration's purely political achievements. Ronald Reagan succeeded brilliantly in making his own engaging personality the central fact of American politics in the 1980s.

Reagan in the White House

Even many people who disagreed with the president's policies found themselves drawn to his attractive and carefully honed public image. Reagan was a master of television and a gifted public speaker. He was the oldest man ever to serve as president, but he seemed vigorous, resilient, even youthful.

When he was wounded in an assassination attempt in 1981, he joked with doctors on his way into surgery and appeared to bounce back from the ordeal with remarkable speed. Four years later, he seemed to rebound from cancer surgery with similar zest. He had few visible insecurities. Even when things went wrong, as they often did, the blame seemed seldom to attach to Reagan himself (inspiring some Democrats to begin referring to him as "the Teflon president").

Reagan was not much involved in the day-to-day affairs of running the government; he surrounded himself with tough, energetic administrators who insulated him from many of the pressures of the office and apparently relied on him largely for general guidance, not specific decisions. But Reagan did make active use of his office to generate support for his administration's programs, by appealing repeatedly to the public over television and by fusing his proposals with a highly nationalistic rhetoric.

"Supply-Side" Economics

Reagan's 1980 campaign for the presidency had promised, among other things, to restore the economy to health by a bold experiment that became known as "supply-side" economics or, to some, "Reaganomics." Supply-side economics operated from the assumption that the woes of the American economy were in large part a result of excessive taxation, which left inadequate capital available to investors to stimulate growth. The solution, therefore, was to reduce taxes, with particularly generous benefits to corporations and wealthy individuals, in order to encourage new investments. The result would be a general economic revival that would help everyone. Because a tax cut would reduce government revenues (at least at first), it would also be necessary to reduce government expenses. A cornerstone of the Reagan economic program, therefore, was a dramatic cut in the federal budget.

In its first months in office, accordingly, the new administration hastily assembled a legislative program based on the supply-side idea. It proposed $40 billion in budget cuts and managed to win congressional approval of almost all of them. In addition, the president proposed a bold, three-year rate reduction on both individual and corporate taxes. In the summer of 1981, Congress passed it too. Not since Lyndon Johnson had a president compiled so impressive a legislative record in his first months in office.

By early 1982, however, the nation had sunk into the most severe recession since the 1930s. The Reagan economic program was not directly to blame for the problems, but critics claimed that the administration's policies were doing nothing to improve the situation. In fact, however, the economy recovered more rapidly and impressively than almost anyone had expected. By the middle of 1983, unemployment (which had reached nearly 11 percent in 1982, the highest level in over forty years) had fallen to 8.2 percent. The gross national product had grown 3.6 percent, the largest increase since the mid-1970s. Inflation had fallen below 5 percent. The economy continued to grow, and both inflation and unemployment remained low (at least by the new and more pessimistic standards the nation seemed now to have accepted) through most of the decade.

The recovery was a result of many things. Years of tight money policies by the Federal Reserve Board had helped lower inflation. A worldwide "energy glut," the virtual collapse of the OPEC cartel, and the deregulation of natural gas production had produced at least a temporary end to the inflationary pressures of spiraling fuel costs. And staggering federal budget deficits were pumping billions of dollars into the flagging economy but also, many warned, threatening ultimately to destroy the recovery they were helping to create.

The Fiscal Crisis

By the mid-1980s, the growing fiscal crisis had become one of the central issues in American politics. Having entered office promising a balanced budget within four years, Reagan presided over record budget deficits and accumulated more debt in his eight years in office than the American government had accumulated in its entire previous history. Before the 1980s, the highest single-year budget deficit in American history had been $66 billion (in 1976). Throughout the 1980s, the annual budget deficit consistently exceeded $100 billion (and in 1986 peaked at $221 billion). The national debt rose from $907 billion in 1980 to nearly $3 trillion by 1990.

The enormous deficits had many causes, some of them stretching back over decades of American public policy decisions. In particular, the budget suffered from enormous increases in the costs of "entitlement" programs (especially Social Security and Medicare), a result of the aging of the population and dramatic increases in the cost of health care. But some of the causes of the deficit lay in the policies of the Reagan administration. The 1981 tax cuts, the largest in American history, sharply eroded the revenue base of the federal government and accounted for a large percentage of the deficit. The massive increase in military spending (a proposed $1.6 trillion over five years) on which the Reagan administration insisted added more to the federal budget than its cuts in domestic spending removed.

In the face of these deficits, the administration refused to consider raising income taxes (although it did agree to a major increase in the Social Security tax). It would not agree to reductions in military spending. It could not much reduce the costs of entitlement programs, and it could do nothing to reduce interest payments on the massive (and growing) debt. Its answer to the fiscal crisis, therefore, was further cuts in "discretionary" domestic spending, which included many programs aimed at the poorest (and politically weakest) Americans. There were reductions in funding for food stamps; a major cut in federal subsidies for low-income housing (which contributed to the radical increase in homelessness that by the late 1980s was plaguing virtually all American cities); strict new limitations on Medicare and Medicaid payments; reductions in student loans, school lunches, and other educational programs; and an end to many forms of federal assistance to the states and cities—which helped precipitate years of local fiscal crises as well.

By the end of Reagan's third year in office, funding for domestic programs had been cut nearly as far as the Congress (and, apparently, the public) was willing to tolerate. Congress responded with the Gramm-Rudman-Hollings Act, passed late in 1985, which mandated major deficit reductions over five years and provided for automatic budget cuts in all areas of government spending should the president and Congress fail to agree on an alternative solution. Under Gramm-Rudman-Hollings, the budget deficit did decline for several years from its 1983 high. But much of that decline was a result of a substantial surplus in the Social Security trust fund (which the sharply increased Social Security taxes had produced), not of any larger fiscal successes.

Reagan and the World

Reagan encountered a similar combination of triumphs and difficulties in international affairs. Determined to restore American pride and prestige in the world, he argued that the United States should once again become active and assertive in opposing communism and supporting friendly governments whatever their internal policies.

Relations with the Soviet Union, which had been steadily deteriorating in the last years of the Carter administration, grew still more chilly in the first years of the Reagan presidency. The president spoke harshly of the Soviet regime (which he once called the "evil empire"), accusing it of sponsoring world terrorism and declaring that any armaments negotiations must be "linked" to negotiations about Soviet behavior in other areas. Relations with the Russians deteriorated further after the government of Poland (under strong pressure from Moscow) imposed martial law on the country in the winter of 1981 to crush a growing challenge from an independent labor organization, Solidarity.

Although the president had long denounced the SALT II arms control treaty as unfavorable to the United States, he continued to honor its provisions. But the Reagan administration at first made little progress toward arms control in other areas, despite the growing political power of a popular antinuclear movement in both Europe and the United States. In fact, the president proposed the most ambitious new military program in many years: the Strategic Defense Initiative (SDI), widely known as "Star Wars" (after a popular science-fiction movie). Reagan claimed that SDI, through the use of lasers and satellites, could provide an effective shield against incoming missiles and thus make nuclear war obsolete. The Soviet Union claimed that the new program would elevate the arms race to new and more dangerous levels and insisted that any arms control agreement begin with an American abandonment of SDI.

At the same time, the Reagan administration began, rhetorically at least, to support opponents of communism anywhere in the world, whether or not the regimes they were challenging were directly allied to the Soviet Union. This policy became known as the Reagan Doctrine, and it meant, above all, a new American activism in the Third World. The most conspicuous examples of the new activism came in Latin America. In October 1983, the administration sent American soldiers and marines to the tiny Caribbean island of Grenada to oust an anti-American Marxist regime that was forging a relationship with the Soviet Union. In El Salvador, where first a repressive military regime and later a moderate civilian one were engaged in murderous struggles with left-wing revolutionaries (who were supported, according to the Reagan administration, by Cuba and the Soviet Union), the president provided increased military and economic assistance. In neighboring Nicaragua, a pro-American dictatorship had fallen to the revolutionary "Sandinistas" in 1979; the new government had grown increasingly anti-American (and increasingly Marxist) throughout the early 1980s. The administration gave both rhetorical and material support to the so-called contras, a guerrilla movement drawn from several antigovernment groups and fighting (without great success) to topple the Sandinista regime. Indeed, support of the contras became a mission of special importance to the president, and later the source of some of his greatest difficulties.

In other parts of the world, the administration's bellicose rhetoric seemed to hide an instinctive restraint. In June 1982, the Israeli army launched an invasion of Lebanon in an effort to drive guerrillas of the Palestinian Liberation Organization from the country. The United States supported the Israelis rhetorically but also worked to permit PLO forces to leave Lebanon peacefully. An American peacekeeping force entered Beirut to supervise the evacuation. American marines then remained in the city, apparently to protect the fragile Lebanese government, which was embroiled in a vicious civil war. Now identified with one faction in the struggle, Americans themselves became the targets; a 1983 terrorist bombing of a United States military barracks in Beirut left 241 marines dead. Rather than become more deeply involved in the Lebanese struggle, Reagan withdrew the American forces.

The tragedy in Lebanon was an example of the changing character of Third World struggles: an increasing reliance on terrorism by otherwise powerless groups to advance their political aims. A series of terrorist acts in the 1980s—attacks on airplanes, cruise ships, commercial and diplomatic posts; the seizing of American and other Western hostages—alarmed and frightened much of the Western world. The Reagan administration spoke bravely about its resolve to punish terrorism; and at one point in 1986, the president ordered American planes to bomb sites in Tripoli, the capital of Libya, whose controversial leader Muammar al-Qaddafi was widely believed to be a leading sponsor of terrorism. In general, however, terrorists remained difficult to identify or control.

The Election of 1984

Reagan approached the campaign of 1984 at the head of a united Republican party firmly committed to his candidacy. The Democrats, as had become their custom, followed a more fractious course. Former vice president Walter Mondale established an early and commanding lead in the race by soliciting support from a wide range of traditional Democratic interest groups. But for a time, he lost the initiative to a younger and apparently more dynamic candidate, Senator Gary Hart of Colorado, who presented himself as a leader of a "new generation" and the spokesman for vaguely defined "new ideas." The magnetic and controversial African-American leader, Jesse Jackson, also staged an impressive primary campaign that drew substantial minority support away from Mondale. But with the help of the AFL-CIO and other established groups, Mondale revived his campaign and managed to capture the nomination. He brought momentary excitement to the Democratic Convention in San Francisco that summer by selecting a woman, Representative Geraldine Ferraro of New York, to be his running mate and the first female candidate ever to appear on a major-party national ticket.

The Republican party, by contrast, rallied comfortably behind its revered leader, whose triumphant campaign that fall scarcely took note of his opponents. Reagan's victory in 1984 was decisive. He won approximately 59 percent of the vote, and he carried every state except Mondale's native Minnesota and the District of Columbia. But Reagan was much stronger than his party. Democrats gained a seat in the Senate and maintained only slightly reduced control of the House of Representatives.

The Reagan Scandals

For a time, Reagan's personal popularity deflected attention from a series of scandals that might well have destroyed another administration. Top officials in the Environmental Protection Agency resigned when it was disclosed that they were flouting the laws they had been appointed to enforce. Officials of the CIA and the Defense Department resigned after revelations of questionable stock transactions. Reagan's secretary of labor left office after being indicted for racketeering (although he was later acquitted). Edwin Meese, the White House counsel and later attorney general, finally resigned in 1988 after years of attacks for controversial financial arrangements that many believed had compromised his office.

Unnoticed at first were several larger scandals that surfaced only as Reagan was about to leave office. One involved misuse of funds by the Department of Housing and Urban Development, abuses so widespread that for a time the survival of the agency itself was in question. Another, more serious scandal involved the savings and loan industry. The Reagan administration and Congress had sharply reduced regulatory controls over the troubled savings and loans. Many responded by rapidly, often recklessly, and sometimes corruptly expanding. By the end of the decade, the industry was in chaos, and the government was forced to step in to prevent a complete collapse. Predictions of the eventual cost to the government of the savings and loan debacle ran as high as half a trillion dollars.

But the most damaging scandal of the Reagan years came to light in November 1986. After reports appeared in foreign newspapers, the White House conceded that it had sold weapons to the revolutionary government of Iran, apparently as part of a largely unsuccessful effort to secure the release of several Americans being held hostage by radical Islamic groups in the Middle East. Even more damaging was the administration's revelation that some of the money from the arms deal with Iran had been covertly and illegally funneled into a fund to aid the contras in Nicaragua.

In the months that followed, aggressive reporting and a highly publicized series of congressional hearings exposed a remarkable and previously unsuspected feature of the Reagan White House: the existence within it of something like a "secret government," unknown to the State Department, the Defense Department, even parts of the CIA, dedicated to advancing the administration's foreign policy aims through secret and at times illegal means. The principal figure in this covert world appeared at first to be an obscure marine lieutenant colonel assigned to the staff of the National Security Council, Oliver North. But gradually it became clear that North was acting in concert with other, more powerful figures in the administration. The Iran-contra scandal, as it became known, did serious damage to the Reagan presidency, and the investigations into the affair continued for years. In 1992, the special prosecutor handling the case won an indictment against former secretary of defense Caspar Weinberger.

There were other signs in the late 1980s that the glow of the "Reagan Revolution" was beginning to fade. In October 1987, the American stock market—whose spectacular success had been one of the most conspicuous features of the economic boom—experienced the greatest single-day decline in its history (stocks lost 22 percent of their value); and although stock prices gradually recovered over the next two years, the crash damaged the confidence that had fueled the financial markets. At about the same time, one of the most popular financial innovations of the 1980s, the "leveraged buyout," which had permitted a wave of corporate takeovers financed by huge loans, began to unravel. Some of the nation's largest corporations, unable to carry the enormous debt they had acquired in their takeover efforts, began to flounder or collapse.

The Election of 1988

The fraying of the Reagan administration helped the Democrats regain control of the United States Senate in 1986 and fueled hopes in the party for a presidential victory in 1988. Even so, several of the most popular figures in the Democratic party refused to run. And the early front runner, Senator Gary Hart of Colorado, withdrew from the race in May 1987 after embarrassing revelations of an extramarital relationship with a young model. That left the field to a group of lesser-known candidates and to Jesse Jackson, whose fervent support among African-Americans made him a major force in the party.

The man who emerged from the pack was relatively little known: Michael Dukakis, a three-term governor of Massachusetts who claimed to have helped produce a dramatic revival in the New England economy (a revival frequently described as "the Massachusetts miracle"). Dukakis was a dry, even dull campaigner. But Democrats remained optimistic about their prospects in 1988, largely because of the identity of their opponent, Vice President George Bush.

In nearly thirty years in public life—as a member of Congress from Texas, as ambassador to the United Nations and minister to China, as director of the CIA, head of the Republican National Committee, and finally vice president—Bush had identified himself clearly with no major issue and could take credit for no major accomplishments. He had been an ineffective campaigner in 1980, when he ran unsuccessfully for president, and had attracted derision for his performance in the 1984 campaign, when he was running for reelection as vice president. Capitalizing on his ties to the still-popular Reagan, Bush overcame challenges from other major figures in the party to win the Republican nomination, but he entered the last months of the campaign substantially behind Dukakis.

Beginning at the Republican Convention, however, Bush staged a remarkable turnaround by making his campaign a long, relentless attack on

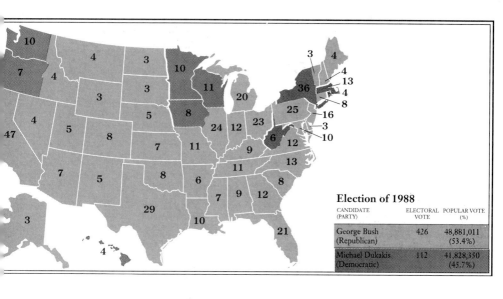

Election of 1988

CANDIDATE (PARTY)	ELECTORAL VOTE	POPULAR VOTE (%)
George Bush (Republican)	426	48,881,011 (53.4%)
Michael Dukakis (Democratic)	112	41,828,350 (45.7%)

Michael Dukakis, tying him to all the unpopular social and cultural stances Americans had come to identify with "liberals." Indeed, the Bush campaign was almost certainly the most negative, and many believed among the most discreditable, of the twentieth century. It was also, apparently, one of the most effective, although the listless, indecisive character of the Dukakis campaign contributed to the Republican cause as well. Having trailed Dukakis by a sizable margin as late as August, Bush won a substantial victory in November. He received 54 percent of the popular vote to Dukakis's 46, and he won 426 electoral votes to Dukakis's 111. But Bush carried few Republicans into office with him; the Democrats retained secure majorities in both houses of Congress.

GEORGE BUSH AND THE POST-COLD WAR WORLD

The Bush presidency was notable for a series of dramatic developments in international affairs and an almost complete absence of initiatives or ideas on domestic issues. For a time, Bush's apparent successes in foreign policy managed to obscure the absence of a domestic agenda. By 1992, however, with the nation in the second year of a serious recession, the president's once-overwhelming popularity had declined substantially.

The End of the Cold War

The broad popularity Bush enjoyed during his first three years in office was partly because of his subdued, unthreatening public image. But it was primarily because of the success of several international initiatives. Late in 1989, he dispatched American troops to Panama to overthrow the unpopular military leader Manuel Noriega. Noriega had worked for years as an informant for the CIA and United States drug agencies. But now he was himself under indictment in the United States for drug trafficking, and his contemptuous defiance of American pressures had embarrassed the government in Washington for two years. The Panama invasion—which installed an elected, pro-American, civilian government in Panama—was highly popular within the United States.

But Bush's early popularity also owed a great deal to a series of genuinely revolutionary transformations in the international order that made 1989 and 1990 one of the truly epochal moments in modern world history. There were many theories as to why the world changed so quickly and dramatically in those years. But the most frequent explanation centered on Mikhail Gorbachev, who succeeded to the leadership of the Soviet Union in 1985 and quickly became the most revolutionary figure in world politics in at least four decades. Benefiting from years of social and economic frustration in his country, Gorbachev transformed Soviet politics by launching two dramatic new policies. *Glasnost* (openness) introduced new levels of personal and political liberties to Soviet life. *Perestroika* (reform, or restructuring) attempted to revive the rigid and unproductive Soviet economy by introducing, among other things, such elements of capitalism as private ownership and the profit motive.

The forces Gorbachev unleashed changed Soviet life more quickly than he had imagined. Various Soviet republics began agitating for independence. Reformers demanded that Gorbachev move even faster to restructure the economy, as shortages in food and consumer goods grew severe. Gorbachev attempted through it all both to lead the reform forces he had helped unleash and, simultaneously, to placate conservative hard-liners who believed he was

CROSSING THE BERLIN WALL, NOVEMBER 9, 1989 Jubilant Germans swarm over the infamous Berlin Wall, which had divided the city since 1961, on the day the East German government opened the gates. A few months later, the wall was gone and Germany was on the way to reunification.

moving too fast. He insisted that he was still a communist and that he was only attempting to perfect the Soviet system.

One dramatic result of the Gorbachev reforms was the collapse of the Soviet empire, which occurred with startling speed in 1989. In the space of a few months, every nation in the so-called Soviet bloc in Central and Eastern Europe—Poland, Hungary, Czechoslovakia, Bulgaria, Romania, and East Germany—either overthrew its government or forced it to transform itself into an essentially noncommunist (and in some cases, actively anticommunist) regime. The Communist parties of Europe all but collapsed. And in every case, Gorbachev and the Soviet Union not only refused to oppose but actively encouraged the changes. Perhaps the most dramatic moment in the transformation of Europe came on November 9, 1989, when the government of East Germany began dismantling the notorious Berlin Wall, for nearly thirty years a symbol of the Cold War, and allowed free passage between the two Germanys. Within a year, German reunification—which only a few months earlier had seemed at best a distant dream—was a reality.

The challenges to communism were not successful everywhere. In May 1989, students in China began staging large demonstrations calling for greater democratization, which the post-Mao government had long been promising but had never delivered. But as the democracy movement grew, hard-line leaders seized control of the Chinese government and sent military forces to crush the uprising. The result was a massacre on June 3, 1989, in Tiananmen Square in Beijing. A still-unknown number of demonstrators, perhaps several thousand, died. The assault crushed the democracy movement, restored hard-liners to power, and inaugurated a period of harsh repression, to which the Bush administration reacted with seeming indifference.

But the events in China had no counterpart elsewhere in the communist world. And in 1991, communism began to collapse at the site of its birth: the Soviet Union itself. An unsuccessful coup by hard-line Soviet leaders on August 19 precipitated a dramatic unraveling of communist power. Within days, not only did the coup itself collapse in the face of resistance from the public and, more important, crucial elements within the military; not only did Mikhail Gorbachev return to power; but the forces of disunion that had been gathering strength for several years made a quantum leap forward. It soon became evident that the legitimacy of both the Communist party and the central Soviet government had been fatally injured. By the end of 1991, every republic in the Soviet Union had declared independence; Boris Yeltsin, the president of Russia, in effect outlawed the Communist party—barring it from owning property or playing any meaningful role in the life of the largest and most important republic in the Soviet Union; and the Soviet government, powerless to stop the fragmentation, had collapsed. On December 25, 1991, Mikhail Gorbachev resigned as president; and the U.S.S.R., nearly 75 years after its birth, ceased to exist.

In the face of these dramatic changes, American foreign policy, which for over four decades had remained securely tied to the premises of "containment," suddenly seemed obsolete. And while a new strategic doctrine to replace containment did not quickly emerge, the pattern of American international behavior began inevitably to change.

The Gorbachev regime had all but repudiated the arms race with the United States in the late 1980s and had been working energetically to produce arms control agreements well before Bush entered office. In 1988, the two superpowers signed a treaty eliminating American and Soviet intermediate-range nuclear forces from Europe. Over the next four years, the United States and the Soviet Union moved rapidly toward even more far-reaching arms reduction agreements, including major troop reductions in Europe and the dismantling of new categories of strategic weapons. At the same time, the nations of the former Soviet Union and the new, noncommunist governments in Central and Eastern Europe were appealing to the West for economic assistance through subsidies, loans, and investments; the United States, beset with its own fiscal and economic difficulties, was slow to respond.

The Gulf War

The events of 1989–1991 left the United States in the unanticipated position of being the only real "superpower" in the world. The Soviet Union and its successor nations were too embroiled in their own problems to play a major international role any longer. Germany and Japan, the emerging economic superpowers, had no significant military strength. China remained largely isolated from international affairs. The Bush administration, therefore, had to consider what to do with America's formidable political and military power in a world in which the major justification for that power—the Soviet threat—was now removed.

The events of 1990–1991 suggested two possible answers, both of which had some effect on policy. One was that the United States would reduce its military strength dramatically and concentrate its energies and resources on pressing domestic problems. And, indeed, there was considerable movement in that direction both in Congress and within the administration. The other was that America would continue to use its power actively, not to fight communism but to defend its economic interests. Once again, that drew the United States into the perilous politics of the Middle East.

On August 2, 1990, the armed forces of Iraq invaded and quickly overwhelmed their small, oil-rich neighbor, the emirate of Kuwait. Saddam Hussein, the militaristic leader of Iraq, soon announced that he was annexing Kuwait and set out to entrench his forces there. After some initial indecision, the Bush administration agreed to join with other nations to force Iraq out of Kuwait—through the pressure of economic sanctions if possible, through military force if necessary. Within a few weeks, Bush had persuaded virtually every important government in the world, including almost all the Arab and Islamic states, to join in a United Nations–sanctioned trade embargo of Iraq. That meant the Iraqis, whose economy was already weak, would be unable to sell any oil on world markets and would be unable to buy any products from abroad or generate hard currency with which to pay their massive debts.

At the same time, the United States and its allies (including the British, French, Egyptians, and Saudis) began deploying a massive military force along the border between Kuwait and Saudi Arabia. The force ultimately reached 690,000 troops (540,000 of them American) and assembled the largest and most sophisticated collection of military technology ever used in warfare.

By late 1990, the Bush administration was clearly losing patience with the sanctions and was preparing for war. On November 29, the United Nations, at the request of the United States, voted to authorize military action to expel Iraq from Kuwait if Iraq did not leave by January 15, 1991. On January 12, both houses of Congress voted to authorize the use of force against Iraq, although many Democrats opposed the resolution, arguing that sanctions should be given more time to work. And on January 16, American and allied air forces began a massive bombardment of Iraqi forces in Kuwait and of military and industrial installations in Iraq itself.

The allied bombing continued for six weeks, meeting only token resistance from the small Iraqi air force and ground defenses. On February 23, allied (primarily American) forces under the command of General Norman Schwarzkopf began a major ground offensive—not primarily against the heavily entrenched Iraqi forces along the Kuwait border, as expected, but into Iraq itself. The allied armies encountered almost no resistance and suffered only light casualties (141 fatalities). There were no reliable figures for the number of Iraqi casualties, but official estimates of deaths ranged as high as 100,000. On February 28, Iraq announced its acceptance of allied terms for a cease-fire, and the brief war came to an end.

The quick and relatively painless victory over Iraq was highly popular in the United States. But the longer range results of the Gulf War were more ambiguous. The tyrannical regime of Saddam Hussein survived, militarily weakened perhaps, but still capable of challenging the United States and its allies when they tried to enforce the terms of the 1991 ceasefire. By late 1992, there was considerable evidence that Iraq's efforts to construct nuclear weapons had not been as decisively thwarted by the allied bombing as the Bush administration had claimed at the time; the Baghdad government was, many believed, now accelerating its efforts to develop an atomic bomb. Kuwait, in the meantime, returned to the control of its prewar government, an undemocratic monarchy increasingly unpopular with its own people.

The Search for a Domestic Agenda

President Bush's popularity reached a record high in the immediate aftermath of the Gulf War. For a time, over 90 percent of those surveyed claimed to approve of the way he was handling his office—the highest approval rating in the history of polling. But as the nation's attention turned back to domestic issues, and as the recession that began late in 1990 persisted into 1992, the president's popularity declined with startling speed. That was in part because of the widespread perception that Bush was uninterested in domestic issues and had no ideas or plans for dealing with them.

The Bush administration faced several obstacles in promoting an effective domestic agenda. First, it inherited a staggering burden of debt and a federal deficit that had been out of control for nearly a decade. Any domestic agenda that required significant federal spending was, therefore, incompatible with the president's pledge to reduce the deficit and his 1988 campaign promise of "no new taxes." Second, President Bush faced a Democratic Congress, which was not, on the whole, disposed to cooperate with him. Third, the president was constantly concerned about the right wing of his own party and, in his eagerness to ingratiate himself with that group, took firm positions on divisive cultural issues such as abortion and affirmative action that further damaged his ability to work with Congress.

Despite this political stalemate, Congress and the White House managed on occasion to agree on significant measures. They cooperated in producing a plan to salvage the floundering savings and loan industry. In 1990, the president agreed to a significant tax increase as part of a multiyear "budget package" designed to reduce the deficit significantly—although in doing so, the president had to repudiate his most prominent 1988 campaign promise. In 1991, after almost two years of acrimonious debate, the president and Congress agreed on a civil-rights bill to combat job discrimination.

But the most serious domestic problem facing the Bush administration was one to which neither the president nor Congress had any answer. The recession that began in 1990 slowly increased its grip on the national economy in 1991 and receded only slightly in 1992. Because of the enormous level of debt that corporations (and individuals) had accumulated in the 1980s, the recession caused an unusual number of bankruptcies. It created a growing frustration among middle-class Americans and growing pressure on the government to address such problems as the rising cost of health care. And as the Bush administration responded to these problems with indecision and passivity, the president's popularity eroded.

The Election of 1992

Because the early maneuvering for the presidential election of 1992 occurred when President Bush's popularity remained high, many leading Democrats declined to run. Bill Clinton, the young, five-term governor of Arkansas, emerged early as the front-runner among the remaining candidates by virtue of a skillful campaign that emphasized broad economic issues over the racial and cultural questions that had so divided Democrats in the past. Clinton survived a bruising primary campaign and a series of damaging personal controversies to capture his party's nomination. George Bush withstood a primary challenge from the conservative journalist Pat Buchanan to become the Republican nominee again. In the meantime, Ross Perot, a blunt, forthright Texas billionaire, launched an independent presidential campaign by appealing to public unhappiness with the political system in general and the fiscal crisis in particular. He produced an astonishing popular response; at several moments in the spring, he led both Clinton and Bush in public opinion polls. In July, as he began to face hostile scrutiny in the press, he abruptly withdrew from the race. But early in October he re-entered and regained much of his earlier support.

After a campaign in which the economy and the president's unpopularity were the major issues, Bill Clinton won a decisive victory over Bush and Perot. He received 43 percent of the vote in the three-way race, to the president's 38 percent (the lowest percentage for an incumbent since Taft in 1912) and Perot's 19 percent (the best showing for a third-party or independent candidate since Theodore Roosevelt in 1912). Clinton won 370 electoral votes to Bush's 168; Perot won none. Democrats retained solid control of both houses of Congress. And a new administration prepared to face the mounting problems of a rapidly changing society.

MODERN TIMES

Much of the anxiety that beset American life beginning in the 1970s, and much of the conservative sentiment that emerged to dominate American politics in the 1980s and early 1990s, was a result of jarring public events that left many men and women shaken and uncertain. But much of it was a result as well of significant changes in the nature and behavior of American society.

The Graying of America

One of the most fundamental changes in American life in the postliberal era was the new profile of the American population. After decades of steady growth, the nation's birth rate began to decline in the 1970s and remained low through the 1980s and early 1990s. In 1970, there were 18.4 births for every 1,000 people in the population. By 1975, the rate had declined to 14.6, the lowest in the twentieth century. And despite a modest increase in the 1980s, the rate remained below 16 throughout the decade. The declining

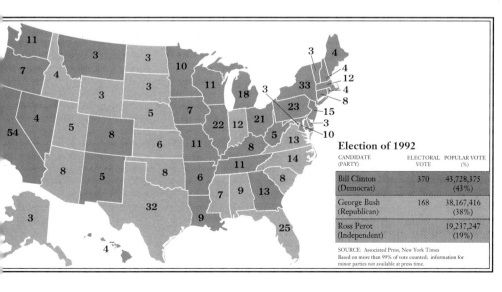

Election of 1992

CANDIDATE (PARTY)	ELECTORAL VOTE	POPULAR VOTE (%)
Bill Clinton (Democrat)	370	43,728,375 (43%)
George Bush (Republican)	168	38,167,416 (38%)
Ross Perot (Independent)		19,237,247 (19%)

SOURCE: Associated Press, New York Times
Based on more than 99% of vote counted; information for minor parties not available at press time.

birth rate and a significant increase in life expectancy produced a substantial increase in the proportion of elderly citizens. Over 12 percent of the population was more than sixty-five years old by 1990, as compared with 8 percent in 1970. That figure was projected to rise to over 20 percent by the end of the century. The median age in 1990 was 32.9 years, as compared with 28 in 1970. The aging of the population had important, if still not fully understood, implications. It was, for example, a cause of the increasing costliness of Social Security pensions. It meant rapidly increasing health costs, both for the federal Medicare system and for private hospitals and insurance companies.

Hispanics, Asians, and the New Immigration

Perhaps the most striking demographic change in America in the 1970s and 1980s, and the one likely to have the farthest-reaching consequences, was the enormous change in both the extent and the character of immigation. The nation's immigration quotas expanded significantly in those years (partly to accommodate refugees from Southeast Asia and other nations), allowing more newcomers to enter the United States legally than at any point since the beginning of the twentieth century. In the 1970s, more than 4 million legal immigrants entered the United States. In the 1980s, that number rose to more than 6 million. When the uncounted but very large numbers of illegal immigrants in those years are included, the wave of immigration in the twenty years after 1970 was the largest of the twentieth century.

Equally striking was the character of the new immigration. The Immigration Reform Act of 1965 (see p. 810) had eliminated quotas based on national origin; from then on, newcomers from regions other than Latin America were generally admitted on a first-come, first-served basis. In 1965, 90 percent of the immigrants to the United States came from Europe. Twenty years later, only 10 percent of the new arrivals were Europeans. The extent and character of the new immigration was causing a dramatic change in the composition of the American population. Already by the end of the 1980s, people of white European background constituted under 80 percent of the population (as opposed to 90 percent a half-century before). It seemed likely that by the middle of the twenty-first century, whites of European heritage would constitute less than 50 percent of the population.

Particularly important to the new immigration were two groups: Hispanics (or Latinos) and Asians. Both had been significant segments of the

A M E R I C A N   V O I C E S

A Vietnamese Immigrant
Describes Her Life in America,
1984

HERE IN AMERICA, I just remain. I don't change my traditional ways. . . . My children have adapted to American customs in hair styles and dress. . . . The older women don't change much, and most of the older men don't change either.

Over here, for older people, we receive money from the government; if not, we would die of starvation because we are older and don't know what to do. In Vietnam, we have less fear of survival, but over here, I'm afraid that when I get older I'll have to go into a nursing home to stay there, because all of my children are working. . . . Old age here is scary. . . .

The difference is that over here children do not obey their parents; in Vietnam, they obeyed us more. Over here, whenever we say something, they like to argue about it. . . . Things we consider to be right they consider wrong. Like a wife they select whom we don't like. They argue with us, against it, saying that it's right for them and that they will take the responsibility for it. They claim it's their *right* and that we don't have the right to tell them what to do. It is just like we are strangers; they won't let us interfere. . . . Our children do not keep the old traditions. They live apart from one another.

SOURCE: Reprinted from *Hearts of Sorrow: Vietnamese-American Lives*, by James M. Freeman, with the permission of the publisher, Stanford University Press. © 1989 by the Board of Trustees of the Leland Stanford Junior University.

American population for many decades: Hispanics since the very beginning of the nation's history, Asians since the waves of Chinese and Japanese immigration in the nineteenth century. But both groups experienced enormous, indeed unprecedented, growth after 1965.

People from Latin America constituted more than a third of the total number of legal immigrants to the United States in every year after 1965—and a much larger proportion of the total number of illegal immigrants. In California and the Southwest, in particular, they became a major presence. There were also substantial Hispanic populations in Illinois, New York, and Florida. High birth rates among Hispanic communities already in the United States further increased their numbers. In the 1980 census, 6 percent of the population was listed as being of Hispanic origin. The 1990 census showed an increase to 9 percent.

In the 1980s and early 1990s, Asian immigrants arrived in even greater numbers than Hispanics. They constituted more than 40 percent of the total of legal newcomers. They came in particularly large numbers from Vietnam, Thailand, Cambodia, Laos, the Philippines, Korea, and India. By 1990, there were more than 7 million Asian-Americans in the United States, more than twice the number of ten years before. Like Hispanics, they were concentrated mainly in large cities and in the West.

Many of the new Asian immigrants were refugees, including Vietnamese driven from their homes in the aftermath of the disastrous war in which the United States had so long been involved. Large numbers of "boat people"—Vietnamese refugees who put to sea in crowded boats without any clear destination—ultimately found their way to the United States, usually after enduring terrible dangers and hardships. But many Asian immigrants were highly educated professionals seeking greater opportunities in the United States.

As with most new immigrant groups, Asian-Americans found adjustment to the very different culture of the United States difficult and disorienting. They also experienced resentment and discrimination. Whites feared Asian competition in economic activities that they had been accustomed to controlling. There were, for example, heated disputes between white and Vietnamese shrimpers on the Gulf Coast in Texas, Mississippi, and Louisiana. Some African-Americans resented the success of Asian merchants in black neighborhoods. In New York, for example, racial tensions led to a black boycott of some Korean grocery stores in African-American neighborhoods in 1990. Resentment of Asian-Americans may have been a result, in part, of their remarkable success. Indeed, some Asian groups (most notably Indians, Japanese, and Chinese) were by the 1980s earning larger average annual incomes than were whites. Chinese- and Japanese-Americans consistently ranked at or near the top of high-school and college classes in the 1980s. That was in part because Asian-American communities contained significant numbers of people who had been involved in business and the professions before coming to America and had arrived with a high degree of expertise. They also placed a high value on education.

Drug Abuse, AIDS, and Homelessness

The new immigrants of the 1980s and 1990s arrived in cities being ravaged by new and deadly epidemics. One was a dramatic increase in drug use, which by the end of the 1980s was penetrating nearly every community in the nation. The enormous demand for drugs, and particularly for "crack" cocaine, spawned what was in effect a multi-billion-dollar industry; and those reaping the enormous profits of the illegal trade fought strenuously and often savagely to protect their positions.

The Bush administration, and virtually all political figures, spoke heatedly about the need for a "war on drugs," but in the absence of significant funding for such programs, public efforts appeared to have little effect. There were signs at the end of the 1980s that drug use was in decline among middle-class people, but the epidemic showed no signs of abating in the poor urban neighborhoods, where it was doing the most severe damage.

The drug epidemic was directly related to another scourge of the cities in the 1980s: the epidemic spread of a new and lethal disease first documented in 1981 and soon named AIDS (acquired immune deficiency syndrome). AIDS is the product of the HIV virus, which is transmitted by the exchange of bodily fluids (blood or semen). The virus gradually destroys the body's immune system and makes its victims highly vulnerable to a number of diseases (particularly to various forms of cancer and pneumonia) to which they would otherwise have a natural resistance. Although those infected with the virus can live for many years without developing the disease, once they do become ill they are virtually certain to die from it. The first victims of AIDS (and in the early 1990s the group among whom cases remained the most numerous) were homosexual men. But by the late 1980s, as the gay community began to take preventive measures, the most rapid increase in the spread of the disease occurred among intravenous drug users, many of them heterosexuals, who spread the virus by sharing contaminated hypodermic needles. By the early 1990s, government agencies were estimating that between 1 and 1.5 million Americans were infected with the HIV virus. (Worldwide, the figure was approximately 10 million.) Nearly 200,000

Americans had actually contracted AIDS, and nearly 130,000 had died. Although by 1990 researchers had discovered several drugs that could delay or limit some effects of AIDS, neither a cure nor a vaccine seemed imminent.

The increasing scarcity of housing for low-income people contributed to another urban crisis of the 1980s and 1990s: homelessness. There had always been homeless men and women in most major cities; but their numbers were clearly increasing at an alarming rate in the face of rising housing costs, severe cutbacks in federal support for public housing, the closing of mental health institutions, reduced welfare assistance, the declining availability of unskilled jobs, and the increasing weakness of family structures. The phenomenon of tens of thousands of homeless people at large in the cities put pressure on municipal governments to provide shelter and assistance for the indigent; but in an age of fiscal stringency and greatly reduced federal aid, cities found it difficult to produce responses adequate to the dimensions of the crisis.

Nonwhites in the Postliberal Era

Nonwhites in America moved along several very different paths in the 1980s and early 1990s. On the one hand, there were increased opportunities for advancement available to those who were in a position to take advantage of them, a result in large part of the legal and political gains of the 1960s and 1970s. On the other hand, as the industrial economy declined and government services dwindled, there was a growing sense of helplessness and despair among the larger groups of nonwhites who continued to find themselves barred from upward mobility.

For the black middle class, which by the 1980s constituted nearly a third of the entire black population of America, the progress was striking. Economic disparities between black and white professionals did not vanish, but they diminished substantially. African-American families moved into affluent urban communities and suburbs—at times as neighbors of whites, often as residents of predominantly black suburban communities. The number of blacks attending college rose by 350 percent in the decade following the passage of the civil-rights acts (as opposed to the 150 percent increase among whites); by the early 1990s the percentage of black high-school graduates going on to college was nearly the same as that of white high-school graduates (although a far smaller proportion of blacks than whites managed to complete high school).

But the rise of a black middle class served also to accentuate the increasingly desperate plight of other African-Americans. This growing "underclass," as some called it, felt the impact of deindustrialization and urban decline with special force. In the early 1990s, more than one-third of all black families lived in poverty. (More than one-fourth of all the Hispanic families counted by the government likewise lived in poverty—as well as many more who remained uncounted.) At the same time, just under 11 percent of white families could be officially classified as poor.

The black family structure suffered from and contributed to the dislocations of urban poverty. There was a dramatic increase in the number of single-parent, female-headed black households. In the early 1990s, over half of all black children were born into single-parent families, as opposed to only 15 percent of white children. In 1960, only 20 percent of black children had lived in single-parent homes.

Nonwhites were victimized by many things in the changing social and economic climate of the 1980s. Among them was a growing impatience with affirmative action and other programs designed to advance their fortunes, as well as a growing reluctance among federal officials after 1980 to move aggressively to enforce affirmative action guidelines. Nonwhites also suffered from a steady decline in the number of unskilled jobs in the economy. They suffered from the deterioration of public education and other social services, which made it more difficult for them to find opportunities for advancement. And they suffered, in some cases, from a sense of futility and despair, born of years of entrapment in brutal urban ghettoes. By the early 1990s, several generations of nonwhites had grown to maturity living in destitute neighborhoods where welfare or crime (especially drug dealing) were the only means of support for some people. Residents of such neighborhoods also lived with the constant threat of gang violence and other mayhem; for young black males in the early 1990s, murder was the leading cause of death. They also lived with an increasing incidence of drug addiction and AIDs.

The frustration of the inner cities created a harsh new politics among some African-Americans—angry, confrontational, and intentionally abrasive. New black leaders emerged from the ghettoes who rejected the accommodationist rhetoric of the civil-rights movement and even the more militant rhetoric of Jesse Jackson. Instead, they argued that white society was incurably racist and insisted that African-Americans must fight for some form of autonomy. At one level, therefore, American society was becoming more successfully integrated than ever before as the white and black middle classes learned to live and work together reasonably harmoniously. At another level, however, the nation was experiencing a new kind of racial polarization, in which large numbers of African-Americans were living in virtual isolation from white society and coming to view it as fundamentally hostile.

The despair that had come to grip much of black America became graphically and tragically evident in the spring of 1992 in response to events in Los Angeles. In 1991, a group of white Los Angeles policemen had been videotaped savagely beating a black man, Rodney King, as they arrested him for a minor crime after an automobile chase. The tape precipitated the prosecution of the officers involved. In late April 1992, a white jury acquitted the policemen of virtually all charges—a decision that produced shock and disbelief among African-Americans (and many white Americans) through-out the nation. It also produced the worst urban violence of the twentieth century.

In south central Los Angeles, the predominantly African-American neighborhood where many of the poorest residents of the city lived, violence began the night of the verdict and continued for several days. By the time it subsided, more than 50 people were dead and hundreds of businesses and homes were gutted by fire. Smaller uprisings occurred in other cities at the same time. The Los Angeles riot drew attention once again to the failure of the United States to solve the problems of race and urban poverty. But in an age of slow economic growth, the prospects for a decisive public response seemed bleak.

The New Religion and the New Right

In the 1960s, many social critics had predicted the virtual extinction of religious influence in American life. But America in the 1970s experienced the beginning of a major religious revival, perhaps the most powerful since the second Great Awakening of the early nineteenth century. It continued in various forms into the 1990s.

The most important feature of this new awakening was the rise of evangelical Christianity. Evangelicals had been gathering strength for many years, and especially since the early 1950s, when fundamentalists such as Billy Graham and pentecostals such as Oral Roberts had begun to attract huge national (and international) followings—largely a result of their effec-tive use of television—for their energetic revivalism. By the 1980s, more than 70 million Americans (nearly a third of the nation) described them-selves as "born-again" Christians—men and women who had established a "direct personal relationship with Jesus." One of them had occupied the White House—Jimmy Carter, who during the 1976 campaign had talked proudly of his own "conversion experience" and who continued openly to proclaim his "born-again" Christian faith during his years in office. For Jimmy Carter, evangelical Christianity had formed the basis for his commitment to racial and economic justice and to world peace. To many others, however, the message of the new religion was very different—but no less political. In the 1980s, some Christian evangelicals became active on the political and cultural right.

The new political right, of which evangelical Christians were only a part, enjoyed rapid growth in the 1970s and early 1980s. The New Right displayed a remarkable organizing zeal—particularly in launching mass-mailing campaigns of staggering size and raising great sums of money to support conservative efforts. It also injected a series of moral and cultural issues into political debate, as the controversy in 1989 and 1990 over federal support for the arts suggested. Several provocative art exhibits—among them a collection of photographs by Robert Mapplethorpe, some of which contained graphic depictions of homosexual behavior—offended conservatives (as well as many others). The controversy over the content of the exhibits soon extended to a dispute over their funding. Both the artists and the museums displaying their work had received grants from the National Endowment for the Arts (NEA), which now came under attack from Senator Jesse Helms of North Carolina and other conservative leaders. For a time, the future of the NEA seemed in danger. Ultimately, Congress agreed to extend its life, but political pressures continued to bedevil the agency.

The power of the New Right in the early 1980s represented the culmination of many decades of steadily growing conservative sentiment, which had triumphed in 1980, when the right became a central force in propelling Ronald Reagan into the White House. But despite its conspicuous strength, the new conservatism was difficult to define. The most active groups within the New Right were not conservatives of traditional stripe—people associated with and supportive of the business community, defending the position of established economic and social elites. They were, rather, middle-class and lower-middle-class people, whose political demands centered more around social and cultural issues than economic ones, who seemed to exhibit not so much a staid conservatism as a right-wing populism.

By the beginning of the 1990s, the power of the New Right seemed to be in decline in some areas. A series of scandals discredited several leading evangelical ministers. Other factions of the New Right also began to experience hard times after the election of the centrist George Bush and during the recession of 1991–1992, when some working people began returning to a concern with traditional economic issues. Still, the right remained a significant force within the Republican party and a constant factor in the calculation of all those (among them President Bush) who hoped to secure a base within it. The surprising strength of the Louisiana politician David Duke, a former Nazi and Ku Klux Klan leader who received 39 percent of the vote in a 1991 gubernatorial race, suggested the tenacity of right-wing positions on race and religion.

Battles Against Feminism and Abortion

Among other things, the New Right continued to display impressive strength in launching an intense assault on feminism. Leaders of the New Right had campaigned successfully against the proposed Equal Rights Amendment to the Constitution. And they played a central role in the most

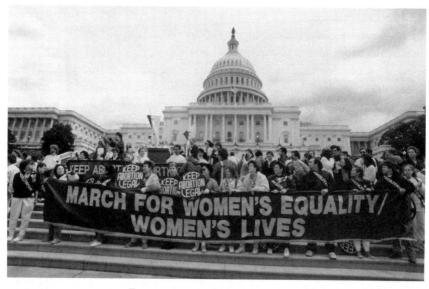

THE ABORTION BATTLE For many years, it was opponents of abortion who staged demonstrations each year in Washington. In the late 1980s, however, as the "right to life" movement made significant political and judicial gains, supporters of "choice" began staging large demonstrations of their own. This one, in March 1989, was part of a much larger march of 300,000 people organized by the National Organization for Women.

divisive issue of the late 1980s and early 1990s: the controversy over abortion rights. (See pp. 850–851.)

For those who favored allowing women to choose to terminate unwanted pregnancies, the Supreme Court's decision in *Roe* v. *Wade* (1973) had seemed to settle the question. By the 1980s, abortion was the most commonly performed surgical procedure in the country. But at the same time, opposition to abortion was creating a powerful grass-roots movement. The right-to-life movement, as it called itself, found its most fervent supporters among Catholics; and indeed, the Catholic church itself lent its institutional authority to the battle against legalized abortion. Religious doctrine also motivated the antiabortion stance of Mormons, fundamentalist Christians, and other groups. The opposition of other antiabortion activists had less to do with religion than with their commitment to traditional notions of family and gender relations. To them, abortion was a particularly offensive part of a much larger assault by feminists on the role of women as wives and mothers. It was also, many foes contended, a form of murder. Fetuses, they claimed, were human beings who had a "right to life" from the moment of conception.

Although the right-to-life movement was persistent in its demand for a reversal of *Roe* v. *Wade* or, barring that, a constitutional amendment banning abortion, it also attacked abortion in more limited ways, at its most vulnerable points. In the 1970s, Congress and many state legislatures began barring the use of public funds to pay for abortions, thus making them almost inaccessible for many poor women. The Reagan and Bush administrations imposed further restrictions on federal funding and even on the right of doctors in federally funded clinics to give patients any information on abortion.

The changing composition of the Supreme Court in the 1980s and 1990s (which saw six new conservative justices named by Presidents Reagan and Bush) renewed the right-to-life movement's hopes for a reversal of *Roe* v. *Wade*. In *Webster* v. *Reproductive Health Services* (1989), the Court upheld a Missouri law that prohibited any institution receiving state funds from performing abortions, whether or not those funds were used to finance the abortions. Hopes were high among anti-abortion forces that the Court would soon repudiate *Roe* v. *Wade* itself. To the surprise of people on both sides of the issue, however, the Court pulled back. In 1992, ruling (in *Planned Parenthood* v. *Casey*) on a Pennsylvania law that imposed still more restrictions on abortion, the Court upheld many of the restrictions but, in a precarious 5 to 4 decision, explicitly reaffirmed the validity of *Roe* v. *Wade* itself. Three justices appointed by Reagan and Bush voted with the majority.

The changing political and judicial climate of the late 1980s mobilized defenders of abortion as never before. They called themselves the "pro-choice" movement, because they were defending not so much abortion itself as every woman's right to choose whether and when to bear a child. It quickly became clear that the pro-choice movement was in many parts of the country at least as strong as, and in some areas much stronger than, the right-to-life movement.

The abortion controversy at times overshadowed other efforts by feminists to protect and expand the rights of women. But such efforts continued. Women's organizations and many individual women worked strenuously in the 1980s and 1990s to raise awareness of sexual harassment in the workplace, with considerable success. Colleges, universities, government agencies, and even many corporations established strict new standards of behavior for their employees in dealing with members of the opposite sex and created grievance procedures for those who believed they had been harassed.

Both the achievements and the limits of the feminists' progress on this issue were evident in the sensational controversy in 1991 over Judge Clarence Thomas, President Bush's nominee for a seat on the Supreme Court. Late in the confirmation proceedings, accusations of sexual harassment from Anita Hill, a law professor and a former employee of Thomas, became public. Thomas's accuser testified before the Senate Judiciary Committee and, in doing so, dramatically polarized both the Senate and the nation. Feminists and others tended to believe the accusations and hailed the accuser for drawing national attention to the issue of harassment; but many Americans, apparently, did not believe her—or at least concluded that the alleged activities should not disqualify Thomas from serving on the Court. Thomas was ultimately confirmed by a narrow margin.

The Changing Left and the New Environmentalism

The New Left of the 1960s and early 1970s did not disappear after the end of the war in Vietnam, but it faded rapidly. Many of the students who had fought in its battles grew up, left school, and entered conventional careers. Some radical leaders, disillusioned by the unresponsiveness of American society to their demands, resignedly gave up the struggle and chose instead to work "within the system." Marxist critiques continued to flourish in academic circles, but to much of the public they came to appear dated and irrelevant—particularly as Marxist governments collapsed in disrepute beginning in 1989.

Yet a left of sorts did survive, giving evidence in the process of how greatly the nation's political climate had changed. Where 1960s activists had rallied to protest racism, poverty, and war, their counterparts in the 1980s and 1990s more often fought to stop the proliferation of nuclear weapons and power plants, save the wilderness, protect endangered species, limit reckless economic development, and otherwise protect the environment.

Public concerns about the environment had arisen intermittently since the beginning of the industrial era and had been growing in intensity ever since 1962, when the publication of Rachel Carson's *Silent Spring* aroused widespread public concern about the effect of insecticides on the natural world. Several highly visible environmental catastrophes in the 1960s and 1970s greatly increased that concern. Among them was a major oil spill off Santa Barbara, California, in 1969; the discovery of large deposits of improperly disposed toxic wastes in a residential community in upstate New York in 1978; and a frightening accident at the nuclear power plant at Three Mile Island, Pennsylvania, in 1979. These and other revelations of the extent to which human progress threatened the natural world helped produce a major popular movement.

In the spring of 1970, a nationwide "Earth Day" signaled the beginning of the environmental movement. It differed markedly from the "conservation" movements of earlier years. Modern environmentalists shared the concerns of such earlier figures as John Muir and Gifford Pinchot about preserving some areas of the wilderness and carefully managing the exploitation of resources. But the new activists went much further, basing their positions on the developing field of ecology, the study of the connections among all components of an environment. Toxic wastes, air and water pollution, the destruction of forests, the extinction of species: these were not separate, isolated problems. All elements of the earth's environment were intimately and delicately linked together, ecologists claimed. Damaging any one of those elements risked damaging all the others. Only by adopting a new social ethic, in which economic growth became less important than ecological health, could the human race hope to survive in a healthy world.

In the twenty years after the first Earth Day, environmental issues gained increasing attention and support. Although the federal government often displayed limited interest in the subject, environmentalists won a series of significant battles, mostly at the local level. They blocked the construction of roads, airports, and other projects (including American development of the supersonic transport airplane, or SST) that they claimed would be ecologically dangerous. By the end of the 1980s, the sense of urgency had grown, as scientists began warning that the release of certain industrial pollutants (most notably chlorofluorocarbons) into the atmosphere was depleting the ozone layer of the earth's atmosphere, which protects the globe from the sun's most dangerous rays. They warned, too, of the related danger of global warming, a rise in the earth's temperature as a result of emissions from the burning of fossil fuels (coal and oil).

The concern for the environment, the opposition to nuclear power, the resistance to economic development—all were reflections of a more fundamental characteristic of the post-Vietnam left. In a sharp break from the nation's long commitment to growth and progress, many dissidents argued that only by limiting growth and curbing traditional forms of progress could society hope to survive.

Some of these critics of the "idea of progress" expressed a gloomy resignation, urging a lowering of social expectations and predicting an inevitable deterioration in the quality of life. Other advocates of restraint believed that change did not require decline: human beings could live more

DOONESBURY Cartoonist Garry Trudeau created his celebrated comic strip in the 1960s while he was an undergraduate at Yale University. In this 1984 cartoon, Trudeau uses his title character, Mike Doonesbury, to illustrate the transformation of 1960s idealists into 1980s "yuppies."

comfortably and more happily if they learned to respect the limits imposed on them by their environment. But in either case, such arguments evoked strong opposition from conservatives and others, who ridiculed the no-growth ideology as an expression of defeatism and despair. Ronald Reagan, in particular, made an attack on the idea of "limits" central to his political success.

The Culture Wars

Few controversies attracted more attention in the late 1980s and early 1990s than the battle over what became known as "multiculturalism." Multicul-turalism meant different things to different people, but at its core was an effort to legitimize the cultural pluralism of the rapidly diversifying Ameri-can population. That meant acknowledging that "American culture," which had long been defined primarily by white males of European descent, also included other traditions: female, African-American, Indian, and increas-ingly in the late twentieth-century Hispanic and Asian. Although such demands were often controversial, especially when they became the basis of assaults on traditional academic curricula, much greater acrimony emerged out of efforts by some revisionists to portray traditional western culture as inherently racist and imperialistic. A prolonged, if somewhat muted, dis-pute over how to commemorate the 500th anniversary of Columbus's first voyage to the "New World" illustrated how sharply ideas of multicultural-ism had changed the way Americans discussed their past. In 1892, the Columbian anniversary had been the occasion of boisterous national cele-bration—and a great world's fair in Chicago. In 1992, it produced agonizing debates over the impact of the European discovery on native peoples; and the only world's fair was in Spain.

Debates over multiculturalism and related issues helped produce an increasingly strained climate in academia and in the larger American intel-lectual world. People on the left complained that the ascendancy of conser-vative politics placed new and intolerable limits on freedom of expression, as the effort to restrict NEA grants to controversial artists suggests. Many on the right complained equally vigorously of a tyranny of "political cor-rectness," by which feminists, cultural radicals, and others introduced a new form of intolerance to public discourse in the name of defending the rights of women and minorities.

The controversies surrounding multiculturalism and "political correct-ness" were illustrations of a painful change in the character of American society. Traditional patterns of authority faced challenges from women, minorities, and others. The liberal belief in tolerance and assimilation was fraying in the face of the growing cultural separatism of some ethnic and racial groups. Confidence in the nation's future was declining, and with it confidence in the capacity of American society to provide justice and opportunity to all its citizens.

The American Future

The American people had suffered many trials and disappointments since the heady days at the end of World War II, when an "American Century" seemed about to dawn, and since the mid-1950s, when the United States appeared poised for a prolonged era of domestic tranquillity, economic abundance, and international preeminence. By the early 1990s, America, like many other nations, was faced with the problems of a faltering industrial economy, an increasingly diverse and contentious population, and growing dangers to the environment that threatened the health of the entire world.

At the same time, however, the great changes in world affairs of the late 1980s and early 1990s seemed to vindicate one of the most important assumptions behind America's 200-year experiment in democracy: that the desire for personal freedom is a basic human impulse that even decades of repressive government cannot extinguish. The dramatically different world order that was emerging from the upheavals of the late twentieth century was filled with dangers. But the United States, despite its many problems, remained what it had long been: one of the stablest, wealthiest, and most resilient societies in modern history. At the dawn of a new era, the United States—whose example had done much to fuel the forces of change—faced the challenge of preserving and extending its own democracy in the face of major new perils and great new opportunities.

APPENDICES

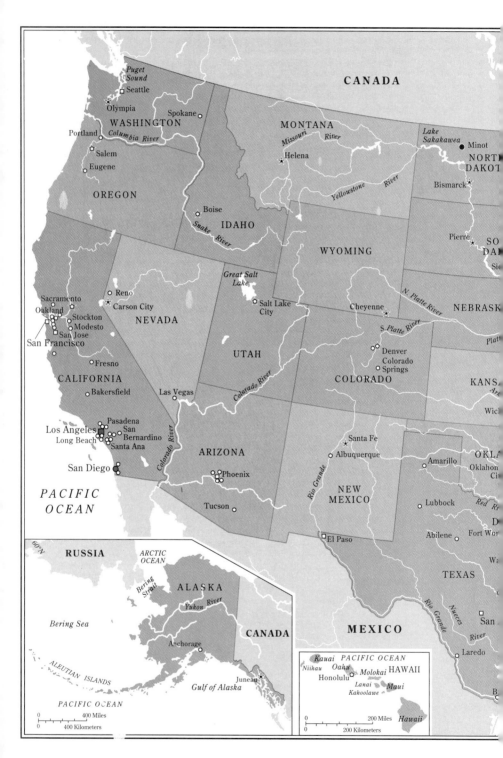

CANADA

Puget
Sound
□ Seattle
★ Olympia
Spokane ○
WASHINGTON
Portland ○   Columbia River
Salem ○
Eugene ○
OREGON

MONTANA
Missouri   River
Helena ●
Lake
Sakakawea
Minot ●
NORTH
DAKOTA
Yellowstone   River
Bismarck ★

Boise ○
IDAHO
Snake   River
WYOMING
Cheyenne ★
N. Platte River
Pierre ★
SOUTH
DAKOTA
Sio

NEBRASKA

Reno ○
Carson City ★
Sacramento ○
Oakland ○
Stockton ○
Modesto ○
San Jose ○
San Francisco
Fresno ○
NEVADA
Great Salt
Lake
Salt Lake
City ○
UTAH
Colorado River
Denver ○
Colorado
Springs ○
COLORADO
S. Platte River
Platte
KANSAS
Ark
Wic

CALIFORNIA
Bakersfield ○
Las Vegas ○
Pasadena ○
Los Angeles ■
Long Beach
San
Bernardino ○
Santa Ana ○
San Diego ○
ARIZONA
Phoenix ○
Tucson ○
Colorado River
Rio Grande
Santa Fe ★
Albuquerque ○
NEW
MEXICO
El Paso □
OKLAHOMA
Amarillo ○
Oklahoma
City
Lubbock ○
Red Riv
Abilene ○   Fort Wor
D

PACIFIC
OCEAN

RUSSIA
ARCTIC
OCEAN
Bering Strait
ALASKA
Yukon   River
Bering Sea
Anchorage ○
CANADA
Juneau ○
Gulf of Alaska
ALEUTIAN ISLANDS
PACIFIC OCEAN

MEXICO

TEXAS
Rio Grande
Nueces
San
River
Laredo
B

Kauai   PACIFIC OCEAN
Niihau   Oahu
Honolulu ○   Molokai   HAWAII
Lanai   Maui
Kahoolawe
Hawaii

60°N

0   400 Miles
0   400 Kilometers

0   200 Miles
0   200 Kilometers

A-2

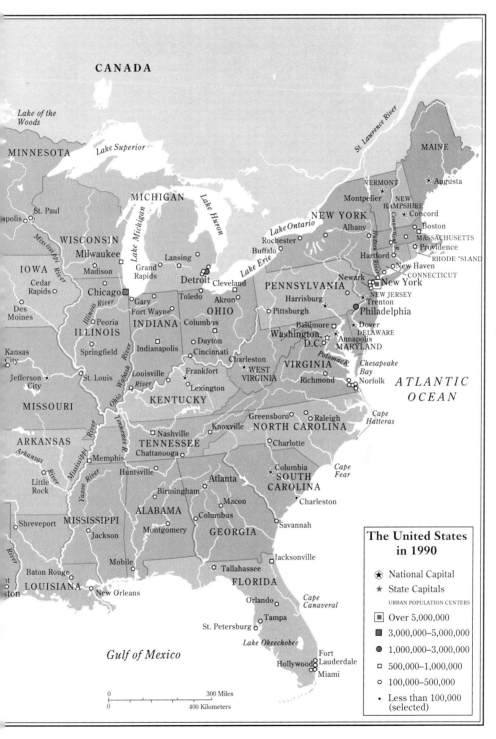

CANADA

Lake of the
Woods

MINNESOTA

Lake Superior

MAINE

Lake Michigan

Lake Huron

MICHIGAN

VERMONT

*Augusta

Montpelier   NEW
             HAMPSHIRE
*Concord

St. Paul

Mississippi River

WISCONSIN

Milwaukee

Lake Ontario

NEW YORK

Rochester o   Albany o

o Boston

apolis o

IOWA

Madison

Grand o
Rapids

Lansing o

Buffalo o

MASSACHUSETTS

o Providence

Cedar
Rapids o

Chicago ■

o Gary

Detroit Cleveland

Lake Erie

Hartford o

o New Haven

RHODE 'SLAND

CONNECTICUT

Des
Moines

Fort Wayne o

Toledo o   Akron o

PENNSYLVANIA

Harrisburg

Newark

New York

NEW JERSEY

Illinois River

o Peoria

INDIANA

OHIO

Columbus o

o Pittsburgh

Trenton

Philadelphia

Kansas
City

ILLINOIS

Springfield o

Indianapolis o

o Dayton

Baltimore o

Washington,

Dover

DELAWARE

Jefferson *
City

St. Louis o

Wabash River

Louisville o

Cincinnati o

Frankfort

Charleston o

D.C.

Annapolis

MARYLAND

Ohio River

o Lexington

WEST
VIRGINIA

VIRGINIA

Potomac R.

Chesapeake
Bay

MISSOURI

KENTUCKY

Richmond o

o Norfolk

ATLANTIC

OCEAN

ARKANSAS

Tennessee R.

o Nashville

Knoxville o

Greensboro o

o Raleigh

NORTH CAROLINA

Cape
Hatteras

Arkansas River

Memphis o

TENNESSEE

Chattanooga o

o Charlotte

Yazoo River

Mississippi River

Little
Rock

Huntsville o

Columbia o

SOUTH
CAROLINA

Cape
Fear

Birmingham o

Atlanta o

o Charleston

MISSISSIPPI

ALABAMA

Macon o

Columbus o

Shreveport o

Jackson o

Montgomery o

GEORGIA

o Savannah

River

Baton Rouge o

Mobile o

Jacksonville □

t
ston

LOUISIANA

o New Orleans

* Tallahassee

FLORIDA

Orlando o

Cape
Canaveral

Gulf of Mexico

o Tampa

St. Petersburg o

Lake Okeechobee

Fort
Lauderdale

Hollywood

Miami

The United States in 1990

⊛ National Capital

★ State Capitals

URBAN POPULATION CENTERS

▣ Over 5,000,000

■ 3,000,000–5,000,000

● 1,000,000–3,000,000

□ 500,000–1,000,000

o 100,000–500,000

• Less than 100,000 (selected)

0   300 Miles
0   400 Kilometers

A-3

United States Territorial Expansion, 1783–1898

(1859) Date of statehood

The United States in 1783

Louisiana Purchase, 1803

—— 1819 Treaty with Spain defined border of Oregon and Louisiana

West Florida annexation, 1810, 1813

Florida: East Florida cession by Spain, 1819;

Texas Annexation, 1845

- - - Texas boundary claimed by U.S., 1845–1848

Oregon Country, 1846

Mexican Cession, 1848

Gadsden Purchase 1853

Alaska Purch 1867

Hawaii Annexation,

ARCTIC OCEAN

GREENLAND (Denmark)

ALASKA (1959)
Purchased from Russia 1867

CANADA

United States claim ceded to Britain 1846

Ceded by Britain 1818

Disputed by United States and Britain 1783–1842

PACIFIC OCEAN

British claim ceded 1846

ME. (1820)

WASH. (1889)

MONT. (1889)

N.D. (1889)

VT. (1791)

N.H. (1

ORE. (1859)

IDAHO (1890)

S.D. (1889)

MINN. (1858)

WIS. (1848)

MICH. (1837)

N.Y. (1788)

MASS. (1

R.I. (175

CONN. (

WYO. (1890)

IOWA (1846)

PA. (1787)

N.J. (1787)

NEV. (1864)

NEB. (1867)

ILL. (1818)

IND. (1816)

OHIO (1803)

W.VA. (1863)

VA. (1788)

DEL.(1787)

MD.(1788)

UTAH (1896)

COLO. (1876)

KAN. (1861)

MO. (1821)

KY. (1792)

CALIF. (1850)

N.C. (1789)

0   400 Miles

0   400 Kilometers

ARIZ. (1912)

N.M. (1912)

OKLA. (1907)

ARK. (1836)

TENN. (1796)

S.C. (1788)

MISS. (1817)

ALA. (1819)

GA. (1788)

ATLANTIC OC

LA. (1812)

TEXAS (1845)

Annexed 1813

Annexed 1810

HAWAII (1959)

PACIFIC OCEAN

HAWAIIAN ISLANDS Annexed 1898

MEXICO

Gulf of Mexico

BAHAMAS

PUERTO (1898)

CUBA

A-4

Documents and Tables

THE DECLARATION OF INDEPENDENCE

In Congress, July 4, 1776,

THE UNANIMOUS DECLARATION OF THE THIRTEEN UNITED STATES OF AMERICA

When, in the course of human events, it becomes necessary for one people to dissolve the political bands which have connected them with another, and to assume, among the powers of the earth, the separate and equal station to which the laws of nature and of nature's God entitle them, a decent respect to the opinions of mankind requires that they should declare the causes which impel them to the separation.

We hold these truths to be self-evident, that all men are created equal; that they are endowed by their Creator with certain unalienable rights; that among these, are life, liberty, and the pursuit of happiness. That, to secure these rights, governments are instituted among men, deriving their just powers from the consent of the governed; that, whenever any form of government becomes destructive of these ends, it is the right of the people to alter or to abolish it, and to institute a new government, laying its foundation on such principles, and organizing its powers in such form, as to them shall seem most likely to effect their safety and happiness. Prudence, indeed, will dictate that governments long established, should not be changed for light and transient causes; and, accordingly, all experience hath shown, that mankind are more disposed to suffer, while evils are sufferable, than to right themselves by abolishing the forms to which they are accustomed. But, when a long train of abuses and usurpations, pursuing invariably the same object, evinces a design to reduce them under absolute despotism, it is their right, it is their duty, to throw off such government and to provide new guards for their future security. Such has been the patient sufferance of these colonies, and such is now the necessity which constrains them to alter their former systems of government. The history of the present King of Great Britain is a history of repeated injuries and usurpations, all having, in direct object, the establishment of an absolute tyranny over these States. To prove this, let facts be submitted to a candid world:

He has refused his assent to laws the most wholesome and necessary for the public good.

He has forbidden his governors to pass laws of immediate and pressing importance, unless suspended in their operation till his assent should be obtained; and, when so suspended, he has utterly neglected to attend to them.

He has refused to pass other laws for the accommodation of large districts of people, unless those people would relinquish the right of representation in the legislature; a right inestimable to them, and formidable to tyrants only.

He has called together legislative bodies at places unusual, uncomfortable, and distant from the depository of their public records, for the sole purpose of fatiguing them into compliance with his measures.

He has dissolved representative houses repeatedly for opposing, with manly firmness, his invasions on the rights of the people.

He has refused, for a long time after such dissolutions, to cause others to be elected; whereby the legislative powers, incapable of annihilation, have returned to the people at large for their exercise; the state remaining, in the meantime, exposed to all the danger of invasion from without, and convulsions within.

He has endeavored to prevent the population of these States; for that purpose, obstructing the laws for naturalization of foreigners, refusing to pass others to encourage their migration hither, and raising the conditions of new appropriations of lands.

He has obstructed the administration of justice, by refusing his assent to laws for establishing judiciary powers.

He has made judges dependent on his will alone, for the tenure of their offices, and the amount and payment of their salaries.

He has erected a multitude of new offices, and sent hither swarms of officers to harass our people, and eat out their substance.

He has kept among us, in time of peace, standing armies, without the consent of our legislatures.

He has affected to render the military independent of, and superior to, the civil power.

He has combined, with others, to subject us to a jurisdiction foreign to our Constitution, and unacknowledged by our laws; giving his assent to their acts of pretended legislation:

For quartering large bodies of armed troops among us:

For protecting them by a mock trial, from punishment, for any murders which they should commit on the inhabitants of these States:

For cutting off our trade with all parts of the world:

For imposing taxes on us without our consent:

For depriving us, in many cases, of the benefit of trial by jury:

For transporting us beyond seas to be tried for pretended offences:

For abolishing the free system of English laws in a neighboring province, establishing therein an arbitrary government, and enlarging its boundaries, so as to render it at once an example and fit instrument for introducing the same absolute rule into these colonies:

For taking away our charters, abolishing our most valuable laws, and altering, fundamentally, the powers of our governments:

For suspending our own legislatures, and declaring themselves invested with power to legislate for us in all cases whatsoever.

He has abdicated government here, by declaring us out of his protection, and waging war against us.

He has plundered our seas, ravaged our coasts, burnt our towns, and destroyed the lives of our people.

He is, at this time, transporting large armies of foreign mercenaries to complete the works of death, desolation, and tyranny, already begun, with circumstances of cruelty and perfidy scarcely paralleled in the most barbarous ages, and totally unworthy the head of a civilized nation.

He has constrained our fellow citizens, taken captive on the high seas, to bear arms against their country, to become the executioners of their friends, and brethren, or to fall themselves by their hands.

He has excited domestic insurrections amongst us, and has endeavored to bring on the inhabitants of our frontiers, the merciless Indian savages, whose known rule of warfare is an undistinguished destruction of all ages, sexes, and conditions.

In every stage of these oppressions, we have petitioned for redress, in the most humble terms; our repeated petitions have been answered only by repeated injury. A prince, whose character is thus marked by every act which may define a tyrant, is unfit to be the ruler of a free people.

Nor have we been wanting in attention to our British brethren. We have warned them, from time to time, of attempts made by their legislature to extend an unwarrantable jurisdiction over us. We have reminded them of the circumstances of our emigration and settlement here. We have appealed to their native justice and magnanimity, and we have conjured them, by the ties of our common kindred, to disavow these usurpations, which would inevitably interrupt our connections and correspondence. They, too, have been deaf to the voice of justice and consanguinity. We must, therefore, acquiesce in the necessity which denounces our separation, and hold them as we hold the rest of mankind, enemies in war, in peace, friends.

We, therefore, the representatives of the United States of America, in general Congress assembled, appealing to the Supreme Judge of the world for the rectitude of our intentions, do, in the name, and by the authority of the good people of these colonies, solemnly publish and declare, that these united colonies are, and of right ought to be, free and independent states: that they are absolved from all allegiance to the British Crown, and that all political connection between them and the state of Great Britain is, and ought to be, totally dissolved; and that, as free and independent states, they have full power to levy war, conclude peace, contract alliances, establish commerce, and to do all other acts and things which independent states may of right do. And, for the support of this declaration, with a firm reliance on the protection of Divine Providence, we mutually pledge to each other our lives, our fortunes, and our sacred honor.

The foregoing Declaration was, by order of Congress, engrossed, and signed by the following members:

John Hancock

New Hampshire	*Massachusetts Bay*	*Rhode Island*
Josiah Bartlett	Samuel Adams	Stephen Hopkins
William Whipple	John Adams	William Ellery
Matthew Thornton	Robert Treat Paine	
	Elbridge Gerry	

Connecticut
Roger Sherman
Samuel Huntington
William Williams
Oliver Wolcott

New York
William Floyd
Philip Livingston
Francis Lewis
Lewis Morris

New Jersey
Richard Stockton
John Witherspoon
Francis Hopkinson
John Hart
Abraham Clark

Pennsylvania
Robert Morris
Benjamin Rush
Benjamin Franklin
John Morton
George Clymer
James Smith
George Taylor
James Wilson
George Ross

Delaware
Caesar Rodney
George Read
Thomas M'Kean

Maryland
Samuel Chase
William Paca
Thomas Stone
Charles Carroll,
    of Carrollton

Virginia
George Wythe
Richard Henry Lee
Thomas Jefferson
Benjamin Harrison
Thomas Nelson, Jr.
Francis Lightfoot Lee
Carter Braxton

North Carolina
William Hooper
Joseph Hewes
John Penn

South Carolina
Edward Rutledge
Thomas Heyward, Jr.
Thomas Lynch, Jr.
Arthur Middleton

Georgia
Button Gwinnett
Lyman Hall
George Walton

Resolved, That copies of the Declaration be sent to the several assemblies, conventions, and committees, or councils of safety, and to the several commanding officers of the continental troops; that it be proclaimed in each of the United States, at the head of the army.

THE CONSTITUTION OF THE UNITED STATES[1]

We the People of the United States, in Order to form a more perfect Union, establish Justice, insure domestic Tranquility, provide for the common defence, promote the general Welfare, and secure the Blessings of Liberty to ourselves and our Posterity, do ordain and establish this CONSTITUTION for the United States of America.

Article I

Section 1.
All legislative Powers herein granted shall be vested in a Congress of the United States, which shall consist of a Senate and House of Representatives.

Section 2.
The House of Representatives shall be composed of Members chosen every second Year by the People of the several States, and the Electors in each State shall have the Qualifications requisite for Electors of the most numerous Branch of the State Legislature.

No Person shall be a Representative who shall not have attained to the Age of twenty-five Years, and been seven Years a Citizen of the United States, and who shall not, when elected, be an Inhabitant of that State in which he shall be chosen.

[Representatives and direct Taxes[2] shall be apportioned among the several States which may be included within this Union, according to their respective Numbers, which shall be determined by adding to the whole Number of free Persons, including those bound to Service for a Term of Years, and excluding Indians not taxed, three fifths of all other Persons.][3] The actual Enumeration shall be made within three Years after the first Meeting of the Congress of the United States, and within every subsequent Term of ten Years, in such Manner as they shall by Law

---

[1] This version, which follows the original Constitution in capitalization and spelling, was published by the United States Department of the Interior, Office of Education, in 1935.
[2] Altered by the Sixteenth Amendment.
[3] Negated by the Fourteenth Amendment.

direct. The Number of Representatives shall not exceed one for every thirty Thousand, but each State shall have at Least one Representative; and until such enumeration shall be made, the State of New Hampshire shall be entitled to chuse three, Massachusetts eight, Rhode-Island and Providence Plantations one, Connecticut five, New York six, New Jersey four, Pennsylvania eight, Delaware one, Maryland six, Virginia ten, North Carolina five, South Carolina five, and Georgia three.

When vacancies happen in the Representation from any State, the Executive Authority thereof shall issue Writs of Election to fill such Vacancies.

The House of Representatives shall chuse their Speaker and other Officers; and shall have the sole Power of Impeachment.

Section 3.

The Senate of the United States shall be composed of two Senators from each State, chosen by the Legislature thereof, for six Years; and each Senator shall have one Vote.

Immediately after they shall be assembled in Consequence of the first Election, they shall be divided as equally as may be into three Classes. The Seats of the Senators of the first Class shall be vacated at the Expiration of the second Year, of the second Class at the Expiration of the fourth Year, and of the third Class at the Expiration of the sixth Year, so that one-third may be chosen every second Year; and if Vacancies happen by Resignation, or otherwise, during the Recess of the Legislature of any State, the Executive thereof may make temporary Appointments until the next Meeting of the Legislature, which shall then fill such Vacancies.

No Person shall be a Senator who shall not have attained to the Age of thirty Years, and been nine Years a Citizen of the United States, and who shall not, when elected, be an Inhabitant of that State for which he shall be chosen.

The Vice President of the United States shall be President of the Senate, but shall have no vote, unless they be equally divided.

The Senate shall chuse their other Officers, and also a President pro tempore, in the absence of the Vice President, or when he shall exercise the Office of President of the United States.

The Senate shall have the sole Power to try all Impeachments. When sitting for that purpose they shall be on Oath or Affirmation. When the President of the United States is tried, the Chief Justice shall preside: And no person shall be convicted without the Concurrence of two thirds of the Members present.

Judgment in Cases of Impeachment shall not extend further than to removal from Office, and disqualification to hold and enjoy any Office of honor, Trust, or Profit under the United States: but the Party convicted shall nevertheless be liable and subject to Indictment, Trial, Judgment, and Punishment, according to Law.

Section 4.

The Times, Places and Manner of holding Elections for Senators and Representatives, shall be prescribed in each State by the Legislature thereof; but the

Congress may at any time by Law make or alter such Regulations, except as to the Places of Chusing Senators.

The Congress shall assemble at least once in every Year, and such Meeting shall be on the first Monday in December, unless they shall by Law appoint a different Day.

Section 5.

Each House shall be the Judge of the Elections, Returns and Qualifications of its own Members, and a Majority of each shall constitute a Quorum to do Business; but a smaller number may adjourn from day to day, and may be authorized to compel the Attendance of absent Members, in such Manner, and under such Penalties, as each House may provide.

Each House may determine the Rules of its Proceedings, punish its Members for disorderly Behaviour, and, with the Concurrence of two thirds, expel a Member.

Each House shall keep a Journal of its Proceedings, and from time to time publish the same, excepting such Parts as may in their Judgment require Secrecy; and the Yeas and Nays of the Members of either House on any question shall, at the Desire of one fifth of those Present, be entered on the Journal.

Neither House, during the Session of Congress, shall, without the Consent of the other, adjourn for more than three days, nor to any other Place than that in which the two Houses shall be sitting.

Section 6.

The Senators and Representatives shall receive a Compensation for their Services, to be ascertained by Law, and paid out of the Treasury of the United States. They shall in all Cases, except Treason, Felony, and Breach of the Peace, be privileged from Arrest during their Attendance at the Session of their respective Houses, and in going to and returning from the same; and for any Speech or Debate in either House, they shall not be questioned in any other Place.

No Senator or Representative shall, during the Time for which he was elected, be appointed to any civil Office under the Authority of the United States, which shall have been created, or the Emoluments whereof shall have been increased, during such time; and no Person holding any Office under the United States shall be a Member of either House during his continuance in Office.

Section 7.

All Bills for raising Revenue shall originate in the House of Representatives; but the Senate may propose or concur with Amendments as on other bills.

Every Bill which shall have passed the House of Representatives and the Senate, shall, before it become a Law, be presented to the President of the United States; If he approve he shall sign it, but if not he shall return it, with his Objections, to that House in which it shall have originated, who shall enter the Objections at large on their Journal, and proceed to reconsider it. If after such Reconsideration two thirds of that House shall agree to pass the bill, it shall be sent, together with the objections, to the other House, by which it shall likewise be reconsidered, and if approved by two thirds of that House, it shall become a Law. But in all such Cases the Votes of both Houses shall be determined by Yeas and Nays, and the Names of the Persons voting for and against the Bill shall be entered on the Journal of each House respectively. If any Bill shall not be returned by the President within ten Days (Sundays excepted) after it shall have been presented to him, the Same shall be a Law, in like Manner as if he had signed it, unless the Congress by their Adjournment prevent its Return, in which Case it shall not be a Law.

Every Order, Resolution, or Vote to which the Concurrence of the Senate and House of Representatives may be necessary (except on a question of Adjournment) shall be presented to the President of the United States; and before the Same shall take Effect, shall be approved by him, or being disapproved by him, shall be repassed by two thirds of the Senate and House of Representatives, according to the Rules and Limitations prescribed in the Case of a Bill.

Section 8.

The Congress shall have Power To lay and collect Taxes, Duties, Imposts and Excises, to pay the Debts and provide for the common Defence and general Welfare of the United States; but all Duties, Imposts and Excises shall be uniform throughout the United States;

To borrow money on the credit of the United States;

To regulate Commerce with foreign Nations, and among the several States, and with the Indian Tribes;

To establish an uniform rule of Naturalization, and uniform Laws on the subject of Bankruptcies throughout the United States;

To coin Money, regulate the Value thereof, and of foreign Coin, and fix the Standard of Weights and Measures;

To provide for the Punishment of counterfeiting the Securities and current Coin of the United States;

To establish Post Offices and post Roads;

To promote the Progress of Science and useful Arts, by securing for limited Times to Authors and Inventors the exclusive Right to their respective Writings and Discoveries;

To constitute Tribunals inferior to the Supreme Court;

To define and punish Piracies and Felonies committed on the high Seas, and Offenses against the Law of Nations;

To declare War, grant Letters of Marque and Reprisal, and make Rules concerning Captures on Land and Water;

To raise and support Armies, but no Appropriation of Money to that Use shall be for a longer Term than two Years;

To provide and maintain a Navy;

To make Rules for the Government and Regulation of the land and naval forces;

To provide for calling forth the Militia to execute the Laws of the Union, suppress Insurrections and repel Invasions;

To provide for organizing, arming, and disciplining the Militia, and for governing such Part of them as may be employed in the Service of the United States, reserving to the States respectively, the Appointment of the Officers, and the Authority of training the Militia according to the discipline prescribed by Congress;

To exercise exclusive Legislation in all Cases whatsoever, over such District (not exceeding ten Miles square) as may, by Cession of particular States, and the acceptance of Congress, become the Seat of the Government of the United States, and to exercise like Authority over all Places purchased by the Consent of the Legislature of the State in which the Same shall be, for the Erection of Forts, Magazines, Arsenals, Dock-yards, and other needful Buildings;—And

To make all Laws which shall be necessary and proper for carrying into Execution the foregoing Powers, and all other Powers vested by this Constitution in the Government of the United States, or in any Department or Officer thereof.

Section 9.

The Migration or Importation of such Persons as any of the States now existing shall think proper to admit, shall not be prohibited by the Congress prior to the Year one thousand eight hundred and eight, but a tax or duty may be imposed on such Importation, not exceeding ten dollars for each Person.

The privilege of the Writ of Habeas Corpus shall not be suspended, unless when in Cases of Rebellion or Invasion the public Safety may require it.

No bill of Attainder or ex post facto Law shall be passed.

No capitation, or other direct, Tax shall be laid unless in Proportion to the Census or Enumeration herein before directed to be taken.

No Tax or Duty shall be laid on Articles exported from any State.

No Preference shall be given by any Regulation of Commerce or Revenue to the Ports of one State over those of another: nor shall Vessels bound to, or from, one State, be obliged to enter, clear, or pay Duties in another.

No Money shall be drawn from the Treasury, but in Consequence of Appropriations made by Law; and a regular Statement and Account of the Receipts and Expenditures of all public Money shall be published from time to time.

No Title of Nobility shall be granted by the United States: And no Person holding any Office of Profit or Trust under them, shall, without the Consent of the Congress, accept of any present, Emolument, Office, or Title, of any kind whatever, from any King, Prince, or foreign State.

Section 10.

No State shall enter into any Treaty, Alliance, or Confederation; grant Letters of Marque and Reprisal; coin Money; emit Bills of Credit; make any Thing but gold and silver Coin a Tender in Payment of Debts; pass any Bill of Attainder, ex post facto Law, or Law impairing the Obligation of Contracts, or grant any Title of Nobility.

No State shall, without the Consent of the Congress, lay any Imposts or Duties on Imports or Exports, except what may be absolutely necessary for executing its inspection Laws; and the net Produce of all Duties and Imposts, laid by any State on Imports or Exports, shall be for the use of the Treasury of the United States; and all such Laws shall be subject to the Revision and Control of the Congress.

No state shall, without the Consent of Congress, lay any duty of Tonnage, keep Troops, or Ships of War in time of Peace, enter into any Agreement or Compact with another State, or with a foreign Power, or engage in War, unless actually invaded, or in such imminent Danger as will not admit of delay.

Article II

Section 1.
The executive Power shall be vested in a President of the United States of America. He shall hold his Office during the Term of four years, and, together with the Vice President, chosen for the same Term, be elected, as follows:

Each State shall appoint, in such Manner as the Legislature thereof may direct, a Number of Electors, equal to the whole Number of Senators and Representatives to which the State may be entitled in the Congress: but no Senator or Representative, or Person holding an Office of Trust or Profit under the United States, shall be appointed an Elector.

[The Electors shall meet in their respective States, and vote by Ballot for two persons, of whom one at least shall not be an Inhabitant of the same State with themselves. And they shall make a List of all the Persons voted for, and of the Number of Votes for each; which List they shall sign and certify, and transmit sealed to the Seat of the Government of the United States, directed to the President of the Senate. The President of the Senate shall, in the Presence of the Senate and House of Representatives, open all the Certificates, and the Votes shall then be counted. The Person having the greatest Number of Votes shall be the President, if such Number be a Majority of the whole Number of Electors appointed; and if there be more than one who have such Majority, and have an equal Number of Votes, then the House of Representatives shall immediately chuse by Ballot one of them for President; and if no Person have a Majority, then from the five highest on the List the said House shall in like Manner chuse the President. But in chusing the President, the Votes shall be taken by States, the Representation from each State having one Vote; a quorum for this Purpose shall consist of a Member or Members from two-thirds of the States, and a Majority of all the States shall be necessary to a Choice. In every Case, after the Choice of the President, the Person having the greatest Number of Votes of the Electors shall be the Vice President. But if there should remain two or more who have equal votes, the Senate shall chuse from them by Ballot the Vice President.][4]

The Congress may determine the Time of chusing the Electors, and the Day

---

[4] Revised by the Twelfth Amendment

on which they shall give their Votes; which Day shall be the same throughout the United States.

No person except a natural-born Citizen, or a Citizen of the United States, at the time of the Adoption of this Constitution, shall be eligible to the Office of President; neither shall any Person be eligible to that Office who shall not have attained to the Age of thirty-five years, and been fourteen Years a Resident within the United States.

In Case of the Removal of the President from Office, or of his Death, Resignation, or Inability to discharge the Powers and Duties of the said Office, the same shall devolve on the Vice President, and the Congress may by Law provide for the Case of Removal, Death, Resignation, or Inability, both of the President and Vice President, declaring what Officer shall then act as President, and such Officer shall act accordingly, until the disability be removed, or a President shall be elected.

The President shall, at stated Times, receive for his Services a Compensation, which shall neither be increased nor diminished during the Period for which he shall have been elected, and he shall not receive within that Period any other Emolument from the United States, or any of them.

Before he enter on the execution of his Office, he shall take the following Oath or Affirmation:—"I do solemnly swear (or affirm) that I will faithfully execute the Office of President of the United States, and will, to the best of my Ability, preserve, protect, and defend the Constitution of the United States."

Section 2.

The President shall be Commander in Chief of the Army and Navy of the United States, and of the Militia of the several States, when called into the actual Service of the United States; he may require the Opinion, in writing, of the principal Officer in each of the executive Departments, upon any subject relating to the Duties of their respective Offices, and he shall have Power to Grant Reprieves and Pardons for Offenses against the United States, except in Cases of Impeachment.

He shall have Power, by and with the Advice and Consent of the Senate, to make Treaties, provided two-thirds of the Senators present concur; and he shall nominate, and by and with the Advice and Consent of the Senate, shall appoint Ambassadors, other public Ministers and Consuls, Judges of the supreme Court, and all other Officers of the United States, whose Appointments are not herein otherwise provided for, and which shall be established by Law: but the Congress may by Law vest the Appointment of such inferior Officers, as they think proper, in the President alone, in the Courts of Law, or in the Heads of Departments.

The President shall have Power to fill up all Vacancies that may happen during the Recess of the Senate, by granting Commissions which shall expire at the End of their next Session.

Section 3.

He shall from time to time give to the Congress Information of the State of the Union, and recommend to their Consideration such Measures as he shall judge necessary and expedient; he may, on extraordinary occasions, convene both Houses, or either of them, and in Case of Disagreement between them, with respect to the Time of Adjournment, he may adjourn them to such Time as he shall think proper; he shall receive Ambassadors and other public Ministers; he shall take care that the Laws be faithfully executed, and shall Commission all the Officers of the United States.

Section 4.
The President, Vice President and all civil Officers of the United States, shall be removed from Office on Impeachment for, and Conviction of, Treason, Bribery, or other high Crimes and Misdemeanors.

Article III

Section 1.
The judicial Power of the United States, shall be vested in one supreme Court, and in such inferior Courts as the Congress may from time to time ordain and establish. The Judges, both of the supreme and inferior Courts, shall hold their Offices during good Behaviour, and shall, at stated Times, receive for their Services, a Compensation, which shall not be diminished during their Continuance in Office.

Section 2.
The judicial Power shall extend to all Cases, in Law and Equity, arising under this Constitution, the Laws of the United States, and Treaties made, or which shall be made, under their Authority;—to all Cases affecting ambassadors, other public ministers and consuls;—to all cases of admiralty and maritime Jurisdiction;—to Controversies to which the United States shall be a Party;—to Controversies between two or more States;—between a State and Citizens of another State;[5]—between Citizens of different States—between Citizens of the same State claiming Lands under Grants of different States, and between a State, or the Citizens thereof, and foreign States, Citizens, or Subjects.

In all Cases affecting Ambassadors, other public Ministers and Consuls, and those in which a State shall be Party, the supreme Court shall have original Jurisdiction. In all the other Cases before mentioned, the supreme Court shall have appellate Jurisdiction, both as to Law and Fact, with such Exceptions, and under such Regulations as the Congress shall make.

The trial of all Crimes, except in Cases of Impeachment, shall be by Jury; and such Trial shall be held in the State where the said Crimes shall have been committed; but when not committed within any State, the Trial shall be at such Place or Places as the Congress may by Law have directed.

[5] Qualified by the Eleventh Amendment.

Section 3.

Treason against the United States, shall consist only in levying War against them, or in adhering to their Enemies, giving them Aid and Comfort. No Person shall be convicted of Treason unless on the Testimony of two Witnesses to the same overt Act, or on Confession in open Court.

The Congress shall have power to declare the Punishment of Treason, but no Attainder of Treason shall work Corruption of Blood, or Forfeiture except during the Life of the Person attained.

Article IV

Section 1.

Full Faith and Credit shall be given in each State to the public Acts, Records, and judicial Proceedings of every other State. And the Congress may by general Laws prescribe the Manner in which such Acts, Records and Proceedings shall be proved, and the Effect thereof.

Section 2.

The Citizens of each State shall be entitled to all Privileges and Immunities of Citizens in the several States.

A Person charged in any State with Treason, Felony, or other Crime, who shall flee from Justice, and be found in another State, shall on demand of the executive Authority of the State from which he fled, be delivered up, to be removed to the State having Jurisdiction of the crime.

No Person held to Service or Labour in one State, under the Laws thereof, escaping into another, shall, in Consequence of any Law or Regulation therein, be discharged from such Service or Labour, but shall be delivered up on Claim of the Party to whom such Service or Labour may be due.

Section 3.

New States may be admitted by the Congress into this Union; but no new State shall be formed or erected within the Jurisdiction of any other State; nor any State be formed by the Junction of two or more States, or parts of States, without the Consent of the Legislatures of the States concerned as well as of the Congress.

The Congress shall have Power to dispose of and make all needful Rules and Regulations respecting the Territory or other Property belonging to the United States; and nothing in this Constitution shall be so construed as to Prejudice any Claims of the United States, or of any particular State.

Section 4.

The United States shall guarantee to every State in this Union a Republican Form of Government, and shall protect each of them against Invasion; and on Application of the Legislature, or of the Executive (when the Legislature cannot be convened) against domestic Violence.

Article V

The Congress, whenever two-thirds of both Houses shall deem it necessary, shall propose Amendments to this Constitution, or, on the Application of the Legislatures of two-thirds of the several States, shall call a Convention for proposing Amendments, which, in either Case, shall be valid to all Intents and Purposes, as part of this Constitution, when ratified by the Legislatures of three-fourths of the several States, or by Conventions in three-fourths thereof, as the one or the other Mode of Ratification may be proposed by the Congress; Provided that no Amendment which may be made prior to the Year One thousand eight hundred and eight shall in any Manner affect the first and fourth Clauses in the Ninth Section of the first Article; and that no State, without its Consent, shall be deprived of its equal Suffrage in the Senate.

Article VI

All Debts contracted and Engagements entered into, before the Adoption of this Constitution, shall be as valid against the United States under this Constitution, as under the Confederation.

This Constitution, and the Laws of the United States which shall be made in Pursuance thereof; and all Treaties made, or which shall be made, under the Authority of the United States, shall be the supreme Law of the Land; and the Judges in every State shall be bound thereby, any Thing in the Constitution or Laws of any State to the Contrary notwithstanding.

The Senators and Representatives before mentioned, and the Members of the several State Legislatures, and all executive and judicial Officers, both of the United States and of the several States, shall be bound by Oath or Affirmation to support this Constitution; but no religious Tests shall ever be required as a qualification to any Office or public Trust under the United States.

Article VII

The Ratification of the Conventions of nine States shall be sufficient for the Establishment of this Constitution between the States so ratifying the same.

Done in Convention by the Unanimous Consent of the States present the Seventeenth Day of September in the Year of our Lord one thousand seven hundred and Eighty seven, and of the Independence of the United States of America the Twelfth. In Witness whereof We have hereunto subscribed our Names.[6]

George Washington
President and deputy and deputy from Virginia

New Hampshire
John Langdon
Nicholas Gilman

Massachusetts
Nathaniel Gorham
Rufus King

Connecticut
William Samuel
  Johnson
Roger Sherman

New York
Alexander Hamilton

New Jersey
William Livingston
David Brearley
William Paterson
Jonathan Dayton

Pennsylvania
Benjamin Franklin
Thomas Mifflin
Robert Morris
George Clymer
Thomas FitzSimons
Jared Ingersoll
James Wilson
Gouverneur Morris

Delaware
George Read
Gunning Bedford, Jr.
John Dickinson
Richard Bassett
Jacob Broom

Maryland
James McHenry
Daniel of
  St. Thomas Jenifer
Daniel Carroll

Virginia
John Blair
James Madison, Jr.

North Carolina
William Blount
Richard Dobbs
  Spaight
Hugh Williamson

South Carolina
John Rutledge
Charles Cotesworth
  Pinckney
Charles Pinckney
Pierce Butler

Georgia
William Few
Abraham Baldwin

Articles in Addition to, and Amendment of, the Constitution of the United States of America, Proposed by Congress, and Ratified by the Legislatures of the Several States, Pursuant to the Fifth Article of the Original Constitution.[7]

[Article I]

Congress shall make no law respecting an establishment of religion, or prohibiting the free exercise thereof; or abridging the freedom of speech, or of the press; or the right of the people peaceably to assemble, and to petition the Government for a redress of grievances.

---

[6] These are the full names of the signers, which in some cases are not the signatures on the document.

[7] This heading appears only in the joint resolution submitting the first ten amendments.

[Article II]

A well regulated Militia, being necessary to the security of a free State, the right of the people to keep and bear Arms shall not be infringed.

[Article III]

No Soldier shall, in time of peace, be quartered in any house, without the consent of the Owner, nor in time of war, but in a manner to be prescribed by law.

[Article IV]

The right of the people to be secure in their persons, houses, papers, and effects, against unreasonable searches and seizures, shall not be violated, and no Warrants shall issue, but upon probable cause, supported by Oath or affirmation, and particularly describing the place to be searched, and the persons or things to be seized.

[Article V]

No person shall be held to answer for a capital or otherwise infamous crime, unless on a presentment or indictment of a Grand Jury, except in cases arising in the land or naval forces, or in the Militia, when in actual service in time of War or public danger; nor shall any person be subject for the same offence to be twice put in jeopardy of life or limb; nor shall be compelled in any criminal case to be a witness against himself, nor be deprived of life, liberty, or property, without due process of law; nor shall private property be taken for public use, without just compensation.

[Article VI]

In all criminal prosecutions, the accused shall enjoy the right to a speedy and public trial, by an impartial jury of the State and district wherein the crime shall have been committed, which district shall have been previously ascertained by law, and to be informed of the nature and cause of the accusation; to be confronted with the witnesses against him; to have compulsory process for obtaining witnesses in his favour, and to have the Assistance of Counsel for his defense.

[Article VII]

In suits at common law, where the value in controversy shall exceed twenty dollars, the right of trial by jury shall be preserved, and no fact tried by a jury, shall be otherwise reexamined in any Court of the United States, than according to the rules of the common law.

[Article VIII]

Excessive bail shall not be required, nor excessive fines imposed, nor cruel and unusual punishments inflicted.

[Article IX]

The enumeration of the Constitution, of certain rights, shall not be construed to deny or disparage others retained by the people.

[Article X]

The powers not delegated to the United States by the Constitution, nor prohibited by it to the States, are reserved to the States respectively, or to the people.

[Amendments I–X, in force 1791.]

[Article XI][8]

The Judicial power of the United States shall not be construed to extend to any suit in law or equity, commenced or prosecuted against one of the United States by Citizens of another State, or by Citizens or Subjects of any Foreign State.

[Article XII][9]

The Electors shall meet in their respective States and vote by ballot for President and Vice-President, one of whom, at least, shall not be an inhabitant of the same State with themselves; they shall name in their ballots the person voted for as President, and in distinct ballots the person voted for as Vice-President, and they shall make distinct lists of all persons voted for as President, and of all persons voted for as Vice-President, and of the number of votes for each, which lists they shall sign and certify, and transmit sealed to the seat of the government of the United States, directed to the President of the Senate;—The President of the Senate shall, in the presence of the Senate and House of Representatives, open all the certificates and the votes shall then be counted;—The person having the greatest number of votes for President, shall be the President, if such number be a majority of the whole number of Electors appointed; and if no person have such majority, then from the persons having the highest numbers not exceeding three on the list of those voted for as President, the House of Representatives shall choose immediately, by ballot,

[8] Adopted in 1798.
[9] Adopted in 1804.

the President. But in choosing the President, the votes shall be taken by states, the representation from each state having one vote; a quorum for this purpose shall consist of a member or members from two-thirds of the states, and a majority of all the states shall be necessary to a choice. And if the House of Representatives shall not choose a President whenever the right of choice shall devolve upon them, before the fourth day of March next following, then the Vice-President shall act as President, as in the case of the death or other constitutional disability of the President.—The person having the greatest number of votes as Vice-President, shall be the Vice-President, if such number be a majority of the whole number of Electors appointed, and if no person have a majority, then from the two highest numbers on the list, the Senate shall choose the Vice-President; a quorum for the purpose shall consist of two-thirds of the whole number of Senators, and a majority of the whole number shall be necessary to a choice. But no person constitutionally ineligible to the office of President shall be eligible to that of Vice-President of the United States.

[Article XIII][10]

Section 1.
Neither slavery nor involuntary servitude, except as a punishment for crime whereof the party shall have been duly convicted, shall exist within the United States, or any place subject to their jurisdiction.

Section 2.
Congress shall have power to enforce this article by appropriate legislation.

[Article XIV][11]

Section 1.
All persons born or naturalized in the United States, and subject to the jurisdiction thereof, are citizens of the United States and of the State wherein they reside. No State shall make or enforce any law which shall abridge the privileges or immunities of citizens of the United States; nor shall any State deprive any person of life, liberty, or property, without due process of law; nor deny to any person within its jurisdiction the equal protection of the laws.

Section 2.
Representatives shall be apportioned among the several States according to their respective numbers, counting the whole number of persons in each State, excluding

[10] Adopted in 1865.
[11] Adopted in 1868.

Indians not taxed. But when the right to vote at any election for the choice of electors for President and Vice-President of the United States, Representatives in Congress, the Executive and Judicial officers of a State, or the members of the Legislature thereof, is denied to any of the male inhabitants of such State, being twenty-one years of age, and citizens of the United States, or in any way abridged, except for participation in rebellion, or other crime, the basis of representation therein shall be reduced in the proportion which the number of such male citizens shall bear to the whole number of male citizens twenty-one years of age in such State.

Section 3.
No person shall be a Senator or Representative in Congress, or elector of President and Vice-President, or hold any office, civil or military, under the United States, or under any State, who, having previously taken an oath, as a member of Congress, or as an officer of the United States, or as a member of any State legislature, or as an executive or judicial officer of any State, to support the Constitution of the United States, shall have engaged in insurrection or rebellion against the same, or given aid or comfort to the enemies thereof. But Congress may by a vote of two-thirds of each House, remove such disability.

Section 4.
The validity of the public debt of the United States, authorized by law, including debts incurred for payment of pensions and bounties for services in suppressing insurrection or rebellion, shall not be questioned. But neither the United States nor any State shall assume or pay any debts or obligation incurred in aid of insurrection or rebellion against the United States, or any claim for the loss or emancipation of any slave; but all such debts, obligations, and claims shall be held illegal and void.

Section 5.
The Congress shall have the power to enforce, by appropriate legislation, the provisions of this article.

[Article XV][12]

Section 1.
The right of citizens of the United States to vote shall not be denied or abridged by the United States or by any State on account of race, color, or previous condition of servitude—

Section 2.
The Congress shall have power to enforce this article by appropriate legislation.

[12] Adopted in 1870.

[Article XVI][13]

The Congress shall have power to lay and collect taxes on incomes, from whatever source derived, without apportionment among the several States, and without regard to any census or enumeration.

[Article XVII][14]

The Senate of the United States shall be composed of two Senators from each State, elected by the people thereof, for six years; and each Senator shall have one vote. The electors in each State shall have the qualifications requisite for electors of the most numerous branch of the State legislatures.

When vacancies happen in the representation of any State in the Senate, the executive authority of such State shall issue writs of election to fill such vacancies: *Provided*, That the legislature of any State may empower the executive thereof to make temporary appointments until the people fill the vacancies by election as the legislature may direct.

This amendment shall not be so construed as to affect the election or term of any Senator chosen before it becomes valid as part of the Constitution.

[Article XVIII][15]

Section 1.
After one year from the ratification of this article the manufacture, sale, or transportation of intoxicating liquors within, the importation thereof into, or the exportation thereof from the United States and all territory subject to the jurisdiction thereof for beverage purposes is hereby prohibited.

Section 2.
The Congress and the several States shall have concurrent power to enforce this article by appropriate legislation.

Section 3.
This article shall be inoperative unless it shall have been ratified as an amendment to the Constitution by the legislatures of the several States, as provided in the Constitution, within seven years from the date of the submission hereof to the States by the Congress.

[13] Adopted in 1913.
[14] Adopted in 1913.
[15] Adopted in 1918.

[Article XIX][16]

The right of citizens of the United States to vote shall not be denied or abridged by the United States or by any State on account of sex.

Congress shall have power to enforce this article by appropriate legislation.

[Article XX][17]

Section 1.

The terms of the President and Vice-President shall end at noon on the 20th day of January, and the terms of Senators and Representatives at noon on the 3d day of January, of the years in which such terms would have ended if this article had not been ratified; and the terms of their successors shall then begin.

Section 2.

The Congress shall assemble at least once in every year, and such meeting shall begin at noon on the 3d day of January, unless they shall by law appoint a different day.

Section 3.

If, at the time fixed for the beginning of the term of the President, the President elect shall have died, the Vice-President elect shall become President. If a President shall not have been chosen before the time fixed for the beginning of his term or if the President elect shall have failed to qualify, then the Vice-President elect shall act as President until a President shall have qualified; and the Congress may by law provide for the case wherein neither a President elect nor a Vice-President elect shall have qualified, declaring who shall then act as President, or the manner in which one who is to act shall be selected, and such person shall act accordingly until a President or Vice-President shall have qualified.

Section 4.

The Congress may by law provide for the case of the death of any of the persons from whom the House of Representatives may choose a President whenever the right of choice shall have devolved upon them, and for the case of the death of any of the persons from whom the Senate may choose a Vice-President whenever the right of choice shall have devolved upon them.

[16] Adopted in 1920.
[17] Adopted in 1933.

Section 5.
Sections 1 and 2 shall take effect on the 15th day of October following the ratification of this article.

Section 6.
This article shall be inoperative unless it shall have been ratified as an amendment to the Constitution by the legislatures of three-fourths of the several States within seven years from the date of its submission.

[Article XXI][18]

Section 1.
The eighteenth article of amendment to the Constitution of the United States is hereby repealed.

Section 2.
The transportation or importation into any State, Territory, or possession of the United States for delivery or use therein of intoxicating liquors, in violation of the laws thereof, is hereby prohibited.

Section 3.
This article shall be inoperative unless it shall have been ratified as an amendment to the Constitution by conventions in the several States, as provided in the Constitution, within seven years from the date of the submission hereof to the States by the Congress.

[Article XXII][19]

No person shall be elected to the office of the President more than twice, and no person who has held the office of President, or acted as President, for more than two years of a term to which some other person was elected President shall be elected to the office of the President more than once.

But this Article shall not apply to any person holding the office of President when this Article was proposed by the Congress, and shall not prevent any person who may be holding the office of President, or acting as President, during the term within which this Article becomes operative from holding the office of President or acting as President during the remainder of such term.

[18] Adopted in 1933.
[19] Adopted in 1961.

This article shall be inoperative unless it shall have been ratified as an amendment to the Constitution by the legislatures of three-fourths of the several states within seven years from the date of its submission to the states by the Congress.

[Article XXIII][20]

Section 1.
The District constituting the seat of Government of the United States shall appoint in such manner as the Congress may direct:

A number of electors of President and Vice-President equal to the whole number of Senators and Representatives in Congress to which the District would be entitled if it were a State, but in no event more than the least populous State; they shall be in addition to those appointed by the States, but they shall be considered, for the purposes of the election of President and Vice-President, to be electors appointed by a State; and they shall meet in the District and perform such duties as provided by the twelfth article of amendment.

Section 2.
The Congress shall have power to enforce this article by appropriate legislation.

[Article XXIV][21]

Section 1.
The right of citizens of the United States to vote in any primary or other election for President or Vice President, for electors for President or Vice President, or for Senator or Representative in Congress, shall not be denied or abridged by the United States or any state by reason of failure to pay any poll tax or other tax.

Section 2.
The Congress shall have the power to enforce this article by appropriate legislation.

[Article XXV][22]

Section 1.
In case of the removal of the President from office or of his death or resignation, the Vice President shall become President.

[20] Adopted in 1961.
[21] Adopted in 1964.
[22] Adopted in 1967.

Section 2.
Whenever there is a vacancy in the office of the Vice President, the President shall nominate a Vice President who shall take office upon confirmation by a majority vote of both Houses of Congress.

Section 3.
Whenever the President transmits to the President Pro Tempore of the Senate and the Speaker of the House of Representatives his written declaration that he is unable to discharge the powers and duties of his office, and until he transmits to them a written declaration to the contrary, such powers and duties shall be discharged by the Vice President as Acting President.

Section 4.
Whenever the Vice President and a majority of either the principal officers of the executive departments or of such other body as Congress may by law provide, transmit to the President Pro Tempore of the Senate and the Speaker of the House of Representatives their written declaration that the President is unable to discharge the powers and duties of his office, the Vice President shall immediately assume the powers and duties of the office as Acting President.

Thereafter, when the President transmits to the President Pro Tempore of the Senate and the Speaker of the House of Representatives his written declaration that no inability exists, he shall resume the powers and duties of his office unless the Vice President and a majority of either the principal officers of the executive departments or of such other body as Congress may by law provide, transmit within four days to the President Pro Tempore of the Senate and the Speaker of the House of Representatives their written declaration that the President is unable to discharge the powers and duties of his office. Thereupon Congress shall decide the issue, assembling within forty-eight hours for that purpose if not in session. If the Congress, within twenty-one days after receipt of the latter written declaration, or, if Congress is not in session, within twenty-one days after Congress is required to assemble, determines by two-thirds vote of both Houses that the President is unable to discharge the powers and duties of his office, the Vice President shall continue to discharge the same as Acting President; otherwise, the President shall resume the powers and duties of his office.

[Article XXVI][23]

Section 1.
The right of citizens of the United States, who are eighteen years of age or older, to vote shall not be denied or abridged by the United States or by any State on account of age.

Section 2.
The Congress shall have power to enforce this article by appropriate legislation.

[23] Adopted in 1971.

PRESIDENTIAL ELECTIONS

Year	Candidates	Parties	Popular Vote	Percentage of Popular Vote	Electoral Vote	Percentage of Voter Participation
1789	**GEORGE WASHINGTON (Va.)***				69	
	John Adams				34	
	Others				35	
1792	**GEORGE WASHINGTON (Va.)**				132	
	John Adams				77	
	George Clinton				50	
	Others				5	
1796	**JOHN ADAMS (Mass.)**	Federalist			71	
	Thomas Jefferson	Democratic-Republican			68	
	Thomas Pinckney	Federalist			59	
	Aaron Burr	Dem.-Rep.			30	
	Others				48	
1800	**THOMAS JEFFERSON (Va.)**	Dem.-Rep.			73	
	Aaron Burr	Dem.-Rep.			73	
	John Adams	Federalist			65	
	C. C. Pinckney	Federalist			64	
	John Jay	Federalist			1	
1804	**THOMAS JEFFERSON (Va.)**	Dem.-Rep.			162	
	C. C. Pinckney	Federalist			14	

A-30

Year	Candidate	Party	Popular Vote	% Popular Vote	Electoral Vote	% Electoral Vote
1808	**JAMES MADISON (Va.)**	Dem.-Rep.			122	
	C. C. Pinckney	Federalist			47	
	George Clinton	Dem.-Rep.			6	
1812	**JAMES MADISON (Va.)**	Dem.-Rep.			128	
	De Witt Clinton	Federalist			89	
1816	**JAMES MONROE (Va.)**	Dem.-Rep.			183	
	Rufus King	Federalist			34	
1820	**JAMES MONROE (Va.)**	Dem.-Rep.			231	
	John Quincy Adams	Dem.-Rep.			1	
1824	**JOHN Q. ADAMS (Mass.)**	Dem.-Rep.	108,740	30.5	84	26.9
	Andrew Jackson	Dem.-Rep.	153,544	43.1	99	
	William H. Crawford	Dem.-Rep.	46,618	13.1	41	
	Henry Clay	Dem.-Rep.	47,136	13.2	37	
1828	**ANDREW JACKSON (Tenn.)**	Democratic	647,286	56.0	178	57.6
	John Quincy Adams	National Republican	508,064	44.0	83	
1832	**ANDREW JACKSON (Tenn.)**	Democratic	687,502	55.0	219	55.4
	Henry Clay	National Republican	530,189	42.4	49	
	John Floyd	Independent			11	
	William Wirt	Anti-Mason	33,108	2.6	7	

* State of residence at time of election.

A-31

PRESIDENTIAL ELECTIONS *(cont.)*

Year	Candidates	Parties	Popular Vote	Percentage of Popular Vote	Electoral Vote	Percentage of Voter Participation
1836	**MARTIN VAN BUREN (N.Y.)**	Democratic	765,483	50.9	170	57.8
	W. H. Harrison	Whig			73	
	Hugh L. White	Whig	739,795	49.1	26	
	Daniel Webster	Whig			14	
	W. P. Magnum	Independent			11	
1840	**WILLIAM H. HARRISON (Ohio)**	Whig	1,274,624	53.1	234	80.2
	Martin Van Buren	Democratic	1,127,781	46.9	60	
	J. G. Birney	Liberty	7,069		—	
1844	**JAMES K. POLK (Tenn.)**	Democratic	1,338,464	49.6	170	78.9
	Henry Clay	Whig	1,300,097	48.1	105	
	J. G. Birney	Liberty	62,300	2.3	—	
1848	**ZACHARY TAYLOR (La.)**	Whig	1,360,967	47.4	163	72.7
	Lewis Cass	Democratic	1,222,342	42.5	127	
	Martin Van Buren	Free-Soil	291,263	10.1	—	
1852	**FRANKLIN PIERCE (N.H.)**	Democratic	1,601,117	50.9	254	69.6
	Winfield Scott	Whig	1,385,453	44.1	42	
	John P. Hale	Free-Soil	155,825	5.0	—	
1856	**JAMES BUCHANAN (Pa.)**	Democratic	1,832,955	45.3	174	78.9
	John C. Frémont	Republican	1,339,932	33.1	114	
	Millard Fillmore	American	871,731	21.6	8	
1860	**ABRAHAM LINCOLN (Ill.)**	Republican	1,865,593	39.8	180	81.2
	Stephen A. Douglas	Democratic	1,382,713	29.5	12	
	John C. Breckinridge	Democratic	848,356	18.1	72	
	John Bell	Union	592,906	12.6	39	

Year	Candidate	Party	Popular Vote	%	Electoral Vote	%
1864	**ABRAHAM LINCOLN (Ill.)**	Republican	2,213,655	55.0	212	73.8
	George B. McClellan	Democratic	1,805,237	45.0	21	
1868	**ULYSSES S. GRANT (Ill.)**	Republican	3,012,833	52.7	214	78.1
	Horatio Seymour	Democratic	2,703,249	47.3	80	
1872	**ULYSSES S. GRANT (Ill.)**	Republican	3,597,132	55.6	286	71.3
	Horace Greeley	Democratic; Liberal Republican	2,834,125	43.9	66	
1876	**RUTHERFORD B. HAYES (Ohio)**	Republican	4,036,298	48.0	185	81.8
	Samuel J. Tilden	Democratic	4,300,590	51.0	184	
1880	**JAMES A. GARFIELD (Ohio)**	Republican	4,454,416	48.5	214	79.4
	Winfield S. Hancock	Democratic	4,444,952	48.1	155	
1884	**GROVER CLEVELAND (N.Y.)**	Democratic	4,874,986	48.5	219	77.5
	James G. Blaine	Republican	4,851,981	48.2	182	
1888	**BENJAMIN HARRISON (Ind.)**	Republican	5,439,853	47.9	233	79.3
	Grover Cleveland	Democratic	5,540,309	48.6	168	
1892	**GROVER CLEVELAND (N.Y.)**	Democratic	5,556,918	46.1	277	74.7
	Benjamin Harrison	Republican	5,176,108	43.0	145	
	James B. Weaver	People's	1,041,028	8.5	22	
1896	**WILLIAM McKINLEY (Ohio)**	Republican	7,104,779	51.1	271	79.3
	William J. Bryan	Democratic-People's	6,502,925	47.7	176	
1900	**WILLIAM McKINLEY (Ohio)**	Republican	7,207,923	51.7	292	73.2
	William J. Bryan	Dem.-Populist	6,358,133	45.5	155	
1904	**THEODORE ROOSEVELT (N.Y.)**	Republican	7,623,486	57.9	336	65.2
	Alton B. Parker	Democratic	5,077,911	37.6	140	
	Eugene V. Debs	Socialist	402,283	3.0	—	

PRESIDENTIAL ELECTIONS *(cont.)*

Year	Candidates	Parties	Popular Vote	Percentage of Popular Vote	Electoral Vote	Percentage of Voter Participation
1908	**WILLIAM H. TAFT (Ohio)**	Republican	7,678,908	51.6	321	65.4
	William J. Bryan	Democratic	6,409,104	43.1	162	
	Eugene V. Debs	Socialist	420,793	2.8	—	
1912	**WOODROW WILSON (N.J.)**	Democratic	6,293,454	41.9	435	58.8
	Theodore Roosevelt	Progressive	4,119,538	27.4	88	
	William H. Taft	Republican	3,484,980	23.2	8	
	Eugene V. Debs	Socialist	900,672	6.0	—	
1916	**WOODROW WILSON (N.J.)**	Democratic	9,129,606	49.4	277	61.6
	Charles E. Hughes	Republican	8,538,221	46.2	254	
	A. L. Benson	Socialist	585,113	3.2	—	
1920	**WARREN G. HARDING (Ohio)**	Republican	16,152,200	60.4	404	49.2
	James M. Cox	Democratic	9,147,353	34.2	127	
	Eugene V. Debs	Socialist	919,799	3.4	—	
1924	**CALVIN COOLIDGE (Mass.)**	Republican	15,725,016	54.0	382	48.9
	John W. Davis	Democratic	8,386,503	28.8	136	
	Robert M. LaFollette	Progressive	4,822,856	16.6	13	
1928	**HERBERT HOOVER (Calif.)**	Republican	21,391,381	58.2	444	56.9
	Alfred E. Smith	Democratic	15,016,443	40.9	87	
	Norman Thomas	Socialist	267,835	0.7	—	
1932	**FRANKLIN D. ROOSEVELT (N.Y.)**	Democratic	22,821,857	57.4	472	56.9
	Herbert Hoover	Republican	15,761,841	39.7	59	
	Norman Thomas	Socialist	881,951	2.2	—	

Year	Candidate	Party	Popular Vote	%	Electoral Vote	% Participation
1936	**FRANKLIN D. ROOSEVELT (N.Y.)**	Democratic	27,751,597	60.8	523	61.0
	Alfred M. Landon	Republican	16,679,583	36.5	8	
	William Lemke	Union	882,479	1.9	—	
1940	**FRANKLIN D. ROOSEVELT (N.Y.)**	Democratic	27,244,160	54.8	449	62.5
	Wendell L. Willkie	Republican	22,305,198	44.8	82	
1944	**FRANKLIN D. ROOSEVELT (N.Y.)**	Democratic	25,602,504	53.5	432	55.9
	Thomas E. Dewey	Republican	22,006,285	46.0	99	
1948	**HARRY S. TRUMAN (Mo.)**	Democratic	24,105,695	49.5	304	53.0
	Thomas E. Dewey	Republican	21,969,170	45.1	189	
	J. Strom Thurmond	State-Rights Democratic	1,169,021	2.4	38	
	Henry A. Wallace	Progressive	1,156,103	2.4	—	
1952	**DWIGHT D. EISENHOWER (N.Y.)**	Republican	33,936,252	55.1	442	63.3
	Adlai E. Stevenson	Democratic	27,314,992	44.4	89	
1956	**DWIGHT D. EISENHOWER (N.Y.)**	Republican	35,575,420	57.6	457	60.6
	Adlai E. Stevenson	Democratic	26,033,066	42.1	73	
	Other		—		1	
1960	**JOHN F. KENNEDY (Mass.)**	Democratic	34,227,096	49.9	303	62.8
	Richard M. Nixon	Republican	34,108,546	49.6	219	
	Other		—		15	
1964	**LYNDON B. JOHNSON (Tex.)**	Democratic	43,126,506	61.1	486	61.7
	Barry M. Goldwater	Republican	27,176,799	38.5	52	

PRESIDENTIAL ELECTIONS (cont.)

Year	Candidates	Parties	Popular Vote	Percentage of Popular Vote	Electoral Vote	Percentage of Voter Participation
1968	**RICHARD M. NIXON (N.Y.)**	Republican	31,770,237	43.4	301	60.6
	Hubert H. Humphrey	Democratic	31,270,533	42.7	191	
	George Wallace	American Independent	9,906,141	13.5	46	
1972	**RICHARD M. NIXON (N.Y.)**	Republican	47,169,911	60.7	520	55.2
	George S. McGovern	Democratic	29,170,383	37.5	17	
	Other		—		1	
1976	**JIMMY CARTER (Ga.)**	Democratic	40,828,587	50.0	297	53.5
	Gerald R. Ford	Republican	39,147,613	47.9	241	
	Other		1,575,459	2.1	—	
1980	**RONALD REAGAN (Calif.)**	Republican	43,901,812	50.7	489	52.6
	Jimmy Carter	Democratic	35,483,820	41.0	49	
	John B. Anderson	Independent	5,719,722	6.6	—	
	Ed Clark	Libertarian	921,188	1.1	—	
1984	**RONALD REAGAN (Calif.)**	Republican	54,455,075	59.0	525	53.3
	Walter Mondale	Democratic	37,577,185	41.0	13	
1988	**GEORGE BUSH (Texas)**	Republican	47,946,422	54.0	426	50.2
	Michael S. Dukakis	Democratic	41,016,429	46.0	112	
1992	**BILL CLINTON (Ark.)**	Democratic	43,728,375	43.0	370	55
	George Bush	Republican	38,167,416	38.0	168	
	Ross Perot	Independent	19,237,247	19.0	0	

POPULATION OF THE UNITED STATES,
1790–1990

Year	Population	Percent Increase	Population per Square Mile	Percent Urban/ Rural	Percent White/ Nonwhite	Median Age
1790	3,929,214		4.5	5.1/94.9	80.7/19.3	NA
1800	5,308,483	35.1	6.1	6.1/93.9	81.1/18.9	NA
1810	7,239,881	36.4	4.3	7.3/92.7	81.0/19.0	NA
1820	9,638,453	33.1	5.5	7.2/92.8	81.6/18.4	16.7
1830	12,866,020	33.5	7.4	8.8/91.2	81.9/18.1	17.2
1840	17,069,453	32.7	9.8	10.8/89.2	83.2/16.8	17.8
1850	23,191,876	35.9	7.9	15.3/84.7	84.3/15.7	18.9
1860	31,443,321	35.6	10.6	19.8/80.2	85.6/14.4	19.4
1870	39,818,449	26.6	13.4	25.7/74.3	86.2/13.8	20.2
1880	50,155,783	26.0	16.9	28.2/71.8	86.5/13.5	20.9
1890	62,947,714	25.5	21.2	35.1/64.9	87.5/12.5	22.0
1900	75,994,575	20.7	25.6	39.6/60.4	87.9/12.1	22.9
1910	91,972,266	21.0	31.0	45.6/54.4	88.9/11.1	24.1
1920	105,710,620	14.9	35.6	51.2/48.8	89.7/10.3	25.3
1930	122,775,046	16.1	41.2	56.1/43.9	89.8/10.2	26.4
1940	131,669,275	7.2	44.2	56.5/43.5	89.8/10.2	29.0
1950	150,697,361	14.5	50.7	64.0/36.0	89.5/10.5	30.2
1960	179,323,175	18.5	50.6	69.9/30.1	88.6/11.4	29.5
1970	203,302,031	13.4	57.4	73.5/26.5	87.6/12.4	28.0
1980	226,545,805	11.4	64.0	73.7/26.3	86.0/14.0	30.0
1990	248,709,873	9.9	70.3	77.5/22.5	80.3/19.7	32.9

NA = Not available.

EMPLOYMENT, 1870–1990

Year	Number of Workers (in millions)	Male/Female Employment Ratio	Percentage of Workers in Unions
1870	12.5	85/15	—
1880	17.4	85/15	—
1890	23.3	83/17	—
1900	29.1	82/18	3
1910	38.2	79/21	6
1920	41.6	79/21	12
1930	48.8	78/22	7
1940	53.0	76/24	27
1950	59.6	72/28	25
1960	69.9	68/32	26
1970	82.1	63/37	25
1980	108.5	58/42	23
1985	108.9	57/43	19
1988	114.9	55/45	17
1990	124.8	54/46	16

PRODUCTION, TRADE, AND FEDERAL SPENDING/DEBT, 1790–1990

Year	Gross National Product (GNP) (in billions $)	Balance of Trade (in millions $)	Federal Budget (in billions $)	Federal Surplus/Deficit (in billions $)	Federal Debt (in billions $)
1790	—	-3	.004	+0.00015	.076
1800	—	-20	.011	+0.0006	.083
1810	—	-18	.008	+0.0012	.053
1820	—	-4	.018	-0.0004	.091
1830	—	+3	.015	+0.100	.049
1840	—	+25	.024	-0.005	.004
1850	—	-26	.040	+0.004	.064
1860	—	-38	.063	-0.01	.065
1870	7.4	-11	.310	+0.10	2.4
1880	11.2	+92	.268	+0.07	2.1
1890	13.1	+87	.318	+0.09	1.2
1900	18.7	+569	.521	+0.05	1.2
1910	35.3	+273	.694	-0.02	1.1
1920	91.5	+2,880	6.357	+0.3	24.3
1930	90.7	+513	3.320	+0.7	16.3
1940	100.0	-3,403	9.6	-2.7	43.0
1950	286.5	+1,691	43.1	-2.2	257.4
1960	506.5	+4,556	92.2	+0.3	286.3
1970	992.7	+2,511	196.6	+2.8	371.0
1980	2,631.7	+24,088	579.6	-59.5	914.3
1990	5,465.1	-100,997.1	1,251.8	-220.3	3,223.3

Suggested Readings

CHAPTER 15 RECONSTRUCTING THE NATION

General Studies. Eric Foner, *Reconstruction: America's Unfinished Revolution, 1863–1877* (1988); Kenneth Stampp, *The Era of Reconstruction* (1965); John Hope Franklin, *Reconstruction After the Civil War* (1961); William A. Dunning, *Reconstruction, Political and Economic, 1865–1877* (1907); W. E. B. Du Bois, *Black Reconstruction* (1935); E. Merton Coulter, *The South During Reconstruction* (1947); Rembert Patrick, *The Reconstruction of the Nation* (1967).

Early Reconstruction. Herman Belz, *Reconstructing the Union* (1969); William B. Hesseltine, *Lincoln's Plan of Reconstruction* (1960); Willie Lee Rose, *Rehearsal for Reconstruction: The Port Royal Experiment* (1964); Louis S. Gerteis, *From Contraband to Freedman* (1973); Richard H. Abbott, *The First Southern Strategy* (1986).

Congressional Reconstruction. William R. Brock, *An American Crisis* (1963); Howard K. Beale, *The Critical Year: A Study of Andrew Johnson and Reconstruction* (1930); Eric McKitrick, *Andrew Johnson and Reconstruction* (1960); Hans Trefousse, *Andrew Johnson* (1989); Michael Les Benedict, *A Compromise of Principle: Congressional Republicans and Reconstruction, 1863–1869* and *The Impeachment and Trial of Andrew Johnson* (1973); Hans L. Trefousse, *The Radical Republicans* (1963) and *The Impeachment of a President* (1975); David Donald, *The Politics of Reconstruction* (1965); La Wanda Cox and John H. Cox, *Politics, Principles, and Prejudice, 1865–1867* (1963); Richard N. Current, *Old Thad Stevens* (1942); Fawn Brodie, *Thaddeus Stevens* (1959); David Donald, *Charles Sumner and the Rights of Man* (1970); Harold Hyman, *A More Perfect Union* (1973); Stanley Kutler, *The Judicial Power and Reconstruction Politics* (1968); Mark W. Summers, *Railroads, Reconstruction, and the Gospel of Prosperity* (1984); Charles Fairman, *Reconstruction and Reunion* (1971); Herman Belz, *A New Birth of Freedom* (1976) and *Emancipation and Equal Rights* (1978); William Gillette, *The Right to Vote* (1965).

The South in Reconstruction. Dan T. Carter, *When the War Was Over: The Failure of Self-Reconstruction in the South, 1865–1867* (1985); Michael Perman, *Reunion Without Compromise* (1973) and *The Road to Redemption: Southern Politics, 1869–1879* (1984); Joel G. Taylor, *Louisiana Reconstructed* (1974); Vernon Wharton, *The Negro in Mississippi, 1865–1890* (1965); Peyton McCrary, *Abraham Lincoln and Reconstruction* (1978); Joel Williamson, *After Slavery: The Negro in South Carolina During Reconstruction* (1965); Thomas Holt, *Black over White* (1977); Roberta Alexander, *North Carolina Faces the Freedmen: Race Relations During Presidential Reconstruction, 1865–1867* (1985); C. Peter Ripley, *Slaves and Freedmen in Civil War Louisiana* (1976); Barbara Fields, *Slavery and Freedom on the Middle Ground* (1985); Michael Wayne, *The Reshaping of Plantation Society: The Natchez District* (1983); William Gillette, *Retreat from Reconstruction* (1980); James D. Anderson, *The Education of Blacks in the South* (1989); Roger Ransom and Richard Sutch, *One Kind of Freedom* (1977); Robert Higgs, *Competition and Coercion* (1977); Crandall A. Shifflett, *Patronage and Poverty in the Tobacco South: Louisa County, Virginia 1860–1900* (1982); Leon Litwack, *Been in the Storm So Long* (1979); Eric Foner, *Nothing but Freedom: Emancipation and Its Legacy* (1983); Peter Kolchin, *First Freedom* (1972);

Allen Trelease, *White Terror* (1967); William S. McFeely, *Yankee Stepfather: General O. O. Howard and the Freedmen* (1968); George Bentley, *A History of the Freedmen's Bureau* (1955); Otto Olsen, *Carpetbagger's Crusade: Albion Winegar Tourgée* (1965); L. N. Powell, *New Masters: Northern Planters During the Civil War and Reconstruction* (1980); William Harris, *Day of the Carpetbagger* (1979); Elizabeth Jacoway, *Yankee Missionaries in the South* (1979); Richard N. Current, *Those Terrible Carpetbaggers* (1988); William C. Harris, *The Day of the Carpetbagger: Republican Reconstruction in Mississippi, 1867–1875* (1979); Sarah Wiggins, *The Scalawag in Alabama Politics, 1865–1881* (1977); Jacqueline Jones, *Soldiers of Light and Love* (1980) and *Labor of Love, Labor of Sorrow: Black Women, Work, and the Family from Slavery to the Present* (1985); James Sefton, *The United States Army and Reconstruction* (1967).

The Grant Administration. Williams McFeely, *Grant* (1981); Margaret S. Thompson, *The "Spider Web": Congress and Lobbying in the Age of Grant* (1985); Allan Nevins, *Hamilton Fish* (1936); William B. Hesseltine, *U. S. Grant, Politician* (1935); David Loth, *Public Plunder* (1938); John G. Sproat, *"The Best Men"* (1968); Ari Hoogenboom, *Outlawing the Spoils* (1961); Irwin Unger, *The Greenback Era* (1964); C. Vann Woodward, *Reunion and Reaction* (1951); K. I. Polakoff, *The Politics of Inertia* (1973); Edwin C. Rozwenc, ed., *Reconstruction in the South*, rev. ed. (1952).

CHAPTER 16 THE NEW SOUTH AND THE FAR WEST

The New South. C. Vann Woodward, *Origins of the New South* (1951), *The Burden of Southern History* (rev. 1968), *American Counterpoint* (1971), *Thinking Back* (1986), and *The Future of the Past* (1989); Jonathan Wiener, *Social Origins of the New South: Alabama, 1860–1885* (1978); Paul Buck, *The Road to Reunion* (1937); Paul Gaston, *The New South Creed* (1970); W. J. Cash, *The Mind of the South* (1941); Orville Vernon Burton, *In My Father's House* (1985); Orville Vernon Burton and Robert C. McMath, Jr., eds., *Toward a New South?* (1982); J. Morgan Kousser and James M. McPherson, eds., *Region, Race, and Reconstruction* (1982).

Southern Politics. C. Vann Woodward, *Reunion and Reaction* (1951) and *Tom Watson: Agrarian Rebel* (1938); Stanley P. Hirshson, *Farewell to the Bloody Shirt: Northern Republicans and the Southern Negro* (1962); Kenneth E. Davison, *The Presidency of Rutherford B. Hayes* (1972); Vincent P. DeSantis, *Republicans Face the Southern Question: The New Departure Years, 1877–1897* (1959); J. Morgan Kousser, *The Shaping of Southern Politics: Suffrage Restriction and the Establishment of the One-Party South, 1880–1910* (1974); Paul Lewinson, *Race, Class, and Party* (1932); V. O. Key, Jr., *Southern Politics and the Nation* (1949); Francis B. Simkins, *Pitchfork Ben Tillman* (1944); Joseph F. Wall, *Henry Watterson: Reconstructed Rebel* (1956); Sheldon Hackney, *Populism to Progressivism in Alabama* (1959); David Potter, *The South and the Concurrent Majority* (1972); Carl Degler, *The Other South: Southern Dissenters in the Nineteenth Century* (1974).

Race, Economics, and Social Structure. Gavin Wright, *Old South, New South* (1986); Melvin Greenhut and W. Tate Whitman, eds., *Essays in Southern Economic Development* (1964); Jacquelyn Dowd Hall et al., *Like a Family: The Making of a Southern Cotton Mill World* (1987); David Carlton, *Mill and Town in South Carolina, 1880–1920* (1982); Don Doyle, *New Men, New Cities, New South: Atlanta, Nashville, Charleston, Mobile, 1860–1910*

(1990); Melton A. McLaurin, *Paternalism and Protest: Southern Cotton Mill Workers and Organized Labor* (1971); Altina L. Waller, *Feud: Hatfields, McCoys, and Social Changes: Appalachia, 1860–1900* (1988); Steven Hahn, *The Roots of Southern Populism: Yeoman Farmers and the Transformation of the Georgia Upcountry* (1983); Steven Hahn and Jonathan Prude, eds., *The Countryside in the Age of Capitalist Transformation* (1985); Roger Ransom and Richard Sutch, *One Kind of Freedom* (1977); C. Vann Woodward, *The Strange Career of Jim Crow* (rev. 1974); Howard Rabinowitz, *Race Relations in the Urban South, 1865–1890* (1978); Cynthia Neverdon-Morton, *Afro-American Women of the South and the Advancement of the Race, 1895–1925* (1989); James M. McPherson, *The Abolitionist Legacy: From Reconstruction to the NAACP* (1975); Robert Higgs, *Competition and Coercion: Blacks in the American Economy, 1865–1914* (1977); Joel Williamson, *After Slavery* (1965), *The Crucible of Race: Black-White Relations in the American South Since Emancipation* (1985), and *A Rage for Order* (1986), an abridgment of *The Crucible of Race;* Neil McMillen, *Dark Journey: Black Mississippians in the Age of Jim Crow* (1989); Louis R. Harlan, *Booker T. Washington: The Making of a Black Leader, 1856–1901* (1972) and *Booker T. Washington: The Wizard of Tuskegee: 1901–1915* (1983); August Meier, *Negro Thought in America* (1963); Francis Broderick, *W. E. B. DuBois* (1959); Elliott M. Rudwick, *W. E. B. DuBois: Propagandist of Negro Protest* (rev. 1969).

The Far West.   Ray Allen Billington and Martin Ridge, *Westward Expansion*, rev. ed. (1982); Robert V. Hine, *The American West*, 2nd ed. (1984); Frederick Merk, *History of the Westward Movement* (1978); Richard White, *It's Your Misfortune and None of My Own: A New History of the American West* (1991); Patricia Limerick, *The Legacy of Conquest: The Unbroken Past of the American West* (1987); Richard Slotkin, *The Fatal Environment: The Myth of the Frontier in the Age of Industrialization* (1985); Rodman W. Paul and Richard W. Etulain, *The Frontier and the American West* (1977); Thomas D. Clark, *Frontier America* (rev. 1969); Howard R. Lamar, *The Far Southwest, 1846–1912* (1966); Henry Nash Smith, *Virgin Land* (1950); Frederick Jackson Turner, *The Frontier in American History* (1920); Ray A. Billington, *Frederick Jackson Turner* (1973).

Miners and Cattlemen.   Rodman W. Paul, *Mining Frontiers of the Far West, 1848–1880* (1963) and *The Far West and the Great Plains in Transition, 1859–1900* (1988); William S. Greever, *Bonanza West: Western Mining Rushes* (1963); Duane A. Smith, *Rocky Mountain Mining Camps* (1967); Lewis Atherton, *The Cattle Kings* (1961); Ernest E. Osgood, *The Day of the Cattleman* (1929); Edward E. Dale, *The Range Cattle Industry*, rev. ed. (1969); J. M. Skaggs, *The Cattle Trailing Industry* (1973); Robert K. Dykstra, *The Cattle Towns* (1968); Andy Adams, *The Log of a Cowboy* (1927); Joe B. Frantz and Julian Choate, *The American Cowboy: The Myth and the Reality* (1955); L. Steckmesser, *The Western Hero in History and Legend* (1965); Odie B. Faulk, *Tombstone: Myth and Reality* (1972); Earl Pomeroy, *The Pacific Slope* (1965); Gunther Barth, *Instant Cities* (1975).

Indians.   Wilcomb E. Washburn, *The Indian in America* (1975) and *Red Man's Land/White Man's Law* (1971); Ralph K. Andrist, *The Long Death: The Last Days of the Plains Indians* (1964); Francis P. Prucha, *American Indian Policy in Crisis* (1976) and *The Great White Father: The United States Government and the American Indians* (1984); William T. Hagan, *The Indian Rights Association: The Herbert Welsh Years, 1882–1904* (1985); Robert M. Utley, *Last Days of the Sioux Nation* (1963), *Frontiersmen in Blue: The United States Army and the Indian, 1848–1865* (1967), *Frontier Regulars: The United States Army and the Indian* (1973), and *The Indian Frontier of the American West, 1846–1890* (1984); Dee Brown, *Bury My Heart at Wounded Knee: An Indian History of the*

American West (1970); Thomas W. Dunlay, *Wolves for the Blue Soldiers* (1982); Margert Coel, *Chief Left Hand: Southern Arapaho* (1981); Loretta Fowler, *Arapahoe Politics, 1851–1978: Symbols in Crisis of Authority* (1982); John Powell, *People of the Sacred Mountain: A History of the Northern Cheyenne Chiefs and Warrior Societies, 1830–1879*, 2 vols. (1981); Angie Debo, *Geronimo* (1976); Mari Sandoz, *Crazy Horse* (1961); James C. Olson, *Red Cloud and the Sioux Problem* (1965); Donald J. Berthrong, *The Southern Cheyennes* (1963); Frederick E. Hoxie, *A Final Promise: The Campaign to Assimilate the Indians, 1880–1920* (1984); Robert Mardock, *Reformers and the American Indian* (1971); Robert F. Berkhofer, Jr., *The White Man's Indian* (1978); Richard White, *The Roots of Dependency* (1983).

Western Women. Julie Jeffrey, *Frontier Women: The Trans-Mississippi West, 1840–1880* (1979); Sandra L. Myres, *Westering Women and the Frontier Experience, 1880–1915* (1982); Polly Welts Kaufman, *Women Teachers on the Frontier* (1984); Joanna L. Stratton, *Pioneer Women: Voices from the Kansas Frontier* (1981); John Mack Faragher, *Women and Men on the Overland Trail* (1979); Glenda Riley, *Women and Indians on the Frontier, 1825–1915* (1984) and *The Female Frontier* (1988); Susan Armitage and Elizabeth Jameson, eds., *The Women's West* (1987); Ruth Moynihan, *Rebel for Rights: Abigail Scott Dunaway* (1983).

Western Agriculture. Walter Prescott Webb, *The Great Plains* (1931); Fred A. Shannon, *The Farmer's Last Frontier, 1860–1897* (1945); Gilbert C. Fite, *The Farmer's Frontier* (1966); Paul W. Gates, *History of Public Land Development* (1968); Everett Dick, *The Sod-House Frontier* (1937); Allan Bogue, *From Prairie to Corn Belt* (1963); John Mack Faragher, *Sugar Creek: Life on the Illinois Prairie* (1986). See also Suggested Readings for Chapter 19.

CHAPTER 17 INDUSTRIAL SUPREMACY

General Histories. John A. Garraty, *The New Commonwealth* (1968); Edward C. Kirkland, *Industry Comes of Age: Business, Labor, and Public Policy, 1860–1897* (1961); Samuel P. Hays, *The Response to Industrialism, 1885–1914* (1957); Ray Ginger, *The Age of Excess* (1963); Carl Degler, *The Age of the Economic Revolution* (1977); Daniel Boorstin, *The Americans: The Democratic Experience* (1973); Thomas C. Cochran and William Miller, *The Age of Enterprise* (1942); Robert Higgs, *The Transformation of the American Economy, 1865–1914* (1971); Robert Wiebe, *The Search for Order, 1877–1920* (1968).

Technology. Roger Burlingame, *Engines of Democracy: Inventions and Society in Mature America* (1940) and *Henry Ford* (1957); Lewis Mumford, *Technics and Civilization* (1934); George Daniels, *Science and Society in America* (1971); Nathan Rosenberg, *Technology and American Economic Growth* (1972); Elting E. Morison, *Men, Machines, and Modern Times* (1966); Judith McGaw, *Most Wonderful Machine: Mechanization and Social Change in Berkshire Paper Making, 1801–1885* (1988); Robert W. Bruce, *Bell* (1973); Frank E. Hill, *Ford* (1954); Allan Nevins, *Ford*, 3 vols. (1954–1962); Peter Temin, *Steel in Nineteenth Century America* (1964); Frederick A. White, *American Industrial Research Laboratories* (1961); Robert Conot, *A Streak of Luck* (1979); Richard N. Current, *The Typewriter and the Men Who Made It* (1954).

Railroads. George R. Taylor and I. D. Neu, *The American Railroad Network, 1861–1890* (1956); John F. Stover, *The Life and Decline of the American Railroad* (1970) and *The*

Railroads of the South, 1865–1900 (1955); Richard C. Overton, *Burlington West* (1941) and *Gulf to Rockies* (1953); Edward C. Kirkland, *Men, Cities, and Transportation*, 2 vols. (1948); Thomas C. Cochran, *Railroad Leaders* (1953); Edward G. Campbell, *The Reorganization of the American Railroad System* (1938); Gabriel Kolko, *Railroads and Regulation, 1877–1916* (1965); Lee Benson, *Merchants, Farmers, and Railroads* (1955); George H. Miller, *Railroads and the Granger Laws* (1971); Robert Fogel, *Railroads and American Economic Growth* (1964); Anthony F. C. Wallace, *St. Clair: A Nineteenth-Century Coal Town's Experience with a Disaster-Prone Industry* (1987).

The Corporation. Alfred D. Chandler, Jr., *Strategy and Structure: Chapters in the History of the American Industrial Enterprise* (1962), *Pierre S. DuPont and the Making of the Modern Corporation* (1971), *The Visible Hand: The Managerial Revolution in American Business* (1977), and *Scale and Scope: The Dynamics of Industrial Capitalism* (1990); Glenn Porter, *The Rise of Big Business* (1973); Glenn Porter and Harold C. Livesay, *Merchants and Manufacturers* (1971); Olivier Zunz, *Making America Corporate, 1870–1920* (1990); Norma R. Lamoreaux, *The Great Merger Movement in American Business, 1895–1904* (1985); Matthew Josephson, *The Robber Barons* (1934); Maury Klein, *The Life and Legend of Jay Gould* (1986); Harold C. Livesay, *Andrew Carnegie and the Rise of Big Business* (1975); Allan Nevins, *Study in Power: John D. Rockefeller*, 2 vols. (1953); David F. Hawkes, *John D.: The Founding Father of the Rockefellers* (1980); Joseph Wall, *Andrew Carnegie* (1970); Bernard Weisberger, *The Dream Maker* (1979).

Ideologies. Edward C. Kirkland, *Dream and Thought in the Business Community, 1860–1900* (1956); Sidney Fine, *Laissez Faire and the General Welfare State: A Study of Conflict in American Thought, 1865–1901* (1956); Irvin G. Wylie, *The Self-Made Man in America* (1954); Daniel T. Rodgers, *The Work Ethic in Industrial America, 1850–1920* (1978); David Thelen, *Paths of Resistance: Tradition and Dignity in Industrializing Missouri* (1986); Louis Galambos, *The Public Image of Big Business in America, 1880–1940* (1975); Richard Hofstadter, *Social Darwinism in American Thought*, rev. ed. (1955); Robert G. McCloskey, *American Conservatism in the Age of Enterprise* (1951); Samuel Chugerman, *Lester F. Ward: The American Aristotle* (1939); Arthur E. Morgan, *Edward Bellamy* (1944); Charles A. Baker, *Henry George* (1955); John L. Thomas, *Alternative America: Henry George, Edward Bellamy, Henry Demarest Lloyd, and the Adversary Tradition* (1983); T. J. Jackson Lears, *No Place of Grace: Antimodernism and the Transformation of American Culture, 1880–1920* (1981).

Labor. Melvyn Dubofsky, *Industrialism and the American Worker, 1865–1920* (1975); Henry Pelling, *American Labor* (1960); Herbert G. Gutman, *Work, Culture, and Society in Industrializing America* (1976); David Montgomery, *Beyond Equality* (1975), *Workers' Control in America: Studies in the History of Work, Technology, and Labor Struggles* (1979), and *The Fall of the House of Labor* (1987); Richard J. Oestreicher, *Solidarity and Fragmentation: Working People and Class Consciousness: Detroit, 1875–1900* (1986); Brian Greenberg, *Worker and Community: Response to Industrialization in a Nineteenth-Century American City, Albany, New York, 1850–1884* (1985); Daniel Nelson, *Managers and Workers: Origins of the New Factory System in the United States, 1880–1920* (1975); Stuart Kaufman, *Samuel Gompers and the Origins of the American Federation of Labor* (1978); Philip Taft, *The A.F. of L. in the Time of Gompers*, 2 vols. (1957–1959); Samuel Gompers, *Seventy Years of Life and Labor*, 2 vols. (1975); Stanley Buder, *Pullman* (1967); Henry David, *The Haymarket Affair* (1936); P. K. Edwards, *Strikes in the United States, 1881–1974* (1981); Sheldon Stromquist, *A Generation of Boomers: The Pattern of Railroad Labor Conflict in*

Nineteenth-Century America (1987); Steven J. Ross, *Workers on the Edge: Work, Leisure, and Politics in Industrializing Cincinnati, 1788–1890* (1985); Roy Rosenzweig, *"Eight Hours for What We Will": Workers and Leisure in an Industrial City, 1870–1920* (1983); Alexander Keyssar, *Out of Work: The First Century of Unemployment in Massachusetts* (1986).

Women. Susan E. Kennedy, *If All We Did Was to Weep at Home* (1979); Barbara Wertheimer, *We Were There: The Story of Working Women in America* (1977); Patricia Cooper, *Once a Cigar Maker: Men, Women, and Work Culture in American Cigar Factories, 1900–1919* (1987); Mary Blewett, *Men, Women, and Work Culture: Class, Gender, and Protest in the New England Shoe Industry* (1988); Tamara Hareven, *Family Time and Industrial Time: The Relationship Between the Family and Work in a New England Industrial Community* (1982); Alice Kessler-Harris, *Out to Work: A History of Wage-Earning Women in the United States* (1982); Susan Levine, *Labor's True Women: Carpet Weavers, Industrialization, and Labor Reform in the Gilded Age* (1984).

The Left. J. H. M. Laslett, *Labor and the Left* (1970); Nick Salvatore, *Eugene V. Debs: Citizen and Socialist* (1982); Mari Jo Buhle, *Women and American Socialism, 1870–1920* (1981); Melvyn Dubofsky, *We Shall Be All: A History of the Industrial Workers of the World* (1969); Gerald N. Grob, *Workers and Utopia* (1961).

CHAPTER 18 THE AGE OF THE CITY

General Histories. Howard Chudacoff, *The Evolution of American Urban Society*, rev. ed. (1981); Blake McKelvey, *The Urbanization of America* (1963); Constance M. Green, *The Rise of Urban America* (1965); Charles N. Glaab and Andrew T. Brown, *A History of Urban America* (1967); Arthur M. Schlesinger, *The Rise of the City, 1878–1898* (1933); Sam Bass Warner, Jr., *The Urban Wilderness* (1972) and *Streetcar Suburbs* (1962); Jon C. Teaford, *City and Suburb: The Political Fragmentation of Urban America* (1979) and *The Twentieth-Century American City: Problem, Promise, and Reality* (1986); Lewis Mumford, *The Culture of the Cities* (1938) and *The City in History* (1961).

Mobility and Race. Stephan Thernstrom, *Poverty and Progress* (1964) and *The Other Bostonians* (1973); Michael Frisch, *Town into City* (1972); Richard Sennett, *Families Against the City* (1970); Clyde Griffen and Sally Griffen, *Natives and Newcomers* (1977); Howard Chudacoff, *Mobile Americans* (1972); Stephan Thernstrom and Richard Sennett, eds., *Nineteenth Century Cities* (1969); Gilbert Osofsky, *Harlem: The Making of a Ghetto* (1966); Allan H. Spear, *Black Chicago* (1967); Kenneth L. Kusmer, *A Ghetto Takes Shape* (1976); David M. Katzman, *Before the Ghetto* (1966); Olivier Zunz, *The Changing Face of Inequality: Urbanization, Industrial Development, and Immigrants in Detroit, 1880–1920* (1982).

Immigration. John Bodnar, *The Transplanted: A History of Immigrants in America* (1985) and *Immigration and Industrialization* (1977); Oscar Handlin, *The Uprooted*, rev. ed. (1973); Thomas Kessner, *The Golden Door: Italian and Jewish Immigrant Mobility* (1977); Josef Barton, *Peasants and Strangers: Italians, Rumanians, and Slovaks in an American City* (1975); Virginia Yans-McLaughlin, *Family and Community: Italian Immigrants in Buffalo, 1880–1930* (1977); Philip Taylor, *The Distant Magnet: European Emigration to the U.S.A.*

(1971); Marcus Hansen, *The Immigrant in American History* (1940); Maldwyn A. Jones, *American Immigration* (1960); David Ward, *Cities and Immigrants* (1965); Barbara Solomon, *Ancestors and Immigrants* (1965); Elizabeth Ewen, *Immigrant Women in the Land of Dollars: Life and Culture on the Lower East Side, 1890–1925* (1985); Ewa Morawska, *For Bread and Butter: The Life-Worlds of East Central Europeans in Johnstown, Pennsylvania, 1890–1940* (1985); Jack Chen, *The Chinese of America* (1980); Francis L. K. Hsu, *The Challenge of the American Dream: The Chinese in the United States* (1971); Moses Rischin, *The Promised City: New York's Jews* (1962); Humbert S. Nelli, *The Italians of Chicago* (1970); John W. Briggs, *An Italian Passage* (1978); John B. Duff, *The Irish in the United States* (1971); Mario T. Garcia, *Desert Immigrants: The Mexicans of El Paso, 1880–1920* (1981); Matt S. Maier and Feliciano Rivera, *The Chicanos: A History of Mexican-Americans* (1972); Harry Kitano, *Japanese-Americans: The Evolution of a Subculture* (1969); Victor Greene, *For God and Country: The Rise of Polish and Lithuanian Ethnic Consciousness in America* (1975); Edward R. Kantowicz, *Polish-American Politics in Chicago* (1975); Nathan Glazer and Daniel P. Moynihan, *Beyond the Melting Pot* (1963); Leonard Dinnerstein and David Reimers, *Ethnic Americans: A History of Immigration and Assimilation* (1975); Milton M. Gordon, *Assimilation in American Life* (1964); Thomas Sowell, *Ethnic America* (1981); Robert D. Cross, *The Church and the City* (1967); John Higham, *Strangers in the Land* (1955) and *Send These to Me* (1975).

Urban Poverty and Reform. Robert H. Bremner, *From the Depths* (1956); James T. Patterson, *America's Struggle Against Poverty* (1981); Thomas L. Philpott, *The Slum and the Ghetto* (1978); Jacob Riis, *How the Other Half Lives* (1890), *Children of the Poor* (1892), and *The Battle with the Slum* (1902); Allen F. Davis, *Spearheads for Reform* (1967); Marvin Lazerson, *Origins of the Urban School* (1971); Stephan F. Brumberg, *Going to America, Going to School* (1986); Selwyn K. Troen, *The Public and the Schools* (1975); David B. Tyack, *The One Best System: A History of American Urban Education* (1974); Barbara Gutmann Rosencrantz, *Public Health and the State* (1972); James H. Cassedy, *Charles V. Chapin and the Public Health Movement* (1962); James F. Richardson, *The New York Police* (1970).

Urban Politics. John M. Allswang, *Bosses, Machines and Urban Voters* (1977); Alexander B. Callow, *The Tweed Ring* (1966); Seymour Mandelbaum, *Boss Tweed's New York* (1965); Lyle Dorsett, *The Pendergast Machine* (1968); Zane Miller, *Boss Cox's Cincinnati* (1968); John Sproat, *The Best Men* (1968).

Social Thought and Urban Culture. Stuart Blumin, *The Emergence of the Middle Class: Social Experience in the American City, 1760–1900* (1989); Lawrence Levine, *Highbrow/Lowbrow: The Emergence of a Cultural Hierarchy in America* (1988); Morton White, *Social Thought in America* (1949); D. W. Marcell, *Progress and Pragmatism* (1974); Charles Forcey, *The Crossroads of Liberalism* (1961); Lawrence Cremin, *The Transformation of the School* (1961); Frank Luther Mott, *American Journalism*, rev. ed. (1962); Larzer Ziff, *The American 1890s: Life and Times of a Lost Generation* (1966); Jay Martin, *Harvests of Change* (1967); Susan Porter Benson, *Counter Cultures: Saleswomen, Managers, and Customers in American Department Stores, 1890–1940* (1986); Godfrey M. Lebhar, *Chain Stores in America* (1962); John F. Kasson, *Amusing the Million: Coney Island at the Turn of the Century* (1978) and *Rudeness and Civility: Manners in Nineteenth-Century Urban America* (1990); Kathy Peiss, *Cheap Amusements: Working Women and Leisure in Turn-of-the-Century New York* (1986); Marc Carnes, *Secret Ritual and Manhood in Victorian America*

(1989); Gunther Barth, *City People* (1980); Allen Guttmann, *A Whole New Ball Game: An Interpretation of American Sports* (1988); Donald R. Mrozek, *Sport and American Mentality, 1880–1910* (1983); Harvey Green, *Fit for America: Fitness, Sport, and American Society* (1986); John A. Lucas and Ronald Smith, *Saga of American Sport* (1978); Dale Somers, *The Rise of Sports in New Orleans* (1972); Eliot Gorn, *The Manly Art: Bare-Knuckle Prize Fighting in America* (1986); Lewis Mumford, *The Brown Decades* (1931); T. J. Jackson Lears, *No Place of Grace: Antimodernism and the Transformation of American Culture, 1880–1920* (1981); T. J. Jackson Lears and Richard Wightman Fox, eds., *The Culture of Consumption* (1983); Christopher Tunnard and H. H. Reed, *American Skyline* (1955).

CHAPTER 19 FROM STALEMATE TO CRISIS

General Histories. Nell Irvin Painter, *Standing at Armageddon: The United States, 1877–1919* (1987); R. Hal Williams, *Years of Decision: American Politics in the 1890s* (1978); John H. Dobson, *Politics in the Gilded Age* (1972); John A. Garraty, *The New Commonwealth* (1969); Harold U. Faulkner, *Politics, Reform, and Expansion* (1959); Samuel P. Hays, *The Response to Industrialism, 1885–1914* (1957); Robert Wiebe, *The Search for Order, 1877–1920* (1967); Sean Denis Cashman, *America and the Gilded Age* (1984); Alan Trachtenberg, *The Intercorporation of America: Culture and Society in the Gilded Age* (1982).

Politics, Reform, and the States. Morton Keller, *Affairs of State* (1977); Stephen Skowronek, *Building a New American State: The Expansion of National Administrative Capacities, 1877–1920* (1982); Martin J. Sklar, *The Corporate Reconstruction of American Capitalism, 1890–1916* (1988); Matthew Josephson, *The Politicos* (1963); David J. Rothman, *Politics and Power: The United States Senate, 1869–1901* (1966); Robert D. Marcus, *Grand Old Party* (1971); H. Wayne Morgan, *From Hayes to McKinley* (1969); Leonard D. White, *The Republican Era* (1958); Ari Hoogenboom, *Outlawing the Spoils* (1961) and *The Presidency of Rutherford B. Hayes* (1988); Walter T. K. Nugent, *Money and American Society* (1968); Allen Weinstein, *Prelude to Populism* (1970); Irwin Unger, *The Greenback Era* (1964); John Sproat, *"The Best Men"* (1968); Geoffrey Blodgett, *The Gentle Reformers* (1966); James Bryce, *The American Commonwealth*, 2 vols. (1888); Paul Kleppner, *The Cross of Culture: A Social Analysis of Midwestern Politics, 1850–1900* (1970) and *The Third Electoral System, 1853–1892* (1979); Richard Jensen, *The Winning of the Midwest: Social and Political Conflict, 1888–1896* (1971); Ruth Bourdin, *Women and Temperance: The Quest for Power and Liberty, 1873–1900* (1980); Michael E. McGerr, *The Decline of Popular Politics* (1986).

Party Leaders. Harry Barnard, *Rutherford B. Hayes and His America* (1954); Kenneth Davison, *The Presidency of Rutherford B. Hayes* (1972); Allan Peskin, *Garfield* (1978); Margaret Leech and Harry J. Brown, *The Garfield Orbit* (1978); Thomas C. Reeves, *Gentleman Boss: The Life of Chester Alan Arthur* (1975); David Jordan, *Roscoe Conkling of New York* (1971); Allan Nevins, *Grover Cleveland: A Study in Courage* (1933); Horace Samuel Merrill, *Bourbon Leader: Grover Cleveland and the Democractic Party* (1957); Harry J. Sievers, *Benjamin Harrison*, 3 vols. (1952–1968); H. Wayne Morgan, *William McKinley and His America* (1963); Lewis L. Gould, *The Presidency of William McKinley* (1981); Margaret Leech, *In the Days of McKinley* (1959); Herbert Croly, *Marcus Alonzo Hanna* (1912); Nick Salvatore, *Eugene V. Debs: Citizen and Socialist* (1982).

The Depression. Samuel McSeveney, *The Politics of Depression* (1972); Donald McMurray, *Coxey's Army* (1929); Carlos A. Schwantes, *Coxey's Army* (1955); Ray Ginger, *The Bending Cross* (1949); Almot Lindsey, *The Pullman Strike* (1942); Ray Ginger, *Altgeld's America* (1958).

Populism. John D. Hicks, *The Populist Revolt* (1931); Lawrence Goodwyn, *Democratic Promise* (1976) and *The Populist Moment* (1978), an abridgement of *Democratic Promise;* Norman Pollack, *The Populist Response to Industrial America* (1962) and *The Just Polity: Populism, Law, and Human Welfare* (1987); Allan Weinstein, *Prelude to Populism: Origins of the Silver Issue* (1970); Richard Hofstadter, *The Age of Reform* (1954); Sheldon Hackney, *Populism to Progressivism in Alabama* (1969); C. Vann Woodward, *Origins of the New South* (1972); Steven Hahn, *The Roots of Southern Populism* (1983); Robert McMath, *Populist Vanguard* (1975); Bruce Palmer, *Man over Money* (1980); Walter T. K. Nugent, *The Tolerant Populists* (1960); Theodore Saloutos, *Farmer Movements in the South, 1865–1933* (1960); Fred Shannon, *The Farmer's Last Frontier* (1945); Peter Argersinger, *Populism and Politics: William Alfred Peffer and the People's Party* (1974); Barton C. Shaw, *The Wool-Hat Boys: Georgia's Populist Party* (1984); Theodore R. Mitchell, *Political Education in the Southern Farmers Alliance, 1887–1900* (1987); C. Vann Woodward, *Tom Watson, Agrarian Rebel* (1938); Francis B. Simkins, *Pitchfork Ben Tillman* (1944).

The Election of 1896. Paul Glad, *McKinley, Bryan, and the People* (1964) and *The Trumpet Soundeth* (1960); Stanley Jones, *The Presidential Election of 1896* (1964); J. Rogers Hollingsworth, *The Whirligig of Politics: The Democracy of Cleveland and Bryan* (1963); Paolo Coletta, *William Jennings Bryan: Political Evangelist* (1964).

CHAPTER 20 THE IMPERIAL REPUBLIC

General Histories. Charles S. Campbell, *The Transformation of American Foreign Relations, 1865–1900* (1976); Robert L. Beisner, *From the Old Diplomacy to the New, 1865–1900* (1975); Julius W. Pratt, *Expansionists of 1898* (1936); Albert K. Weinberg, *Manifest Destiny: A Study in Nationalist Expansion in American History* (1935); Walter LeFeber, *The New Empire* (1963); William Appleman Williams, *The Tragedy of American Diplomacy*, rev. ed. (1972); Ernest May, *Imperial Democracy* (1961) and *American Imperialism: A Speculative Essay* (1968); David F. Healy, *U.S. Expansionism: Imperialist Urge in the 1890s* (1970); John Dobson, *America's Ascent: The United States Becomes a Great Power, 1880–1914* (1978); H. Wayne Morgan, *America's Road to Empire* (1965); J. A. S. Grenville and George Berkeley Young, *Politics, Strategy and American Diplomacy: Studies in Foreign Policy, 1873–1917* (1966); Milton Plesur, *America's Outward Thrust: Approaches to Foreign Affairs, 1865–1890* (1971); David M. Pletcher, *The Awkward Years: American Foreign Relations under Garfield and Arthur* (1962).

The Spanish-American War. David F. Trask, *The War with Spain in 1898* (1981); Frank Freidel, *The Splendid Little War* (1958); Joyce Milton, *The Yellow Journalists* (1989); Walter Millis, *The Martial Spirit* (1931); Louis A. Perez, Jr., *Cuba Between Empires, 1868–1902* (1983); Philip S. Foner, *The Spanish-Cuban-American War and the Birth of American Imperialism*, 2 vols. (1972); Graham A. Cosmas, *An Army for Empire: The United States Army in the Spanish-American War* (1971); Richard S. West, Jr., *Admirals of the*

American Empire (1948); Richard Challener, *Admirals, Generals, and American Foreign Policy, 1889–1914* (1973); Willard B. Gatewood, Jr., *Black Americans and the White Man's Burden, 1898–1903* (1975) and *"Smoked Yankees": Letters from Negro Soldiers, 1898–1902* (1971); Edmund Morris, *The Rise of Theodore Roosevelt* (1979); Gerald F. Linderman, *The Mirror of War: American Society and the Spanish-American War* (1974).

Imperialism and Anti-Imperialism. Robert L. Beisner, *Twelve Against Empire* (1968); E. Berkeley Tompkins, *Anti-Imperialism in the United States, 1890–1920: The Great Debate* (1970); Thomas J. Osborne, *"Empire Can Wait": American Opposition to Hawaiian Annexation, 1893–1898* (1981); Kendrick A. Clements, *William Jennings Bryan* (1983); Frederick Merk, *Manifest Destiny and Mission in American History* (1963); Julius W. Pratt, *America's Colonial Empire* (1950); James H. Hitchman, *Leonard Wood and Cuban Independence, 1898–1902* (1971).

The Pacific Empire. Peter Stanley, *A Nation in the Making: The Philippines and the United States* (1974); Paul M. Kennedy, *The Samoan Tangle* (1974); Glenn May, *Social Engineering in the Philippines* (1980); Merze Tate, *The United States and the Hawaiian Kingdom* (1965); Richard E. Welch, Jr., *Response to Imperialism: The United States and the Philippine-American War, 1899–1902* (1979); Leon Wolff, *Little Brown Brother* (1961); Stuart Creighton Miller, *"Benevolent Assimilation": The American Conquest of the Philippines, 1899–1903* (1982); John Morgan Gates, *Schoolbooks and Krags: The United States Army in the Philippines, 1898–1902* (1971); Daniel B. Schirmer, *Republic or Empire? American Resistance to the Philippine War* (1972); Stanley Karnow, *In Our Image: America's Empire in the Philippines* (1989).

America and Asia. James C. Thomsen, Jr., Peter W. Stanley, and John Curtis Perry, *Sentimental Imperialists: The American Experience in East Asia* (1981); Marilyn B. Young, *The Rhetoric of Empire* (1968); Warren Cohen, *America's Response to China*, rev. ed. (1980); Akira Iriye, *Across the Pacific* (1967) and *Pacific Estrangement: Japanese and American Expansion* (1972); Robert McClellan, *The Heathen Chinese: A Study of American Attitudes Toward China* (1971); Jane Junter, *The Gospel of Gentility: American Women Missionaries in Turn-of-the-Century China* (1984); Charles Neu, *The Troubled Encounter* (1975); Paul Varg, *The Making of a Myth: The United States and China, 1897–1912* (1968) and *Missionaries, Chinese, and Diplomats* (1958); Patricia Hill, *The World Their Household: The American Women's Foreign Mission Movement and Cultural Transformation* (1985).

CHAPTER 21 THE RISE OF PROGRESSIVISM

Progressivism: Overviews. Richard Hofstadter, *The Age of Reform: From Bryan to FDR* (1955); Robert Wiebe, *The Search for Order, 1877–1920* (1967); Gabriel Kolko, *The Triumph of Conservatism* (1963); James Weinstein, *The Corporate Ideal in the Liberal State, 1900–1918* (1969); Arthur Link and Richard L. McCormick, *Progressivism* (1983); John Whiteclay Chambers, *The Tyranny of Change* (1980); Nell Irvin Painter, *Standing at Armageddon: The United States, 1877–1919* (1987).

The Muckrakers. Harold S. Wilson, *McClure's Magazine and the Muckrakers* (1970); C. C. Regier, *The Era of the Muckrakers* (1932); David Chambers, *The Social and Political Ideas of the Muckrakers* (1964); Justin Kaplan, *Lincoln Steffens* (1974); Leon Harris, *Upton Sinclair* (1975); Louis Filler, *The Muckrakers*, rev. ed. (1980).

Progressive Thought. Arthur Ekirch, *Progressivism in America* (1974); Morton White, *Social Thought in America* (1949); D. W. Marcell, *Progress and Pragmatism: James, Dewey, Beard and the American Idea of Progress* (1974); Charles Forcey, *The Crossroads of Liberalism: Croly, Weyl, Lippmann* (1961); Richard Abrams, *The Burdens of Progress* (1978); Sudhir Kakar, *Frederick Taylor* (1970); David W. Noble, ed., *The Progressive Mind*, rev. ed. (1981); Carl Degler, *In Search of Human Nature: The Decline and Revival of Darwinism in American Social Thought* (1991).

Social Work and the Social Gospel. Allen F. Davis, *Spearheads of Reform: The Social Settlements and the Progressive Movement, 1890–1914* (1968) and *American Heroine: The Life and Legend of Jane Addams* (1973); Roy Lubove, *The Progressives and the Slums: Tenement House Reform in New York City* (1962); Jane Addams, *Twenty Years at Hull House* (1910); C. H. Hopkins, *The Rise of the Social Gospel in American Protestantism* (1940); Henry May, *Protestant Churches and Industrial America* (1949); William R. Hutchinson, *The Modernist Impulse in American Protestantism* (1982); Robert M. Cruden, *Ministers of Reform: The Progressives' Achievement in American Civilization, 1889–1920* (1982); Paul Boyer, *Urban Masses and Moral Order, 1820–1920* (1978); Timothy Miller, *Following in His Steps: A Biography of Charles M. Sheldon* (1987).

Education and the Professions. Burton Bledstein, *The Culture of Professionalism* (1976); Thomas L. Haskell, *The Emergence of Professional Social Science* (1977); Paul Starr, *The Social Transformation of American Medicine* (1982); Regina Markell Morantz-Sanchez, *Sympathy and Science: Women Physicians in American Medicine* (1985); Kenneth M. Ludmerer, *Learning to Heal: The Development of American Medical Education* (1985); David Tyack and Elizabeth Hansot, *Managers of Virtue: Public School Leadership in America, 1820–1980* (1982); Lawrence Veysey, *The Emergence of the American University* (1970); Barbara Miller Solomon, *In the Company of Educated Women: A History of Women in Higher Education in America* (1985); Ellen Fitzpatrick, *Endless Crusade: Women Social Scientists and Progressive Reform* (1990); Barbara Harris, *Beyond Her Sphere: Women and the Professions in American History* (1978).

Municipal Reform. Zane Miller, *Boss Cox's Cincinnati* (1968); John D. Buenker, *Urban Liberalism and Progressive Reform* (1973); James B. Crooks, *Politics and Progress: The Rise of Urban Progressivism in Baltimore* (1968); Melvin G. Holli, *Reform in Detroit* (1969); J. Joseph Huthmacher, *Senator Robert F. Wagner and the Rise of Urban Liberalism* (1971); Oscar Handlin, *Al Smith and His America* (1958); Michael Kazin, *Barons of Labor: The San Francisco Building Trades and Union Power in the Progressive Era* (1981).

Women, Reform, and Suffrage. Eleanor Flexner, *Century of Struggle* (1959); Nancy Cott, *The Grounding of Modern Feminism* (1987); Karen Blair, *The Clubwoman as Feminist* (1980); Anne F. Scott, *Making the Invisible Woman Visible* (1984); Nancy Shrom Dye, *As Equal as Sisters: Feminism, the Labor Movement, and the Women's Trade Union League of New York* (1981); Sheila M. Rothman, *Woman's Proper Place* (1978); Ellen C. Lagemann, *A Generation of Women: Education in the Lives of Progressive Reformers* (1979); Rosalind Rosenberg, *Beyond Separate Spheres: Intellectual Roots of Modern Feminism* (1982); Jacquelyn Dowd Hall, *The Revolt Against Chivalry* (1979); Elaine Tyler May, *Great Expectations: Marriage and Divorce in Post-Victorian America* (1980); Mari Jo Buhle, *Women and American Socialism* (1983); Aileen S. Kraditor, *Ideas of the Woman Suffrage Movement* (1965); Alan P. Grimes, *The Puritan Ethic and Woman Suffrage* (1967); David Morgan, *Suffragists and Democrats: The Politics of Woman Suffrage in America* (1972); Ellen C. DuBois, *Feminism and Suffrage: The Emergence of an Independent Women's Movement in*

America, 1848–1869 (1978); Ruth Rosen, *The Lost Sisterhood: Prostitutes in America, 1900–1918* (1982); William O'Neill, *Divorce in the Progressive Era* (1967) and *Everyone Was Brave: The Rise and Fall of Feminism in America* (1969); David M. Kennedy, *Birth Control in America: The Career of Margaret Sanger* (1970); Linda Gordon, *Woman's Body, Woman's Right: A Social History of Birth Control* (1976); Elyce J. Rotella, *From Home to Office: U.S. Women and Work, 1870–1930* (1981).

Racial Issues. Louis Harlan, *Booker T. Washington: The Making of a Black Leader* (1972) and *Booker T. Washington: The Wizard of Tuskegee, 1901–1915* (1983); Elliott Rudwick, *W. E. B. Du Bois* (1969); August Meier, *Negro Thought in America, 1880–1915* (1963); Donald Spivey, *Schooling for the New Slavery: Black Industrial Education* (1978); Charles F. Kellogg, *NAACP* (1970); James M. McPherson, *The Abolitionist Legacy: From Reconstruction to the NAACP* (1975); George Fredrickson, *The Black Image in the White Mind* (1968); Joel Williamson, *The Crucible of Race: Black-White Relations in the American South Since Emancipation* (1985); John Dittmer, *Black Georgia in the Progressive Era, 1900–1920* (1977); Paula Giddings, *When and Where I Enter: The Impact of Black Women on Race and Sex in America* (1984); Cynthia Neverdon-Morton, *Afro-American Women of the South and the Advancement of the Race, 1885–1925* (1989).

State-Level Reform. George E. Mowry, *California Progressives* (1951); David P. Thelen, *The New Citizenship: Origins of Progressivism in Wisconsin* (1972), *Robert M. La Follette and the Insurgent Spirit* (1976), and *Paths of Resistance: Tradition and Dignity in Industrializing Missouri* (1986); Sheldon Hackney, *Populism to Progressivism in Alabama* (1969); Robert S. Maxwell, *La Follette and the Rise of Progressivism in Wisconsin* (1944); Russel B. Nye, *Midwestern Progressive Politics* (1951); Richard M. Abrams, *Conservatism in a Progressive Era: Massachusetts* (1964); Robert F. Wesser, *Charles Evans Hughes: Politics and Reform in New York State, 1905–1910* (1967); Irwin Yellowitz, *Labor and the Progressive Movement in New York State* (1965); Richard L. McCormick, *From Realignment to Reform: Political Change in New York State, 1893–1910* (1981); Dewey Grantham, *Southern Progressivism: The Reconciliation of Progress and Tradition* (1983); C. Vann Woodward, *Origins of the New South* (1951).

National Issues. Ruth Bourdin, *Women and Temperance: The Quest for Power and Liberty, 1873–1900* (1980); James T. Timberlake, *Prohibition and the Progressive Movement* (1963); Joseph Gusfield, *Symbolic Crusade: Status Politics and the Temperance Movement* (1963); John Higham, *Strangers in the Land* (1955); James Weinstein, *The Decline of Socialism in America* (1967); Robert Wiebe, *Businessmen and Reform* (1962); Sidney Fine, *Laissez Faire and the General Welfare State* (1956); Melvyn Dubofsky, *We Shall Be All* (1969); Michael E. McGerr, *The Decline of Popular Politics: The American North, 1865–1928* (1986).

CHAPTER 22—THE BATTLE FOR NATIONAL REFORM

General Histories. George E. Mowry, *The Era of Theodore Roosevelt* (1958); Arthur Link, *Woodrow Wilson and the Progressive Era, 1910–1917* (1954); John Milton Cooper, Jr., *The Warrior and the Priest: Woodrow Wilson and Theodore Roosevelt* (1983). See also Suggested Readings for Chapter 21.

Theodore Roosevelt. Edmund Morris, *The Rise of Theodore Roosevelt* (1979); Henry F. Pringle, *Theodore Roosevelt* (1931); William H. Harbaugh, *Power and Responsibility* (1961), published in paperback as *The Life and Times of Theodore Roosevelt*; John Morton Blum, *The Republican Roosevelt* (1954); G. Wallace Chessman, *Theodore Roosevelt and the Politics of Power* (1969); John A. Garraty, *The Life of George W. Perkins* (1960); Horace S. Merrill and Marion G. Merrill, *The Republican High Command* (1971).

William Howard Taft. Henry F. Pringle, *The Life and Times of William Howard Taft*, 2 vols. (1939); Paolo E. Coletta, *The Presidency of Taft* (1973); Donald E. Anderson, *William Howard Taft* (1973); James L. Penick, *Progressive Politics and Conservation: The Ballinger-Pinchot Affair* (1968); Harold T. Pinkett, *Gifford Pinchot: Private and Public Forester* (1970); George Mowry, *Theodore Roosevelt and the Progressive Movement* (1946); Norman Wilensky, *Conservatives in the Progressive Era: The Taft Republicans of 1912* (1965).

Woodrow Wilson. Arthur S. Link, *Woodrow Wilson*, 5 vols. (1947–1965); John Morton Blum, *Woodrow Wilson and the Politics of Morality* (1956); Alexander George and Juliette George, *Woodrow Wilson and Colonel House* (1956); Edwin A. Weinstein, *Woodrow Wilson: A Medical and Psychological Biography* (1981); John Morton Blum, *Joseph Tumulty and the Wilson Era* (1951); L. J. Holt, *Congressional Insurgents and the Party System, 1909–1916* (1967).

National Issues. Samuel P. Hays, *The Gospel of Efficiency: The Progressive Conservation Movement, 1890–1920* (1962); Elmo P. Richardson, *The Politics of Conservation* (1962); O. E. Anderson, *The Health of a Nation* (1958); Craig West, *Banking Reform and the Federal Reserve, 1863–1923* (1977).

Roosevelt's Foreign Policy. Howard K. Beale, *Theodore Roosevelt and the Rise of America to World Power* (1956); Richard Challener, *Admirals, Generals, and American Foreign Policy, 1898–1914* (1973); David H. Burton, *Theodore Roosevelt: Confident Imperialist* (1969); Julius W. Pratt, *Challenge and Rejection: The United States and World Leadership, 1900–1921* (1967); Richard Leopold, *Elihu Root and the Conservative Tradition* (1954); Akira Iriye, *Pacific Estrangement: Japanese and American Expansion, 1897–1911* (1972); Charles E. Neu, *An Uncertain Friendship: Roosevelt and Japan, 1906–1909* (1967); Charles Vevier, *United States and China* (1955).

America and the Caribbean. Dana G. Munro, *Intervention and Dollar Diplomacy in the Caribbean, 1900–1921* (1964); Louis A. Perez, Jr., *Cuba Under the Platt Amendment* (1988); Dwight C. Miner, *Fight for the Panama Route* (1966); Walter LaFeber, *The Panama Canal* (1978); David McCullough, *The Path Between the Seas* (1977); Walter Scholes and Marie Scholes, *The Foreign Policies of the Taft Administration* (1970).

Wilson's Foreign Policy. Arthur Link, *Wilson the Diplomatist* (1957) and *Woodrow Wilson: Revolution, War, and Peace* (1979); Robert Freeman Smith, *The United States and Revolutionary Nationalism in Mexico, 1916–1932* (1972); Kenneth Grieb, *The United States and Huerta* (1969); Robert Quirk, *An Affair of Honor: Woodrow Wilson and the Occupation of Veracruz* (1962) and *The Mexican Revolution, 1914–1915* (1960); David Healy, *Gunboat Diplomacy in the Wilson Era: The U.S. Navy in Haiti, 1915–1916* (1976); Dana Munro, *Intervention and Dollar Diplomacy in the Caribbean, 1900–1914* (1964).

CHAPTER 23 AMERICA AND THE GREAT WAR

The Road to War. Ernest R. May, *The World War and American Isolation* (1959); Patrick Devlin, *Too Proud to Fight: Woodrow Wilson's Neutrality* (1974); Jeffrey J. Sanford, *Wilsonian Maritime Diplomacy* (1978); Manfred Jonas, *The United States and Germany* (1984); John Milton Cooper, Jr., *The Vanity of Power: American Isolation and the First World War* (1969); Ross Gregory, *The Origins of American Intervention in the First World War* (1971); Daniel Smith, *Robert Lansing and American Neutrality* (1958); C. Roland Marchand, *The American Peace Movement and Social Reform* (1973); Thomas A. Bailey and Paul B. Ryan, *The Lusitania Disaster* (1975); Barbara Tuchman, *The Zimmerman Telegram* (1958).

Military Histories. Edward M. Coffman, *The War to End All Wars* (1969); Harvey A. De Weerd, *President Wilson Fights His War* (1968); A. E. Barbeau and Florette Henri, *The Unknown Soldiers: Black American Troops in World War I* (1974); J. Garry Clifford, *The Citizen Soldiers* (1972); Russell Weigley, *The American Way of War* (1973); Frank Freidel, *Over There* (1964); David Trask, *The United States in the Supreme War Council* (1961); John Whiteclay Chambers, *To Raise an Army* (1987); Donald Smythe, *Pershing* (1986).

Wartime Diplomacy. Arno Mayer, *Political Origins of the New Diplomacy* (1959); George F. Kennan, *Russia Leaves the War* (1956) and *Russia and the West Under Lenin and Stalin* (1961); W. B. Fowler, *British-American Relations, 1917–1918* (1969); Carl Parrini, *Heir to Empire: United States Economic Diplomacy, 1916–1923* (1969).

Domestic Impact. David M. Kennedy, *Over Here* (1980); Neil A. Wynn, *From Progressivism to Prosperity: World War I and American Society* (1986); Jordan Schwarz, *The Speculator* (1981); Robert D. Cuff, *The War Industries Board: Business-Government Relations During World War I* (1973); Valerie Jean Conner, *The National War Labor Board* (1983); George Nash, *The Life of Herbert Hoover: The Humanitarian, 1914–1917* (1990); Daniel Beaver, *Newton D. Baker and the American War Effort, 1917–1919* (1966); Seward Livermore, *Politics Is Adjourned* (1966); Charles Gilbert, *American Financing of World War I* (1970); George T. Blakey, *Historians on the Homefront* (1970); J. R. Mock and Cedric Larson, *Words That Won the War* (1939); Stephen Vaughn, *Holding Fast the Inner Lines: Democracy, Nationalism, and the Committee on Public Information* (1979); Richard Polenberg, *Fighting Faiths: The Abrams Case, the Supreme Court, and Free Speech* (1987); Zechariah Chaffee, Jr., *Free Speech in the United States* (1941); William Preston, Jr., *Aliens and Dissenters: Federal Suppression of Radicals, 1903–1933* (1963); H. C. Peterson and Gilbert Fite, *Opponents of War, 1917–1918* (1957); Harry N. Scheiber, *The Wilson Administration and Civil Liberties, 1917–1921* (1960); Donald Johnson, *The Challenge to America's Freedoms* (1963); John Higham, *Strangers in the Land* (1955); Frederick C. Luebke, *Bonds of Loyalty* (1974); Alfred W. Crosby, Jr., *Epidemic and Peace, 1918* (1976); Allan M. Brandt, *No Magic Bullet: A Social History of Venereal Disease in the United States* (1985); Maurine W. Greenwald, *Women, War, and Work* (1980); Barbara J. Steinson, *American Women's Activism in World War I* (1982); Carol S. Gruber, *Mars and Minerva* (1975); Charles Chatfield, *For Peace and Justice: Pacifism in America, 1914–1941* (1971); Sondra Herman, *Eleven Against War* (1969); Charles DeBenedettis, *Origins of the Modern Peace Movement* (1978); Otis L. Graham, Jr., *The Great Campaigns* (1971); Ellis W. Hawley, *The Great War and the Search for a Modern Order* (1979).

Wilson and the Peace. Arthur S. Link, *Wilson the Diplomatist* (1957); N. Gordon Levin, Jr., *Woodrow Wilson and World Politics* (1968); Lloyd Ambrosius, *Woodrow Wilson and the American Diplomatic Tradition* (1987); Arthur Walworth, *Wilson and the Peacemakers* (1986); Robert H. Ferrell, *Woodrow Wilson and World War I* (1985); Arno Mayer, *Wilson vs. Lenin* (1959) and *Politics and Diplomacy of Peacemaking* (1965); Peter Filene, *Americans and the Soviet Experiment* (1967); Christopher Lasch, *The American Liberals and the Russian Revolution* (1962); Lloyd C. Gardner, *Safe for Democracy: The Anglo-American Response to Revolution, 1913–1923* (1984); Inga Floto, *Colonel House at Paris* (1980); John A. Garraty, *Henry Cabot Lodge* (1953); Ralph Stone, *The Irreconcilables* (1970); Warren F. Kuehl, *Seeking World Order* (1969); Denna Fleming, *The United States and the League of Nations* (1932); Arthur Link, *Woodrow Wilson: War, Revolution, and Peace* (1979); Gene Smith, *When the Cheering Stopped* (1964); George Kennan, *Decision to Intervene* (1958); John L. Gaddis, *Russia, the Soviet Union, and the United States* (1978); William C. Widenor, *Henry Cabot Lodge and the Search for an American Foreign Policy* (1980); Robert E. Osgood, *Ideals and Self-Interest in American Foreign Relations* (1953).

Postwar America. Burl Noggle, *Into the Twenties* (1974); Stanley Coben, *A. Mitchell Palmer* (1963); Robert K. Murray, *The Red Scare* (1955); Roberta Strauss Feuerlicht, *Justice Crucified: The Story of Sacco and Vanzetti* (1977); David Brody, *Steelworkers in America* (1960) and *Labor in Crisis* (1965); Francis Russell, *A City in Terror* (1975); Robert L. Friedheim, *The Seattle General Strike* (1965); James Grossman, *Land of Hope: Chicago, Black Southerners, and the Great Migration* (1989); William M. Tuttle, Jr., *Race Riot: Chicago in the Red Summer of 1919* (1970); Elliott Rudwick, *Race Riot at East St. Louis* (1964); Robert V. Haynes, *A Night of Violence: The Houston Riot of 1917* (1976); Kenneth Kusmer, *A Ghetto Takes Shape* (1976); Alan Spear, *Black Chicago* (1967); David Cronon, *Black Moses* (1955); Amy J. Garvey, *Garvey and Garveyism* (1963); Judith Stein, *The World of Marcus Garvey* (1986); Theodore Vincent, *Black Power and the Garvey Movement* (1971); Wesley M. Bagby, Jr., *The Road to Normalcy* (1962); Stuart I. Rochester, *American Liberal Disillusionment in the Wake of World War I* (1977).

CHAPTER 24 THE NEW ERA

General Studies. William Leuchtenburg, *The Perils of Prosperity* (1958); John D. Hicks, *Republican Ascendancy* (1960); Arthur M. Schlesinger, Jr., *The Crisis of the Old Order* (1957); Ellis Hawley, *The Great War and the Search for a Modern Order* (1979); Donald R. McCoy, *Coming of Age* (1973); John Braeman, ed., *Change and Continuity in Twentieth Century America: The 1920s* (1968); Frederick Lewis Allen, *Only Yesterday* (1931); Isabel Leighton, ed., *The Aspirin Age* (1949); George Soule, *Prosperity Decade* (1947).

Labor, Agriculture, and Economic Growth. Alfred Chandler, *Strategy and Structure* (1962); Louis Galambos, *Competition and Cooperation* (1966); Louis Galambos and Joseph Pratt, *The Rise of the Corporate Commonwealth: U.S. Business and Public Policy in the Twentieth Century* (1988); Irving Bernstein, *The Lean Years: A History of the American Worker, 1920–1933* (1960); David Brody, *Steelworkers in America* (1960) and *Workers in Industrial America* (1980); Lizabeth Cohen, *Making a New Deal: Industrial Workers in Chicago, 1919–1939* (1990); Gerald Zahavi, *Workers, Managers, and Welfare Capitalism: The Shoe Workers and Tanners of Endicott Johnson, 1890–1950* (1988); Peter Gottlieb, *Making Their Own Way: Southern Blacks' Migration to Pittsburgh, 1916–1930* (1987);

Robert Zieger, *Republicans and Labor* (1969); Leslie Woodcock, *Wage-Earning Women* (1979); Gilbert Fite, *George Peek and the Fight for Farm Parity* (1954); Theodore Saloutos and John D. Hicks, *Twentieth Century Populism* (1951).

The New Culture. Daniel Boorstin, *The Americans: The Democratic Experience* (1973); Ed Cray, *Chrome Colossus* (1980); James J. Flink, *The Car Culture* (1975) and *The Automobile Age* (1988); Bernard A. Weisberger, *The Dream Maker* (1979); Lary May, *Screening Out the Past* (1980); Robert Sklar, *Movie-Made America* (1975); Sumiko Higashi, *Virgins, Vamps, and Flappers: The American Silent Movie Heroine* (1978); Susan J. Douglas, *Inventing American Broadcasting* (1987); Erik Barnouw, *A Tower of Babel*, vol. 1 (1966); Philip T. Rosen, *The Modern Stentors: Radio Broadcasting and the Federal Government, 1920–1933* (1980); Robert Creamer, *Babe* (1974); Kenneth S. Davis, *The Hero: Charles A. Lindbergh* (1959); Randy Roberts, *Jack Dempsey, The Manassa Mauler* (1979); Robert Lynd and Helen Lynd, *Middletown* (1929); Stanley Coben, *Rebellion Against Victorianism* (1991); Paul Carter, *Another Part of the Twenties* (1977); Kathy Peiss, *Cheap Amusements* (1986); Stewart Ewen, *Captains of Consciousness* (1976); Roland Marchand, *Advertising the American Dream* (1985); Stephen Fox, *The Mirror Makers: A History of American Advertising and Its Creators* (1984); Daniel Horowitz, *The Morality of Spending: Attitudes Toward the Consumer Society in America, 1875–1940* (1985); Ronald Edsforth, *Class Conflict and Cultural Consensus: The Making of a Mass Consumer Society: Flint, Michigan* (1987).

Women and Family. Nancy Cott, *The Grounding of American Feminism* (1987); Alice Kessler-Harris, *Out to Work: A History of Wage-Earning Women in America* (1982); Sheila Rothman, *Woman's Proper Place* (1978); William Chafe, *The American Woman* (1972); Linda Gordon, *Woman's Body, Woman's Right* (1976); J. Stanley Lemons, *The Woman Citizen: Social Feminism in the 1920s* (1973); Winifred Wandersee, *Women's Work and Family Values, 1920–1940* (1981); Susan Strasser, *Never Done: A History of American Housework* (1982); Ruth Schwarz Cowan, *More Work for Mother* (1983); Phyllis Palmer, *Domesticity and Dirt* (1989); Lois Scharf, *To Work and to Wed* (1980); Paula Fass, *The Damned and Beautiful* (1977); Helen Lefkowitz Horowitz, *Campus Life: Undergraduate Cultures from the End of the Eighteenth Century to the Present* (1987); Susan Porter Benson, *Counter Cultures* (1986); Lois Banner, *American Beauty* (1983); John D'Emilio and Estelle B. Friedman, *Intimate Matters: A History of Sexuality in America* (1988); W. Andrew Achenbaum, *Shades of Gray: Old Age, American Values, and Federal Policies Since 1920* (1983); Howard P. Chudacoff, *How Old Are You? Age in American Culture* (1989); David H. Fischer, *Growing Old in America* (1977).

Intellectuals. Roderick Nash, *The Nervous Generation: American Thought, 1917–1930* (1969); Robert Crunden, *From Self to Society: Transition in American Thought, 1919–1941* (1972); Malcolm Cowley, *Exiles Return* (1934); Edmund Wilson, *The Twenties* (1975); Frederick J. Hoffman, *The Twenties* (1949); Houston Baker, Jr., *Modernism and the Harlem Renaissance* (1987); Nathan I. Huggins, *Harlem Renaissance* (1971); David L. Lewis, *When Harlem Was in Vogue* (1981); Kenneth M. Wheeler and Virginia L. Lussier, eds., *Women and the Arts and the 1920s in Paris and New York* (1982); John Stewart, *The Burden of Time* (1965); Paul Conkin, *The Southern Agrarians* (1988); Cleanth Brooks, *William Faulkner: The Yoknapatawpha Country* (1963).

Cultural Conflict. Norman Clark, *Deliver Us from Evil* (1976); Joseph Gusfeld, *Symbolic Crusade* (1963); Andrew Sinclair, *The Era of Excess* (1962); Herbert Asbury, *The Great Illusion* (1950); John Higham, *Strangers in the Land* (1963); David Chalmers, *Hooded Americanism* (1965); Kenneth Jackson, *The Ku Klux Klan in the City* (1965); Ray Ginger,

Six Days or Forever? (1958); Norman Furniss, *The Fundamentalist Controversy* (1954); William G. McLoughlin, *Modern Revivalism* (1959); George M. Marsden, *Fundamentalism and American Culture* (1980); Lawrence Levine, *Defender of the Faith, William Jennings Bryan: The Last Decade, 1915–1925* (1965).

Politics and Government. Robert K. Murray, *The Politics of Normalcy* (1973) and *The Harding Era* (1969); Eugene Trani and David Wilson, *The Presidency of Warren G. Harding* (1977); Burl Noggle, *Teapot Dome* (1962); James N. Giglio, *H. M. Daugherty and the Politics of Expediency* (1978); Francis Russell, *The Shadow of Blooming Grove* (1968); Andrew Sinclair, *The Available Man* (1965); Donald McCoy, *Calvin Coolidge* (1967); William Allen White, *A Puritan in Babylon* (1940); James Gilbert, *Designing the Industrial State* (1972); John Hoff Wilson, *Herbert Hoover: Forgotten Progressive* (1975); David Burner, *Herbert Hoover* (1979); Robert F. Himmelberg, *The Origins of the National Recovery Administration: Business, Government, and the Trade Association Issue, 1921–1933* (1976); Ellis Hawley, *Herbert Hoover as Secretary of Commerce: Studies in New Era Thought and Practice* (1974); LeRoy Ashby, *Spearless Leader* (1972); Richard Lowitt, *George W. Norris*, vol. 2 (1971); David P. Thelen, *Robert M. La Follette and the Insurgent Spirit* (1978); George B. Tindall, *The Emergence of the New South* (1967); Christine Bolt, *American Indian Policy and American Reform* (1987); William Harbaugh, *Lawyer's Lawyer* (1973); David Burner, *The Politics of Provincialism* (1967); Alan Lichtman, *Prejudice and the Old Politics* (1979); Kristi Andersen, *The Creation of a Democratic Majority, 1928–1936* (1979); Oscar Handlin, *Al Smith and His America* (1958); Paula Elder, *Governor Alfred E. Smith: The Politician as Reformer* (1983); Elisabeth Israels Perry, *Belle Moskowitz: Feminine Politics and the Exercise of Power in the Age of Alfred E. Smith* (1987); Frank Freidel, *Franklin D. Roosevelt: The Ordeal* (1954) and *Franklin D. Roosevelt: The Triumph* (1956).

CHAPTER 25 THE GREAT DEPRESSION

The Coming of the Depression. Michael Bernstein, *The Great Depression: Delayed Recovery and Economic Change in America, 1929–1939* (1987); Robert Sobel, *The Great Bull Market* (1968); John Kenneth Galbraith, *The Great Crash* (1954); Milton Friedman and Anna Schwartz, *The Great Contraction* (1965) or Chapter 7 of *A Monetary History of the United States* (1963); Peter Temin, *Did Monetary Forces Cause the Great Depression?* (1976); Broadus Mitchell, *Depression Decade* (1947); Lester V. Chandler, *America's Greatest Depression* (1970); Charles Kindelberger, *The World in Depression* (1973); Susan E. Kennedy, *The Banking Crisis of 1933* (1973).

The Impact of the Depression. Irving Bernstein, *The Lean Years* (1960); Arthur M. Schlesinger, Jr., *The Crisis of the Old Order* (1957); Robert S. McElvaine, ed., *Down and Out in the Great Depression: Letters from the Forgotten Man* (1983); Studs Terkel, *Hard Times* (1970); Federal Writers' Project, *These Are Our Lives* (1939); Tom Terrill and Jerrold Hirsch, *Such as Us* (1978); Ann Banks, *First-Person America* (1980); Janet Poppendieck, *Breadlines Knee-Deep in Wheat: Food Assistance in the Great Depression* (1986); Donald Worster, *Dust Bowl* (1979); Walter Stein, *California and the Dust Bowl Migration* (1973); James N. Gregory, *American Exodus: The Dust Bowl Migration and Okie Culture in California* (1989); William Mullins, *The Depression and the Urban West Coast, 1929–1933* (1991).

Depression Culture and Society. Robert Lynd and Helen Merrell Lynd, *Middletown in Transition* (1935); Frederick Lewis Allen, *Since Yesterday* (1940); Richard Pells, *Radical Visions and American Dreams: Culture and Social Thought in the Depression Years* (1973); Warren Susman, *Culture as History* (1984); Richard Krickus, *Pursuing the American Dream* (1976); Gilman Ostrander, *American Civilization in the First Machine Age* (1970); Andrew Bergman, *We're in the Money: Depression America and Its Films* (1971); Alice Goldfarb Marquis, *Hopes and Ashes: The Birth of Modern Times, 1929–1939* (1986); David P. Peeler, *Hope Among Us Yet: Social Criticism and Social Thought in the Depression Years* (1987). See Suggested Readings for Chapter 26 for literature on blacks, Hispanics, Indians, and labor during the Depression.

Women and the Depression. Julia K. Blackwelder, *Women of the Depression: Caste and Culture in San Antonio, 1919–1939* (1984); William Chafe, *The American Woman* (1972); Lois Scharf, *To Work and to Wed: Female Employment, Feminism, and the Great Depression* (1980); Joan Jensen and Lois Scharf, eds., *Decades of Discontent: The Women's Movement, 1920–1940* (1983); Susan Ware, *Holding Their Own: American Women in the 1930s* (1982); Jeane Westin, *Making Do: How Women Survived the '30s* (1976).

The Hoover Presidency. Albert Romasco, *The Poverty of Abundance* (1965); Joan Hoff Wilson, *Herbert Hoover* (1975); David Burner, *Herbert Hoover* (1978); Harris Warren, *Herbert Hoover and the Great Depression* (1959); Jordan Schwarz, *The Interregnum of Despair* (1970); Herbert Hoover, *The Great Depression* (1952); James S. Olsen, *Herbert Hoover and the Reconstruction Finance Corporation* (1977) and *Saving Capitalism: The Reconstruction Finance Corporation and the New Deal, 1933–1940* (1988); Martin Fausold and George Mazuzun, eds., *The Hoover Presidency* (1974); Martin Fausold, *The Presidency of Herbert C. Hoover* (1985); William J. Barber, *From New Era to New Deal: Herbert Hoover, The Economists, and American Economic Policy, 1921–1933* (1985).

Politics and Protest. John Shover, *Cornbelt Rebellion* (1965); Roger Daniels, *The Bonus March* (1971); David Beito, *Taxpayers in Revolt* (1989); Donald Lisio, *The President and Protest* (1974); Harvey Klehr, *The Heyday of American Communism: The Depression Decade* (1984); Mark Naison, *Communists in Harlem During the Depression* (1983); Robin D. G. Kelley, *Hammer and Hoe: Alabama Communists During the Great Depression* (1990); Arthur M. Schlesinger, Jr., *The Crisis of the Old Order* (1957); David Burner, *The Politics of Provincialism* (1967); Thomas Kessner, *Fiorello H. LaGuardia and the Making of Modern New York* (1989); Frank Freidel, *The Triumph* (1956) and *Launching the New Deal* (1973); Eliot Rosen, *Hoover, Roosevelt, and the Brains Trust* (1977); Rexford G. Tugwell, *The Brains Trust* (1968).

CHAPTER 26 THE NEW DEAL

General and Biographical Studies. William E. Leuchtenburg, *Franklin D. Roosevelt and the New Deal* (1963) and *In the Shadow of FDR* (1983); Robert S. McElvaine, *The Great Depression* (1984); Anthony J. Badger, *The New Deal* (1989); Arthur M. Schlesinger, Jr., *The Age of Roosevelt*, 3 vols. (1957–1960); Paul Conkin, *The New Deal* (1967); Edgar Robinson, *The Roosevelt Leadership* (1955); James MacGregor Burns, *Roosevelt: The Lion and the Fox* (1956); Gerald Nash, *The Great Depression and World War II* (1979); Frank Freidel, *Franklin D. Roosevelt*, 4 vols. (1952–1973) and *Franklin D. Roosevelt: A Rendezvous with Destiny* (1990); Geoffrey Ward, *Before the Trumpet: Young Franklin Roosevelt,*

1882–1905 (1985) and *A First-Class Temperament: The Emergence of Franklin Roosevelt* (1989); Kenneth Davis, *FDR: The Beckoning of Destiny* (1972), *FDR: The New York Years: 1928–1933* (1985) and *FDR: The New Deal Years, 1933–1937* (1986); Joseph P. Lash, *Eleanor and Franklin* (1971); J. H. Wilson and Marjorie Lightman, eds., *Without Precedent: The Life and Career of Eleanor Roosevelt* (1984); Steve Fraser and Gary Gerstle, eds., *The Rise and Fall of New Deal Liberalism* (1988); Harvard Sitkoff, ed., *Fifty Years Later: The New Deal Evaluated* (1985); John Braeman et al., eds., *The New Deal*, 2 vols. (1975); Katie Louchheim, *The Making of the New Deal* (1983); Peter Fearon, *War, Prosperity, and Depression* (1987).

New Deal Politics and Programs. Frank Freidel, *Launching the New Deal* (1973); Raymond Moley and Eliot Rosen, *The First New Deal* (1966); Herbert Feis, *Characters in Crisis* (1966); Otis Graham, *Encore for Reform* (1967); Ellis Hawley, *The New Deal and the Problem of Monopoly* (1966); Donald Brand, *Corporatism and the Rule of Law* (1988); Bernard Bellush, *The Failure of the NRA* (1975); Sidney Fine, *The Automobile Under the Blue Eagle* (1963); Peter H. Irons, *The New Deal Lawyers* (1982); Susan Ware, *Beyond Suffrage* (1981) and *Partner and I: Molly Dewson, Feminism, and New Deal Politics* (1987); Thomas K. McCraw, *TVA and the Power Fight* (1970); Michael Parrish, *Securities Regulation and the New Deal* (1970); Ralph F. De Bedts, *The New Deal's SEC* (1964); Mark Leff, *The Limits of Symbolic Reform: The New Deal and Taxation, 1933–1939* (1984); Albert U. Romasco, *The Politics of Recovery: Roosevelt's New Deal* (1983); Searle Charles, *Minister of Relief* (1963); George McJimsey, *Harry Hopkins: Ally of the Poor and Defender of Democracy* (1987); John Salmond, *The Civilian Conservation Corps* (1967); Bonnie Fox Schwartz, *The Civil Works Administration, 1933–1934* (1984); James T. Patterson, *America's Struggle Against Poverty, 1900–1980* (1981); Mimi Abramowitz, *Regulating the Lives of Women* (1988); William R. Brock, *Welfare, Democracy, and the New Deal* (1987).

Agriculture. David Hamilton, *From New Day to New Deal: American Farm Policy from Hoover to Roosevelt, 1928–1933* (1991); Van L. Perkins, *Crisis in Agriculture* (1969); Richard S. Kirkendall, *Social Scientists and Farm Politics in the Age of Roosevelt* (1966); Christina Campbell, *The Farm Bureaus* (1962); Gilbert Fite, *George M. Peek and the Fight for Farm Parity* (1954); David Conrad, *The Forgotten Farmers* (1965); Paul Mertz, *The New Deal and Southern Rural Poverty* (1978); Lowell K. Dyson, *Red Harvest: The Communist Party and American Farmers* (1982); Bruce Shulman, *From Cotton Belt to Sunbelt* (1991).

Depression Dissidents. Arthur M. Schlesinger, Jr., *The Politics of Upheaval* (1960); George Wolfskill, *Revolt of the Conservatives* (1962); Donald Grubbs, *Cry from the Cotton* (1971); Donald McCoy, *Angry Voices* (1958); R. Alan Lawson, *The Failure of Independent Liberalism* (1971); Alan Brinkley, *Voices of Protest: Huey Long, Father Coughlin, and the Great Depression* (1982); David H. Bennett, *Demagogues in the Depression* (1969); Leo Ribuffo, *The Old Christian Right: The Protestant Far Right from the Great Depression to the Cold War* (1983); Glen Jeansonne, *Gerald L. K. Smith: Minister of Hate* (1988); Abraham Holzman, *The Townsend Movement* (1963); Charles J. Tull, *Father Coughlin and the New Deal* (1965); T. Harry Williams, *Huey Long* (1969).

The "Second New Deal." J. Joseph Huthmacher, *Senator Robert Wagner and the Rise of Urban Liberalism* (1968); W. D. Rowley, *M. L. Wilson and the Campaign for Domestic Allotment* (1970); Sidney Baldwin, *Poverty and Politics: The Farm Security Administration* (1968); Roy Lubove, *The Struggle for Social Security* (1968); Paul Conkin, *Tomorrow a*

New World (1971); Jane deHart Matthews, *The Federal Theater* (1967); Jerre Mangione, *The Dream and the Deal* (1972); William F. McDonald, *Federal Relief Administration and the Arts* (1968).

The Late New Deal. James T. Patterson, *Congressional Conservatism and the New Deal* (1967); Frank Freidel, *FDR and the South* (1965); George Wolfskill and John Hudson, *All But the People* (1969); Leonard Baker, *Back to Back* (1967); Richard Polenberg, *Reorganizing Roosevelt's Government* (1966); Barry Karl, *Executive Reorganization and Reform in the New Deal* (1963); James T. Patterson, *The New Deal and the States* (1969); Charles Trout, *Boston: The Great Depression and the New Deal* (1977); Herbert Stein, *The Fiscal Revolution in America* (1969); Dean May, *From New Deal to New Economics* (1981); Theodore Rosenof, *Patterns of Political Economy in America* (1983).

Blacks, Hispanics, Indians. Harvard Sitkoff, *A New Deal for Blacks* (1978); Nancy Weiss, *Farewell to the Party of Lincoln: Black Politics in the Age of FDR* (1983) and *The National Urban League* (1974); John B. Kirby, *Black Americans in the Roosevelt Era* (1980); Raymond Wolters, *Negroes and the Great Depression* (1970); Ralph Bunche, *The Political Status of the Negro in the Age of FDR* (1973); John Dollard, *Caste and Class in a Southern Town*, 3rd ed. (1957); Dan T. Carter, *Scottsboro* (1969); Robert L. Zangrando, *The NAACP Crusade Against Lynching* (1980); Abraham Hoffman, *Unwanted Mexican Americans in the Great Depression* (1974); Francisco E. Balerman, *In Defense of La Raza* (1982); Rodolfo Acuña, *Occupied America*, rev. ed. (1981); Carey McWilliams, *Factories in the Field* (1939); Sarah Deutsch, *No Separate Refuge: Culture, Class, and Gender on the Anglo-Hispanic Frontier in the American Southwest, 1880–1940* (1987); Donald L. Parman, *The Navajos and the New Deal* (1976); Laurence M. Hauptman, *The Iroquois and the New Deal* (1981); Laurence C. Kelly, *The Assault on Assimilation: John Collier and the Origins of Indian Policy Reform* (1983); Vine DeLoria, Jr., *The Nations Within* (1984); Clifford Lytle, *American Indians, American Justice* (1983); Kenneth R. Philp, *John Collier's Crusade for Indian Reform, 1920–1954* (1977); Graham D. Taylor, *The New Deal and American Indian Tribalism* (1980).

Labor. Irving Bernstein, *Turbulent Years* (1970) and *A Caring Society: The New Deal, the Worker, and the Great Depression* (1985); Gary Gerstle, *Working-Class Americanism: The Politics of Labor in a Textile City, 1914–1960* (1989); Bruce Nelson, *Workers on the Waterfront: Seamen, Longshoremen, and Unionism in the 1930s* (1988); Joshua Freeman, *In Transit: The Transport Workers Union in New York City, 1933–1966* (1989); Lizabeth Cohen, *Making a New Deal: Industrial Workers in Chicago, 1919–1939* (1990); Melvyn Dubofsky and Warren Van Tine, *John L. Lewis* (1977); Daniel Nelson, *American Rubber Workers and Organized Labor, 1900–1941* (1988); Robert H. Zieger, *John L. Lewis: Labor Leader* (1988) and *American Workers, American Unions, 1920–1985* (1986); Christopher L. Tomlins, *The State and the Unions* (1985); George G. Suggs, Jr., *Union Busting in the Tristate: The Oklahoma, Kansas, and Missouri Metal Workers Strike of 1935* (1986); John W. Hevener, *Which Side Are You On? The Harlan County Coal Miners, 1931–1939* (1978); David Brody, *Workers in Industrial America* (1980); Jerold Auerbach, *Labor and Liberty* (1966); Sidney Fine, *Sit-Down* (1969); Bert Cochran, *Labor and Communism* (1977); Peter Friedlander, *The Emergence of a UAW Local* (1975); John Barnard, *Walter Reuther and the Rise of the Auto Workers* (1983); Ronald W. Schatz, *The Electrical Workers* (1983); David Milton, *The Politics of U.S. Labor: From the Great Depression to the New Deal* (1980); August Meier and Elliott Rudwick, *Black Detroit and the Rise of the UAW* (1979).

CHAPTER 27 THE GLOBAL CRISIS, 1921–1941

The 1920s. L. Ethan Ellis, *Republican Foreign Policy, 1921–1933* (1968); Merlo J. Pusey, *Charles Evans Hughes*, 2 vols. (1963); Joan Hoff Wilson, *American Business and Foreign Policy, 1920–1933* (1968) and *Ideology and Economics* (1974); William Appleman Williams, *The Tragedy of American Diplomacy* (1962); Frank Costigliola, *Awkward Dominion: American Political, Economic, and Cultural Relations with Europe, 1919–1933* (1984); Akira Iriye, *After Imperialism* (1965); Warren Cohen, *America's Response to China* (1971) and *Empire Without Tears* (1987); Roger Dingman, *Power in the Pacific* (1976); Thomas Buckley, *The United States and the Washington Conference* (1970); Robert H. Ferrell, *Peace in Their Time* (1952); Joseph Tulchin, *The Aftermath of War* (1971); William Kamman, *A Search for Stability* (1968); Michael J. Hogan, *Informal Entente: The Private Structure of Cooperation in Anglo-American Economic Diplomacy, 1918–1928* (1977); Melvyn P. Leffler, *The Elusive Quest* (1979).

The Hoover Years. Robert H. Ferrell, *American Diplomacy in the Great Depression* (1970); Elting Morison, *Turmoil and Tradition* (1960); Alexander DeConde, *Hoover's Latin American Policy* (1951); Raymond O'Connor, *Perilous Equilibrium* (1962); Armin Rappaport, *Stimson and Japan* (1963).

New Deal Diplomacy. Robert Dallek, *Franklin D. Roosevelt and American Foreign Policy, 1932–1945* (1979); Lloyd Gardner, *Economic Aspects of New Deal Diplomacy* (1964); Frank Freidel, *Launching the New Deal* (1973); Beatrice Farnsworth, *William C. Bullitt and the Soviet Union* (1967); Robert Browder, *The Origins of Soviet-American Diplomacy* (1953); Peter Filene, *Americans and the Soviet Experiment, 1917–1933* (1967); Edward E. Bennett, *Recognition of Russia* (1970); Walter LaFeber, *Inevitable Revolutions* (1983); Bruce J. Calder, *The Impact of Intervention* (1984); Lorenzo Meyer, *Mexico and the United States in the Oil Controversy* (1977); Bryce Wood, *The Making of the Good Neighbor Policy* (1961); Irwin F. Gellman, *Good Neighbor Diplomacy: United States Policies in Latin America, 1933–1945* (1979); David Green, *The Containment of Latin America* (1971); Dorothy Borg, *The United States and the Far Eastern Crisis of 1933–1938* (1964).

Isolationism and Pacifism. Selig Adler, *The Uncertain Giant* (1966) and *The Isolationist Impulse* (1957); Robert Divine, *The Reluctant Belligerent* (1965); William Langer and S. Everett Gleason, *The Challenge to Isolation* (1952) and *The Undeclared War* (1953); Manfred Jonas, *Isolationism in America* (1966); Wayne S. Cole, *America First* (1953), *Senator Gerald P. Nye and American Foreign Relations* (1962), *Charles A. Lindbergh and the Battle Against American Intervention in World War II* (1974), and *Roosevelt and the Isolationists, 1932–1945* (1983); Warren I. Cohen, *The American Revisionists* (1967); Thomas C. Kennedy, *Charles A. Beard and American Foreign Policy* (1975); Richard Lowitt, *George W. Norris*, 3 vols. (1963–1978); John K. Nelson, *The Peace Prophets* (1967); Lawrence Wittner, *Rebels Against War* (1984); Charles Chatfield, *For Peace and Justice: Pacifism in America, 1914–1941* (1971); Charles DeBenedetti, *Origins of the Modern American Peace Movement, 1915–1929* (1978) and *The Peace Reform in American History* (1980).

The Coming of World War II. Arnold Offner, *The Origins of the Second World War* (1975); Bernard F. Donahoe, *Private Plans and Public Dangers* (1965); Garry Clifford and Samuel R. Spencer, Jr., *The First Peacetime Draft* (1986); Waldo H. Heinrichs, Jr., *Threshold of War* (1988); Manfred Jonas, *The United States and Germany*

(1984); James Leutze, *Bargaining for Supremacy* (1977); Michael S. Sherry, *The Rise of American Airpower* (1987); Joseph Lash, *Roosevelt and Churchill* (1976); Warren Kimball, *The Most Unsordid Act: Lend-Lease, 1939–1941* (1970); David Reynolds, *The Creation of the Anglo-American Alliance, 1937–1941* (1982); David F. Schmitz, *The United States and Fascist Italy, 1922–1944* (1988); Roger Dingman, *Power in the Pacific* (1976); Akira Iriye, *Across the Pacific* (1967), *After Imperialism: The Search for a New Order in the Far East, 1921–1933* (1965), and *The Origins of the Second World War in Asia and the Pacific* (1987); Hebert Feis, *The Road to Pearl Harbor* (1950); Jonathan Utley, *Going to War with Japan* (1985); James MacGregor Burns, *Roosevelt: The Soldier of Freedom* (1970); Roberta Wohlstetter, *Pearl Harbor: Warning and Decision* (1962); Gordon Prange, *At Dawn We Slept* (1981) and *Pearl Harbor* (1986); Martin V. Melosi, *The Shadow of Pearl Harbor* (1977).

CHAPTER 28 AMERICA IN A WORLD AT WAR

War and American Society. John Morton Blum, *V Was for Victory* (1976); Richard Polenberg, *War and Society* (1972); Mark J. Harris et al., *The Homefront* (1984); Alan Clive, *State of War: Michigan in World War II* (1979); Gerald D. Nash, *The American West Transformed: The Impact of the Second World War* (1985); Richard R. Lingeman, *Don't You Know There's a War On?* (1970); Studs Terkel, *"The Good War": An Oral History of World War II* (1984).

War Mobilization and Wartime Politics. Donald Nelson, *Arsenal of Democracy* (1946); Bruce Catton, *War Lords of Washington* (1946); David Brinkley, *Washington Goes to War* (1987); Eliot Janeway, *Struggle for Survival* (1951); Joel Seidman, *American Labor from Defense to Reconversion* (1953); Nelson Lichtenstein, *Labor's War at Home* (1982); Howell John Harris, *The Right to Manage* (1982); Leslie R. Groves, *Now It Can Be Told* (1962); Oscar E. Anderson, Jr., *The New World* (1962); Chester Bowles, *Promises to Keep* (1971); Lester V. Chandler, *Inflation in the United States, 1940–1948* (1951); Richard Steele, *Propaganda in an Open Society* (1985); Patrick S. Washburn, *A Question of Sedition: The Federal Government's Investigation of the Black Press During World War II* (1986); Alan Winkler, *The Politics of Propaganda* (1978); Philip Knightley, *The First Casualty* (1975); James MacGregor Burns, *Roosevelt: The Soldier of Freedom* (1970); Godfrey Hodgson, *The Colonel: The Life and Wars of Henry Stimson* (1990); Ellsworth Barnard, *Wendell Willkie* (1966); Maurice Isserman, *Which Side Were You On? The American Communist Party During World War II* (1982).

The War and Race. Louis Ruchames, *Race, Jobs, and Politics* (1953); Neil Wynn, *The Afro-American and the Second World War* (1976); Herbert Garfinkel, *When Negroes March* (1959); Richard M. Dalfiume, *Desegregation of the U.S. Armed Forces* (1969); Domenic J. Capeci, Jr., *The Harlem Riot of 1943* (1977) and *Race Relations in Wartime Detroit* (1987); Philip McGuire, ed., *Taps for a Jim Crow Army: Letters from Black Soldiers in World War II* (1982); August Meier and Elliott Rudwick, *CORE* (1973); Mauricio Mazon, *The Zoot-Suit Riots* (1984); Roger Daniels, *The Politics of Prejudice* (1962) and *Concentration Camps, USA* (1971); Audrie Girdner and Anne Loftis, *The Great Betrayal* (1969); Bill Hosokawa, *Nisei* (1969); Peter Irons, *Justice at War* (1983); Thomas James, *Exiles Within: The Schooling of Japanese-Americans, 1942–1945* (1987).

Women and the War. Ruth Milkman, *Gender at Work: The Dynamics of Job Segregation by Sex During World War II* (1987); Susan M. Reverby, *Ordered to Care: The Dilemma of American Nursing, 1850–1945* (1987); Karen Anderson, *Wartime Women: Sex Roles, Family Relations, and the Status of Women During World War II* (1981); D'Ann Campbell, *Women at War with America* (1984); Sherna B. Gluck, *Rosie the Riveter Revisited* (1987); Maureen Honey, *Creating Rosie the Riveter: Class, Gender, and Propaganda During World War II* (1984); Margaret R. Higgonet et al., *Behind the Lines: Gender and the Two World Wars* (1987); Susan Hartmann, *The Homefront and Beyond: American Women in the 1940s* (1982); Leila Rupp, *Mobilizing Women for War* (1978).

Wartime Military and Diplomatic Experiences. James MacGregor Burns, *Roosevelt: The Soldier of Freedom* (1970); Robert Divine, *Roosevelt and World War II* (1969) and *Second Chance* (1967); Albert Russell Buchanan, *The United States and World War II*, 2 vols. (1962); Fletcher Pratt, *War for the World* (1951); Margaret Hoyle, *A World in Flames* (1970); Kenneth Greenfield, *American Strategy in World War II* (1963); Samuel Eliot Morison, *Strategy and Compromise* (1958), *History of United States Naval Operations in World War II*, 14 vols. (1947–1960), and *The Two Ocean War* (1963); Winston S. Churchill, *The Second World War*, 6 vols. (1948–1953); Chester Wilmot, *The Struggle for Europe* (1952); Charles B. McDonald, *The Mighty Endeavor* (1969); Stephen Ambrose, *The Supreme Commander* (1970) and *Eisenhower: Soldier, General of the Army, President-Elect* (1983); Michael Howard, *The Mediterranean Strategy in World War II* (1968); Dwight D. Eisenhower, *Crusade in Europe* (1948); Forrest Pogue, *George C. Marshall*, 2 vols. (1963–1966); D. Clayton James, *A Time for Giants: Politics of the American High Command in World War II* (1987); Max Hastings, *Overlord: D-Day and the Battle for Normandy* (1984); Russel F. Weigley, *The American Way of War* (1973); Cornelius Ryan, *The Last Battle* (1966); John Toland, *The Last Hundred Days* (1966); Ronald Schaffer, *Wings of Judgment: American Bombing in World War II* (1985); David S. Wyman, *The Abandonment of the Jews: America and the Holocaust, 1941–1945* (1984); Warren Kimball, *The Juggler: Franklin Roosevelt as Wartime Statesman* (1991); Gaddis Smith, *American Diplomacy During the Second World War* (1964); E. J. Kind and W. M. Whitehill, *Fleet Admiral King* (1952); Barbara Tuchman, *Stilwell and the American Experience in China* (1971); John W. Dower, *War Without Mercy: Race and Power in the Pacific War* (1986); John Toland, *The Rising Sun* (1970); Ronald Spector, *Eagle Against the Sun: The American War with Japan* (1985); William Manchester, *American Caesar* (1979).

Atomic Warfare. Martin Sherwin, *A World Destroyed* (1975); Gar Alperovitz, *Atomic Diplomacy* (1965); Robert Jungk, *Brighter Than a Thousand Suns* (1958); Nuel Davis, *Lawrence and Oppenheimer* (1969); Gregg Herken, *The Winning Weapon* (1980); W. S. Schoenberger, *Decision of Destiny* (1969); Robert Donovan, *Conflict and Crisis* (1977); John Hersey, *Hiroshima* (1946); Herbert Feis, *The Atomic Bomb and the End of World War II* (1966); Richard Rhodes, *The Making of the Atomic Bomb* (1987); Leon V. Sigal, *Fighting to a Finish* (1988).

CHAPTER 29 AMERICA AND THE COLD WAR

Origins of the Cold War. Walter LaFeber, *America, Russia, and the Cold War, 1945–1967* (1967, rev. 1980); Stephen Ambrose, *Rise to Globalism*, 5th ed. (1988); Bernard Weisberger, *Cold War, Cold Peace* (1984); Adam Ulam, *The Rivals: America and Russia*

Since World War II (1971); John Lewis Gaddis, *Strategies of Containment* (1982), *The United States and the Origins of the Cold War, 1941–1947* (1972), and *The Long Peace* (1987); John L. Snell, *Illusion and Necessity* (1967); Gaddis Smith, *American Diplomacy During the Second World War* (1965) and *Dean Acheson* (1972); Herbert Feis, *Churchill, Roosevelt, and Stalin* (1957); William Taubman, *Stalin's American Policy* (1982); William McNeill, *America, Britain and Russia* (1953); Diane Clemens, *Yalta* (1970); Herbert Feis, *Between War and Peace: The Potsdam Conference* (1960); Athan G. Theoharis, *The Yalta Myths* (1970); W. L. Neumann, *After Victory* (1969); George C. Herring, Jr., *Aid to Russia* (1973); Daniel Yergin, *Shattered Peace* (1977); Thomas G. Paterson, *Soviet–American Confrontation* (1974), *On Every Front: The Making of the Cold War* (1979), and *Meeting the Communist Threat* (1988); Gregg Herken, *The Winning Weapon* (1980); Martin Sherwin, *A World Destroyed* (1975); Gar Alperovitz, *Atomic Diplomacy: Hiroshima and Potsdam*, rev. ed. (1985); Robert A. Pollard, *Economic Security and the Origins of the Cold War* (1985).

Truman's Foreign Policy. Robert Donovan, *Conflict and Crisis* (1977); Lloyd Gardner, *Architects of Illusion* (1970); Joyce Kolko and Gabriel Kolko, *The Limits of Power* (1970); George F. Kennan, *American Diplomacy, 1900–1950* (1952) and *Memoirs, 1925–1950* (1967); David Mayer, *George Kennan and the Dilemmas of U.S. Foreign Policy* (1988); Anders Stephanson, *Kennan and the Art of Foreign Policy* (1989); Dean Acheson, *Present at the Creation* (1970); Fraser J. Harbutt, *The Iron Curtain: Churchill, America, and the Origins of the Cold War* (1986); Thomas Schwartz, *America's Germany: John J. McCloy and the Federal Republic of Germany* (1991); Richard J. Barnet, *The Alliance* (1983); Laurence Kaplan, *The United States and NATO* (1984); Hadley Arkes, *Bureaucracy, the Marshall Plan and National Interest* (1973); Michael Hogan, *The Marshall Plan* (1987); Imanuel Wexler, *The Marshall Plan Revisited* (1983); Akira Iriye, *The Cold War in Asia* (1974); Robert M. Blum, *Drawing the Line: The Origin of the American Containment Policy in East Asia* (1982); John King Fairbank, *The United States and China*, rev. ed. (1971); Edwin O. Reischauer, *The United States and Japan*, rev. ed. (1965); Warren I. Cohen, *America's Response to China*, rev. ed. (1980); Michael Schaller, *The U.S. Crusade in China* (1979), *Communists* (1971), and *The American Occupation of Japan: The Origins of the Cold War in Asia* (1985); Lisle Rose, *Roots of Tragedy* (1976); Gary May, *China Scapegoat* (1979); Christopher Thorne, *Allies of a Kind* (1978); Bruce R. Koniholm, *The Origins of the Cold War in the Middle East* (1980); William R. Louis, *The British Empire in the Middle East* (1984); Michael B. Stoff, *Oil, War, and American Security* (1980).

Truman's Domestic Policies. Alonzo Hamby, *Beyond the New Deal* (1973); Robert Donovan, *Conflict and Crisis* (1977) and *Tumultuous Years* (1982); Richard L. Miller, *Truman: The Rise to Power* (1986); Roy Jenkins, *Truman* (1986); William E. Pemberton, *Harry S. Truman* (1989); Barton J. Bernstein, ed., *Politics and Policies of the Truman Administration* (1970); Andrew J. Dunar, *The Truman Scandals and the Politics of Morality* (1984); Robert H. Ferrell, *Harry S. Truman and the Modern American Presidency* (1983); Donald R. McCoy, *The Presidency of Harry S. Truman* (1984); Susan Hartmann, *Truman and the 80th Congress* (1971); Stephen K. Bailey, *Congress Makes a Law* (1950); Gary Reichard, *Politics as Usual* (1988); Richard O. Davies, *Housing Reform During the Truman Administration* (1966); R. Alton Lee, *Truman and the Steel Seizure Case* (1977); Allen J. Matusow, *Farm Policies and Politics in the Truman Years* (1967); Arthur F. McClure, *The Truman Administration and the Problems of Postwar Labor* (1969); R. Alton Lee, *Truman and Taft-Hartley* (1967); Christopher L. Tomlins, *The State and the Unions* (1985); William Berman, *The Politics of Civil Rights in the Truman Administration* (1970); Donald

McCoy and Richard Ruetten, *Quest and Response* (1973); Richard M. Dalfiume, *Desegregation of the U.S. Armed Forces* (1969); Maeva Marcus, *Truman and the Steel Seizure* (1977); William O'Neill, *American High* (1986); John P. Diggins, *The Proud Decades* (1988).

Cold War Politics. James T. Patterson, *Mr. Republican* (1972); Irwin Ross, *The Loneliest Campaign* (1968); Norman Markowitz, *The Rise and Fall of the People's Century* (1973); Maurice Isserman, *If I Had a Hammer . . .: The Death of the Old Left and the Birth of the New Left* (1987); Allen Yarnell, *Democrats and Progressives* (1974); Steven M. Gillon, *Politics and Vision: The ADA and American Liberalism, 1947–1985* (1987); Richard Norton Smith, *Thomas E. Dewey and His Times* (1982); Richard Pells, *The Liberal Mind in a Conservative Age: American Intellectuals in the 1940s and 1950s* (1985).

The Korean War. Bruce Cumings, *The Origins of the Korean War* (1980) and Cummings, ed., *Child of Conflict: The Korean–American Relationship, 1943–1953* (1983); Glenn D. Paige, *The Korean Decision* (1968); Joseph C. Goulden, *Korea: The Untold Story of the War* (1982); John Spanier, *The Truman–MacArthur Controversy* (1959); Allen Whiting, *China Crosses the Yalu* (1960); Carl Berger, *The Korean Knot* (1957); Ronald Caridi, *The Korean War and American Politics* (1969); Robert Leckie, *Conflict* (1962); Robert R. Simmons, *The Strained Alliance* (1975); Charles W. Dobbs, *The Unwanted Symbol* (1981).

Countersubversion. David Caute, *The Great Fear* (1978); Edward Shils, *The Torment of Secrecy* (1956); Allen Weinstein, *Perjury* (1978); Ronald Radosh and Joyce Milton, *The Rosenberg File* (1983); Walter and Miriam Schneer, *Invitation to an Inquest*, rev. ed. (1983); Richard Freeland, *The Truman Doctrine and the Origins of McCarthyism* (1971); Athan Theoharis, *Seeds of Repression* (1971); Alan Harper, *The Politics of Loyalty* (1969); Michael R. Belknap, *Cold War Political Justice: The Smith Act, the Communist Party, and American Civil Liberties* (1977); Stanley Kutler, *The American Inquisition* (1982); Larry Ceplair and Steven Englund, *The Inquisition in Hollywood* (1983); Mary Sperling McAuliffe, *Crisis on the Left* (1978); Harvey Levenstein, *Communism, Anticommunism, and the CIO* (1981); Thomas C. Reeves, *The Life and Times of Joe McCarthy* (1982); David Oshinsky, *A Conspiracy So Immense* (1983); Michael Paul Rogin, *The Intellectuals and McCarthy* (1967); Robert Griffith, *The Politics of Fear* (1970); Richard Fried, *Men Against McCarthy* (1976) and *Nightmare in Red* (1990); Richard Rovere, *Senator Joe McCarthy* (1959); Victor Navasky, *Naming Names* (1980); William O'Neill, *A Better World* (1983); Joseph Starobin, *American Communism in Crisis* (1972).

CHAPTER 30 THE AFFLUENT SOCIETY

General Studies. William Leuchtenburg, *A Troubled Feast* (1979); Carl Degler, *Affluence and Anxiety* (1968); John Brooks, *The Great Leap* (1966); Godfrey Hodgson, *America in Our Time* (1976); William Chafe, *The Unfinished Journey* (1986); Eric Goldman, *The Crucial Decade and After* (1960); John P. Diggins, *The Proud Decades* (1989); Douglas T. Miller and Marion Novak, *The Fifties* (1977); William O'Neill, *American High* (1986).

The Postwar Economy. John K. Galbraith, *The Affluent Society* (1958) and *The New Industrial State (1967); Loren J. Okroi, Galbraith, Harrington, Heilbroner* (1986); C. Wright Mills, *The Power Elite* (1956); Harold G. Vatter, *The U.S. Economy in the 1950s* (1963); Robert Heilbroner, *The Limits of American Capitalism* (1965); Joel Seidman, *American Labor from Defense to Reconversion* (1953); John Hutchinson, *The Imperfect Union* (1970).

Culture and Society. William Graebner, *The Age of Doubt: American Thought and Culture in the 1940's* (1991); Paul Carter, *Another Part of the Fifties* (1983); Marty Jezer, *The Dark Ages: Life in the U.S. 1945–1960* (1982); George Lipsitz, *Class and Culture in Cold War America* (1981); Douglas T. Miller and Marion Novak, *The Fifties* (1977); Herbert Gans, *The Levittowners* (1967); Kenneth Jackson, *The Crabgrass Frontier* (1985); Ruth Cowan, *More Work for Mother: The Irony of Household Technology* (1983); Elaine Tyler May, *Homeward Bound: American Families in the Cold War* (1988); Eugenia Kaledin, *Mothers and More: American Women in the 1950s* (1984); Edward J. Epstein, *News from Nowhere* (1973); David Halberstam, *The Powers That Be* (1979); Tom Wolfe, *The Right Stuff* (1979); Walter A. McDougall, . . . *the Heavens and the Earth: A Political History of the Space Age* (1985); R. L. Rosholt, *An Administrative History of NASA* (1966); Walter Sullivan, ed., *America's Race for the Moon* (1962); Barbara B. Clowse, *Brainpower for the Cold War: The Sputnik Crisis and the National Defense Education Act of 1958* (1981); Paul Boyer, *By the Bomb's Early Light* (1986); David Riesman, *The Lonely Crowd* (1950); William Whyte, *The Organization Man* (1956); C. Wright Mills, *White Collar* (1956); Bruce Cook, *The Beat Generation* (1971); John Tytell, *Naked Angels* (1976); Ann Charters, *Kerouac* (1973); Dennis McNally, *Desolate Angel* (1979); Arthur M. Schlesinger, Jr., *The Vital Center* (1949); Daniel Bell, *The End of Ideology* (1960); Howard Brick, *Daniel Bell and the Decline of Intellectual Radicalism* (1986); Richard H. Pells, *The Liberal Mind in a Conservative Age* (1985); David Potter, *People of Plenty* (1954); Richard Hofstader, *The Age of Reform* (1954); Mary Sperling McAuliffe, *Crisis on the Left* (1978); Daniel Bell, ed., *The Radical Right* (1963).

The Eisenhower Presidency. Stephen Ambrose, *Eisenhower the President* (1984); Piers Brendon, *Ike* (1986); Robert F. Burk, *Dwight D. Eisenhower* (1986); Fred Greenstein, *The Hidden-Hand Presidency* (1982); Charles C. Alexander, *Holding the Line* (1975); Herbert S. Parmet, *Eisenhower and the American Crusades* (1972); Peter Lyon, *Eisenhower: Portrait of a Hero* (1974); Dwight D. Eisenhower, *The White House Years*, 2 vols. (1963–1965); Emmet John Hughes, *The Ordeal of Power* (1963); Sherman Adams, *Firsthand Report* (1961); Richard Nixon, *Six Crises* (1962); Nicol C. Rae, *The Decline and Fall of the Liberal Republicans* (1989); Gary Reichard, *The Reaffirmation of Republicanism* (1975); David W. Reinhard, *The Republican Right Since 1945* (1983); Mark H. Rose, *Interstate: Express Highway Politics, 1941–1956* (1979).

Foreign Policy. Robert Divine, *Eisenhower and the Cold War* (1981); Townsend Hoopes, *The Devil and John Foster Dulles* (1973); Louis Gerson, *John Foster Dulles* (1967); Stephen Ambrose, *Ike's Spies* (1981); Cecil Currey, *Edward Lansdale: The Unquiet American* (1988); Michael Beschloss, *MAYDAY* (1986); Chester Cooper, *Lost Crusade* (1970); Frances Fitzgerald, *Fire in the Lake* (1972); John T. McAlister, Jr., *Vietnam: The Origins of Revolution* (1969); George Herring, *America's Longest War* (1979); Chester Cooper, *The Lion's Last Roar* (1978); Hugh Thomas, *Suez* (1967); Mira Wilkins, *The Maturing of Multinational Enterprise* (1974); Kermit Roosevelt, *Counter-coup* (1980); Burton Kaufman, *The Oil Cartel Case* (1978); Richard Immerman, *The CIA in Guatemala* (1982); Walter LaFeber, *Inevitable Revolutions* (1983); Stephen G. Rabe, *Eisenhower and Latin America* (1988); Robert A. Divine, *Foreign Policy and U.S. Presidential Elections*, 2 vols. (1974) and *Blowing in the Wind: The Nuclear Test Ban Debate, 1954–1960* (1978); Blanche W. Cooke, *The Declassified Eisenhower* (1981); Richard A. Melanson and David A. Mayers, eds., *Reevaluating Eisenhower* (1986); Burton I. Kaufman, *Trade and Aid* (1982); Howard Ball, *Justice Downwind: America's Nuclear Testing Program in the 1950s*

(1986); Gregg Herken, *Counsels of War* (1985); Richard G. Hewlett and Jack M. Hall, *Atoms for Peace and War, 1953–1961* (1989); Richard Smoke, *National Security and the Nuclear Dilemma* (1988).

Legal and Constitutional Issues. Philip Stern, *The Oppenheimer Case* (1969); Michael Straight, *Trial by Television* (1954); Paul Murphy, *The Constitution in Crisis Times* (1972); Alexander Bickel, *Politics and the Warren Court* (1965) and *The Supreme Court and the Idea of Progress* (1970); Philip Kurland, *Politics, the Constitution, and the Warren Court* (1970); John Weaver, *Earl Warren* (1967).

Civil Rights. Richard Kluger, *Simple Justice* (1975); Stephen J. Whitfield, *A Death in the Delta: The Story of Emmett Till* (1988); Anthony Lewis, *Portrait of a Decade* (1964); Martin Luther King, Jr., *Stride Toward Freedom* (1958); William Chafe, *Civilities and Civil Rights* (1980); Harvard Sitkoff, *The Struggle for Black Equality, 1954–1980* (1981); John W. Anderson, *Eisenhower, Brownell, and the Congress* (1964); Robert F. Burk, *The Eisenhower Administration and Black Civil Rights* (1984); Numan V. Bartley, *The Rise of Massive Resistance* (1969); Elizabeth Huckaby, *Crisis at Central High* (1980); David Garrow, ed., *The Montgomery Bus Boycott and the Women Who Started It: A Memoir of Jo Ann Gibson Robinson* (1987); Robert J. Norrell, *Reaping the Whirlwind: The Civil Rights Movement in Tuskegee* (1985); Howell Raines, *My Soul Is Rested* (1977).

CHAPTER 31 THE ORDEAL OF LIBERALISM

General Studies. Godfrey Hodgson, *America in Our Time* (1976); Charles R. Morris, *A Time of Passion* (1984); Allen J. Matusow, *The Unraveling of America* (1984); Theodore H. White, *America in Search of Itself* (1982); William Chafe, *The Unfinished Journey* (1986).

Kennedy and Johnson. Theodore H. White, *The Making of the President, 1960* (1961); Arthur M. Schlesinger, Jr., *A Thousand Days* (1965); Theodore Sorensen, *Kennedy* (1965); Richard N. Goodwin, *Remembering America* (1988); Herbert Parmet, *Jack* (1980) and *JFK* (1983); Henry Fairlie, *The Kennedy Promise* (1973); David Burner, *John F. Kennedy and a New Generation* (1988); Lewis Paper, *The Promise and the Performance* (1975); Bruce Miroff, *Pragmatic Illusions* (1976); Garry Wills, *The Kennedy Imprisonment* (1982); Thomas Brown, *JFK: The History of an Image* (1988); *The Report of the Warren Commission* (1964); William Manchester, *The Death of a President* (1967); Anthony Summers, *Conspiracy* (1980); Edward J. Epstein, *Inquest* (1966) and *Legend* (1978); Henry Hurt, *Reasonable Doubt* (1985); Doris Kearns, *Lyndon Johnson and the American Dream* (1976); Eric Goldman, *The Tragedy of Lyndon Johnson* (1968); Ronnie Dugger, *The Politician* (1982); Robert Caro, *The Years of Lyndon Johnson: The Path to Power* (1982) and *Means of Ascent* (1990); Lyndon B. Johnson, *Vantage Point* (1971); George Reedy, *The Twilight of the Presidency* (1970); Jim Heath, *Decade of Disillusionment* (1975); Vaughn D. Bornet, *The Presidency of Lyndon B. Johnson* (1983); Paul K. Conkin, *Big Daddy from the Pedernales* (1986).

Domestic Policies. Tom Wicker, *JFK and LBJ* (1968); Jim Heath, *John F. Kennedy and the Business Community* (1969); Victor Navasky, *Kennedy Justice* (1971); James Sundquist, *Politics and Policy* (1968); Sar Levitan, *The Great Society's Poor Law* (1969); Sar

Levitan and Robert Taggart, *The Promise of Greatness* (1976); Daniel Knapp and Kenneth Polk, *Scouting the War on Poverty* (1971); Robert H. Haveman, ed., *A Decade of Federal Antipoverty Programs* (1977); Greg J. Duncan, *Years of Poverty, Years of Plenty* (1984); Charles Murray, *Losing Ground* (1984); Frances Fox Piven and Richard Cloward, *Regulating the Poor* (1971); Nicholas Lemann, *The Promised Land: The Great Black Migration and How It Changed America* (1991); Hugh Davis Graham, *Uncertain Trumpet* (1984); Allen J. Matusow, *The Unraveling of America: A History of Liberalism in the 1960s* (1984); James T. Patterson, *America's Struggle Against Poverty, 1900–1980* (1981); Henry J. Aaron, *Politics and the Professors* (1978); John E. Schwarz, *America's Hidden Success* (1983).

Race Relations. David Lewis, *King* (1970); Carl Brauer, *John F. Kennedy and the Second Reconstruction* (1977); Martin Luther King, Jr., *Why We Can't Wait* (1964); David Garrow, *Protest at Selma* (1978), *The FBI and Martin Luther King* (1981), and *Bearing the Cross* (1986); Taylor Branch, *Parting the Waters* (1988); William Chafe, *Civilities and Civil Rights* (1980); Hugh Davis Graham, *The Civil Rights Era* (1990); Nancy Weiss, *Whitney M. Young, Jr., and the Struggle for Civil Rights* (1989); Steven Lawson, *Black Ballots: Voting Rights in the South, 1966–1969* (1976); Abigail Thernstrom, *Whose Votes Count? Affirmative Action and Minority Voting Rights* (1987); Harris Wofford, *Of Kennedys and Kings* (1980); Stephen Oates, *Let the Trumpet Sound* (1982); Doug McAdam, *Freedom Summer* (1988); Stokely Carmichael and Charles Hamilton, *Black Power* (1967); Alex Haley, *The Autobiography of Malcolm X* (1966); Benjamin Muse, *The American Negro Revolution* (1969); Eugene Wolfenstein, *The Victims of Democracy: Malcolm X and the Black Revolution* (1981); Robert Fogelson, *Violence as Protest* (1971); Joe R. Feagin and Harlan Hahn, *Ghetto Revolts* (1973); *Report of the National Advisory Commission on Civil Disorders* (1968); Paul Burstein, *Discrimination, Jobs, and Politics* (1985).

Foreign Policy. Richard Walton, *Cold War and Counterrevolution* (1972); Louise Fitzsimmons, *The Kennedy Doctrine* (1972); Roger Hilsman, *To Move a Nation* (1965); Philip Geyelin, *Lyndon B. Johnson and the World* (1966); Richard Barnet, *Intervention and Revolution* (1968); Haynes Johnson, *The Bay of Pigs* (1964); Peter Wyden, *Bay of Pigs* (1969); Trumbull Higgins, *The Perfect Failure: Kennedy, Eisenhower, and the CIA at the Bay of Pigs* (1987); Elie Abel, *The Missile Crisis* (1966); Graham Allison, *Essence of Decision* (1971); Robert Kennedy, *Thirteen Days* (1969); Herbert Dinerstein, *The Making of a Missile Crisis* (1976); Dan Kurzman, *Santo Domingo* (1966); Jerome Slater, *Intervention and Negotiation* (1970); Richard D. Mahoney, *JFK: Ordeal in Africa* (1983); Warren Cohen, *Dean Rusk* (1980); Gerald T. Rice, *The Bold Experiment: JFK's Peace Corps* (1985).

Vietnam. George C. Herring, *America's Longest War*, rev. ed. (1986); Stanley Karnow, *Vietnam* (1983); R. B. Smith, *An International History of the Vietnam War: The Kennedy Strategy* (1985); *The Pentagon Papers*, Senator Gravel edition (1975); David Halberstam, *The Best and the Brightest* (1972); Neil Sheehan, *A Bright Shining Lie* (1988); Guenter Lewy, *America in Vietnam* (1978); John Galloway, *The Gulf of Tonkin Resolution* (1970); Alexander Kendrick, *The Wound Within* (1974); Norman Podhoretz, *Why We Were in Vietnam* (1982); Leslie Gelb and Richard Betts, *The Irony of Vietnam: The System Worked* (1979); Larry Berman, *Planning a Tragedy* (1982) and *Lyndon Johnson's War* (1989); George McT. Kahin, *Intervention* (1986); Gabriel Kolko, *The Anatomy of a War* (1985); Wallace J. Thies, *When Governments Collide* (1980); Michael Herr, *Dispatches* (1977); Lawrence Baskir and William Strauss, *Chance and Circumstance* (1978); Gloria Emerson,

Winners and Losers (1976); Mark Baker, *Nam* (1982); Al Santoli, *Everything We Had* (1981); Wallace Terry, *Bloods* (1984); William Broyles, Jr., *Brothers in Arms: A Journey from War to Peace* (1986); Thomas Powers, *Vietnam: The War at Home* (1973); Irwin Unger, *The Movement* (1974); Peter Braestrup, *Big Story* (1977, abridged ed. 1978); Don Oberdorfer, *Tet* (1971); Bruce C. Palmer, Jr., *The 25-Year War* (1984); Col. Harry Summers, *On Strategy* (1981); Thomas C. Thayer, *War Without Fronts* (1985); Robert W. Komer, *Bureaucracy at War* (1986); Ronald Spector, *Advice and Support* (1983).

1968. David Caute, *The Year of the Barricades* (1988); Lewis Chester, Godfrey Hodgson, and Lewis Page, *American Melodrama* (1969); David Farber, *Chicago '68* (1988); Charles Kaiser, *1968 in America* (1988); Godfrey Hodgson, *America in Our Time* (1976); Arthur M. Schlesinger, Jr., *Robert Kennedy and His Times* (1978); Norman Mailer, *Miami and the Siege of Chicago* (1968); Ben Stavis, *We Were the Campaign* (1969); Marshall Frady, *Wallace*, rev. ed (1976); Theodore White, *The Making of the President, 1968* (1969).

CHAPTER 32 THE CRISIS OF AUTHORITY

General Studies. William O'Neill, *Coming Apart* (1971); Ronald Berman, *America in the Sixties* (1968); Allen J. Matusow, *The Unraveling of America* (1984); Peter N. Carroll, *It Seemed Like Nothing Happened* (1982).

The New Left and the Counterculture. James Miller, *"Democracy in the Streets": From Port Huron to the Siege of Chicago* (1987); Maurice Isserman, *If I Had a Hammer . . .: The Death of the Old Left and the Birth of the New Left* (1987); Milton Viorst, *Fire in the Streets* (1979); Todd Gitlin, *The Whole World Is Watching* (1981) and *The Sixties: Years of Hope, Days of Rage* (1987); Irwin Unger, *The Movement* (1974); Lawrence Lader, *Power on the Left* (1979); Kirkpatrick Sale, *SDS* (1973); Sara Evans, *Personal Politics* (1979); W. J. Rorabaugh, *Berkeley at War* (1989); Peter Clecak, *Radical Paradoxes* (1973); Kenneth Keniston, *Young Radicals* (1968); Lewis Feuer, *The Conflict of Generations* (1969); Paul Goodman, *Growing Up Absurd* (1960); Theodore Roszak, *The Making of a Counter Culture* (1969); Charles Reich, *The Greening of America* (1970); Ronald Berman, *America in the Sixties* (1968); Joan Didion, *Slouching Towards Bethlehem* (1967) and *The White Album* (1979); John Diggins, *The American Left in the Twentieth Century* (1973); Richard Flacks, *Youth and Social Change* (1971); Morris Dickstein, *Gates of Eden* (1977); Jon Wiener, *Come Together: John Lennon in His Time* (1984).

Indians and Hispanics. Larry W. Burt, *Tribalism in Crisis: Federal Indian Policy, 1953–1961* (1982); Charles F. Wilkinson, *American Indians, Time, and the Law*, rev. ed. (1987); Wilcomb Washburn, *Red Man's Land/White Man's Land* (1971); Vine Deloria, Jr., *Behind the Trail of Broken Treaties* (1974) and *Custer Died for Your Sins* (1969); D'Arcy McNickle, *Native American Tribalism* (1973); Stan Steiner, *The New Indians* (1968); Peter Iverson, *The Navajo Nation* (1981); Rodolfo Acuña, *Occupied America*, 2nd ed. (1981); Julian Samora, *Los Mojados* (1971); Oscar Lewis, *La Vida* (1969); Matt Meier and Feliciano Rivera, *The Chicanos* (1972); Ronald Taylor, *Chávez and the Farm Workers* (1975).

Feminism. Susan M. Hartmann, *From Margin to Mainstream: Women and American Politics Since 1960* (1989); Cynthia Harrison, *On Account of Sex* (1990); Winifred Wandersee, *On the Move: American Women in the 1970s* (1988); William Chafe, *The American*

Woman (1972); Sheila Rothman, *Woman's Proper Place* (1978); Jo Freeman, *The Politics of Women's Liberation* (1975); Gayle Yates, *What Women Want* (1975); Betty Friedan, *The Feminine Mystique* (1963); Carol Gilligan, *In a Different Voice* (1982); Alice Kessler-Harris, *Out to Work: A History of Wage-Earning Women in the United States* (1982); Donald Matthews and Jane Sherson De Hart, *Sex, Gender, and the Politics of ERA* (1990); Robin Morgan, ed., *Sisterhood Is Powerful* (1970); Ethel Klein, *Gender Politics* (1984); Kristin Luker, *Abortion and the Politics of Motherhood* (1984); Rosalind Petchesky, *Abortion and Women's Choice* (1984); Marian Faux, *Roe v. Wade* (1988); Nancy Cott, *The Grounding of Modern Feminism* (1987).

Nixon and the World. Franz Schurman, *The Foreign Policies of Richard Nixon* (1987); Richard Stevenson, *The Rise and Fall of Détente* (1985); Robert S. Litwak, *Détente and the Nixon Doctrine: American Foreign Policy and the Pursuit of Stability* (1984); Henry A. Kissinger, *White House Years* (1979) and *Years of Upheaval* (1982); Gareth Porter, *A Peace Denied* (1975); William Shawcross, *Sideshow: Nixon, Kissinger, and the Destruction of Cambodia* (1978); Roger Morris, *Uncertain Greatness* (1977); Seyom Brown, *The Crisis of Power* (1979); David Landau, *Kissinger: The Uses of Power* (1972); Marvin Kalb and Bernard Kalb, *Kissinger* (1974); Seymour Hersh, *The Price of Power* (1983); Tad Szulc, *The Illusion of Peace* (1978); Roger Hilsman, *The Crouching Future* (1975); Harland Moulton, *From Superiority to Parity* (1973); John Newhouse, *Cold Dawn* (1973); John Stockwell, *In Search of Enemies* (1977); Thomas Powers, *The Man Who Kept the Secrets* (1979); Michael Oksenberg and Robert Oxnam, eds., *Dragon and Eagle* (1978); William Quandt, *Decade of Decision* (1977); Robert Stookey, *America and the Arab States* (1975).

Nixon's Domestic Policies. Herbert Parmet, *Richard Nixon and His America* (1989); Stephen Ambrose, *Nixon: The Triumph of a Politician, 1962–1972* (1989); William Safire, *Before the Fall* (1975); Raymond Price, *With Nixon* (1977); Daniel P. Moynihan, *The Politics of a Guaranteed Income* (1973); Vincent Burke and Vee Burke, *Nixon's Good Deed* (1974); R. L. Miller, *The New Economics of Richard Nixon* (1972); R. P. Nathan et al., *Monitoring Revenue Sharing* (1975); John Ehrlichman, *Witness to Power* (1982); Bob Woodward and Scott Armstrong, *The Brethren* (1980); Theodore H. White, *The Making of the President, 1972* (1973); Richard Barnet, *The Lean Years* (1980); Joan Edelman Spero, *The Politics of International Economic Relations* (1977); J. C. Hurewitz, ed., *Oil, the Arab–Israeli Dispute, and the Industrial World* (1976).

Nixon and Watergate. Garry Wills, *Nixon Agonistes* (1970); Fawn Brodie, *Richard Nixon* (1981); Bruce Mazlish, *In Search of Nixon* (1972); Jonathan Schell, *The Time of Illusion* (1975); Stanley J. Kutler, *The Wars of Watergate* (1990); Richard M. Nixon, *RN: The Memoirs of Richard Nixon* (1978); Theodore H. White, *Breach of Faith* (1975); Anthony Lukas, *Nightmare* (1976); Bob Woodward and Carl Bernstein, *All the President's Men* (1974) and *The Final Days* (1976); John Dean, *Blind Ambition* (1976); Richard Cohen and Jules Witcover, *A Heartbeat Away* (1974); Arthur M. Schlesinger, Jr., *The Imperial Presidency* (1973).

CHAPTER 33 THE UNFINISHED NATION

The Ford Presidency. Gerald Ter Horst, *Gerald Ford* (1975); Robert T. Hartmann, *Palace Politics* (1980); Richard Reeves, *A Ford Not a Lincoln* (1976); Gerald Ford, *A Time to Heal* (1979); James L. Sundquist, *The Decline and Resurgence of Congress* (1981); A. James

Reichley, *Conservatives in an Age of Change: The Nixon and Ford Administrations* (1981); Edward and Frederick Schapsmeier, *Gerald R. Ford's Date with Destiny: A Political Biography* (1989).

The Carter Presidency. Jimmy Carter, *Why Not the Best?* (1975) and *Keeping Faith* (1982); Rosalynn Carter, *First Lady from Plains* (1984); Erwin Hargrove, *Jimmy Carter as President* (1989); Jules Witcover, *Marathon* (1977); James Wooten, *Dasher* (1978); Clark Mollenhoff, *The President Who Failed* (1980); Jack Bass and Walter Devries, *The Transformation of Southern Politics* (1976); Hamilton Jordan, *Crisis* (1982); Haynes Johnson, *In the Absence of Power* (1980); Steven Gillon, *The Democrats' Dilemma: Walter F. Mondale and the Liberal Legacy* (1992); Charles O. Jones, *The Trusteeship Presidency* (1988); Zbigniew Brzezinski, *Power and Principle* (1983); Cyrus Vance, *Hard Choices* (1983); Gaddis Smith, *Morality, Reason, and Power* (1986); James Bill, *The Eagle and the Lion* (1988); Walter LaFeber, *Panama Canal* (1978); A. Glenn Mower, Jr., *Human Rights and American Foreign Policy* (1987); William B. Quandt, *Camp David* (1986).

The New Right. Peter Steinfels, *The Neo-Conservatives* (1979); Sidney Blumenthal, *The Rise of the Counter-Establishment* (1986); Burton Yale Pines, *Back to Basics* (1982); David W. Reinhard, *The Republican Right Since 1945* (1983); John K. White, *The New Politics of Old Values* (1988).

The Reagan Presidency. Theodore H. White, *America in Search of Itself* (1982); William Boyarsky, *The Rise of Ronald Reagan* (1968); Anne Edwards, *Early Reagan* (1987); Garry Wills, *Reagan's America* (1987); Hedrick Smith et al., *Reagan: The Man, the President* (1980); Hedrick Smith, *The Power Game* (1988); Lou Cannon, *Reagan* (1982); Robert Dallek, *Ronald Reagan: The Politics of Symbolism* (1984); Ronnie Dugger, *On Reagan* (1983); Richard Reeves, *The Reagan Detour* (1985); Laurence I. Barrett, *Gambling with History* (1984); Rowland Evans and Robert Novak, *The Reagan Revolution* (1981); Fred I. Greenstein, ed., *The Reagan Presidency* (1983); John L. Palmer and Isabel V. Sawhill, eds., *The Reagan Experiment* (1982); Joan Claybrook, *Retreat from Safety* (1984); Jonathan Lash, *A Season of Spoils* (1984); Jane Mayer and Doyle McManus, *Landslide: The Unmaking of the President, 1984–1988* (1988); George Gilder, *Wealth and Poverty* (1981); Frank Ackerman, *Reaganomics* (1982); Thomas Byrne Edsall, *The New Politics of Inequality* (1984); Sidney Weintraub and Marvin Goodstein, eds., *Reaganomics in the Stagflation Economy* (1983); Michael J. Piore and Charles F. Sabel, *The Second Industrial Divide* (1984); David Stockman, *The Triumph of Politics* (1986); William Greider, *The Education of David Stockman and Other Americans* (1982); Donald T. Regan, *For the Record* (1988); Nancy Reagan, *My Turn* (1989).

Reagan and the World. Alexander Haig, *Caveat: Realism, Reagan and Foreign Policy* (1984); Strobe Talbott, *Deadly Gambits* (1984) and *The Master of the Game: Paul Nitze and the Nuclear Peace* (1988); Walter LaFeber, *Inevitable Revolutions*, rev. ed. (1984); Raymond Bonner, *Weakness and Deceit: U.S. Policy and El Salvador* (1984); Tom Buckley, *Violent Neighbors* (1984); Robert O. Pastor, *Condemned to Repetition: The United States and Nicaragua* (1987); Bob Woodward, *Veil: The Secret Wars of the CIA* (1987); Seweryn Bialer and Michael Mandelbaum, eds., *Gorbachev's Russia and American Foreign Policy* (1988); John Newhouse, *War and Peace in the Nuclear Age* (1989).

Politics After Reagan. Thomas Ferguson and Joel Rogers, *Right Turn* (1986); Adolph L. Reed, Jr., *The Jesse Jackson Phenomenon* (1986).

Postliberal Society and Culture. Peter N. Carroll, *It Seemed Like Nothing Happened* (1982); Peter Clecak, *America's Quest for the Ideal Self* (1983); Jim Hougan, *Decadence: Radical Nostalgia, Narcissism, and Decline in the Seventies* (1975); Christopher Lasch, *The Culture of Narcissism* (1978); Edwin Schur, *The Awareness Trap* (1976); Kirkpatrick Sale, *Power Shift* (1975); John Woodridge, *The Evangelicals* (1975); Marshall Frady, *Billy Graham* (1979); Jonathan Schell, *The Fate of the Earth* (1982); Randy Shilts, *And the Band Played On: Politics, People, and the AIDS Epidemic* (1987); John Langone, *AIDS: The Facts* (1988); Frank Levy, *Dollars and Dreams: The Changing American Income Distribution* (1987); Studs Terkel, *The Great Divide* (1988).

Gender and Family. Andrea Dworkin, *Right-Wing Women* (1983); Barbara Ehrenreich, *The Hearts of Men: American Dreams and the Flight from Commitment* (1983); Susan M. Bianchi, *American Women in Transition* (1987); Elizabeth Fox-Genovese, *Feminism Without Illusions: A Critique of Individualism* (1991); Mary Francis Berry, *Why ERA Failed* (1986); Jane Mansbridge, *Why We Lost the ERA* (1986); Kristin Luker, *Abortion and the Politics of Motherhood* (1984); Rosalind Pechesky, *Abortion and Woman's Choice* (1984); Winifred D. Wandersee, *On the Move: American Women in the 1970s* (1988); Jonathan Kozol, *Rachel and Her Children: Homeless Families in America* (1988); Ruth Sidel, *Women and Children Last* (1986); Harrell R. Rodgers, Jr., *Poor Women, Poor Families* (1986); Hilda Scott, *Working Your Way to the Bottom: The Feminization of Poverty* (1985).

Nonwhites in the 1970s and 1980s. Derrick Bell, *And We Are Not Saved: The Elusive Quest for Racial Justice* (1987); Douglas Glasgow, *The Black Underclass* (1980); Leslie W. Dunbar, ed., *Minority Report* (1984); Marian Wright Edelman, *Families in Peril* (1987); William Julius Wilson, *The Truly Disadvantaged* (1987); Frank D. Bean and Marta Tienda, *The Hispanic Population of the United States* (1987); James D. Cockcroft, *Outlaws in the Promised Land: Mexican Immigrant Workers and America's Future* (1986); David M. Reimers, *Still the Golden Door* (1985); John Crewden, *The Tarnished Door* (1983); Stan Steiner, *The New Indians* (1968); Vine Deloria, Jr., *American Indian Policy in the Twentieth Century* (1985).

Illustration Credits

Index

Note: *Pages followed by the letter* m *refer to maps.*

About the Author

ALAN BRINKLEY is professor of American history at Columbia University. Educated at Princeton and Harvard, he has served on the faculties of the Massachusetts Institute of Technology, Harvard University, the City University of New York Graduate School, and Princeton University. He is the author of *Voices of Protest: Huey Long, Father Coughlin, and the New Deal,* which won the 1983 American Book Award for History; coauthor of *American History: A Survey;* and the writer of many articles, essays, and reviews in both scholarly and nonscholarly periodicals.

A Note on the Type

The text of this book is a digitized version of Janson, a typeface long thought to have been made by the Dutchman Anton Janson, who was a practicing type founder in Leipzig during the years 1668–1687. However, it has been conclusively demonstrated that this family of type is actually the work of Nicholas Kis (1650–1702), a Hungarian, who most probably learned his trade from the master Dutch type founder Dirk Voskens. Janson is an excellent example of the influential and sturdy Dutch types that prevailed in England up to the time William Caslon developed his own incomparable designs from them.